Daniel McAnulty
Senior Editor
mcanulty@mit.edu

Analucia Berry
Treasurer & Layout Editor
analucia@mit.edu

Kate Thompson
Managing Ed
mkt@mit.edu

MW00909036

Around MIT

Approximately The Thirty-Third Edition
August 2004

Chapter Coordinators:
Katherine H. Allen
Amittai Axelrod
Mariana Baca
Analucia Berry
Andrew Brooks
Augusta Dibbell
James Harvey
Guy Hoffman
Grace Kenney
Josh Lifton
Daniel McAnulty
Alex Rolfe
Yang Ruan
Janet Ryu
Jen Selby
Kate Thompson

Contributors:
Punyashloka Biswal
Kevin Chen
Emily Cofer
Sarah Dagen
Laura Dean
Roger Dingledine
Joe Foley
Anna Folinsky
Anna Gladstone
David Glasser
Asanka Herath
Jenny Hu
Headley Jacobus
Scott Johnston
Aparna Jonnalagadda
Christina Laskowski
Conor Lenahan
Issel Anne Lim
Lex Nemzer
Karolina Netolicka
Marcos Ojeda
Paige Phillips
Jerrad Pierce
Rob Radez
Hannah Reitzel
Javed Samuel
Elizabeth Smith
Richard Tibbetts
Yelena Tsitkin
Tao Yue

Thanks To:
Elizabeth Barnes, Cynthia Stanton
and Daniel Barkowitz of the
Financial Aid Office
Rich Berlin and the Office of
Campus Dining
Irene Brisson
Emer Garland of MIT Public
Relations Services
Jeff Lieberman
Andrea Lockerd
Fran Miles of Student Life Programs
Laura Stuart and Dr Kristine Girard
of MIT Medical
Sarah Wenzel of the MIT Librarians
Theodric Young of WMBR
Oren Zuckerman
Orit Zuckerman
The Academic Resource Center
The ASA Executive Board
The Graduate Departments and
Departmental Administrators
The Wright Flyer hackers

Guy Hoffman
Publicity Manager
ghoffman@mit.edu

Cover photo: Wright Flyer hack on the Great Dome, December 2003. Photograph courtesy of Erik Nygren.

Erin Price
Advertising Manager
aerynne@mit.edu

Andrew Brooks
Distribution Manager
zoz@mit.edu

Welcome to a new home.

I can still remember my first night at MIT. Arriving from the sticks of Pennsylvania on an airplane in the afternoon, I was given more pamphlets, papers, and propaganda than I could have known what to do with. In an unfamiliar city — with the wonderful benefits of a roof, a bed, and a lamp — I curled up in the corner, absorbing this barrage of information while the notion slowly dawned on me that I was now able to spend my time doing whatever I wished. In the midst of this warmly spectacular realization, I came across a book that called itself a "Guide to the Institute" nestled among the papers. Within its pages I found a strange combination of bureaucracy and humanity, alternating between indecipherable rules and regulations and wonderfully witty commentary on the local area and on the unique MIT jargon and viewpoints that I had already begun to encounter. I stayed up very late into the night, reading and re-reading the sections about MIT life, imagining all the things I didn't know about the place I had come to, and looking forward to all the things I would find out when the sun rose again.

From 1998 to 2002, How To Get Around MIT, the student compiled guidebook, took a brief hiatus and was carried on by MIT administrators in the form of the "Guide to the Institute" that I stumbled across in Fall 2000. (The book you currently hold, however, was written entirely by students and alums and published using only money from area advertisers and book sales.) Though the non-student issues read very differently in parts, much of the text of certain sections, such as the Glossary and Moah 'Bout Boston, were left untouched. Reading those sections of HowToGAMIT sometimes still brings back that incredible feeling of newness — the awe of a strange new home and an undiscovered country. At the same time, it reminds me of the many friends I've made, of the countless people who accepted me into their home when I was a new student and who made my life more exciting and enjoyable than I could have imagined it being.

This book is an attempt, on the part of all the contributors, to make those kinds of experiences possible for as many people as possible. Simply by living here you are part of something huge; a machine of innumerable facets; and when the weight of life and all its complexities becomes overwhelming, sometimes merely standing in a new location is all it takes for the wonderment of the landscape to sink back in.

I'd like to thank all the people without whose efforts this book could never have been made, most especially Kate Thompson and Analucia Berry whose efforts spread to every corner, nook, and cranny of the book and editing process. Thanks to Erin Price without whose ad-selling skills we'd have never gone to press, Guy Hoffman for his design savvy and the wonderful cover, and last but most certainly not least thanks to Zoz for getting the HowToGAMIT ball rolling again two years ago, his indefatigable efforts to keep it going, and for his always impressive outright publishing know-how.

daniel e mcanulty
senior haus
aug 5, 2004

Contents

Telephone Numbers

Common Phone Numbers

The following pages list some of the most often called numbers around the Institute and outside. Remember that Massachusetts uses 10-digit dialling.

MIT, 77 Massachusetts Ave., Cambridge, MA 02139
Telephone: 617-253-1000
Emergency — from any MIT phone, dial 100

From off campus:

3-xxxx => 617-253-xxxx

5-xxxx => 617-225-xxxx

8-xxxx => 617-258-xxxx

2-xxxx => 617-452-xxxx

Campus Police (CP) and MIT Ambulance	W31-215	3-1212
Medical Department (9am-5pm)	E23-189	3-4481
Weekends, Holidays, Nights		3-1311
Nightline		3-8800
Mental Health Department	E23-368	3-2916

If you can't find what you are looking for here, Athena has a directory of useful numbers, both on-campus and off (such as restaurants). To use it, enter `add sipb ; rolodex <name to look up>` at the `athena%` prompt. For more tie lines that allow you to internal-dial to off-campus locations, see `web.mit.edu/is/tel/tielines.html`

Dorms

Ashdown Desk	305 Memorial Drive	3-2961
Baker Desk	362 Memorial Drive	3-3161
Bexley Desk	46-52 Massachusetts Avenue	8-9863
Burton Desk	410 Memorial Drive	3-3261
East Campus Desk	3 Ames Street	3-2871
Eastgate (Manager)	60 Wadsworth Street	3-7463
Edgerton Desk	143 Albany Street	3-4933
French House (Lounge)	476 Memorial Drive	8-6388
German House Desk	476 Memorial Drive	3-6561
Green Hall (Manager)	350 Memorial Drive	3-3675
MacGregor Desk	450 Memorial Drive	3-1461
McCormick Desk	320 Memorial Drive	3-5961
New House Desk	471-475 Memorial Drive	3-6561
Next House Desk	500 Memorial Drive	3-8761
Random Hall Desk	282-290 Massachusetts Avenue	8-6344
Russian House Desk	476 Memorial Drive	3-6561
Senior Haus Desk	70 Amherst Street	3-3191

Sidney-Pacific Desk	70 Pacific Street	2-4753
Simmons Hall Desk	279-243 Vassar Street	3-5107
Spanish House Desk	473 Memorial Drive	3-6561
Tang Desk	550 Memorial Drive	3-1773
The Warehouse (NW30) Desk	224 Albany Street	3-6588
Westgate (Manager)	540 Memorial Drive	3-5146

Independent Living Groups

Alpha Chi Omega	478 Commonwealth Avenue, Boston	617-450-0030
Alpha Delta Phi	351 Massachusetts Avenue, Cambridge	617-576-2792, -93, -94
Alpha Epsilon Pi	155 & 165 Bay State Road, Boston	617-247-3170
Alpha Phi	479 Commonwealth Avenue, Boston	617-859-9223
Alpha Tau Omega	405 Memorial Drive, Cambridge	617-577-1110
Beta Theta Pi	119 & 120 Bay State Road, Boston	617-247-2011
Chi Phi	32 Hereford Street, Boston	617-247-8355
Delta Kappa Epsilon	403 Memorial Drive, Cambridge	617-494-8250
Delta Psi (No. 6 Club)	428 Memorial Drive, Cambridge	617-252-3786
Delta Tau Delta	416 Beacon Street, Boston	617-247-3687
Delta Upsilon	526 Beacon Street, Boston	617-536-3931
Epsilon Theta	259 St. Paul Street, Brookline	617-734-9211
Fenway House	34 The Fenway, Boston	617-437-1043
Kappa Sigma	407 Memorial Drive, Cambridge	617-494-0330
Lambda Chi Alpha	99 Bay State Road, Boston	617-266-7021, -236-1328
Nu Delta	460 Beacon Street, Boston	617-437-7300
Phi Beta Epsilon	400 Memorial Drive, Cambridge	617-494-8677
Phi Delta Theta	97 Bay State Road, Boston	617-247-8691
Phi Kappa Sigma	530 Beacon Street, Boston	617-536-3683
Phi Kappa Theta	229 Commonwealth Avenue, Boston	617-437-7795
Phi Sigma Kappa	487 Commonwealth Avenue, Boston	617-267-2199
pika	69 Chestnut Street, Cambridge	617-492-6983
Pi Lambda Phi	450 Beacon Street, Boston	617-267-4935
Sigma Chi	532 Beacon Street, Boston	617-262-3192
Sigma Kappa	480 Commonwealth Avenue, Boston	617-437-1233
Sigma Nu	28 The Fenway, Boston	617-536-9925
Sigma Phi Epsilon	515 & 518 Beacon Street, Boston	617-536-1300
Student House	111 Bay State Road, Boston	617-247-0506
Tau Epsilon Phi	253 Commonwealth Avenue, Boston	617-262-5090
Theta Chi	528 Beacon Street, Boston	617-267-1801
Theta Delta Chi	372 Memorial Drive, Cambridge	617-494-8300
Theta Xi	64 & 66 Bay State Road, Boston	617-536-8587
WILG	355 Massachusetts Avenue, Cambridge	617-547-0205
Zeta Beta Tau	58 Manchester Road, Brookline	617-232-3257
Zeta Psi	233 Massachusetts Avenue, Cambridge	617-661-4111 x100

Information

Directory Assistance (MIT Operator)		0
Emergency Closings		3-SNOW (3-7669)
Harvard (info)		186-5-5000
Harvard numbers (from Institute phones)	617-49x-xxxx =>	186-x-xxxx
Information Office	7-121	3-4795
Mass. General Hospital (from Institute phones)	617-726-xxxx =>	1936-xxxx
Network Status		3-DOWN (3-3696)
Residential Life Programs	W20-549	2-4280
Wellesley (switchboard)		187-1000
Wellesley numbers (from Institute phones)	781-283-xxxx =>	187-xxxx

Official Stuff

Athletics Office	W35	3-4498
Careers Office	12-170	3-4733
Concourse	16-135	3-3200
Counseling and Support Services	5-104	3-4861
Experimental Study Group	24-612	3-7786
Faculty Club	E52-6th	3-2111
Financial Aid Office	11-320	3-4971
Graduate Students Office	3-138	3-4860
Ombudsperson	10-213	3-5921
Registrar's Office	5-119	3-4784
Student Services Center (Bursar's Office)	11-120	8-8600
Student Employment	11-120	3-4973
Terrascope	16-177	3-4074
Office of Academic Services	7-133	3-6776

Activities

APO Community Service Fraternity	W20-415	3-3788
Association of Student Activities (ASA)	W20-401	3-2696
Graduate Student Council (GSC)	50-222	3-2195
Lecture Series Committee (LSC)	W20-469	3-3791
MIT Science Fiction Society	W20-473	8-5126
Student Art Association	W20-429	3-7019
Student Information Processing Board (SIPB)	W20-557	3-7788
The Tech	W20-483	3-1541
Undergraduate Association (UA)	W20-401	3-2696
WMBR Radio (on-air DJ)	50-030	3-8810

Miscellaneous

Athena On-Line Consulting (OLC)	N42-lobby	3-4435
Building Repair & Maintenance		3-4948 (F-IXIT)

Campus Activities Complex (CAC)	W20-500	3-3913
Child Care (Center for Work and Family)	16-151	3-1592
Technology Children's Centers:	Eastgate	3-5907
	Lincoln Lab	781-861-3850
	Stata (32-100)	3-1720
	Westgate	3-4340
CopyTech	11-004, E52-045	3-2806
Department of Facilities	NE49-2200	3-6859
Information Systems HelpDesk		3-1101
Intramural (IM) Office	W35-2975	3-7947
Telephone Repair	E19-741	3-4357 (3-HELP)

Outside Numbers

American Automobile Association	617-443-9300
Better Business Bureau	508-652-4800
Cambridge Hospital	617-665-1000
City Hall (Cambridge)	617-349-4000
City Hall (Boston)	617-635-4000
Consumer Affairs Hotline	617-727-7780 (or 1-888-283-3757)
Directory Assistance	411
Domino's Pizza	617-424-9000
Fire Department (Cambridge)	617-349-4900
Fire Department (Boston)	617-343-3550
Emergency	**911**
Greater Boston Legal Services	617-371-1234
Massachusetts General Hospital	617-726-2000
MBTA Schedules (6:30a-8p M-F, 7:30a-6p Sa-Su)	617-222-3200
General Information	617-222-5000
MIT Switchboard	617-253-1000
Emergency Closings	617-253-7669 (617-253-SNOW)
Information	617-253-4795
Network Status	617-253-3696 (617-253-DOWN)
Police (Cambridge)	617-349-3300
Police (Boston)	617-343-4200
Emergency	**911**
Somerville Hospital	617-591-4500
Sports Scoreboard (Recording)	617-265-6600
Time and Temperature (Recording)	617-637-8687 (617-NER-VOUS)
Weather (Recording)	617-936-1234
Women's Center (Boston Medical Center)	617-414-4893

Emergency Information

For any emergency:
dial 100 from an Institute phone or **dial 617-253-1212** from a cellular phone.
All calls from a cellular telephone to 911 go to the State Police in Framingham and are then transferred to the city where the emergency is — not the MIT Police.

Fire, Medical, Police, Ambulance

Call x100 for emergency medical or police service. Emergency medical care is provided by the student-run ambulance service 24 hours a day. The Campus Police can also be reached at x3-1212. Those who live off-campus should call their local emergency number (911 in most places) *and* call the CPs at 617-253-1212. MIT Medical's 24-hour Urgent Care Line is x3-1311.

Physician, Surgeon, Psychiatrist

The Medical Department (building E23, x3-1311) always has a physician, an obstetrician/gynecologist, a pediatrician, a surgeon, and a psychiatrist on call. A physician is on site at all times. The psychiatrist can be consulted about anything from home troubles to drug problems.

Nightline

Call x3-8800 (DEF TUV TUV OPER OPER) from 7pm to 7am, September through May, to talk about anything. Nightline has male and female students available all night, and all calls are both anonymous and confidential. If something is bothering you, call.

Arrest

If you are arrested, call the Campus Police (x3-1212). In nearly all cases, the Campus Police will help you seek release from custody on personal recognizance, on bail, or through arrangements with a bondsman. Don't plead guilty — ask for a "continuance." (The Campus Police will explain this and more when you call.)

Dean-on-Call

There is always a dean on call, even after office hours. To reach him or her for any reason, call Campus Police (x3-1212) and ask for the dean-on-call.

Money

The Institute can arrange to get you money in an emergency. Details are in the **Finances** chapter. After hours, contact the Dean-on-Call (see above), who can clear you for money from the Campus Police emergency fund. If you're off campus the money may even be wired to you.

Physical Plant

Call x3-4948 (F-IXIT) anytime for problems, from electrical failures to floods.

SafeRide

The Parking and Transportation Office runs four "SafeRide" vans which run from 6pm to 3am (4am on Thursdays, Fridays and Saturdays). Two go to living groups in Cambridge, and two to FSILGs in Boston. Use this service, especially when you're on campus alone late at night and need to get home. Phone numbers are x3-2997 and x8-6510, see the **Transportation** chapter for more details.

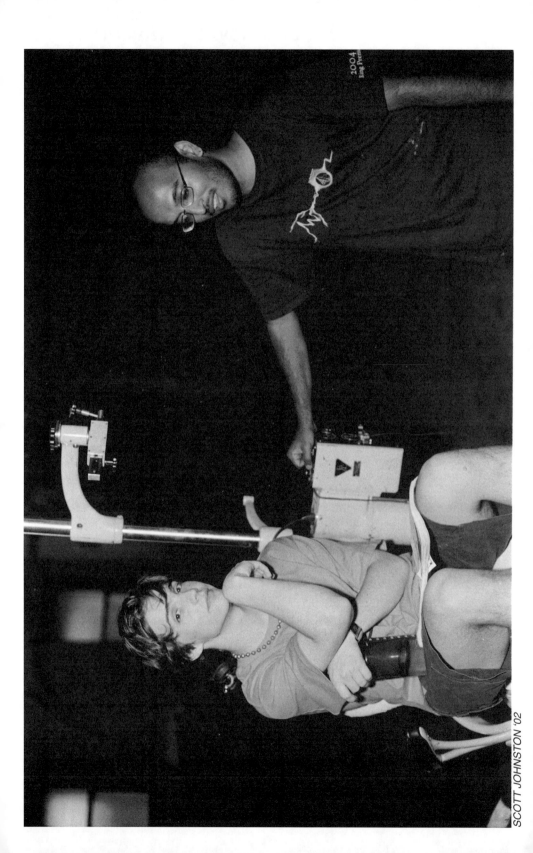

"Help!"

Sometimes the Institute can seem to be a pretty cold place, especially when things aren't going well and you're looking for a place to turn for help. Fortunately MIT takes its responsibility to provide support services very seriously, which means there are lots of safety nets around if you know where to look for them.

Don't be afraid to ask!!! Often the hardest step in solving your problem is just asking for help. If the first contact doesn't get you what you want, *try someone else*. There are many services for students here. Besides the resources below, don't forget about your advisor, housemaster, graduate resident tutor, friends, or an instructor you trust as sources of advice. Department heads are a valuable resource for graduate students.

Offices of the Deans for Student Life and Undergraduate Education

ODSUE is split into two Deans' Offices, under which a large number of offices are organized. If you have a problem or are faced with a serious question, or even a small one, the ODSUE is a good place to go. The Deans have an extensive knowledge of both the Institute and student problems. The Deans are willing to talk with students; that's their job. They can direct you to helpful resources, relay comments or complaints to the appropriate people, or initiate a look into (and sometimes a change of) established policies on your behalf. Although the staff of each section works primarily in its respective area, feel free to talk to any of them. It is likely, though, that you will get greater satisfaction from a Dean whose duties or interests match your problem.

ODSUE is concerned with the students' living and learning environments. It concerns itself with students' interests and welfare and with their growth both as individuals and as members of the academic community. It is the purpose of ODSUE to support and to complement the academic program at MIT.

Each Dean has a number of offices under them:

Dean for Undergraduate Education
Robert P. Redwine
Room 4-110, 617-253-6056
web.mit.edu/due/

Admissions
Careers Office
Edgerton Center
Office of Academic Services
Office of Minority Education
Registrar's Office
ROTC
Student Financial Services
Student Services Information Technology
Teaching and Learning Laboratory

Dean for Student Life
Larry G. Benedict
Room 4-110, 617-253-4052
web.mit.edu/dsl/

Administrative Services
Athletics, Physical Education and Recreation
Community Development & Substance Abuse
Counseling and Support Services
Enterprise Services (including Audio Visual,
    Campus Activities Complex, CopyTech,
    Endicott House, MIT Card Office and
    Parking & Transportation)
Housing
Religious Life
Student Discipline
Student Life Programs

Under the Dean for Undergraduate Education (DUE)

Admissions
web.mit.edu/admissions/www/
3-108, x3-4791

Remember these guys?

Careers Office
web.mit.edu/career/www/
12-170, x3-4733

Career Services provides information and guidance about jobs, careers and professional schools for undergraduates, graduate students, post-docs and alumni.

Edgerton Center
web.mit.edu/edgerton/
4-405, x3-4629

The Edgerton Center gives students a chance to experience hands-on learning. Located on Strobe Alley (the fourth floor of building 4), the Edgerton Center has several classes, runs the student machine shop, and supports student engineering teams.

Edgerton classes include the Strobe Project Lab and several seminars that vary by semester. The Strobe Project Lab (6.163) is an extremely popular Institute Lab with limited enrolment. (The makeup of the class is determined by lottery at the first lecture.) About five seminars are offered each semester. In the past, seminars have addressed topics such as Sports Product Development, Practical Electronics, and Turning Ideas into Inventions.

The student engineering groups the Edgerton Center supports include the Solar Car Team, Battlebots, Formula SAE, the Rocket Team, the Mars Gravity project, the Tech Model Railroad, and the Easy Rider Motorcycle Club.

Office of Academic Services
web.mit.edu/acserv/
7-133, x3-6776

The OAS combines the offices and services of several administrative bodies. As a unit, the OAS includes the Academic Information and Communication office, the Faculty and Alumni Support office, and the Academic Resource Center. The new organization brings together many of the staff and services that support the MIT educational program and makes it easier for staff to collaborate on activities that support faculty in their roles as teachers and advisors. Many of the academic programs that are part of the general undergraduate program are supported through OAS, including Freshman Advising and Seminars, the Undergraduate Research Opportunities Program, January IAP, Orientation Programs, and the Writing Requirement.

Office of Minority Education
web.mit.edu/ome/
4-113, x3-5010

The OME actively pursues the building of a more effective undergraduate academic support structure throughout the Institute for all undergraduates, with a special concern for underrepresented minorities (African-American, Mexican-American, Native American and Puerto Rican/Hispanic). Programs and activities generated by the office are based on a commitment to have all students fully engage the educational opportunities within the Institute. The specific programs and resources are offered to maximize the opportunities for underrepresented minority groups, to encourage their pursuit of graduate degrees and professional careers, and to educate the MIT community toward that end.

Project Interphase is a summer academic orientation program which provides an opportunity for incoming underrepresented minority students to learn about the Institute and its resources prior to the fall term. Project Interphase has several objectives: (1) to assist freshmen in developing and sharpening their knowledge of and faculty with those quantitative skills and verbal concepts that are essential for successful academic performance at MIT, (2) to encourage individual development of study habits and discipline for a smooth transition into the first year, and (3) to introduce students to MIT, its support services, and the surrounding community under conditions somewhat moderated from those which characterize the fall and spring semesters. The program includes seven weeks of chemistry, humanities, math, and physics courses, as well as a comprehensive review of all the academic programs and options open to freshmen. As of 2003, Interphase now accepts non-minority students as well.

The OME **Tutorial Services** was founded by members of the Black Students' Union. Although now administered by the OME, it is still coordinated by students. It is open to all students, but is especially intended to augment the academic assistance minority students receive from the departments, to enhance their success at MIT.

Tutors in the program and OME staff work with the departments to offer the best resources to students through this evening program. The staff is composed of undergraduate and graduate students who are hired for their expertise in particular courses and their commitment to the academic success of undergraduates. The Program operates in the Tutorial Services Room, 12-124, 7 days a week: Sunday through Thursday, 2pm-10pm, Friday and Saturday 2pm-6pm, and additional hours during exam periods and by special request. The 24-hour TSR line is x3-8406, and the TSR Listen Only Information Line is 617-252-3804.

A Seminar Series called **XL** introduces students to the academic and non-academic resources within the MIT community. The seminars serve to: (1) promote an effective undergraduate experience, (2) provide valuable contacts and resources, and (3) explore postgraduate and professional pathways. Check with the OME about new programs.

Secrets and Strategies for Academic Success (SSAS) is a series of monthly presentations that informs students of resources they can use to enhance their MIT educational experience. "Time Management" and "How to Choose a Major" are examples of topics included.

The OME's Industrial Advisory Council for Minority Education (IACME) sponsors a **Mentor Program**, which pairs freshmen and sophomores with an engineer or scientist working in industry. OME also has a **Buddy Program** to pair freshmen one-on-one with upperclassmen, to help their adjustment to MIT and expand their social networks. Other programs and social functions can be found on the OME web page.

Finally, OME conducts research on the retention and adjustment of minority students in order to learn more about the variables and conditions in the environment which influence their matriculation at MIT. Studies are also conducted with other departments and offices within the Institute to address different facets of students' adjustment, such as the use of Institute resources.

Registrar's Office
web.mit.edu/registrar/
5-111 and 5-119

The Registrar's office has two major divisions: Schedules and Records. The Records half maintains the enrollment records; they are the place to go if you need an official transcript or a replacement diploma. The Schedules half deals with all things scheduling, from the Academic Calendar to classroom reservations. WebSIS (student.mit.edu) lets you plan your classes, check your grades, pay your tuition bill, and maintain your personal information (name, address, emergency contacts, *etc.*). Most routine matters don't require a trip to the Registrar's office.

ROTC
web.mit.edu/armyrotc/, web.mit.edu/afrotc/, navyrotc.mit.edu
W59, x3-4475

MIT hosts the Boston ROTC units for the Navy, Army and AirForce. Each is a separately run program, but all provide full or partial scholarships to finish your degree. If you are interested visit the websites, or you can go to the Heinz Building (W59) where all three units are located to talk to the staff for any of the three.

Student Financial Services
web.mit.edu/finaid/
11-120, 11-220, and 11-320; x8-8600

The SFS office integrates the former Student Financial Aid Office and the Bursar's Office. Designed specifically to accommodate students' needs for efficiency, the office draws upon the work of four teams: the Service Delivery Team (service representatives who respond to questions in the Student Services Center), the Loan Services Team, the Student Record Team, and the Communications and Fund Management Team (Donor Relations). For students' convenience, the Office of Student Employment has also moved to the Student Services Center. The central location in Building 11 provides a one-stop approach to service and streamlines the steps it takes to solve financial questions.

Student Services Information Technology
web.mit.edu/ssit/
11-420, x8-6421

The mission of Student Services Information Technology is to provide high quality information services support to a wide ranging set of users within DUE/DSL and MIT. This support focuses on the automation of business processes and information systems to provide students, faculty and administrators with timely and accurate information and support. SSIT is responsible for administrative and desktop computing support for DSL/DUE staff; support and development of MITSIS (MIT's Student Information System) for administrative users; and support and development of WebSIS (`websis.mit.edu`), the students' online access to their own information.

Teaching and Learning Laboratory
`web.mit.edu/tll/`
5-122, x3-2850

TLL works with teachers (Professors, Lecturers, TAs, *etc.*) to improve the quality of instruction at MIT.

Under the Dean for Student Life (DSL)

Administrative Services
`web.mit.edu/dsl/admin/index.html`
W20-507, x8-9692 or x3-7272

Administrative Services "provides support to the DSL so that it is able to fulfill its mission of creating a more positive experience for the MIT student." This involves providing administrative support services to DSL departments, offices, committees, and recognized student groups in order to help them enhance their overall effectiveness. If you can infer from that what this office actually does, you may be suitable for a staff position.

Athletics, Physical Education and Recreation
`web.mit.edu/athletics/www/`
W32-109, x3-4291

MIT's physical education programs, varsity and intramural athletics, club sports, and community recreation. See the **Athletics** chapter for more information.

Campus Activities Complex
`web.mit.edu/campus-activities/www/`
W20-500, x3-3913

The Campus Activities Complex (CAC) offers event coordination, building management, tenant services and support services for major Institute events and conferences. The CAC manages and stewards the use of five multipurpose buildings as centers for social, cultural, educational, religious, and recreational interaction: Stratton Student Center (W20), Kresge Auditorium (W16), the Religious Activities Center (W11), MIT Chapel (W15), and Walker Memorial (50), as well as a host of other spaces on campus such as lobbies 10 and 13 and the barbecue pits. If you need a place for an event or activity, these are the people to contact. Spaces need to be reserved in advance; how far in advance depends on the space, but for large facilities like Kresge it can be months. For more information, see *Reserving Facilities* in the **MIT Facilities** chapter.

Office of Campus Dining
`web.mit.edu/dining/`
W20-507, x3-4875

The Office of Campus Dining (OCD) provides oversight to all food operations on MIT campus and for local restaurant deliveries using the TechCash plan (see *MIT Card Office* regarding TechCash). The Office has extensive feedback mechanisms working with student governments, groups and individually interested students with dining related requests, comments and concerns. Questions and comments can be sent through the Campus Dining web site or to `foodstuff@mit.edu`. Check out the *Campus Dining* section of **Miscellaneous**.

Community Development & Substance Abuse
web.mit.edu/cdsa/
26-161, x3-3276

The Office of Community Development and Substance Abuse Programs is tasked with "promoting a campus culture of informed, responsible decision making". Basically, the office is a marketing department, producing posters, brochures and other advertising material such as the popular (but according to recent studies at the Harvard School of Public Health, largely ineffective) "social norms" marketing campaigns that attempt to convince students that their peers are drinking much less than they might think. In addition to their straightforward propaganda function, CDSA also offers alcohol and drug education for students and staff, and sponsors social activities on campus that do not involve alcohol. Support for students with actual substance abuse problems is provided by Counseling & Support Services and the Mental Health department of MIT Medical.

Counseling and Support Services
web.mit.edu/counsel/www/
5-104, x3-4861

Also known as the Counseling Deans, the staff of Counseling and Support Services are there to assist you with any and all problems you might be having at MIT. For detailed information, please see the *Counseling Deans* section later in this chapter and in the **Academics** chapter.

Housing
web.mit.edu/housing/
Undergrad housing: E32-200, x3-2811
Grad and family housing: E32-238, x3-5148
Off-campus housing: E32-214, x3-1493

If you want to sleep, shower, or call a place home while you're at MIT, you'll need somewhere to live. (If you don't want to do any of these things, go read the *Burnout* section.) With the exception of FSILGs (which fall under the office of Student Life Programs), the Housing office deals with all things housing — undergrad dorms, grad dorms and off-campus housing. Its primary purposes are making sure people have places to live and maintaining the dorms (which they like to call Residence Halls). For more information on residences at MIT, see the **Housing** chapter.

MIT Card Office
web.mit.edu/mitcard/
E32-117, x3-3475

The MIT Card office produces the MIT identification card for students, faculty, employees, affiliates and visitors. The MIT card is used for security and access privileges to dorms, parking garages, libraries, athletic facilities, labs and offices. It is also used as a debit card ("TechCASH") for financial point of sale transactions such as dining, vending machines and retail outlets, CopyTech, and residential laundries. Spouses and partners of MIT students or employees are also able to obtain an MIT Card. For more information on what the MIT card can do for you, and for eligibility requirements, see the web site. The Card Office's hours are 8:30am to 4:30pm, Monday through Friday.

Religious Life
web.mit.edu/dsl/religious_life.html
W11, x3-2981

The department of Religious Life is primarily made up of the MIT Board of Chaplains and 30+ active MIT student religious groups. The MIT Board of Chaplains represent many of the world's religions, serving both their own religious communities and the MIT community. They are available for counseling, private talks, and program development. Many of the religious groups these chaplains represent meet weekly for worship, prayer, or study. A list of religious counselors appears later in this chapter.

Office of Student Discipline
web.mit.edu/discipline/
E32-133, x3-7848

The Office of Student Conflict Resolution and Discipline handles both academic and personal complaints against students. If you are considering filing a complaint against another student, or someone has (or may have) made a complaint against you, the website contains helpful information on policies and procedures. The website also has information on several options for anonymous reporting and anonymous action. The office also offers mediation to help people in conflict try to reach a constructive resolution. This service is completely voluntary and confidential.

Student Life Programs
web.mit.edu/slp/
W20-549, x2-4280

All aspects of residential life, aside from actually placing students in housing, fall under the auspices of SLP. The unit is supposed to encourage teamwork and collaboration within and between all offices and with faculty and students, which means it is basically just another layer of bureaucracy to deal with when trying to get anything done. SLP is working to organize itself to optimally carry out the recommendations of the Task Force on Student Life and Learning. This seems to involve behaving like some kind of bacterium, as the residential life and student life glob is continually dividing, merging and replicating. After being combined some years ago into "RLSLP", as of July 2002 it re-split into the Department of Student Life Programs and the Department of Housing. On-Campus housing (dorms) and Off-Campus housing (mostly apartments) fall under the Housing office, but Fraternities, Sororities, and Independent Living Groups (which are in the nebulous area between on- and off-campus) are served by SLP.

SLP are the people to contact for information on planning concerts, dances, mixers, and the like. Before you do, check out *The Guidebook To Planning Events @MIT* on the web at web.mit.edu/campus-activities/guidebook/Page0001.htm to see what sort of police, licensing, contracts, metal detection and other hoops you will have to jump through. There are more regulations involved in throwing a simple party than you could probably think of off the top of your head in a ten-minute brainstorming session, so start planning early.

Other Useful Offices

Academic Resource Center (ARC)
web.mit.edu/arc/
7-103 and 7-104

The Academic Resource Center is another figurehead for a large number of useful programs. Similar to the Student Services Center, ARC is an office of first resort. They can assist you in finding information and resources on: academic advising, academic programs, first year student pilot programs and academic initiatives, the Independant Activities Program (IAP), new student programs (including Orientation, undergraduate academic performance standards, undergraduate research (i.e. UROPs), undergraduate seminars and the training of freshman advisors, associate advisors and Resident Associate Advisors. If they can't help you, they know who can.

Student Services Center
web.mit.edu/ssc/
11-120, x8-8600

Academic registration records as well as the undergraduate financial aid program are all centrally located in 11-120. If you have paperwork problems or financial issues, this is the place to go. At the SSC you can make payments to your student account, meet with your financial aid counselor, order a transcript, sign direct loan notes, pick up and turn in those indispensable Add/Drop forms, add or remove yourself from the degree list, pick up old paychecks and generally get things done. The SSC is open from 9am to 5pm every weekday except Wednesday, when it's open from 10am to 5pm. Other than at the beginning of term and similar deadline days, lines to speak to someone human are seldom long.

Burnout

Quote #1: "I'm thinking about double-majoring." This is a common saying by freshmen, especially during their first August here.

Quote #2: "I'm now convinced that the only way MIT students graduate in four years is repression." This is a quote from a member of the Class of 2003.

Freshmen arrive here enthusiastic about academics. High school seniors come here even with (or perhaps because of) MIT's reputation as a pressure-cooker, because they get — or think they will get — an incredible feeling of self-satisfaction from learning or creating. MIT attempts to cram 6 to 8 years worth of material in a four-year span — an experience that is exhilarating, but also draining. Recuperation time after a period of overwork may vary from needing a relaxing weekend to needing an entire care-free summer to get that enthusiasm back.

Some students, however, will *never* get that enthusiasm back. Long-term stress over a couple of years can do this. An MIT course load induces tunnel-vision, often causing students to pre-empt their own happiness for apparently more important, immediate concerns. Some will be able to drudge through their last few terms just to get that coveted $160,000 MIT degree, and will decide to pursue careers that have nothing to do with their major. Others may be even more unfortunate, reaching the point of burnout; when the same stimuli (paper deadlines, upcoming exams, end-of-term projects) that once motivated, now do the exact opposite.

Burnout is serious, and symptoms can be similar to depression. Along with general unhappiness, concentrating on work — or anything even remotely stressful — feels impossible. If work is turned in at all, it will be likely turned in late. MIT students commonly believe learning is their "purpose," and the inability to do work will make those burned out feel disabled or worthless. Keep in mind that the circumstances that push a student to the edge of burnout may be as much the result of problems in one's personal life (family, friends, relationships) as feeling unsatisfied in one's academic life.

While you're at MIT, keep the following suggestions and questions in mind:

1. As you plan your schedule, talk to as many upperclassmen in your major as possible. How good is the professor in such and such class? Some professors here are phenomenal, and will make you want to work your ass off and continue on to graduate school. Others will talk more to the chalkboard then to their students. Do *not* pick your classes using only the *MIT Bulletin* to see what you need to take next to graduate.

2. Do you like your classes? Most students go through growing pains because of the heavy course load. However, if you're a junior and still hate the classes in your major, don't think it's too late to change departments. Remember, just because you thought you wanted to be course 10 when you came here doesn't mean you (or really any freshman) knew exactly what course 10 was back then. Some students have such a serious case of tunnel-vision that they don't realize until their senior year how much they hate their department. Also, realize that MIT has a fairly narrow list of majors. If your interests have changed, and you're not happy, consider transferring.

3. If feeling overworked, can you take fewer classes? For some majors, you will only need about 3.5 classes every term. For other majors, taking an extra term or year to graduate is not the worst possible thing imaginable — especially if your mental or physical health is at risk.

4. Realize that, no matter how bad you may feel, other MIT students have felt and do feel the same way. There is nothing wrong with seeking help. If you feel troubled, talk to one of the resources in this chapter — most importantly a dean from Counseling and Support Services (`web.mit.edu/counsel/www/`). It's their job to help you. They can give advice on both personal and academic problems. They can also tell you the procedures for taking a term (or two) off or transferring to another school. (For more information about leaves of absence see the **Academics** chapter under withdrawals.) MIT is not necessarily the best academic or social environment for everyone. Even those students who graduate from MIT happy had hardly any idea what they were getting themselves into when they first came here.

Counseling Deans

The staff in Counseling and Support Services (5-104, x3-4861, web.mit.edu/counsel/www/) assist both undergraduate and graduate students with a wide range of issues ranging from the sublime to the mundane. The principal function of the office is to provide individual personal counseling services. This office is equipped and designed to solve continuing major problems as well as to offer quick solutions to short-term problems. International students, women, gay students, minority and disabled students also receive special assistance with programs and ideas especially concerned with their respective groups. The services offered by this division of the Office of the Dean of Student Life are so diverse that you may seek help there without anyone having the slightest idea what specifically brought you to the office until you explain your concern. This is done so that students will have no hesitation about seeking support when they need it.

Students can call or visit the office to talk about their questions, plans or problems. Whether your concerns are academic, administrative, career, financial, family, residential, social, legal, or personal, the people in this office are interested in hearing from you. Your problems will be kept strictly confidential. The staff of this office maintains close working relations with the psychiatric service (see the *Mental Health* section before you jump to conclusions) and Nightline (the student hotline, described in the *Nightline* section in this chapter).

The counselors in CSS handle withdrawals, readmissions, and excused absences from final examinations. They can also get your professors to give you some leeway on due dates if you need time to handle your problem. Students are often referred to this office by their instructors, advisors, housemasters, and by fellow students who have been helped by the office. Because the counseling deans meet with the Committee on Academic Performance and have a cooperative relationship with many Institute offices including Student Financial Aid, the Bursar's Office, the Registrar, and the Medical Department, many students find it helpful to discuss issues related to these other offices with the counseling deans.

Counseling and Support Services has special concerns for disabled students, for gay, lesbian, bisexual and transgender students, for minority students, and for women students. If you have a disability, see Dean Arnold Henderson to help implement special arrangements which may be necessary to deal with this environment. Each case is given individual attention and concern.

This section also supports the academic and personal well-being of women students and minority students by developing and coordinating specific programs and by responding to the concerns of individual students. The goal is to be sure that the MIT environment is supportive of minorities and women, and attractive to prospective students from these groups. Dean Ayida Mthembu is particularly involved with this aspect of the office.

Mental Health

The Institute mental health staff (E23-368, x3-2916) are good people to talk with. Whether you have problems (*any* problems), opinions on some subject, an idea you want to run up a flagpole or just want to see what makes them tick, invite one to your living group for a dinner or go see them.

There are about twenty clinicians on the staff; as with the Deans, it's OK to ask for a particular clinician if you know him or her. The wait on a visit is generally one week from the time you make the appointment. If you really need to talk to someone immediately, you can always find a clinician to see you on the same day you call, but you must make it clear to the receptionist that you need to see someone right away. Alternatively, you can see a therapist during walk-in hours, without an appointment, any weekday. Just come to the Mental Health Service on the third floor of E23 between 2pm and 4pm any weekday.

Most of the people who consult the mental health staff are psychologically indistinguishable from the general MIT population, and can *in no way* be classified as sick or disturbed. If some problem is bothering you, even if it is identical to those that everyone else faces, don't hesitate to visit the mental health service. They can keep small difficulties from becoming larger, or merely facilitate the solving of problems that you can mostly solve yourself.

Mental health records are kept separate from all others, including regular Medical Department records. The clinician *cannot* legally discuss you with anyone outside the staff unless you sign a release; even then you can specify the type of information to be released. The system is designed to maintain confidentiality. Only the mental health staff can use them — not the president, not the FBI, not the CIA, not *anybody* else (except maybe Der Führer von Homeland Defense, but that remains to be seen). This system protects patient and doctor alike.

If for any reason you don't hit it off with one clinician, feel free to contact another. You can switch without apology or explanation. Nobody will ask any questions.

A psychiatrist is on call 24 hours a day through the MIT Medical Department (Building E23, x3-1311 or x3-2916). See **Emergency Information**.

If the MIT Mental Health Department does not fit your needs, they can provide you with a list of off-campus possibilities covering a range of cost options. (If you have the MIT Student Health Insurance, it will cover at least part of the cost of seeing a therapist.)

Nightline x3-8800
Nightline is the main student-run help service on campus. It operates every night during the school year from 7 PM-7 AM. You can call Nightline at **617-253-8800**.

Nightline is both a counseling and an information service. If you're having problems with academics or your roommate; if you need information concerning birth control or drop date; or if you just need someone to talk to, give them a call. *All phone calls to Nightline are strictly anonymous and confidential.*

Nightline is staffed exclusively by MIT students; each night there will be at least one female and one male staffer on duty. The staff members are volunteers who have received training in peer counseling and crisis counseling and have experience dealing with an enormous range of issues, but they *are not* professionals. While Nightline is not meant to be a substitute for professional counseling services, Nightline staffers can direct you to the right professionals to talk to if you decide you'd like to pursue counseling. More importantly, Nightline staffers are there to listen — if you just need to vent about MIT, if you need to settle an obscure bet about the area (in square miles and/or meters) of San Juan, or if there's been something seriously upsetting you for a while and you just want to get it off your chest.

If you feel that you might be interested in becoming one of the Nightline staff, give them a call — **Def Tuv Tuv Oper Oper**.

Other Resources

In addition to the services mentioned in this chapter, don't overlook your personal resources — graduate resident tutors or housemasters in your living group (that's what they're paid for!), friends, a coach or professor you trust. People are usually a lot more willing to listen than you might imagine — many of them may have been through the same thing.

Also, the secretaries in many of the offices around the Institute know a tremendous amount about MIT. By speaking with one of them first, you will probably save yourself a lot of running around.

Religious Counselors

Religious Counselors are warm and friendly people who can help you view your problems from a different angle. A number of faiths maintain full-time clergymen on campus at the Religious Counselors' building (W2A, 312 Memorial Dr.). Adherents to other faiths can usually find clergy in the Boston area, but they should also feel free to talk to any of the people listed below. See *Religion* in the **Activities** chapter for more information.

The following religious groups maintain clergy on campus:

American Baptist	Rev. John Wuestneck	617-452-1780
Assemblies of God	Rev. Mike Olejarz	617-253-2327
Buddhist	Ven. Tenzin LS Priyadarshi	617-324-6030
Campus Crusade for Christ	Rev. George Hinman	
Church of Jesus Christ of Latter Day Saints	Dr. Lewis Clark Christian	617-547-6188
Episcopal	Rev. Amy McCreath	617-253-2983
Jewish(Hillel)	Rabbi Ben Lanckton	617-253-2982
	Rabbi Gershon Segal	617-253-2982
	Miriam Rosenblum	617-253-2982
Lutheran	Rev. Johanna Kiefner	617-253-2325
Methodist	Rev. John Wuestneck	617-252-1780
Muslim	Suheil Laher	617-252-1781
Presbyterian	Rev. John Wuestneck	617-452-1780
Roman Catholic	Father Paul Reynolds	617-452-1779
Southern Baptist	Rev. Michael Dean	617-253-2328
United Church of Christ	Rev. John Wuestneck	617-452-1780
Vedanta Society	Cyrus Mehta	617-253-2327
	Swami Tyagananda	617-536-5320

Self-Help

The MIT lifestyle can be incredibly stressful, and it's easy to be overwhelmed sometimes. Often when you are struggling with a worry or difficulty, you may feel it is too trivial to talk it over with one of the people mentioned in this chapter. Although none of the counseling resources mentioned will consider *any* problem too trivial to talk with them about, sometimes it can still be difficult to make that first phone call or appointment. It can seem like there's a general attitude of extreme self-sufficiency here at MIT, but that doesn't mean you should have to suffer through a problem or a stressful time on your own.

As a general rule, the time to consider seeking help is when (or before!) your problem is beginning to interfere with everyday functioning (it may actually be easier to reach out before it gets to this point). Are you skipping classes and having serious trouble concentrating? Has there been a big change in your eating or sleeping patterns? Are you feeling so low or down that you're having trouble getting out of bed in the morning, or finding it difficult to get excited about activities or accomplishments you used to find stimulating? If any of these things sound like you, *talk to someone*. It may be too much to try and deal with how you feel and the demands of MIT at the same time. You might feel a great deal better if you could just share the burden with someone. Reach out before things get any worse.

If you're not yet quite comfortable with any of the resources listed here (or if you're trying to decide whom to turn to), the following suggestions may help in the meantime:

1. Try taking a mini-vacation from MIT: a bus trip out to Wellesley, an afternoon at the Aquarium or a museum, a weekend away if you can manage it. (A list of museums and such is in the **Sightseeing** chapter.) If you're under a lot of stress, your first reaction to time off is probably "I can't afford the time!" But sometimes you can't afford *not* to. If you return refreshed, you may get more work done in the long run. If you can't *physically* get away, try letting yourself do something for fun that you've been putting off for a while. Read a book that's not related to your work, or really *enjoy* one of the magazines that have been piling on your desk. Hang a "do not disturb" sign on your door and take a nap. Buy all the ingredients for a favorite dish and cook it for yourself. Don't feel guilty for not doing work, everyone deserves some time off. In other words, punt.

2. Try to exercise. If you're feeling down, it can be really hard to motivate yourself, but it can work wonders. Run, dance, swim, ride a bike, walk. Enjoy the Esplanade.

3. Make a list of ten good things about yourself. Force yourself to put ten things down, even if it's "I had perfect attendance in eighth grade" or "My eyes are a nice shade of brown." For one week, add three more things to the list every night before you go to bed.

4. Try starting a journal. Write things in it that you can't tell anyone. Start as many sentences as you can with "I feel...". Make a point to write in it every couple of days. Then go back and reread it often; you may be surprised.

5. Do something nice for someone else. Write to a past high school or MIT instructor and tell them how much their class meant to you. Send someone you love flowers or a nice card for no special reason. Cut a clipping from the newspaper that you think would be of interest to someone you haven't seen in a while and drop it to them in the mail. Buy a friend's favorite flavor of ice cream and hide it in their freezer with a note. Give a friend a compliment. If it feels good, consider doing some kind of volunteer work. Be a Big Brother or Sister or help out a shelter for homeless people. There are also many service organizations on campus that would be happy to have another person helping with their projects. Consult the Public Service Center in 4-104 at x3-0742.

6. Talk to a friend you trust. Ask an upperclassman (or underclassman!) if they've ever confronted a similar problem and how they handled it. Continue asking around and try not to get discouraged. You'd be surprised what others have gone through.

7. Buy a joke book. Read out of it every day until you get one good belly laugh. Before the next day's reading, tell the joke that made you crack up to someone else.

8. Do something childish once in awhile. Find a playground and swing on a swing. Go shopping in a toy store. Visit the Children's Museum. Buy a box of 64 crayons and a pad of white paper. Use them. Blow soap bubbles. Skip down Mass. Ave. while singing.

9. Spend some time thinking about the long-term priorities of your life. Try to get a little closer to deciding what you want to be and what you want to accomplish with your life. Buy a copy of R. N. Bolles' *What Color Is Your Parachute?*; or talk with your friends or someone in the Career Services and Preprofessional Advising (12-170, x3-4733) about your strengths. Try to include some of the things that will move you closer to your long-range goals in your life.

The sooner that your difficulty is intercepted, the less damage it will do to your social and academic life — and your mental health. If none of these suggestions really seems to help, consider turning to one of the other resources in this chapter.

Social Workers

There are five social workers in residence (E23-344, x3-4911), who are good at mobilizing and integrating the resources available for solving various personal and family problems. They can suggest and contact agencies that may be needed. They can also help with substance abuse problems. They specialize in helping foreign students (and their families) adjust to living in the United States.

Drugs

Although many people do go through MIT without being exposed to it, there is some drug activity at MIT, and for some people their first exposure to drugs may occur here at MIT. If you have a problem within your living group, see someone in confidential authority there, like a graduate resident tutor. Often a word or two in the right ear will solve the problem. By all means, if the problem persists after that, go through official channels — the Dean's Office can help without causing problems.

If your interest is more speculative, three words of advice:

1. "Just Say No" is more than a trite slogan. Make sure you know exactly what you're doing, and don't try anything just because "everyone else is doing it."

2. *Don't* assume the Campus Police will protect you from the Cambridge authorities. Contrary to common opinion, there is no "buffer zone" between students and the outside world.

3. Don't force anything. See what the scene is like before getting involved.

On a personal level, the Counseling Deans (5-104, x3-4861) offer confidential drug counseling. To supplement their services, the Science Library maintains technical reports on drug safety while the Campus Police (W31, x3-1212) is always available to answer legal questions. *Straight Talk About Drugs on Campus* is available from the Campus Police. Even straighter talk is contained in an underground student publication called *DaMIT: Drugs at MIT*. It was first published following the tragic and avoidable death of Richard "DickGuy" Guy, a friend and comrade to many, and is a coherent, responsibly written source aimed at protecting people who have already decided to experiment. If you find the pamphlet useful (`fortytwo.mit.edu/archive/damit.htm`), its authors ask that you do your fellow students a favor by making extra copies and leaving them around, as these pro-bono student publications have a tendency to fade away if not kept track of. The above webpage also provides an interesting response by three MIT Medical physicians, linked at the bottom of the page, that is worth reading in conjunction with the pamphlet. You can also consult the Mental Health Service (x3-2916).

Adverse Reactions

In an emergency, call the Medical Department's Urgent Care Line at x3-1311 — the psychiatrist on call will go over if possible. Campus Police will also provide help (restraint, transportation, reassurance) if called. The Dean-on-Call (reached through the Campus Police, x3-1212) or Nightline are other resources if you just need to talk or you're not sure what to do. *In any case, make sure the person in trouble is never left alone — being so may cost his or her life.* For most cases, overnight care may be given at the Inpatient Unit without formal hospitalization.

Addiction

Don't worry about legal penalties; the addiction is penalty enough. See someone in the Dean's Office, Mental Health, or Internal Medicine, and break the habit. Remember that psychiatric records are completely confidential. Not even your primary care physician sees them.

Awareness

Drug Education Information is available through the Health Education Office (E23-205, x3-1316). Books, pamphlets, and other various materials are available to students as well as a list of local area resources.

Sex

One of the best sources of written information is *Our Bodies, Ourselves for the New Century*, available at almost any bookstore. The cover says that it is "written by and for women," but it is recommended for everyone. Also, the Medical Department has several pamphlets dealing with special topics. Stop by and browse (E23-205). Members of the Mental Health Service also have experience as sexual counselors (x3-2916).

Don't rush to have sex just because you're now at college. There can be a lot of pressure, especially if "everyone" in your living group is sexually active. While it may seem that way, appearances can be deceptive. Remember the old adage: "Teenage sex is like e-commerce; everyone thinks everyone else is doing it, but not that many people are actually doing it, and those who are doing it aren't doing it well." If you're not sure, you're probably not ready. Nightline (x3-8800) can help you think things through, as well as offer advice on birth control and protection from sexually-transmitted diseases.

Pregnancy

If you have even the slightest suspicion that you are pregnant, get a pregnancy test immediately. (Pregnancy tests are free from the MIT Medical Department and many Boston clinics.) Prompt action will save you lots of trouble later. If you decide on an abortion, the procedure is safer and cheaper earlier; if you decide to carry to term, early care will help your child later. Even though it may be very difficult, it's important to remember that *you gain nothing from waiting and worrying*. If you're worried or scared and want to talk things through, Nightline (x3-8800) is an anonymous and confidential resource (again, Nightline staffers have been trained in counseling and have a large knowledge base about resources available to the MIT community), or call the MIT Medical Department or a clinic (see the Yellow Pages) and refer to *Our Bodies, Ourselves for the New Century* for further information.

If you are pregnant, you still have options. You can choose to keep the child, put it in foster care (*e.g.*, with a relative until you are out of school), give the child up for adoption, or have an abortion.

Abortion

Abortion is a procedure which terminates pregnancy. If done during the first trimester, the actual procedure is very brief and can be performed as an outpatient procedure.

Never opt for an illegal abortion. Abortion has been legal in the United States for three decades, despite some conservative groups' very vocal opposition, and abortions performed at certified clinics are quite safe. The Medical Department's Obstetrics/Gynecology Service (x3-1315) offers completely confidential counseling and referrals. The Member Services Office (x3-5979) can tell you about health insurance coverage. The social workers at Planned Parenthood (1055 Commonwealth Ave., 617-616-1660) can also direct you to good legal abortion centers and provide information and counseling.

Birth Control

Anybody connected with MIT can obtain contraceptive information and prescriptions from the Medical Department regardless of age or marital status. As always, such matters are confidential between the patient and the physician.

The Dean's office started a program of distributing condoms in dormitories. Dispensers may be located in bathrooms or stairwells; your graduate resident tutor or resident advisor should be able to offer specifics. Your GRT/RA should also have a supply of condoms on hand in case the dispensers are empty.

Workshops on safer sex are available for presentation to interested student groups. Call the Medical Department's Health Education Service (x3-1316) for more information.

Sexually Transmitted Diseases

Sexually transmitted diseases (STD's) are at or near epidemic levels throughout the US. The most dangerous STD is AIDS, Acquired Immune Deficiency Syndrome. This deadly virus is transmitted only by the exchange of body fluids, such as blood or semen. There is *no known cure* for the disease, but it *is* possible to reduce the risk of developing it by practicing "safer sex" (use a condom) and limiting the number of sexual partners you have. Groups with a particularly high risk of contracting the virus are intravenous drug users and people who have had unprotected sex. If you suspect that you may have HIV or may have been exposed to it, you can see an internist at the Medical Department. Testing for HIV infection is done confidentially at MIT, at no charge; the results are *not* placed in your medical record. You can also get a confidential screening for the HIV antibody at Mass. General Hospital (MGH, 617-726-2000) or the Fenway Community Health Center (617-267-0900). For more information, referrals, or counseling, call the Massachusetts HIV Counseling and Testing Hotline (800-235-2331, Mon.-Fri. 9am-9pm, Sat. 10am-2pm). The Med Department can also help, of course, with examinations and information.

Most other STDs are curable *if treated early*. If you suspect you have one, contact the Medical Department and get checked; lab tests are quick and accurate. If you do have one, it's your responsibility to tell *all* of your partners and encourage them to get tested. Remember, STD's are often without early symptoms in females though they can have serious consequences for both genders years later. Some people advise getting tested every year for everything if you are sexually active. The tests are covered by your MIT insurance and take almost no time at all.

Counseling

Planned Parenthood, physicians, psychiatrists, social workers, and a clinical sociologist as well as clinics, religious counselors, and social service groups can be useful for helping you make your decisions about sexual activity. MIT has five social workers in residence (see *Social Workers*). The social workers and the Dean's Office can be particularly helpful in dealing with monetary problems.

Rape

If a rape has just occurred, go immediately to a safe location and call the Campus Police (617-253-1212, or 100 from any Institute phone), 911, or a friend whom you trust for transportation to a medical facility. The Campus Police have female officers trained in rape crisis available at all times — just ask. The Boston Area Rape Crisis Center (BARCC, 617-492-7273), located in Cambridge, is an excellent organization that provides a number of services to rape survivors, including a 24 hr. hotline (English: 1-800-841-8371; Spanish: 1-800-223-5001), counseling services, and legal services. BARCC also has medical advocates on-call who can accompany you to the hospital and provide you with information and support the entire time you are at the hospital.

Even though it may be extremely difficult to do so after such a traumatic experience, it is important to seek medical treatment as soon as possible. Beth Israel Deaconess, the Cambridge Hospital and Boston Medical Center all have special medical teams for rape victims. They will typically do a general exam and check for internal injuries. You may also choose to be tested for pregnancy, STDs and foreign substances if you believe you were drugged. You have the right to refuse or reject any part of the medical exam. Getting a medical exam does not make a committment to pressing charges, however evidence gathered at a hospital may be held for at least six months at your request, whether or not you decide to file a complaint. Reporting a rape is your choice.

If you are going to press charges, it is important *not* to wash, change clothing, or straighten up anything before calling the police or going to the hospital. If you decide not to go to the police immediately, write down everything about the assault you can remember, if you can. Keep these details in case you change your mind.

If you have been raped in the past there are a number of resources available to help you deal with the experience and its after effects. Rape is a serious trauma and it is important to get help in dealing with it, but you are the only one who can decide when you're ready to begin talking about your experience. If and when you do decide to begin talking to someone about your experience, the mental health staff at the Med Center are always available. BARCC is also an excellent resource, providing long term counseling, hotline services, and support groups with over 20 years of experience. If you're not yet comfortable with any of these resources, Nightline (x3-8800) may be a convenient way to begin talking in an anonymous, confidential context (remember, Nightline staffers are trained to deal with all sorts of issues). Talking about it may help you decide if you're ready to seek out any of the other resources available to you.

Acquaintance Rape

If some one you know forces you to have sex against your will or without your consent, it is rape. Whether or not you agreed to go to their room, or whether you had anything to drink, *no still means no*. If you were unable to give consent because you were unconscious or incapacitated, it's still rape. It may be difficult to call it that for many reasons — it may be difficult to come to terms with what happened, or you may be reluctant to identify some one you know as a rapist. What ever the case may be, it's important that you find support.

If you have more questions or would like to become involved with sexual violence prevention groups on campus, you can contact Stop Our Silence (sos-admin@mit.edu).

Missing Persons

If you can't find someone after going through all the usual channels (friends, neighbors, GRTs etc.), call Campus Police (x3-1212) and the Housemaster of your dorm, if you live in one. Be prepared to supply all the resident information on the missing person. Don't call the person's home unless it's absolutely necessary. The Dean's Office will handle it.

Harassment

"Some of the people in my dorm refuse to stop making crude and tasteless racial jokes in my presence. They recently pulled a few hacks which embarrassed and humiliated me. I am fed up with their brand of humor!"

"One of my professors propositioned me. Even though I told him that I'm not interested, he keeps hinting around that it might make a difference in my grade."

"I make no secret of my homosexual preferences, and I don't try to impose my beliefs on others. However, my frankness has made me the target of all kinds of abuse and insults. I've had to move out of my dorm..."

If you are being unreasonably bothered by any person or group of people, *tell someone*. You do not have to just suffer silently and put up with or ignore such behavior. The Institute has a very strict policy on harassment, which is defined as "verbal or physical conduct which has the intent or effect of unreasonably interfering with an individual's educational and/or work performance at MIT, or creating an intimidating, hostile or offensive educational or work environment on or off campus." The *intent* and *effect* are both important because if someone is hurting you, even if they don't mean to, they should be made aware of it and stopped.

If you can't get the offensive behavior to stop on your own, *speak with someone at the Institute about it*. In addition to any of the resources mentioned earlier in this chapter, you might like to talk to one of the Ombudspersons (x3-5921), who are great to talk to and will take your problem very seriously.

If the harassment is taking place over the Athena system, send mail to stopit@mit.edu. Stopit deals with all types of violations of the *Athena Rules of Use*, of which harassment is one.

If you would like more information before you talk to someone, look up harassment in the index of the *MIT Course Catalog*.

Prejudice

If you feel mistreated in any way for reasons of racial, ethnic, or sexual bias, speak to Mary Rowe (10-213, x3-5921), Special Assistant to the President (Ombudsperson). If you feel you have been the victim of discrimination in employment or other opportunities, take your complaint to the Affirmative Action/Equal Opportunity and Diversity Programs Office (E19-215, x8-8718).

MIT has an *Affirmative Action Plan* presenting the Institute's objectives and procedures for ensuring equal opportunity for minorities and women in employment (both) and in letting contracts. Copies of this plan are on file in the Information Center (7-121, x3-4795), and in the various Personnel Offices, and, undoubtedly, in the Affirmative Action/Equal opportunity and Diversity Programs Office.

Massachusetts also maintains an agency to deal with cases of suspected discrimination, the Massachusetts Commission Against Discrimination (One Ashburton Place, Rm. 601, Boston, 617-994-6000, www.state.ma.us/mcad/).

Nighttime Safety
MIT is an urban school!

There have been cases of armed robbery, rape, and assault on campus. Some years ago, two MIT students were assaulted on Memorial Drive at 9:30pm and one was murdered. More recently, other students have been assaulted and robbed on the Harvard Bridge. There have also been many muggings in the Main Street/Kendall Square area. Don't ever carry large sums of money alone, especially after dark. Avoid unlit or isolated areas such as Briggs Field or even the parking garages. Let someone know where you'll be and when you expect to return. On returning to campus from outlying communities, give some thought to well-lit routes. Wherever you go after dark, try to have a few friends with you if possible and, for goodness' sake, when the soundtrack music becomes tense and increases in volume, be careful rounding blind corners.

If requested, the Campus Police (x3-1212) will escort late working students and employees from main buildings to dorms or parking lots at night. The **SafeRide** vans run every night from 6pm until 3 or 4am depending on the day, and the police are willing to send a car for you until the morning. When in doubt, *call them*. It's not worth the risk. The Campus Police have a wide variety of crime prevention and safety information available from their Crime Prevention Unit. Stop by anytime.

Women's Resources

Since males outnumber females at MIT, women here may have different experiences and problems than they would in other places. All services that are open for males are also available for women; in addition, a few activities and services especially for women are available.

The Margaret Cheney Room (3-310, x3-4880) is a suite of rooms especially set aside for female students. It has a grand piano, complete kitchen equipment, beds, study areas, and showers. It serves as a meeting place for women's activities and women in general. Women students can obtain access to the combination by bringing their MIT I.D. to the Counseling and Support Services in Room 5-104, x3-4861. Locker space is also available from the same office. Various women's groups use the Cheney Room for their meetings and social gatherings. In order to reserve the rooms for such activities, call x3-4861.

If you are female and have a problem (medical, social, academic, psychological), all the couseling and medical services of the Institute are open to you. However, if you prefer counseling or treatment by a female, you can get it. Try talking to Lynn Roberson of CSS (x3-4861). Be warned of "women prejudiced against women"; it does happen sometimes.

MIT Medical has a significant number of women doctors with training in various specialties including internal medicine, dermatology, and obstetrics/gynecology. Gynecology is covered by MIT Students' Medical Insurance. Birth control advice and contraceptives are available on a confidential basis to those who want them. For more information call the Medical Department. They will also provide referrals for abortions.

If you should find yourself discriminated against because of your sex, (or any other reason), notify Mary Rowe (10-213, x3-5921), Special Assistant to the President (Ombudsperson), who is specifically concerned with the quality of life for all women and men connected with MIT.

Women's groups at MIT include:

Association of MIT Alumnae (W59-221, `alumweb.mit.edu/groups/amita`) AMITA serves as an organization through which current students may meet with alumnae to discuss careers, chat informally, etc. AMITA may be contacted through the Alumni Association.

Society of Women Engineers (W20-447, x3-2096, `web.mit.edu/swe/www/`) SWE is an international organization of engineers and scientists dedicated to supporting the professional interests of women. The MIT SWE section supports the objectives of the national organization with career guidance, professional development, and friendly support. They are a social and personnel support group for women of all disciplines. SWE has office hours from Tuesday through Thursday from 3pm-5pm during the school year.

Spouses&Partners@MIT (`web.mit.edu/medical/spousesandpartners/`, E23-368, x3-1614,) is a support and self-help program sponsored by MIT Medical for American and international spouses of students, staff, faculty, and visiting scientists. It helps members develop a social network and make connections with people and resources in order to find jobs, further education, do volunteer work, and/or develop careers.

Women's Advisory Board is a committee of representatives of women's groups at MIT which serves as a lobbying group for improvements or decisions affecting MIT women. Representatives are chosen by women's groups. For more information contact Mary Rowe (10-213, x3-5921).

Women's Athletic Leagues There are a large number of MIT women's athletic leagues: ice hockey, rugby, soccer, tennis, volleyball. There's even a team for women who have never played organized sports before that calls itself the Ultimate Team. They are all listed at `web.mit.edu/life/category/women.html` (along with a number of other organizations listed in this section).

Women's Forum (`web.mit.edu/committees/womensforum/`) Members include all women at MIT. They meet at noon on the first and third Mondays of the month to discuss a wide variety of topics and offer a good opportunity for faculty, employees, spouses, and students to get together. (x3-7741).

MIT Women's League (`web.mit.edu/womensleague/`) includes all wives of faculty, administrative and research staff and all female staff members. They have a meeting room (Emma Rogers Room, 10-340) and an adjoining office (10-342, x3-3656). In addition to having special programs, members are involved in a number of projects that benefit the community at large (*e.g.*, furniture exchange, English classes for foreign wives, Christmas Convocation, Seminar Series, and the Newcomer Welcoming Committee).

Stop Our Silence (`web.mit.edu/stop/www/`) is an MIT student group dedicated to promoting education about and prevention of sexual violence. While not explicitly a women's organization — after all, rape is not solely a feminist issue — SOS does provide a forum where women can voice their concerns about sexual violence. SOS organizes Take Back the Night Rallies, supports the Clothesline Project at MIT, and organizes speakers and screenings periodically.

There are many more women's groups on campus; a few of them have been indexed at web.mit.edu/life/category/women.html, but there are many more that aren't listed.

Off-campus women's organizations include:

Boston Women's Health Book Collective (34 Plympton St., Boston MA 02118, 617-451-3666, www.bwhbc.org) has written the book *Our Bodies, Ourselves for the New Century* and has an ongoing interest in health care and services.

Women's Law Collective (620 Massachusetts Ave, Cambridge, MA; 617-492-5110) is a group of women attorneys who handle private legal matters. They also test litigation on problems affecting women. If they accept your case, their services are free.

Check with the **Center for New Words** (www.newwordsbooks.com, 186 Hampshire St., Cambridge; 617-876-5310) for other local feminist publications, clubs *etc.*

Lost and Found

If you lose something in a dorm, ask at the desk. Everywhere else on campus, found items are sent to the Campus Police at W31-215, x3-9753. If you lose something (as opposed to considering it stolen), you can report it at web.mit.edu/cp/www/admin.shtml. The CPs will contact you if the item turns up.

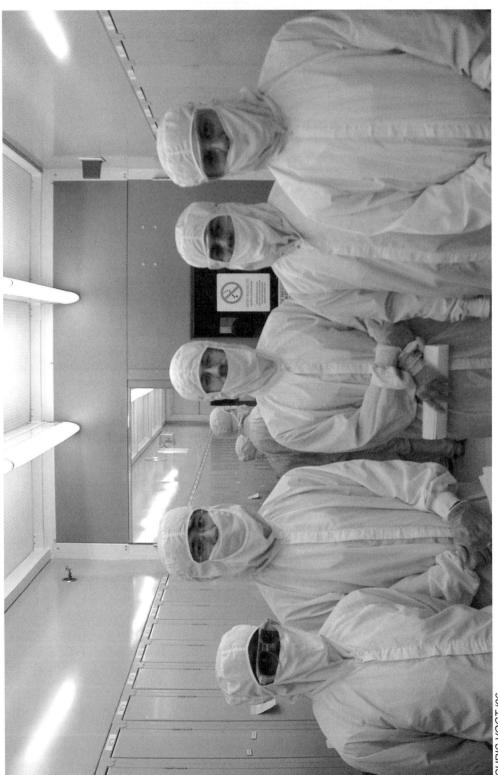

Medical Resources

MIT Medical Department

MIT Medical, in the Health Services Center (E23), is a multispecialty group practice employing 24 full-time and 50 part-time physicians as well as other medical professionals. MIT Medical services are available to all members of the MIT community including students, faculty and staff.

MIT Medical clinicians provide primary care in internal medicine, surgery, and pediatrics, amongst other services. Most medical specialties are also available on campus: a pharmacy, a full-time optometry service including contact lens services, and diagnostic testing facilities including a laboratory and radiology (x-ray) department. A dental service that offers treatment for students and their spouses is available on a fee-for-service basis.

All visits to MIT Medical are by appointment except in emergencies. The regular hours are from 8:30am to 5:00pm Monday through Friday, except during holidays. A few departments, such as the Ophthalmology Department and the Mental Health Department, regularly keep somewhat later hours, staying open until 6:00 or 7:00 in the evening. Same-day appointments are usually available for patients who are sick, so be sure to call your doctor's office. **Emergency medical care is available through Urgent Care 24 hours a day, 7 days a week. Telephone x3-1311 (617-253-1311 from off campus) to contact the clinician on duty for advice.** Clinicians do not make house calls, but if someone is too ill to come to the Health Services Center without assistance call the Campus Police at 100 or x3-1212 to contact the 24-hour student ambulance service.

MIT Medical services and contact information:

After-Hours Service	x3-1311	Nutrition *	x3-1546
Allergy	x3-4460	Obstetrics/Gynecology	x3-1315
Audiology *	x3-7870	Occupational Health	x3-8552
Billing Office	x8-5336	Ophthalmology	x3-4351
Cardiology	x3-4904	Optical Shop	x8-5367
Claims and Member Services	x3-5979	Orthopedics *	x3-2974
Dental	x3-1501	Patient Advocate	x3-4976
Dermatology	x3-4295	Patient Billing	x8-5336
Ear, Nose, Throat *	x3-7870	Pediatrics	x3-1505
Eye	x3-4351	Personal Assistance Program	x3-4911
Gastroenterology *	x3-1681	Pharmacy	x3-1234
Health Plans Office	x3-4371	Podiatry *	x3-1681
Health Promotion and Wellness	x3-1316	Prescription Refill Line (24hrs.)	x3-0202
Health Screening	x3-1777	Pulmonary Medicine	x3-4355
Inpatient Service	x3-5486	Surgery	x3-1302
Internal Medicine	x3-4481	Support Groups	x3-2916
Laboratory *	x3-4239	Urgent Care	x3-1311
Medical Director	x3-1716	Urology *	x3-4356
Medical Records	x3-4906	X-Ray/Mammography *	x3-4905
Mental Health	x3-2916		
Neurology *	x3-3956	*Referral by MIT Physician Required*	

The quality of care given at the Medical Center can be fairly good, despite the oft-repeated adage "They test you for pregnancy and mono, and if those are both negative they tell you it's nothing." If you are not happy with how you are treated, call the Patient Advocate at x3-4976 or email advocate@mit.edu.

A major goal of MIT Medical is to make high quality medical care accessible to the entire MIT community. Members of the student community can choose a personal physician whom they can consult whenever an illness, problem, or question arises. To choose or change your personal phsyician, contact Patient Registration at x3-6286. If you are not sure who your primary care physician is, call x3-4481. If the appropiate personal physician is not available and the need is urgent, the patient will be seen by another physician, nurse practitioner, or physician's assistant, with subsequent referral if needed. In this way, patients who call or come to Medical for care are seen by a health professional on the same day.

An 18-bed Inpatient Service is operated by MIT Medical for patients who cannot be cared for at home but for whom hospitalization in a general hospital is inappropriate. Children are not admitted to the Inpatient Service, but if necessary are referred to a nearby hospital offering pediatric care. Patients requiring major surgery or treatment for serious illness are sent to one of the Boston or Cambridge hospitals where their care is usually supervised by one of the MIT Medical physicians or surgeons. The Inpatient Service can be reached at x3-5486.

MIT Medical's Center for Health Promotion and Wellness is located in E23-205. The four health educators at the Center offer free information on a variety of topics, including stress management, nutrition, sexual health, relationships, sleep, alcohol, and drugs. Students may privately discuss health concerns with a health educator either by appointment, phone-call or e-mail. They can be reached at x3-1316. Health educators are also available to do workshops for dorms, FSILGs or student groups. The Health Promotion and Wellness website has further useful information at web.mit.edu/medical/a-center.html

Whether a patient will be billed directly for services at the Health Services Center depends on the health program in which the student, affiliate, or employee is enrolled. Most of the medical services provided on campus are available to students at no cost. Call patient billing (for students, x3-4303) if you have any questions about charges. You probably received a chart which lists all the free services, but if you lost it or did not receive it go to web.mit.edu/medical/p-student.html for the online list. The cost of off-campus medical care and hospitalization is extremely high in the Boston area. For this reason, it is extremely important that everyone maintain adequate health insurance. (See *Health Insurance* and *Dental Insurance*, below.)

Brochures describing MIT Medical, the Student Health Program, the Affiliate Health Program, and the MIT Health Plans for employees are available in the Member Services Office (E23-191, x3-5979). Your questions or suggestions for improvement within the Department are always welcome and can be directed to any staff member or to the Patient Advocate (x3-4976).

Area Hospitals and Clinics

Mass. General Hospital (55 Fruit St., Boston, 617-726-2000; MBTA: Charles/MGH; www.mgh.harvard.edu). Nearest hospital to MIT. General walk-in clinic 8.30am to 8pm Monday-Friday, most clinics by appointment. Regular hospital facilities. 24-hour emergency care. By car from campus, cross the Longfellow Bridge and turn in left after you pass under the elevated T line.

Children's Hospital (300 Longwood Ave., Boston, 617-355-6000; MBTA: Longwood or Longwood Medical; web1.tch.harvard.edu). Usually accepts patients up to age 21. General medical and surgical inpatient service, and extensive outpatient clinics. Handles everything from dental care to plastic surgery. 24-hour emergency service.

Brigham & Women's Hospital (75 Francis St., Boston, 617-732-5500; MBTA: Longwood or Brigham Circle; www.brighamandwomens.org). Obstetrics and Gynecology, orthopedics, neuroscience, diagnostics, outpatient care.

Cambridge Hospital (1493 Cambridge St., Cambridge, 617-665-1000; MBTA: Harvard then #69 bus; www.challiance.org). Primary care, outpatient clinics, pediatrics, 24-hour emergency including psychiatric. By car from campus, go up Hampshire St. from One Kendall Square, turn left onto Cambridge Street and follow the signs.

Mount Auburn Hospital (330 Mt. Auburn St., Cambridge, 617-492-3500; MBTA: Harvard; www.mtauburn.caregroup.org). General services, inpatient and outpatient clinics, walk-in clinic 8am to 7pm Monday-Friday and 10am to 5pm Saturday/ Sunday; 24-hour emergency, specialists on call.

McLean Hospital (115 Mill St., Belmont, 617-855-2000; MBTA: Harvard then #73 bus; www.mclean.harvard.edu). Extensive mental health services including substance abuse, bipolar and psychotic disorders and eating disorders.

Somerville Hospital (230 Highland Ave., Somerville, 617-591-4500; MBTA: Davis then #88 bus; www.challiance.org). Primary care, outpatient clinics, pediatrics.

Health Insurance

Massachusetts law requires that students have comprehensive health insurance. MIT students are automatically covered by the Student Health Plan, paid for through tuition. The Student Health Plan covers most services provided at MIT Medical. This insurance can also be purchased for spouses and children of MIT students. See web.mit.edu/ medical/p-student.html for more details on cost and enrolment.

For coverage (*e.g.* hospitalization) outside of MIT Medical, students are automatically enrolled in the MIT Student Extended Insurance Plan unless they choose to waive this coverage because they are already covered under their family's plan. If you are already covered, you need to show proof of coverage by the beginning of each semester (August 1 and February 1) to waive MIT's insurance before being charged for it. The decision to waive is important and should be considered carefully. Compare the benefits offered by MIT's policy and your family's. Students often find out too late that their coverage is not adequate. Questions regarding any facet of medical insurance can be directed to the MIT Health Plans Office (E23-308, x3-4371), or visit web.mit.edu/ medical/p-student for more information.

Faculty, staff, employees, and their families may be eligible for either the Traditional or Flexible MIT Health Plan. Both are prepaid comprehensive programs of medical care. Medical services for the MIT Health Plans are provided by MIT Medical. Outside hospitalization, apart from emergency care, is provided at any Blue Cross/Blue Shield affiliated local hospital, such as Mass. General, Mt. Auburn and Cambridge Hospitals for general procedures, Brigham and Women's Hospital for obstetric and gynecological care, and the Children's Hospital for pediatric care. The Flexible plan gives you the option to use almost any doctor or hospital outside the MIT Health Plan network when you pay part of the cost. If you are interested, you should talk to the MIT Health Plans Office at (E23-308, x3-4371).

Dental Insurance

Health insurance plans, including the extended plan offered by MIT, do not generally cover dental care except in very dire situations. However, thanks to years of advocacy by the GSC, as of August 2003 MIT graduate and undergraduate students have several options for affordable dental care. These options span the two methods by which a student may choose to receive dental care: purchasing dental insurance or paying for dentistry as needed through walk-in care.

In the category of dental insurance, MIT students are now able to purchase the Boston University Student Dental Plan, which costs $175 per year (or $130 per semester) and utilizes student dentists from the Boston University dental school. More information regarding the Boston University Student Dental Plan can be found at `dentalschool.bu.edu/sdp/`

If walk-in care is preferred, the choices available are the MIT, Harvard and BU dental centers. Certified dentists practice at MIT Dental (`web.mit.edu/medical/services/s-dental.html`), and provide services at costs comparable to market value, with a discount of 10 percent (as of March 2003) given to MIT students. Harvard Dental Center (`www.harvarddentalcenter.harvard.edu`) provides three choices for dental care based on who provides service — a faculty dentist, a post-doctoral student training for a dental specialty, or a pre-doctoral dental student — with the first being the most expensive at market value and the last being the least expensive. Although the dental care provided by the pre-doctoral dental students is much less expensive than the faculty practice, they cannot perform x-rays, orthodontics or certain other more complicated procedures.

The final, and in many ways most attractive, option is to take advantage of the deal negotiated by the GSC and the MIT Benefits Office in 2003. MIT students can now obtain a ten percent discount at Boston University Dental Health Center for walk-in care. With this option, services are performed by post-doctoral students who are not restricted in the types of procedures they can perform in the way that pre-doctoral students are. It is difficult to compare the costs of various dental care providers because there is no fixed price for most procedures, and the cost depends on the specifics of the dental work that is done. However, based on average values, and with the 10% discount that MIT students now receive, dental care at the BU Dental Health Center is cheaper than any of the alternatives listed above, including the pre-doctoral teaching practice from Harvard Dental

School. Information regarding both the MIT and BU dental programs is gathered on the GSC website: web.mit.edu/gsc/www/studentlife/health/dental.

Mental Health Service

MIT Medical's Mental Health Service is staffed by nine psychiatrists, four psychologists, seven Licensed Independent Clinical Social Workers and five clinical nurse specialists. The service is open from 8:30am to 7pm Mondays through Thursdays, and Fridays from 8:30am to 5pm. The service also offers walk-in hours Monday through Friday from 2pm-4pm, during which you can see a clinician without having made an appointment for that day. There is always one clinician on duty and reachable at x3-2916, even during nights and weekends.

To make an appointment, call x3-2916 or stop by the office located at E23-368. When patients make an initial appointment, they are offered a 20-minute, same-day phone consultation with a mental health clinician, which helps the service match patients with the most appropriate clinician. An initial appointment is made within a week. Any information discussed with a mental health clinician is confidential and can only be disclosed with your consent. If you would rather speak to someone outside MIT, the mental health staff will provide referrals to off-campus clinicians, although you may not always be referred to a psychiatrist. If an admission is necessary, patients are generally referred to inpatient facilities at McLean Hospital. For more information, see web.mit.edu/medical/services/s-mentalhealth.html. See also the sections on *Counseling Deans* and *Nightline* in the **Help!** chapter.

Pediatric Services

MIT Medical's Pediatric Service (x3-1505) is staffed by five pediatricians, a pediatric nurse practitioner and a lactation consultant. The service is available to the children of MIT students, faculty, staff, and employees. Office visits are available Monday through Friday from 8:30am to 5pm. Some visits are covered by health insurance or an optional Child Health Fee, and some visits are on a fee-for-service basis. See web.mit.edu/medical/services/s-pediatrics.html for more information on what is covered, and the *Children's Services* section of the **MIT Facilities** chapter for more resources for children and families.

Student Emergency Medical Services

The Student Emergency Medical Services (SEMS) group is an ASA-approved student group dedicated to providing emergency medical support resources to the MIT Community. As part of that effort, they seek to train undergraduate and graduate students, as well as MIT faculty and staff, in emergency medical skills. SEMS also operates a student-run ambulance for all emergency calls within the MIT community, providing transport to MIT Medical and all Boston-area hospitals. It is widely acknowledged that MIT students, undergraduates in particular, may be more comfortable calling for help if they know that help is being offered by fellow students. Visit the SEMS home page at www.people.fas.harvard.edu/~malan/sems/www/ for further information.

HIV Testing

AIDS (Acquired Immune Deficiency Syndrome) is caused by HIV (Human Immuno-deficiency Virus). While there are drugs which can treat the symptoms of AIDS or slow the spread of HIV, there is no actual cure. HIV is transmitted through contact with infected bodily fluids — the most frequent modes of transmission are having sex with or sharing needles with an infected person. While some stereotypes regarding AIDS as a disease of homosexual men and drug users still exist, the truth is that today, AIDS is increasingly an epidemic affecting minorities, women, and heterosexuals. If you engage in sexual activity, you are at risk for contacting AIDS — practice safe sex. The Health Promotion and Wellness Office can provide you with a great deal of information on safe sex practices. Obviously, AIDs is not the only sexually transmitted disease — others are far more common, if generally less lethal. The Health Promotion and Wellness office offers information on other STDs, and you can request free STD testing from your personal physician.

If you think that you have been exposed to HIV, opportunities for testing abound. However, it is important to note that anonymous testing is not available at most medical facilities. Most Boston-area medical facilities offer "confidential" testing — should you test positive, your name will be confidentially reported to the department of health, although the results of the test will not be added to your medical record unless you specifically request it. In true "anonymous" testing, your name is not known even to the test center, where you will be referred to by a unique code. Anonymous testing is not available in all states, although Boston does have locations that offer this service. It is also important to realize that HIV tests will not accurately detect whether or not you have been infected for at least several weeks after possible exposure. All commonly used tests for HIV depend on the identification of HIV antibodies within the body, and most people take between three weeks and two months to begin producing antibodies. There are no guarantees regarding when individuals will begin to produce HIV antibodies after exposure to the virus. During this period, however, people are still capable of transmitting the virus to others. Other tests — viral load tests and nucleic acid tests designed to detect HIV genetic material — can yield results before the body begins producing antibodies, but they are much more expensive, more prone to error, and are not necessarily offered by most testing organizations.

MIT Medical offers confidential (not anonymous) HIV testing — contact your personal physician if you would like to get HIV testing at the Med Center. If you would prefer confidential tested at a non-MIT-affiliated site, the Bisexual Resource Center maintains a list of local confidential test sites at `www.biresource.org/health/boston_testing_clinics.html`. You can also call the National AIDS Hotline (1-800-342-2437) or the AIDS Action Comittee (800-235-2331, `www.aac.org`) for similar information. Project TRUST, at the Boston Medical Center, is a state-sponsored facility that offers free anonymous testing, although demographic information is gathered. The Boston Medical Center is located at 840 Harrison Avenue, on the CT1 bus line. More information about Project TRUST is available at `www.bmc.org/HIV-AIDS/Project%20TRUST.htm`.

Forget Dear Abby...

Ask a MedLink!

Have a health-related question, especially one you don't want to ask your doctor, your friends, or your parents? Ask your questions confidentially and see answers in The Tech.

Just send an email to **askamedlink@mit.edu**

Or submit a question anonymously using the form at
http://web.mit.edu/medlinks/www/askamedlink.htm

Look for Ask a MedLink in The Tech, starting this fall.

MedLinks is a residentially-based peer health advocacy program comprised of student representatives who work to help students connect with medical and campus support resources. All MedLinks receive training in a variety of health-related issues, First Aid, and CPR. MedLinks can also dispense single doses of common over-the-counter medications, disposable thermometers and a variety of first aid supplies. For more information about MedLinks visit: http://web.mit.edu/medlinks/www/

Law

The pillars reported us to some outback nazi law-enforcement agency and now they've run us down like dogs.

— *Hunter S. Thompson*

Ignorance of the law is no excuse. This section contains a brief overview of the more relevant laws and regulations which affect MIT students. It is divided into Institute Law, which pertains to MIT's internal regulations, and Outside Law, which covers some of the relevant Massachusetts law. On campus, one must deal with student committees, the Campus Police, the Office of the Dean of Students and Undergraduate Education (ODSUE), and various official MIT administrative groups. Off campus, one is at the mercy of many levels of government and law enforcement.

Mind you gentle reader, ignorance of the law, includes a misunderstanding of the law. Please do not presume that because you've read the brief outline in this guide, overheard someone else's opinion, or read the General Laws of Massachusetts cover to cover that you truly understand the meaning and content of a given law. With the complexities of the modern legal code, including court precedence, non-intuitive redefinitions of common phrases, and the complex interaction between laws, should you think you need the sort of legal knowledge you and your life sentence can depend on, please contact a lawyer. In fact, carry a lawyer's number in your wallet at all times.

Institute Law
web.mit.edu/policies/

Most of the statutes that govern MIT faculty and staff and some of those that pertain to students are outlined in the *MIT Policies and Procedures* (P&P). It's worth looking over at least once. Theft, careless risk of causing harm to persons and misuse of Institute property are as unacceptable as in any other community. Willful harm to persons (see *Harassment* in the **Help!** chapter) or destruction of property is a very serious offense. If you are interested in making a complaint against someone, there are several means of making such a complaint, many of which are outlined in P&P, Section 9.6, "Complaint and Grievance Procedures".

Campus Police
W31-215; Emergency Phone: 100; Phone: x3-1212
Address: 120 Massachusetts Avenue
Web: web.mit.edu/cp/www/

Campus Police (new official name: "The Police at MIT") policy is to keep the peace, not necessarily to make sure that evil gets punished. They can be consulted unofficially and are happy to answer any questions that you may have. If you get in trouble either on campus or off, give the Campus Police a call. They provide legal advice to students who are arrested and will contact Institute (or outside) lawyers should you need one. The Campus Police provide bicycle and laptop registration and lost-and-found services. Some of these services are available online at web.mit.edu/cp/www/admin.shtml. They also run a variety of outreach and theft prevention programs.

The Campus Police patrol and provide emergency medical services to all parts of campus and the FSILGs in Boston and Brookline. They have a staff of 65 sworn police officers and supervisors and 3 civilian personnel who provide administrative support services. All MIT police officers are required to have at least three years of police experience before coming to MIT and all must have successfully completed basic training at a police academy. Each officer is a trained EMT and a sworn deputy sheriff in Middlesex, Norfolk and Suffolk counties. All officers also have full powers as state police with regard to crimes occurring on campus.

The Chief of Police is John DiFava. Formerly the Colonel of the Massachusetts State Police, he was called in to run security at Logan Airport after the airliner attack on the New York World Trade Center. He joined the MIT Police shortly afterwards.

Cheating

Section 10.2 of P&P, "Procedures for Dealing with Student Academic Dishonesty", describes many of the situations considered by the MIT community to be academically dishonest and their possible consequences. Cheating on tests and plagiarism are considered major offenses, and lesser "grey area" activities such as working together on problem sets and reviewing previous years' assignments may constitute minor (yet still punishable) offenses. On the other hand, many professors encourage *collaboration*, as long as each student writes up his or her own solution. Policies vary by professor and class and are normally listed on the course syllabus; make sure you understand the policy of each of your classes. Activities as seemingly harmless as lending a friend a copy of your work have been disciplined many times in the past; some courses utilize software to analyze the structure and content of electronically submitted problem sets.

All cases of academic dishonesty are handled by the professor and student(s) involved. Complications that make the dispute intractable to this form of mediation are referred to the faculty member's department or the Office of the Dean for Students and Undergraduate Education (ODSUE) or the Committee on Discipline (COD). Standard penalties are grade reduction, extra or replacement assignments, or a faculty warning letter that is kept in a confidential file at ODSUE. In the last case, this letter may be used against you should further offenses occur. In the worst cases, all expulsions must be approved by the President.

In short, don't cheat.

The Committee on Discipline
web.mit.edu/discipline/

The Committee on Discipline is the main body at MIT which deals with Institute regulations. It is composed of both faculty members and students, and handles complaints against students from faculty members, MIT employees, and other students. No person making a complaint against another may sit on the Committee. The procedures of the Committee on Discipline are given in the *Committee on Discipline Rules and Regulations*, available online at the COD website.

As stated in said Rules and Regulations, "The Committee has the authority to impose any sanction it deems appropriate," although suspensions and expulsions require the approval of the President.

Notes for the Accused: You'll be notified by the ODSUE telling you of what you're accused and by whom. You should consult the ODSUE, which will tell you to find a counselor and inform you of the procedure. You can also contact any member of the Committee on Discipline directly.

If you are accused of a criminal offense, according to the COD FAQ (also linked from the main webpage), "MIT's policy is to wait until the criminal process is completely finished from investigation to a decision in court before the COD meets." The COD may come to a different conclusion than a court of law.

COD proceedings are closed and confidential in almost all cases. See *Privacy*.

Judicial Committees
Dorms: `web.mit.edu/dormcon/judcomm`
IFC: `ifc.mit.edu/documents/`

Most of the living groups have a house judicial committee known as JudComm. These student-elected groups generally deal with disputes or complaints among the residents of a living group. The Interfraternity Council (IFC) has a JudComm to deal with matters of concern among fraternities, and the Dormitory Council itself also has a JudComm. Go to a member of JudComm if you're concerned about a problem in your living group.

Privacy and Files
P&P, Section 11. You have the right to review Institute files about you, except those assembled before November 19, 1974 in which the author has been assured of confidentiality. You also have the right to challenge the contents. The school cannot release personal information, excluding directory information, about you to outside people (including parents, if you are over 18, and employers) without your consent. The only exception is in the case of court orders or subpoenas.

Certain specific student information (including grades, financial information, and records of disciplinary infractions) can be released to Institute officials if it is deemed necessary that they have that information. The Institute may also release some student information to another school if you are enrolled there concurrently or if you are applying to it.

Information in your advisor's file is considered confidential, but is not legally so. Medical records — physical and mental — are legally private. Your medical information cannot be shared with your parents, advisors, or others without your consent. Medical records cannot be released without your written consent. HIV test results will not be released without your specific written consent.

For more information, check out the *Student Information Policy* at `web.mit.edu/policies/sip/`

Student/Faculty Liaisons
Section 4.4 of P&P states that, "Potential conflicts of interest of a particularly sensitive nature may arise out of sexual relationships, especially in the context of educational or employment supervision and evaluation." Although no precise guidelines are given here, P&P 7.2 makes it clear that no members of the same family may be in a

46   Law

supervisor-employee type work relation. Should a situation arise, students are encouraged to seek the counsel of their faculty advisors, the faculty in residence, the Graduate Student Organization, or the Office of the Dean of Student Life.

Outside Law

Outside the Institute you have to worry about various governmental types. You can receive information about city laws from the agency involved, simply by phoning and explaining what you need to know (Cambridge City Hall, 617-349-4000; Boston City Hall, 617-635-4000). The Dewey Library at MIT (E53) maintains an up-to-date copy of the state's legal code. You can also inquire about the law by phoning Consumer Affairs at 617-973-8787. Their specialties are tenant and consumer problems, but they will refer you to proper agencies to handle any troubles. The Massachusetts General Laws are available on the web at `www.state.ma.us/legis/laws/mgl/` if you want to search them yourself.

Age of Consent

There is some dispute over whether relevant law pertaining to the age of consent and statutory rape is MGL Chapter 272 Section 4 or MGL Chapter 265 Section 23, and hence whether the age of consent is 16 or 18. Now might be a good time to call that lawyer whose number we suggested you keep in your wallet.

Alcohol

It is illegal in Massachusetts for anyone under twenty-one years of age to purchase alcohol, or to receive it from anyone other than a guardian. It is also illegal to falsely represent one's age in order to obtain alcohol. Large fines are imposed by the Commonwealth for violating the above.

Arrest

If you are arrested, call Campus Police (617-253-1212). In nearly all cases, the CPs will help the student in seeking release from custody on the student's personal recognizance, on bail, or through arrangements with a bondsman. Don't plead guilty — just ask for a "continuance." (Campus Police will explain all this and more if you call.)

Automobile Problems

If an automobile dealer fails to service your car under the terms of its warranty, complain to the Mass. Attorney General (Consumer Protection Division, 617-727-8400).

Drunk Driving

Should you be suspected of drunk driving, the police will detain you, read you your rights, tow your car, and take you handcuffed to a police station. It is important to know your rights. If you are at all confused, call the Campus Police (617-253-1212) to ask for advice.

When accused, the police will offer you the chance to take a breathalyzer test. If you refuse, the result is suspension of license for not less than 120 days and not more than 2 years, effective immediately. If you accept the test, and your blood alcohol level is over 0.08, your license will be suspended for a minimum of 90 days and a maximum of 15 months. Note that if you are less than 21 years old, the blood alcohol level for which you count as legally intoxicated is significantly reduced to 0.02. Charts are available online to let an individual determine his or her approximate limits, but these are rough guides at best.

First-time convictions for drunk driving may face fines of up to $5000, imprisonment for up to 2.5 years, license revocation for up to one year, and be required to participate in the 40-hour First Offenders Driver Alcohol Education Program, among other penalties. It's estimated that the average cost of a drunk driving conviction to the perpetrator is $7317. Things just get bleaker from there.

In summary, there is *never* a good excuse for drunk driving. Call a cab or a friend.

False Fire Alarms

Persons turning in false fire alarms from anywhere, including dormitories, are liable for up to a $500 fine. Years ago, a fireman was killed answering a false alarm here. *Don't do it.*

Firearms and Other Weapons

The possession of any type of firearm (including air pistols and air rifles) in Massachusetts is strictly regulated. Failure to have a Firearms Identification Card (FID) or a License to Carry will result in a mandatory one-year imprisonment for the first offense and 5 years for the second. Furthermore, possession of a firearm on the grounds of a college or university without specific authorization from the particular school carries a penalty of $1000 fine and/or one year imprisonment. *Get those permits immediately!* For details, and more information about Massachusetts Gun Law, call the Rangemaster of the MIT Pistol and Rifle Range (x3-3296).

In order to carry a concealed handgun, you'll need a Class A license. In order to possess a handgun which you do not carry on your person (*i.e.* for recreational range shooting or home defense), you'll need to obtain a Class B license.

If you find it necessary to carry Mace or other self-defense sprays, it is necessary to obtain an FID or FID for Mace Only. These are "shall-issue", in that with the exception of a few specific disqualifications, they must be issued to an applicant.

In order to obtain any of the above licenses with the exception of the FID for Mace Only, you'll need to take a handgun safety class. These have been offered through the MIT Pistol Club in recent years.

Disqualifications for the possession of a Class A or Class B firearm license or either FID include violent crime, various crimes against property, violation of a restraining order, and various motor vehicle offenses. A few less intuitive examples include driving under the influence, shoplifting, and destruction of property. The precise disqualification is under the judgement of the licensing authority.

Additionally, should you be caught "disturbing the peace" in possession of knives having a blade length in excess of 1.5 inches, throwing knives, brass knuckles, nunchaku, zoobow, shuriken, spiked armbands, or weighted chains, among other items, you'll face not more than 2.5 years. The law in our fine state disallows many non-lethal personal defense devices such as tasers and collapsible batons.

Jury Duty

Even if you remain a legal resident of your home state, as an inhabitant of Massachusetts for more than 180 days (which you probably will be) you are eligible to be called for jury duty. This is not all that horrible a thing, since you can postpone it for up to a year (meaning that it doesn't have to interfere with your classes) and since Massachusetts has a "one day/one trial" system.

You show up at 8:30am to sign in for your day in the jury pool, and they brief you on the process. If they pick you, you serve for the trial (which is typically less than three days) and are done. If you aren't selected to serve on a jury, they'll often let you go home at lunch time.

Legal Problems/Legal Aid

Call the Dean's Office (OSDUE, 4-110, 617-253-4052), or Campus Police (627-253-1212). They will either help you directly or refer you to the appropriate people. Greater Boston Legal Aid Services (617-371-1234) will help you get in contact with the right people to help you. Conversation with the Dean's Office is confidential.

Patents and Copyrights

If you think you have a patentable invention/discovery, contact the Technology Licensing Office (NE25-230, x3-6966) for information on the Institute's policies and procedures and the requirements and regulations of the US Patent & Trademark Office. This office will also provide information on the laws and procedures for copyright, including policies with respect to student theses. If you have developed your discovery or invention using MIT resources or grants, MIT requires that you at least file a disclosure with the TLO so they can evaluate MIT's rights concerning the intellectual property. MIT's licensing terms are fairly reasonable and they will pay for the patent application which is often very expensive. Waivers are sometimes available for items that you might wish to pursue elsewhere.

Regarding the idea itself, you should talk with someone in your field (the Patent Administration Office can recommend someone) about the possible existence of previous patents similar to yours. The whole procedure is extremely complex, but the rewards of having a patent of your own make a preliminary investigation worthwhile. For quick checks, or extensive searches of existing patents, look up VERA at libraries.mit.edu/vera/ for access to online patent databases, both US and International.

Miscellaneous Laws

Seat belts are mandatory in Massachusetts, both for drivers and passengers, with fines for non-compliance.

Bicycles must obey all applicable motor vehicle laws. Busts have occurred in Central Square for vehicular infractions on bikes.

Smoking is prohibited in all bars and restaurants in Boston. As of October, 2004, Cambridge also prohibits smoking in bars, restaurants, and public places. With respect to dorms, Cambridge Law prohibits smoking in public areas, but allows students to smoke in private rooms. Each dorm has a different smoking policy, some being smoke free, and others allowing it in certain areas. Check `web.mit.edu/housing/undergrad/residences.html` if this concerns you.

Many forms of gaming and gambling are illegal in Massachusetts. These include playing cards in public for money or other goods.

Notaries Public

Check with the Information Office (7-121, x3-4795) or the Institute Directory for a current list of notaries at MIT. If you have a Fleet account, you can go to the bank in w20; outside MIT, your bank should provide a notary public free of charge. Some students and other MIT affiliates happen to be notaries public; send mail to `notarypublic@mit.edu` to reach those that have added themselves to this mailing list.

Voting

To register, go to the Election Commission of the city where you live: Cambridge Election Commission, 51 Inman Street, First Floor, (617-349-4361); Boston City Hall, Government Center (617-635-4000); Brookline Town Hall, 333 Washington St. Also the student government has occasionally sponsored registration drives, particularly on Registration Day; look for announcements.

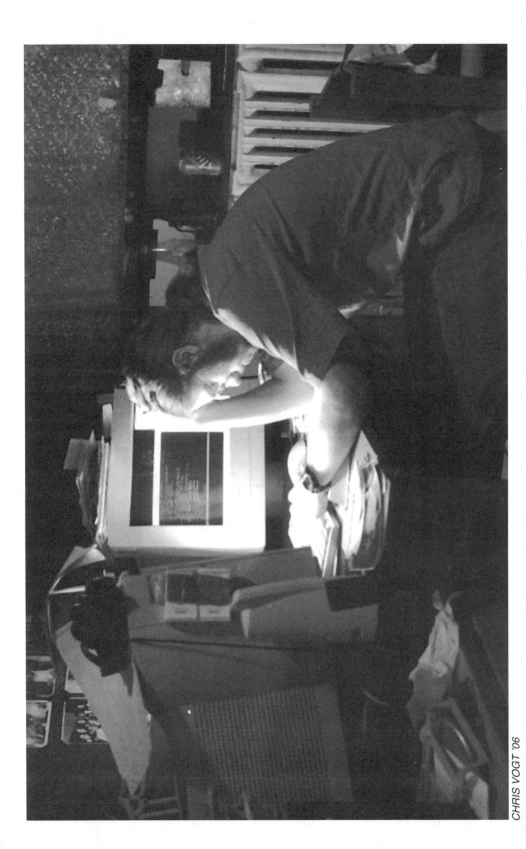

Academics

This chapter attempts to provide answers to a variety of questions dealing with Institute academics. Other useful sources of information include the Faculty's Term Regulations (http://web.mit.edu/faculty/termregs/), which govern everything from what time classes start to the rules for holding a test in the evening. The Academic Guide is a fairly comprehensive source of information for undergrads; this and more can be found at http://web.mit.edu/acadinfo/. The Graduate Students' Office maintains Graduate Policies and Procedures at http://web.mit.edu/gso/gpp/. For more information, make use of resources listed in the **MIT Publications** chapter.

Add/Drop

Adding and dropping courses is fairly easy, but has hard deadlines. Courses can be added until Add Date, usually the fifth week of term (October 8 for Fall 2004, March 4 for Spring 2004). After the first week of classes, to add a course you must get your advisor's and the instructor's signatures. Courses dropped before Add Date do not affect your record in any way (with the exception that you are no longer eligible to take an Advanced Standing exam for that class). After Add Date, courses can be dropped until Drop Date (10th week), which is generously late compared to other schools (November 17 in Fall 2004, April 21 in Spring 2005). Courses dropped between Add Date and Drop Date stay on your internal record with a "DR" grade, but do not appear on your external record. Although DRs on your record shouldn't have any effect on your life, you should drop unattended courses as soon as possible, lest you forget about them. Dropping after Drop Date requires a lengthy petition to the CAP, which generally accepts well-worded excuses of laziness and forgetfulness at most once in a student's time at MIT.

Advanced Standing

Getting credit for course material you already know is not difficult. For incoming freshmen, Advanced Placement (AP) and International Baccalaureate (IB) credit can often be applied towards advanced standing. Check with department-specific policies on AP and IB advanced standing credit at web.mit.edu/firstyear/2008/subjects/ap.html. Even when AP or IB credit is not recognized, for many subjects all that is needed is a passing grade on an Advanced Standing exam. See the instructor and your advisor for details. Incoming students should contact the AP staff in the Academic Resource Center (7-104, x3-6771) with any questions.

Advanced Standing exams allow you to receive credit for a course with which you're already familiar without having to take the course. These long-treasured exams are offered in early February, May, August, and December. You must file a petition with the Registrar three weeks before the exam period begins and get the course instructor's approval. Freshmen are graded pass/no record for exams taken during their first term, and A/B/C/no record for the remainder of the year; upperclassmen are given letter grades. A freshman failing an exam will not have a fail recorded on the permanent transcript. Advanced standing exam grades are never computed into your cumulative average.

If you are considering testing out of a course, *don't* register for it (not even as a listener). Registration in a subject automatically makes you ineligible to take the Advanced Standing exam; this disqualification is independent of whether or not you remained registered or actually did attend classes. If you accidentally do this, a petition will be necessary to resolve the problem. Pre-registration alone does not disqualify you from taking a subject's Advanced Standing exam.

Grad students seeking advanced-placement credit generally make informal arrangements with the instructor and department rather than take an exam. Most departments allow you to use some subjects taken at other schools to fulfill graduate degree course requirements or the minor requirement.

Advisors

Freshman Advisors can help you with many of your problems during your first year at MIT. Get to know your advisor. Most are faculty, but your advisor may be a staff member from any department. Freshman can also choose to register for an advising seminar, where you meet weekly with your advising group. Associate Advisors are upperclassmen that have volunteered their time to help advise freshmen in conjunction with freshman advisors. If you're interested in becoming an associate advisor, talk to someone in the Academic Resource Center (7-103).

All freshmen that declare a major at the end of the first year will then be assigned an advisor in their department. If you know a particular faculty member in your department, you can request him or her as an advisor. Students who do not declare a major before their sophomore year will be assigned a faculty advisor by the ARC.

Your faculty advisor can be very helpful. Remember: he or she is your link to your department and to the faculty committees (CAP, etc.). If you are not doing well, his or her intervention can be very helpful. Keep in touch, especially since many advisors are busy with their own work and thus will not chase you down to see how you are doing throughout the term. It is possible to use your advisor as a rubber-stamp signature on various forms, but you'll have a much better and easier time if you take the initiative and actually discuss your plans and problems with your advisor on a regular basis. This will also qualify him or her to write your grad-school recommendations.

Changing Advisors

If you're having trouble with your advisor or have met another member of the faculty you would like to have as your advisor, you can change advisors. It is usually not too difficult. Freshmen and undesignated sophomores should talk to the people in the Academic Resource Center (7-104, x3-6771). They are very helpful. Upperclass students with majors should speak to their department undergraduate headquarters.

Co-op, with industry

Most engineering majors have organized cooperative study plans with industry, Course VI-A being the most noteworthy. Check with your advisor or look in the Course Bulletin for details. The tuition differs from the regular tuition in some departments. Check at department headquarters for more information.

Committees

Faculty committees (often containing student representatives) make many decisions on academic policy. Committee membership lists are available in the *MIT Directory* under "Standing Committees of the Faculty" or at web.mit.edu/committees/. The most important committees are listed below.

1. **Committee on Academic Performance** (CAP, 7-104, x3-4164) handles most petitions, including those concerning pass/fail, dropping a course after the drop date, and deadlines for finishing incompletes. They also decide whether to place a student on academic probation.

2. **Faculty Policy Committee** (FPC) maintains a broad overview of the Institute's academic programs, deals with a wide range of policy issues of concern to the Faculty, and coordinates the work of Faculty committees.

3. **Committee on the Undergraduate Program** (CUP) is responsible for encouraging experimental innovation in undergraduate education and formulating proposals for changes in undergraduate educational policy. It exercises oversight responsibility for undergraduate education, including the freshman year and interdepartmental programs, giving special attention to long-term directions. The Committee exercises authority to approve and supervise limited educational experiments.

4. **Committee on Graduate School Policy** (CGSP) is concerned with academic performance, degree candidacies, fellowships and scholarships, etc. It is composed of students and representatives of the graduate committee from each department and program. See your department's representative or the Office of the Dean of the Graduate School (3-132, x3-1957) for more information.

5. **Committee on Curricula** (COC, 5-111, x3-3309) handles requests for exemptions and substitutions in general Institute requirements. It also handles proposals for changing requirements.

These committees are always looking for potential active student members. Although they require a very serious commitment, being on one of them is a good way to leave your mark on MIT. Undergraduate student members are nominated through UA NomComm for most committees. For more information email NomComm at ua-nomcomm-chairs@mit.edu or see web.mit.edu/ua/www/committees/nomcomm/. Graduate student members are nominated through the GSC Nominations Committee. Interested students must contact gsc-vice-president@mit.edu and fill out an application. See web.mit.edu/gsc/www/about/reps/instituterps/ for directions and more details.

Complaints/Suggestions

Your advisor is the first person to turn to. Other natural choices are the department head and other professors within the department. The department's feedback committee, if it exists, can also prove useful. Other resources include departmental student groups, the Executive Officer, or even the secretaries at Headquarters. (These last offer information rather than brute-force pull. However, that information may prove invaluable and is unavailable elsewhere.)

Cross-Registration

Sometimes a course that you want to take is not offered at MIT. But not to worry — cross-registration programs with Harvard and Wellesley open the door to many fields not available at the Institute.

Harvard

Cross-registration at Harvard at the Faculty of Arts and Sciences (FAS) or any professional school except the Business School is now open to all MIT students. Cross-registration is generally restricted to upperclassmen, but exceptions are sometimes made for freshmen (especially for foreign language courses not offered at MIT, such as Arabic or Korean). Pursuing a minor or even a major composed mostly of Harvard classes is possible, but be sure to check with your advisor and department that you can get the credit you want before registering. Generally, you "are not supposed to" take an MIT-equivalent subject at Harvard unless you have a serious schedule conflict between the MIT version of the course and another MIT course. Since most cross-registering students take HASS-type courses which rarely have exact equivalents, this rule is not well enforced.

Check `www.harvard.edu/www/academics/catalogs.html` for Harvard catalog listings. See Bette Davis (x3-4443, 14N-408) for cross-registration forms and other information. You can also check with the Harvard University Information Center at Holyoke Center in Harvard Square.

The deadline for cross-registering depends on the school (*check ahead!*), but for the FAS it falls around late September . For graduate students, forms can be picked up at Student Services; undergrads can pick up their forms at the HASS office. FAS's calendar is different from that of MIT: classes for the fall term start two weeks after MIT's and have finals in January; spring term classes start a week before MIT's, and have finals in late May, often after MIT's finals. *You must take your Harvard final at the same time they do, so make sure you are able to take it when it is scheduled!* To call Harvard, dial x186 + the Harvard extension. Harvard information is x186-5-5000.

Two more notes: (1) The cross-registering forms are the worst that MIT bureaucracy can offer (and that's saying something) — don't expect to complete them in an hour! (2) The first week of classes at Harvard are the "shopping period", meaning that you check out classes without worrying about assignments, so don't worry about committing to a class until after then.

Wellesley

In the Student Services Center (11-120) you will find information sheets on cross-registration, bus schedules, Wellesley catalogs, course evaluations by MIT students, and more. Information about the exchange is also posted on the exchange bulletin board near the Admissions Office.

Wellesley classes begin about a week before MIT classes do, so it is important to begin attending Wellesley classes no later than the first week of MIT classes. You must cross-register at Wellesley during the first week of classes. MIT needs you to list the Wellesley subject on your original registration form or fill out an add card.

A free bus service is run between MIT and Wellesley Monday through Friday afternoons. The cross registration bus schedule is based on a combination of MIT and Wellesley class schedules. Be sure to allow enough time for transportation between classes. Note that some Wellesley classes are taught at MIT.

Policies concerning use of Wellesley subjects to meet general Institute and departmental requirements are described on the information sheets. Information about course prerequisites, the meaning of "limited enrollment", or anything else can be gotten from the Wellesley instructor. To call Wellesley dial x187 + the Wellesley extension, or 617-283 plus the Wellesley extension from a non-campus phone. For extension information call x3-0320.

For more information, see *Wellesley* in **Colleges Around Boston**.

Degree requirements

See *Graduation and Degrees*.

Disabilities

The MIT Disabilities Services Office (DSO, 7-145, x3-1674, `dso-www@mit.edu`) is responsible for providing appropriate accommodations to students with temporary or permanent disabilities, including learning, psychiatric and physical disabilities, ADHD, and RSI. You must document your disability at the DSO to receive accommodations. Depending on the disability, the DSO can arrange for textbooks on tape, textbook readers, or enlarged or Braille course material, and can help students find note-takers for a class or bring a tape recorder to classes. For exams, the DSO can help you get extended time, exams on tape, an exam reader, a scribe, a private room, or clarification of exam questions. For detailed information and directions, see the DSO student handbook, available in the DSO office or at `web/dso/www/general_sec11.html`

The Adaptive Technology for Information and Computing (ATIC) lab (7-143, x3-7808, `atic@mit.edu`) has equipment for students with disabilities. The lab has computers with voice recognition, alternative mice, digitizing tablets, as well as an OCR scanner, Braille translation, voice synthesis, screen magnification, and tactile imaging devices. ATIC services are free and the lab is open 24 hours a day for students established as ATIC lab users.

Domestic Year Away

You can spend a year studying at another college in the United States provided that certain conditions are met. The school you want to attend must accept you and be of "established merit," and your department must certify that the school has unique resources unavailable at MIT, Wellesley, or Harvard. Your program of study there should involve a workload comparable to MIT's, and its objectives must be consistent with your overall MIT degree program.

You won't have to reapply to MIT to get back in. Financial aid is available for those who would normally be eligible. The Student Financial Aid Office will determine your need at the other school and what your need would have been at MIT and will give you the *smaller* award. You can get more information from the Careers Office (12-170, x3-4733). Deadlines for submitting the worksheet ("Worksheet for Planning Study Abroad/

Domestic Study Away", available from the Careers Office office in 12-170) are mid-May for fall term study away, and late November for spring term study away.

End-of-Term Regulations

For all undergraduate courses, no tests are allowed after the Last Test Date, defined as the Friday before the last week of classes (December 3 in Fall 2004, May 6 in Spring 2005). In a course with a final exam, no assignments can be due after the Last Test Date. In a course without a final, one assignment may be due between the Last Test Date and the last day of the course. No term papers are allowed to have due dates during finals week. If your instructor decides to "be nice" and extends a paper's due date to finals week, the extension might disappear if the CAP finds out about it.

In graduate courses with final exams, no tests or assignments may be due after the Last Test Date. In graduate courses without final exams, one assignment or test may be given between the Last Test Date and the last day of class. Such an in-class test's length is limited to one class period or 1.5 hours, whichever is shorter. See `web.mit.edu/faculty/termregs/end_of_term.html` for more detailed information on end-of-term regulations.

It is not uncommon for professors, especially those new to MIT, to be unaware of this policy or to accidentally violate it. (It also happens, but is rare, that a professor will intentionally violate the policy.) If you think there is a problem, first talk to the professor (possibly with other members of the class) and/or your TA. If you are not satisfied with the result, call the ARC (x3-6771) or email `exam-termregs@mit.edu` to complain to the chairman of the faculty.

Exploratory Subjects

Sophomores have the option of designating up to one subject per term "Exploratory;" this designation may be made at any time up until Add Date. Exploratory subjects may be changed to listener status at any time up until the following Reg Day, even after a grade has been issued. Any class, including a GIR or major requirement, may be designated exploratory.

Note: Exploratory status has only been around since Fall 2003, so not everyone has had time to become familiar with it. Some academic advisors and course administrators have been telling students that they cannot take major requirements exploratory. While major requirements cannot be taken on Junior/Senior P/D/F, this is not the case for exploratory subjects. If you have trouble designating a class exploratory, contact the ARC (7-104, x3-6771).

Finals

Final exam schedules come out in mid-term, and are available at the ARC, the Information Center (7-121), and the Registrar's Office web site (`registrar.mit.edu/exams.html`). If you have conflicting finals, follow the instructions on the Conflict Form on the back of the schedule. (See the section on *End-of-Term Regulations* to see what is permissible during the last week of a class with a final.)

Call the ARC (7-104, x3-6771) or check the web site if you forgot (or never found out) where your final is supposed to be. The Schedules Office (5-111, x3-4788) has the most up-to-date information, and they handle conflicts. Often, living groups will have the exam schedule posted at the front desk. If you will be more than 45 minutes late, you must get permission from the CSS (Counseling and Support Services) office (5-104, x3-4861) to enter the exam room.

If you cannot take a final at the scheduled time, all is not lost. Undergrads should go to the CSS Office (beforehand if possible) and explain the circumstances which prevent you from taking the exam (a personal visit is strongly preferred to a call). If your reason is accepted, and the instructor has issued an O (absent from final or last two weeks of class up to that time), the Dean's Office will issue a grade of OX (absentee exemption). It is *your* responsibility to make up that final. If you had been doing failing work throughout much of the term, the instructor still has the right to give you an F instead of an O. If you are sick, be sure to go to the Medical Department before the exam. If your reason is not accepted, the O remains as such on your record — it is equivalent to an F and is averaged into your GPA.

Disasters, both big (family emergencies, accidents) and small (sleeping through a test), sometimes happen during finals week. If you unexpectedly miss all or part of a final, your first priority should be to find (or otherwise contact) the professor as soon as possible to explain your situation. Professors can be very understanding, and sometimes arrangements can be made for the final to be taken before the end of finals week. If this is not possible, you can request an OX (see above). The instructor issues the O (missed final), and the X (excused) is issued by CSS. Note that CSS only gets involved if the missed final cannot be made up later in exam week. If you have a medical emergency during finals week, you unfortunately must somehow relay your condition to CSS and your instructor to deal with your exam — Medical cannot write excuse letters.

A postponed final is normally taken early in the next semester. This means that if you miss a second-term final, you must retain all of your knowledge of the course through the summer and part of the fall term. So it might be better to take the final on time if you are not too sick. Be realistic about your capabilities though, because if you do badly, it is nearly impossible to have the grade changed.

Graduate students who need to reschedule a final should talk with their instructor. Also, you can check with the Graduate School Office (3-138, x3-4860).

If you have a tendency to go to pieces or otherwise fail to perform maximally on finals, talk with your instructor beforehand; afterwards plead for an incomplete.

Foreign Study

If you are interested in studying abroad, you should start to plan as soon as possible. Junior Year Abroad is generally the easiest way to go. Student status and dorm priority are generally unaffected. Financial aid is available as for Domestic Year Away. Contact the Careers Office (12-170, x3-4733) for more information. If you are interested in studying at Cambridge University, England, the Cambridge-MIT Institute (CMI), intended primarily for MIT juniors, is currently in full swing — see the web page at web.mit.edu/cmi/ue/exchange.html for more details.

For study abroad elsewhere, you are generally expected to apply directly to the college you would like to attend, or through a program outside of MIT. Be sure to start the process well in advance and be aware of the admissions deadlines; keep in mind that you may be required to obtain recommendations from professors and other application materials of that nature. The Careers Office has a selection of study abroad books and information which you can browse to find information about programs and universities. For more information, see the Study Abroad web site at `web.mit.edu/career/www/Abroad/study.html` and contact the Careers Office to make an appointment to speak with a study abroad officer.

The opportunities for foreign graduate study are in some ways greater. OCSPA has some reference materials. The Graduate School Office (3-138, x3-4860) also has information on DAAD, Churchill, Fulbright-Hays, Marshall, and other foreign scholarships. `web.mit.edu/gso/financialaid/grants.html` has a lot of useful information.

Freshman Troubles

Not everyone's freshman year is a non-stop joyride. You may encounter one or more of the following difficulties:

Advisor problems

If you don't like your advisor, you can get a new one at the Academic Resource Center (7-104, x3-6771). Tell the ARC people what you want in an advisor. Don't hesitate to request a change if you feel one is necessary. You *can* change advisors more than once as well, although they will not be happy about it and will try to dissuade you as they prefer you to work out your problems with your advisor instead of just switching to a new one. (See *Advisors* above.)

Fifth-week flags

If you are getting a D or an F after the fifth week of classes (usually right after the first round of tests) your instructor will send you a fifth-week flag (your advisor and GRT also get copies). Getting one doesn't mean you'll fail, it's just a heads-up. Whatever you do, don't go into hiding. Talking to your instructor will often help — go to office hours or make an appointment to talk to your professor or TA. Showing effort can go a long way.

Failure (i.e., not passing)

Don't panic. Normally you will merely have to repeat the course if you want to get credit for it. Pleading sometimes helps. Possibly your fifth-week flags did not give you a clear idea of where you stood. Talk to your professor. Remember that freshman failing grades are not recorded on your external transcript (but they might influence the CAP at the end of the term).

Seminar problems

If you don't like — or think you won't do well in — your freshman advising seminar, you can drop it. However, since most seminars are oversubscribed, give your seminar a decent chance. You probably won't be able to switch to another. No matter how much these seminars have been advertised as "fun" courses, they are sometimes treated as an indicator of your creativity and research potential; remember that in some departments the weeding-out process for graduate school starts first-term freshman year. Beware that a few "freshman" seminars have, on occasion, assumed background beyond that of the average freshman. (One year, a number-theory seminar assumed substantial familiarity with group theory.) If that's the case, talk to your seminar leader. Probably everyone else is floundering, too. You can obtain a listing of the seminars for the next term at the Academic Resource Center (7-104 , x3-6771).

Course Problems

If you really don't like your professor, go to the undergraduate department office or to the departmental headquarters and explain why you would rather be in another section. Don't use the negative approach; instead, explain why another section would be better for you. If there is only one section, you can drop the course (and wait for next term) or grin and bear it.

If you have any problems at all, whether they concern problem set difficulties or room temperature, talk to the instructor. He or she wants feedback (in most cases) and will react favorably to the simple fact that you have gotten off your tail and said something — even if it is critical. Just do things tactfully, and you will be surprised at how well received you'll be.

If that doesn't work, try your advisor or other faculty members in the appropriate department. Go straight to the department head if necessary. Try the Deans, especially the ARC (7-104, 3-6771), and then the counseling staff (5-104, x3-4861); they are all experienced in dealing with classroom complaints.

Don't worry that your comments might be too trivial to waste someone's time with. If something bothers you, it probably bothers other people, too. If you're really unsure, sound out another student, a dean, or a random faculty member and see what happens. Normally, all you have to do is ask. If your problems involve the course material, you have several paths available to you. Tutorials (if they exist) provide personalized help — it's best to attend them throughout the term and avoid the crowded cram sessions on the day before the exam. Your TA might also be able to arrange a help session. Students and GRTs/RAs in your living group may have taken the course in question; they might have old quizzes and homework as well as an understanding of the material. Undergraduate offices also often have facilities to help out. The Office of Minority Education (4-113, x3-5010, web.mit.edu/ome/) offers tutoring for all students. Above all, going to office hours given by professors and TAs is often helpful. Professors' office hours are often sparsely attended, offering privacy and a chance to get to know your professor better.

Schedule Conflicts

If you have two or more conflicting subjects scheduled, check with the Schedules Office (5-111, x3-4788). If you can't get into a different section, dropping one of the courses and waiting until the next term is usually the best solution. Discuss the problem with each one of the instructors. Beware of attempting to divide your class time between the two subjects, as many classes have participation and attendance requirements, particularly foreign language and smaller HASS classes.

The schedule given on your schedule card is taken from the master list given in your registration booklet. During the first week of classes, many courses will not pay attention to the section assignments and you can simply show up at the most convenient section. However, this is not true for all courses; many have special procedures to change sections. After the first week, you generally need departmental approval to change your section.

Grade Challenging

Problem sets, quizzes, and exams are often marked by TAs or graders. If you have any questions about the accuracy of a mark, ask the grader; if you cannot resolve the problem, talk with the instructor. Normally he or she will be quite willing to look at your side of it.

If you feel a course grade is unfair, first talk to the instructor, and then, if necessary, to the department head. The CAP is willing to act as an intermediary in case of disagreements but cannot override a department's decision. The instructor must fill out a Special Report Sheet and send it to the Registrar before the grade change can officially take place. All such changes, including making up I's and OX's, must be done before you get your degree. (An OX is the grade given if you are excused from a final with the Dean's Office approval — given, for example, because of illness). (See *Finals* above.)

Grades

No pluses or minuses show up on your official transcript or are factored into your GPA. For all external purposes, a B+ is the same as a B-, except perhaps in your heart. Hidden grades, such those that you received during your first freshman term, appear on your offical transcript as Pass/No Record (or whatever is appropriate) and are not factored into your GPA. Internal advisors (such as CAP) may see the grade modifiers and hidden grades that are on your internal transcript.

That said, some medical schools require that you submit your hidden grades and grade modifiers in order to apply. The Registrar's Office will not release a copy of your internal transcript to an outside party. However, you can arrange for letters containing your internal grades from individual departments to be sent either to you, or to the Careers Office, and then to be forwarded to medical schools.

There are several grades that you may receive for a class:

A, B, C: Self-explanatory.

D: Passing, except for freshmen. Some courses require a grade of better than a D for their prerequisites. (Generally, prerequisites are flexible, but they generally suggest what you should have a working knowledge of before you take a class. If you get a D in a class, it might be a sign that your working knowledge in that field might be a bit lacking.)

P: A passing grade for freshmen, for classes graded P/D/F, or for classes taken on Junior/Senior P/D/F.

F: Fail. Do not pass go, do not collect $200. Zero grade points (out of 5, a D will get you 2). Generally, you don't get credit for the class, but if you fail one class in your major in your final semester that's not part of a GIR, and you made an honest effort to pass the class, F is for effort, and it's still possible to graduate in some circumstances.

DN, FN: No Record. You would have had a D or an F, but you're a freshman, so the course won't appear on your transcript.

O: Absent. You were doing all right, but missed a something big at the end of term (like a final, or final paper or project). This gets treated like an F unless it gets changed to an OX by CSS.

OX: Absence excused by CSS. The instructor must give you an opportunity to earn a passing grade. It is your responsibility to contact him and get this process started.

I: Incomplete. You're missing some minor part of the class, and a passing grade is expected when the work is completed. You cannot graduate with an I on your transcript (It will show as an F).

J: Used for Thesis/UROP/Co-op work that extends into another semester. When you get your grade for the final term of Thesis/UROP/Co-op work on that project, it carries over to all of your J grades for that project.

U: Grade for Thesis work that has been deemed unsatisfactory.

T: Temporary. Used for classes like 18.02A that finish in a different term than they start in.

Graduate Schools

Reasonably thorough collections of graduate school catalogs can be found in the Humanities Library (14S) and the Careers Office (12-170, x3-4733). The latter also has independent references on school reputations, financial aid, and degrees awarded. In addition, the office has some applications for the GMAT, LSAT, MCAT and GRE. The Graduate School Office (3-138, x3-4860) also has GRE application forms and information. Reference copies of test bulletins are kept in the Careers Office (12-170). Register to take the GRE and other such exams spring term your junior year.

Isaac Colbert, Dean of the Graduate School, can be helpful to talk to if you want to come to MIT for graduate study. When applying to grad schools, it's usually best to specify the doctorate under "degree to be studied for." This and other rules of thumb may be gleaned from your advisor and other faculty if you ask for help.

Getting a Recommendation

Recommendations may be at least as important as your GPA. You should have a good working relationship with at least one faculty member and ask for recommendations early. Make sure that you ask people for their approval before using them as a reference. It helps to know that you'll get a good recommendation. (Unlike many in the "real world", MIT people tend to be brutally honest in their recommendations.)

Admission to MIT Graduate School

For some departments (particularly Chemistry and Biology) it is harder for MIT undergrads to get into MIT than for grads from other institutions of comparable quality. The reason is that departments want to avoid "inbreeding". Consult the department, the Admissions Office, and the Graduate School Manual for more information and help.

It is possible to be admitted as an interdisciplinary graduate student. You still have to find a department that will admit you, but some flexibility is allowed. It will take a lot of talking to get you what you want, and at least one professional ally. Don't delay.

Prelaw, Premed, and Educational Counseling

The Committee on Preprofessional Advising and Education serves the special needs of students interested in entering the medical, legal, and teaching professions (and related areas in public administration). The Committee itself consists of three advisory councils, one in each field. If you are wondering what it feels like to be a professional in one of these areas, the members of the advisory councils will be glad to tell you.

The Careers Office (12-170, x3-4733) publishes special handbooks for the medical, legal, and teaching professions (and related areas in public administration). It also provides graduate school catalogs, applications for entrance exams (MCAT, LSAT, etc.), and academic counseling and sponsors seminars given by professionals and representatives of graduate schools. Students interested in teaching should contact the MIT/Wellesley Teacher Education Program (`education.mit.edu/tep/`). MIT students can gain teaching certification through Wellesley.

Graduate cross-registration

MIT has cross registration programs with a number of schools. Most of these programs are very limited (e.g., at Brandeis only Course XI grad students may cross register), but don't let these restrictions stop you. Build a good case for yourself, convince your advisor of its merit, and you at least have a chance. With perseverance and careful planning, things can go the way you want them to. More information is available in the Graduate Student Manual, from Dan Engelhardt at the Student Services Center, or from the appropriate coordinator:

School	MIT Coordinator
Boston University (African Studies)	Departments of Economics and Political Science
Brandeis (Social Welfare)	Department of Urban Studies and Planning
Harvard	Registrar's Office, 5-119, x8-6409
Wellesley	Student Services Center, 11-120
Woods Hole Oceanographic Institute	Participating MIT Departments: Biology; Earth, Atmospheric, and Planetary Sciences; Civil and Environmental Engineering; Electrical Engineering and Computer Science; Materials Science and Engineering; Mechanical Engineering; and Ocean Engineering. Information regarding these programs in Oceanography and Applied Ocean Science and Engineering may be obtained from the MIT Joint Program Office, Room 54-911, x3-7544.

Graduation and Degrees

You must submit an application to be a degree candidate in order to graduate. The application is included in your registration material. MIT does not automatically grant your degree as soon as all your requirements have been met. It is possible to graduate with one deficiency if it occurred in a departmental subject for which you were registered in the final term and you made an honest effort to complete the course. Even then, graduation is not automatic. Your department will have to petition the Committee on Academic Performance (CAP) and make a well-informed plea. Double-majors may not graduate with a deficiency.

Before you receive your diploma, all library books must be returned, all keys to rooms and labs must be returned to the Office of the Superintendent of Facilities or to the appropriate professor, and all financial matters must be cleared. The Student Accounts office will notify you of the deadline dates for all the formalities.

Prior to graduation, any student employed by the Institute must file a Termination Clearance form with the Payroll Office, with signatures certifying that he or she has returned all keys, books, supplies, etc. Some labs have their own special termination procedures for teaching assistants.

Two Bachelor's Degrees

If you wish to seek two Bachelor's degrees, you must fulfill requirements in two departments while accumulating an additional 90 units (about one year's worth). You may petition the Committee on Curricula (through the Registrar's Office) for a double major only after completing two semesters on grades. They say that you must petition at least two terms before graduating; but they have been known to relax this requirement if you have been making a demonstrable effort towards the second degree. The petition must list the two degrees and the expected graduation date. Consult your advisors in both departments to find out about the deadline for application and to obtain approval of your entire program.

Make sure you contact both departments about your joint thesis if you plan to present one.

Bachelor's and Master's Degrees

Some departments will award an SB and an SM simultaneously. You must be accepted for graduate study at least one term before the degree is awarded; that requires a petition. Check with your advisor for details. If you want a Bachelor's degree in one department and a Master's in another, you are on your own. Don't give up, though — it has been done.

Two Master's Degrees

You do not necessarily have to take additional credit units for two Master's degrees. However, there are requirements about splitting up the units between the two departments. You can do a joint thesis for two Master's degrees; a petition must be filed at least two terms before graduation.

Degrees, Interdepartmental

Many departments have concentrations which allow much work in another area (II-A, VI-1 Bio option, etc.). Check with your advisor.

Degrees, Unspecified

Many courses sponsor very flexible programs that can be adjusted to suit your personal preferences up to a certain limit. Since all departments have the option of offering unspecified degrees, your advisor or department head can help you set up a program. But remember that you still must fulfill the general Institute requirements, even if they don't seem to fit into your personalized educational program.

How to Get Around Requirements

If you want to make substitutions for Institute requirements, you have to petition the COC. Getting out of a departmental requirement will require working things out with your advisor and the department head. Talk to the people involved before writing your petition. Your advisor and the deans can be of help. Try to find out about policies and precedents, and build up a believable case, which may take a major creative effort in borderline cases.

Don't be afraid to try; the results can be worth it. Petition forms are available from your advisor, the Student Services Center and the ARC. Your petition will be more effective if you justify yourself in two sentences on the petition itself. Items which are petitioned for most frequently are substitutions for humanities and lab requirements. Often other subjects may be substituted for certain requirements in the department. Make sure you have the approval of the instructor in the subject you want to substitute. If your petition is refused, you can appeal to the same committee and they may change their minds if you are persuasive enough.

IAP

Independent Activities Period (IAP) is a unique MIT experience. It is the time in between fall and spring terms — about four weeks in January. During this time there are many activities, seminars, and some accelerated courses. It is a time to explore some of the things which have always interested you but that you haven't had time for. If you have some skill or knowledge that you would like to share with others, you can teach your own course or sponsor your own activity. Past topics taught by professors and students alike include wine tasting, machining, algebraic topology, sightseeing, and a real-time role-playing game. There is no real limit to what you can do. Regular IAP activities include the Mystery Hunt, LSC science-fiction movie marathon, and Charm School.

Information about organization, registration, and funding (it exists!) is available online at web.mit.edu/iap/.

Credit for IAP

You are generally limited to twelve units of credit for IAP. Anything else requires a petition to the COC or CGSP. The freshman credit limit does not apply to IAP credit. If you're looking for IAP credit activities, look for listings in the IAP guide that have a big "C" by them.

Incompletes

Incompletes must be completed by the end of the fifth week of the succeeding term, unless the instructor explicitly grants you an extension (which at most extends to the last day of classes of that term). Any further extension requires the approval of the CAP, which is given only in special circumstances (for instance, if the lab equipment you need is not available during the appropriate term). If you withdraw from MIT before making up the Incomplete, talk to the CAP about when to make it up; if the Incomplete requires scarce MIT equipment, remember that you are not officially allowed to use such equipment when not registered. The CAP encourages readmitted students to make up Incompletes.

Incompletes not completed remain Incompletes; they are not computed into your average. *However*, they are often treated by graduate schools as "F"s. Departments and the CAP will consider the number of Incompletes in your record if your academic performance is being reviewed.

It is a good idea to ask your professor ahead of time for an Incomplete (but don't ask if you haven't already done two thirds of the course work), explain the reasons for it, and tell him when you plan to finish the subject. (If he is not going to give you an Incomplete, better to know before the term ends.) Many professors will go out of their way to be accommodating, even to the point of calling you up to see if you are still working on the Incomplete; others will screw you to the wall.

Inventing Your Own Course

New courses have been invented in the past, and can be quite rewarding for both teachers and students. A strong commitment and faculty backing are essential, and the alternative freshman programs, such as ESG or Concourse, may be of assistance. The Educational Studies Program (ESP, W20-467, x3-4882) provides an organization for teaching Saturday courses to high school students. Starting an IAP course is much easier and can be done through a department or independently. Contact the IAP office (7-104, x3-1668).

Junior/Senior P/D/F

Junior/Senior P/D/F is an underutilized gem available to upperclassmen. Juniors and Seniors can opt to take up to two courses (total) graded Pass/D/F, where a "Pass" equals a C or better. Credit is given for P and D grades. Junior/Senior P/D/F is intended to allow students to take courses outside their main field(s) of study without worrying about grades. It also gives upperclassmen a way of "dropping" a difficult or time-consuming course to P/D/F rather than outright dropping of the subject. As such, courses taken P/D/F unfortunately cannot be used for General Institute, major, or minor requirements. Junior/Senior P/D/F can be initiated up until Add Date.

Light Load

Regular students planning to register for a light load (fewer than 32 units) must get approval from their advisors and a counseling dean (5-104). If the forms are signed by add date, the CAP will take this into account at its end-of-term meeting and will not take action because of a low registration. There is also the possibility of saving money by paying tuition on a per-unit basis while still being considered a regular student. Taking more than two terms of light load is discouraged and requires a CAP petition.

Listener Status

There are two ways to sit in on a subject: the first is getting permission to sit in on a class and learn informally; the second is registering officially to listen to a class. If you do register to listen, you will not be allowed to advance-place the course later on. For the summer term, or whenever you pay tuition on a per-unit basis, the listening rates are the same as for regular students' tuition. It is possible to change status to a regular student during the term (up to the add date). See your advisor for the necessary paperwork.

Pass/Fail

Pass/Fail grading is generally available only to first-term freshmen (in which case it is more accurately described as Pass/No Record) and to students in seminars or UROP programs. An instructor may petition the COC to have his/her entire subject made Pass/Fail but cannot allow individual students to take the course Pass/Fail unless one of the above options applies to them.

First-term freshmen will receive only Pass/No Record grading on their grade reports for their first term; if they achieve a "C" standard or above, their external grade report will simply show a pass, and if they manage only a "D" or an "F", it will only be recorded on their "hidden" internal record and not their official transcript. In the second term, this idea is extended to A/B/C/No Record; a grade of "A", "B" or "C" is recorded on the official transcript, whereas "D" and "F" go no further than the hidden internal record.

Problems

If something is wrong and you can't find adequate help from your advisor, the ARC, the Counseling Deans (5-104, x3-4861), or anywhere else, go to Mental Health (E23-368, x3-2916). These people specialize in helping when you're in trouble. Wherever you go for help, don't give up if you have a bad first experience. Although misunderstandings and miscommunications sometimes happen, there are many helpful, caring people at the Institute who will respect you and take what you tell them seriously.

Registration

Pre-Registration

Unless you are a new undergraduate, you need to pre-register for your courses. As with everything at MIT designed to make things easier for people other than students, don't be late or you will have to pay a large fine! During pre-registration you can choose the courses you think you will be taking in the next term, if you really want to think about it way ahead of time. If you are planning to register for courses that tend to fill up or require a lottery to enter, you really should pre-register for them; many times your chances of getting in are dependent on whether or not you've pre-registered.

Thanks to the wonder of modern computing's ability to inconvenience, you must pre-register via WebSIS at `websis.mit.edu` (provided you have the right sort of web browser; the certificates required are incompatible with a number of popular browsers, and the pre-registration process makes superfluous use of JavaScript, so you must enable that horrible option if you have been clueful enough to turn it off).

If you'd like to reserve specific times in the day for non-academic activities, scroll to the bottom of the pre-reg page and choose your times. This won't guarantee that you won't be assigned a class during those hours, but the program will try its best.

Lotteried courses include HASS-Ds, courses which are generally oversubscribed, and Sloan (Course 15) courses. Generally by pre-registering you are automatically entered in the lottery; for Sloan courses, you need to enter by going to `sloanbid.mit.edu`.

The deadlines for pre-registration are bafflingly early (December 30 for Spring 2005, May 31 for Fall 2005), so pay attention to avoid a hefty, unjust fine. However, you can change your pre-registration up until a couple of weeks before term begins, so many people who aren't going to take any limited-enrollment classes just pre-register for any old thing and make up their minds later (usually on Reg. Day, since for those people there's no point in pre-registering at all other than to avoid the fine). For more information, see `https://student.mit.edu/cgi-docs/sfprwpra.html` (don't forget the 'https' or you'll get an out-of-date page; also, you'll need web certificates).

Note concerning lotteried classes: if you don't get in, a lot of times talking with the professor will make a big difference. Often, oversubscribed classes dwindle significantly very shortly into term, and perseverance can pay off. As a rule, it never hurts to go to the first day of a class you're interested in.

Actual Registration

Registration Day (or Reg. Day, as it's more commonly known) for Fall 2004 is Tuesday, September 7th. For Spring 2005, it is Monday, January 1st. It's the day before the first day of classes.

Continuing Students:

On Registration Day, all continuing students should meet with their advisors. Don't wait until the last minute to do this! You may find that your advisor is gone, or very busy, and then you might have to run around looking for someone else who can sign your form. Many advisors post a sign-up sheet outside their door and you are expected to sign up for a time slot in advance. If you have big questions or problems it's a good idea to email your advisor ahead of time, and possibly meet before Reg. Day.

Your advisor will have your registration form, which will list the classes that you submitted for pre-registration. You may add or delete classes by crossing them out or writing them on the form; this will save you the trouble of having to fill out an Add or Drop form later. (On the other hand, filling out add/drop forms is very easy, so don't think that you have to know exactly what you want to take by Reg. Day. It's not a bad idea to sign up for more classes than you expect to take and then decide which ones to drop once you know better what they're like.) When you are done choosing your courses, sign your form, ask your advisor to sign your form, and turn it in at the specified location.

For most students, registration forms should be turned in at Johnson Athletic Center (for fall term) or DuPont Gymnasium (for spring term) between noon and 5pm on Registration Day. A few departments have made special arrangements for you to turn it in elsewhere — for example, your department headquarters. When in doubt, ask your advisor.

Freshman Registration:

Incoming freshmen will receive their registration materials and meet with their advisors during Orientation. If you are a freshman, you must turn in your signed Registration form at the Student Services Center (11-120).

Freshmen have a credit limit of 54 units in the fall and 57 units in the spring, which can only be exceeded by 6 units if taking Seminar XL, or by 3 units if enrolled in Mission 2008 (12.000).

There are several special programs for freshmen, *for more information, contact the following people:*

Concourse: Cheryl Butters, 16-135, x3-3200, cbutters@mit.edu

Experimental Study Group (ESG): Holly Sweet, 24-612, x3-7786, hbsweet@mit.edu

Terrascope: Debra Aczel, 16-177, x3-4074, daczel@mit.edu

Media Arts and Sciences (MAS): Michael Bove, E15-368B, x3-0334, vmb@media.mit.edu

Special Students:

Special students should bring their admittance letter to the Student Services Center (11-120) no later than the first week of classes, where they should complete registration and provide other information.

Transfer Student Registration:

Transfer students should meet with their advisors during Orientation or on Registration Day to receive their Registration forms. When meeting with your advisor, you should discuss your transfer credit as well as sign up for classes.

Transfer students, like continuing undergraduates, should drop their signed registration form at Johnson Athletic Center or DuPont Gymnasium between noon and 5pm on Registration Day.

Late Registration:

If your registration form is not turned in by the end of registration week, you will have to pay a $40 late fee. If you have not registered by Add Date you will have to petition and pay a $100 late fee.

Registration Hold

It is possible that your registration will be put on hold for a variety of reasons. If your registration is on hold, your advisor will not receive your registration form and you will have to talk to the office that placed the hold. Below are the types of registration holds you may encounter and the appropriate offices to contact. Once your hold has cleared, you can pick up your registration form at the Student Services Center, have it signed by your advisor, and turn it in.

Financial Hold: Student Services Center, 11-120, x8-8600

Medical Hold: Health Screening, E23-South Arcade, call x3-1777 for appointments

Immigration Hold: International Students Office, 5-133, x3-3795

Housing Hold: Graduate Housing, E32-133, x3-5148

Checking Registration

Check your registration. No, really. I know you signed up for 4.301, and you know it, but does the registrar? Maybe, or maybe not. Be sure to check WebSIS a few weeks into term.

Registrar's Office, 5-119, x8-6409

The Registrar will send you notification of your registration status periodically throughout the term (more-or-less after Registration Day and before and after Add and Drop Dates). Check these carefully and be sure to have them corrected immediately if necessary. You can also check your registration status and grades online at websis.mit.edu (you will need certificates, and thus a browser that supports the ones MIT uses).

Be sure to keep a copy of everything you can, especially end-of-term grade reports. The Registrar's computer has been known to "forget" you registered for a 24-unit lab, *etc.*

Requirements

Requirements and other information for the Class of 2008 can be found at web.mit.edu/firstyear/2008/subjects/.

For other undergraduate students, see web.mit.edu/acadinfo/undergrad/academic-guide/sec2.html.

For graduate students, see web.mit.edu/admissions/www/graduate/degreerequirements.html.

Sophomore Standing

At the end of your first term at MIT, if you have completed more than 25% of your undergraduate credits (including at least one HASS CI-HW), you will be notified of your eligibility for sophomore standing. Generally, only students who enter MIT with a good deal of AP credits or transfer credits have amassed sufficient units to receive this offer.

There are arguments for and against taking sophomore standing. If you remain a freshman, you will still be graded on an A/B/C/No Record scale. The 57-unit credit limit also makes it more difficult to unintentionally overload yourself. Finally, sophomore standing is an irrevocable decision. If you choose sophomore standing, though, the credit limit will be lifted, permitting you to take 5 (or more) classes. You also will be able to declare a major and choose an advisor within your course. In making the decision, you should consider what your hidden grades in your fall classes were. (Ask your advisor or the ARC in 7-104).

If you elect to take sophomore standing, you will need to fill out a form, available from Karen Blose in the Academic Resource Center (7-104, x3-9765). You can declare your major immediately or leave yourself an "undesignated sophomore". If you choose to declare a major, you must meet with the departmental administrator of your course to choose an advisor. The deadline for these forms is Add Date. Sophomore standing does not make you eligible to move off-campus, or to leave the RBA program. Further information is available at the ARC and on the following webpages: web.mit.edu/firstyear/2008/rightnow/soph_stand.html (this page only exists during late fall term) and web.mit.edu/acadinfo/undergrad/academic-guide/sec8.html.

Special Projects

If you have an idea you want to work on or something you want to study, it is possible to get Institute backing. You may even be able to get credit or satisfy Institute requirements while doing your own thing. Petitions for fulfillment of Institute requirements go to the Committee on Curricula (COC); for fulfillment of department requirements, talk to the department.

First, dig up an idea. (Example: writing a guidebook for the MIT community; that's how this book originally got started, back in the day.) Several established ways of doing so are:

1. Check with the UROP office (7-104, x3-7306, web.mit.edu/urop/) or check their bulletin board in the main corridor for current research offerings. Although most

projects take place on campus, it is also possible to have an off-campus project at hospitals, corporations, non-profit organizations, or government agencies. See the UROP web site or booklet for more ideas and for the rules and regulations regarding project work. Also, see the *UROP* section of this chapter.

2. Ask at department headquarters/graduate offices for references on current research.

3. Find a professor you want to work with and ask him or her for project ideas. Most faculty members have lots of ideas on which they themselves don't have time to work.

4. Drop in at a lab you're interested in and ask someone about what's going on. In most cases, you'll get an enormously thorough description; people are very willing to talk about their work.

5. Check out the Edgerton Center. They support a lot of hands-on projects, like the Solar Car team and Strobe Lab. It's full of people who are eager to help you find something interesting.

Second, find a way to do your own thing. A few suggestions are:

1. Register for a "projects" or "special problems" subject in your (or any other) department. The best types are those with credit "to be arranged." You must find a faculty sponsor. If the project works out well, you can do a careful write-up and petition to make it your thesis.

2. Try to make your project a part-time job with a professor or try to make it a summer job, possibly by getting a hold of grant money. Consult your advisor or department head for suggestions on how to go about it.

3. Check with the interdepartmental labs. A fairly thorough listing is in the Course Catalog. Whatever your idea, if you're really interested in pursuing it you should be able to find help and sponsorship somewhere in the Institute. If at first you don't succeed, keep trying; there are plenty of places to go for advice. The person who turned you down may change his or her mind and offer assistance the next month.

Special Students

Special students, by definition, are not considered to be working toward a degree. Special students pay tuition based upon the number of units they register for; they must be readmitted each term. They usually are not eligible for financial aid, campus housing, or cross-registration. Subjects taken by a special student can be used toward a degree if the student is subsequently admitted as a regular student.

If you're considering changing your status from a regular student to a special student, contact the counseling deans (5-104, x3-4861). Otherwise, you can apply for admission as a special student by contacting the Office of Admissions (3-108, x3-4791).

Study Abroad

See *Foreign Study*.

Summer Session

The summer session is open to all students who completed the preceding spring term and who have not yet graduated. Regular students can pre-register online through `websis.mit.edu`.

Others can apply for admission as a Special Student through the Office of Admissions (see *Special Students*). Non-MIT students cannot register for MIT summer session without being admitted to the Institute under the same admission standards as those for the regular school year.

The summer catalogue is issued in March and is available on the web at `web.mit.edu/catalogue/summer/`. The number of courses offered in the summer is limited, but it usually includes some large freshman and sophomore courses (these days it seems mostly mathematical, such as 18.03 and 18.06) and Sloan courses. Tuition is paid on a per-unit basis, although minimum and maximum rates do exist. For more information about Summer Session, see the academic guide, `web.mit.edu/acadinfo/undergrad/academic-guide/`.

Summer is a good time to do research. It can be done for credit, pay or volunteer. If you do it for credit, however, you will have to pay for it, depending on how many units you register for. Check with the UROP Office (7-104, x3-7306) for more information and help, and ask your department about ongoing projects which you might find attractive.

Theses

Theses are available form the MIT Libraries and some are even available online. For information about obtaining a copy of an MIT thesis, see `theses.mit.edu`.

Copies of *Specifications for Thesis Preparation*, published by the Libraries, are available from your department, the Institute Archives (14N-118) and the web at `libraries.mit.edu/archives/` under Quick Links.

Your advisor or department should be able to answer most questions. Thesis supplies and high quality copying are available from CopyTech — see *Copying and Printing Services* in the **MIT Facilities** chapter.

Transferring Credit

It is possible to receive MIT credit for work done at other institutions. If an exact MIT equivalent exists, fill out a Request for Additional Credit form with a recorded grade of "S". To obtain a real letter grade for a course taken outside MIT, consider taking an advanced-standing test rather than transferring the credit. (Make sure you look at the MIT problem sets and exams first to get an idea of what you'll be expected to be capable of.)

There are transfer credit examiners in each department and Humanities sections. You should check with them *before* taking a course to make sure you will get the credit you want. If no equivalent exists here, see the most closely-related MIT department. Any questions about the granting of credit for work done before you entered MIT as a freshman should be directed to the Director of Advanced Placement in the Admissions Office.

List of Department Transfer Credit Examiners: `web.mit.edu/firstyear/trans-fer/credit/examiners.html`

Information for Transfer Students and Freshmen: `web.mit.edu/firstyear/trans-fer/credit/`

Freshmen

Arrange to have AP scores and transcripts that award college credit sent to the Director of Advanced Placement (Admissions Office, 3-108, x8-5505).

Transfer Students

When you arrive at MIT, see Linda DiSilva in the Transfer Admissions Office to receive your Transfer Credit Sheet. This sheet will list the credit that your received over the summer. You will also be provided with a list of transfer credit examiners for the various departments. Visit the appropriate transfer credit examiners during Orientation and bring with you the subject materials from any courses for which you wish to receive credit (including syllabi, names of texts used, and papers).

Graduate and Special Students

Graduate level subjects completed satisfactorily at other universities may be accepted toward requirements for an advanced degree but do not contribute to the residency requirement. If the subject has an MIT equivalent, submit an Additional Credit sheet; if not, you must request credit through a petition that must be approved by the departmental graduate registration officer. Courses previously taken by a Special Student may be used later in partial fulfillment of requirements for a graduate degree. In either case, the registration officer should indicate the amount of A-level or other credit accepted.

UROP

The Undergraduate Research Opportunities Program (UROP) is rooted in ideas presented in a lecture by Edwin Land in 1959, when he argued that every student should have a faculty guide to help the student explore his/her own connections to learning and inventing. Land, the founder of Polaroid Corporation, used to sneak into New York University labs at night to try out his ideas about the polarization of light, because he didn't have anything like UROP to help him.

These days a lot of students think about UROP simply as a way to get an interesting research job, and the program works quite well for this. Many students find that UROP leads to thesis work, to graduate school, and to careers. In fact, the people at UROP say they will let you do "anything you want, as long as you can get a faculty member to supervise you (and the department to approve)."

Thus, while there are hundreds of undergraduates building their research skills while working on projects for high-powered MIT faculty, there are also a goodly number developing their own projects in science, technology, and the humanities.

You can start a UROP any time during your four years at MIT. If you are a first-year student, UROP has a program called the UROP Mentor Program, which will match you up with an experienced upperclassman on a UROP project during the Independent Activities Period in January. You are not eligible for pay during this time, but you will be given priority for UROP funding should you participate in a UROP project at a later time.

When looking for a UROP, don't hesitate to talk to professors who are doing research that interests you. Part of their job is to teach you, and most are quite happy to talk about their latest projects and interests. Also consider looking outside of your department. Many projects end up crossing disciplinary boundaries, and you could find the perfect research for you in labs whose main work is in a completely different field.

For more information about UROPs, stop by the UROP office (7-104, x3-7306), or see `web.mit.edu/urop/` or check their bulletin board in the Infinite Corridor for current research offerings.

Credit for UROP

First, you need to arrange with a faculty supervisor such details as the nature of the project and the number of units to be awarded. Next, you need to compose a UROP Proposal and complete the cover sheet. Have it signed by your supervisor and submitted to the UROP coordinator in your faculty supervisor's department.

Register for UROP credit as you would for any class. If you want to receive pass/fail credit, register for the UR subject number (e. g., 1.UR, 14.UR). If you wish to receive a grade, register under the suitable subject number for undergraduate research in the department (usually 1.URG, 2.URG, etc.). A UROP may be added after Add Date if it really starts after Add Date. And don't forget to remind your faculty supervisor to submit a grade at the end of the term — if your research isn't finished, a grade of "J" may be awarded to indicate satisfactory research activity continuing beyond one semester. Paid and volunteer UROPs will earn you non-degree URN credit. This will be registered by the UROP office when your faculty supervisor notifies them. You should not register for this credit yourself.

Undesignated Sophomore Status

The Academic Resource Center (7-104, x3-6771) works with students who have not designated a major. The people there will talk to you about selecting a major and choosing or changing advisors. They can often help with problems of course and career selection. If you choose a major and then change your mind, don't worry. It is possible for sophomores to un-designate.

For more information about undesignated sophomore status, or for help choosing a major, contact the Academic Resource Center or see their web site at `web.mit.edu/arc/`.

Warnings

Undergraduates

A CAP Warning is issued in the case of a student whose performance during the past term is considered unsatisfactory and whose status at the Institute may be jeopardized if his or her performance does not improve during the next term. A warning can also be issued when, in the opinion of the department and the CAP, the student is not making sufficient progress towards an academic degree. ("Sufficient progress" includes completion of Institute and department requirements, as well as accumulation of credits at a reasonable rate.)

Students on CAP Warning are given a maximum credit limit for the subsequent term. Generally, the limit is 48 units for freshmen and 51 units (not to exceed four subjects) for upperclassmen. In some instances, the Committee and student's department may decide upon a higher or lower credit. The letter notifying the student of his or her Warning status specifies the exact credit limit voted. The academic advisor and department also receive copies of this letter.

A Warning does not appear on a student's external transcript, it appears only on the internal grade report.

If you have a problem or are facing a warning, talk to some of the Committee members or to the staff of the CAP, located in room 7-104. Most of these people are quite reasonable individuals. There is no set cut-off point for getting a warning or escaping it. The CAP will always review your academic record if you pass less than 39 units worth of classes, for freshmen, and if your term GPA is 3.0 or less (on a 5 point scale), for upperclassmen. The normal procedure for each department is to have a grades meeting at the end of each term, at which recommendations are made to the CAP about each student. Therefore, if you think there is something the faculty of your department should know, *tell them* via your advisor or professors before the end of the term.

Your advisor is your representative and advocate at these meetings, as well as before the CAP. If you are having problems, make sure that he or she knows the full situation if (or better yet, before) you get into trouble. If it's too late for that, call your advisor as soon as possible to provide your side of the story. If you have been ill, be sure you have thorough medical records to show the CAP, as your claims will not be considered without documentation. If you are claiming you have had emotional problems, you may be required to get verification from a psychiatrist.

If you have any questions, contact the CAP in room 7-104, or by e-mailing cap-help@mit.edu. In general, the committee is quite reasonable and tries to help students as much as possible.

Graduate Students

Graduate students may receive a warning from the Committee on Graduate School Policy if their cumulative average is somewhere below the 3.5 to 4.0 range. However, the Committee is not required to warn you. If your poor performance continues, your department will probably recommend kicking you out — it is *vital* that both the CGSP and your advisor clearly understand the circumstances which are causing your problems.

Withdrawal

If you have been on Warning at some point and are now doing poorly, the Committee on Academic Performance may, after consulting your advisor, require you to withdraw. Virtually no one flunks out due to lack of intelligence; if you're having trouble, there's probably some other factor at work.

If you're headed for a withdrawal, *don't panic*. Visit the counseling deans (5-104) or Mental Health (E23-368). Feel free to ask any questions in the CAP office (7-104). The

Careers Office (12-170, x3-4733) can help you find a permanent job (or a temporary one if you intend to reapply for admission).

Transfer

If you plan to transfer to another school, remember that most universities require a minimum GPA of 4.0 (out of 5) for transfer students. If yours is substantially below that, don't be surprised if you are not admitted as a transfer student. If you really think you can't do MIT work, transfer out before the end of your sophomore year; for sophomores, high school grades are the major basis for the admissions decision, and a low MIT GPA won't matter as much. Contrary to archaic wisdom, taking classes at another university prior to admission (e. g. Summer School) will not help your chances of getting a transfer – taking those grades into consideration is known as "provisional admission", and is expressly forbidden under the rules of school accreditation. If you're confident of admission, you can still take the classes and try to transfer the credit in after being accepted, however. The best advice to maximize your chances of getting in if you've decided to transfer is to do your best to finish up your current term with a decent GPA.

Readmission after Required Withdrawal

Normally students seeking readmission after their first required withdrawal apply through the Counseling Deans (5-104). Students with more than one required withdrawal must apply for readmission through the CAP.

It is important to note that the character of the CAP can change quite a bit. The CAP's membership changes partially every year and the committee making decisions about your readmission may have very different attitudes than the one that asked you to leave. When applying for readmission through the CAP, you should submit every existing piece of evidence showing you will be a productive, disciplined, and enthusiastic student. This includes job recommendations, transcripts, and a medical report if you think your past problems were medical in origin. See the ARC for help in writing an effective application.

If applying for readmission through the counseling deans, talk to other students who have gone through Dean's Office readmission before selecting any particular dean. For example, in the past, some deans have tried to restrict a student's choice of major without much investigation into the student's strengths and weaknesses. Be aware that many people regard pure mathematics and physics as unsuitable for someone who has had academic problems.

For graduate students, an application for readmission must be approved by the relevant department. If you're gone more than five years, the request must be approved both by the departmental graduate committee and by the Dean for Graduate Students.

Voluntary Withdrawal and Leave of Absence

If you want to leave school, even if only temporarily, you should contact the counseling deans in room 5-104 for advice and help with all the procedural hassles. If you're not sure whether to take a term or so off, consider talking to one of the deans, your advisor, friends, your personal physician, or members of the Mental Health Service.

Also, the Placement Office can help you in finding a temporary or permanent job. When you request a leave of absence, you will be asked to indicate when you plan to return, but you can change your return date later. Readmission of undergraduates who have withdrawn in good standing is not hard and is done through the Student Life side of ODSUE, particularly Counseling and Support Services. You won't lose financial aid, and housing spaces are often available. In general, a Leave of Absence is preferable to a Voluntary Withdrawal for short-term absences. Though it is limited to 4 semesters, readmission is automatic with a Leave of Absence, while Counseling and Support Services must approve readmission for Voluntary Withdrawals, which may be of any length.

A word about Wainwright Bank and Socially Responsible Banking:

Ever wonder what your bank does with your money? At Wainwright Bank your deposits help fund homeless shelters, special needs housing, environmental protection, HIV/AIDS services, food banks, breast cancer research, and more. In fact, Wainwright depositors have financed over $350 million in socially responsible community development loans right here in your neighborhood. Think Globally. Act Locally.

MARCOS OJEDA '05

MIT Facilities

MIT is in many lines of business; perhaps you have encountered its educational subsidiary. In addition to facilities directly related to education, the Institute has machine shops, art studios, graphic services, and all the comforts of a large resort community. Whatever your heart desires it is probably available right on campus.

Finding exactly what you want, however, is not always easy. You might start with the Information Office (7-121, x3-4795). You can also take a fantastic voyage through the pages of your MIT phone book or ask the internet.

We list here only a few of MIT's more interesting, easily accessible facilities, as well as some related services in the area. Institute museums and art galleries are found in **Sightseeing**.

Athletic Facilities
See *Athletic Facilities* under **Athletics**.

Audio-Visual
MIT Audio-Visual (4-017, x3-2808, `web.mit.edu/av/www/`) rents out projectors and projectionists, tape recorders, public address equipment, overhead and opaque projectors and other AV equipment. They tend to be pricier than outside vendors, but can usually get you what you need on short notice. MIT AV also runs the projection screen in the infinite corridor, which can be an easy way to advertise to pedestrians on campus. See the *Advertising* section in the **Miscellaneous** chapter.

Barbecue Pits
There are four barbecue pits located between Kresge Auditorium and the Kresge Parking Lot on Amherst Street. These pits are reservable through the Campus Activities Complex (W20-500). Each pit serves approximately 50 people and the CAC will provide 2 tables for food preparation for each pit that is reserved. If you are interested in renting additional tables and chairs, contact the CAC. A campus police detail is required if you are planning to serve alcohol and the event must be registered in addition to the space reservation if more than 100 people are expected to attend.

Many dormitories on campus also have BBQ pits that are reservable only by residents. Talk to the dormitory front desk staff for details.

Children's Services
The **MIT Center for Work, Family and Personal Life**, located in 16-151, is one of the best family resources on campus. They can help you locate childcare, schools, summer camps, playgroups and babysitters and can assist in other family matters associated with relocating. They have information on scholarships, sliding fee scales and tax savings programs for childcare. They can also help graduate student spouses living on campus in Eastgate or Westgate become licensed child care providers and put them in touch with parents on campus. For more information, call x3-1592, email `worklife@mit.edu`, or check out their website at `web.mit.edu/hr/worklife/`

There is a variety of private childcare options in the area, ranging from in-home care and licensed care in private homes to large childcare centers. In general, you should expect to pay between $6 and $9 an hour for a childcare center and between $10 and $14 per hour for childcare in your home. For full time care in a childcare center, you may pay up to $1900 per month for infants, with the cost decreasing with age. Childcare centers tend to fill before or during the summer months for the coming school year, so you should begin your search for a childcare provider early.

The **Technology Children's Centers (TCC)** are located in Eastgate, Westgate and the Stata Center (Bldg 32) and offer on campus full- and part-time care for children ranging from 8 weeks to five years old. Center hours are from 8:30am to 5:45pm. Tuition costs vary with schedule and age. For more information and applications, call x3-1217, email `tccinfo@mit.edu` or look at `web.mit.edu/mitchildcare/`. There is a $50 nonrefundable application fee. However, this fee also allows you apply to other childcare centers managed by Bright Horizons as well. Note that there can be a waitlist for spots at any particular location.

MIT also operates a center in Lexington, the **MIT Lincoln Laboratory Children's Center** is located just over a mile away from Lincoln Laboratory at Minuteman Regional High School. They offer childcare for up to 104 children ranging in age from 8 months to 6 years. For more information, call 781-981-6391 or check out their website at `www.ll.mit.edu/careers/lincc.html`.

During the hot summer months, the **MIT Summer Day Camp** (`web.mit.edu/daycamp/`) is also available for boys and girls between the ages of 6 and 14. It consists of four 2-week sessions between late June and mid August, and operates from 9:00am to 3:40pm. An extra hour of care is also available. The camp offers arts & crafts, basketball, dance, drama, gymnastics, sailing, soccer, swimming, tennis, and other electives. The new and improved athletic facilities, experienced staff, and enriching environment will provide campers with the ultimate camp atmosphere. For more information, contact the Day Camp office (W35-297, 617-253-2913).

Computers

Information Systems and Technology (IS&T) offers a variety of computing products and services for a fee, though these would typically be engaged on a departmental or research group level rather than an individual one. For more information about IS&T see `web.mit.edu/is/`. IS&T manages many computer resources at MIT that are free to students and staff. See the **Athena** chapter.

All MIT students, faculty, and on-campus staff members are eligible for Athena accounts. If you have your MIT ID (and the keywords provided in your summer orientation packet if you're a student), then you can go to `web.mit.edu/accounts/` and click on the Registration link. You can also register at the Athena User Accounts Office (N42 front desk). People without IDs, or those with other affiliations to MIT, should get their supervisors or a faculty/staff member to email `accounts@mit.edu` about sponsoring the account.

The **MIT Computer Connection** (x3-7686), located in N42, is essentially the campus computer store. They recommend Apple, IBM, Sun and Dell computers and offer educational discounts on computers, software, and computer supplies which can be purchased through `dell.com` or `govconnection.com`. They are happy to answer any questions related to purchasing a computer and even offer current Athena configurations. Prices, availability, and package deals vary almost weekly, so be sure to check it out if you are considering purchasing one of these machines, even if you stopped by only a short time before. Selection can sometimes be less than you want, but educational prices are unbeatable. Hours are Mon 12:00pm-4:30pm, Tue-Fri 10am-4:30pm. See the **Shopping** chapter for more information on purchasing computers or software.

Perhaps the most widely used computer facilities on campus are the computer clusters. Athena clusters, with machines running UNIX, can be found all over campus and each cluster has at least one black and white printer; try not to abuse the printers. There is a color Athena printer at the W20 Copytech that you can use free of charge for moderate use. The **New Media Center** in 26-139 is a cluster of Macintosh computers intended for multimedia work, not general use. They are outfitted with much of the latest media creation software and hardware. The door combination is not the same as the regular Athena cluster combination, and can be obtained by typing `tellme nmccombo` at the Athena prompt. For those who embrace Microsoft, the Athena cluster in 37-312 has the largest room dedicated to computers running WinAthena: all the luxuries of Windows with the convenience of still being able to access your Athena account. For more information on network computing at MIT, see the **Athena** chapter. Many academic departments also have their own computer clusters. These clusters may run any number of operating systems and frequently have software that is specific to that department. Finally, Macintosh workstations with scanners are available for an hourly fee at **CopyTech** in 11-004 and W20. They can print color and black and white, including transparencies. Call to reserve, or just show up. See *Copying and Printing Services*, below.

The **Student Information Processing Board (SIPB)** in W20-557 is a volunteer student organization involved in many aspects of computing at MIT. The student members are available to answer questions any time the office is open. Call x3-7788, email `sipb@mit.edu` or stop by in person. The SIPB office has a general scanner and a photographic negative scanner that may be used for short periods of time. They also offer some Athena documentation including "inessential guides", copies of the Athena pocket reference and cluster cards (provided by I/S). There are also Athena mini-courses during orientation and IAP. If it's an odd time for people to be awake, like before noon, call to see if anyone is in the SIPB office before heading over.

Finally, computing help may be obtained from **OLC** or the **Help Desk**. Athena On Line Consulting (OLC) is MIT's official support group for Athena related questions. For help, you may visit their office in N42, call them at x3-4435 or read their stock answers for common Athena related questions at `web.mit.edu/answers/`. MIT Information System's Computing Help Desk provides free support for Macintosh and Windows systems. The Help Desk phone lines are open Monday to Friday from 8am to 6pm; walk-ins are welcome in the office in N42 from 9:15am to 5pm. For Mac questions, call 617-253-1101; for Windows questions call 617-253-1102. The Computing Help Desk also maintains a set of stock answers for common Macintosh and Windows at `itinfo.mit.edu/answer`. You can also reach the Help Desk by email at `computing-help@mit.edu`.

Copying and Printing Services

The **Copy Technology Centers** are the in-house copy facilities at MIT. CopyTech services include self-service copying with a variety of paper choices, drop-off production service, color copies, self-service computer workstations with consultations, computer to 35mm slide service, Velo/GBC/Fastback/Hardcase bindings, business cards, fax service, wedding invitations, laminations, scan-to-PDF and burn-to-CD services. Thesis and school supplies are available for purchase. Athena documentation and a large-format color printer can be found in the Main Campus CopyTech center. The CopyTech Express in the Student Center has a poster service. The locations in 11-004 and E52 are also distribution points for supplemental course readers.

There are three campus locations: Main Campus building 11-004, open Mon-Fri 8am to 7pm, call x3-2806; East Campus building E52-045, open Mon-Fri 8am to 5pm, call x3-5203; Student Center (W20), open Mon-Fri 10am to 11pm, Sat & Sun 12pm to 5pm, call x8-0859. 24-hour self-service copiers and Athena Quickstations are also available at the W20 location. Forms of payment include cash, requisition, MIT card, check and Visa/MC. CopyTech likes to try to help student groups get what they need within a budget, so ask. See also `web.mit.edu/ctc/www/`

There are satellite CopyTech photocopiers located around the Institute which have 24 hour access, but require an account number to use. If you are a graduate student or working on a departmental project, talk to your advisor about getting an account number. There are also photocopiers in the various libraries and at some dormitory desks.

The Tech (W20-483, x3-1541) has many computers with Quark XPress and Adobe imaging applications, useful for many publishing purposes besides turning out a newspaper. In the downtime between issues, it may be possible for you to arrange use of them.

LSC (W20-469, x3-3791) has offset presses which accommodate paper up to 17" x 23". When you need to print in large quantities, LSC can be less expensive than photocopying. LSC movie publicity is a product of these presses, and the results can be quite good. Check with the LSC Publicity Director (`lsc@mit.edu`) if you're interested.

Endicott House

Endicott House, located in Dedham, is a 25 acre estate which hosts special events and serves as a conference center. It is open to any group associated with MIT but is not for private entertainment purposes. It is not cheap. For reservations and more information, call the director at 781-326-5151 or go to the website: `www.mitendicotthouse.org`

Faculty Club

The MIT Faculty Club, located on the sixth floor of the Sloan Building at 50 Memorial Drive (Bldg. E52), has 8 function rooms and is capable of hosting a myriad of special events including business meetings, private dinners, receptions, wedding banquets and more. The Faculty Club, which is also home to MIT Catering and the sales office for both, offers an elegant hotel-like setting with beautiful views of the Boston skyline. Food ranges from simple buffets to the most elegant banquets. Reservations should be made months (or years, in the case of graduation) in advance by calling 617-253-2111. For more information see web.mit.edu/dining/catering/mitfacultyclub/

Glass Blowing

The MIT Glass Lab is located in the basement of the infinite corridor, in room 4-003. Extracurricular classes are offered to the MIT community throughout the school year. There is a class that serves as an introduction to the basics of glass blowing. A typical student will learn how to make a paperweight, a cup, a vase, and various other simple forms. There is a 6-8 week class in the Fall, a 4 week class over IAP, where preference is given to freshmen, and a 6-8 week class in the Spring. Classes are filled by lottery only. To enter the lottery, you must come to the lottery meeting. An announcement about the lottery meeting will be sent to glassblowing@mit.edu. You can blanche yourself onto this list or use mailmaint to do so. More information about the glass lab can be found at web.mit.edu/glasslab/

Hobby Shop

The Hobby Shop (W31-031) is located in the basement of the Armory (enter du Pont, go toward the recreation locker rooms, downstairs across from the equipment desk and then around the corner from the pistol and rifle range). In this well-equipped woodworking and metal shop, members are encouraged to build whatever they need with instruction and advice from the professional staff. Recent machine additions include an OMAX waterjet machining center and a CNC lathe. Furniture, musical instruments, thesis experiments, invention prototypes, bed lofts and more have all been built in the shop. Credit seminars are offered in the fall and spring terms with non-credit classes during IAP and the summer. Novices are welcome. The membership fee is $17/term for students and student spouses and $40/term for staff. During fall and spring terms the Hobby Shop is open Mon/Tue/Fri 10am-6pm, Wed/Thu 10am-9pm. During IAP and summer the hours are subject to change. For more information visit their website: web.mit.edu/campus-activities/hobbyshop/ or contact Ken Stone at x3-4343, email: kenstone@mit.edu.

If your project requires precision machining of metal components, you probably want a machine shop rather than the Hobby Shop; see the *Machine Shop* section of this chapter for information about the student machine shop.

Kresge

Kresge Auditorium has the largest seating capacity on campus. It is used for shows, bands, the orchestra, and lectures. The scheduling for the auditorium is done the Monday after Thanksgiving for the coming school year and is booked fairly solidly. In addition to the auditorium, there is a Little Theatre and two rehearsal rooms. Reservations can be made through the CAC in W20-500.

Language Learning and Resource Center (LLARC)

The LLARC, located in 16-644, has an extensive collection of audio, video and computing materials for all levels of languages taught at MIT. Most language classes will require you to visit the LLaRC at some point during the term. The LLaRC also offers a wide variety of materials to teach beginning and intermediate levels of languages from Arabic to Vietnamese. Other tapes, including prose, poetry, plays, and musical "ear-training exercises" are available. Some materials may require the use of an MIT ID. For more information see `llarc.mit.edu` or call x3-9779.

Libraries

The Libraries' web site has a wealth of information: `libraries.mit.edu`. Brochures describing the libraries, their hours, and their services are available at each unit.

Five divisional libraries — Barker, Dewey, Humanities, Rotch, and Science — as well as several branch libraries make up the MIT Libraries. It's not as complicated as it sounds; each of the divisional libraries houses major subject collections that relate to MIT's five schools. Barker has the engineering collection, the Dewey Library holds social sciences and management, the Humanities Library supports the humanities and some social sciences, as well as a general fiction collection, Rotch covers architecture and urban planning, and the Science Library has the science collections. The Humanities and Science Libraries share space in the Hayden Library Building. The Hayden Library includes a 24 hour study room, accessible with your MIT ID when the library is closed. There's a separate library for Music, where you can listen to tapes, records, and CDs, as well as watch videos and DVDs. (CDs and scores may also be checked out.) The major library units are as follows:

Aeronautics and Astronautics	33-111	x3-5665
Barker Engineering	10-500	x3-5663
Dewey (Management and Social Science)	E53-100	x3-5676
Document Services	14-0551	x3-5650
Hayden Circulation	14S-100	x3-5671
Humanities	14S-200	x3-5683
Institute Archives and Special Collections	14N-118	x3-5136
Lewis Music	14E-109	x3-5689
Lindgren (Earth, Atmospheric and Planetary Sciences)	54-200	x3-5679
Rotch (Architecture and Urban Studies)	7-238	x8-5590
Rotch Visual Collections	7-304	x3-7087
Science	14S-134	x3-5685
Schering-Plough	E25-131	x3-6366

Use **Barton**, the online catalog, to discover what the Libraries own (`libraries.mit.edu/barton/`). Check out materials with your MIT ID card. If you want to have a book that is located in one library delivered to another MIT library more convenient for you, you may request it through "Your Account" in Barton or through BookPage (`libraries.mit.edu/mitonly/bookpage.html`).

The "Your Account" feature in Barton also allows you to renew books (up to three times per item); place holds on items checked out by other library users; request stored material; and view your account to see fines owed, books on loan, and requests pending. The feature is not certificates-based so you need to remember the password. You may ask at any circulation desk for a search to be done for a book that you didn't find on the shelves; you may also recall books that someone else has checked out.

Shortly before the due date, you will receive an email reminding you that checked-out books are due. You will also receive an email that books are overdue. Fines are charged on overdue material and range from $0.50/day to $3.00/hour depending on the borrowing period. Fines for overdue recalled books are $2.00/day. Fines should be paid *when the book is returned*; if not paid within 30 days, the charges will be transferred to your Bursar account (fines billed in this way will become a minimum of $5.00 each).

Computers

Each library has at least one Athena terminal for general use. There are also Athena clusters located in Barker, Hayden and Rotch libraries. These clusters all have black and white printers which are just like regular Athena printers.

Online resources

The MIT Libraries have built up an impressive collection of online journals and resources. As of printing there were nearly 300 databases and over 4000 e-journals ranging from "Abstract and Applied Analysis" to "Zoological Journal of the Linnean Society". Many contain the complete back issues as well as current editions. There is also an extensive selection of electronic reference sources including the Oxford English Dictionary and the Encyclopedia Britannica. E-books are also available, such as the O'Reilly "critter" series.

If you are on campus, or have certificates installed on your computer, you may use the majority of the on-line resources to which the libraries subscribe from anywhere you may be. These include e-books, e-journals, databases and encyclopediae. All electronic resources can be accessed from VERA (Virtual Electronic Resource Access): libraries.mit.edu/vera/

Photocopies

All libraries have copy machines and printers; the charge is $0.10/page. Most copiers use MIT Library Copy Cards, which are for sale in Aeronautics and Astronautics, Barker, Dewey, Hayden and Rotch Libraries as well as at Document Services (14-0551). For more information, see libraries.mit.edu/docs/copiersfaq.html

Reserve books

"Reserve" collections of books required for courses are scattered among various libraries. Reserve books may circulate for a two-hour period or for overnight. Heavy fines are charged *by the hour* if you return them late. If you need to keep a reserve book out longer, check to see if there is a copy in the regular collections.

Barker Engineering Library (10-500) has a beautiful reading room (with comfy seats) inside the Great Dome. Dewey Library (E53-100) has current business, political and news magazines and current business newspapers. The Institute Archives and Special Collections (14N-118) has manuscript and archival collections, MIT theses, and rare books. The Humanities Library has best sellers, leisure reading, mystery and travel collections, general magazines and newspapers. The Lewis Music Library has a large collection of music books and scores along with CDs, videos, and DVDs covering classical, jazz, film, electronic, popular, folk, and world music. The listening stations in the Music Library are some of the best individual study areas at the Institute, but remember that your fellow students may need to use them for music-related coursework. The Official Airline Guide and other information on airline history is available in the Aero/Astro Library. Rotch

Library often has interesting art and architecture exhibits, as does Rotch Visual Collections, where slides are housed. The Science Library contains USGS and foreign topographic maps. Geologic maps, nautical charts, and globes, are in Lindgren Library (which also contains a large meteorite). Barker and Hayden Libraries have public Athena clusters.

Reading rooms
The Stratton Student Center houses a reading room on the 5th floor. The room contains a collection of donated magazines and is available for quiet study 24 hours a day, 7 days a week.

There are also quite a few departmental and laboratory reading rooms, often containing materials unobtainable elsewhere. Many of them have thousands of items in specific fields. See `libraries.mit.edu/ordering/independent-libs.html` for a list.

Some dormitories support their own small libraries. Check with the main desk. Also, many faculty members have personal libraries from which some students may borrow.

MITSFS
The MIT Science Fiction Society Library (W20-473, x8-5126), a student-maintained facility, has the world's largest open-stack SF collection with 90% of all science fiction published in English. Hours are irregular (though usually posted on the door) and browsing is encouraged. You must be a member to borrow books, but non-members can read books freely within the library. Membership for a year costs $12 and decreases if you are willing to pay for multiple years up front. Life and Permanent memberships are also available. For more information, see `web.mit.edu/mitsfs/`

Outing Club
The MIT Outing Club (W20-461, x3-2988) has a small reference library of outdoor guidebooks, instruction books, safety books, expedition histories, outdoor periodicals, and New England and New York USGS topographic maps.

Religious books
The Religious Activities Center (W11) has Catholic, Protestant, Muslim, and Jewish collections. Many of these collections are run by student groups. For example, the Hillel Library has 3000 volumes of Judaica in several languages.

Other Libraries Around Boston
If the MIT Libraries do not have something you want for your coursework or research, you may be able to get it through the Interlibrary Borrowing Service (`libraries.mit.edu/ilb/`) or the Boston Library Consortium. Members of the Consortium are Boston College, Boston Public Library, Boston University, Brandeis University, Brown University, Marine Biological Laboratory (at WHOI), Massachusetts State Library, Northeastern University, Tufts University, University of Connecticut, University of Massachusetts Amherst/Boston/Dartmouth/Lowell/Medical Center, University of New Hampshire, Wellesley College and Williams College. You may apply for a Consortium card at Barker, Dewey, Humanities, Rotch and Science Libraries Reference Desks.

Harvard University has a tremendous library system with more than 90 distinct libraries, but it is difficult to get stack privileges. For information on getting access to Harvard

Libraries, see `libraries.mit.edu/ordering/harvard.html`. However, the easiest way to use another university library is often to get a friend there to take out books for you.

Wellesley College Libraries loan books to MIT students. The hours are Mon-Thu 8:15am-midnight, Fri 8:15am-7pm, Sat noon-7pm, and Sun noon-midnight. You can take out as many books as you want and they may stay out for four weeks. Fines range between $0.25 per day and $2 per hour and may be cut in half if you pay when you return overdue books. For information on the Wellesley shuttle bus, see the **Colleges Around Boston** chapter.

Boston Public Library at Copley Square (with branches everywhere) is a large research library. It also has many circulating books and stereo records (which are normally in rather poor shape unless you get them when they're new), out-of-town newspapers and periodicals, and loads of reference material. It's open Mon-Thu 9am-9pm and Fri-Sat 9am-5pm. To get your card, show your MIT ID and fill out an application form. Suburbanites are also eligible for cards.

Cambridge Public Library (449 Broadway, 45 Pearl St., other branches, and bookmobiles) is large and easy to use (open stacks). It usually has several copies of current bestsellers. Reserve one and wait your turn. If you don't live in Cambridge you must show a BPL or other library card to get a card. If you do live in Cambridge, you'll need a photo ID and some other item (like an apartment lease, bill or postmarked envelope) that bears your current address.

Brookline has a public library (361 Washington St. and branches) whose collection is similar to Cambridge's. To register for a Brookline card, bring a Minuteman Library Network Card (if you have one), or a hometown library card, a picture ID and some other item (like an apartment lease, bill or postmarked envelope) that bears your current address. Hours are Mon-Thu 10am-9pm, Fri-Sat 10am-5pm and Sun 1pm-5pm.

All the suburbs and towns around Boston have their own libraries. Collections are normally aimed at the general reader and all have special children's sections. Some have film and lecture programs. There are several special-topic libraries around Boston; some have formidable defenses against entrance by common students. Check with the MIT librarians if you're interested or have special needs.

Machine Shop

The Edgerton Center runs a well-equipped Student Shop in 44-023, including manual and CNC milling machines, lathes, band saws, drill presses, a belt sander and many hand tools. Completion of a training program is required before using the shop and training is conducted monthly in the evenings. Hours vary, so be sure to check the web site at `web.mit.edu/Edgerton/www/Shop.html` before heading in. For additional information contact Fred Cote, x8-7728, `fpcote@mit.edu`.

The Student Shop is only available to students; if you cannot use it for whatever reason and still need access to a machine shop, your best bet is to check within your department. Most departments have a shop with basic machine tools; the Chemistry Department has a glassware shop. Check around for equipment you need and then ask. Rules vary with the shops, but all of them expect you to furnish your own stock.

While the Student Shop is generally the best place to go to do your own metal-working, it doesn't have a waterjet cutter or a CNC lathe. If you need access to these, the Hobby Shop is your best bet; see the *Hobby Shop* section of this chapter for details.

Music Practice Rooms

Practice rooms *per se* are rare. The ones in Building 4 are under the (strict!) control of the Music Department. Most dormitories own pianos and a few are scattered within the living groups. There are several pianos in the Student Center including three practice rooms on the 4th floor. The rooms are under card access and you need to get privileges. Music stands are not provided, so you will need to bring your own.

Observatories

The **George R. Wallace, Jr., Astrophysical Observatory**, located in Westford, MA, is a teaching facility used for classes (*e.g.*, 12.410J/8.287J, Observational Techniques of Optical Astronomy) and for individual research projects. All scheduling is done through the office of the director, Prof. J.L. Elliot (Course XII, x3-6308). The Observatory is 40 miles from Cambridge, in Westford. It has one 24" and one 16" Cassegrain telescope, and several 14-inch and 8-inch telescopes. The 24" is sometimes difficult to get time on, while the other scopes are accessible for projects of any merit. There are overnight and meal facilities, a workshop, a darkroom and computer facilities. Instruments include a high-speed CCD photometer, several small CCD systems, photographic cameras and a spectrograph. The Wallace website is `web.mit.edu/org/w/wallace/`

The **MIT Haystack Observatory** is also located in Westford, MA, and has both a radio astronomy program conducted by the Northeast Radio Observatory Corporation (a consortium of 12 northeastern universities, including Harvard and MIT) and a radar imaging program conducted by MIT's Lincoln Laboratory. Facilities include a 37 meter Cassegrainian radio telescope and Long-Range Imaging Radar, and students are encouraged to request time not just for research but as a general educational opportunity. The Haystack Observatory is part of a larger MIT research complex which also includes facilities at Millstone Hill and the Firepond (operated by Lincoln Laboratory). For more information, see: `web.haystack.mit.edu`

Finally, for hands-on astronomy closer to home, students can take 12.S23 (a fall seminar) and get some observation experience using 12-inch optical telescopes, using the naked eye, film or CCD cameras from the roof of building 37. IAP versions are occasionally offered so check the IAP course offerings.

Printing

See *Copying and Printing Services*.

Problems with Buildings

The Department of Facilities (usually referred to as Physical Plant or PhysPlant) is responsible for all MIT academic and administrative buildings. If there is a problem such as lack of light, heat, or water, go to their website: `web.mit.edu/facilities/`

and fill out the "Repair" form. For an emergency or a repair required after 5:00 PM, call the maintenance line (known to students as FIXIT) at x3-4948 (F-IXIT). In buildings managed by CAC, DAPER and Housing, please inform those staff or building managers first before contacting PhysPlant, except in an emergency.

Pubs

MIT has three pubs on campus — the **Muddy Charles,** the **Thirsty Ear** and the **R&D Pub**. The Muddy Charles is located in the Walker Memorial Building on the first floor, on the Memorial Drive side. The pub employs MIT graduate students for bartending staff and is a popular destination for staff and stressed-out graduate students trying to relax after work. The hours are Mon-Thurs 11:50am-1:50pm and 4:00pm-11:00pm, Fri 11:30am-11:00pm. They have a good selection of draught and bottled beers, and serve some counter food. Food can also be ordered in from Pritchett (upstairs) or from any restaurant that will deliver. As a special bonus, on Fridays in the Summer, the patrons of the Muddy may sit on the East Verandah of Walker overlooking the tennis courts. ID is checked at the door.

The Thirsty Ear is located in the basement of Ashdown House (305 Memorial Drive, enter from the courtyard), and used to be operated by residents. Its status for the fall of 2004 is unclear as the MIT administration tried to close it during the spring. Check the web page at web.mit.edu/thirsty-ear/ for up-to-the-minute information.

The **R&D Pub**, located in Building 32, will be open from 4pm to 10pm M-F serving beer, wine and light fare. It is slated to open the week of August 30th, 2004.

Religious Services

MIT provides both the MIT Chapel and Religious Activities Center as sites for diverse religious services. The MIT Chapel is open daily from 7am to 11pm for private meditation when there is no other service going on. Services of many faiths are held throughout the week; scheduling is done through the Campus Activities Complex. For more information, see *Religious Organizations* in the **Activities** chapter.

Reserving Facilities

Most of the classroom facilities on campus can be reserved through the Schedules Office which is part of the Office of the Registrar. In general, you need to be an academic department, faculty, an administrative office or an ASA-recognized student group to reserve any kind of room. You may email your request to schedule@mit.edu, fax your request to x3-7459, mail your request to room 5-111 or simply walk in and ask to schedule a room. Be sure to include your group name, purpose of event, contact person (with phone number and mailing address), requested dates and times, number of rooms and room requirements if applicable.

The Campus Activities Complex will allow academic departments, MIT-affiliated programs, and ASA-recognized student groups to reserve CAC facilities including rooms in the Student Center, Kresge Auditorium, the Religious Activities Center, the MIT Chapel, Lobby 10, Lobby 13, Walker Memorial, Kresge Barbecue Pits, Wong Auditorium and Tang Center (E51). The CAC will also allow you to reserve booths in Lobby 10 and the Student Center Lobby. CAC provides logistical planning and support to your program. To make a reservation, go to the CAC office in W20-500 and fill out the appropriate forms.

Athletic facilities may be reserved by students and athletic membership holders at the following numbers:

Basketball, Volleyball & Badminton Courts	x8-6199
Outdoor Field Space (Softball, Soccer, etc.)	x8-6199
Squash Courts	x8-6199 or x2-3690
Tennis Courts (Indoor)	x3-1451
Tennis Courts (Outdoor)	x8-6199

Some athletic facilities (Rockwell Cage, Johnson Athletic Center, du Pont Gym) may also be reserved for large non-athletic events. For more information, contact the Athletic Facility Reservations Office (W35-297W, x3-4916). See the **Athletics** chapter for further details on athletic facilities.

Finally, some facilities on campus are reservable only through academic departments. Examples include departmental conference rooms and very specialized lecture halls. Contact the departmental administrator for details. Dormitory facilities can be reserved at the front desk, although you typically must be a resident of that dorm to make a reservation.

Student Art Association

The Student Art Association is open to anyone in the MIT community, although preference is given to students. SAA has superb facilities for ceramics, drawing, jewelry, painting, silk-screening, Chinese brush painting, calligraphy, etching, and a host of other arts. It also has an excellent darkroom and general photographic facilities. Classes in ceramics, photography, and drawing are offered during fall, spring, and summer terms, and IAP. There are fees for classes ($5-70, although most are between $60-70) as well as for the use of the facilities. The office is on the fourth floor of the Student Center (W20-429).

Student Center (W20)

The Stratton Student Center is a constantly fluctuating hub of activity for students. It was originally opened in 1965 and renovated in 1988. Now it is being converted into an environmentally friendly "green" building with the addition of 24 solar panels on the roof to generate electricity for the MIT power grid.

Current Student Center offerings include lounges where students can hang out, study or watch TV, small and large reservable meeting spaces, a large performance space, practice rooms, an art gallery, an Athena cluster, a huge quiet study area and a game room. The Game Room is open daily from 8am-12am and provides diversions such as air hockey, bubble hockey, Dance Dance Revolution, pool tables, video games and pinball. The Student Center is also home to a huge number of student activity offices on the fourth floor and the new Latino Cultural Center in the basement.

Retail services in the Student Center in the basement include Alpha Cleaners & Tailoring, MIT Computer Connection, MIT Optical, STA Travel, New Tech Barber, Technicuts, and a US Post Office. The post office is in a very convenient location, staffed by one very grouchy and two very efficient postal employees. Go there a few times and you'll figure out who to avoid. If you have to get a post office box, get one in the Kendall Square Post Office; the Student Center Post Office loses mail at twice the rate. CopyTech Express, Fleet Bank and the MIT Coop are located on the 1st floor. There is also an MITFCU ATM outside of LaVerde's. Vendors selling interesting things occasionally occupy the 1st floor lobby.

There are various dining options in the Student Center. LaVerde's Market and Alpine Bagels are located on the 1st floor (along with a third, yet unamed, dining option). Lobdell food court occupies most of the 2nd floor and hosts a variety of activities and microorganisms when not being used as a dining facility.

For more information on Student Center vendors, check out the **Miscellaneous** and **Shopping** chapters.

A student-run 24-hour coffeehouse on the 3rd floor used to serve snacks, baked goods, frozen burritos and pizza, instant soup and, of course, coffee for the desperate and destitute among the student body busily tooling the night away. The surly staff and surlier coffee were legendary across campus, and the comfortable, cozily shabby furniture, large tables perfect for spreading out schoolwork, unpredictable music and separable back room made it a favourite student hangout prior to its unfortunate renovation in 2000. Sadly, the Institute's alleged commitment to student life didn't extend to financially subsidizing the Coffeehouse to the extent that proved necessary, and it was finally forced to close down in December of 2002. (The newly-yuppified space is still there but the coffee, food and staff are not). We live in hope that it will reopen some day.

The Coffeehouse closure illustrates the importance of students taking an interest in the direction of the Student Center. The Campus Activities Complex (CAC) runs the Student Center, but has mechanisms in place for students to contribute input and feedback. The CAC Advisory Board consists of students and alumni from all parts of campus who give advice and direction to all major CAC initiatives (mission, program changes, strategic planning, *etc.*). The student members are supposed to represent your voice, so make sure they do so by emailing them your opinions at cacab@mit.edu. To send feedback to the CAC directly, either use the form on their website at web.mit.edu/campus-activities/ or go to W20-500 and talk to them in person.

Walker Memorial (Building 50)

Walker was the original student center of MIT. The building served community dining through Morss Hall and Pritchett (which includes a pool table and TV). Morss Hall is now a major event site, schedulable through the Campus Activities Complex (CAC). Walker houses a number of student activities including the Graduate Student Council, WMBR radio station, the Outing Club's Boulder Wall, the A Cappella Production Facility and the Muddy Charles Pub. Walker also contains the original gymnasium which is often used as a testing/registration site and can be reserved for dance rehearsal through the CAC.

Athena

"Where's the any key?"

Athena, named for the Greek goddess of wisdom, is the main computing environment on campus. Although most students now arrive with their own computers, Athena remains a highly visible aspect of MIT student life.

Begun as Project Athena, it was a major, Institute-wide experiment in the use of computer technologies to improve education at MIT. Project Athena pioneered or refined some of the foundations of UNIX and network computing today, including the X Window System, Kerberos security and Zephyr instant messaging. Now the Athena Computing Environment is the largest single, centrally managed installation of heterogeneous, networked workstations in the world. Athena supports 17 public clusters containing over 350 workstations. Athena workstations are also located in classrooms, laboratories, libraries, living groups, and staff areas. Many are privately owned by faculty and students.

Athena offers computing resources to all undergraduates, graduate students, and faculty. Every student has an account on Athena.

Clusters of computers are scattered about campus. There is a combination for the keypress locks, which is the same for all the public clusters — type "tellme combo" at an athena% prompt. The most visible clusters are the large cluster on the fifth floor of the Student Center and the two "Fishbowl" clusters, one in Building 12 near the Building Four Coffee Shop, and the other in Building 56 on the first floor. There are also about a dozen Quickstations around campus, which are useful if you need to be logged in for a short time (less than ten minutes).

NOTE: This is not meant to be an extensive guide to Athena, merely an introduction. For more extensive help, pick up an Athena Pocket Reference or some of the other printed Athena documentation at the CopyTech in the basement of Building 11, and come to some Athena Minicourses (See web.mit.edu/minidev/www/ for the schedule.)

Getting an Account

Find an open computer with a "Welcome to Athena" screen, press a key, click the mouse on the "Register for an Account" option, and follow the instructions. If you have any problems contact OLC in the basement of the Student Center (W20-021B, x3-4435) or Athena User Accounts in N42 (N42-140, x3-1325). It usually takes a day or two for your account to become active. Incoming students with network access can now open Athena accounts prior to arriving on campus at web.mit.edu/register/.

Be sure you like your username, as it's nearly impossible to change it. Remember that you're going to be using this email address for the next few years and you don't want to be embarrassed telling recruiters or admissions offices what your email address is. There's also a good chance that if you use Athena a lot, your username will become your nickname, so choose wisely. Ten years ago, almost all MIT students were introduced to the internet through Athena, but nowadays most are already proficient. Don't make the mistake of selecting an Athena usename in the same fashion as you might have chosen an AOL screen name. It's equally important to choose a good password. Passwords should be changed at least once a term by typing "`passwd`" at the `athena%` prompt. Good passwords usually have both uppercase and lowercase letters as well as numerals and nonalphanumeric characters. A guide to choosing a good password can be found at `web.mit.edu/answers/accounts/ accounts_choose_password.html`. Never tell anyone your password as they can mess up your files or change your password so that you can't log in; furthermore, it is expressly forbidden and you may be faced with disciplinary action. If someone should somehow manage to change your password, or you forget it, go to N42 with a picture ID and Athena User Accounts will get you out of your fix.

Logging in

At an open computer with a "Welcome to Athena" screen, press a key, type in your username, and then type your password. For security reasons, your password won't be displayed on the screen.

Using Athena

When you log in, you will see a main terminal window with a prompt, `athena%`, at which you type commands. There will also be a bar at the bottom of the screen with several icons on it. This is the GNOME bar, which provides a menu to applications and graphical management of windows. People who have only used Apple or Microsoft operating systems will feel right at home. Several programs, such as the **Mozilla** web browser and the **StarOffice** office suite, behave very similarly to their Macintosh and Windows counterparts and have very low learning curves. However, Athena has its roots in the UNIX family of operating systems. Many tasks are still best performed in text windows or from the command line. To get another terminal window from the command line, type "`xterm &`".

Filesystem and Basic Commands

The UNIX filesystem is structured into a hierarchical directory structure, the same organization that Mac and Windows folders represent. Pathnames are given using the forward slash (`/`) character, not the backslash (`\`) or colon (`:`).

Athena uses the Andrew File System (AFS) to provide file access from any Athena station. Student groups and courses have Athena "lockers" where their files can be stored. Lockers have a quota, one gigabyte as of September 2004. Your own locker is given the same name as your username. You can get to another locker by typing "`attach <lockername>`." This locker will then show up mounted on your current workstation at `/mit/<lockername>`. "`add <lockername>`" will attach a locker and add it to your path so that you can quickly run a program located in a locker. You can give selected people access to your files by setting permissions. Type "`olc answers`" and select the AFS option to learn more about setting permissions.

More About Your Locker

When you first get your Athena account, you will find several files and directories already created in your locker:

`Public` — A world-readable directory where you can place files that you want everyone to be able to access.

`Private` — For your private files. Note that the contents of your home directory (and by default any directories you create there) can have their filenames listed by anyone but the files themselves cannot be read. Files in the `Private` directory can not even be listed by anyone besides you.

`www` — For web publishing. This is the canonical place to set up your home page, which can be accessed by a URL of the form `web.mit.edu/<username>/www/` or `www.mit.edu/~<username>/`

`OldFiles` — Your backup directory. Your locker will be automatically backed up every night and the backups made available to you in this directory, which is read-only. If you accidently delete something which existed the previous day, you can copy it back out of `OldFiles`. Only the previous night's backup is made available in this way — if you wait another day to look for the file, it will be gone from the backup as well. The size of your `OldFiles` directory does not count towards your locker quota. See `web.mit.edu/answers/unix/unix_oldfiles.html` for more information.

In addition to these, your locker contains a number of "dotfiles" (files that begin with a period, *e.g.* ".cshrc"). The period keeps them from being listed unless you type "`ls -a`". These files contain important configuration and customization information. See `web.mit.edu/olh/Dotfiles/Dotfiles.html` for more information about them.

Files

Files can be accessed through application programs, which often have graphical file browsers similar to their Mac or Windows counterparts. However, both files and programs can be managed from the command line. To run a program, type the name of it at the `athena%` prompt. To quit the program, in general, type ctrl-c (press the control key and the c key at the same time) in the terminal window you ran the program from. If the program opens up a new shell (or window), and you will want your prompt back, type an '`&`' after the program name.

[To use the following examples, replace `<filename>`, `<directory name>`, etc., with the appropriate filename, directory name, etc. Comprehensive manual pages on a command can be obtained by typing "`man <command name>`".]

Directory Commands:

   `ls` lists the files and subdirectories in that directory.

   `ls -a` also lists your "dotfiles" -- files which the computer accesses when you log in.

   `cd <directory name>` changes directories.

   `mkdir <directory name>` creates a directory which you can then put files in.

File Commands:

   `more <filename>` displays text files in an terminal window, one screenful at a time.

   `delete <filename>` gets rid of file (truly gone after three days).

   `undelete <filename>` retrieves a mistakenly deleted file.

mv <old filename> <new filename> moves a file, effectively renaming it. If <new filename> is an existing directory, the file will be moved inside it.

cp <filename> creates a copy of the file.

grep <word> <filename> searches for a word in a file.

Email

MIT offers access to mail through two common methods, POP3 (Post Office Protocol) and IMAP (Internet Message Access Protocol). The important difference between them is that POP3 downloads the messages to your locker, while IMAP lets you read your mail on the server. Some prefer IMAP as it allows them to access their email from many locations and computers without logging in to Athena; once mail is downloaded using POP3, it is removed from the mail server. Others prefer POP3 because the Athena quota is larger than the mail server quota and Athena offers greater flexibility in managing saved mail. MH (also xmh and exmh which use MH) uses POP3 to access mail, while Evolution, Pine and WebMail use IMAP.

For a long time, **MH** (Mail Handler) was the only supported mail client on Athena. Many people still prefer to use it instead of graphical or full-screen text mail clients. MH is rather unique in that all its commands are performed from the command line. Here is a brief summary of MH commands:

inc incorporates your new mail so that you can read it.

Each message is assigned a number, which is displayed at the beginning of the line when it is incorporated. Commands, such as show and rmm, when not followed by a number, will apply to the current message, which is marked with a plus sign '+'.

scan lists all the mail messages you have received and their numbers.

show <message #> displays your mail message, similar to more.

next displays the mail message with the next number.

rmm <message #> deletes the mail message.

comp allows you to compose an email message to send using the emacs editor. Put the address or Athena username of who you're sending it to after the To: prompt. Cc: is for carbon copies to other people, with multiple addresses separated by commas. A topic for the letter can be put on the Subject: line. Begin your letter on the line after the "--------". Don't erase this line! When finished, save, exit and type 'send'.

repl is similar to comp, this is to send a reply to a specific message back to its sender.

forw will include a message so that you can send it on to someone else.

For those who prefer a dedicated mail interface, **Evolution** and **Pine** are the supported mail clients on Athena. Evolution includes a contact manager and personal planner and resembles Microsoft Outlook in many ways. It is rather intuitive to use, and comprehensive help is available from the program's Help menu. Pine is a text-based program but quite easy to learn. More information can be obtained at www.washington.edu/pine/

WebMail (`webmail.mit.edu`) provides web-based access to your MIT email account, convenient for email access on the road.

Of course, your MIT email account can also be checked from your home computer using a variety of programs.

Spam filtering is implemented at the mail server using **SpamAssassin**, but you must configure your email client to work with it. More information on spam filtering, as well as other email functionality such as auto-response and email forwarding, can be found at `web.mit.edu/is/topics/email/index.html`

Zephyr

Zephyr is Athena's instant messaging system. Through zephyr, you can send messages to other Athena users who are logged in. You can also participate in discussion groups (zephyr classes and instances), often centered around various living groups and student activities. Zephyr is often used from the command prompt:

`zwrite <username>` sends a message to another user logged in at the same time.

`zlocate <username>` tells if a user is logged on and receiving zephyrs.

You can use a text editor to create a file called "`.anyone`" in your home directory containing usernames of your friends. Then, type "`znol`" to find out which of these people are logged in and to be notified when anyone on your list logs in or out. A graphical alternative to `znol` is `xzul` -- type "`add sipb; xzul &`" to open it and pop up a list in a separate window.

Messages sent to you will pop up on your screen by default. Clicking *anywhere* on the message except the title bar will close it. Be careful not to click a zephyr away before you've read it, as there is no record of it anywhere. If you click on the border of the zephyr, or the bar above it, you can move it while keeping it on the screen. Holding down the shift key and highlighting text in the zephyr copies the text. Popup zephyrs are quite bearable for people who use zephyr occasionally, but heavy users of zephyr often turn to the **Owl** zephyr client instead. Macintosh and Windows zephyr clients exist, with **MacZephyr** being more mature as you might expect. These can be obtained from `itinfo.mit.edu/product?name=zephyr`

The *Inessential Guide to Zephyr*, available from SIPB, gives a broader overview of zephyr, but is somewhat technical in nature. Often, the best source of information about zephyr is an experienced upperclassman.

Text Editing and Word Processing

Emacs is a full-screen visual text editor, developed by free software advocate Richard Stallman as a replacement for the `vi` editor while he was at MIT. It's extremely extensible and customizable; you can web-surf, read your email, send zephyrs, or do just about any computing function without ever quitting Emacs. The most important, though, is how to quit and save your document! This is done by hitting ctrl-x followed by ctrl-c, and answering the question at the prompt.

Framemaker is a fancy "What You See Is What You Get" word processor and is easy enough to learn to do basic processing. It does not run on Linux-Athena workstations. **StarOffice** is widely used and supported on these machines. **Applixware** is also available.

LaTeX is a text formatter. It is more flexible and powerful than WYSIWYG text layout software, but is harder to learn. Many people use it to write large documents such as theses and anything that requires precise control of mathematical formulae.

There is documentation available and minicourses on each of these. When you don't have time for a lot of options and just want to jot down some text, **Pico** is a very simple text editor that does not have very many features but is fast to load and easy to use.

Printing
All of the clusters have printers. `cview printers` will give a list of all the printers and the clusters they're located in, as well as how many jobs each one is currently processing.

`lpr -P<printer name> <filename>` will print out a text or PostScript file.

`xdpr -P<printer name>` will print a window dump. When the cursor changes to a crosshair, click in the window you wish to print out. Clicking in the root (background) window will print out the entire screen.

`lpq -P<printer name>` can be used to check the status of the printer, including which jobs are ahead of yours, and whether or not the printer is working.

`lprm -P<printer name>` will cancel the first pending printing request belonging to you. You can cancel specific print jobs with `lprm -P<printer name> <job ID>`. `lprm -P<printer name> <username>` will cancel all your jobs.

When you pick your stuff up from the printer, you can easily tell what is yours by the presence of a header page with your name on it. These header pages are designed to be as un-wasteful as possible: they have things like graph paper or music staffs on them.

Thesis printers are available in the main CopyTech Center in 11-004 and in the CopyTech Express in the Student Center (W20).

Screensaving
It is generally considered a good idea to screensave if you want to leave your terminal for a little while. While Athena has a default screensaver to protect the screens, this does not protect your files from random passers-by. Before you go, type "`xlock`" at the `athena%` prompt, or select "Lock" from the GNOME menu. This protects your account in that you need to enter your password before you can get to your account. *Do not leave your workstation unattended for more than 20 minutes.* Not only is it rude to people who may need the computer, but they will actually be able to log you out after 20 minutes.

Help
Help in learning how to use Athena is readily available. Athena is a powerful and fun environment, and we encourage you to explore and learn. Typing `help` at the `athena%` prompt will open a web browser with the 'Athena On-Line Help' page, which

has links to many topics and answers to help you. Browsing through can teach you many things. You can call Athena Consulting at x3-4435, stop by their office at N42, or ask them a question over Athena by typing "olc" at the athena% prompt and following the instructions. Answers to frequently asked questions on Athena can be accessed by typing "olc answers" at the athena% prompt or on the web at web.mit.edu/answers/. SIPB (Student Information Processing Board), located in W20-557 outside the Student Center cluster, is a group of students who help to create and maintain many services on Athena. They can often answer questions about Athena software. Information Systems conducts a series of Athena Minicourses which focus on specific topics, such as Getting Started on Athena, and using editors such as Emacs, LaTeX, and Framemaker, as well as many other useful things on Athena. You can find their complete schedule at web.mit.edu/minidev/www/.

Mailing lists

Much information within MIT is shared via mailing lists, from class announcements to social activities. Athena provides tools to allow you to subscribe and unsubscribe from mailing lists, as well as manage mailing lists of your own. The basic command for manipulating mailing lists is blanche. Typing "blanche" by itself gives you a complete list of commands, but the most commonly used are as follows:

blanche <list name> -a <your username> adds yourself to a mailing list.

blanche <list name> -d <your username> removes you from a mailing list.

If you have trouble using blanche, a menu-driven interface to the same features can be accessed with the mailmaint command or by accessing the WebMoira site at web.mit.edu/moira/ with your web browser.

Never email a list asking to be removed! The list members cannot remove you and will just become upset with the unnecessary mail. The blanche command will not immediately stop you from receiving list mail — it takes at least 4 hours for mailing list database updates to propagate. If you are still receiving mail, contact Athena User Accounts or OLC for help. If you wish to contact the administrator of a mailing list, use the address <list name>-request instead of sending mail to the list itself. If someone does mail a list asking to be removed, send them a discreet personal message — don't cc: it to the whole list, or you'll be just as bad.

Personal web pages

Your Athena account can be used to host a personal web site that anyone on the internet can access. Your web site is contained in the www directory in your Athena account — anything you put in there can be accessed over the web. You can place HTML and graphics files in there, or even sound and video as long as your disk quota can handle it. Many people find this useful for keeping in touch with friends back home or directing people who want to know more about them such as potential employers. If you create an index.html file in the directory, people will not be able to list the contents of the directory, they will just receive that page. Once you have built your web site, visit web.mit.edu/is/web/reference/create/faq/announce-page.html for information on how to get your web site listed in the MIT online directory and the MIT Community home page list.

Quota

All Athena users have a disk space quota, although it is quite large and most people will not fill it immediately. To check how much quota you have left, type "`quota -v`" at the `athena%` prompt.

Games

One of Athena's most important purposes is to provide a distraction when we should all be doing more productive things. The best way in which it does this is by providing a variety of computer games to play. Don't monopolize computers during busy periods by playing games, though!

`add games; ls /mit/games/bin` will give you a list of games. Most are executables that you just have to type their names to get them to run. Have fun!

Logging out

It's really important to logout before you leave. Click on the Logout button in the lower right corner of your screen, and confirm that you wish to leave, or type logout at the `athena%` prompt, making sure it listens to you before you go.

Residential Computing

All students can have their own computers in their dorm rooms connected to MIT's residential network (MITnet). The network supports almost any kind of computer and operating system: Macintosh, Unix, even Windows. To be able to connect to MITnet, which includes a direct connection to the Internet, simply go to `rcc.mit.edu` and fill out the form there. A Residential Computing Consultant (RCC) will then help you get your computer set up, which usually just consists of giving it the correct IP address.

Once you have your own computer connected to the network, you can use its own software to access various Athena features such as printers and your e-mail. The online help and your RCC can help you out with setting this up if you have problems.

You can bring many parts of Athena to your personal computer through programs available at `web.mit.edu/software/` for on-campus download:

- **Kerberos** implements the basic Athena authentication package and is required for most of the other tools.

- **BetterTelnet** and **NiftyTelnet** (Macintosh) and **HostExplorer** and **SecureCRT** (Windows) allow you to log onto Athena remotely. You do not get the GNOME bar, but you do get an Athena prompt.

- **Virex** (Mac) and **VirusScan** (Windows) are officially supported anti-virus software.

- **X-Win32** is an X server for Windows. Combined with HostExplorer/SecureCRT, you can run **MATLAB** or other specialized graphical programs on Athena without leaving your dorm room. Mac OS X users can download a variety of free X servers from other locations — Apple's version at `www.apple.com/macosx/x11/` is one of the most popular.

- **KLPR** gives you access to Athena printers. Very useful for people without printers of their own, or when the high quality of a laser is preferred to inkjet output.

- **MacZephyr** and **WinZephyr** allow you to participate in the zephyr messaging system, and offer a more convenient interface than the text-only mode of receiving zephyrs in your terminal window.

- **TSM** is a network backup program. Useful for those who don't want to be bothered with backing up onto CD-Rs or DVD-Rs every once in a while. (Files stored in your Athena locker are backed up automatically, but files on your computer are your own concern.) The backup service costs $7.50 a month per computer.

Some notes on etiquette

If you end up using a graphical client to read your e-mail on your personal computer, it is worth keeping a few things in mind, particularly with regard to mailing lists (every MIT student will find themselves on at least a few mailing lists before they know it!). Most people at MIT use plain text mail readers on Athena, so it is considered very bad form to send mail using HTML or 'Rich Text,' and even worse to send e-mail attachments such as pictures or word processor documents. Unsuspecting people who do this often get savagely "flamed," so it's best to avoid it from the outset! If you are using Eudora to read your mail, avoid HTML mail by answering that you want your message to be in plain text when it asks. It is also easy to set the preferences to always use plain text by choosing Options... from the Tools menu, selecting the Styled Text panel and choosing "Send plain text only." With Microsoft Outlook it is a similar process — in a new message window choose 'Plain Text' from the Format menu, or turn plain text mail on permanently by choosing Options... from the Tools menu, clicking the Send tab, and setting Mail Sending Format to "Plain Text." You should also turn Quoted-Printable encoding off while you are at it, or all your quotation marks and apostrophes etc. will be rendered as gibberish and your message will be more likely to be automatically rejected as junk mail by various automated antispam systems.

If you have a file you want to share with other MIT people, use your `Public` directory. Move the file into this directory and then direct interested parties there — this helps avoid clogging up people's mailboxes and Athena quotas. Some people read their mail over slow networks from overseas so you can't predict when you'll be causing someone problems by sending an attachment — just give everyone a break and keep the e-mails text only.

How to Get Around the Paper Forest

The Institute publishes not only thick volumes on the advances in high-energy physics and information theory, but also publishes thousands of pages of guides and policies that describe and govern the way things are (or at least should be) around here. Luckily, almost all of these publications can be found online, although some of them require MIT certificates to view. This section lists some of the most useful of these documents, and where to find them.

When You Arrive

MIT Facts

The MIT administration maintains a website with everything it ever wanted you to know about itself. It contains listings of labs, professors, and other good public relations things, mostly laundry-list style. Though mostly maintained for those who *want* to donate to MIT, it may be a good way to get a quick overview of everything the Institute sponsors. The address is `web.mit.edu/facts/`

First-Year

The Academic Resource Center maintains a website for all students entering MIT. There are sections for freshmen, for transfer students, and for graduate students, as well as info for faculty advisors. The website contains fairly comprehensive listings of all the things new students should know about, including registration, course selection, academic requirements, advising, housing, student life, and much more. The address is `web.mit.edu/firstyear/20xx/` (where xx is equal to your graduating year, for example 08).

Picking Classes

Course Catalog

The MIT Bulletin: Courses and Degree Programs is published in print every year in September. It contains information on requirements for undergraduate and graduate degrees, interdisciplinary study and research, departmental programs, and descriptions of subjects. To obtain a copy, go to the Student Services Center (11-120) or to the Coop, in Kendall Square or in the Student Center, where you can have one mailed to you. They will also be handed out during the week before Reg Day. An online version is available at `web.mit.edu/catalogue/`

HASS Guide

The *Humanities, Arts, and Social Sciences Guide* (HASS) is published each term and contains information on all humanities courses above and beyond the catalog description. It's very useful and usually accurate. Print copies are available in the Student Services Center (11-120) and an online version is at `web.mit.edu/hass/www/guide.html`. Procedures for selecting HASS classes are a little different for first-semester freshmen, who can visit `web.mit.edu/hass/www/frosh/` for details.

Seminars

Various departments offer a number of seminars each semester for undergraduates with interest in a subject but with little or no background. The Academic Resource Center maintains a listing of all the seminars being offered each semester; you can find these listings online at `student.mit.edu/catalog/mUndergraduate_Seminars.html`, or visit the ARC in 7-103 and 7-104.

Summer Session

The *Summer Session Catalogue Issue* of the *MIT Bulletin* is published annually in April. It contains complete information concerning academic activities during the Summer Session. To obtain a print copy, contact the Reference Publications Office in E28-100 or at x3-2635. The *Summer Session Catalogue* is published on the web at `web.mit.edu/catalogue/summer/`

IAP (January Semester)

The *Guide to IAP Activities* is a catalogue of activities taking place during the January Independent Activities Period. The guide is online at `web.mit.edu/iap/` and while officially published in December, the website may be updated as early as October.

Cross-Registration

MIT students may cross-register for classes at Harvard or at Wellesley College for no additional cost. This is done usually, but not always, for HASS (humanities, arts, and social sciences) subjects. The Student Services Center (11-120, x8-8600) has lots of information about these programs, as well as people available to answer questions Monday-Friday 9am-5pm. A website that briefly describes the procedures for cross-registering is at `web.mit.edu/ssc/crossreg.html`

Picking Classes - The Insider Info

Student Subject Evaluations

The MIT Office of Academic Services gives out surveys to students in every subject at the end of each semester, and makes a summary of these evaluations for each course available to the MIT community. They are published on the web at `https://web.mit.edu/acadinfo/sse/`, but need to be accessed from an on-campus computer. The `https://` must be included to access the site. There is one form for Science/Engineering subjects, and another for HASS subjects. Both include averaged student ratings for each instructor, for the text, for assignments, and for various other materials, as well as sample comments. The Institute maintains this guide now mostly for instructors to improve their subjects, but it may be useful to students selecting subjects at the beginning of the semester. Some Course-specific subject evaluation guides are also available. One of the largest, the *Underground Guide to Course VI*, is available from Eta Kappa Nu at `hkn.mit.edu/ug.html` — print copies are available in the Course VI undergraduate office (38-476).

How to Do Research At MIT

UROP

The Undergraduate Research Opportunities Program Office makes available information for undergraduate students about participating with MIT faculty members in a wide range of research and project activities both on- and off-campus. Visit the UROP office in 7-104 or browse their website at `web.mit.edu/urop/index.html`. The site contains general information about the UROP program, about finding a UROP, and about getting funding or credit, as well as some listings by professors who are looking to hire a UROP.

Student Thesis Guides

Many departments publish guides for students who are attempting to write a thesis as part of their degree requirements. They are meant specifically for students who are working in that particular department, but include general information about the formal thesis guidelines and completion schedule. One such example is: www.eecs.mit.edu/ug/thesis-guide.html.

Research

For information and current news about research funding, policies and procedures, and other topics relevant to research and other scholarly activities, visit web.mit.edu/osp/www/. (Office of Sponsored Programs, E19-750, x3-4734)

How to Do Non-Study Stuff

Event Planning

The *Guidebook to Planning Events @MIT* lists available facilities, policies for reserving them, applicable MIT regulations, and even ways to get the word out. When planning an event, keep in mind that there are more rules than you can probably imagine, and some events may involve such things as Campus Police supervision, metal detectors at the entrance, and entertainment licenses from the City of Cambridge. If you're ever in charge of planning an event for your club or living group, read this to avoid trouble with the authorities. The Guidebook is available from the Campus Activities Complex, (W20-500, x3-8585). A pdf version can be downloaded from web.mit.edu/campus-activities/www/downloads/SLP_Guidebook.pdf

Student Activities Request for Funding Guide

This outlines the process which allows groups to request funds from administrative offices or departments primarily within the Dean for Student Life Office, if funds from student government sources are insufficient. It can be found at web.mit.edu/slp/finances/supp-funding-guide.html. (SLP, W20-549, x3-4734)

Staying Safe

Safety

The Environment, Health and Safety Office (web.mit.edu/environment/ehs/) puts out a long list of guides ranging from Biosafety through Chemical Safety to General Safety.

Spending Money at MIT

Financial Policies and Reports

A list of all publications produced by the Controller's Accounting Office can be found at web.mit.edu/cao/www/cao_pubs.htm. This includes information on travel, petty cash and the cashiers' office, the treasurer's report, retirement plan information, the accounting and purchasing system and various forms.

Laboratory and Office Supplies

Electronic Catalogue (ECAT) is MIT's web-based purchasing system for purchasing directly from selected MIT partner vendors. (web.mit.edu/ecat/)

Purchasing Policy

Procurement Policy and Procedures is a brief handbook on purchasing regulations. (NE49-4122, x3-7241, web.mit.edu/controller/procurement/)

Thou Shalt (Not)

Undergraduate Guide

The *Academic Guide for MIT Undergraduates and their Advisors* is published every few years by the Committee on Academic Performance. It is intended to be a summary of information concerning the grading system, Institute requirements, registration procedures, and other administrative aspects of MIT, including detailed information concerning policies and procedures followed by the CAP. It can be found online at web.mit.edu/acadinfo/undergrad/academic-guide/intro.html or at the Academic Resource Center (7-104, x3-4164).

Graduate Policies

Graduate Policies and Procedures is the definitive statement of organization, policies, and procedures applicable to graduate instruction. An online version is available at web.mit.edu/gso/gpp/index.html. Also useful may be the Graduate Student Office (3-138) and the website it maintains at web.mit.edu/gso/. The GSO provides many academic and other services to Institute graduate students.

Faculty Rules

Rules and Regulations of the Faculty is the official statement of the organization, operation, rules and regulations of the faculty. It is available online at web.mit.edu/faculty/rules/. In addition, the Term Regulations, containing information on faculty rules relevant to students such as restrictions on exam and assignment scheduling, can be found at web.mit.edu/faculty/termregs/

Personnel Policy Manual

The regulations governing MIT employees. (Human Resources Department, x3-4251, web.mit.edu/hr/policy/)

Employee Benefits

Numerous publications, forms, and tools for MIT's employees are available at web.mit.edu/hr/benefits/forms.html (Human Resources Department, E19-215, 400 Main St, x3-4251)

Handicapped Access

Handicapped Access

The Disabilities Services Office (7-145, x3-1674) offers various services to members of the MIT community with disabilities; information can be found at web.mit.edu/dso/www/. The office also publishes *Access to MIT: A guide to facilities for the handicapped*, available at the Personnel Office (E19-226) and the Information Office (7-121). The *DSO Student Handbook* is online at web.mit.edu/dso/www/general_sec11.html. The handbook includes information about note-taking services, Braille materials, and procedures for requesting other specific accommodations for disabled students.

Finding People

The MIT website has an excellent people search engine for all currently listed MIT affiliates. Additional printed directories are intended for authorized use by Institute personnel only. They should not be made available for advertising, placement, or other commercial use.

Faculty and Staff Directory

The Faculty and Staff Directory gives office and home telephone numbers and addresses of faculty, staff, and employees, and is published each year in October. It is available to faculty members and those who do business with the Institute, but is not distributed to students. (Reference Publications Office, E28-100, x3-2635, `web.mit.edu/referencepubs/`)

The Student Directory

The Student Directory is published at the beginning of each academic year, and includes names, home addresses, telephone numbers, e-mail addresses and local addresses of MIT students. Copies of the student directory are distributed to student residences on campus and to franternities, sororities and living group houses. Students living off campus can obtain a copy from the Information Center in room 7-121 by showing MIT identification. (Reference Publications Office, E28-100, x3-2635, `web.mit.edu/referencepubs/`)

The Alumni Register

The Alumni Register is a complete roster of all alumni and alumnae, published periodically. The 2002 Alumni Register may have been the last printed, hardback version published (Alumni Association, 10-110, x3-8200, `alum.mit.edu/as/shopping/register.html`). The *Alumni Directory* can be accessed online at `alum.mit.edu`.

How is MIT Doing
Quench your curiosity

MIT Corporation Reports to the President

The Secretary of the Corporation annually submits a summary report of the activity of the Corporation and its committees. (`web.mit.edu/corporation/report.shtml`, MIT Office of the Corporation, 7-203, x3-2058)

The Report of the Treasurer to the MIT Corporation

Published annually in October, this is a report of operations, gifts, plant facilities, and investments of the preceding fiscal year. It includes a five-year trend analysis and a description of the distribution of investment income to funds. (Office of the Treasurer of the Corporation, 238 Main St., Suite 200, 617-253-4900)

Reports to the President

A compilation of annual reports submitted to the President from MIT's major academic and administrative units. (`web.mit.edu/annualreports/`, Reference Publications Office, E28-100, x3-2635)

MIT Geography

As far as MIT is concerned, Massachusetts Avenue runs north-south, and the Charles River runs east-west. While this is convenient, it isn't particularly true, as Cambridge enjoys a peculiar immunity from reason. The Charles River runs north-south, east-west and (again) north-south near MIT; and both Mass. Ave. and the Red Line (which supposedly follows Mass. Ave.) angle around so much that nobody even bothers to give objective directions to anywhere.

In this section, "north" means "up Mass Ave towards Central Square"; "south" means "towards the river, where the Hahvard bridge is"; "east" means "also towards the river, but where the Longfellow Bridge is"; and "west" means "also also towards the river, but along Vassar Street."

MIT's main campus is quite compact and often confusing to navigate, with tunnels, passageways, and cleverly-hidden hallways. If you're new to the place, you could try walking around and getting lost once or twice just to get the hang of it, or you could get an overview by taking an Information Center tour. Tours are given at 10am and 2pm. For details, call the Info Center (7-121, x3-1875).

Nearly everything at MIT is referred to by number, and places are no exception. The general formula for a room number is X-YZZ, where X is the building number, Y indicates the floor where the room is located, and ZZ is the number of the room on that floor.

Exceptions abound for everything. Building 54 is 21 stories tall, and so its upper rooms have 4-digit numbers: 54-100 is on the first floor, 54-1100 would be on the eleventh. However, the "first" floor of 54 occupies the 3rd & 4th stories of the building - apparently because Cambridge building codes restrict the number of floors in a building, but not the height. (There's another place on campus that has 4-digit room numbers, but that's left as an exercise for the reader.)

All buildings at MIT are numbered according to their location. This is not to imply that the numbering makes sense, but rather that there is a method to it. Building numbers have an indicative prefix:

• M or none: Main Campus. The area enclosed by Ames St, the train tracks, and Mass Ave. Athena Clusters on main campus are prefixed with an M, as in "m38 cluster"; this occasionally carries over in conversation.

• W: Buildings west of main campus, but south of the train tracks.

• NW: Buildings west of Mass Ave but north of the train tracks.

• N: Buildings north of the train tracks, but between Mass Ave, and Main Street.

• NE: Buildings north of Main Street but west of 3rd Street.

• E: Buildings east of Ames Street and south of Main Street, plus E70.

Two anomalies are Building 46, which straddles the train tracks and thus the N/M boundary; and Building E70, which is north of Main Street (and of NE18, NE20, and NE25) but isn't called NE70.

Plenty of other strange situations exist, due to the layout of Cambridge proper: N57 is farther west than a lot of W and NW buildings; NE49 is farther west than half of main campus and the N buildings; the same train tracks are both east of half the NE buildings and south of all the N buildings; *etc, etc.*

Some building numbers have suffixes, usually denoting nearby or connected subdivisions (7 & 7A, for example). An exception is Building 14, which doesn't really exist above ground; it is the composition of buildings 14N, 14E, 14S, 14W and the courtyard enclosed by the buildings. Building 32 is also notable in that the suffix letter appears as part of the room number, rather than the building number (32-G*yyy* not 32G-*yyy*).

Tunnels exist between buildings 14 & 18; 18 & 54; 54 & 56; 26 & 32; 66 & 68; 68 & E17/E18/E19; New House & MacGregor; and between the parallels of East Campus (for EC residents); and between New House and MacGregor (for New House residents only). See map for details.

Basements otherwise connect where two buildings meet. They can be handy in bad weather or to avoid "rush hour traffic" at the top of the hour. Be careful of floor changes — in going from one building to the next, a ramp or a few steps may mean you've gone up or down a floor. The Infinite Corridor traffic (buildings 7-3-10-4-8) can be bypassed on the 2nd, 3rd, or basement levels. It may be more convenient, depending on your destination, to walk through Killian Court, or along the street outside building 13.

Notice that buildings to the East (2,4,6,8) and West (1,3,5,7) of Killian Court are symmetric... except for Lobby 7.

The doors to the following buildings are always unlocked: 7, 8, 16, 39, and W20, the Student Center. Doors are usually kept open until 11pm in buildings 13, 14, 24, 56, Kresge and the Chapel.

Tips:

• You can get from 77 Mass Ave to within 100 feet of the Kendall T stop without ever going outside.

• Tired of waiting for the slow elevators in Lobby 10 or Lobby 7? If you want to go to the 4th floor of the main buildings, take the lobby 16 elevators to the 5th floor and turn left. You will find yourself on the 4th floor of the main buildings.

Can't get there from here:

• The 2nd floor of 13 does not connect to the main buildings.

• The 1st floor of 9 does not connect to the main buildings.

• The 3rd floor of 9 does not connect to building 7. It used to, until the Rotch library was built. It's worth a visit.

• Be careful of the elevators in 4 and 6. The door on one floor is blocked by a file cabinet. Try to figure out which floor.

• The 1st and 2nd floors of 36 do not connect to 32.

• There are no tunnels between dorms and academic buildings, despite what the upperclassmen may tell you.

• Your MIT ID card will not let you access Buildings 18 or 68, nor the upper floors of 16 or 54, unless you work there.

Where is...

- the Secret Ninja Courtyard: the courtyard bounded by 8, 6, 2 and 4. Accessible from the basement level.
- the Secret Ninja Parking Lot: the courtyard bounded by 7, 5, 3 and 1. Accessible via road, or the basement level.
- the Fishbowl: Student Services Center area (named after the Fishbowl Cluster which was removed to make way for the SSC).
- Transparent Horizons: The sculpture between the two parallels of East Campus and 66.
- Fred T. Dorm ("Fred", for short): East Campus
- the Great Sail: Alexander Calder's large metal sculpture between Walker, 14, 18, and the West Parallel of EC (properly known as the Big Sail).
- the Dot: The circle of grass in front of the Green Building (officially named McDermott Court).
- the Green Building: 54
- the Bio Building: 68
- Walker: 50
- Hayden: 14
- Networks: Courses
- Courses: Alpine Bagel Company
- Tosci's: the empty space in the front of W20 where Arrow Street Crepes was.
- Newbury Comics: the formerly empty space on the first floor of the student center, currently occupied by the arcade (which used to be in the basement).
- the Stata Center: 32
- the Two Towers: 32-D (Minas Tirith) and 32-G (Minas Morgul).
- the Z-Center, Dupont, and Johnson: the sweaty complex west of W20.
- Briggs field: the giant field west of Kresge.
- the nuclear reactor (NW12): the blue dome west of Mass Ave, just north of the train tracks.
- the MIT Museum (N52): at the corner of Mass Ave and Front Street.

`whereis.mit.edu` and `floorplans.mit.edu` can be useful references for other such questions.

Recent changes to MIT's campus

Building 20 was demolished in 1998, and Building 32 erected on the same spot. E10 and E20 were torn down in 2001 to make way for E14; the Media Lab Extension project, which has been postponed for lack of funds. Building 45 was recycled earlier this year to make way for Building 46 — the McGovern Institute for Brain & Cognitive Science — which is due to open in 2005. The "(Far) East Campus Project", currently unscheduled, is slated to create a "vibrant community" for Sloanies.

Building 32 (the Stata Center) is complicated. The building officially consists of two nine-story towers sharing a two-story base, and also includes three underground floors with 678 parking spaces. However, the lower two floors of the towers (that is, the third and fourth floors of 32) are also connected, though only the fourth floor rooms are numbered with their tower designations. The towers, much like the overall complex, are named after major donors: the eastern tower after Bill Gates, the western one after Alexander Dreyfoos, and are numbered 32-G and 32-D. Amusingly, the two towers are also called Minas Morgul (32-G) and Minas Tirith (32-D) by their inhabitants.

There are five exterior entrances to Building 32: on Vassar Street by 36; between 36 and 26; just west of 57 (the Alumni Pool); and two on the eastern side. The first floor is largely open, and is supposed to evoke a small town of sorts. This "Student Street" is slated to include a café, a gym, dance studios, an information center, child care, and (much like all small towns) a few classrooms. There will also be a new pub (**the R&D**) on the fourth floor, which is supposed to replace **The Thirsty Ear**. It remains to be seen whether or not one can get a $1.25 beer in a $300 million building.

Bathrooms

Here are a few guidelines for finding a bathroom quickly. On the main corridor, lavatories are stacked vertically, men's above women's and vice versa. They normally occur at the junction of two buildings — for instance, 3-101, which is a women's room. In the other main buildings, a similar situation applies, with bathrooms occurring at the ends of buildings or just before (or after) a corner. Example: 1-101 is a men's room. In the newer buildings, men's and women's rooms are usually close together and either centrally or peripherally located. The notable exception is Building 14 with men's rooms at the western end, women's rooms at the eastern end, and none on the first floor. Check the corridors for water fountains. Where there is a fountain, a bathroom usually isn't far away.

Card Readers

Many doors on campus have card readers that will allow you to use your MIT card to unlock the door. The card readers have three lights on them. A flashing green light means the lock is inactive, and the door can be opened by pushing or pulling as appropriate. A solid yellow light means you must swipe your card to open the door. A pattern that flashes red-green, yellow means that the door is being held open. If you swipe your card, and see a green light (usually accompanied by an audible click), the door has been unlocked by your card. If you swipe your card and see a red light, it means that you are not authorized to use that door. Contact the card office (E32-117, x3-3475, mitcard@mit.edu) if you think you should be able to use this door. If you see a rapidly flashing red light after swiping, it means your card could not be read correctly, or that the reader is broken.

Phones

There are three types of phones located around campus. Blue Light Phones, or Emergency Phones, will connect you to the Campus Police emergency line when they are picked up or the button is pressed. Your location will be immediately transmitted to the police, so if you are experiencing an emergency and can't talk to the person at the other end, stay in the area and the CPs will arrive shortly. Campus phones (identifiable by their lack of coin slots) will let you call any 5-digit MIT number, including institutions that have MIT "tie lines". See the **Useful Phone Numbers** chapter or web.mit.edu/is/tel/tielines.html for instructions on how to dial places such as Wellesley, Harvard, and Mass. General Hospital. There are also regular pay phones located around campus.

Tunnels

Below is a map of the main underground tunnels at the Institute. They can be useful for going from place to place when it's raining, or for moving wheeled equipment without encountering stairs (tunnels tend to change elevation via ramps instead). PhysPlant offers subterranean tours of campus through MITAC (50-005, x3-7990, web.mit.edu/mitac/), or just explore on your own with the map.

Vending Machines

Vending machines are located along the basement of the Infinite Corridor, and in other scattered places in the Institute. Large clusters of vending machines are located at the following locations: Lobby 16, the basement of 10, the basement of the 2/14 intersection, and the 3rd floor of E51.

Coffee machines are located in 16-1, 14-0, 10-0 and, cruelly, on the third floor of W20 — where the 24-hour Coffeehouse used to be.

If you have problems with a vending machine or need a refund, call the answering service at x3-2707.

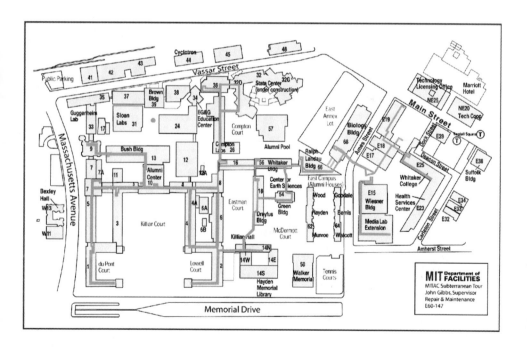

Finances

Paying the 'Tuting Piper

The most important bills you will be paying for the next four (five, six, seven...) years are those to MIT. At least they seem that way. Here are some helpful hints in dealing with the *real* heart of MIT.

Financial Statements

MIT Student Account Statements reflect the charges and payments of your MIT expenses ranging from tuition to library fines. As of July 2004, paper bills are no longer sent to students, parents, or sponsors. Instead, they are posted on MITPAY, MIT's online billing system. The Student Account Statement should be available on the 10th of each month, with payment due on the first of the next month.

Students can access MITPAY through WEBSIS: `student.mit.edu`.
"Authorized Payers" can access MITPAY at `web.mit.edu/sfs`

By default, only students are allowed to access their MITPAY account. If your parents pay the bills, you need to make your parent or sponsor an Authorized Payer: Log in from WEBSIS, click the "Authorize Payers" link, then create a login and password for your sponsor. Remember, unpaid bills may hold up your registration or even your degree, so it pays to keep on top of your finances.

Tuition

For the fall term, tuition is charged in the middle of July and due in the middle of August. For the spring term, tuition is charged in the middle of December and is due in the middle of January. "Anticipated Funds" on your MITPAY statement indicate expected loans, scholarships, sponsored payments and graduate tuition awards. Some of these funds require additional steps (and thus paperwork) before they can be applied to your account, so make sure you follow up on awards that you know are coming.

Unless you make other arrangements, account charges must be paid in full each month or a 1.5% interest charge will be applied to the balance (MIT extended medical insurance is exempt from late charges as of Fall term 2003-2004).

Account Counselors

If you think the Institute screwed up your financial statement, contact Student Account Services (11-120, x8-8600, `web.mit.edu/bursar/`), part of the Student Services Center, or your student account counselor. If the discrepancy is in the form of an incorrect charge, you should also contact the office that assessed it because only that office can authorize a correction to your account. A formal dispute of a charge must be received by your student account counselor in writing within sixty days of the billing date of the statement with the disputed charge. However, before you jump to hasty conclusions, remember that the timing on many of these invoices is random and the bill you receive may include a debt that you have already paid.

116   Finances

Your student account counselor is assigned by the first letter of your last name:

A-G	Mary Murray	maryjo@mit.edu	x3-3339
H-O	Sophya Gudelman	gudelman@mit.edu	x3-4131
P-Z	Amanda Romero	aromero@mit.edu	x3-3335

These are people you should get to know, particularly if you have an unusual situation. Their purpose is to help you navigate the complicated bureaucracy, so if you have a question, ask! They are in 11-120 and available during normal business hours without an appointment (although you need to check in at the desk).

Where to Make a Payment

Payments to the Institute can be made at the Cashiers' Office (10-180, web.mit.edu/caw/www/) or the Student Services Center (11-120, web.mit.edu/ssc/). Payments can also be mailed to MIT, P.O. Box 3972, Boston MA 02241-3972, or wired, but if you wire the money make sure you email ssc@mit.edu to confirm the amount sent, the name of the sending organization and the date sent. Payment is not accepted via credit card or foreign currency. Payments for each term are due about a month before classes begin. An alternative to paying in full by the due date is the MIT Payment Plan. The plan allows you to pay your student account balance in four monthly installments per term; you must sign up for this plan with your financial aid representative *before* the payment is due. Beginning in Fall term 2003-2004, the MIT extended medical insurance charge will not be subject to a finance charge if you pay in installments.

If you haven't paid an outstanding prior term balance by Registration Day, a visit to Student Accounts will be in order. This may require unending patience due to long lines and long-winded explanations; best to avoid this madness if possible. For more information on the Student Services Center, see the **Help!** chapter.

Financial Aid, Undergraduate

Money for undergraduates normally comes in package deals: part scholarship, part loan, part term-time job. The amount of each is determined by the people in the Financial Aid Office (11-320, x3-4971, web.mit.edu/finaid/), also part of Student Financial Services, from data you and your parents provide on several different required forms.

FAFSA

The Free Application for Federal Student Aid (FAFSA) can be filled out on paper, though they have a decent web form (www.fafsa.gov) and heavily encourage its use. You will need to order a PIN (personal identification number) from them several weeks in advance if you want to fill out the form entirely online---otherwise you will be sent a card to sign once your form is otherwise complete. Your parents have to sign this form as well, so they should also order a PIN. Expect to spend 1-2 hours on this form if your taxes (and your parents' taxes) are complete and accessible.

PROFILE

Required for US Citizens only, The College Scholarship Service's PROFILE also has both a paper and a web form (profileonline.collegeboard.com/index.jsp) but the CSS PROFILE does not require a PIN. It does, however, require pages and pages of tedious data entry---be prepared with all the data you needed for the FAFSA, plus detailed information about your and your parents' finances and your immediate family.

In addition, MIT now has The College Scholarship Service process most of the paperwork MIT would otherwise require: you may be required to send them your parents' or your own tax forms. Expect to spend 2-4 hours on this form if you have all the required data, plus 30-60 minutes a few weeks later putting together the packet of required tax forms and auxiliary data.

Foreign Students

Although you escape the tedious and intrusive PROFILE, foreign students are required to fill out a special "For Students From Foreign Countries" application.

In addition, if one or both of your parents earn an income in a currency other than U.S. dollars, you will need to submit the MIT Foreign Income and Expense Supplement.

Other Forms

Self-Help and Outside Award Form --- If you receive work-study or student loans, you will be asked to fill out this form once your FinAid package has been determined. It will ask you to decide how to divide your "self-help" allocation between loans and work-study. 10 minutes

Student Information Review Form --- This for students who receive grants, to attempt to match special grant funds to students who qualify. You will be asked about your interests, student activities, future potential careers, volunteer work, and whether you have family ties to particular organizations. 15 minutes

Effort Adjustment Form --- If you earn more than is expected at your summer job, you may wish to submit this form. It allows you to reduce your "self-help" (term-time work or loans) by an amount you specify. 5 minutes

Undergraduate Outside Award Update Form --- If you receive outside awards, you'll need to submit this form to let MIT know. Your grant money (if any) will not be reduced by outside award monies---it will only reduce your "self help"---unless you receive grants that exceed your self-help expectation. See the *External Scholarships* section below for more information on how to find scholarships.

All of these "other" forms will be mailed to you if you need them, and should be returned to:

Student Financial Services
Room 11-320
Massachusetts Institute of Technology
77 Massachusetts Avenue
Cambridge, MA 02139-4307

The financial aid forms are usually mailed to continuing aid recipients in February. If you haven't received aid but would like to try, go to the Financial Aid Office (11-320, web.mit.edu/finaid/) and request an application. For returning students, these forms are usually due sometime in April. *Make the deadlines!* Deadlines will be published for the coming school year. For undergraduates, need is the only criterion that determines how much aid you get and how it is split up. If you still need more money, there are additional loans available to students that can help fill the gap.

Remember, *all* undergraduates must file a form declaring their draft status (*e.g.*, female, registered, etc.) before they are eligible to receive aid every year.

Caution: Your Federal work-study eligibility does *not* guarantee you a job when you arrive at MIT. It means that MIT expects you to contribute that amount to your support by working (or some other suitable means, *e.g.*, loans) while at MIT. Your earnings are taxable, so you must file several forms to prevent taxes from being taken out of your paycheck.

If you have any questions about any of the financial aid process, or need help, contact your Financial Aid Counselor Like Loan Counselors, they are assigned by the first letter of your last name, and are in the Student Services Center (11-120)

A-Ch	Elizabeth Barnes	barnes@mit.edu	x8-5775
Ci-G	Carmen Velez	cvelez@mit.edu	x8-5606
H-La	Elva Green	egreen@mit.edu	x8-0717
Lb-O	Kenneth Hayes		
P-Sr	Jason Shumaker	jasons@mit.edu	x3-8467
Ss-Z	Yvonne Gittens	gittens@mit.edu	x8-5610

External Scholarships

External scholarships are often worth applying for. Look online at FastWeb (www.fastweb.com), CollegeNet (www.collegenet.com), CollegeBoard (apps.collegeboard.com/cbsearch_ss/scholarshipSearch.jsp), and others. Also look for books at your local library — it should have a few that list scholarships and provide tips for applying. Most scholarships have deadlines; you might have already missed them. Apply for them now and save yourself from the same problem next year. Don't apply for a scholarship that requires an application fee; it's almost always a scam. Also check the professional societies like IEEE, ASME and SWE. Many of them offer MIT section scholarships in addition to the national scholarships. In addition to helping pay your tuition, they are also academic honors and can help you get into grad school.

Of particular interest to women is Intel's annual Women in Science and Engineering scholarship. Any female sophomore or junior from one of the engineering schools is eligible, but it often goes to someone in Course 6. The WISE scholarship covers full tuition and a small stipend for up to 3 years. The winner of the scholarship is also declared an Intel Scholar, and is guaranteed an internship at Intel if they want one, but they are not *required* to work for Intel (unlike some other industrial scholarships, such as Microsoft's). Application is a two-stage process: first an essay, then the finalists are interviewed. Intel selects the winner. The application process takes place in the fall, and the winner is notified sometime in December or the beginning of IAP. The only requirements for keeping the scholarship for the full term are that you maintain a certain GPA and remain enrolled full-time.

Financial Aid, Graduate

Between 80% and 85% of grad students are receiving some sort of financial aid through MIT, their government, an outside foundation, or some other means. There are Research Assistantships (RA's), Teaching Assistantships (TA's), Federal Traineeships, industrial grants, MIT awards and other random sources of income for graduate students. These can be supplemented by loans from the Federal Government (Perkins, Ford/Stafford, etc.) or by MIT Technology Loans. Some of these kinds of support (*e.g.*, RA, TA) are obtained from the department, while some come through the Graduate School Office. Other sources such as state and federal loans come through dealings with the Financial Aid Office. If you get a TAship and are a US citizen or permanent resident, MIT requires you to fill out a Free Application for Federal Student Aid (FAFSA, `www.fafsa.ed.gov`).

The Graduate Students Office (3-138, `web.mit.edu/gso/`) and your own department's headquarters have all the information needed to apply for financial aid, including information on industrial and foundation grants. Most financial aid programs have early application deadlines, so get to work early. For graduate students, academic performance is important for financial aid.

Unfortunately, neither MIT nor the individual departments can afford to provide financial aid to all deserving students. For this reason, you should apply for graduate fellowships whenever possible. (Contributing to your funding will decrease the financial strain on your lab and may spare you from writing more than your fair share of grant proposals.) In general, it is better to apply for a 12-month Federal fellowship than a 9-month fellowship, as your chances of getting it are just as good and it is much less trouble to decrease your award than it is to try and increase it. Also, some fellowships have very special requirements or are not available for international students. Read all of the fine print. If you have any questions, the Graduate School Office should be able to help you out.

The National Science Foundation's Graduate Research Fellowship offers partial tuition and full stipend funding for up to three years. You must be a college senior or first year graduate student to apply. For more information see `www.ehr.nsf.gov/dge/programs/grf/`. Other fellowships are offered by the Heinz Foundation, NASA, the National Science Foundation, Sigma Xi (the national research honorary society), the US Department of Education, the US Department of Energy and the US Department of Defense. For more information see `web.mit.edu/gso/financialaid/extfellowships.html`

Graduate awards (RAs, TAs, etc.) are processed by the academic department granting the award. Stipends are also awarded by the departments, although they are processed through the MIT Payroll Office. You should ask your department any questions you have about stipends and supplementary RAships or TAships that you have. You are responsible for any charges or fees not covered by your graduate award, so read your financial statements very carefully and ask questions sooner than later. Your graduate finances, especially if you have a fellowship, can be very confusing at first.

You will find that your department is instrumental in almost all financial support decisions. It also has an intimate grasp of what opportunities are available, both inside and outside MIT. Be sure to keep in touch with both your advisor and department headquarters.

Loans

Both undergraduates and graduates apply for loans at the Financial Aid Office (11-320, x3-4971, web.mit.edu/finaid/). You must complete a Graduate Loan Application and, if a US citizen or permanent resident, a Free Application for Federal Student Aid (FAFSA) for consideration for loan funding. Although scholarships are disbursed on a scheduled basis, loans can often be arranged to fill unforeseen gaps in your budget. Jobs are sometimes provided for the same purpose. If you are granted a loan, be sure to go to the Student Services Center in 11-120 and sign for it at the beginning of the term. Otherwise, it may go away or you may be charged finance charges on the balance on your Bursar's bill.

Emergency Loans (Cash Advances)

During Office Hours

Undergrads: Go to the Financial Aid Office (11-320, x3-4971) to request a loan (which may be approved within a few minutes). Then go to Student Account Services (11-120, x8-8600, open Mon,Tue,Thu,Fri 9am-5pm, Wed 10am-5pm), and finally to the Cashiers' Office (10-180, x3-3340, open Mon-Fri 9am-11:40am, 12pm-4pm). Alternately, you can start at Counseling and Support Services (5-104, x3-4861).

Grads: You can get an advance on your fellowship money if necessary; go to the Graduate Students Office (3-138, x3-4860). If you are not on a fellowship or need a loan, use the procedure described above for undergraduates.

After Hours

Contact the Dean-on-Call (see the **Emergency** chapter), who can clear you for money from the Campus Police emergency fund. If you're off campus the money may even be wired to you.

So the Financial Aid Office Screwed You...

1. Go to the Student Services Center in 11-120 and ask to see your Financial Aid Representative. They cannot lower the amount of the aid package. They might even increase it. It's worth a try if you have a legitimate complaint. The Financial Aid Office (11-320, x3-4971, web.mit.edu/finaid/) won't help you until you have the appropriate magic paperwork, although they can suggest what information may be helpful. Start a log of every conversation you have with anyone about your financial aid. Include their name, contact information, date and time and details of the conversation. Keep photocopies of all documents. You are entitled to copies of your financial aid record, but they will be loath to give them to you once they are in the file.

2. Look for outside scholarships or funding. See the appropriate *Financial Aid* section.

3. Get in on your state loan program; check with the Financial Aid Office. In most cases, the loan will be interest-free until you get out of school, grad school, the Peace Corps, or military service.

4. Have your parents get a loan from a bank.

5. Try to get a term-time job. Check at the Student Employment Office (11-120, x3-4973, web.mit.edu/seo).

Special Payments

If you are an undergraduate taking fewer than 32 units, you can arrange to pay tuition on a per-unit basis. Get the necessary paperwork, a "Tuition Adjustment — Light Load" form, from the Student Services Center (11-120, x8-8600). This should be done before the tuition billing date (mid-July or mid-January) of the term that you intend to be on light load. Tuition will be charged for all subjects taken as a Listener and is charged on a pro-rated basis for subjects dropped during the term. If you wait too long before doing the paperwork (it must be handed in to the Student Services Center or the Registrar's Office (5-119, x8-6409) prior to the end of the fifth week of the term) you will have to pay full tuition. This option is not generally available to international students or students in engineering internship or cooperative programs, and can only be done for a maximum of two terms in the course of an undergraduate degree.

The Deans' Office can also help you if you feel that you have run into extraordinary difficulties and you don't want to pay full tuition (*e.g.*, family emergency that caused you to leave school for seven weeks, then return just in time to flunk your classes). Each case receives individual treatment, and the deans are understanding in cases of genuine problems. Check with the Student Services Center (11-120, x8-8600).

Employment, School Year

Finding a job is not too difficult; finding one you like may be a little harder. During the school year, over 3,000 undergraduates seek and locate part-time employment on campus, ranging from working desk in the dormitories to operating the MIT nuclear reactor. The libraries, dormitories, and dining halls usually hire during the first week of each semester. Be on the alert for sign-up meetings and get started early or you will miss your chance. However, even if you do miss the initial sign-up, you can always place yourself on their waiting lists. Openings do appear during the term. If working in Lobdell doesn't appeal to you, check the Student Employment Office (11-120, within the Student Services Center). They maintain listings of jobs within MIT and the Boston area. They provide contacts — *you* must follow them up.

You can usually find something you like if you try hard enough. Like most things in life, you get out of it what you put into it. Research projects are also a good supply of jobs. The work ranges from drudgework to something you can do a thesis on (often within the same job). The Undergraduate Research Opportunities Program (UROP) website lists hundreds of professors and labs and their areas of research. Find professors in fields that interest you and start asking. Also check the UROP bulletin board in the Infinite Corridor outside of the Admissions Office (3-108). If you would like to do a UROP project with a professor who is not listed, make an appointment to see him or her. There may still be research positions available. It may take a while, but you should be able to find something. Funding can come from the professor's research grant, UROP (check the website for details), or the College Work-Study Program (CWSP). Since eligibility for CWSP varies, check with the Financial Aid Office. Very often some combination of these is used. For more information go to the UROP Office (7-104, x3-7306, web.mit.edu/urop).

Four jobs that are almost always available:

1. Admissions tour guides. Apply at the Information Desk in 7-121. They hire at the very beginning and end of term.

2. Psychology experiments. Check 9.00 lectures, or look for flyers on bulletin boards and in the Med. Center.

3. Dietary experiments. Slow, bad tasting, and restrictive, featuring complete measurement of dietary input and output, big money. Check posters on bulletin boards. Some studies, for less compensation, are for shorter duration and are less restrictive.

4. Campus publications are always looking for people to sell ads — it's hard work but you get to make your own hours.

Graduate students are considered full time employees, and many fellowship programs will not allow students to take a second job. Check the details of your funding source before applying for employment if this applies to you.

Employment, Summer

Decide what you want to do over the summer before the end of Fall term, so that you can visit hometown firms over the winter vacation and beat the rush (but not by much).

If you're preparing a resumé, be clear and precise. Don't undersell yourself, but don't make claims you can't substantiate. Use your good sense and you should be able to present a good resumé that will enhance your job chances. Be sure to have some good references in mind. (See *Getting a Recommendation* in **Academics**.) The Office of Career Services and Preprofessional Advising (12-170, x3-4733, web.mit.edu/career/www/) will assist you in preparing your resumé.

Check your abilities. Do you speak a foreign language? Can you program computers? There are often vacancies available for people with esoteric skills, even when the general job market is bad. You might even try looking for a foreign job.

Go to career fairs---and not just to get the free t-shirts. Bring a bunch of copies of your resumé, hand them out, and follow up. Especially with smaller companies, it's important to remind them you still exist. Pay attention to when they will be on campus again (many of them come back for information sessions and to interview students) and try to be there.

The Office of Career Services and Preprofessional Advising (12-170, x3-4733, web.mit.edu/career/www/) sponsors interviews with companies who sometimes are looking for summer workers. It also provides access to MonsterTrak, an online service with job listings.

If you are a freshman, you should consider the 6-unit seminar Freshman/Alumni Summer Internship Program (FASIP). Participants learn about career planning and job search skills and are put in contact with alumni who are interested in hiring and mentoring MIT freshmen. Look for information before the Spring Semester, when the program starts.

Sophomores can participate in Undergraduate Practice Opportunities Program (UPOP), a program that assists in finding a summer position and provides some academic credit.

UPOP consists of three parts: an intensive week of pre-employment training during IAP, 10-12 weeks of summer employment, and a written report and oral presentation in the fall. Look for information before IAP.

Some large cities have MIT alumni clubs that may invite you to a gathering over winter vacation. A good many of these alumni are likely to be in business with jobs available for students from their alma mater. Check with these gatherings if you're looking for an interesting summer job.

You can usually find a summer job related to your major in Boston or Cambridge if you start looking early. The Alumni Office (10-110, `web.mit.edu/alum/`) has lists of alumni and where they work. Try contacting them and seeing if they can offer you a summer job. Don't be intimidated by contacting MIT alumni---often they will be thrilled to talk to someone from the 'Tute, even if they don't have anything to offer you.

The Student Employment Office (SEO, 11-120, `web.mit.edu/seo/`) builds listings of summer jobs. If you are a US citizen or permanent resident, have completed your financial aid application for the following year and have financial need, you should consider community service as a summer job. Many non-profits in the Boston area hire MIT students for the summer, so it is possible that you could find a summer job with a non-profit in your hometown.

Many students start or continue research projects during the summer. UROP helps fund many of these jobs. Their application deadline comes in mid-April. See *Employment, School Year*.

There are some openings with the state or federal civil services. Unskilled or semi-skilled government work isn't the greatest thing in the world, but it's available and it won't tax your mind. Check out their web page (`www.usajobs.opm.gov`) or call (1-478-757-3000) for more information. For state civil services, check with the particular state.

If you're around Boston and can't find a job, try some of the odd jobs listed at `boston.craigslist.org`. They might provide interesting non-academic employment (*e.g.*, carpentry, electric wiring).

Employment, Permanent

No matter what you intend to do, get started early. Junior year is certainly not too early to start thinking about graduation and what you plan to do afterwards. Go to some of the Career Fairs and seminars sponsored by various student groups.

The Office of Career Services and Preprofessional Advising (12-170, x3-4733, `web.mit.edu/career/www/`) serves both students and alumni. They sponsor meetings between students and recruiters. Check their office for schedules. They also publish a *Placement Manual* and distribute the *College Placement Annual* (helpful even for summer employment) and have an extensive library of job contacts. *Take advantage of this office!*

Your department should be able to offer career guidance, and your advisor should be capable of helping you sort out possibilities, with special knowledge of your abilities and preferences. Also try the professional societies such as IEEE, ASME, and AIChE. Some student groups and professional societies like Eta Kappa Nu, the Electrical Engineering Honor Society (hkn.mit.edu), publish books of student resumés which they give or sell to companies. Be sure to have your resumé included if possible.

The Industrial Liaison Program (E38-400, x3-2691, web.mit.edu/ilp/) keeps in close touch with companies around the world. Though its main function is industrial liasion, not career counseling, industrial liaison, you might try to get an advisor in ILP. Try hard.

Banks

When looking at banks, pay attention to location, minimum balances, account fees, checking fees and ATM fees. By law, you cannot be charged banking fees if you are under 18. Your local bank should also have at least one Notary Public whose services you can use free of charge (if it's your bank). "Direct deposit" is a way for your paychecks to be automatically deposited into your bank account. Ask for information at the Payroll Office (E19-510). Fleet offers a discount on monthly fees to those who participate.

ATMs

Automated Teller Machines (ATMs) will allow you to get cash 24 hours a day. You should be able to get an ATM card from your bank and it should be protected by a personal identification number (PIN). Your ATM card should work in every ATM. However, it is very likely that if you use your card in another bank's machine you will be charged one fee from the bank that owns the ATM and another fee from your bank for using another bank's ATM. Many area banks participate in the SUM network, so they waive ATM fees for cardholders of other SUM-network banks. Find out if your bank participates, and if it does, look for these ATMs to save a few bucks.

ATM Card vs. Debit Cards

A direct debit card will allow only "point of sale" transactions. The card will transfer money from your bank account directly to the vendor's bank account. This requires you to enter your PIN. A deferred debit card looks similar to a credit card (it may have a Visa or MasterCard logo) and allows "off-line" transactions. This means that instead of typing your PIN, you sign a receipt and the transaction is stored for later processing. Many ATM cards function as a direct debit card and you don't have to do anything special to get one. The deferred debit card is what most people think of as a debit card, but because "off-line" transactions can take place your entire account can be cleaned out by thieves with little or no problem and you do not have the same theft protection on a debit card that you do on a credit card.

Local Banking Options

MIT Federal Credit Union (NE48, aka 700 Technology Square, x3-2844, www.mitfcu.org) is not a bank per se, but is the best option for MIT students and employees for many banking services including savings, checking and loans. Many people have an MITFCU account even if they maintain a regular bank account as well. See the Credit Union section for more details. MITFCU participates in the SUM network, and has ATMs in the Student Center, E19, and Building 10. They will be adding ATMs in Stata and Technology Square in August 2004.

Cambridge Trust (617-876-5500, www.cambridgetrust.com) is a smaller bank in the area whose closest branches are in Kendall Square across from the Coop, in University Park across from Star Market, in Harvard Square and in Porter Square. Their most useful account is the ATM Convenience Account which has no minimum balance, no monthly fees and allows up to 8 checks per statement cycle with no additional fees. They are part of the SUM ATM network, but many of their accounts charge $1.00 for using a SUM but non-Cambridge Trust ATM. They also offer internet banking, direct deposit and candy at the counter. They are close, convenient, and friendly - many customers rave about the old-fashioned personalized service.

Fleet (617-434-2200, fleet.com) is in some ways the most convenient bank for MIT students. Their closest locations are in the Student Center and Kendall Square, which is to say you can't get any closer. They offer a package deal that includes checking, savings and credit and have the largest number of ATMs in the area. However, they are notorious for poor service and onerous fees, hidden and otherwise. Beware of bouncing a check there: they are rumored to open a credit card in your name to float the transaction.

Wainwright Bank (1-888-428-BANK, wainwrightbank.com) is another smaller bank in the area whose closest branches are in Kendall Square on Broadway, in Central Square and in Harvard Square. They offer a free Student Checking account with no minimum balance and no limit on the number of transactions. They also offer a free debit card and overdraft privilege service, as well as free internet and telephone banking. They are a member of the SUM ATM network. Service is friendly. Of note are Wainwright's social initiatives: over $300 million of its customers' deposits have been committed to financing local social justice initiatives such as homeless shelters, affordable housing, HIV/AIDS housing and services, environmental protection, breast cancer research, immigration services and legal services for low-income citizens.

Nexity (nexity.com) is a completely online bank. Their interest rates are well above the national average. They refund all of your ATM fees. The no interest, no minimum checking account offers unlimited checks. For $5 per month, you also get online bill paying. Overdraft protection is offered and customer service is reported to be excellent. The major disadvantage is that there is no bank to go to (and thus no Notary Publics or other useful banking services).

Other banks in the area that offer no interest, free checking include **Century Bank**, **Eastern Bank** and **Sovereign Bank**. Overdraft protection is offered at all three banks.

Cashiers' Office

The Cashiers' Office is located in 10-180 on the Infinite Corridor and is easily recognizable by the mural of a dollar bill painted on its outside wall. It is open Mon-Fri 9am-11:40am, 12pm-4pm. There you can make cash payments to your Student Account, pay for transcripts, obtain thesis receipts, and cash checks (see below). The Cashiers' Office sells non-discounted T Passes during the last four working days of the month, American Express Traveler's Checks at a 1% fee, Harvard Shuttle Tickets, and MIT Hobby Shop Cards. Finally, you can pick up pay checks, petty cash reimbursements (under $50) and petty cash envelopes (9am-11:15am and 2pm-3pm). An MIT ID is required for almost everything.

Cashing Personal Checks

You can cash personal checks up to $100 (or larger, with the approval of the Bursar or Assistant Bursar) at the Cashiers' Office (see *Cashiers' Office* above). A valid MIT ID is required, there is a 35-cent charge, and no third-party or payroll checks are accepted.

Of course, the bank at which your account is held will cash checks drawn against it free of charge. Banks are generally open 9am-4pm Monday through Friday, and some feature extra hours each day and/or Saturday.

Many supermarkets in the area cash checks for a service charge if you have a courtesy card for that store. Apply for one at the customer service booth. The limit on how much you can cash varies from $25 to $100 for a personal check, more for a paycheck.

Credit Cards

A credit card, for the few unfamilar with the term, is a way to purchase things on credit. At the end of the month, all of your purchases will appear on a bill. You may choose to pay off the bill completely and on time (this is highly recommended) in which case you will have zero balance and no fees or penalties. You may choose to pay only the minimum required payment or some portion of the bill in which case the company will charge you interest on the balance that you carry over to the next month. The credit card companies make their money by charging you fees (like late fees) and interest on your unpaid balance and these fees can ruin your finances and your credit report if you let them.

Why get a credit card as a college student? The most basic reason is because they are easy to get then, and having one helps you build a credit rating which you will need in the future. They are also a good way to keep track of your spending, allow you to make emergency purchases, and can give you a float between when you need to spend your money and when your next pay check comes in. They are also the main way of purchasing goods and services online, and are often used to hold reservations such as hotel rooms. Often credit cards will also come with additional benefits like travel insurance and rewards benefits.

With a credit card comes the possibility of credit card theft. Check your statement carefully each month and keep all of your receipts to compare it to. If there are charges that you did not make, call your credit card company and report the inaccuracies. You may have to file paperwork, but you shouldn't have to pay for charges that you did not make. If your credit card is lost or stolen, report it immediately. There is a legal limit of $50 per card that you can be liable to pay, but the trouble and inconvenience associated with forged charges and getting a new card make it worthwhile to keep careful watch on your cards. After you report the loss of a credit card to the bank, you cannot be charged for purchases made on it, even below the liability limit. It is a good idea to keep a list of all credit cards and numbers in a safe place so you can report a stolen card.

The standard credit cards are American Express (which has no credit limit but requires you to pay off your bill every month), American Express (Amex) Blue, which has a seldom-used "smart chip" and doesn't require you to pay off your bill every month, Visa, Mastercard, and Discover (which is popular with students due to its cashback feature).

There are also credit cards from stores like Macy's, Sears, and Filenes. Many of these stores offer two versions of their credit card. The first version only works for the store where you accepted the card. For example, your Macy's card will act as a credit card but only at Macy's. You get substantial discounts and promotions if you hold a store card. However, the second version is not a Macy's card but a Macy's Visa card which acts like a credit card everywhere Visa is accepted and also gives you discounts at Macy's. Be sure which you are getting when you sign up. If it turns out you got the wrong one, call the company and they should correct the situation.

Regardless of which credit card you choose, it will be offered by a company like US Bank, First USA, MBNA or Fleet and not from Visa or Mastercard directly. Some of these companies will approach you and others you will have to approach. The MIT Alumni card and the credit card offered through the MIT Coop are from First USA (the latter is one of the easiest credit cards to get — look for their booth in the Student Center at the start of the term). Cards offered through professional societies like IEEE and ASME are from MBNA. The MIT Federal Credit Union also offers a Visa card (see *Credit Union* below). For the most part, you should be able to get a credit card with just your name, address and Social Security number. If they ask you for copies of your Social Security card, bills, or other interesting forms of verification, you may want to think twice. Other questions to ask when applying for a credit card are:

- Is there an introductory rate, what is it and how long does it last?
- After that, what will my rate be?
- Is there an application fee?
- Are there processing fees?
- Is there an annual fee?
- Is there a late fee?
- Is there an over-the-limit fee?
- Are there any other fees, like account termination fees or balance transfer fees?
- When and how can a variable rate be changed?
- When and how can a fixed rate be changed?
- What is the grace period before interest is applied?
- How will you inform me of any changes in my contract?
- Will the company inform me if I am about to go over my limit?
- If I go over my limit, what happens?
- What is the company policy if I have trouble paying my bill?

Read the fine print that comes with your card and you may save yourself a lot of trouble later on.

Credit Union

The MIT Federal Credit Union (MITFCU) is a federal corporation, not a part of the Institute. It is similar to a small savings and loan bank, but instead of having to serve two conflicting masters (customers and shareholders), a Credit Union has loyalty only to its members. All MIT students, both graduate and undergraduate, and employees on the MIT payroll are eligible to become members by buying one share in the Union. They offer full bank services (including ATM, phone and internet banking, and a Visa card with an initial limit of $500), no account charges, and higher interest rates than regular banks. They are part of the SUM ATM network and give you 8 free withdrawals at other banks' ATMs, in addition to unlimited free transactions at their own 3 ATMs on campus. On top of all that, their new facilities in 700 Technology Square (NE48) include a coffee station, an internet cafe and a wireless access lounge, so waiting is painless. The only drawback of the Credit Union is that the office hours are even narrower than regular banks (8:30am-3:00pm).

They also offer good loan rates. Your payroll may be deposited directly into your credit union account. The Credit Union Office (NE48, aka 700 Technology Square, x3-2844) has more detailed information about all of this and an explanatory pamphlet, as does their website (`www.mitfcu.org`).

Insurance

The most important point is to find a reputable insurance company. This, among other things, means going to a state-licensed agent who represents a well-known company. On many items, rates don't vary at all in Massachusetts. Buy your insurance elsewhere if you can. Beware of agents who add "service charges" on top of the normal bill. Be cautious also about mail solicitations. Above all, don't be afraid to ask questions and make sure you know all the details before signing.

For information on automobile insurance, see *Insurance* in the **Transportation** chapter. For information on medical insurance, see the **Medical Resources** chapter.

Life Insurance

If you do decide to buy life insurance, Savings Bank Life Insurance (available at any bank with the words "Savings Bank" in the title) is the best deal you can get as a Massachusetts resident. You can also get life insurance through professional societies like IEEE and ASME.

Unless you already have dependents, there are few reasons to insure yourself. If you should die before you have paid off your Federal educational loans, they will be waived automatically, and your parents will not be hit with an unexpected debt (other loans, however, particularly commercial loans, may pursue against your estate). Don't be taken in by promises of preferential rates later when you sign up for full insurance; by the time you need it you will have a much better idea of what you want. Check with a lawyer if you want further details.

Personal Property

In general, if you are still part of your family's household (*i.e.*, you are still a dependent) then your personal property, including bikes and stereos, will be covered by any standard homeowner's policy. If you are not covered in this way, you can take out a tenant's policy which is generally a "$50 deductible" policy (*i.e.*, you pay the first $50 of any loss). The premiums vary from about $50-100 for about $7,000 worth of insurance (generally a minimum), so check what you own and decide if it's worth insuring. Certain items, such as computers, might have to be insured by means of floaters, as part of homeowner's insurance.

For insuring computer equipment you may wish to check out Safeware (`www.sourcedata.com`) or InsurePC (`www.insurepc.com`). For renter's insurance for dorms, check out the Fireman's Fund (`www.firemansfund.com`) and National Student Services, Inc. (`www.nssinc.com`).

Remember to report any thefts to the Campus Police (W31-215) so a police report will be available if you file an insurance claim. This will also allow them to increase patrols in the affected areas.

MIT Property

MIT-owned equipment that has been registered either through the Property Office or through the Treasurer's Office is covered by Institute insurance. Property owned by individuals or by the government is not covered (unless it has been specifically authorized for use on MIT projects).

Operation Identification

To reduce the chance of theft (and increase the chance of having your possessions returned if they are stolen), the Campus Police periodically run laptop registration drives. A metal tag is placed on the top of your computer, or other small electronic device, that if removed leaves an indelible tattoo. A schedule of dates for registration can be found at web.mit.edu/security/www/stophome.html, or check with the Campus Police booth at the Activities Midway.

To prevent theft of other items, the Campus Police have electric scribers that can be used to engrave your valuables. They recommend you use your driver's license number (including state abbreviation) or your Social Security Number, but putting your SSN anywhere that people might see it is a bad idea, so resist any suggestions to use your SSN. When you engrave your valuables, the CPs will give you Operation Identification stickers for your door/windows (letting potential thieves know that your property is protected, or perhaps just that it is valuable enough to be worth protecting) and they will also register the property that you have engraved in the provided inventory booklets.

In both cases, the goal is to discourage theft by making stolen items much more difficult to sell.

Purchasing

You may find that you need to buy things for MIT while a student. (This is different than buying things for yourself with MIT's money, which is to be avoided.) The most common methods of payment are interdepartmental transfer (in which one part of MIT transfers money to another part of MIT), purchase order (which is a lot of paperwork and nuisance so your vendor gets paid), MIT purchasing credit card (which is wonderful but difficult to obtain and cannot be used for flowers, explosives, travel expenses, alcohol and other desirable things), and reimbursement. Reimbursement is by far the most common for students.

To get reimbursed, take your receipt to whoever manages your account, whether it be a student treasurer, a departmental financial officer, or administrative assistant. If the purchase was under $50, they will give you a petty cash slip which you can take to the Cashiers' Office where they will give you cash for it. If the purchase was over $50, MIT will cut you a check and either force you to pick it up or mail it to you. This process can take several weeks. You should keep photocopies of all of your receipts to make sure you get accurately reimbursed for all of them, especially if being reimbursed by check as the Payroll Office is notoriously error-prone. The Student Life Programs office has documentation on how they deal with different types of financial transactions for student groups which may be enlightening: web.mit.edu/slp/finances/transactions.html#documentation

Note that Institute funds can not be used to buy alcohol for student-run organizations (including residences). Check with your department before purchasing alcohol for department events if you want to be reimbursed.

Tax Exemption

MIT is a non-profit organization and thus is exempt from paying taxes, including sales tax, and MIT will refuse to reimburse you for sales tax that you have paid. To avoid paying sales tax, get a tax exemption form from whoever manages your account. Some stores will want to keep your tax exemption form; others will simply have you fill out another form; and some won't accept it at all, which is irritating, but these are often stores that have seen the forms abused. Remember that you do not pay tax on groceries in Massachusetts or on mail-order or catalog purchases from out-of-state.

Taxes

Massachusetts has a 5% sales tax on all goods excluding food (but including prepared meals) and clothing. However this tax does not apply to students eating at MIT dining facilities. The nearby state of New Hampshire does not have sales tax, prompting occasional field trips across state lines. Massachusetts also has a state income tax. RA and TA stipend payments are considered taxable salaries for federal and state purposes and are subject to withholding. Stipends from Fellowships (except for amounts used for tuition, fees, books, supplies and equipment) are also taxable but not subject to withholding. You may be able to file as a state resident for tax purposes, which is easier than filing the non-resident forms. Get the 1NR form and check: you can be a resident of more than one state for tax purposes.

You should file income tax forms, particularly if you haven't filled out forms to prevent withholdings on your earning. If you file your tax forms, you will likely get your withholdings back. Federal Income Tax forms are generally available in local banks. Massachusetts Income Tax forms are available in post offices. Dewey library often has forms as well. Downloadable PDF forms for both federal and state taxes are available online; if you can't find the necessary forms, call (see below for web site addresses and phone numbers).

Federal: Check with the Internal Revenue Service in room 775, in the JFK Building downtown (Government Center, Boston), call 1-800-829-1040, or check the website (www.irs.gov). Most students can get by with the Form 1040EZ which can be downloaded from their website, or e-filed.

State: The Department of Revenue is at 51 Sleeper St, Boston and can be reached at 1-800-392-6089. The web page is www.dor.state.ma.us.

International Students: Read up on the web page or contact the IRS. Your nation of citizenship may be party to a tax treaty with the United States, in which case you may not have to have US payroll tax deducted from your income. See also *Foreign Citizens* in the **Miscellaneous** chapter.

MARCOS OJEDA '05

Housing

Living conditions can be very important to both your social and academic success while at the Institute. Accordingly, great care should be taken in deciding where to live, as transfers can be exceedingly difficult and time-consuming (see *Moving* later in this chapter). Making an educate decision initially will save you a great deal of hassle and stress later.

There are four types of housing available to MIT students — dormitories, on-campus apartments, FSILGs (fraternities, sororities and MIT-affiliated independent living groups), and off-campus apartments. Undergraduates with housing problems should contact the Undergraduate Housing Office (E32-200, x3-2811, residence@mit.edu). Graduate students and students with families should contact the Graduate and Family Housing Office (E32-238, x 3-5148, graduatehousing@mit.edu) with their problems or concerns. For off-campus housing information consult the Off-Campus Housing Service (E32-214, x3-1493).

Undergraduates are guaranteed four years of Institute (dormitory) housing, unless they choose to leave for an FSILG or off-campus apartment. Graduate students are not so fortunate; securing graduate housing is a matter of chance, as demand far outstrips supply. As of 2002, MIT forbids freshmen undergraduates from living in FSILGs or off-campus.

Undergraduate Dormitories

Having historically operated with far more autonomy than might be expected from official university housing, MIT's undergraduate dormitories span a diverse range of student cultures and attitudes. Most students find that selecting a dormitory is the most important decision they make in their first term at MIT.

Picking The Best One For You

You should have been mailed a guide to residences during the summer before your arrival on campus. In order to get another copy try emailing residence@mit.edu or calling x3-2811. The descriptions in the residence guide you're sent are usually written by students, but they are occasionally edited by the authorities without disclaimer. While the residence guide and the student-produced i3 movies that come with it are useful in forming rough impressions of the characters of the dorms , it is impossible to capture the whole spirit of a living group in two pages of text and five minutes of video. The only way to truly judge whether or not a dorm is right for you is to visit and spend some time absorbing the atmosphere and the personalities of the residents.

Choosing your dorm is a five-step process. The first four steps take place before you arrive on campus. First, you will be asked to carefully look over the propaganda sent to you over the summer (i.e. the residence guide and CD of i3 videos). In late June, you will be asked to rank the dorms in order of preference. In early July, the Undergraduate Housing Office will run a lottery to assign all freshmen to an initial dorm. Once the Undergraduate Housing Office assigns you to a dorm, the student Room Assignment Chairs (RAC) of that dorm will assign you to a temporary room.

After you are assigned a dorm and room in the summer housing lottery, you will arrive on campus to explore the dorms in person. Take advantage of all the activities and free food offered during the Residence Exploration period of Orientation ("Rush"). It's an experience not to be missed - you'll spend several days as the focus of attention with all of the upperclassmen doing their damndest to entertain you. (You'll never eat that well again.) Once you've explored your living options in person, you will be asked to enter a second lottery. In this lottery, you can choose to either list up to three dorms you'd prefer to live in or you can "squat" the dorm you were assigned over the summer. If you choose to squat your summer dorm assignment, you are guaranteed a slot in that dorm; however, you will probably not be able to stay in your temporary room. Most dorms require all freshmen to participate in what is called In-House Rush. In-House Rush occurs the night before the final freshmen moving day. Most dorms have markedly different sub-communities within them, often delineated by floor, suite, or entry. In-House Rush is an evening of events designed to help you choose which of those sub-communities you'd perfer to join. Once you go through In-House Rush, the RAC of your permanent dorm will assign you a room based on your preferences. Althought it may seem overly complicated, the long and involved rooming process at MIT helps to ensure that you will find the best place for you to live, learn, and enjoy yourself during your time at MIT. Take advantage of all your opportunities to explore your first year residence options!

Residence Based Advising Programs

McCormick Hall and Next House both have mandatory Residential Based Advising (RBA) programs for their freshmen. RBA means that your freshman advising group (whether part of a seminar or not) is composed entirely of residents of your dorm and has an associate advisor who lives in your dorm alongside you. The benefits of the program include lots of free food and well-trained associate advisors. The primary disadvantage is that you are committed to your assigned dormitory for your entire freshman year. You cannot enter the Final Housing Lottery after Orientation and it is nearly impossible to transfer to another dorm until your sophomore year. Make sure you're really psyched about the program before placing McCormick or Next in your top three choices for your freshman dorm in the summer housing lottery. For more information on the RBA programs at these dorms, read the information on RBA in the *Guide to First Year Residences* that's mailed to you over the summer before your freshman year or check out web.mit.edu/firstyear/rba/

Graduate Dormitories

On-campus graduate housing is not easy to obtain. Although a new graduate dorm, Sidney-Pacific, has recently opened, spaces in grad dorms are still dear.

New first-year graduate students are assigned to graduate housing based on their stated preference and some element of chance through a lottery system. The initial period of housing is for one year; after that, if you want to continue to live in graduate housing you must enter the Continuing Student Lottery. If by some miracle you get a low enough number to get continuing housing, you are set for the rest of your time on campus — you do not have to enter the lottery again in subsequent years.

If you are disabled or have special needs, it can affect your on-campus housing. You should include a letter about your condition and information from your physician with your housing application or send it to the Graduate and Family Housing Office.

Limited parking is available, but no one is guaranteed a parking spot. You are "strongly discouraged" from bringing a car to campus.

Ashdown House

Ashdown is one of the more social graduate student residences, with regular activities and the Thirsty Ear pub located in the basement. It is also the closest to Main Campus. However, all first year residents will get a double or a triple room, and it takes some involvement in the dorm (taking an officer position, working desk, *etc.*) to get a single the following year. The dorm is co-ed and houses 420 students; rooms are furnished.

Edgerton House

Edgerton is a co-ed, apartment style dormitory and holds 190 students. It is located near University Park and is about a 10-minute walk from campus. It is not furnished, but a refrigerator and stove are provided. It is more expensive than a dormitory-style residence such as Ashdown.

Green Hall

Green Hall is a small, all-women's dormitory. It is located on Dorm Row on West Campus, a short walk from Main Campus. 46 female graduate students are housed in furnished rooms. The dorm residents tend to get to know each other and the housemasters well, and the rent reflects the dormitory quality of the building.

NW30

This is a new graduate residence, which was created inside a renovated Instrumentation Lab warehouse to the northwest of campus — hence the common moniker "The Warehouse". It is a co-ed, apartment-style dorm that houses 120 first-year graduate students in furnished, air-conditioned apartments with kitchenettes. The floors are tiled. Housing contracts for the Warehouse do not include the summer — you must move out for the months of June through August, inclusive.

Sidney-Pacific

This is the newest graduate residence, which opened in Fall 2002. It is co-ed and houses about 700 graduate students, so it is the largest MIT residence hall and the center of grad. student life for the S-P/Edgerton/Warehouse area. It is also the farthest from Main Campus (but close to Star Market). A lot of effort is being put into organizing a social structure that will cater to such a large population, so it hopefully won't feel as isolating as other large communities. The entire building is air-conditioned and has been designated as non-smoking. The apartments are at the lower end of the price scale and are furnished. Sidney-Pacific also features Senior Segue, a program designed to alleviate undergraduate housing problems by moving seniors into grad housing. Students who join the Senior-Segue program are guaranteed first-year grad housing if they enter an MIT graduate program (including M. Eng.)

Tang Hall

Tang Hall is located at the far end of Dorm Row on West Campus, past the last undergraduate dorm. It is a co-ed, 24-storey apartment tower that houses 404 first-year graduate students in apartment-style suites resembling isolation cubes. Rooms are the cheapest of the apartment residences, and are furnished, but you have to supply your own lights. The building is not air-conditioned and in the summer the rooms become unbearable ovens if you don't buy your own (the windows don't open very far in order to force desperate graduate students to come up with more creative ways to end the torture). Despite the best efforts of the Tang Hall Residents' Association, most social interaction occurs in the elevator.

Married Student Housing

MIT housing for married students is in Eastgate and Westgate. The application process for these units involves a separate lottery from the single occupancy residences and results in two years of housing rather than one. For information concerning this process, the availability of openings, and a description of their physical facilities, consult the Graduate Housing Office, E32-200, x3-5148, or visit them on the web at `web.mit.edu/housing/grad/`

Fraterities, Sororities, and Independent Living Groups

While not necessarily on-campus, it should be noted that another form of MIT-affiliated housing is available to grad students — the FSILG system. The unpopular Freshmen On Campus decision has left many FSILGs with empty beds and increasingly empty coffers. All of the ILGs (barring the Women's Independent Living Group) actively solicit grad students, and several fraternities and sororities do so as well. Living in a FSILG offers some unique advantages to grad students — a community that is much more cohesive and vital than anything grad dorms have to offer, a meal plan, housing that is cheap, year-round, and guaranteed. On the other hand, you will be required to carry out any house duties, the living environments of FSLIGs generally offer no more privacy than a dorm, and, most obviously, you will find yourself more involved in undergrad rather than grad student life. Contact information for specific ILGs is available on the LGC website (`web.mit.edu/lgc/www/houses/`); contact information for specific frats is available at the IFC website (`ifc.mit.edu/members.php`); contact information for sororities is available at the Panhel website (`web.mit.edu/Panhel/www/members.html`).

Dormitory Facilities

Both undergraduate and graduate dormitories share the same range of basic facilities, although the graduate dorms are less amenable to painting and other room modifications.

Bicycles

Most dorms have a semi-secure place to lock up your bike. However, lots of people use these areas; some may be careless and leave gates unlocked, reducing the security to the level of any back street in Cambridge. New and/or expensive bikes are safer for each additional lock between them and the bike market. See the **Transportation** chapter for more information.

Cooking

Many students at MIT enjoy cooking for themselves. The advantages include cheaper (and less greasy food) as well as choosing what, where, and when you eat. You can easily save more than 50% over MIT food prices, and a thrifty student can cut the cost (and unhealthy gain in body weight — a.k.a. "Freshman Fifteen") by 2/3 or more. One disadvantage is that cooking (and subsequent cleaning up) requires a significant investment in time. Many students find that getting together with friends to cook can save a lot of time and money as well as being a good way to double-time your socialization and body-maintenance.

In many dorms, the Institute has provided cooking areas. However, dorm facilities for cooking range from lounge microwaves to complete kitchens. Be sure to check the cooking facilities of any dorm you are considering, even if you currently don't plan to cook for yourself. Aramark (MIT's previous monopoly on-campus food provider, notorious nationwide for bad food) has changed quite a few minds in this respect. In dorms containing kitchen facilities, refrigerator space is included with the room rent. Used fridges are also not hard to come by. Small refrigerators can be purchased for $30-$60. Check the ads in *Tech Talk*, the walls of the Institute, or the Yellow Pages. Don't give up hopes of cooking for yourself because of lack of kitchen space — quite a few students make do with nothing but illicit microwave ovens and rice cookers in their rooms. The Institute officially frowns on cooking in dorm rooms, however.

Front Desks and House Management
The desk staff and house manager handle a wide variety of problems arising from the physical considerations of the dorm. In addition to dealing with mail and lockouts, many front desks offer additional services such as sale of soft drinks or rental of athletic equipment. Most desks have listings of services provided, either posted or available for inspection. Ask. Complaints about desk staff should be made to the desk captain or house manager.

Heat
During the summer months, Boston can become quite hot and humid. Many students wish to install air conditioners in their rooms if they are staying in a dorm for the summer (see *Summer Residences* for more information). In most cases, installing A/C is okay, but you should always check with your house manager to make sure it is allowed. Some dorms, like Senior Haus and New House, have central air and you will not need to install a window unit to keep cool.

During the winter months, it can become quite cold in Boston. All dorms, in theory, have heating units in the rooms or central heating. However, in some older dorms, such as East Campus, the old steam heating systems are loud and unruly at times. Some residents prefer to find alternative methods of keeping warm in the winter as a result of the clanky radiators.

Humidity
During the winter, low humidity seems to be quite common in dormitories. If you continually wake up in the morning with a sore throat, try placing a few cans or dishes of water on the radiator. You'll be surprised how fast the water goes away, and even more surprised by what it leaves behind. Small, cheap humidifiers (under $20) are available in local drugstores. Some ultrasonic humidifiers have recently been considered dangerous; read *Consumer Reports* (available in the MIT Libraries) before you buy.

Liability for Damages
You can be assessed for a share of any damages in your suite or floor that cannot be pinned on an individual. This bill must be paid before you can get your degree.

Locked Yourself Out of Your Room
With the advent of new doors and real locks in some dormitories, it has become much more difficult for the locked-out resident to pick his or her own lock. If the time-hon-

ored MIT card or coat hanger doesn't work, go to the desk and sign out a spare key (which is easier, and less suspicious-looking). If the desk is closed, find the night watchman, or call Housing Operations at x3-1500 and ask for Unit 12 to come to help you with a lockout.

Painting a Room

The Institute sporadically provides free paint in certain predetermined colors to residents of East Campus, Senior Haus, and Bexley. This distribution is officially on a yearly basis. Other dorms may have similar arrangements. Sometimes new painting policies spring up at the concoction of the house governments and house managers. Check with your house manager or your house government to confirm your dorm's current policy if you're interested in painting your room. To get paint, go to your house desk and choose your hues; the paint will be delivered there. Alternatively, many residents prefer to buy their own paint, especially if they have an intricate design or odd color in mind. Always check with the manager before touching a brush to the wall, as you may be forced to pay to have the walls returned to their original color once you move out. One thing to remember if you plan to order institute paint - order it very early, as it takes its sweet time to arrive.

Pets

Pets, with the exception of fish, are not allowed in most dormitories. The exceptions to this rule are East Campus, Senior Haus, Bexley and Random Hall, which allow cats in certain areas. Check with the house government of each of these dorms to find out if you are allowed to have a cat. Tolerance of any animal's stay is subject to the approval of all members of the living group as well as compliance with pet regulations put in place by the Housing Office or the dormitory. If you want to keep your beloved pet, make sure that it is properly registered, and that your neighbors are not disturbed by noise, smell, or sand trays.

Remodeling a Room

Non-destructive remodeling is OK in most cases as long as the room can be restored to its original state. The newer dorms tolerate rather less self-expression, and painting or building a loft (or even moving your unwieldy and overpriced custom Simmons furniture without official help) may be considered serious offenses. All lofts must be approved by the house manager, since there are fire code issues involved.

Telephones

All dorm rooms now have real phone service. MIT's phone system (5ESS digital PBX switching system) allows dorm residents to make local and long distance calls from MIT phones. The 5ESS system was installed in the summer of 1988, and in spring of 2000 MIT helped Lucent stay alive by purchasing a 5ESS-2000 system. For those interested in such things, 5ESS stands for Fifth-generation Electronic Switching System, boasts five nines of reliability (99.999% uptime), and is used to switch telephones in small cities.

To call someone at MIT, dial the last five digits of their number: 3-xxxx, 5-xxxx, 8-xxxx or 2-xxxx. For local calls outside MIT, dial 9 followed by the ten-digit number (you must include the area code for all calls). Local calls are included in your dorm rent. For toll-free calls, dial 9-1-800 and the number.

From outside of MIT, replace 3-xxxx with 617-253-xxxx, 5-xxxx with 617-225-xxxx, 8-xxxx with 617-258-xxxx, and 2-xxxx with 617-452-xxxx. See the **Useful Telephone Numbers** chapter for additional abbreviations and MIT tie lines.

Long distance calls are processed by PaeTec Communications (`www.campuslink.com`). To make a domestic call, dial 9 + area code + seven digits; at the tone, enter your ID code. For international calls, dial 9 + 011 + country code + city code + telephone number; at the tone, enter your ID code. You can pick up your ID code at Registration from the PaeTec Campuslink representatives. For problems related to the phone system, dial x3-3654. For some rowdy telephone fun, try going to the 5ESS telephone support page `web.mit.edu/is/tel/` and learning some of the cooler features of the phone system (like three-way calls and concealing your phone number from caller ID). Ironically, the features may not work with a fancier phone, so if you get hooked you'll want to keep using your Institute phone.

Valuables
Easily-removable valuables such as jewelry, money, and yuppie appliances like "personal digital assistants" or iPods should never be left unguarded in a dorm room, even for a short period of time. On lower floors, keep TVs, stereos, CD players, reel-to-reels, etc. out of easy sight through your window — no point in inviting trouble. Don't forget, MIT is in a big city and that means a noticeable crime rate, even on Dorm Row. The Campus Police can loan you an electric scribe to scratch your name on your valuables as part of Operation Identification.

Varying Room Costs
The Institute gives recognition to the unequal desirability of rooms by charging slightly different rents for different rooms in some dorms. Factors that cause rents to vary include crowding, number of people using kitchen and bathroom facilities, common space, closets, view, elevator service, trash collection, type of rodent infestation, *etc*. The exact cost of your room will show up on your bill from MIT. For more information on room rents, see `web.mit.edu/housing/`

Waterbeds
Waterbeds are allowed in dormitories, provided that the floors are deemed strong enough to support them safely. You'll need to get the house manager to approve the model and inspect the installation. As long as you treat the waterbed with care and don't puncture it accidentally, there should be no problems. However, the standard lease for apartments specifically forbids waterbeds. If you plan to move from a dorm to an apartment, check to see if you can take the waterbed with you.

Wild Animals
Despite appearances, the squirrels and mutant rats living in the East Campus courtyard and its surroundings are not tame. Don't leave food lying around your room in cardboard containers or plastic bags — the squirrels will gnaw through the window frame if they smell anything. Also, some of the biggest cockroaches in the East, and not to mention assorted mice, caterpillars, mosquitoes, and other vermin, inhabit most dorms, especially during the summer. They won't cause many problems, as long as you keep the windows closed or install a good screen. Anti-roach devices are available

at some dorm desks. Do yourself and your dorm mates a favor and clean up spilled foodstuffs immediately.

Fraternities, Sororities and Independent Living Groups

MIT's independent living groups are diverse by any standard. Links to most groups' websites can be found at web.mit.edu/life/category/lg.html, but the only way to get to know a house is to visit it and meet the people who live there. FSILGs are currently rushing upperclassmen shortly after Orientation and during IAP, although the difficulties that FSILGs have had since the institution of the Freshmen On Campus rule mean that this schedule is subject to change. If you have questions, you can try to contact someone in the FSILG you're interested in - contact information for ILGs is available on the Living Group Council website (web.mit.edu/lgc/www/houses/); contact information for specific frats is available at the Interfraternity Council website (ifc.mit.edu/members.php); contact information for sororities is available at the Panhel website (web.mit.edu/Panhel/www/members.html).

Rush Week (R.I.P.)

MIT looked into its magic hat and determined that today's freshmen are no longer capable of living in FSILGs when they first arrive. It also decided that Rush, which depends on a purely temporary rooming assignment upon first arrival, and a more permanent reassignment a week later, was too much paperwork for its administrators and too much stress for overprotective parents. Thus, MIT has been eradicating Rush (or "REX," as administrators want it called) by leaps and bounds. Fortunately, thanks to students' efforts, the concept of Rush — that is the ability to choose where you will live, still exists. However, the time during orientation which was given to frosh to spend exploring and experiencing different dorms has been cut back to a mere handful of odd hours. It remains to be seen what will happen under this new system. Various student groups, such as the Dormitory Council (DormCon, web.mit.edu/dormcon/www/) and ILTFP (iltfp.mit.edu), have been working hard to see that freshmen retain the right to choose their housing based on actual interaction with members of living groups during Rush-like events rather than the woefully inadequate propaganda mailed out over the summer.

Problems

If you are having problems with your fraternity, talk to the FSILG advisor, Laura Martin (W20-549, x3-7549). She can discuss your options (including depledging) and the merits of each. It is more important to live in a way that makes you happy than to simply bow to social pressure.

Off-Campus Housing (Apartments)

The housing situation around Boston is *bad*. Rents are high, quality is low, and tenant rights are not well established. Most apartments will be unfurnished and not air conditioned. Some will come without refrigerators. In most cases, utilities such as electricity, heat and water are not included. Also, some landlords will not rent to families with children or allow pets, so allow extra time to find an apartment if you have such needs. Have references from former landlords and your bank prepared ahead of time, treat the search for housing with great care, and get all the help you can find.

If you think you want to live in an apartment, or even if you already have one, go to the Off-Campus Housing Service (E32-214, x3-1493). They offer rental information for houses and apartments, available roommate situations, lists of rooms for rent in private homes, and lists of short-term accommodations. They also can give you information on legal services, local public schools, public transportation, bus schedules, route maps, maps of Boston, Cambridge, Arlington and Somerville, and furniture resources (sales and rental). Finally, they host "Roommate Get-Togethers" so students can meet potential roommates before the start of the Fall term, and will even let you make free local telephone calls to agents and landlords. Pick up a copy of their *MIT Guide to Neighborhoods and Rental Housing Market* in person or check it out online on their website at web.mit.edu/housing/och/. Also ask for *A Guide to Security Deposits* and *Shopping for an Apartment*, which are sources of information on the legal and contractual side of renting. Since OCHS's services are restricted to MIT affiliates, new students may want to bring their admission letter with them to verify that they are students.

It can be difficult to judge the safety of a neighborhood for a prospective resident and this can be made worse by the pressures inherent in searching for housing on short notice. To avoid unwittingly moving into a high-crime neighborhood, make sure you visit the MIT Police in W31-215. Their Crime Prevention Unit can provide you with information about local neighborhoods as well as general crime prevention and home security tips.

To get off-campus housing, you will have to:

1. **Find an apartment.** OCHS operates a service for helping people find roommates and/or vacant rooms, and they maintain listings of vacant apartments. Plan on checking the lists early and often (for example starting in June for a September lease), as the best offerings are taken quickly. There are commercial outfits which can match you with non-MIT roommates as well.

2. **See the apartment.** Sign *nothing* until you are sure that the apartment is suitable and habitable. Don't trust any verbal agreements. Also *do not pay* for anything before seeing the apartment.

3. **Sign an application form and make a deposit.** The larger realty companies require this. It is primarily to ensure that you can pay. However, they can refuse your tenancy for very simple reasons, such as being a student, although grounds such as race, sex, age, nationality, or possession of children are illegal. Once you sign the application, the landlord can force you to sign the lease, so read the lease first. Be aware that there is no corresponding obligation for the landlord — he is not under contract until the lease is signed. Don't sign more than one application, or you could find yourself in serious trouble.

4. **Sign the lease.** If your lease follows the standard form of the Greater Boston Real Estate Board, or one of the forms used by the large realty firms, it will consist of several pages of obfuscatory small print. If you rent from an individual, the form will (hopefully) be short and simple. Either way, *read it*. If something isn't specified, you can be sure it will work to your disadvantage. You may be liable for rent even if the rate goes up halfway through the year. At the end of the year, you may be forced to rent for another twelve months unless you give notice some specified time period in advance. The people who work in OCHS will be happy to examine the lease for you, and explain

what the clauses mean and where you may have trouble. A lease is a contract. It can be enforced.

Prices vary widely. Expect to pay at least $950 per month for a 1-bedroom apartment, $1400 for a 2-bedroom apartment, $2000 for an unfurnished house and at least $500 per bedroom if you are in a roommate situation. You will probably have to make a security deposit of one to two months' rent. Leases usually run from September 1 to August 31 (though some run from June 1 to May 31), so remember that you are also promising to rent for the following summer. You can reduce your cost of housing by signing a lease during the winter, but it is much harder to find housing in the winter months and is not recommended. Subletting is legal only if the landlord agrees in writing, in which case you are still responsible to him.

It is also possible to rent an apartment with no lease on a month-to-month, or even week-to-week basis; such an arrangement is called a Tenancy-At-Will. In this case the lease may be terminated by either side as long as written notice is given in advance, usually by the rental period plus one day. Often, you become a tenant at will just by paying another month's rent without having renewed your lease. It is very important to make an agreement with your landlord, in writing, about the terms of your tenancy-at-will. Tenancy-At-Will is most commonly applied to get an apartment that is off the standard lease cycle (renewal during the summer) back onto that cycle, when the tenant's housing situation is unclear or when the property is up for sale.

Real Estate Agents

Real estate agencies, licensed by the state of Massachusetts, can help you streamline your apartment search by showing you available apartments in an unfamiliar area, thus saving you time, money and effort. They may charge you up to one month's rent for their services. Keep in mind that they *must* be licensed in order to collect a realtor's fee. To verify that your realtor is licensed go to www.state.ma.us/reg/boards/

Be careful when choosing a realtor. Many of them will show you the apartments that they are trying to get rid of rather than the apartments that you have asked to see. This will include showing 3-bedroom accommodations when you have asked to see 2-bedrooms. They may try to convince you that an apartment suits your needs when it doesn't, or that it is in your price range when it isn't. They may even pressure you to put money down when you are not ready. Don't be intimidated. Your choice of apartments will affect your quality of life, and it is worth an extra few days of searching or a better realtor.

Online Resources

Websites that you may find useful in locating an apartment include www.bostonapartments.com, www.justrentals.com, www.aptguides.com, boston.craigslist.org and www.housingoptions.com.

Temporary Housing

In the event you need temporary housing (after arriving at MIT or while between apartments), there are several resources available to you. First, the Off-Campus Housing Service has a list of hotels, motels and other accommodations located in the area ranging in cost between $60 and $350 per night. For incoming students only, dormitories have rooms

Housing   143

available from June 12th to August 12th (with advance reservation) ranging from $25 to $35 per night. (This option is not available for families with children over the age of 6.) For more information, contact Bailey Hewit-Moray (`bailey@mit.edu`). In August and September, there are a very limited number of free beds on campus, barracks-style, for emergency arrivals. They are only for single students on a first-come, first-served basis. For more inforamtion, contact the OCHS at x3-1493, or email Eleonore Zamora at `eleonore@mit.edu` or Linda Patton at `general@mit.edu`.

Moving

Generally, the difficulties involved in moving from one mode of residence to another are considerable. You can't move from a dorm to an FSILG unless invited. Finding an off-campus apartment can be a hassle, and once you're out of the dormitory system, it's difficult to get back in. It is advisable to think out your moves carefully. For undergraduate living options, your best resource and authority is Denise Vallay in the Housing Department (E32-200, x3-2811). Contact her with questions, complaints and to settle administrative details. For graduate student living options contact Tony Gray in the Housing Department (E32-238, x3-5148).

Within Your Dorm

It is, comparatively, trivial to switch rooms or halls/entryways within your current dorm. Consult your house's Room Assignment Chair (RAC) for transfers to vacant rooms. In arranging a swap, make sure you are not violating any priority system.

Between Undergraduate Dorms

It used to be that the simplest way to transfer between undergrad dormitories during the term was a one-for-one switch; finding someone in your target dorm to trade spaces with you. However, that procedure is no longer used by the Housing Office. For this reason, there are often 'unofficial' switches that occur. Be very careful and make sure you know which Housing Department policies that you're violating in order to determine whether or not you're willing to risk the consequences of getting caught — including denial of further Institute housing. A good procedure if you are interested in this sort of switch is to: first, feel out the situation with students completely; talk with rooming assignment chairs, hallmembers and graduate resident tutors of the place you want to move to in order to make sure that they will be OK with it. Secondly, never mention your housing situation in any way, shape or form to anybody even half-way official.

If you plan to officially change dorms during a term, you must fill out the application at: `web.mit.edu/housing/undergrad/application.html`. Unless you have "compelling reasons", which can be mental, physical, or financial reasons for immediate attention, you will be put on a list. Depending on the dorm you want to transfer to and how competent the Housing Department is feeling, getting off that list and being granted an actual transfer can take from no time at all to the rest of the term. Be aware that due to crowding (which administrators keep claiming is "temporary"), it may be particularly difficult to transfer into or out of certain dorms during the middle of the term.

If your request for a within-term transfer is not granted, you can always request a dorm transfer by entering the transfer lotteries run at the end of each term. Notice of these lotteries is sent out to each dorm by its RACs and House Manager, who will notify residents of dates regarding the lottery. Entering the lottery entails filling out a housing request web form in which you will rank one to three potential transfer dorms by preference. The lottery will then be run much like the freshman lotteries and you will either be reassigned to one the dorms you listed or (at worst) stuck where you were. If you enter a transfer lottery and are granted a transfer, you *must* move. You may, however, refuse transfers granted from regular transfer requests made to the Housing Office during term. The Housing Office prefers people to enter the transfer lotteries, as it simultaneously rearranges everyone wanting a transfer, which is both easier for Housing, and conveniently makes it more likely that you'll be able to move into the dorm of your choice.

Between Graduate Dorms
MIT policy currently does not allow transfers between graduate dormitories. Transfers between apartments in a single-student dormitory may be granted, but are unlikely due to the limited availability of graduate housing. Transfers between apartments in family graduate housing will cost you $100 to even apply and are relatively strictly restricted.

From an FSILG to a Dorm
If you decide during your pledge year that you wish to move from an FSILG to a dormitory, the Institute's housing policy guarantees you a space. After that first year, there are no guarantees. Check with Denise Vallay, (E32-200, x3-2811). If you leave an FSILG, you must pay whatever you owe them before obtaining a dorm room. If you have already paid for housing at an FSILG, you should, in return, expect a proportionate refund — but the system varies from house to house.

Leaving the Undergraduate Dorms in Midterm
If you get a room in the dormitory system, you are considered financially responsible for that room unless you leave the Institute. In all other cases, a rent refund is not guaranteed; talk to Denise Vallay in the Housing Department (E32-200, x3-2811). If you withdraw from the Institute you must leave the housing system. During the first 12 weeks of the term, you get a proportionate refund.

Returning to an Undergraduate Dorm
If you want to return to the dorm system after time away from MIT, you should talk to the appropriate people in Counseling and Support Services (5-104, x3-4861) and/or to Denise Vallay in the Housing Department (E32-200, x3-2811) and apply early. Chances of getting a spot are much better fall term than spring. Being granted a slot in undergraduate housing after leaving MIT is not guaranteed in all cases. If you retain your MIT student status while absent from the Institute (for example, Domestic Year Away or CMI), you do not generally lose your place in the dorm system, provided that you notify the proper authorities in advance. Keep in mind, though, that if you leave for a study-abroad program, you are not guaranteed to return to the dorm from which you left. If you take a leave of absence for medical, personal or academic reasons, talking to the correct people in CSS can go a long way in getting you on-campus housing in a dorm when you return.

Moving Out
Depending on how much stuff you've acquired in your current place, moving between apartments can be anything from an unpleasant ordeal to a post-apocalyptic nightmare.

Packing

Whether you are hiring movers or moving yourself, packing early and well will save you a lot of time and effort. Pack in structural containers like boxes or plastic bins. Try not to use bags except for bedding, as they cannot be stacked and may rip. Boxes can be obtained for free from grocery stores, liquor stores, MIT recycling areas and the `reuse-ask` mailing list. CopyTech will give you empty printer paper boxes for 50 cents each, and Athena clusters often prove fruitful as well. Boxes and plastic bins of various sizes can be purchased from many hardware and basic department stores. Moving crates can be bought or rented from `www.rentacrate.com`. When packing, make sure that you label all containers with your name, contents and destination. Use many small boxes instead of a few large boxes when packing. Pack all fragile things separately in bubble wrap or newspaper, or pack them along with your clothes using socks and T-shirts for padding. Just before you move, pack a suitcase or backpack with important items like medication, toiletries and a few days worth of clothes in case your stuff gets lost or in case you run out of time to unpack immediately.

Any possessions that you have decided to get rid of in the process of packing and moving should be donated to the Salvation Army (or other charitable organiziation) or posted to `reuse@mit.edu`. Waste not, want not.

Before You Move

Try to get a key to your new place ahead of time. Former tenants can leave quite a mess behind that the landlord should (but may not have) cleaned for you. If you feel the need to decontaminate your apartment yourself, go over and scrub it before you move. It's a lot harder to mop with boxes every where. You may wish to set up your utilities before you move in. It can take up to a week or more to get internet and cable installed, so make your appointment well in advance.

Moving Yourself

U-Haul (844 Main Street, 617-354-0500) and **Budget** (220 Mass Ave, 800-367-0522) both rent moving vans and trucks starting at $19.95. They will also rent furniture covers, cushioning materials, rope, dollies and storage space. If you have to park a moving van or truck on the street, check with the local parking office. They can often block off a portion of the curb for you to use during your moving day.

Moving Companies

If you have decided to hire a moving company, try **Nick's (Friendly) Moving Company** (617-491-7700 or 800-286-NICK) at 495 Columbia St. Suite B, Somerville. They have a 2-hour minimum, $100/hour peak rate and people report being very happy with their service. (They also answer the phone on Sundays). If you need an alternative, try **Gentle Giant Movers** (800-287-3030) or check the Yellow Pages.

When choosing a moving company, ask about the hourly rate and the minimum. They should ask you questions about how much stuff you have and make a recommendation about the size of truck and number of movers you will need. Three movers work more efficiently than two. Ask for three if you can — the price will work out the same and the time may significantly decrease. Make sure that you have water and an adequate tip ready for them. It's best to move fragile or expensive things yourself.

Student Law

Most organized living groups and living group associations (*e.g.*, IFC, DormCon) have judicial committees, and rules and regulations which they enforce. These are student organizations enforcing student rules; consequently their power is limited, though they are backed by higher sources of power at the Institute. Their regulations are printed and usually given to incoming members of the group. These rules are often quite flexible and subject to waiver for special cases. See also the **Law** chapter.

If you have received a judgement that you think is unfair or incorrect, there are usually several ways to appeal, either within the local system, through the Undergraduate Association or Graduate Student Council Ombudsman, the Dean for Student Life Office, or the Committee on Discipline. Usually you should use the appeals procedures of the group involved first before trying any higher power.

Summer Housing

Many people prefer not to go home for the months of June, July, and August. For such people, the situation is far from hopeless, though new summer dormitory housing rules requiring a UROP or other "official" sponsorship are making things worse. Most dormitories stay open, although they may consolidate summer residents to fill only parts of the building. The rest of the space will be filled at times with alumni here for Alumni Weekend, conventioneers, special programs, or other visitors. Be warned that any (noisy) renovations will occur during the summer. This has been more of a problem for dorms on the east side of campus in recent years. Also be warned that over the past few years, some administrators have been attempting to limit or eradicate student summer housing and instead use dorms solely as lucrative temporary conference/convention/visitor housing. While student groups such as DormCon have (so far) successfully argued that the damage to student community and the inconvenience to students and the housing system is prohibitive, the entire process is currently under review. To sign up for summer housing, you must fill out the requisite forms at `web.mit.edu/housing/undergrad/summer.html`. (Summer housing deadlines are available on the Housing website, and will also be forwarded to dorm residents by RACs or House Managers during spring term.)

The rent for summer housing in dormitories is comparable with the regular rent; details and special rules are explained in emails which are sent to the dormitories in the spring and on the Housing website, `web.mit.edu/housing/`. Some FSILGs offer a better deal. Rather than have their rooms standing empty, they will take in people for the summer at low rents (though sometimes including obligatory house chores such as cleaning bathrooms). Other FSILGs are just as expensive as the dorms. Summer sublets off campus are often available — check ads and bulletin boards. Subletting rooms in gradate residence halls also occurs. Check `web.mit.edu/housing/grad/sublet/` for information on this pilot program started in the summer of 2003. Make any summer housing arrangements early, since cheap sublets and FSILG spaces fill up quickly.

wmbr.org | recrutiment@wmbr.org | 617-253-8810

Activities

Procrastination is one of the main activities at the Institute: work is often so overwhelming that one doesn't know where to begin. As a result, MIT has a very extensive choice of co- and extra-curricular activities that will keep your mind away from those annoying problem sets. From student government and service through sports and theatre, they span the whole range. Look through the list below, but remember that there are many unofficial groups (as well as plenty of official ones that for whatever reason aren't listed) in addition to the ones printed here, so ask around, and be sure to check out the Activities Midway. There's something for everyone, but if you can't find a group for an activity you're interested in, you can always start your own.

Descriptions were provided by the groups. Contact information often includes the web page of the group or an email address; the best way to join a group is to visit the web page and show up to the next meeting or activity. Also, check in the back of the Student Directory, in the UA office, or on the ASA (web.mit.edu/asa/www/lists/) and Campus Life (web.mit.edu/campus-life.html) web sites for a current and complete listing of student groups. The Activities Midway, held on August 29th, is also a good place to learn about what activities are offered. Most activities are open to anyone who is interested, and prior experience is rarely required, so punt away!

Student Government

Dormitory Council (DormCon)

```
office: W20-401
email: dormcon-exec@mit.edu
website: web.mit.edu/dormcon/www
```

DormCon: We got your campus life RIGHT HERE! DormCon is the assembly of the undergraduate dormitory governments. DormCon advocates the interests of all undergraduate dorm residents, making sure that their voices are heard around the Institute. DormCon addresses many important issues such as Dorm Rush/ REX, RBA, and campus dining. DormCon also funds various dorm initiatives. The meetings are open to all and are held on a bi-weekly basis.

Graduate Student Council (GSC)

```
office: 50-220
phone: x3-2195
email: gsc-officers@mit.edu
website:  gsc.mit.edu
```

The Graduate Student Council's mission is to provide for the academic, social and professional needs of the graduate student community. The GSC represents all MIT graduate students, and as a unified voice advocates for the improvement of graduate student life. The Council is comprised of elected representatives from all departments, graduate residences, and the graduate student body at-large. In addition, there are ten standing committees and boards, and a variety of Presidential and Faculty Committees on which the GSC is represented, such as the Committee on Graduate School Programs, the Faculty Policy Committee, and the Corporation Joint Advisory Committee. Furthermore, the GSC organizes and encourages social, academic, cultural and other co-curricular activities that engage graduate students throughout their stay at the Institute. A few of the GSC committees are described below.

Academics, Research and Careers (ARC) Committee

```
gsc-arc-chair@mit.edu
```

This committee is here to help students with their professional development. It offers programs and seminars that address student needs that may not be emphasized in the regular academic curriculum. It also co-hosts the Career Fair with the undergraduate senior class and the Society of Women Engineers.

Activities Committee

```
gsc-ac-chair@mit.edu
```

Our mission is to create FUN events. GSC Activities connects all graduate students to events like Red Sox games, skiing trips, free wings at the Muddy Charles Pub on Wednesdays and more. If you don't see anything that you like, feel free to get involved and start up something.

Housing and Community Affairs (HCA) Committee

`gsc-hca-chair@mit.edu`

The HCA Committee is concerned with issues such as housing, stipends, safety, health services, parking, athletics, and related matters. In essence, we are here to look out for your basic needs, so if you have concerns about any of these areas please contact us.

Orientation Committee

`gsc-oc-chair@mit.edu`

The Orientation Committee plans events to welcome over 2,000 incoming graduate students to MIT. We are committed to helping new and continuing students expand their social network and experience professional and individual growth during their tenure. It is an excellent opportunity to meet new people.

Interfraternity Council (IFC)

office: W20-450
phone: x3-7454
website: ifc.mit.edu

As the governing body of 28 member fraternities, the Interfraternity Council brings together the many different fraternities at MIT for both community building events and policy changes. As an on-campus governing body, the IFC represents its constituency to the MIT administration, as well as providing invaluable mediation and self-regulation to its member organizations.

Panhellenic Association

office: W20-450
phone: 617-869-7996
email: sororities@mit.edu
website: web.mit.edu/panhel/www/

Sororities at MIT pride themselves at being different from sororities at other schools, and anything else at MIT. Consisting of over 400 women, MIT Panhellenic (the group of the 5 sororities) is the largest women's group on campus. The Panhellenic Association coordinates and liaises between the individual sororities.

Undergraduate Association (UA)

office: W20-401
phone: x3-2696
email: ua@mit.edu
website: web.mit.edu/ua/www/

The Undergraduate Association represents the undergraduate population at MIT. Through the UA Senate, undergraduates are able to serve as representatives for their respective dormitories and to participate directly in the legislative process. You can also become involved in one of the numerous UA committees which plan and develop events and programs to improve student life. In the UA, we hold "Students above all".

All the following groups fall under the jurisdiction of the UA. You may get in touch with any one of them by calling the UA at x3-2696, or feel free to drop by the UA office on the fourth floor of the Student Center, W20-401.

The Undergraduate Association Senate

The UA Senate is the highest ranking legislative body of the Undergraduate Association. With representatives from all the dormitories and from the fraternity system, the Senate speaks on behalf of the undergraduate student body.

Judicial Review Board (JudBoard)

JudBoard is the highest ranking judicial body of the Undergraduate Association. Its members interpret the UA Constitution and adjudicate conflicts over Senate legislation.

Nominations Committee (NomComm)

The Nominations Committee of the Undergraduate Association has two major activities - placing qualified students onto the governing committees of the faculty and administration and supporting those student representatives once they are there. Contact them if you would like to be a part of an Institute committee.

Association of Student Activities (ASA)

email: asa-exec@mit.edu
website: web.mit.edu/asa/www/ ASA

The ASA, a joint committee of the UA and the GSC, provides advice and assistance to new and existing student groups; members of the group hold officer training workshops, distribute office space, and help other student groups attract new members. They are the organization to contact if you want to start your own student group.

Finance Board (FinBoard)

email: finboard-request@mit.edu
website: web.mit.edu/finboard/

The UA Finance Board is a group of ten undergraduates in charge of funding student groups through the UA. FinBoard's job is to review the budget requests from student groups and recommend the allocation of funds. Throughout the semester, FinBoard members also help student groups with the funding process, from application to reimbursement.

General Interest Groups

Anime Club

email: anime-inquiry@mit.edu
website: web.mit.edu/anime/www/

The MIT Anime Club provides regular showings of Anime and an online library of Anime-related text and scanned pictures to its members and the MIT community.

Assassins' Guild

email: high-council@mit.edu
website: web.mit.edu/assassin/

We could tell you about ourselves, but then we'd have to kill you. Just kidding; we're actually a group of people who play live-action role-playing games, lasting from single-night games to ten-day-long sagas.

mitBEEF

e-mail: mitbeef-exec@mit.edu
URL: web.mit.edu/mitbeef

mitBEEF aims to educate the MIT community about the production and consumption of beef products and cows, and to increase general bovine awareness. To this end, we hold meatings at which we prepare beef in a variety of ways, go beef-caroling, and organize events such as the Great American Meat-In. Moo.

Caving Club

office: W20-461
phone: x3-2988,
email: caving-request@mit.edu
website: web.mit.edu/spelunk/www/

The caving club organizes caving and rappelling trips to caves in Massachusetts, New York, Vermont, and West Virginia. We also hold practice sessions for SRT (single rope techniques) sporadically during the school year and summer. No experience is required for the fall-semester beginner trips or for rope practices, but experience on a rope is required for trips to vertical caves.

Chess Club

website: web.mit.edu/chess-club/www/

The MIT Chess Club is a place for advanced players and beginners to play and improve their chess skills. For beginners, there are fun tournaments and lessons by advanced players of the club. Advanced players attend lectures given by former national champion Larry Christiansen. Some strong members of the team also travel to participate in intercollegiate competitions.

Club Z

email: clubz@mit.edu
website: web.mit.edu/clubz/

The group sponsors substance-free activities that range from pie-eating contests to providing jazz bands for great music. The events are free and there's always some sort of free food involved too! Club Z creates new opportunities for people throughout the MIT community to meet and interact with one another. We strive to create a comfortable environment that brings together a diverse group of people from all over MIT.

Debate Team

office: W20-423
email: debate-request@mit.edu
website: web.mit.edu/debate/www/

The members of the MIT Parliamentary Debate Society participate in weekly debate tournaments at colleges and universities across America and around the world.

Easyrider Motorcycle Club
```
email: easyrider-request@mit.edu
website: web.mit.edu/easyrider/
```
"Easy Rider - The MIT Motorcycle Club" was founded in 1998 to foster the interaction between motorcyclists at MIT. We now have over 80 members. Together, we go on day rides in the New England area, and also on more extended trips. In addition, we have various social events on campus, such as BBQs and movie nights, where we exchange tips and tricks about motorcycling and enjoy biker life. Experienced rider or motorcycle novice, cruiser or sport bike - everyone's welcome!

Electronic Research Society (MITERS)
```
office: N52-115
phone: x3-2060
email: miters-request@mit.edu
website: web.mit.edu/miters/www
```
We do all kinds of fun stuff. MITERS ("might-urs") is a workshop for building projects and playing with them, open all day and night on the first floor of the MIT Museum building. An anarchistic utopia of inventor/artist/techjunk junkies and a Pac-Man playing robot. During warm months we sponsor SwapFest, which is enjoyed by thousands every year.

Epicurean Club
```
email: chefs@mit.edu
website: web.mit.edu/epicurean/www/
```
The Epicurean Club is MIT's culinary club, with activities ranging from gourmet cooking of various types of foods ethnic and otherwise, to wine, cheese, chococate, and dessert tastings. Learn about the different culinary traditions in different cultures, or share your passion in all things epicurean with other like-minded gourmands. Subscribe to chefs@mit.edu and join us in our next event! Culinary skills not mandatory, but enthusiasm for fine foods and fun gatherings is highly recommended!

Experiencing Health Policy
```
email: sandhyas@mit.edu
```
This is a student-run group focused on promoting awareness of important current issues in health policy. Speakers will be invited during the school year to speak on various related topics. Also, interested students will have the opportunity to spend a week during IAP in Washington, DC, visiting organizations like the NIH, the World Health Organization and other major influences in the field of health policy.

MIT Formula SAE Team (FSAE)
```
office: 7 Emily St
email: fsae@mit.edu
website: web.mit.edu/fsae
```
0-60 in 4 seconds, 1.5 lateral g's. Sound like fun? The MIT FSAE Team is a group of graduate and undergraduate students who design, build and race cars. We create a new vehicle each year to compete at the national FSAE competition in Detroit (one of the most prestigious engineering competitions in the world). If you love cars, if you are interested in a hands-on team project, or simply if you want to learn you should check us out.

Go Club
```
email: mitgoclub-officers@mit.edu
website: web.mit.edu/mitgoclub/www/
```
Go is a challenging two-player strategy game. Also known as Wei-Qi and Baduk, Go is very popular in Asia and Europe, and increasingly so in America. The MIT Go Club is dedicated to promoting Go within the MIT community by introducing beginners to the game, and by fostering the face-to-face playing of Go. All levels of players are welcome, from complete beginners to high-level players.

Innovation Club
```
phone: 617-621-8575
email: innovationclub-exec@mit.edu
website: web.mit.edu/innovation/
```
Mirroring MIT's motto of "mens et manus," the MIT Innovation Club seeks both to understand innovation as a science and to practice generating and implementing new ideas. The club seeks to understand how people innovate through its Innovation Lecture Series and Innovation Odyssey. To practice innovation, the club initiates Technology Testbeds at MIT, and conducts brainstorms.

MIT Student Juggling Club

email: Juggleofficers@mit.edu

website: web.mit.edu/juggle/www

The purpose of the MIT Student Juggling Club is to foster and share an enthusiasm for juggling and the circus arts among students and other members of the MIT community. We meet evry Friday from 4-6PM in lobby 10 and we welcome anyone no matter what their experience or ability, even if you just want to watch. We have supplies available for anyone to use.

We participate in fairs, parties, and other activities, and we sponsor shows for the MIT community. Stop by and well teach you how to juggle, devil stick, Diablo, or begin working on a 9 ball cascade!

Laboratory for Chocolate Science

email: chocolatiers-request@mit.edu

Q: What would you do with 10 kg of chocolate chips?

A: Whatever you want.

The Laboratory for Chocolate Science is dedicated to learning everything we can about our favorite substance, and the best way of learning is through doing. Any member is invited and encouraged to run activities, and the scope is limited only by your imagination. Teach a class, run an experiment---we won't care if a little chocolate is wasted. It's all for a good cause, and there is always more...

We have a strict non-discrimination policy: white, dark and milk chocolate lovers are all welcome.

Mars Society

office: W20-445

phone: x5-8888

email: mars@mit.edu

website: web.mit.edu/mars/

The Mars Society is dedicated to establishing a permanent human presence on the planet Mars, a potential springboard for boundless intellectual, social, and spatial growth of human civilization. We pursue this goal through research and educational projects as enablers for both public and private space programs. We host the annual MarsWeek conference at MIT.

MIT Model UN

If you are interested in world affairs, meeting fellow college students from across the country, broadening your horizons past science and technology, taking weekend trips to exciting places, staying in 5 star hotels, having fun, and developing skills in managing people, then you should check out MIT's Model UN club. We welcome interested persons of all skill levels. Come join us and learn about how the world really works.

Outing Club (MITOC)

office: W20-461

phone: x3-2988

email: mitoc-request@mit.edu

website: web.mit.edu/mitoc/www/

MITOC provides a forum for members to meet one another and pursue outdoor trips. We organize several trips per year to the White Mountains, Acadia, Vermont, etc. MITOC members participate in hiking, climbing, biking, kayaking, canoeing, skiing, and camping. The outing club owns two cabins in New Hampshire, and has a large quantity of outdoor gear for rent.

Queer Women Looking for Life in Tech School (QWiLLTS)

office: 50-306

email: qwillts-admin@mit.edu

website: web.mit.edu/qwillts/

A Social and Discussion group for all Queer, Lesbian, Bisexual, and Questioning Women Students (and their Supporters too!). We plan dinners in the Rainbow Lounge, movie and game nights, go bowling and clubbing, plan discussions with queer women faculty, and facilitate discussions on topics of political, social and cultural interest.

Science and Engineering Business Club

email: sebc_request@mit.edu

website: web.mit.edu/sebc/

SEBC serves as an unbiased, student-based educational resource and network for undergraduate students, graduate students, and post-doctoral fellows seeking careers in business.

Science Fiction Society (MITSFS)
```
office: W20-473
phone: x8-5126
email: mitsfs@mit.edu
website: web.mit.edu/mitsfs/www/
```
We have the world's largest open-shelf collection of science fiction. Anyone can come and browse whenever the Library is open, and members can borrow from our circulating section. Membership is open to all, and dues are reasonable - approximately equal to buying two paperbacks a year. Meetings are held at 5:30 on Fridays during term, are fun and silly and are usually followed by a dinner trip.

Society for Creative Anachronism (SCA)
```
email: sca@mit.edu
website: web.mit.edu/sca/www/
```
This is the MIT borough of the Society for Creative Anachronism, a world-wide living history organization dedicated to reviving the best aspects of the Middle Ages: the glory, the pageantry, and the chivalry.

Solar Electric Vehicle Team
```
website: web.mit.edu/solar-cars/www/
```
The MIT SEVT is a student team that designs, builds, exhibits, and races solar and electric vehicles across the country and around the world.

Strategic Games Society (SGS)
```
office: 50-316
email: sgs@mit.edu
website: web.mit.edu/sgs/www/
```
Dedicated to the playing of all varieties of strategic games, depending on the tastes of those who show up on any particular weekend.

Students for the Exploration and Development of Space (SEDS)
```
office: W20-445
email: mitseds-officers@mit.edu
website: web.mit.edu/mitseds/www/
```
SEDS not only stands for Students for the Exploration and Development of Space, it stands for good times. At SEDS, we participate in a melange of mind-enhancing experiences - observation trips to Wallace Observatory, Spacetable discussions with pipin' hot pizza, and movie nights. We are varied in age and major, and we are Moonballrific.

Team Up 4 Education
```
email: tu4e@mit.edu
```
Team Up 4 Education is student group dedicated to mentoring local high school athletes and improving their ability to gain admission to and succeed in college. Our group of volunteers provide SAT tutoring in the spring, college application preparation in the fall, time management and study skills sessions, and visits to local area colleges.

TechLink
```
phone: X8-0397
email: techlink-officers@mit.edu
website: web.mit.edu/techlink/
```
TechLink began in 1999 as a joint venture between the MIT Sloan Senate and the MIT Graduate Student Council. Our mission is to provide opportunities for social interaction across school and departmental lines, for the purpose of personal and professional development.

Tech Model Railroad Club (TMRC)
```
office: N52-118
phone: x3-3269
email: tmrc-officers@mit.edu
website: tmrc.mit.edu
```
TMRC is building a large and amazing HO-scale model railroad on campus, with hand-built track and scenery. We're also designing and building one of the most advanced computerized model railroad control systems in the world. Come learn to lay track, build scenery and cars, and make the trains go! Wednesdays 7pm-10pm, Saturdays 5pm-10pm.

Technology and Policy Student Society (TPSS)
    website: web.mit.edu/tpss/
    TPSS is a group of primarily Technology and Policy Program (TPP) students and Technology, Policy Management (TMP) PhD students. Our activities aim to stimulate discussion and awareness about technology policy issues and to provide career guidance and contacts in the field. Among other activities, TPSS hosts a lunch-talk series to foster campus-wide discussion and awareness of critical technology policy issues.

Undergraduate LBGT Community (ULC)
    office: 50-306
    phone: x3-5440,
    email: ulc-request@mit.edu
    website: web.mit.edu/faqs/www/
    We are fun and interesting. We are social and outgoing. We are the undergraduate lesbian, bisexual, gay, and transgender community. ULC provides a safe, friendly, and comfortable environment for undergraduate students to meet and socialize. We organize study breaks, parties, movie nights, trips, outings to nice restaurants,and other events. Email to join; your email address will be kept confidential.

Westgate Community Association
    email: westgate-officers@mit.edu
    website: web.mit.edu/westgate
    The Westgate Community Association (WCA) is an ASA recognized group; its members are Westgate residents (students, their spouses/partners and families).

The purpose of the Westgate Community Association (WCA) is to
1. represent Westgate residents to the housing office, Graduate Student Council (GSC) and other MIT groups
2. To provide social programs for Westgate families with and without children
3. To establish Westgate house rules and regulations
4. To provide guidance and advocacy concerning various housing issues to Westgate Residents
5. To increase the quality of life of Westgate residents

The governing board of WCA is the Westgate Executive Committee (WEC) and the current positions are president, treasurer/secretary, Parents' Resource Coordinators for Families With Children (PRC), Couples' Resource Coordinators for Families Without Children (CRC) and Recycling/Floor Representative Organizer (RFRO).

World's Best Hovercraft Club
    email: hover-officers@mit.edu
    website: web.mit.edu/hovercraft/
    Have you ever dreamed of flying? So did we. The World's Best Hovercraft Club was created by a man who wanted to turn that dream into a reality. After much hard work, we created our first hovercraft and flew merrily over the Charles River. If you would like to be a part of our next hovercraft building adventure, just send us an email!

Activism Groups

Amnesty International
    email: mitai-request@mit.edu
    website: web.mit.edu/amnesty/
    Part of a world-wide human rights movement independent of political factions and ideologies, hoping to preserve the rights of those in need around the world through large-scale letter-writing campaigns.

College Democrats
    email: mit-cds-request@mit.edu
    website: web.mit.edu/mit-cds/
    Our group is committed to promoting the ideals of the Democratic Party and encouraging student involvement and interest in politics. To accomplish this, we organize canvassing trips, voter registration drives, study break discussions, and special events (i.e. speakers, debates, etc.). We are constantly in need of volunteers, and anyone on the MIT campus is welcome to join!

College Republicans
    email: republicans-request@mit.edu
    website: web.mit.edu/republicans/www/
    We are a group of conservative students who advocate conservative and Republican ideas on campus and battle the barrage of liberalism at MIT. We get people out to vote, bring in conservative speakers, challenge

people to think differently, and encourage people to support America and our troops. In addition, we hope to start a conservative newspaper on campus.

Gays, Lesbians, Bisexuals, Transgenders and Friends at MIT (GaMIT)

```
office: 50-306
phone: x3-5440
email: gamit-admin@mit.edu
website: web.mit.edu/gamit/www/
```

GaMIT ensures a queer-positive environment at MIT, providing many resources for all LBGT people and their allies. We range from deeply closeted to in-your-face activists, using our united strength to bring about change. We provide support to anyone who wants to come out (or not), stage a protest, hold an event, or exchange ideas in support of the LBGT community.

Greens

```
office: 50-309
email: greens@mit.edu
website: web.mit.edu/greens/
```

We are the MIT chapter of the Green Party. We are involved in progressive political activism ranging from the Cambridge City Council to world trade agreements.

Jewish Student Activism (JSA)

```
email: jsa@mit.edu
```

JSA is a place for those who are interested in promoting awareness of ancient Jewish traditions and Jewish heritage. JSA sponsors activities, seminars, and information sessions about both modern and ancient Jewish issues and topics. JSA provides support for pro-Israel activism.

Pro-Choice

```
email: pro-choice-request@mit.edu
website: web.mit.edu/pro-choice/www/
```

We are an organization on campus dedicated to support women facing unwanted pregnancies and provide an alternate voice to the anti-abortionists at MIT. We are involved in support of women who need access to various resources pertaining to their reproductive rights, information distribution to further understandings of choice issues, and activism to increase awareness of such choice issues.

Pro-Life

```
office: W20-401
email: pro-life-acl@mit.edu
website: web.mit.edu/pro-life/
```

MIT Pro-Life is a student organization devoted to fostering respect for human life from the moment of conception, and to promoting educational support for the pro-life position. Our pro-life efforts are mainly educational and campus-oriented. Our goal is to be a resource for MIT students to examine in depth the social, medical, and legal aspects of the pro-life response to abortion.

SaveTFP

```
email: savetfp@mit.edu
website: web.mit.edu/savetfp/
```

So who is SaveTFP? Just a bunch of MIT students, trying to make the best of our four years here without letting it get the best of us. As students, we realize what a unique and remarkable culture we have at MIT and work to save it. Our goal is simple: preserving and enhancing the good things about MIT.

Share A Vital Earth (SAVE)

```
email: save-request@mit.edu
website: web.mit.edu/save/www/
```

SAVE is the environmental club at MIT. Members are involved in advocating, publicizing, and educating about various issues including rainforests, vegetarianism, and recycling. Their top priority is reducing MIT's environmental impact by reducing waste. Think globally, act locally.

Social Justice Cooperative (SJC)

```
email: peace-request@mit.edu
website: web.mit.edu/justice/
```

The SJC is a progressive political organization that, through political and direct action, promotes a more democratic society, nonviolence, and human rights for all while resisting governmental oppression, corporate globalization, racism, sexism, and other forms of discrimination.

Students for Global Sustainability
    email: sfgs-exec@mit.edu
    website: web.mit.edu/sfgs/
Students for Global Sustainability (SfGS) is an organization dedicated to thinking globally and acting locally. The MIT SfGS is a chapter of the World Student Community for Sustainable Development (WSC-SD). The WSC-SD is an international partnership of six student communities seeking to promote sustainable development in the research, education and day-to-day collaborations among tomorrow's scientists, engineers and policy-makers.

Students for Israel (MITSI)
    email: mitsi-officers@mit.edu
    website: web.mit.edu/mitsi/www/
The purpose of the MIT Students for Israel (MITSI) is to be a postive, proactive, pro-Israel force on MIT's campus. MITSI members have varied political views, but we agree on one key point: our support for the state of Israel. MITSI therefore works to increase support and awareness of Israel by organizing speakers, educational and cultural activities, training sessions, and more.

Students for Labor Justice
    email: labor-info@mit.edu
    website: labor.mit.edu
Students for Labor Justice is a group dedicated to the struggle for workers' rights and economic justice on our campus, in our local community and around the world. Next year, we are planning two campaigns. The Fair Trade Coffee Campaign will work to spread the word about fair trade products and ensure fairly traded coffee is available in all campus dining establishments. The Anti-Sweatshop Initiative will build demand for "sweat-free" apparel on campus and monitor the Institute's progress on its commitment to fair labor standards for workers making MIT-licensed products

Service Groups

Alpha Phi Omega
    office: W20-415
    phone: x3-3788
    email: apo-mvp@mit.edu
    website:web.mit.edu/apo/
Alpha Phi Omega (APO) is a co-ed national service fraternity. Throughout the semester, we do community service around MIT and Boston. Among our regular projects are Registration Day, Book Exchange, and weekend projects at various scout camps. Come join us in the spirit of leadership, friendship, and service!

Alternative Spring Break
    email: asb-exec@mit.edu
    website: web.mit.edu/asb/www/
ASB is MIT's student-run community service group that coordinates trips to locations around the US and abroad during spring break. Participants get the opportunity for hands-on experience working with communities in need by offering their enthusiasm and optimism. Past trips include teaching in inner-city schools in DC, building houses in Kentucky, and investigating cultural diversity in Puerto Rico.

ARCTAN (American Red Cross Team and Network)
    office: W20-441
    phone: 617-375-0700 x305
    email: arctan-info@mit.edu
    website: web.mit.edu/arctan/www/
ARCTAN is MIT's official liaison society to the American Red Cross. ARCTAN runs the MIT Disaster Action Team and holds blood drives on campus a few times each year, and offers opportunities to volunteer health and safety services, international services, English as a second language, youth programs, the Boston food pantry and disaster relief. Anyone associated with MIT is welcome to join and commitments are extremely flexible.

Arnold Air Society
    office: W59
    email: aas-cc@mit.edu
    website: web.mit.edu/aas/
Arnold Air Society is a professional, honorary service organization advocating the support of aerospace power. "Service" is perhaps the foremost in the minds of members, because of the society's continuing contri-

butions to our campuses (MIT, Harvard, Wellesley, Tufts), and our communities. Projects include: volunteering at the Boston Marathon, MIT giving tree, and getting to know the Veterans of our community.

BrainTrust
```
email: braintrust-exec@mit.edu
website: web.mit.edu/braintrust/www/
```
MIT BrainTrust is a student group that seeks to serve the community through neuroscience. Our activities, which include panel discussions and community parties, are organized to educate the public about the realities of brain-related injuries and diseases, and foster interaction among researchers, clinicians and patients, the individuals who contribute to different facets of neuroscience. We welcome students from all departments.

Cancer Society
```
email: cancer@mit.edu
website: web.mit.edu/cancer/
```
Cancer-free MIT is a goal that we hope to attain by anti-smoking campaigns, promotion of existing cancer databases and proliferation of books and pamphlets. We work closely with the American Cancer Society to raise awareness and resources to fight the disease. Our job is to make this accessible to the campus. We hope to spread this to community at large through volunteering within hospital oncology clinics and hosting lectures on the subject.

Circle-K
```
email: circlek@mit.edu
website: web.mit.edu/circle-k/www/
```
Circle K International is the world's largest collegiate co-ed service organization. Simply stated, the objective of its members is to provide altruistic service to the campus and community while having fun, building long-lasting friendships, and developing leadership skills. Circle K does annual and one-time events as well as fundraising. New project ideas are always welcome!

Educational Studies Program (ESP)
```
office: W20-467
phone: x3-4882
email: esp@mit.edu
website: web.mit.edu/esp/
```
ESP is dedicated to running experiments in education. Students can design and teach a class to motivated middle and high school students; topics have ranged from quantum physics to comic books to improvisation. Our recurring programs include: Splash, a weekend extravaganza of classes and workshops in the fall; HSSP, a 10 session series of mini-courses in the spring and summer; and low-cost SAT prep classes in the fall and spring.

FIRST Robotics Club
```
email: first-admin@mit.edu
```
The FIRST Robotics Club meets primarily during IAP (January) to design and build a robot for the FIRST Robotics competition. MIT students act as mentors to high school students from local schools and help make the robot work. For information on the competition, visit www.usfirst.org.

Graduate Student Volunteer Corps
```
email: gsvc_off@mit.edu
website: web.mit.edu/gsvc/www/home.html
```
The Graduate Student Volunteer Corps is a great way to meet other MIT graduate students, learn about the organiziations that keep Cambridge and Boston going, and help to improve the world around you. Some of our recent events included taking care of urban trees, working on a house for Habitat for Humanity, and putting together Braille books for blind children.

Habitat for Humanity
```
email: habitat-info@mit.edu
website: habitat.mit.edu
```
A group of students striving to eliminate poverty housing by building and renovating houses in the community and by raising awareness of the millions of people who live without adequate shelter.

Hunger Action Group
```
email: hunger-request@mit.edu
website: web.mit.edu/hunger/www/
```
The MIT Hunger Action Group does volunteer work intended to combat hunger. The group volunteers at local soup kitchens, participates in the Boston Walk for Hunger and salvages food from Star Market for donation to homeless shelters.

IDEAS Competition
```
office: 4-104
phone: x8-7344
email: ideas-admin@mit.edu
website: web.mit.edu/ideas/
```
The IDEAS Competition provides MIT students with an opportunity to develop innovative solutions for community needs. IDEAS projects can be local, national or international and are eligible for development grants as well as final awards of up to $5,000. Students can participate as competitors or join the IDEAS staff to help run the competition.

Lecture Series Committee (LSC)
```
office: W20-469
phone: x3-3791
email: lsc@mit.edu
website: lsc.mit.edu
```
LSC runs on-campus movies (using 35mm theater quality equipment) every weekend during term. Admission is $3. LSC members volunteer as ushers and projectionists, sell refreshments, or distribute publicity and get free admission for themselves and a guest. We also sponsor lectures; recent speakers include Douglas Adams, Harlan Ellison, Buzz Aldrin, Scott Adams, Andrew Jarecki, and Neil Gaiman. LSC has been serving the MIT community since 1944.

Setu
```
email: setu@mit.edu
website: setu.mit.edu
```
The mission of Setu is to bring socio-economic development of the underserved communities in South Asia through technology-related projects. Past Setu projects include starting a computer literacy center and a women's empowerment center in India, and a mobile science lab in Pakistan. In Fall 2003, we are offering a course on appropriate technology focussed on rural India.

Smile At MIT
```
email: smile@mit.edu
website: web.mit.edu/smile/
```
Smile At MIT is a student chapter of a nonprofit organization known as Operation Smile. This organization carries out free reconstructive surgery on persons with deformities worldwide, allowing people to live lives free from shame. Smile At MIT focuses on raising funds and promoting awareness of Operation Smile. Members may also apply to participate in Operation Smile's annual student leadership conference and medical missions.

Student Ambassadors
```
website: alum.mit.edu/students/ambassador/
```
The Student Ambassadors are a small group of students dedicated to the positive promotion of MIT. In providing perspectives on life at the Institute, we serve as liaisons between the current MIT student community and two important groups: alumni and prospective students. We do this through public speaking, leading tours, attending conferences, and hosting VIPs.

Student Emergency Medicine Society
```
office: W31-215
email: sems-officers@mit.edu
website: web.mit.edu/sems/www/
```
SEMS is dedicated to providing emergency medical support resources to the MIT community. As part of that effort, we seek to train undergraduate and graduate students, as well as MIT faculty and staff, in emergency medical skills. It is our feeling that MIT students, undergraduates in particular, may be more comfortable calling for help if they know that help is being offered by their peers, students like themselves.

Student Information Processing Board (SIPB)
```
office: W20-557
phone: x3-7788
email: sipb@mit.edu
website: www.mit.edu/sipb/
```
SIPB is a volunteer student group concerned with computing at MIT. Members consult students with computing problems at almost any time, day or night, write software documentation, and run servers. They also lobby on behalf of student computing interests.

United Trauma Relief
    website: web.mit.edu/utr/www/

We are a student-based humanitarian aid organization dedicated to the prevention and alleviation of suffering that results from poverty, disease, and war throughout the world. We work on various projects, campaigns, and fundraisers for medical treatment access, natural disasters, refugees, and local issues. We are always open to new ideas for humanitarian aid projects.

Publications and Campus Media

Counterpoint
    office: W20-443
    email: counterpoint@mit.edu
    website: counterpoint.mit.edu

Counterpoint is the MIT/Wellesley Journal of Campus Life. They welcome discussion of a wide variety of topics from all points of view; they publish monthly, and feature interesting articles that focus on the subtleties of life at Wellesley and MIT, rather than the latest news.

Radio Society (W1MX)
    phone: x3-3776
    website: web.mit.edu/w1mx/

America's oldest college amateur radio station, the group covers the entire range of interests in amateur radio; activities include DX, traffic nets, RTTY, MARS, OSCAR, and casual operating by individuals. The group assists with ham radio license exams and Swapfest, an electronics flea market.

Rune, MIT Journal of Arts and Letters
    office: W20-477
    email: rune@mit.edu
    website: web.mit.edu/rune/

Rune exists primarily to foster artistic interests through an annual selection of literary and visual works that is published for the entire MIT community. Students, staff, and affiliates are welcome to submit to our magazine and/or contribute as staff members.

Student Cable Group
    email: mit-student-cable@mit.edu
    website: mitv.mit.edu

The Student Cable Programming Group produces a wide range of television programming available on MIT Cable Channel 36. Students play every role in television production—from direction to acting to technical work. Besides creating original programming, the group televises lectures and other large events. Everyone is welcome to create their own show.

The Tech
    office: W20-483
    phone: x3-1541
    website: www-tech.mit.edu

The Tech, founded in 1881, is MIT's oldest and largest newspaper. It is published on Tuesdays and Fridays during the regular school year, weekly during the month of January, and monthly during the summer. The staff is composed of undergraduate and graduate students and alumni, and is always looking for interested writers and photographers, as well as technology, business, and production staffers.

Technique
    office: W20-451
    phone: x3-2980
    website: web.mit.edu/yearbook/

Technique is the yearbook of MIT. Each year our staff of photographers, designers and writers creates and publishes a work of art, a photographic and literary memoir of MIT. We maintain the best black and white darkroom on campus and an impressive array of photographic equipment. Stop by one of our Saturday afternoon meetings to browse through ancient yearbooks, get some film, and start having fun!

The Thistle
```
office: 50-309
email: thistle-acl@mit.edu
website: web.mit.edu/thistle/www/
```
The Thistle is a newspaper published by the MIT alternative news collective which deals with contemporary social and political issues from a progressive/radical perspective. We are a group of MIT undergraduates, graduate students, staff, and other interested community members committed to fighting racism, sexism, classism, homophobia, and other forms of oppression. We usually publish twice a semester.

Voo Doo
```
office: 50-309
email: voodoo@mit.edu
website: web.mit.edu/voodoo/www/
```
Voo Doo is the only intentionally humorous publication on the MIT campus. Criticized in the past for being "not funny", the Voo Doo editors and staff redoubled their efforts and now consist of bitter, jaded reprobates whose life ambition seems to be to stir up trouble. Voo Doo is usually published once a term, with other material and publicity stunts appearing whenever we feel like it. Submissions of cartoons, comics, drawings, photographs, opinion columns, prose, stories, jokes, and suggestions for irresponsible pranks are accepted year-round.

WMBR Radio
```
phone: x3-4000
phone: x3-8810 (on-air DJ)
website: wmbr.org
```
WMBR is the MIT campus radio station, which offers the opportunity to learn all about music and the music industry, radio engineering, audio production techniques, hands-on electrical engineering skills, news reporting, or even how to manage a small corporation. The station broadcasts between 20 and 24 hours a day in a variety of formats.

Arts, Music, Theater, and Dance Groups

Anointed
```
phone: 617-233-0300
email: anointed@mit.edu
```
Looking for a way to express yourself and your compassion for Christ? MIT's Anointed is the answer! Anointed is a Christian inter-denominational dance group at MIT. We are open to all people, regardless of dance experience or gender. All are welcome. We supply the dance garments and instruments, you supply the creativity. We are an ASA funded group that is student lead, and Christ focused. We meet weekly for dance practice and minister through dance on the MIT campus and throughout the greater Boston-Cambridge Community.

Argentine Tango Club
```
email: tango@mit.edu
website: web.mit.edu/tango/www/
```
The MIT Argentine Tango Club presents an opportunity to the community to encounter the world of Tango. The club organizes classes and free guided practices for the student population that might otherwise not be able to afford taking part in the Tango culture. Social events like dances and movie nights featuring Tango performances are also organized every term.

Ballroom Dance Club
```
email: bdc-officers@mit.edu
website: web.mit.edu/bdclub/
```
The MIT Ballroom Dance Club is a group that provides ballroom classes in a fun and casual atmosphere where no commitment or partners are necessary. Our weekly workshops cover many styles of ballroom at three levels of difficulty, but we primarily focus on social dancing. Our monthly dance parties are also a great way to practice and meet other dancers.

Ballroom Dance Team
```
email: mitbdt-rookie-coordinator@mit.edu
website: ballroom.mit.edu
```
The MIT Ballroom Dance Team consists of about 60 students, alumni, and staff who love to dance. We take classes in tango, rumba, waltz, cha-cha and more, and participate in competitions throughout the Northeast;

we also hold social dances and free beginner workshops. MITBDT is about having team spirit, making friends, and learning to be sexy, graceful, and confident on the dance floor.

Chamak
```
email: chamakboard@mit.edu
website: web.mit.edu/chamak/www/
```
Chamak is an Indian fusion dance team aimed to fuse Indian classical, traditional, and modern dance with American forms of dance such as hip-hop and R&B. Currently, this selected group has performed all around the Metropolitan area. Chamak also represents the exceptional South Asian talent at MIT by performing at many universities throughout the nation who sponsor dance competitions and exhibitions.

Chorallaries
```
office: W20-437
email: choral-info@mit.edu
website: web.mit.edu/choral/www/
```
The Chorallaries of MIT is the Institute's original co-ed a cappella group, which competes, records professional CDs, and goes on tour. We perform off campus and on, including the "Bad Taste" show, a cherished MIT tradition of vulgar skits and lewd songs.

Concert Band
```
office: W20-413
email: bavicchi-lives@mit.edu
website: web.mit.edu/band/
```
The MIT Concert Band, founded in 1948, is a student-run musical ensemble. We play a variety of pieces for wind and concert band, including standards and original works. Each year, the group performs several concerts in Kresge Auditorium and goes on tour in the spring. We are always open to new members at all levels of musical proficiency.

Concert Choir
```
email: cc-auditions@mit.edu
website: web.mit.edu/21m401/www/
```
Concert Choir is a choral group, open by audition to all students at MIT. We perform major works as well as lesser-known pieces. Recent performances include Rachmaninoff's Vespers, Brahms' Motets, and Beethoven's Mass in C. Rehearsals are Mondays and Thursdays from 6pm-8:30pm; informal auditions take place at the first rehearsal of each term. Concert Choir can be taken for fun or credit.

Dance Theater Ensemble
```
website: web.mit.edu/dte/www/
```
The MIT Dance Theater Ensemble (DTE) is a co-curricular dance ensemble supported by the MIT Theater Arts Program and the MIT Council of Arts. DTE performs original work as well as works by visiting guest artists and by our faculty advisor, Thomas DeFrantz. DTE holds informal auditions for all students and MIT affiliates at the beginning of each semester.

Dance Troupe
```
email: dt-officers@mit.edu
website: web.mit.edu/dancetroupe/www/
```
Love to dance? Join MIT Dance Troupe, a student-run organization dedicated to bringing diverse styles of dance to everyone in the MIT community. We offer various technique classes to members, and we produce one full length concert every semester. Membership is open to all MIT affiliates, regardless of experience.

Dramashop
```
office: Kresge Basement, across from Rehearsal Room A
phone: x3-2908
email: ds_officers@mit.edu
website: web.mit.edu/dramashop/www/
```
MIT's only co-curricular theater group. Four major productions a year. Student designers, actors, techies, playwrights, and directors working hand-in-hand with MIT's theater faculty. And we need you. Whether you're a theater junkie, or have never set foot on or behind a stage. It's easy to get involved - come take part in our student-written, student-directed, student-acted One-Acts this fall!

Gilbert and Sullivan Players

phone: x3-0190
website: web.mit.edu/gsp/www/

A group of actors, instrumentalists, and stage crew dedicated to performing the works of Gilbert and Sullivan. The repertory group produces one new major show each term, and holds numerous informal sing-throughs.

Guild of Bellringers

email: guild-of-bellringers-contact@mit.edu
website: web.mit.edu/bellringers/www/

The MIT Guild of Bellringers rings handbells and tower bells, at MIT and in Boston. We're responsible for ringing the eight bells of the Old North Church in a traditional British style called change-ringing, which we also practice on handbells. We also have weekly handbell ensemble meetings where we play more familiar music, from folk songs to Gershwin. Beginners are always welcome.

Imobilare

email: imobilare-exec@mit.edu
website: web.mit.edu/imobilare/www/

Imobilare represents Hip Hop Culture for MIT and the nearby community. Members take part in this urban culture through practice of its elements: Break Dance, Turntablism, MC-ing, Beatboxing, or Graffitti. Imobilare is a growing community open to everyone, which has its members positively channeling their energies and expressing their creativity, while fostering an appreciation for Hip Hop's unique history.

Kinaesthetics Lab

email: kinaesthetics-officers@mit.edu
website: web.mit.edu/kinaesthetics/www/

Kinaesthetics Lab is a student choreography group whose goal is to study the creation of dance as an artistic process. We hope to raise awareness of dance as an art form, and to promote support for the serious pursuit of choreography and dance at MIT. No experience is necessary to join KL.

Lindy Hop Society

email: swing@mit.edu
website: web.mit.edu/swing

The Lindy Hop Society is MIT's swing dance club. We hold a free dance every Wednesday evening. We welcome everyone from the complete beginner to Frankie Manning to come and learn, practice, dance and socialize.

Lion Dance

office: W20-439
website: web.mit.edu/lion-dance/www/

The MIT Lion Dance Club is a lion dance group based in Boston. We have been performing all over the East Coast for over eight years now (since 1994). We became an official club at MIT in 1997. It is a lot of fun, particularly working with children. In general, we usually perform around Chinese New Year and IAP.

Logarhythms

email: logs@mit.edu
website: web.mit.edu/logs/www/

The Logarhythms are the male a cappella singing group at MIT, founded in 1949. Since then the Logs have roamed the width of the US (and England too), performing for high schools, alumni, colleges, and even on television and radio.

Muses

office: W20-401
email: musesrule@mit.edu
website: web.mit.edu/muses/www/

While battling distractions of swooning men, the Super Hot Muses entertain the masses with melodious voices and infectious fun. They've sung on sidewalks, subways and the Empire State Building, serenaded Professor Lewin during 8.02 lecture, and recorded a CD nominated for best female collegiate a cappella album.

Musical Theater Guild

```
office: W20-453
phone: x3-6294
email: mtg-board@mit.edu
website: web.mit.edu/mtg/
```

The largest and oldest student theater group, dedicated solely to the production of stage musicals. The group holds four productions a year, which are planned and run entirely by students.

Oori

```
email: oori@mit.edu
website: web.mit.edu/oori/www/
```

We are the Korean traditional drumming group that you may have seen playing in front of the student center or other locations around campus! We welcome all new members to our weekly practices and will provide you with a drum and the skills needed to play it. Performances include cultural festivals, such as MIT's Grains of Rice and Korean Culture Night, as well as Boston-sponsored events such as Wide Horizons, a day camp for Korean adoptees.

OrigaMIT

```
email: origamit-officers@mit.edu
website: web.mit.edu/origamit/www/
```

OrigaMIT is an informal club for members of the MIT community interested to explore the art and mathematics of folding. The meetings are an opportunity for members to exchange ideas, techniques, and designs, and are often prefaced with a short presentation of concepts or a demonstration of instructions for an origami model. No prior experience with origami is required.

Plush Daddy Fly

```
email: plush-officers@mit.edu
website: web.mit.edu/plush/www/
```

A Sketch Comedy group that performs once at the end of every term, and sometimes randomly in the middle (like opening for Colin Mocherie), for the purposes of attracting members of the opposite sex and putting off finals studying. We're inspired by Mr. Show, Saturday Night Live, MadTV, homonyms, Sea World, etc. Looking for writers/actors/funny people for try-outs in early Fall.

Resonance of MIT

```
email: resonance-request@mit.edu
website: web.mit.edu/resonance/www/
```

Resonance is an all-MIT co-ed a cappella group. We have a blast performing contemporary songs that range from Metallica to Madonna, complete with choreography and skits featuring the Ladies' Man and cucumbers. We work hard to make great music, but we also love spending time together outside of our twice-weekly rehearsals. We just released our very first CD, First Harmonic.

Roadkill Buffet

```
email: rkb@mit.edu
website: web.mit.edu/roadkill/www/
```

Roadkill Buffet is MIT's only improv comedy troupe. There is no script, no costumes, and no safety net. There are a dozen minds racing to give our audience quality improvisational theater, which is made up on the spot. Auditions are held in early September. Even if you have no experience with improv; you can be a part of Roadkill Buffet.

Shakespeare Ensemble

```
office: W20-423
phone: x3-2903
email: ensemble-request@mit.edu
website: web.mit.edu/ensemble/www/
```

"Sword-fighting, murder, betrayal, romance, envy, fairies, cross-dressing, debauchery, adultery, blackmail, hallucinations, treason, and sack! And that's just the cast parties!" - Rachel, member 3 years. "I joined because I got bitten by a theater bug. I've stayed because the Ensemble has been fueling the fever ever since." - Jenn, 4 years. "Check out the ladies!" - Dan, 2 years. Theater. Shakespeare. Actors. Techies. Learning. Friends. Fun. Come join us for our Fall 2004 production of Taming of the Shrew: student-run, student-designed, and student-acted with a local professional director! Email ensemble-request@mit.edu for more information about actor auditions and tech signups.

Student Art Association
```
office: W20-429
website: web.mit.edu/dsa_0002/www/
```
The Student Art Association offers studio facilities and courses in working in many artistic media, including ceramics, photography, drawing, painting, stained glass, and more.

Techiya
```
email: techiya-request@mit.edu
website: web.mit.edu/techiya/www/
```
Techiya is MIT's only Jewish, Hebrew, and Israeli a cappella group. We are co-ed and sing a variety of modern and traditional Jewish music in Hebrew, English, and Yiddish. We hold auditions in September after the Activities Midway for anyone interested - undergrad or grad, Jewish or not. We perform on and off campus, record studio albums, and have fun celebrating Jewish culture.

Tech Squares
```
phone: x3-7000
email: squares@mit.edu
website: web.mit.edu/tech-squares/
```
At Tech Squares, we put the "Modern" in Modern Western Square Dancing. Square dancing will boggle your mind - literally! Got 2 left feet? No problem, it's the brainpower that counts. Think square dancing is outdated? Think again - we challenge any stereotype you've got! On top of that, you get to meet cool people, eat free food, even get PE credit!

Toons
```
email: toons-request@mit.edu
website: www.the-toons.com
```
The Toons is a co-ed a cappella group comprised of MIT and Wellesley college students who get together, harmonize, and have fun. Our style includes everything from 50s and 60s music to the present. We perform home concerts at MIT and Wellesley each semester. We also love to travel and perform at other colleges and anywhere else we are invited.

Cultural Groups

African Students' Association
```
email: africans-acl@mit.edu
website: web.mit.edu/africans/www/
```
The African Students' Association seeks to promote African awareness on campus. Through various cultural performances, film festivals and photo exhibitions we aim to introduce the MIT student population to the beautiful traditions of Africa. We host discussions and workshops to address the political and socio-economic issues around the continent while seeking to bring out the full potential of Africa.The Association takes pride in its role of producing tomorrow's African and world leaders. While we discuss real and important issues we ensure that our events remain interesting and fun.

Arab Student Organization
```
website: web.mit.edu/arab/www/
```
Holds social events and lectures to allow the members of the Arab community to come together, and to share Arabic culture with the MIT community. The emphasis is on spreading culture not politics. Anyone can join the group; meetings are once a month.

Armenian Students' Organization
```
website: web.mit.edu/armenia/www/
```
Aimed at sharing and promoting Armenian culture at MIT. The club holds several social functions throughout the year and is open to the entire MIT community.

Asian American Association
```
email: aaa-exec@mit.edu
website: web.mit.edu/mitaaa/www/
```
The MIT Asian American Association (MITAAA) is dedicated to the promotion of the Asian American experience by providing a series of social, cultural, political, and educational events. MITAAA serves to represent the diverse interests of Asian American students, Asian students from abroad, and non-Asian students who are interested in learning more about the Asian American experience.

Association of Taiwanese Students
    email: mitats-request@mit.edu
    website: web.mit.edu/mitats/www/
Our members are anyone who likes to have fun and/or learn about Taiwanese and traditional Chinese culture. We have 3 master chefs, 2 painters, and a renowned singer. We offer spectacular holiday celebrations, workshops, professional athletic training, karaoke and dim-sum runs, superior T-shirts and quality free food.

Australian and New Zealand Club
    email: anz-request@mit.edu
    website: web.mit.edu/anz/www/home.html
Dedicated to promoting the exotic cultures of Australia and New Zealand, and acting as a resource for Aussies and Kiwis overseas. If you don't know what Australian Rules football is, who Crocodile Dundee and Mad Max are, or what Foster's is really Australian for, you need to join.

Bangladeshi Students Association
    email: bd-exec@mit.edu
    website: web.mit.edu/bangladesh/www/
The MIT Bangladeshi Students' Association provides a focal point for all the Bangladeshis on campus. We organise various activities both to bring together the Bangladeshi community, and to disseminate our culture to the entire MIT community. Such activities include participation in the International Fair, cultural shows, welcome socials for new and returning students, dinners, movies, etc.

Bhangra
    email: bhangra-request@mit.edu
    website: web.mit.edu/bhangra/www/
Bhangra is a vibrant, energetic, and colorful folk dance originating in Punjab in the Indian subcontinent. MIT Bhangra Club holds free classes, open to everyone, all skill levels, and all backgrounds. Class participation often leads to dance troupes performing at various cultural events and competitions throughout the year.

Black Students' Union
    office: 50-105
    email: bsu-exec@mit.edu
    website: web.mit.edu/bsu/www/
The purpose of the Black Students' Union is to provide support for Black students and to promote social interactions between students, faculty, and alumni. This organization also serves to aid in efforts to improve welfare of the Black community as a whole.

Black Women's Alliance
    email: black-women-request@mit.edu
    website: web.mit.edu/black-women/www/
Our purpose is to provide a forum to address the needs and concerns of Black women undergraduate students at MIT; to promote the awareness of Black women's issues in the MIT community through activities designed to increase the visibility of Black women on campus and to encourage interaction with other campus groups; to promote scholarship, activism, unity, friendship, and community.

Brazilian Students Association
    website: web.mit.edu/brazil/home.html
The MIT Brazilian Students Association strives to disseminate Brazilian culture throughout MIT via its 70-plus student members. The club also participates in activities in the Brazilian community in the greater Boston area.

Chinese Choral Society
    email: cccs-officers@mit.edu
    website: web.mit.edu/cccs/www/
CCS is a fun group formed by students and professionals who love choral music as well as Chinese culture and tradition. We produce bi-quarterly concerts a year and participate actively in a variety of other shows and events. We have great relationships with local Chinese communities and other schools.

Chinese Student and Scholar Association (CSSA)
    office: W20-439
    website: web.mit.edu/cssa/www/
The Chinese Student and Scholar Association (CSSA) at MIT is a non-profit and non-political student organization. Its purpose is to help students adjust to the new environment as well as to promote friendship, culture exchange and interactions among all students on campus.

Chinese Students Club
```
email: mitcsc@mit.edu
website: web.mit.edu/csc/www/
```
Promotes interaction between Chinese students and those who wish to learn more about Chinese culture. CSC encourages an international understanding of the Chinese heritage and fosters a friendship with Chinese people through intellectual, cultural, and social activities.

Club Argentino
```
email: argentinos@mit.edu
website: web.mit.edu/argentina/
```
This is a club where people from Argentina meet in order to get in touch with other Argentines in Boston. We have irregular meetings, which we advertise by way of our mailing list.

Club Francophone MIT
```
email: francophone-request@mit.edu
website: francophone.mit.edu
```
Club Francophone is a group for MIT students interested in the French language and the francophone cultures of the world. Members range in fluency from neophyte to native. Club activities consist of cultural and social events that include film and museum outings and on-campus screenings, French tables, lectures, cooking parties and tastings, and intensive group discussions about phenomenological existentialism.

Colombian Student Association
```
email: colombians-officers@mit.edu
website: web.mit.edu/colombianos/www/
```
The Colombian Association of MIT is a student organization with the purpose of promoting the Colombian culture at MIT and in the Boston area. During the last academic year we were involved in diverse social, academic, cultural, and sports events. Our events included the MIT-International Fair, the Colombian Colloquiums and the Colombian Party. Our members come from different Colombian regions as well as from other countries.

European Club
```
office: W20-443
phone: x8-0756,
email: contact@euroclub.mit.edu
website: euroclub.mit.edu
```
The MIT European Club welcomes members from many countries and professional disciplines who share a European background or an interest in Europe. We organize a broad array of social gatherings, outings and athletic activities, such as dessert parties, barbecues,hiking weekends, beach trips, theater and concert visits, ski trips, a tennis competition and weekly pub tours! In addition, our yearly Career Fair attracts many major companies offering jobs in Europe.

Filipino Students Association
```
website: web.mit.edu/mitfsa/www/
```
The Filipino Students Association offers friendship and services to Filipinos who are away from home and to others who are interested in Philippine affairs and culture. We also network with Filipino students from other Boston-area universities and with the local Filipino community.

Hansori
```
website: web.mit.edu/hansori/www/
```
Hansori, meaning a unified or a great voice in Korean, is a group of Korean undergraduates and graduates with deep enthusiasm in finding their identity by learning their culture and history. Hansori's activities include study of modern Korean history, publication of its own magazines, installation of Korean software on Athena, and performing Poong Mool. These activities are aimed at the eventual formation of a more harmonious and culturally-rich community at MIT.

Hellenic Students' Association
```
email: proedreio@mit.edu
website: web.mit.edu/hellenic/www/
```
The purpose of the Hellenic Students' Association is to promote fellowship among members of the Greek student community. The association is bringing together about 150 students from Hellas, Cyprus and the Diaspora. It is a very active group, organizing large annual events such as the Easter Celebration as well as parties, informal meetings, and participating in the events of the larger Greek community of Boston such as

the Independence Day parade. The association aims at promoting Hellenic Ideas and Culture, not only to people of Hellenic descent, but to a potentially wider audience. Towards that goal several lectures are organized, as well as other events such as traditional dancing lessons. Furthermore, the HSA welcomes and helps out the newly admitted students and serves as the representative of the Greek/Cypriot student body of MIT as a whole. To join, send email to the executive committee (above), contact Anna Pisania [apisania@mit.edu, 617 253 6489] or visit the HSA website (also above).

Hong Kong Students Society
website: web.mit.edu/hkssmit/www/

An association that allows students interested in the exciting city of Hong Kong to gather together for barbecues, picnics, study breaks, and joint-school banquets. Anyone interested is welcome to join.

International Film Club (ifilm)
email: ifilm@mit.edu
website: web.mit.edu/ifilm/www/

The main activity of the International Film Club is to screen movies each week, on Wednesdays and Thursdays, preceded by a short introduction.

International Students Association
email: isa-web@mit.edu
website: web.mit.edu/isa/

The ISA tries to increase the MIT community's awareness of international students. They organize seminars to bring Americans and internationals together, and to provide information on international student concerns, such as how to get jobs in the United States.

Iranian Studies Group at MIT
email: iranian@mit.edu
website: web.mit.edu/isg/

The Iranian Studies Group at MIT (ISG) is a non-partisan organization with the aim of promoting an analytical understanding of the long-term social, economic, political and cultural issues related to the development of the Iranian society through consultation with and dialogue amongst intellectuals, experts and the larger public.

Japanese Association of MIT (JAM)
email: nihonjinkai-request@mit.edu
website: http://mit.edu/jam/

JAM organizes various social, cultural, and leisure events to promote interaction between Japanese students, researchers, staff, and faculty members at MIT, their family members, and people interested in Japan. Every year, we typically organize Fall and Spring Parties and barbeque cook-outs. We also participate in the MIT intramural sports league for softball, basketball, and ice hockey, play in an annual Japanese softball tournament, and organize regular tennis get-togethers. Membership applications are always welcome on-line!

Japanese Society of Undergraduates
email: jsu-officers@mit.edu
website: http://web.mit.edu/jsu

Japanese Society of Undergraduates is an informal club for anyone interested in the Japanese culture. Our typical activities include movie showings, study breaks, cooking, dinner outings, etc. We also participate in MIT events such as the International Fair and Grains of Rice.

Korean Students' Association
email: ksa-exec@mit.edu
website: web.mit.edu/ksa/www/

The Korean Students' Association exists as a non-political club to provide opportunities for Korean undergraduates at MIT to explore their common ethnic and cultural backgrounds and to promote the understanding of the Korean people and culture.

La Union Chicana por Aztlan (LUChA)
website: web/lucha/www/

LUChA is dedicated to providing academic, social, and cultural support to those who wish to associate with the Mexican-American community at MIT. The organization, among other things, fights for the advancement of Chicanos in education, provides a sense of community for Chicanos at MIT, and maintains an active role in the MIT minority community.

Lebanese Club

```
office: 9-355
phone: x3-4420
email: lebanon-request@mit.edu
website: web.mit.edu/lebanon/www/
```

The Lebanese Club's aim is to foster a sense of community among the Lebanese students at MIT by having social and cultural activities and promote the Lebanese culture and traditions among the MIT community.

Mitaly

```
email: mitaly@mit.edu
website: web.mit.edu/mitaly/www/
```

The purpose of MITaly is to spread, promote and advance the Italian culture at MIT. MITaly serves also as a network for Italian students at MIT and for whoever is interested in our country, its language and culture. MITaly events can be enjoyed by non-Italian speakers, useful to students of the Italian language, and meeting moments for Italians.

MIT Organization of Serbian sTudents (MOST)

```
email: most_sef@mit.edu
website: web.mit.edu/most/www/
```

MOST (Serbian: bridge) is a student cultural group presenting and promoting Serbian cultural heritage to the wider MIT community, and encouraging friendship among the members and nonmembers alike. All people of good will are welcome.

National Society of Black Engineers

```
email: nsbe-eboard@mit.edu
website: web.mit.edu/nsbe/www/
```

We're the MIghTy chapter of NSBE, the largest student-run organization in the country. As a professional organization, dedicated to academic excellence, cultural awareness, and community involvement, we still know how to have fun... If that's something you're into, then NSBE-MIT is definitely for you. Our membership is open to everyone; we would love to see you become part of our organization.

Pakistani Students at MIT (PakSMIT)

```
email: paksmit-exec@mit.edu
website: web.mit.edu/paksmit/www
```

Pakistani Students at MIT (PakSMIT) exists as a club to provide opportunities for both Pakistani students studying at MIT to explore their common ethnic and cultural Background and for MIT community to better understand Pakistani culture and interact with Pakistani people. Come, join us and discover Pakistan, an enchanting land.

Pangaea

```
email: pangaea-exec@mit.edu
website: web.mit.edu/pangaea/www/
```

Pangaea is a student group seeking to enrich the MIT community by promoting cross-cultural exchange around campus. We advocate multicultural awareness and the active appreciation of diversity through creative social and cultural activities — such as movie/dinner nights, discussions, multicultural concerts, guest speakers, and newsletters. Ultimately, we want members of the MIT community to step outside established boundaries and explore.

Persian Students' Association

```
email: persian-officers@mit.edu
website: web.mit.edu/persian/www/
```

MIT PSA is a non-political group interested in promoting Persian and Iranian culture. MIT PSA actively celebrates important Persian occasions and hopes to provide a platform for Iranian-American and Iranian students to interact.

Rainbow Coffeehouse (Graduate Student GLB Coffeehouse)

```
email: glb-coffee-officers@mit.edu
website: web.mit.edu/glb-coffee/www/
```

The Rainbow Coffeehouse is a socio-cultural organization run by graduate students, and aimed at providing a safe space to LBGT community at MIT. Our bi-monthly events include dinners, socials, queer-themed movie nights, picnics and hiking trips. The coffeehouse events are not only open to the entire MIT student community but also to LBGT students from other universities around Boston.

Russia Business and Technology Initiative
website: mitrussia.mit.edu

The Russia Business and Technology Initiative is an MIT student effort that aims to promote interaction between MIT and Russian institutions (academic, governmental and commercial) in the spheres of Business and Technology, and to foster the spirit of entrepreneurship in Russia, specifically in the high technology sector.

Sangam (Indian Student Association)
website: web.mit.edu/sangam/www/

Sangam is one of the oldest student organizations on campus. Our aim is to provide a platform to Indian students for social, cultural, and political exchange. We also aspire to help the incoming students from India acclimate in their new environment. Come join us and have a peek into the rich culture and heritage of India, authentic Indian food, and some quality fun times!

Singapore Students Society (MITSSS)
email: sss-com@mit.edu
website: web.mit.edu/mitsss/www/

The MIT Singapore Students' Society is a cultural organisation whose main purpose is to promote cultural exchange between Singapore students at MIT and students from other countries. It also serves as a platform for Singaporeans in the Boston metropolitan area to interact and have fun.

Society of Hispanic Professional Engineers
email: shpe-request@mit.edu
website: web.mit.edu/shpe/www/2002/popindex.html

MIT SHPE is recognized as a professional organization, and as such, we provide the fundamentals needed to make wise career choices. SHPE's mission is to achieve educational, economic, and social equity for Hispanic individuals by supporting the development of Hispanic engineers and scientists. We provide these opportunities through workshops and conferences.

South Asian American Students (SAAS)
website: web.mit.edu/saas/www/

SAAS is thelargest group representing South Asia on MIT's campus. SAAS is open to all students interested in getting a taste of South Asian culture. Our organization consists of Indians, Bangladeshis, Pakistanis, Sri Lankans, and others. We were founded with the purpose of celebrating the diversity of South Asian culture and promoting social interaction between South Asian students and those of other backgrounds.

Turkish Student Association (TSA)
email: tsa-isleri@mit.edu
website: web.mit.edu/tsa/www/

We organize fun events to introduce the Turkish culture to the MIT community. Our past events have included weekly Turkish movie screenings, study breaks with Turkish food, and camping trips to nearby locations. You are welcome to join our activities.

Vietnamese Student Association
email: vsa@mit.edu
website: http://web.mit.edu/vsa/www/

The MIT VSA is a fun and friendly group of undergraduate and graduate students all sharing the common interest of staying involved with the Vietnamese culture. We highlight each month with a boisterous family-like get-together complete with delicious Vietnamese food. Additionally, we seek meaningful contributions through community service and introducing others to Vietnamese culture. Look for us in events such as Night Market, Grains of Rice, the International Fair, and other diversity or multicultural events.

Religious Groups

Asian Baptist Student Koinonia (ABSK)
website: web.mit.edu/absk/www/

We are a Christian Fellowship at MIT devoted to our lord Jesus Christ and to each other. We strive to build relationships in order to realize God's love for us more. We hold weekly Bible studies and many other activities.

Asian Christian Fellowship
    office: W-11
    email: mitacf-request@mit.edu
    website: web.mit.edu/mitacf/www/
MITACF is a community of students at MIT devoted to demonstrating the realness of God in all that we do, living out the connection between faith and daily living. The purpose of MITACF is to establish, assist, and encourage students who attest the lord Jesus Christ as God incarnate.

Atheists, Agnostics, and Humanists
    email: mitaah-officers@mit.edu
    website: web.mit.edu/mitaah/
MITAAH serves as a unique opportunity for freethinkers to meet and learn from each other and explore secular outlooks on life. The group provides an open and supportive environment for students skeptical of religious claims, while educating the MIT community about secular ideas through lectures and other events.

Bahai Association
    email: mitbahai@mit.edu
    website: web.mit.edu/mitba/www/
The Association is an MIT student organization that promotes the principles of the Bahai Faith, an independent religion with followers all over the world. Membership in the Association is open to students, faculty, and staff of all religious persuasions. One of our main activites is the annual IAP lecture series on science, religion, and society.

Baptist Student Fellowship
    phone: x3-2328
    email: bsf-request@mit.edu
    website: web.mit.edu/bcm/www/
The Baptist Student Fellowship is a group of Christians from a variety of backgrounds meeting weekly for small group Bible studies, prayer, and special events. Join us for retreats, socials and other gatherings with BSF groups around the city. Groups meet in English and Korean. Also, we sponsor community activities like free English classes for international students and spouses.

Black Christian Fellowship
    website: web.mit.edu/bcf/www/
We are a diverse group of people who share one common bond: a love for Christ. We come from many parts of the United States and abroad to praise God and learn more about him while at MIT. Our ministry is dedicated to taking God's word and applying it to our daily lives on campus.

Campus Crusade for Christ
    email: mitccc-officers@mit.edu
    website: web.mit.edu/mitccc/www/
A Community of students committed to Jesus Christ growing together in him, offering every MIT student the opportunity to consider the claim of Christ, and sharing God's love with the world.

Campus Crusade for Cthulhu
    office: 50-020
    email: cthulhu@mit.edu
    website: web.mit.edu/cthulhu/www/
The organization is dedicated to the research and investigation of the Old Ones, Elder Gods, and Things Man Was Not Meant to Know.

Chi Alpha Christian Fellowship
    email: jake05@mit.edu
    website: http://web.mit.edu/xa/www/2004_spring/
Chi Alpha is a Christian Fellowship focused on training young men and women to grow up to be spiritually mature and effective Christians. We do this by having small group Bible studies and discussion groups on "hot" topics, outreach opportunities, leadership training seminars, semesterly New England-wide student led retreats, and most of all, great fellowship and lots of fun. Contact: email jake05@mit.edu or IM the team at AOL screen name XAatMIT.

172 Activities

Chinese Bible Fellowship
```
email: jessicac@mit.edu, jcpsm46@mit.edu
website: web.mit.edu/mitcbf/www/
```
CBF is a campus ministry of Chinese Bible Church of Greater Boston. We are comprised of students desiring to obey and serve our lord Jesus Christ through obedience to his word. Joining together in fellowship, we seek to grow in Christ and "spur one another on toward love and good deeds" (Heb. 10:24).

Cross Products
```
office: W20-439
email: xprod-request@mit.edu
website: web.mit.edu/crossp/
```
The Cross Products is MIT's only Christian a cappella singing group. We are an auditioned group made up of about 10-16 members who have a desire to glorify God through music and want to reach out to our peers and those in our community by holding concerts and singing/serving on campus and throughout the city.

Gospel Choir
```
email: gospel-adm@mit.edu
website: web.mit.edu/mitgoscho/www/
```
The Gospel choir is an on-campus ministry, founded nearly three decades ago, that is dedicated to spreading the gospel of Jesus Christ through song. Our primary goal is to use traditional and contemporary gospel music to spread the word of Jesus Christ. We welcome members of any race, religion or background to experience and minister the glorious knowledge of Christ through song.

Grad Hillel
```
office: W11-039
phone: 3-2982
email: hillel_grads@mit.edu
website: http://web.mit.edu/hillel/www/ grad-hillel.html
```
Grad Hillel is an association of Jewish graduate students from all parts of the MIT community. Grad Hillel sponsors programs, dinners, outings, and social events to enrich the lives of Jewish graduate students. Popular annual events include "Music Under the Stars" in the MIT sukkah, the Yom Kippur break-the-fast, and our "traveling" monthly Shabbat dinners.

Hillel
```
office: W11-040
phone: x3-2982
email: hillel-board@mit.edu
website: web.mit.edu/hillel/www/
```
MIT Hillel is home to Jewish life on campus. We sponsor one or more events every day which range from larger events such as Jews on Ice (a skating party) and the Latke-Hamentashen Debate to community services opportunities, daily classes, Shabbat and holiday meals, daily services, and more. Visit our sukkah on Kresge Oval and the famous "test tube menorah" lighting in Lobby 10. We provide numerous opportunities for you to schmooze with Jews.

Hindu Students Council
```
email: hscweb@mit.edu
website: web.mit.edu/hsc/www/
```
The MIT Hindu Students Council is a forum that provides a variety of opportunities to learn about Hindu heritage. We hold weekly meetings and discussions, celebrations of Hindu festivals, service projects, and many other events to bring together students interested in Hinduism.

Latter-Day Saint Student Association
```
email: ldssa-officers@mit.edu
website: web.mit.edu/ldssa/
```
The Latter-day Saint Student Association (LDSSA) at MIT encompasses a spiritual community of LDS students, families, staff, and friends who foster personal, social, religious, and academic growth through Christ-like living. As an association organized by The Church of Jesus Christ of Latter-day Saints, we hold activities that promote these goals within the bounds of an MIT student schedule, such as weekly Family Home Evenings and monthly socials. The Boston Institute of Religion offers classes on campus through the LDSSA for in-depth scriptural and doctrinal study. These free events encourage students to interact outside of academic circles, develop lasting friendships, and maintain a balance between spiritual and seculardevelopment. All interested students, staff, and MIT affiliates are invited to participate in our events and learn more about LDS beliefs.

Lutheran Episcopal Ministry
```
office: W11
phone: x3-2983
email:  mccreath@mit.edu
website: web.mit.edu/lem/
```
We gather in the MIT Chapel on Wednesdays at 5:10pm to celebrate the Eucharist. After the service, we enjoy a meal prepared by LEMmings and a program on such topics as prayer, faith and science, or ethical questions. We offer weekly Bible study groups, outreach projects, periodic retreats, field trips, special seasonal worship, and social events. All are welcome, regardless of religious background, race, nationality, or sexual orientation.

Muslim Students' Association
```
office: W11
email: msa-ec@mit.edu
website: web.mit.edu/mitmsa/
```
The MIT Muslim Students' Association is a close-knit and friendly community which serves to assist MIT's Muslims in their practice of Islam and endeavors to promote understanding between Muslims and people of other faiths on campus. The Muslim Students' Association holds various social and religious events throughout the year.

Orthodox Christian Fellowship
```
email: orthodox-acl@mit.edu
website: web.mit.edu/ocf/
```
We are a diverse group of Eastern Orthodox Christians from a variety of ethnic backgrounds interested in learning about and living the traditional New Testament Faith. We hold discussions during weekly meetings, host speakers on relevant topics, and have social outings as well.

Pagan Students Group
```
website: web.mit.edu/psg/www/
```
PSG is a support group for Pagans in the MIT community. In addition to organizing meetings or rituals at new and full moons and on the eight solar holidays, we work to improve the image of paganism in our community. Paganism is an affirmation of the beauty and sacredness of life on this earth, and of our unity with it.

St. Paul Youth Ministries
```
email: stpaul@mit.edu
```
Our ministry is a new Catholic ministry at MIT whose purpose is to minister to the youth in the Boston area by giving retreats to the students at local schools. We're currently a fairly small group consisting of mosty MIT students, but also a handful from Harvard and Wellesley. We like to focus on promoting spiritual development among members of the group by going on group retreats at least once a term and also through weekly meetings during which we pray, have Bible study and plan future retreats and other group activities. We welcome all those interested and invite you to email the group list or `joel_f@mit.edu` for any additional information.

Tech Catholic Community
```
office: W11
phone: x3-2981
email: catholic@mit.edu
website: web.mit.edu/tcc/www/
```
The Tech Catholic Community at MIT is an international community of Catholics committed to reaching out in love to the larger MIT and worldly communities. Gathering our unity and strength primarily through the celebration of the Eucharist, we strive to share and grow in our faith and extend welcome to all who are seeking God's truth in their lives.

United Christian Fellowship
```
email: mitucf-req@mit.edu
website: web.mit.edu/ucf/www/
```
United Christian Fellowship is a group dedicated to better understanding the teachings of Jesus Christ and their application to an effective everyday life. Our desire is to form a community in which both the committed and the curious feel welcome and loved. We are the multi-ethnic branch of InterVarsity Christian Fellowship's undergraduate outreach at MIT, in partnership with Asian Christian Fellowship and Black Christian Fellowship.

Victory Campus Ministries
```
email: vcm-info@mit.edu
website: web.mit.edu/vcm/www
```
Victory Campus Ministry exists to be an instrument at MIT for building godly friendships, developing leaders in all areas of society, and reaching out to the MIT community with the love and gospel of Jesus Christ. We believe that everyone has a God given purpose and we are dedicated to helping people find their destiny in God. Join us for in-depth bible studies and meetings with students from other colleges around Boston.

Sports Groups

American Jiu Jitsu Self Defense
```
office: 13-3102A
phone: x3-4623
email: jitsu-off@mit.edu
website: web.mit.edu/jiu-jitsu/www/
```
We practice the American Jiu Jitsu system of Self Defense. We are open to everyone, independent of athletic ability, strength, size, and previous experience. Our art consists of strikes, blocks, throws, locks, escapes, verbal techniques, ground work, police techniques, weapons defense, stick work and more.

Archery Club
```
email: archery-officers@mit.edu
website: web.mit.edu/archery/www/
```
The Archery Club is a group of MIT affiliated people who enjoy the sport of Archery. Some people are interested in learning how to shoot, some just want to practice, others have higher aims of becoming competitive. No equipment or experience is necessary.

Badminton Club
```
email: mitbac-officers@mit.edu
website: web.mit.edu/mitbac/www/
```
The MIT Badminton Club consists of students who are interested in playing badminton regularly. No experience is necessary, only the will and desire to play. We participate in a badminton league that takes place in the Spring and we also go to tournaments throughout the year.

Cheerleading
```
email: cheer-captains@mit.edu
website: web.mit.edu/cheer/
```
MIT Cheerleading is a co-ed squad which requires no experience to join. We cheer at home football and basketball games and attend various local competitions. Practices involve tumbling, stunting, dancing, and practicing game and competition routines. Although many of our members have never cheered before, our 2004 competition season was highly successful, while still being fun for all of us. Come show your friends that yes, MIT really does have cheerleaders!

Cycling Club
```
email: cycling-club-request@mit.edu
website: web.mit.edu/cycling-club/www/home.html
```
The cycling club encourages cyclists of all abilities to join us on our group rides through eastern Massachusetts. We practice both mountain biking and road biking, and some members participate in collegiate racing.

Figure Skating Club
```
email: skating-admin@mit.edu
website: web.mit.edu/skatingclub/www/
```
We provide an enjoyable, supportive, and safe environment for figure skaters of all ability levels. The club offers weekly group lessons, organizes an annual Skating Show and hosts a USFSA Intercollegiate Competition. We practice at MIT's Johnson ice rink which is open from October to March.

Isshinryu Karate-do
email: isshinryu@mit.edu
website: web.mit.edu/isshinryu/
Traditional Okinawan Karate. See website for workout times. No cost to MIT students/faculty/staff. We're a small club concentrating on forms and technique rather than combat or board breaks. If you've never studied a martial art, or don't think you'd be good at it, try a workout with us. Improve your balance, strength, flexibility, stamina, coordination, awareness, and much more.

Judo Club
email: judo@mit.edu
website: web.mit.edu/judo/
Judo is a grappling martial art - meaning throws, joint locks, chokes, and pinning, but no kicking or punching - that emphasizes efficient technique and the mutual welfare of participants. This means Judo can be practiced with full force and complete safety. Judo has been an Olympic sport since 1964. Our club is both instructional and competitve, consisting mostly of beginners.

Karate Club
phone: x3-4874
email: karate-request@mit.edu
website: web.mit.edu/karate/www/
The MIT Karate Club is a traditional martial arts group affiliated with Shotokan Karate of America (SKA). Our club is open to all members of the MIT community; we invite you to come by and try our practice to get a taste of karate and our group.

Kendo Club
email: kendo_officials@mit.edu
website: web.mit.edu/kendo/
We practice kendo (the way of the sword), the art of Japanese fencing, also known as "hitting our friends with sticks". Beginners are welcome anytime, and no equipment is needed to start; please see our website for our practice schedules.

Korean Karate Club
email: mitkkc-officers@mit.edu
website: web.mit.edu/mitkkc/
We practice Chung Do Kwan, a traditional style of Tae Kwon Do. We feature no-contact sparring, so all offensive techniques are done with full power and speed, but stop short of the target, thereby minimizing injuries. It's a great way to work off MIT stress, stay in shape, gain self-esteem and learn self-defense while having fun, too.

Men's Rugby Club
email: mitrfc@mit.edu
website: www.mitrugby.org
The MIT Men's Rugby Club is an open club with Undergrads, Grads, Faculty and Staff playing matches in the Spring and Fall on each Saturday. Trainings are Tuesday & Thursday 6pm on Briggs Field. Rugby at MIT has been played for over 100 years. It offers a great sport with running, passing, kicking and tackling. Rugby friends last a lifetime. New and used players welcome.

Scuba Club
office: W20-461
phone: x3-2988
email: scuba-officers@mit.edu
website: web.mit.edu/scuba-club/www/
The MIT Scuba Club is an organization of divers with various affiliations to MIT. We host talks, plan dives, have cookouts and other activities that are open to certified divers and those who are interested in learning this sport.

Sloan Crew
email: sloan-crew-request@mit.edu

Sloan Crew is a club team that is a great mix of competitive and fun. We practice four times per week during the fall and spring, with coaching. We run a learn-to-row program and an experienced program. Experienced rowers compete in races throughout the seasons, including the Head of the Charles; our novices race in November and in the spring.

Synchro
email: tenley@mit.edu

Curious about synchronized swimming? Many of us were too when we started this group in Spring 2003. Some of us have been involved with this beautiful and powerful team sport for many years, while others have only just started to discover it.

Table Tennis Team
email: cly@mit.edu

website: web.mit.edu/cly/www/mit-tt/

The MIT Table Tennis Team aims to promote competitive table tennis among MIT students. We compete against other schools (e.g. Harvard, Northeastern) and have had great success in the past.

Tae Kwon Do Club
email: tkd@mit.edu

website: web.mit.edu/tkd/

With over 25 years of continuous operation, the MIT Tae Kwon Do Club is MIT's oldest martial arts club. We place great emphasis on both the physical and mental aspects of traditional Tae Kwon Do. Maintaining a respectful, supportive environment allows us to push ourselves to our limits and then learn how to expand those limits. Free for beginners.

Tech Snow
email: team-manager@mit.edu

website: web.mit.edu/snowboard/

Tech Snow is a club dedicated to promoting snowboarding. Together, our members compete, help each other learn, and just have a good time riding. All levels of snowboarders are welcome - from absolute beginners just looking to have fun to experienced riders who want to start collegiate competition.

Women's Crew
website: web.mit.edu/techcrew/www/

The team practices year-round, with most of the competitions taking place during the Spring semester. Most members of the team have no experience prior to MIT, and pick up the sport as a group during their first semester on the team. Crew offers an opportunity for anyone, from small coxswains who command the shells, to lightweight rowers to openweights.

Women's Ice Hockey Club
email: club-hockey-officers@mit.edu

website: www.mit.edu/afs/athena/activity/c/club-hockey/www/about.html

We're a group of mostly grad students, some undergrads, and a few alums that practices three times a week and plays games against club teams from other colleges. Beginners are welcome and the only requirements to get started are a stick, a pair of skates, and the desire to have some fun on the ice.

MIT Women's volleyball club (ChickVB)
website: web.mit.edu/chickVB

email: wvc-officer@mit.edu

WAVE
website: web.mit.edu/wave/index.html

email: wave-officers@mit.edu

MIT is fortunate to have two different women's volleyball clubs, offering players with at a wide range of levels an opportunity to compete and have a great time playing volleyball. ChickVB is a competitive women's volleyball club, practicing year-round and competing in tournaments during the spring and fall semesters. Members of ChickVB have significant volleyball experience, most playing in college or competitive club programs prior to MIT. Tryouts are held in the beginning of the fall semester each year. WAVE offers a more laid-back volleyball atmosphere, with emphasis on teaching and improving volleyball skills. WAVE also practices year-round and competes in tournaments in the spring and fall. Members of WAVE range from people who've never played volleyball before to those who have been playing in clubs for 10 years. Everyone is welcome! Please see our websites or email our officers if you're interested in playing.

Departmental and Honorary Societies

American Nuclear Society
website: web.mit.edu/ans/www/
A 14,000+ worldwide membership organization devoted to the advancement of nuclear technology. Membership in the Society offers the opportunity to network and become acquainted with all levels of the nuclear community.

Biological Engineering Division Student Board
office: 56-639
email: beboard@mit.edu
website: web.mit.edu/beboard/
The Biomedical Engineering Society is a student run organization devoted to serving the MIT community in utilizing the biomedical engineering resources around campus and around the world. Our goal is to promote education and collaboration by working closely with faculty to serve as a gateway to research, employment and academic opportunities in biomedical engineering. The academic home of BMES is the Biological Engineering Division (BE), and thus BMES serves as a nexus of communication between students and faculty regarding the planned new undergraduate degree in Biological Engineering. The BE SB degree proposal will be going through MIT committee review in fall 2004, and BMES is the place to hear the latest on the course offerings and possible implementation of the degree. The Biomedical Engineering Society also gives students an opportunity to work directly with some of the world's leading bioengineering researchers and to be at the forefront of some of the most innovative techniques in development today by establishing connections between students, faculty, industry and other universities. Some other BMES activities include industrial site tours, a monthly lecture series, exclusive internship opportunities, a members' resume book, mentorship programs, student-faculty luncheons and the publication of a quarterly newsletter, the BioTECH.

Eta Kappa Nu (HKN)
website: hkn.mit.edu/
National Electrical Engineering honor society.

Harvard-MIT Mathematics Tournament (HMMT)
email: hmmt-request@mit.edu
website: web.mit.edu/hmmt
The Harvard-MIT Math Tournament is an annual math tournament for high school students. It is run entirely by MIT and Harvard students, and will be taking place at MIT on February 19, 2005. We expect to have over 500 participants this year. You can write problems, take part in organizing the competition, or simply help out on the day of the contest. Please e-mail us if you're interested!

Minority Association of Pre-health Students(MAPS)
email: ij3zeof@mit.edu
phone: 617-225-9245
The Minority Association of Pre-health Students is an organization dedicated to increasing the number of minority undergraduate students matriculating to medical school. The MIT Chapter was founded in 2003 and focuses on exposing undergraduate students of color to the realities of medical school and the medical field. Through forums, study breaks, and various service events, we aim to inform our members of what it means to be a minority in medicine. MAPS is part of a larger student organization called the Student National Medical Association. SNMA members, who are typically medical students, offer guidance to undergraduate students interested in pursuing careers in medicine. They provide MAPS members with information on how to choose a curriculum and how to excel academically. In addition, SNMA members work with MAPS members advising them about the medical school application process and the MCAT. More importantly, SNMA members serve as mentors to undergraduate students helping them successfully matriculate into medical school. MAPS is open to the entire pre-med community.

Pi Tau Sigma
website: web.mit.edu/pts/www/
National Honorary Mechanical Engineering Fraternity.

Society of Physics Students
website: web.mit.edu/sps/www/
SPS is a professional physics organization for undergraduate students. The goals are to promote a community within the group of people who are interested in physics, and to try to bring physics to the larger com-

munity in which we live (this includes both MIT and larger communities like Cambridge). This organization is not limited to physics majors; anyone interested may join.

Society of Women Engineers (SWE)

```
office: W20-447
phone: x3-2096
website: web.mit.edu/swe/www/
```

SWE is a diverse organization dedicated to encouraging women to pursue and achieve their full potential in science and engineering related fields. SWE currently has about 350 members and its events are mostly organized by its 20 executive officers. SWE's activities include the annual Fall Career Fair and Career Fair Banquet, company tech talks, outreach activities at local high schools, Beaverdash - a campus-wide engineering design competition, faculty-student dinners, careers related conference, and study breaks! SWE also has its own members' resume CD and awards scholarships for leadership and excellence every year.

Tau Beta Pi

```
phone: x3-4644
website: web.mit.edu/tbp/www/
```

Tau Beta Pi is the oldest and largest engineering honor society in the United States. The chapter here at MIT sponsors community service projects, cultural events, and an annual career fair open to the MIT community. Members are selected in their junior or senior year based on academic excellence, personal intergrity, and service.

Undergraduate Math Association

```
office: 2-108 (Math Dept. Office)
email: Dave Pritchard (daveagp@mit.edu)
website: web.mit.edu/uma/www
```

We are the official math club of MIT, dorks among dorks. We host a weekly mathematics lecture series featuring talks about interesting subjects in mathematics and lots of pizza, while larger events have included a student/faculty mixer in the winter and a Pi Day Party in the spring. We also sell the best nerdy t-shirts you'll find at MIT. The UMA is open to all undergraduate students, regardless of major, mathematical ability, or dorkiness quotient.

Athletics

The MIT Department of Athletics, Physical Education and Recreation (DAPER) offers programs that stress participation and enjoyment as well as the pursuit of athletics excellence. Participants and coaches are very dedicated, resulting in outstanding teams. All members of the MIT community are welcome to use the athletic facilities and to receive trained assistance in developing their full potential. The programs offered include intercollegiate and intramural sports, physical education classes, private and group instruction in various sports, and recreational facilities of exceptionally high quality. See *Children's Services* in the **Facilities** chapter for athletic facilities for children.

Who's Who in Athletics

The Department of Athletics, Physical Education and Recreation is located on the 2nd floor of the Zesiger Center (W35-297, x3-4498, web.mit.edu/athletics/www/)

Candace Royer (W35-298, x3-4497, clroyer@mit.edu), Department Head/Director of Athletics, is responsible for overseeing MIT's physical education, intercollegiate, intramural, and club sports programs.

John Benedick (W35-292, x3-9892, h2ocoach@mit.edu) is the Assistant Director of Athletics/Sports Administration. He is the person to contact about general varsity athletics questions.

Dan Martin (W35-299, x 3-5003, djmartin@mit.edu) is the Assistant Department Head and Director of Facilities and Operations in DAPER. He is the person to contact if you have a problem with the facilities or equipment.

Walter Alessi (W35-288, x3-8178, waalessi@mit.edu) is the Coordinator of Intramural Sports, as well as the men's soccer and men's lacrosse coach.

Sandy Lett (W35-297W, x3-4916, slett@mit.edu) is the Administrative Assistant/Scheduling, Facilities, & Operations in Physical Education. She can help with updating your PE records or questions about PE registration.

Billy Donovan (W35-297H, x8-6199, wjdono@mit.edu) is the Equipment Manager. He can make life rough on teams or individuals who don't return equipment on time. He can also make life easier if you're nice, so smile.

Thomas Cronan (W35-115A, x3-4908, cronan@mit.edu) is the Head Athletic Trainer and Coordinator of Sports Medicine.

Contact information for other DAPER administrators can be found at http://web.mit.edu/athletics/www/staff-directory.html.

Tim Moore (W35-293, x2-4364, mooretj@mit.edu) is the General Manager of the Zesiger Sports and Fitness Center. If you have questions concerning membership in Department of Athletics, Physical Education, and Recreation (DAPER) facilities, operational hours, programs, services, and events, he can help you find answers. Contact information for other Zesiger Center personnel can be found at http://web.mit.edu/zcenter/gen_info/contact_us.html.

Athletic Facilities

Use of MIT athletic facilities is open to any member of the MIT community who has a valid MIT ID Card. MIT card activation for use of DAPER facilities is provided at no additional fee for current MIT undergraduates and graduate students, because they have already paid for this service via the "Student Life Fee" whether they use the athletics facilities or not. The prices for MIT student families, Wellesley students, alumni, faculty and staff can be found at http://web.mit.edu/zcenter/gen_info/cs_membership.html. Six-month or one-year athletic memberships may be purchased at the main entrance to the Zesiger Center (W35) located in Zesiger-Johnson Lobby. A temporary Day Pass may be issued to a non-Institute student for $5 or to all others for $10. Other temporary passes are available for a week, a month, or the summer, with prices varying based on MIT affiliation.

Towel service and day lockers are provided for all athletic card holders. Zesiger locker rooms are equipped with showers, suit dryers and hair dryers, and provide direct access to the pool.

The **Zesiger Sports and Fitness Center** (W35) is a brand-new, state-of-the-art facility that links the Johnson Athletic Center, Rockwell Cage, and the du Pont Athletic Center. The "Z" Center offers a 50-meter swimming pool with platform and spring diving boards and a 25-meter training pool. You will find recreational swim hours available in one or both pools during all hours of operation. To find the recreational swim schedule you can go to http://web.mit.edu/zcenter/aquatics/schedule.html. The pool also is the host to the MIT swim team, water polo team, PE swimming and diving classes, and other activities. The Aquatic Center offers a variety of swimming, diving, water sport, and water fitness classes, as well as recreational activities and events.

The Zesiger Center is also home to a 12,000 square foot fitness center on the 2nd and 3rd floors including free weights, Nautilus machines and cardiovascular exercise machines (treadmills, exercise bikes, StairMasters, rowing machines and elliptical trainers). Other features include 6 squash courts and a multi-activity court, which can be used for volleyball, soccer, aerobics, recreational basketball, and roller hockey. Programs and services include: fitness center orientations, fitness assessments, personal training, group exercise classes, massage, recreational activities and events. For hours information, go to http://web.mit.edu/zcenter/gen_info/z_hours.html.

The first floor of the **Howard Johnson Athletic Center** (W34) is home to the MIT ice rink from mid-October until Spring Break. PE classes are offered in beginning skating, figure skating, ice hockey and others. The rink is open to DAPER facilities members during open recreational skating hours. Figure and hockey skates can be rented for a minimal fee. The second floor of the Johnson Athletic center is home to MIT's 200 meter indoor track. For facilities hours of operation, call x2-3690 or go to web.mit.edu/athletics/www/facilities.html.

Facilities in the Johnson Athletic Center are also used for large gatherings such as the annual 2.007 competition, the activities midway, exams and graduation.

The **du Pont Athletic Center and Gymnasium** (W32 and W31) located on the corner of Massachusetts Avenue and Vassar Street contains a small weight room, a wrestling room, a fencing room, and an exercise room used for a number of PE and club activities including martial arts and aerobics. The du Pont Gymnasium is used for volleyball, gymnastics, ballroom dance competitions and basketball, and often hosts registration during the fall and spring terms.

The **MIT Pistol and Rifle Range** is located in the basement of the du Pont Athletic Center. Fifteen points are available in the pistol range and 16 points are available in the rifle range. Both ranges connect to a common room whose entrance is near the equipment desk. Air pistols, air rifles and .22 caliber rim fire may be shot at the range. MIT has both a pistol team and a rifle team, which compete at the national level. Pistol PE classes are offered twice a term. Previous experience is not a requirement for either the team or the PE class. The range is not open to general members of the MIT community, although there is an MIT pistol and rifle club which exists primarily for alumni. For details on the various programs, contact the Range Master (x3-3296).

Squash courts can currently be found in two locations. There are six courts at du Pont, and six new international size squash courts with electronic scoreboards in the Zesiger Center. To make reservations for the Zesiger Center courts you can call x2-3690 and for the du Pont courts you can call x8-6199. Reservations can be made up to 24 hours in advance.

There are several sets of **tennis courts** located on the MIT campus. The Katz Outdoor Tennis Courts on Briggs Field across from Baker House are open from 7am until 11pm daily and can be reserved in season by calling x8-6199. Near Walker Memorial there are four paved courts which may be reserved by going to the East Campus desk. Don't call; you must sign up in person. The four indoor tennis courts in the J.B. Carr Center (the tennis bubble) may be reserved by students only, no more than 48 hours in advance, for the hours of 2pm-6pm at no charge. At other times, and for non-students at all times, a fee per court will be charged. Call x3-1451 for reservations. For all the courts it is a good idea to make reservations as early as possible because they go fast.

Rockwell Cage (W33) has a floor surface which can be set up for volleyball, basketball, badminton, gymnastics and archery. Courts can be reserved by calling x8-6199.

Henry G. Steinbrenner Stadium has an excellent Mondo surface 400 meter (1/4 mile) track which is great for running on if you don't mind going around and around. Field events, football, soccer, lacrosse, and field hockey are played inside the oval.

Briggs Field is located between Vassar Street and Amherst Alley on the west side of campus. It's the place to go for baseball, softball, soccer, lacrosse, rugby, field hockey, ultimate frisbee, and intramurals. Call x8-6199 for reservations. In particular, there is an MIT Community Summer Softball League with several dozen MIT-affiliated teams that play at a variety of skill levels. Contact the League commissioner, Shawn Hillier (hillier@mit.edu) for more information.

The **Jack Barry Turf** is in between the Steinbrenner Stadium and the Katz outdoor tennis courts. It has lights for night play and is used for a number of sports including soccer, lacrosse, field hockey, ultimate frisbee, and football. For reservations call 8-6199.

The **Alumni Pool** and **Wang Fitness Center** (Building 57), which had been closed for renovations during construction of Building 32, re-opened on June 7th. The facility now contains two new aerobics rooms with suspension flooring and Spin Bikes. There is towel service available and plenty of showers and locker space. For hours, call 3-2914.

The **MIT Sailing Pavilion**, located at 134 Memorial Drive across from Walker Memorial, has over 100 sailboats and hosts the MIT sailing team. Sailing classes are available during the summer and as PE classes during the school year. To take advantage of the resources and facilities that the sailing pavilion has to offer, you must be a member of the MIT Nautical Association. Membership is free with an MIT athletics card. Guests may be taken out as the crew of a card holding member at no charge but they must be able to swim at least 100 yards and be accompanied by a card holder at all times. Card holders under the age of 21 are required to take the Small Boat Swim Test. This consists of swimming at least 100 yards (4 lengths of the pool) and treading water for 10 minutes. Card holders over 21 are required to sign a form indicating that he or she can swim at least 100 yards and can tread water for 10 minutes. For more information please call x3-4884, email `sailing-request@mit.edu` or visit `web.mit.edu/mit-sailing/www/`.

H.W. Pierce Boathouse (W8, across from Burton Conner, x3-9676) is the center for sweep-rowing and sculling. It has an indoor rowing tank and weight rooms. An introductory sculling lesson is required before you may take out any boat. PE classes are offered in rowing during the summer for additional instruction. You must have passed the Small Boat Swim Test to take out any boat.

Walker Memorial (Building 50) has a gymnasium on the third floor. The space is used for academic testing Monday through Friday and thus will have tables and chairs set up where you want to be playing basketball, but there are open recreation hours from 7pm-11pm on Friday and Saturday. (You may find that the doors continue to be unlocked after 11pm.) While there are basketball hoops in the gym, it is mostly just a large open space and no other equipment is available or provided.

Student dance groups may reserve the Walker Gym through the CAC for one two-hour increment per week on Saturdays or Sundays from 7am to 6pm during the academic year. If a dance group opts to use the Walker Gym for rehearsal space, the group will not be permitted to hold a rehearsal in any other CAC space on Saturday or Sunday. Walker Gym is not an event space, so workshops, instruction and performances may not be held there. It also does not have a sound system, mirrors, or any other luxuries. Other dance rehearsal spaces reservable through the CAC include W20-407, W20-491, and Rehearsal Rooms A and B in Kresge (W16-033 and W16-030). The nearly-completed Stata Center has a new dance room with hardwood floors and big mirrors which can be reserved through DAPER.

The Walker Memorial Dance Studio is a facility located on the river side of the 2nd floor and is reservable through the Department of Music and Theatre Arts in the School of Humanities. There is a lounge with beautiful hardwood floors just outside the dance studio. This space cannot be reserved and cannot officially be used for rehearsal. The T Club Lounge in du Pont and the du Pont Dance Studio (W31-225) have mirrors and sound systems and can be reserved for groups or individuals through the Athletic Department. The McCormick Hall Dance Studio (W4) has mirrors but no sound system and must be reserved by a resident. Permanent (term long) reservations for dance groups may be obtained for the McCormick Dance Studio with the sponsorship of a resident and with the approval of the house government. The Ashdown Dance Studio (W1) has mirrors and a boom box. It can be reserved by a resident and non-residents must be on a guestlist at front desk to use the facilities.

Finally, the MIT Outing Club has a rock-climbing wall in Walker Memorial on the 3rd floor river side (Room 50-303). They have rental shoes available for a donation of $1. Hours vary so check the website for details: `http://mitoc.mit.edu/wall/index.shtml`. Add yourself to `climbing-wall@mit.edu` or send email to `climbing-wall-request@mit.edu` for more information.

Varsity Sports

There are 42 varsity sports at MIT. A few sports have a freshman team. Teams generally practice 5-7pm on weekdays. Some teams will have morning practices. Interested in being on a team? Go to the Athletics Gateway during Orientation or call up the coach today. (Keep in mind that you must be in good academic standing and be carrying a minimum of 36 units in order to be eligible for varsity sports.) A listing of varsity sports, their seasons, and their coaches can be found in the official MIT website at `web.mit.edu/athletics/` through the drop-down menu on the left near the top of the page.

The current varsity sports are:

Baseball (M)	Golf (M)	Softball (W)
Basketball (M & W)	Gymnastics (M & W)	Squash (M)
Crew, Lightweight (M & W)	Ice Hockey (M & W)	Swimming & Diving (M & W)
Crew, Heavyweight (M)	Lacrosse (M & W)	Tennis (M & W)
Crew, Open (W)	Pistol (Coed)	Track and Field, Indoor (M & W)
Cross Country (M & W)	Rifle (Coed)	Track and Field, Outdoor (M & W)
Fencing (M & W)	Sailing (Coed & W)	Volleyball (M & W)
Field hockey (W)	Skiing (M & W)	Water Polo (M)
Football (M)	Soccer (M & W)	Wrestling (M)

Student spectators are welcome, free of charge, at all MIT sporting events. Parking for large events is also often available. Sports events for the week are listed in the Institute Calendar in *Tech Talk*. You can also check the sports pages of *The Tech* and the "Sports Today" columns of the Boston newspapers.

Intramurals

A very extensive intramural program is open to students, faculty, instructors, alumni(ae) and lecturers who meet eligibility requirements. Teams can be organized by just about any group of people, including labs, clubs, and living groups. For many sports there are different leagues for different levels of athletic prowess. The IM Council (W35-288, x3-5782) coordinates all IM competition.

Essential to many IM games is the referee. You, too, can officiate and get paid for your efforts. Officiating courses are offered by the physical education department, but you can ref without taking them. Talk to the manager. Managers are also needed to keep Intramurals alive and well. Don't assume that there is always going to be someone else to do it. IM notices are posted on a bulletin board next to the equipment desk in du Pont.

The current intramural sports are:

Badminton	Pool (Billiards)	Tourney Tennis
Basketball	Roller Hockey	Track and Field
Bowling	Rugby	Track Relays
Foosball	Soccer	Ultimate Frisbee
Football (flag)	Softball	Unihoc
Football (touch)	Squash	Volleyball
Ice Hockey	Table Tennis	Water Polo
Octathon	Team Tennis	

Physical Education

One way the Institute promotes active lifestyles for students is through the Physical Education requirement, which encourages weekly physical activity within the academic course load. The Physical Education curriculum offers an enormous variety of classes including aerobics and fitness, aquatics, dance, racquet sports, martial arts, boating, individual and team sports, and outdoor/adventure activities. Many students try activities that are completely new to them through physical education classes and then continue their participation through club sports, intramurals, and intercollegiate sports. This is especially true for activities such as pistol, squash, fencing, rowing and sailing, in which few freshmen have participated prior to attending MIT. Physical Education classes are taught by the same Faculty-Coaches who serve as Varsity coaches so that all students receive the same expertise in their physical education classes that varsity athletes receive on the playing fields. The learning environment is exceptional and is utilized and appreciated by all members of the MIT community.

Classes usually meet 2 hours a week for six weeks. Registration for classes is through a web-based lottery system found at student.mit.edu. It is possible to resister late for classes if space is available.

Club Sports

In addition to Varsity and IM sports, MIT has a healthy athletics club community. For more information, see web.mit.edu/athletics/www/club_sports.html.

The current club sports are:

Archery	Ice Hockey (W)	Sport Taekwondo
American Jiu-Jitsu	Isshinryu Karate-do	Synchronized Swimming
Self Defense	Judo	Table Tennis
Aikido	Karate	Tae Kwon Do
Ballroom Dance	Kendo	Triathlon
Cycling	Kokikai	Ultimate Frisbee (W & M)
Cheerleading Crew (Sloan)	Korean Karate	Volleyball
Boxing	Rugby (W & M)	Waterpolo (W)
Badminton	Shotokan Karate	
Danzan Ryu Jujitsu	Snowboarding	
Figure Skating	Soccer (male grad students)	

Community Leagues

In many sports there are leagues for people simply interested in playing. Teams are formed by groups from departments, labs or mere coincidence, and everyone in the MIT community is welcome. The two largest such leagues at present are the **Community Hockey League** and the **Summer Softball League**. Impromptu groups for squash, tennis and handball are also very common, especially at the staff and faculty level. Check with your friends to see if a team already exists which you can join. Contact the Club Sports Council at `csc-officers@mit.edu`

Other Classes

The Boston and Cambridge areas also offer a wide variety of opportunities to participate in athletics.

Both the Cambridge YMCA (`http://www.cambridgeymca.org`) and YWCA (`www.ywca.org`) offer classes in martial arts, yoga, racquetball and others. As with all "Y" activities, you must be a member to take a class.

Private schools in the martial arts abound. *Caveat emptor.* According to a knowledgeable member of the MIT Shotokan club, many area schools care more about the dollars they receive than the instruction they give. Ask qualified people before committing yourself. The MIT Shotokan club has a sixth degree black belt instructor in once a week; he can give you expert advice.

Beaches

The **Boston Harbor Islands** may not be the place for sun bathing, but they are your best bet for sandy and rocky beaches with a beautiful view and excellent sightseeing. A ferry departing near the Boston Aquarium will take you to Georges Island which features Fort Warren and some breathtaking views of Boston Harbor. From Georges Island, you can take a water taxi (free of charge) to a number of smaller islands which also feature historical ruins, rocky and sandy beaches, wildlife preserves and picturesque hiking. A round trip ferry ticket costs $10 for adults and group rates are available. For more information see `bostonislands.org`.

The Division of Urban Parks and Recreation (`www.mass.gov/mdc/`), formerly known as the Metropolitan District Commission (MDC), operates a number of beaches in the Boston Area. Constitution Beach and Winthrop Beach in East Boston may be reached by taking the MBTA Blue Line to Orient Heights. Revere Beach in North Boston may be reached by taking the MBTA Blue Line to the Revere or Wonderland Stops. Wollaston Beach in South Boston may be reached by taking the MBTA Red Line to the Wollaston Stop and then walking along Beach Street or taking the Wollaston Beach/Ashmont Bus #217. These beaches are typically unimpressive and the water undeniably cold, but they are easily accessible without a car.

Beaches on the North Shore include the following: Crane Beach, off Route 1A in Ipswich, has a varying fee per car depending on what time of the year it is (prices from $5-20 dollars, check `www.thetrustees.org/pages/294_crane_beach.cfm` for more details); Wingaersheek Beach in Ipswich Bay, $15 per car during the week, $20 on weekends; Plum Island, a long and beautiful beach with limited but cheaper parking (usually $3 to $6); Nahant, nice and close but (as a consequence) often crowded, on a peninsula just north of Boston. Unfortunately, the water on these North Shore beaches wouldn't melt an iceberg.

The South Shore has a number of options. One is **Nantasket Beach**. **Duxbury Beach** is 35 miles south of Boston off Route 3. Further south are **Cape Cod** with infinite beaches and **Nantucket** and **Martha's Vineyard** islands.

On Cape Cod there are several noteworthy peculiarities. First, the rush day for this place is Sunday, when all of Boston deposits itself on the Cape. Since the road facilities for getting on and off the Cape are limited, massive jam-ups result in the evening when everyone tries to go home simultaneously. The obvious solution is to go on a weekday, but, if that proves impossible, the rush can be avoided by starting at about 6am and heading home no later than 2:30pm, which takes quite a bit of willpower. Also, the best beaches in terms of water conditions are **Nauset** and **Coast Guard** on the eastern shore of the Cape. Since they, like everything else, quickly get crowded, you may have to walk one or two miles from the parking lot (north on Nauset, south on Coast Guard) to avoid solidly packed people. The **Cape Cod National Seashore** is undeveloped but much less crowded.

Ferries run to the islands. The best way to get around once you're on an island is by bicycle. They can be rented on the island, but since quality varies widely, you're better off bringing your own.

The Division of Urban Parks and Recreation maintains public beaches for fresh-water swimming at Upper Mystic Lake in Winchester and Houghton Pond in the Blue Hills Reservation in Milton. Walden Pond in Concord has a public beach run by the state. It can get very crowded on weekends; go at non-peak times. Concord can be reached by commuter rail — Walden is a good walk away from the station.

Bicycling
Biking can be dangerous. Watch out for cars (and joggers as well). Be sure to wear a helmet, and remember that it is illegal to ride at night without a light. (Yes, Mom.) If you don't have a bike already, you can rent one from a bike shop.

There are several bike paths in the area maintained by the Department of Environmental Management, Division of Forests and Parks, go here for PDF maps of all DEM trails: www.mass.gov/dem/parks/trails.htm. Also see the **Transportation** chapter for more information on maintaining a bicycle at MIT.

Bowling
Many Bostonians believe that bowling (some call it candlepins) consists of trying to knock down a bunch of wooden dowels with three undersized balls. If this is what you want, there are dozens of alleys in the area. Try **Sacco's Bowl Haven** (45 Day Street, Somerville, 617-776-0552) in Davis Square for an old fashioned atmosphere that is easily accessible by the MBTA Red Line; or check the Yellow Pages. If you want tenpins (which is what the rest of America calls "bowling") it is a little harder; there are currently few nearby places to go. A couple are **Boston Bowl** (820 Wm. T. Morrisey Blvd., Dorchester, 617-825-3800), open 24 hours, and **Lanes & Games** (195 Concord Turnpike, Cambridge, 617-876-5533).

Canoeing

There is an excellent place to canoe within reach of public transportation. The Charles River Canoe and Kayak Service, open April through October, has three locations: near the MBTA Riverside station (617-965-5110), near the Eliot Bridge in Allston/Brighton (617-462-2513), and Cochituate State Park in Natick (508-647-1700). This organization rents canoes on the surprisingly beautiful upper Charles River. South Bridge Boat House (978-369-9438), within walking distance of the Concord railroad station (less than an hour's ride from North Station), also rents canoes on the Concord River, with access to the Assabet and Sudbury Rivers. The MIT Outing Club (W20-461, x3-2988) rents canoes and runs flat and white water trips. The Appalachian Mountain Club also sponsors trips and publishes a guide to canoeing in New England.

Dance

In addition to dance facilities on campus, there are a number of dance studios in the area.

The Dance Complex (536 Massachusetts Ave., Cambridge, 617-547-9363, www.dancecomplex.org) located in Central Square, offers a wide variety of dance styles at many levels as well as hosting performances of local choreographers. Classes are priced between $8 and $13 on a drop-in basis as well as discounted multiple class cards.

Green Street Studios (185 Green St., Cambridge, 617-864-3191, www.greenstreetstudios.org) in Central Square offers excellent ballet and modern classes, as well as a variety of other dance forms. Classes range from $10 to $15 for drop-in and varying prices for multiple class cards. They also present many concerts in an intimate atmosphere. (The entrance is a bit hidden, look for a roll down green metal loading window with a graffitied sign.)

Jeannette Neill Dance Studio (261 Friend St. 5th floor, Boston, 617-523-1355, www.jndance.com) near the North Station T-stop offers mainly jazz classes as well as ballet and hip hop. Classes are typically $12 drop-in, and short term class cards can be purchased for a discount.

Fresh Pond Ballet (1798A Massachusetts Ave., Cambridge, 617-491-5865, www.freshpondballet.com) in Porter Square offers ballet classes including pointe work. Classes are $12 drop-in or $90 for a 10-class card.

Jose Mateo's Ballet Theatre (Old Cambridge Baptist Church, 400 Harvard St., Cambridge, 617-354-7467) — actually approachable from Mass. Ave. just below Harvard Square — offers beginning through intermediate/advanced ballet classes for $12 drop-in with class cards available. The facilities are in an old church which is absolutely beautiful: free standing mirrors, marley floor and clerestory windows.

Fishing

In order to go freshwater fishing, you need a license. You can get it from the Division of Fisheries and Wildlife, (you can buy one online at www.state.ma.us/dfwele/) and some sporting goods stores. You may be able to get a special non-resident 7-day license. For saltwater fishing, no license is needed. Call 617-626-1590 for freshwater information and 617-626-1520 for saltwater information.

Golf

The Boston area does not have many good golf courses, and most are rather far from MIT. You can find some information at www.boston.com/sports/golf/. The better courses include Brookline Municipal (expensive unless you live in Brookline), George Wright in Boston, and Ponkapoag in Canton (which has 36 holes and low greens fees). There are also a number of privately-owned courses with daily fees; these are usually more expensive but better kept. **Stowe** has 36 different holes and **Powderhorn** is a good par 3 course in Lexington.

Hiking, Mountain Climbing, Backpacking, Etc.

New England abounds in beautiful mountains and interesting trails. The **White Mountain National Forest** in New Hampshire, the **Green Mountains** in Vermont, **Baxter State Park** and **Acadia National Park** in northern Maine are areas especially worth visiting. Although the mountains in the Northeast are small by Western standards (the highest, Mt. Washington, is 6233 ft.), they should not be belittled. Treeline is about 4500 ft., so there are many open ridges, and many of the trails are steep and rough. Severe New England weather (Mt. Washington holds a record for its 231 mph gust) adds to the challenge. Even during the summer the weather in the mountains is violent and highly unpredictable. Take a map, compass, and adequate clothing before venturing out there.

The **Appalachian Mountain Club** (www.outdoors.org) maintains hiking trails and shelters throughout the Northeast. They publish maps and guidebooks to the area which are sold there, at outdoor specialty shops, and at The Coop.

The place to go for information on almost any kind of outdoor activity (hiking, backpacking, rock climbing, canoeing, bicycling, cross-country skiing, snowshoeing, or ice climbing) is the **MIT Outing Club** (MITOC, W20-461, x3-2988). They sponsor trips, have up-to-date information and good advice, and even rent equipment to members and people on club-sponsored trips. They have two cabins in New Hampshire (one in Intervale and one near Plymouth). They are often used for club trips and may be rented by other MIT groups. MITOC also administers a newly-built climbing wall in room 50-303; check their web site at web.mit.edu/activities/mitoc/main.html for hours and other information. New members are always welcome.

Other organizations that run trips and give beginner's classes are **AMC** and the **Massachusetts Sierra Club** (www.sierraclubmass.org).

The **MIT Scuba and Skin Diving Club** (web.mit.edu/scuba-club/www/) makes several dive outings a year.

The **MIT Skydiving Club** (web.mit.edu/skydive/www/) makes trips to Jumptown in Orange, MA, where the club owns a skydiving rig for members' use. They also occasionally help pay for classes.

When preparing to purchase equipment for any of the above activities, it's a very good idea to contact someone in the appropriate MIT club for advice.

Ice Skating

There are also several ice-skating rinks in the area, including an outdoor one in the **Boston Common** (during the winter).

Johnson Athletic Center (x3-4498) has free skating during lunch and on weekends during the term, as well as other times during IAP.

The Johnson Rink offers skate sharpening for $4, though the sharpener is not in every day, so you may have to leave your skates for a bit. **Skating Club of Boston** (www.scboston.org) has a sharpener come in part time. **The Charlestown Rink** (617-242-9728) can also sharpen skates.

Jogging

Whether you're a seasoned athlete or just trying to get in shape, Boston is a great place to run. You need to know where to go and how far you went. For an excellent map/mileage chart for jogging in the Boston area see: www.cambridgerunning.org/fun/chlstbl.html

Boston bridge circuits are scenic trails with the added convenience of starting and ending in the same place. The basic idea is to start at Lobby 7, head towards a bridge, and run along the Esplanade (a beautifully landscaped walk/bike trail along the Charles) to another bridge, and back to Lobby 7.

How to get to the bridges from Lobby 7

Harvard Bridge: Step outside Lobby 7, facing Mass. Ave. If you look left, you can see Memorial Drive. Run along Mass. Ave. towards Memorial Drive, and Mass. Ave. will go over the Charles river. This is the Harvard Bridge.

BU Bridge: Cross Memorial Drive to the Charles River side. Follow Mass. Ave. west past the west campus dorms and the crew boat houses. The BU Bridge will be on your left.

Science Museum/Memorial Drive: Cross Memorial Drive to the Charles River side. Follow Memorial Drive east, past the sailing pavilions, and under the highway. Turn right, onto the path along the river. When you get to a street, turn right. Follow the sidewalk over the bridge. The Science Museum will be on your right.

Longfellow Bridge: Do NOT cross Memorial Drive. Follow Memorial Drive east, past EAsT camPUS, Senior Haus, and the 100 Memorial Drive apartments. Keep going straight for a few blocks. Cross the street onto the Longfellow Bridge.

How to get to the Esplanade from the bridge

Harvard Bridge: On the left side of the bridge, about 3/4 of the way across, there is a ramp that heads down towards a path along the river. This is the Esplanade. Follow the path west to the BU Bridge or east to the Science Museum or Longfellow Bridge.

BU Bridge: On the left hand side, about 3/4 of the way across the bridge, there is a steep stairway down from the bridge to a small road. Take the stair down and follow the small road past the BU library. There will stairs to a bridge over the highway. Take this bridge over the highway to the Esplanade. Follow the path east to the Harvard Bridge, Longfellow Bridge, or the Science Museum.

Science Museum/Memorial Drive: Go straight past the Science Museum, over the bridge, and follow the sidewalk into a sharp right turn. Take another right past the tennis courts into a parking lot, and you're on the Esplanade. Follow the path west to the Longfellow Bridge, Harvard Bridge, or BU Bridge.

Longfellow Bridge: On the right hand side, about 3/4 of the way across the bridge, there are stairs to a bridge that goes over the highway. Take this bridge to the Esplanade. Follow the path east to the Science Museum, west to the Harvard Bridge or the BU Bridge.

Distances

Science Museum — Longfellow: 1.83 miles
Harvard — BU: 2.72 miles
Harvard — Longfellow: 2.82 miles
Harvard — Science Museum: 3.77 miles
BU — Longfellow: 4.78 miles
BU — Science Museum: 5.73 miles

When jogging, use your common sense; crime can happen anywhere. You should also beware of Boston drivers, who are not often looking where they are going. Jogging at night is not recommended.

Rollerskating

There aren't many roller rinks in the area, but there is **Roller World** at 425 Broadway (Route 1) in Saugus, MA. For information call 781-233-9507 or visit `www.roller-world.com`.

Skating outdoors can also be fun, but be on the look-out for runners and bikers. The Esplanade, the Common, and between the river and Memorial Drive in Cambridge are all good places to skate. A number of places will rent you skates, check the Yellow Pages.

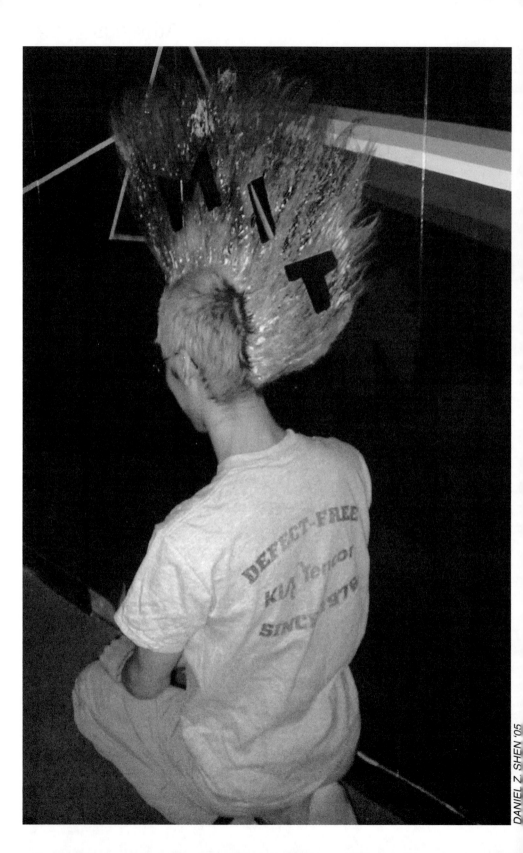

Miscellaneous

In this chapter are collected the small items which don't seem to fit in any other category. Subjects are arranged alphabetically.

Address Change

If you change your home (permanent) address, you must update the address information on WebSIS (`student.mit.edu`) or fill out a new address card in the Registrar's office (5-111 and 5-119). If you live in on-campus housing, your term address is supposed to be kept track of automatically when you move, but it's still worth checking periodically.

If you move off campus, many dorm desks will forward your mail to you. The process to initiate mail forwarding, the length of time it is good for and the reliability of it will vary from dorm to dorm. At the very least, expect to leave a set of adhesive address labels for them to use. Because dorm mail is typically treated as business mail (aggregate delivery), the post office is also unreliable for forwarding mail from dorms.

If you move from one off campus address to another, you can fill out a change of address form at your local post office (such as the one located in the basement of w20) to ensure that your mail follows you.

Advertising and Publicity

There are a quite a few common ways to publicize events on campus. Most common is simply postering various bulletin boards around the 'tute. The postering policy can be found at `www.mit.edu/afs/athena/org/c/community/policies/asaposter.html`. Generally, 'don't hog bulletin board space' seems to cover it, but apparently MIT students are just as good as the officials at generating voluminous rules. Officially, the poster boards are cleared Thursday at midnight every week, though the actual time will vary. They are often cleared one other night per week, probably Monday or Tuesday.

Placing a spotlight on MIT's main website can be very effective, if you time your exposure correctly. You can request a spotlight at `web.mit.edu/site/request.html`. It involves an editorial decision on the part of the web admins, so it's not a solution for every event. is designed with much more attention to public relations than usefulness to the MIT community, so items that will appeal to people both outside and inside MIT have a greater chance of being featured. Be warned, you have to feature the despised new MIT logo on your page to have even a prayer of getting a spotlight.

You can reserve a booth in Lobby 10 or in the Student Center lobby. Both locations are overseen by the CAC in W20-500. *The Guidebook to Planning Events @MIT* may answer many of your questions: `web.mit.edu/campus-activities/guidebook/Page0001.htm`. You can also hang a drop poster in the Student Center, or place a poster on those asinine metal things that replaced drop posters in Lobby 7. If you want a poster in the Student Center, you need to reserve it through the CAC, see above to contact them. If you want a poster in Lobby 7, you should reserve it through the Information Center in 7-121. Call 3-4795 or email `lcorbett@mit.edu` to request an application or check your reservation status. Materials to make the posters can be obtained for a small fee through APO on the 4th floor of the Student Center — `web.mit.edu/apo/www/dropposter-info.shtml` has information about these supplies.

Emailing large groups of mailing lists is frowned upon, particularly mailing lists that you are not subscribed to. Technical hacks like becoming root to mail all the usernames at mit.edu are also regarded as lame, and probably will only enrage people, rather than entice them to your event. If you are organizing a recurring activity, make a mailing list, and invite people to sign up for more information. Don't underestimate word of mouth, either. People do fun things because they hear other people talk about fun things. Of course, this only works if people actually respect your opinion.

LSC slides (see `lsc.mit.edu/info/slides.shtml`) are effective, easy, and fun. Allusions to the movie(s) of the week are always a good idea. You can also buy slide space on the projector run by MIT Audio Visual in the Infinite Corridor — see `web.mit.edu/av/www/MoreHtml/Corridor_3.htm` for details. They're only visible by people heading East down the Infinite, but a lot of people do that each day.

Ads in *The Tech* (see `www-tech.mit.edu/Business/`) can be expensive, but *The Tech* has a little-known policy of offering each ASA-recognized student group a free page of advertising each term — if it's a student group activity you're promoting, make use of this. There are numerous other MIT publications that publish less frequently, but may be more effective for your needs. And perhaps more fun. You can advertise in *Voo Doo Technique, Tech Talk* and many others. You can even advertise in the next issue of *How To Get Around MIT*. Finally, you can advertise on the MIT Audio Visual Services projectors in buildings 3 and 4. Currently (August 2004) weeklong rotating time spot costs $65 for one projector or $100 for both. Demand is high, so try to book in advance.

Blood Drives

There are five blood drives at MIT each year: two fall term, two spring term and one over the summer. Typically each drive continues for 3 or 4 days. For all drives, appointments may be made; there will be a booth in lobby 10 or in the Student Center the week before each drive, or you can send e-mail to `blood-drive-signup@mit.edu` or sign up on the web at `web.mit.edu/blood-drive/www/`. The blood drive hours vary from day to day; look at the web site for the hours during a particular drive. All drives are run by MIT ARCTAN (American Red Cross Team And Network) for the American Red Cross. The blood drives are big organizational efforts that require the help of many, and MIT ARCTAN always welcomes new volunteers. If you are interested in helping, send e-mail to `blood-drive-managers@mit.edu`.

MIT Campus Dining

MIT is unique in that it is one of the few universities around the country that does not have a mandatory meal plan. Although the administration is slowly but steadily taking away the right to choose, students in most dorms still decide what, where and when to eat. Better yet, they can eat at reasonable times (read: 24 hours a day) and to only pay for what they consume.

You can cook for yourself or with friends, order pizza, Chinese, Indian, Italian, or Giant Cookies, venture off campus to sample some of the local restaurants or take advantage of the on-campus dining network.

There are 20 MIT campus dining locations, including 3 convenience stores. If you have an MIT ID, you can dine at any campus dining location that takes the MIT card. This means, in particular, that you don't have to live in a dorm to eat at its dining hall; undergrads, grads, faculty and staff are welcome.

House (Residential) Dining

Baker, Simmons and Next House all have dorm dining halls that are open from 5pm-9pm every day except Friday and Saturday. Simmons also features **Ping Ping Chai** from 9pm to 1am every day except Friday. The McCormick dining hall is currently undergoing renovations and will open for the 2004-2005 school year.

The Residential Dining Discount Program (now referred to as "Preferred Dining Membership") is MIT's only meal plan. The base cost is $225 per term, which gets you a 50% discount on most purchases at the four House Dining locations and the Simmons late night cafe. Convenience retail items like bottled juices, cup yogurt and candy bars are excluded. Other campus dining locations like Lobdell, Forbes Cafe, Pritchett and the coffee shops and cafes scattered around campus are also excluded. You need to eat about 57 of the 75 semesterly meals in order to break even (at a total cost of $450 for the semester.)

All students in Simmons Hall and all incoming freshmen in Baker, Next House and McCormick are automatically enrolled as Preferred Dining Members and must continue their participation as long as they are residents in those dorms. For them, this is a mandatory meal plan. Preferred Dining Membership is also available to all MIT students, faculty and staff regardless of where you live. It is recommended that you enroll before the beginning of the term, however you can enroll on a prorated basis if you choose to participate after the term has started.

Main Campus Dining

On the east side of campus, **Pritchett Grill** on the 2nd floor of Walker Memorial is open Monday through Friday from 4pm - 9pm and Saturday and Sunday 11am - 11pm. Morss Hall (always just called "Walker" by students), on the first floor of the Walker Memorial building, is now officially closed and has been replaced with two dining options in Building 32 (Stata): The **Forbes Family Cafe** on the first floor; and the **R&D** pub, located on the fourth floor.

The Forbes Family Cafe is open 7:30am to 10pm. Its main lunch service runs from 11:00am to 3pm and includes stone oven pizza, rice bowl dishes and other ethnic foods, specialty bread deli sandwiches, soups and extensive grab and go options. At the request of many students, faculty and staff it also serves Starbucks coffee and their specialty drinks and bubble tea from Ping Ping Chai. The R and D pub will be open from 4pm to 10pm M-F serving beer, wine and light fare. Both are slated to open the week of August 30th, 2004.

MIT has two pubs in addition to the R and D: the Muddy Charles in Walker Memorial and the Thirsty Ear in the basement of Ashdown. See the *MIT Facilities* chapter for more information.

Other dining places include the **Lobdell Food Court** (Mon-Thur 11am-3pm, Fri 11am-2 pm), and **Alpine Bagels** / **Cambridge Grill** (Mon-Fri 7am-11pm, Sat-Sun 9am-11pm), both in the Student Center (W20). Arrow Street Crepes, formerly in the front of w20, closed at the end of the 2003-2004 school year and its replacement has not yet been chosen. The Building 4 Coffee Shop and Bosworth's coffee shop in Lobby 7, both on the first floor of the Infinite Corridor, and the Bio Cafe in Building 68 are also reasonably convenient for a quick bagel between your morning classes. Of course, everyone else on campus is thinking the same thing, so expect to spend awhile in line. The Dome Cafe on the fourth floor of building 7 has hot panini sandwiches. Refresher Course in E52 is another breakfast and lunch option for those in Sloan. Ping Ping Chai also operates the Punji Juice Bar in the Z-Center, which serves smoothies, bubble tea, other "healthy beverages" and "energy snacks."

Convenience Stores

MacGregor has a newly renovated and improved convenience store that is open till 2am. Pritchett, in Walker Memorial also has a convenience store which is open 4pm-9pm every day. Hours for dining locations shift sometimes, mostly for holidays and breaks so check the campus dining website web.mit.edu/dining for updated information.

LaVerdes's Market, on the first floor of the student center, is a small grocery store with extensive deli options (subs, sandwiches, bagels, soups, salads, sushi, waffles and the occasional hot meal). They are open 24 hours a day Sunday - Thursday during term, and 7am - 11pm on weekends and during the summer. Groceries at LaVerde's are more expensive than at the nearby Star Market and their (non-catered) coffee isn't good, but their deli gets a sizeable portion of the student body through the semester, and the hours are unbeatable.

Food Trucks

A fast, cheap, and filling alternative to the campus dining facilities is to visit the food trucks. Food trucks usually operate during the lunch period, roughly 11am-2pm, and are very popular with students and staff.

A couple of trucks (including a falafel truck and a Chinese food truck) hang out on Mass. Ave. near the Student Center. Two more Chinese trucks, one yellow and one silver, generally park by Tech Square (on Main Street by the train tracks). All of these trucks are Cambridge street vendors and can be open as late as 3 or 4pm.

Four food trucks can be found next to the parking lot between Main Street and Building 68. Although these food trucks do not accept the MIT card, they are hired and supervised by MIT Campus Dining and are inspected by MIT periodically to help ensure food safety. Food types range from falafel to pizza to Vietnamese, with line length at any given time being a good indicator of popularity since the lines all move fast. Don't let the fact that the food is being prepared in a truck bother you, they are generally good and an MIT staple — not to mention a great excuse to get out in the sunshine when the weather is nice.

Marty B's Mobile Meals serves food in front of 77 Mass Ave (Lobby 7) and offers sandwiches, hamburgers, salads and entrees. It is open 7pm-midnight Wednesday and Thursday, and 7pm until 2am(ish) Friday and Saturday. Hours may increase to meet demand. As the new truck opened right before press time, we have no student reviews yet. However, the MIT CP's were quoted in *The Tech* as "really liking" the food — and who are you to doubt the taste of men and women with guns?

Kosher and Halal Meals

Campus Dining offers a number of Kosher Meal Plan options. You can use your TechCASH account to purchase kosher meals or enroll in a Kosher Plan, which will save you money over the walk-in price. Kosher Meal Plans are available in meal "blocks" which you use at your discretion throughout the semester. The Any 50 Plan for example, is a block of 50 meals that can be used at any of the approximately 70-75 kosher meals served each semester, including Shabbat and holiday meals. The larger the block you enroll in, the lower your cost per meal and the greater the number of guest meals you receive. If you live in a residence hall and are required to purchase a Preferred Dining Membership your membership fee may be applied toward the purchase of a Kosher Meal Plan.

For Muslim members of the MIT community, a halal dinner menu is offered at Baker Dining as a regular part of their service.

TechCASH (aka "The Card")

MIT offers a declining balance account offically named TechCASH but usually referred to as "the card," which allows you to use your MIT ID to make meal purchases at all campus dining locations. You will have had a mealcard account established in your name prior to arriving at MIT. However, you must put money in your account before you can use your MIT ID to make purchases. The amount you deposit is entirely up to you, but recommendations on deposit levels that will appropriately cover your meal expenses can be found at the Campus Dining web site. Purchases are deducted from your account just like an ATM debit card.

Your card account remains open for your entire MIT career unless you close it or it remains inactive for more than 120 days. Unlike most schools where it's "use it or lose it", card account balances at MIT are always reimbursed in full at the end of each term. You or a family member can add funds to your account online at any time. You can also withdraw funds to your bursar's account, suspend your card's TechCASH function or close your account at any time though the MIT Card Office. See `web.mit.edu/dining/mealplans/TechCashPlan.html` for more information.

Do It Yourself

Don't forget, you can always form a cooking group and boycott campus dining completely (unless you live in a dorm where you're required to buy into the campus dining way of life.) Cooking is, by far, the best way to avoid the freshman 15. Many campus dorms have kitchens which you can use to prepare your meals. You can supplement this by getting a small refrigerator for your room. Also, many FSILGs have professional chefs or cooking groups which may be open to friends of the house. More information on cooking in dormitories can be found in *Housing*. A list of local grocery stores can be found in **Shopping**.

Food for Thought

During vacations they close down almost everything; it seems that students don't have to eat anything if they aren't taking classes. However, Baker Dining is open for dinner during IAP as are the first floor operations in the Stratton Student Center.

MIT is constantly renovating spaces and changing management, vendors, hours, prices and locations in order to improve campus dining (that, or confuse the hell out of the students). If you think that different is not necessarily better, Campus Dining has a number of feedback mechanisms located at `web.mit.edu/dining/feedback/index.html`. The UA has a Dining Committee too. You can email MIT Campus Dining at `foodstuff@mit.edu` and or take one of the online surveys.

Employees' Educational Benefits

Children of faculty and staff are eligible for full scholarships at MIT and scholarships of up to 50% MIT tuition at accredited colleges. Loans are also available for children's college expenses. The Benefits Office (E19-215, x3-0500, `web.mit.edu/hr/benefits/edassist.html`) has details. Regular employees are eligible for partial or total reimbursement for educational costs connected with their careers at MIT.

Experiments on Humans

If you are participating as a subject in an experiment, whether it's run by an MIT person or anyone else, you can contact the Committee on the Use of Humans as Experimental Subjects (E32-335, x3-6787, `web.mit.edu/committees/couhes/`) to check whether it poses a hazard to either your physical or mental well-being. Any experiment conducted at MIT that might put the subject at risk — physically, psychologically, or otherwise — must be cleared with the Committee. Check with the Medical Department (x3-4481) for details.

Foreign Citizens

The first place for international students to go with questions or problems is the **International Students' Office** (5-133, x3-3795; `web.mit.edu/iso/www/`). If they can't help you, they should be able to refer you to someone who can. Foreign staff members should consult with the **International Scholars' Office** (4-105, x3-2851, `web.mit.edu/scholars/`). The MIT Center for Work, Family and Personal Life, (16-151, x3-1592, `web.mit.edu/hr/worklife/`) is very helpful to newcomers and their families having difficulty adjusting to the cultural milieu of the United States. An international open house takes place during the week before registration to acquaint newcomers and their families with available resources at MIT and in the Boston area. It is jointly sponsored by MIT Medical and the International Students' Office.

It is the responsibility of each international student to:

1. Keep passport valid at all times
2. Pursue a full course of study during the academic year
3. Keep I-20 or IAP-66 (also called DS-2019) valid at all times (Do not let it expire)
4. Observe employment restrictions (see section on employment)

SEVIS (Student and Exchange Visitor Information System) is a new computerized system to track international students in the US and make sure you stay in legal status. Your information from MIT WebSIS (`student.mit.edu`) is reported to SEVIS, so make sure to keep that information up to date. Whenever you want to exit and re-enter the US, you must have someone from the International Student Office (ISO) sign your I-20 form. This isn't necessary for short trips to Canada or Mexico. The ISO may take up to a week to process your form just before vacation, so try to do this well in advance. Each signature is valid for six months.

America and Americans

North America contains the largest area of uniform culture in the world. Many Americans have never met someone from another culture and are likely to be ignorant of yours. There will be almost as many aspects of your culture that will disturb Americans, as there are aspects of American culture that bother you. Don't hesitate to ask questions; for the most part you will get friendly answers. It won't hurt to try to explain your culture as well.

Americans tend to be less physical or uninhibited than people from European cultures, but more than Asian or African ones. Personal space is important here. People stand at a certain distance when talking, or walk a certain distance apart. This is normal and not a mark of unfriendliness. Many gestures such as hugging and kissing, which are used socially in some cultures, are considered inappropriate outside a close relationship. However, displaying these signs of affection in public is very common compared to more conservative cultures. Men tend to stay further apart than women.

Americans have an informal, active way of life, and to many people they may appear to be very abrupt. Formal introductions are not usually needed; if you want to be friends with the person next door, introduce yourself. Dress is very flexible. Rarely, if ever, is formal attire required; it can always be rented if need be. If you have any doubts, ask. Conversations and telephone calls usually come right to the point. There are very few formalities observed. People usually call each other by their first name. This is not a sign of disrespect. Call your professors Prof. [Last Name], unless they ask you otherwise. If you get a job, chances are your boss will ask you to call him/her by their first name.

Despite the lack of elaborate formalities, people are very careful about being "politically correct". Be careful what words you use especially when you talk about race or gender, but also about people's religion, age, wealth and many other concepts. The converntions are often tricky and counter-intuitive: for example, it is not okay to say "colored people", but it is perfectly fine to talk about "people of color". In time you will figure out what is okay and what is not, just be aware that this is probably a much bigger issue in US than anywhere else.

Americans for the most part don't line up neatly. They tend to bunch up. However, everyone seems to know who's first and crowding is definitely frowned upon. Sales people and officials are not, nor do they consider themselves, inferiors or servants of the public, and they act accordingly. With a pleasant smile and a gracious attitude on your part, you will find them most anxious to help. Tips are usually expected where personal service is involved (e.g. dining out, taxi, food delivery) 15% is an average value, and not tipping is considered rude. If dining in groups bigger than 6, the tip is usually included in the bill; in this case remember not to over-tip.

The drinking age in the US is 21, and many restaurants and shops will ask you for an ID if you want to buy alcohol. Furthermore, many bars and clubs are 18+ or 21+, so it's always good to check the age restriction before you go. Bars and clubs almost always check IDs. Most places will accept a foreign passport; they may or may not accept a foreign driver's license. It is a good idea to eventually get either a Massachusetts Driver's License or Liquor ID.

Driver's Licenses

Drivers from a number of countries may drive for one year in the US on their home licenses. The end of the year is designated as the earlier of (1) the end of the academic year or (2) one calendar year from the date of entry into the US. The year of eligibility begins each time you legally re-enter the US. If your driving license is not printed in English, you might be required to carry an International Driving Permit (IDP). You don't need to be a US citizen to get a US driver's license. If you plan to stay in the US after you graduate, you should try to get a driver's license as soon as you can. The reason is that car insurance is very expensive and goes down for every year that you own your driver's license. Getting a driver's license in Massachusetts does not require taking a driving course. However, you need to provide your own car to take the test. If you don't have a friend who can lend you a car, you can arrange the test through a driving school. The driving school will generally charge $80-$100 for this service. The US has no standardized ID card, so the primary form of identification is the driver's license. If you do not drive, you can get a Massachusetts ID. For more details, consult the International Students Office, Campus Police, or the Registry of Motor Vehicles (www.mass.gov/rmv/license/). Also see the **Transportation** chapter.

Employment

Before taking a job, talk with someone at the International Students' Office since permission to be employed is not automatically granted under the terms of F and visas. Before taking on any paid work, you must obtain a Social Security number (more information below) and file an I-9 form with the Student Employment Office. In order to apply for an SSN, you will need to obtain a Social Security letter from the ISO and apply in person at a local office of the Social Security Administration.

You are eligible to work part-time (20 hours a week) during term and full-time (40 hours a week) in the summer. During your first year in the US, you can only work for, i.e. be paid by, MIT. (Even if a job is physically on-campus but isn't paid by MIT, it is considered off-campus for these purposes.) Subsequently, you may work off-campus with ISO authorization in your field of study. On campus part-time work usually doesn't require any further authorization if you are being paid by MIT directly. On-campus work not directly paid for by MIT (e.g. work with stores in the Student Center) needs to be authorized by an International Student Advisor. F-1 and J-1 students are also eligible for full time on-campus MIT paid work during annual vacations. To work at a US company in summer, you can two options. You may register for an MIT academic program which integrates industry experience (e.g. the VI-A program in EECS). This form of employment uses your Curricular Practical Training work quota, and needs to be authorized by the ISO. Alternatively, you may apply for Optional Practical Training and find an internship on your own in your field of study. This must be approved by U.S. Citizenship and Immigration Services (USCIS). Approval takes up to 90 days, so plan early. Note that OPT is not company-specific, so you can apply for it even before you know where you'll be working. There is a limited amount of time for which you can work at a company under an F1 or J1 visa, but you have to clear the paperwork with the ISO in advance. Other types of employment should be discussed with an International Student Advisor.

Spouses on F visas may *not* accept paid employment. Some students holding J-1 visas and their spouses (J-2) are permitted employment only if they need to work for self-support.

Job listings

The Student Employment Office (11-320) has listings posted on the job boards outside the Student Services Center (11-120), and on their website (`web.mit.edu/seo/`).

The UROP office also maintains on-campus employment opportunities (see below).

MIT Libraries employ many students each year. Often, students just need to contact a library directly to obtain information. Listings are also available on the MIT Libraries web site, `libraries.mit.edu/about/jobs.html`

MIT's *Tech Talk* newspaper also publishes job listings.

The Career Services Office (12-170, x3-4733, `web.mit.edu/career/www/`) has listings for international students interested in jobs in their native country.

Social Security

Anybody who earns income in the US is required to pay taxes on that income, except F-1 and J-1 students if they are non-resident aliens for tax purposes and if their employment is directly related to their purpose for being in the US.

It is very important to obtain a Social Security number. The Immigration Information sessions held during Orientation by the International Students' Office provide information about how to obtain one. You will need to obtain a Social Security letter from the ISO and apply in person at a local office of the Social Security Administration.

If you are not eligible to work (e.g.: F-2, J-2 (without EAD), H-4 or O-3), and need to file taxes, you need to obtain an Individual Taxpayer Identification Number (ITIN). Contact the International Scholars' Office for more information (4-105, x3-6624).

Taxes

All taxpayers must file a tax "return" (form) each year with the Internal Revenue Service (IRS), the United States government agency which handles federal taxes, and may also be required to file with the state tax agencies. This applies even if you are not earning any income. The U.S. tax system is based on a system of self-assessment. Therefore, it is the individual's responsibility to understand the requirements.

The specific procedure for filing a tax return depends on your visa, immigrant status, and dependent(s). A tax worksheet and handouts, as well as IRS publications, are available in the International Scholars Office (4-105) to help individuals determine the correct category. Tax forms for international students are available in the Student Services center (in March).

The International Students Office holds tax workshops in March. Contact the ISO for information. If you've been in the US for 5 years or longer (you are considered a resident for tax purposes), you should attend the tax workshop sponsored by the Dean of Graduate Students (contact the Graduate Students' Office, 3-138, x3-4860).

If you are an international student earning less than $8000 a year, you can file a form to prevent Massachusetts Taxes from being withheld from your salary. As an international student, you do not need to pay Social Security Tax. Check your paycheck to make sure it is not being withheld. If you are not eligible to work but need to file taxes, you need to obtain an individual Taxpayer Identification Number (TIN). Contact the International Scholars Office for more information on any of the above.

English for Foreign Citizens

The MIT Women's League (10-342, x3-3656) gives English classes for students or faculty wives. Visit the Language Lab (14N-305, x3-4771) and the International Students' Office, where you can be referred to other opportunities to improve your English. The Language Conversation Exchange (x3-1614, web.mit.edu/medical/lce/) is an informal, one-to-one partnership for practicing a language and for getting acquainted with someone from another culture.

Host Families

Many families in the area host MIT foreign students each year under the Hosts to International Students Program (HISP). We hope you and your host family will enjoy seeing each other. However, if you do not want to see your host family on a particular occasion, refuse their invitation politely. First-year students can change their host families if desired. If you want a host family or want to become one, the staff at the International Students' Office will explain the procedure for you.

Insurance

In the MIT Student Health Program, outside hospitalization insurance is compulsory for foreign students. If you have questions concerning MIT medical insurance, check with the Student Health Insurance Office (E23-308, x3-4371). Also see the **Medical Resources** and **Finances** chapters. Campus Police can help you with auto insurance, etc. See the **Transportation** chapter for more details.

Passports and Visas

Check the pamphlet Passports and Visa Information Sheet, which you should have received upon arrival here. If you no longer have your copy, get another from the International Students' Office. MIT issues you an I-20 form when you are admitted so that you can apply for a visa. The I-20 does not guarantee a visa, and does not, by itself, let you enter the US. You receive your I-94 form or arrival-departure record when you enter the US. A part of it gets attached to the visa page on your passport, and is detached every time you leave. There is no need to renew visas when they expire if you do not leave the country, but I-94s always have to be valid. Check with the International Students' Office for renewal procedures.

Political Action

You are free to participate in any sort of political action as long as it does not violate the laws of the United States. Immigration officials think twice about renewing the visa of someone arrested for political activity, whether or not he was later convicted;

consequently, activities near and beyond the limits of the law should not be undertaken lightly. All political views are legal, but there are limits to what can be done in pursuit of a cause. You should realize that most Americans do not wish to get involved in foreign politics, nor even think too carefully about their country's existing involvement in them.

UROP for International Students

There are offerings in the Undergraduate Research Opportunities Program (UROP) of particular interest to international students. Check with the UROP Office (7-104, x3-7306, `web.mit.edu/urop/`) and the UROP Directory.

National and Cultural Groups

See the *Cultural Groups* section of the **Activities** chapter in this book for a brief introduction. For an up-to-date listing of contact/chairpersons, check this year's *Student Directory*.

ID Cards

Your MIT ID is increasingly useful, and correspondingly, increasingly inconvenient to lose. It's used for access to your dormitory, should you live on campus, your meal plan, should you choose to regularly eat on campus, access to labs and offices, athletic facilities, libraries, and numerous other services and discounts.

There were a number of concerns about security and privacy when the MIT Card was introduced in 1994. Some issues have been addressed, but not all of them. A discussion of the initial security issues can be found at `www.ai.mit.edu/people/andre/mit_card/`. The Tech carried a number of articles on the subject, including one from 1985, `www-tech.mit.edu/V105/N27/slg.27o.html`, where the MIT Card was looked on as the Holy Grail. Currently, according to the MIT Card Office Privacy Policy (`web.mit.edu/mitcard/privacy.html`), card accesses to all doors on campus are logged for only 14 days. The records are used to troubleshoot devices and cards, and may be released to the MIT police as part of a criminal investigation, if requested in writing. Some people also have concerns with the photos on the card being used for multiple reasons. The policy of distribution for the photo can be found on the same page.

The MIT Card is slowly being upgraded from being a magnetic strip media card to being a radio frequency identifier (RFID) proximity card. Currently (August 2004), the Simmons dorm card readers are proximity card readers, with more being installed as budgets and time allow. All new and replacement cards will contain the RFID tag.

The MIT Card started out as an ID card, and it is still used that way. It is also used as the exterior key for dorms, only providing access to residents. In the interest of promoting student communities, a MIT Card guest list for non-residents was suggested, but has not been adopted. Various offices and labs around the Institute are accessible by the Card. Your professor or supervisor can make a request to add you to the access list. Your MIT Card also functions as your library card at any MIT library.

You may request campus parking and/or take advantage of the subsidized T-Pass program with your MIT ID. See the Transportation section for more details. You may take advantage of the discounted cultural and recreational services offered by MITAC, the MIT Activities Committee (50-005). See Resources in the Entertainment section for more details. Your card also allows you access to the athletic facilities once it has been activated. Bring your MIT ID to the Johnson Equipment Desk in the Zesiger-Johnson Lobby (W35) to initiate membership. See the Athletics section for more details.

The use of TechCash, the money you access by using your MIT Card, has increased tremendously in the past few years. You can now use your MIT Card at all of the on-campus dining facilties (not including the food trucks) including LaVerde's Market and MacGregor Convenience, plus Domino's Pizza, Passport (70 Pacific Street) and Polcari's Restaurant in Kendall Square. In addition, you can use your card to purchase books at both MIT COOP locations, the MIT Press Bookstore and Quantum Books, get a haircut at the New Tech Barber, see a movie at LSC, photocopy your thesis at CopyTech, buy an ice cream sandwich from a vending machine or do your laundry in a dormitory. For a full list of locations where Tech Cash is accepted, see `web.mit.edu/mitcard/techcash/locations.html`. You can manage your account or create a new account online at `web.mit.edu/mitcard/`, either adding money via a credit card or your Bursar account. You can add money incrementally, and it will stay in your account from term to term.

Many dorms and offices around MIT will ask you to leave your card as collateral in exchange for borrowing equipment. This is against the policy of the MIT Card office, and theoretically insecure. Unfortunately, it is also very difficult to avoid. If you are particularly paranoid, ask if you can leave your driver's license. The MIT Card office also requests that you not lend your card to people so that they can access your dorm or buy some food.

Incoming Freshmen and transfer students will automatically receive ID cards during Residence and Orientation week. Incoming Graduate students must meet certain eligibility requirements (see: `web.mit.edu/mitcard/idpolicies.html#Eligibility`) to receive an MIT ID Card. These students should visit the MIT Card Office (E32-117) after arriving on campus to receive an ID card. You will need to present a valid picture ID (a driver's license, passport, etc.) when requesting an MIT Card.

Lost or Stolen Cards

If you lose your card, first check with the Campus Police to see if they have it in the lost and found. Contact the MIT Card office in E32-117 (x3-3475). Also notify them whether you had a Campus Dining Plan or a Payroll Deduction Plan on your card.

A replacement card can be obtained from the MIT Card office between 8:30am and 4:30pm on weekdays. A replacement fee of $15 will be charged, and can be paid by check to the Card Office, cash, Bursar account deduction (students), or payroll deduction (employees). There is no fee if the card was stolen and a police report is presented.

If you are a student living on campus and you discover your card is missing after business hours, call x3-1500 and page unit 12 to the number where you can be reached and they will let you into your building.

Marriage

Congratulations! And good luck.

1. You can have the ceremony performed in the MIT Chapel if you wish. Call x3-3913.

2. Financial Aid usually will not increase the grants you are getting, nor will it give you one if you are not already receiving MIT support. Under normal circumstances, your spouse is expected to work to earn the equivalent of his/her support. But by all means stop by the Financial Aid Office and talk with the people there; maybe you are a special case. Some fellowships have increased stipends if you "acquire" dependents. The spouse's income and assets could decrease graduate financial aid.

3. The Deans, social services staff and religious counselors are available to talk things over with you and can be very helpful in discussing aspects of married student life.

4. Blood tests must be taken and the certificate must be presented with the application. MIT Medical can provide testing (E23-189) and an appointment to have the doctor approve the certificate (allow 2-3 days). The blood test must be less than 30 days old when the marriage application is filed.

5. Both parties must go to a City Hall (any city in Mass.) and file an application. A fee will be charged by the city. (Cambridge charges $10, Somerville $20, Boston $15.) The license can be picked up in 3 days and it must be used within 60 days. A Justice of the Peace or a member of the clergy can validate the license.

6. If waiting a week is too long or your future spouse is scared of needles, Rhode Island has no blood test requirement or waiting period (though it may be hard to arrange the crucial third element of having Elvis perform the ceremony). Just call for an appointment, and bring your birth certificates and $24. Contact information can be found at `www.riwedding.com/marriage_license.asp` for a number of city's clerks.

7. The chaplains and Student Assistance Services in the Dean for Student Life Office can answer questions.

8. If you want on-campus married student housing, get on the waiting list as soon as you can; you are not guaranteed married student housing. Talk to the Dean of Housing.

Same-Sex Marriage

As of this printing, marriage of same-sex couples is legal in Massachusetts. However the repercussions of this change and itseffect on such issues as residency, immigration, financial aid, and health care have not yet been established. For up to date information on this issue, we recommend checking the webside of Gay & Lesbian Advocates & Defenders (`www.glad.org`).

Metropolitan District Commission

The Metropolitan District Commission (MDC) is an entity charged with handling certain services for Boston and the outlying suburbs. The parks, MDC police, water supply, MDC "parkways," many pools, skating rinks, tennis courts, and sewers are managed by the MDC.

MIT Card
See *ID Card*.

Pets
Pets can help smooth away some of the stress you'll accumulate from the seemingly endless problem sets and lab projects. It's hard to stay on edge after watching fish swimming around their aquarium or teaching a kitten how to attack your roommate's pants. However, pets are also a big responsibility. They need to be fed regularly, they need their wastes taken care of, and most importantly, they need some tender loving care. Having a pet means that you need to plan ahead for your vacations — somebody needs to take care of that animal while you're gone. It also means that you need to think about what you're going to do when/if you move off-campus. It's often harder to find housing for you and your pet than just yourself. Never get a pet with the assumption that you can just pass it off to your hall when you move out. Not only does it damage the psyche of the animal (an angry cat can create a vicious swath of urine-soaked destruction), but it places a real burden on the people who have to deal with your negligence.

Where can I get a new pet?
There are a variety of sources that can help you find the pet you want. You may be able to bring a pet from home, if your living situation allows for this (see *Living with Fluffy*). For info on the logistics of doing this, see *Travels with Muffy*.

If you can't bring a pet from home, you can always adopt a pet from the Boston Animal Care and Adoption Center (**MSPCA**; www.mspca.org; 390 S. Huntington Ave, Boston; 617-522-5055) or the **Animal Rescue League of Boston** (www.arlboston.org/Main/index.aspx; 10 Chandler St, Boston; 617-426-9170) . This will require a bit of effort because they want to make sure that the pet will be well taken care of before giving it to you. They will also want the pet to be neutered and up to date on all shots. (You should make sure this happens, regardless of where you get your pet from.) Note that the MSPCA will allow you to adopt a pet to a dorm residence but the Animal Rescue League will not. The links below allow you to browse through availiable pets for either site online.

The mailing list reuse@mit.edu will get emails, generally at the end of the school year, giving away pets. These are usually small pets (fish, rodents). You're unlikely to find the type of pet you want in a short time. You can also try www.petfinder.com, boston.craigslist.org, word of mouth, or go in person to local shelters.

You can also purchase a pet. **Petco** (119 First St, Cambridge; 617-868-3474) sells rodents, reptiles, fish, and birds. You can also look through the yellow pages or www.whitepages.com to find pet shops in the area. Local reptile lovers and salt water fish owners have said good things about **Boston Tropical Fish & Reptile** (located across the street from the Twin Cities Plaza at 243 Monsignor O'Brien Hwy; 617-623-4244), which sells both reptiles and the mice they eat.

Living with Fluffy
Housing for pets varies from place to place. If you live on campus, options are rather limited. You can find the rules and regulations at web.mit.edu/dormcon/pets/.

MIT allows fish anywhere. Bexley, East Campus, Random, and Senior House allow cats in certain areas. All other types of pets are forbidden.

Even if you live in a pet friendly dorm, there are often additional dorm-specific rules to follow. Having a pet requires the consent of those living around you; your housemates may feel that there are enough pets in their living space. Each dorm has a maximum number of cats permitted in the building. Cats are also usually confined to a small area, such as a hall or suite. If you want a cat in Institvte housing, you need to talk to your dorm government (and/or your hall chairs) to find out the specific rules *before* bringing your pet to campus.

If you live off campus, you'll need to talk to your landlord about having pets. Policies vary from place to place and person to person. They can even vary between tenants at the discretion of the landlord between leases. Finding a landlord that is ok with cats is somewhat challenging; finding one that accepts dogs is significantly harder. You might be able to negotiate paying a higher security deposit for the chance to have a pet. However, it is very likely that you have no choice but to pay higher rent.

Pet Supplies

Shaws (Star Market) sells food, litter, and other supplies in their pets aisle. Buy a container to keep your food/litter in and then refill it from bulk bags. The bags are much cheaper, and the container will prevent your pet from chewing through the bag. **Petco**, over by the Galleria, is probably cheaper and has a better selection of pet supplies. Snake owners can buy mice for consumption at Boston Tropical Fish & Reptiles.

Travels with Muffy

Depending on where (and how) you are going, you may be able to take your pet with you, but your options are limited. Most major bus companies (including Greyhound and Peter Pan) as well as Amtrak trains do not allow pets on board. Larger pets will need to be checked. If you have a small dog or cat, you can usually make arrangements for it to travel with you in the cabin. However, don't expect to just show up to Logan with your furry soul mate and walk on the plane. There are a number of issues you will need to deal with if you haven't travelled with your pet before. There are many resources on the web dedicated to this topic, such as `www.petsonthego.com`.

When flying, the first thing you should do is find out the specific policies of your airline. Make a reservation for your pet when you book your ticket. There is generally a fee of $50-$75 for bringing your pet on board. Airlines generally limit the number of pets that can be in the cabin per flight. Some airlines don't allow pet reservations; rather, they operate on a "first come, first fly" policy. Find out what health certificates or other documentation your pet needs to get through the dreaded security checkpoints. The standard requirement is a travel health certificate from a vet, dated within 10 days of the flight. Note that this means you may have to get a new one for the return trip. Airlines also have specific rules governing acceptable types of travel bag for your pet.

Many airlines will also allow you to ship a pet. This will cost around $100-200 and may also require a vet visit. Each airline has a slightly different set of restrictions; contact your airline well ahead of time. If you are shipping a pet internationally, be prepared to deal with the bureaucratic quagmire of quarantine regulations. For much more detailed information about traveling with your pet check out *Traveling with Animals*, from the USDA Animal Welfare Information Center (www.nal.usda.gov/awic/companimals/travelpets.htm), International Air Transport Association Travelers' Pets Corner (www.iata.org/cargo/operations/liveanimals/pets.htm). For information about pet-friendly travel and vacation options check www.petsonthego.com.

A healthy pet is a happy pet

There are two types of pet clinics; shelters that mainly provide one time services and places that also offer routine care. Get your pet neutered at one of the cheaper places (Alliance for Animals clinic is great), but find a vet that you can stick with as time goes on.

In the following listings, note that the nuetering cost is only for the procedure: it doesn't include the price of all the shots a new pet will need.

Alliance for Animals Metro Action Clinic (232 Silver St South, Boston; MBTA: Broadway; 617-268-7800) Costs: Neutering: $40 for cats and dogs between 8-16 weeks and $77 for dogs over 4 months Shots: ~$60 (includes testing for diseases as well). The Metro Action Clinic is a volunteer-based non-profit group that offers cheap neutering, spaying, and immunizations. The staff is very friendly and competent, but usually busy between 7am-8:30am and 4pm-5pm (animal pickup and dropoff times). This isn't a great place for a primary vet, but is an excellent choice for getting a new pet neutered and immunized. Be forewarned — there isn't any parking.

Angell Memorial Hospital (350 South Huntington Ave, Boston, 617-522-7282) Angell is a large veterinary hospital that can handle all sorts of animals and emergency procedures. This might be the best place to call if your pet isn't one of the "normal" ones or if you need emergency care right away. They can offer extended-payment programs for those who need a bit more time.

Back Bay Veterinary Clinic (324 B Newbury St Boston; 617-247-2273) This is a rather upscale clinic over on Newbury Street. They are one of the few places that can accept birds. Their professional, helpful, and competent manner is reflected in their price tag.

Boston Animal Shelter (26 Mahler Road, Roslindale; MBTA: Forest Hills; 617-635-1800) Costs: Rabies Vac: $5 The Boston Animal Shelter offers low cost clinics for rabies shots between March and June. Call ahead for more details on specific times.

Boston Cat Hospital (665 Beacon St, Boston; MBTA: Kenmore; 617-266-7877) Costs: Neutering: $102 for male and $225 for female. Shots: about $45. Office visit: $43. This is a great place to take your cat. The staff is nice and the location is clean, but the prices are a bit high. The staff is wonderful and they know exactly how to make your kitty purr with happiness and health, so to speak.

Cambridge Veterinary Care (1724 Massachusetts Ave. Cambridge; www.cambridgevet.com; 617-661-6255) and **Dr. Weiner's Pet Care Center** (272 Huntington Ave., Boston; MBTA: Symphony Hall; 617-266-9269) Cambridge Veterinary Care and Dr. Weiner's Pet Care Center are the two offices of Dr. Bruce Weiner. The Cambridge location has a very small waiting area but is very clean and fairly well stocked with prescription food and other pet stuff. There have been some mixed reviews, but generally this is a very good choice for your pet's regular care, as they are well-organized and keep excellent records of your pet's medical history. It is not a problem to schedule an appointment on short notice. The prices are a bit high; a routine annual checkup with rabies and all other vaccines and standard tests can run over $300.

Petco (119 First St, Cambridge, across from the Cambridgeside Galleria; 617-868-3474) Costs: shots for a new pet: around $30 Petco offers cheap shot clinics for your pets every other Saturday from 10-11am. You can't get your pet neutered, but you can ask the vet questions while they give your pet a once-over.

Porter Square Veterinarian (360 Summer St, Somerville; MBTA: Davis; 617-628-5588) Costs: Neutering: depends, usually between $100-200 Shots: around $50. Office visit: $46. The Porter Square Veterinary Clinic is large and clean. Oddly enough, it is located in Davis Square. The staff is very friendly and incredibly competent, but the quality care is a bit pricey. However, they often understand that college students can't afford unlimited X-rays of their pet's broken leg and will try to lower the cost as much as possible. An expensive place to get your pet neutered. An excellent veterinarian for accidents and problems your older pet may develop.

What to do when your pet passes on
Losing a pet can be difficult. If you need somebody to talk to, you can always make an appointment with MIT Mental Health (x5-2916) or one of the Counseling Deans in CSS.(x3-4861). Friends can also provide a support network to keep your spirits up.

As for the deceased pet, you'll need to find a way to dispose of the body. The easiest way to do this is to call the Cambridge Public Works Department. They have a 24-hour emergency line at 617-349-4860. You can also look for their website at www.cambridgema.gov/ ~TheWorks/. If you want to bury your pet, keep in mind that MIT strongly frowns upon students using MIT property as a cemetery. More elaborate schemes such as a Viking funeral pyre on the Charles are also discouraged. If you really need a service or ceremony to honor your pet, we recommend that you dispose of the body through Public Works and then have a small ceremony with some caring friends.

Post Offices
There's a Post Office in the basement of the Student Center. Their hours are Mon-Fri 7:30am-5pm. Other post offices are in Kendall Square (by the Fleet Bank) and the main Cambridge post office across from City Hall (up Mass. Ave.). The Post Office at South Station is open 24 hours.

Postdoctoral Fellows and Associates
Eligibility for various aspects of MIT life will depend on whether you are a Fellow or an Associate. Fellows receive funding from an outside agency, and are considered MIT Affiliates for subjects such as health care. Associates are paid by MIT, and may be eligible for staff benefits. Both types should receive an MIT card and be able to use it for all the regular things requiring one, such as using the libraries.

Other aspects will depend on which part of the bureaucracy you are dealing with, and whether they classify you as student, faculty or staff. These aspects may include, but not be limited to, parking, federal withholding tax, car registration and athletics facilities usage. Generally, being classified as a student is an advantage, especially in the case of getting an athletics card: student access is free, staff or faculty access is $375 per year. Good luck.

Weather & School Cancellations

NOAA's weather service (x3-1234) gives predictions for the next forty-eight hours. On Athena, type `add weather; weather bos -f` for the NOAA forecast. MIT rarely closes for inclement weather; if it does, the decision is usually made around 6am. Don't call the MIT switchboard because it will be swamped. Instead, call 617-253-SNOW (SNOW = 7669) for a recorded message.

At night, the light on top of the old Hancock Tower gives the weather forecast for the next eight hours. The significance of the colors can be remembered by the following handy rhyme:

Steady blue, skies are too;

Flashing blue, clouds are due.

Steady red, rain ahead;

Flashing red, snow instead.

(Except in summer, when it means that the Red Sox game is cancelled.)

MIT's
Oldest and Largest
Newspaper

The Weather
Today: Cloudy
Tonight: Cloudy
Tomorrow: Cloudy
Details, Page 360

THE TECH WANTS YOU
AS OMBUDSMAN

A newspaper ombudsman advocates for the readers and has broad responsibilities, including writing an independent unedited column, responding to reader inquiry, and keeping the paper on its toes.

May 10, 2003	*The Tech* elects an ombudsman.
Apr 6, 2004	Ombudsman prints full-page exposé detailing: • entire sentences added to a published letter, • student government officials serving on the editorial board (which writes endorsements!) • and more.
Apr 7, 2004	Chairman suspends the ombudsman.
Apr 21, 2004	*The Tech* violates its Constitution by failing to review the suspension within two weeks.
Apr 23, 2004	Editor in chief resigns.
Apr 25, 2004	*The Tech* violates its Constitution by impeaching its ombudsman without required notice.

Now more than ever, *The Tech* is the campus' only real source for news. It should be keeping a sharp eye on the administration, and doing accurate and investigative reporting. *The Tech* needs a watchdog to keep it on the ball. Be that canine! Email *join@the-tech.mit.edu.*

Transportation

Getting from point A to point B in Boston can be more difficult than that first 8.01 exam. This chapter covers every mode of transportation in the Boston area, as well as tips on getting to the airport and finding your way around the area, and different methods of long-distance travel.

Airplanes

Airplanes are useful, especially for those whose families live far away. People who intend to make a reservation for a "supersaver" flight for winter break should start searching for cheap fares in October. Air travel websites such as www.travelocity.com, www.expedia.com or www.orbitz.com allow you to compare fares from many different airlines, saving you both time and money – they are the best option for pricing simple flights. You can also check airline websites for reservations and information. If your exact dates and times don't matter, www.priceline.com and www.hotwire.com let you place bids on journeys and see if the airlines accept – this can net some deals that can't be matched any other way, especially at the last minute. For students, www.studentuniverse.com has been recommended for cheap overseas flights, hostel information etc. Flying with a companion can also be a good way to save money on plane tickets.

If you are going to New York, flying may be cheaper than you might imagine, though it's hard to beat the current bus prices at $10 each way (see **Bus** section below). The **USAir Shuttle** departs hourly for NY and the **Delta Shuttle** departs every hour on the half hour. However, reservations are now necessary for non-business class seats. The plane fare to Washington is often a very good value, as the bus and train options take much longer and cost almost as much as a cheap plane ticket. USAir and American offer direct flights to DCA, Dulles, and BWI.

Note: If you are flying a long distance and have to make a connection in New York City, make sure you set up your connection such that you both arrive and depart from the same airport. New York uses three major airports which are quite far apart, and it will cost you a lot of time, money and inconvenience to go from one to another.

The following is a list of airline websites and information numbers, as well as the Logan terminal letter for each airline.

Note: All international flights at Logan *arrive* at Terminal E. Most international flights also depart from Terminal E, but not all of them do.

Aer Lingus	E	800-474-7424	www.aerlingus.ie
Air Canada	C	888-247-2262	www.aircanada.ca
Air France	E	800-237-2747	www.airfrance.com
Air Jamaica	E	800-523-3515	www.airjamaica.com
Air Tran	D	800-247-8726	www.airtran.com
Alaska Airlines	B	800-252-7522	www.alaskaair.com
Alitalia	E	800-223-5730	www.alitalia.it

Airline	Terminal	Phone	Website
America West	B	800-235-9292	www.americawest.com
American Eagle	B	800-433-7300	www.aa.com
American (except int'l arrivals)	B	800-433-7300	www.aa.com
American (int'l arrivals only)	E	800-433-7300	www.aa.com
American Trans Air (ATA)	B	800-225-2995	www.ata.com
British Airways	E	800-247-9297	www.british-airways.com
Cape Air	C	800-352-0714	www.flycapeair.com
Continental	C	800-525-0280	www.continental.com
Delta Air Lines	C	800-221-1212	www.delta.com
Delta Express	C	866-2-FLYDLX	www.flydlx.com
Delta Shuttle	B	800-221-1212	www.delta.com
Icelandair	E	800-223-5500	www.icelandair.com
KLM	E	800-374-7747	www.klm.com
Lufthansa	E	800-645-3880	www.lufthansa.com
Midwest Express	C	800-452-2022	www.midwestexpress.com
Northwest	E	800-225-2525	www.nwa.com
Qantas	B	800-227-4500	www.qantas.com.au
Song	C	800-221-1212	www.flysong.com
Swiss	E	877-359-7947	www.swiss.com
TACA	E	800-535-8780	www.taca.com
United	C	800-241-6522	www.ual.com
US Airways Shuttle	B	800-428-4322	www.usairways.com
US Airways	B	800-428-4322	www.usairways.com
US Airways Express	B	800-428-4322	www.usairways.com
Virgin Atlantic	E	800-862-8621	www.fly.virgin.com

Airport

Logan International Airport (Massachusetts Port Authority, 1-800-23-LOGAN, www.massport.com/logan/ is the nation's nineteenth busiest airport and the world's thirty-fifth busiest airport based on passenger volume. Travel time from MIT to Logan runs about 45 minutes by MBTA, though it varies depending on the time of day. It can take anywhere from 15 minutes to an hour by car or taxi, depending on traffic conditions. Budget at least 30 minutes to be safe and avoid rush hour if possible. A cab between MIT and the airport generally runs around $25-$30.

Logan Airport has five terminals (A-E). Terminal A is currently (August 2004) closed indefinitely for renovations (just like everything else in Boston).

Terminals B, C and D are primarily used for domestic travel, but have a few international departures. Terminal E has all international arrivals with most international and a few domestic departures. The terminals wrap around the Central Parking complex and are connected to it and each other by (moving) walkways. Terminal B also has its own separate parking area.

Shuttle buses provide free service between airline terminals and the Airport T Station on the MBTA Blue Line. Shuttle bus 11 is for transport between all terminals, but does not stop at Airport Station. Shuttle Bus 22 serves Terminal B and the Airport Subway Station. Shuttle bus 33 serves Terminals C, D, and E to the Airport Subway Station. Shuttle bus 55 serves all Terminals to the Airport Subway Station during non peak hours (4-7am, 10pm-1am). Shuttle bus 88 serves all terminals and the Satellite Parking Lots 24 hours a day. All other shuttles supposedly run between 7am and 10pm, but some of them have been spotted running later, so your guess is as good as mine.

The T is the best and most inexpensive way to get to the airport, provided you don't have much luggage to carry. From MIT, take either the Red Line to Park Street or the #1 Dudley bus to the ICA/Convention Center station. Once on the Green Line, take it to Government Center. Transfer to the Blue Line and get off at the Airport stop. A free Massport bus takes you to your terminal. (See above for which bus to take.) Leave early during rush hour as the T tends to become very hectic. The Silver Line leg to the airport is scheduled to open in late 2004, running between South Station and Logan Airport.

A number of campus shuttles are available during holidays and at the end of term. The Parking and Transportation Office runs $6.00 shuttles to the airport at Thanksgiving, winter break and spring break. The UA has sponsored shuttles in the past. Keep an eye open for specific times.

Travel Agents

STA Travel (W20-024, 617-225-2555, www.statravel.com) in the basement of the Student Center caters to students, and can be especially useful if traveling abroad. They can get you specially negotiated student deals on air fare, budget hotels and hostels, and tours and packages. They have a small selection of travel backpacks and an impressive selection of Lonely Planet and other travel guides. Hours are 9:30am-5:30pm Mon-Fri. STA Travel also has a 24-hour full service number at 800-777-0112 that can be incredibly helpful for those firmly embedded in the "student lifestyle" — you can make basically all of your travel arrangements over the phone while normal people sleep. For travel agencies that serve MIT in an official role, and useful information regarding MIT travel policies, check the Controller's Accounting Office's travel page at web.mit.edu/cao/www/travel.htm

Bicycles

A two-wheeler can be a good answer to traffic and parking problems — if the thought of facing Boston drivers doesn't scare you off. Cyclists are legally expected to obey all traffic laws (although many don't, angering drivers, especially cabbies, to no end and making for general mayhem on the streets). Cambridge Police aggressively enforce bicycle laws, especially relating to lights and sidewalks, so obeying the law is your best bet.

It is advisable to put a full set of reflectors on your bike along with a headlight (they're required by law) and to wear a safety helmet (how much is your head worth?). Extra precautions should be taken when you ride at night such as additional reflectors and lights.

The **MassBike-MetroBoston Club** (Boston, 617-542-BIKE, www.massbikeboston.org) works on legislation to help commuting cyclists. Among other things, they help new commuting cyclists with a bike-buddy service and with workshops. Call them for information on their services, such as discounts at local bicycle stores and tours. See also *Bicycles* in the **Shopping** chapter.

The **Charles River Wheelmen** (131 Mount Auburn St., Cambridge, www.crw.org) organize frequent bike trips and sports events. See Prof. David Wilson (7-040, x3-5121) if you are interested in the more esoteric aspects of cycling such as researching bike dynamics or developing new bike routes.

Some dormitories have bike repair facilities. Generally these are for the use of dormitory residents only. Also, the MIT Outing Club sometimes holds bicycle repair sessions and organizes bike trips.

On-campus parking, bicycles

There are indoor or covered bicycle parking areas located in the breezeway under building 39, in the basement of Buildings 3 and 13, and in most of the dormitories. The area in Building 13 has a card-key system. You can register for a card-key at Campus Police headquarters for $5.00. Other bicycle areas are located throughout the campus, but don't take it for granted that a high-traffic area is safe: it probably isn't.

The wide variety of bicycle racks is the result of several experimental designs tried by the late Physical Plant and Planning Offices (both now reside in the Department of Facilities) and others.

One place where bicycles should *never* be parked is on the handrails of the steps of the Hermann Building (E53) (or any other handrails). There have been several accidents involving blind people falling over bicycles left there, and Facilities has been known to cut chains and remove bicycles from improper locations. In addition, campus regulations prohibit the securing of a bicycle to a stair handrail or in a hallway, and the Campus Police will attach a lock to bicycles illegally parked or attached to something. You will then have 24 hours to go to W31-215 and pay them $25 to have the lock removed. After 24 hours, both your lock and their lock will be removed, your bike will be impounded and you will have to pay $50 to retrieve your bike. They have no objections to the use of light poles, no-parking signs, or trees as long as safety hazards are not created. In addition, *never* park your bike on any wheelchair ramp, including the ramps in front of the Student Center.

Theft

Theft is a tremendous problem. Both Boston and Cambridge are so well supplied with bicycle thieves that the chance of leaving even a cruddy bicycle unlocked overnight and finding it the next day is miniscule. Things are somewhat better during the day, but not much.

The only bike locks which stand much of a chance of saving your bike are U-shaped locks, such as the **Citadel** and **Kryptonite**. Both are available at the **Bicycle Workshop** (see the **Shopping** chapter) and come with insurance if you read the enclosed brochure and register your bike with the Campus Police. Prices range from $30 to $50. Beware of cheap locks, as you're getting what you pay for — the Campus Police suggest spending 10% of the cost of the bike on the lock. Also keep in mind that Boston thieves will frequently take wheels, seats, and anything not locked on, so attach the lock to something stationary via the frame and *both* wheels if possible.

Bicycles should be registered with the Campus Police (online at `web.mit.edu/cp/www/otherserv/bikereg.html`) and with the Cambridge Police in Central Square (register by email, details at: `www.ci.cambridge.ma.us/~CPD/bikes.html`). It no longer costs the quarter it used to and it can help to recover your bike if it is stolen. Be sure to record your bike's serial number, as that is the only way to positively identify it and Cambridge police will not look for it without one. The Campus Police will also help you engrave an identifying number on your bike as part of Operation Identification.

Bicycle Repair

So you abandoned your bike all winter, and now you'd like to ride it while the weather is decent? One particularly handy bike repair shop is just a short ride away. Broadway Bicycle School (351 Broadway, Cambridge, 617-868-3392, `broadwaybicycleschool.com`) wants to teach you how to repair your bike. They'll rent you workspace and tools in 5-minute increments ($9 per hour), and will be happy to answer questions, though if it's a detailed step-by-step instruction, they do charge $18 per hour.

Campus Police Bicycle Auction

If you're interested in the idea of a bicycle as the cheapest fast form of transportation, the cheapest way to get a bike is to keep your eyes open for the Campus Police Bicycle Auction, which happens every Fall (sometimes Spring) during which rather rickety bicycles sell for very, very cheap. They often need a great deal of repair, so be prepared to spend more on fixing it than buying it. However, if the bike costs less than $10, as many of them do, it can still be a great deal.

Transporting your bicycle

Bicycles are absolutely forbidden on MBTA buses except for the crosstown routes (designated CT), which have bike racks. Ask the bus driver how to use them. Bikes are allowed on the Blue, Red, and Orange Lines. On weekdays, bikes are allowed during off-peak periods, which are between 10am and 2pm, and after 7:30pm. Bikes are permitted all day on weekends. Bicycles are allowed on the commuter rail at all times except rush hour during the weekdays. (Inbound in the morning and outbound in the evening. Schedules are marked in grey to designate rush hour periods.)

If you are traveling on Amtrak, you can bring your bike for about $4 if you box it. Certain trains can accept bicycles without requiring a box, but a reservation must be made. Be sure to show up at the station a half hour early and try to be on hand when the bike is loaded and unloaded. Make sure there are baggage rooms at the stations at both ends of the trip and avoid the trains which have no baggage cars.

Major airlines have widely varying policies for dealing with bicycles. www.bikeaccess.net provides a collection of tips for dealing with different airlines and other methods of transport. One tip: ask a local bike shop for one of their extra bike boxes.

Buses

Boston's major bus terminal is maintained by the MBTA at South Station on the Red line. Calling bus lines is a pain and a half; your best bet is to buy a ticket online at one of the various bus companies (**Greyhound**, **Peter Pan**, etc.) which you can do as little as two hours in advance (www.greyhound.com, www.peterpanbus.com). It takes at least 45 minutes to get there and have your tickets printed out, so try to leave at least an hour before your bus is scheduled to board.

There's also the option of the **Chinatown Bus**, which as of 2004 costs only $10 one way from Boston's Chinatown to New York's and is a good way to get out of town. You can buy a ticket online at www.ivymedia.com/fungwah/ should you feel the need. However, the ticket doesn't actually reserve a seat for you, so it's unclear what the advantage is. Buses leave on the hour and are easily found on Beech Street in Boston, and at the corner of Canal and Bowery in NYC. Arriving 15 minutes in advance during the off-season seems to be enough, as there are enough buses to make it likely you'll get a seat. During the summer it may be harder to find tickets, buy them in advance if it's imperative you reach you destination at a certain time. There are a number of companies operating the same route, so make sure to get on the bus run by the company you bought the ticket from. Most of the buses tend to make a stop at McDonald's or Roy Rogers en route. If the price war ever ends, you can expect the tickets to go up to $15–$25 one way, depending on the time of day travelling. Greyhound once participated in the price war, but gave up at the $20 point ($40 round trip, $25 one-way only in the Boston to New York direction). It can be worth the extra dollars if your ultimate destination is further from Chinatown, as the New York terminus for Greyhound and Peter Pan is the Port Authority Bus Terminal.

Bonanza Bus Line (www.bonanzabus.com) makes hourly trips to and from Providence, Rhode Island, 15 times a day for $15 round trip, which can be a reasonable alternative if the MBTA commuter rail schedule doesn't suit you.

Buses, Charter

If you want to organize a field trip for a large number of people, you can book a charter bus. In general, try to book buses 3 to 4 weeks in advance. Have the times of the trip and the complete address of the origin and destination of the trip when you call for the reservation. Mention non-obvious details that the bus driver may not know — for example, that the entrance to 320 Memorial Drive is on Amherst Alley, not Memorial Drive. Remember to tip the bus driver ~$20 per trip. Call the week before and the day before the trip to confirm the reservation. Make sure that you take a head count before the bus leaves for the destination and have a copy of the directions to the destination on you. (You never know when the driver is going to get lost.) Take a head count again before you return home. Some charter bus companies to try are **Boston Coach** (800-672-7676), **Coach USA** (800-334-6464), **Crystal Transport** (617-787-1544), **Paul Revere** (617-951-0808), **Peter Pan** (800-237-8747), and **Yankee** (617-268-8890). Make sure to get more than one price quote as prices can vary greatly.

The MIT Parking and Transportation office also offers its fleet of vans and buses for charter by MIT community members for MIT functions. All of the vehicles will come with drivers employed by Standard Parking. For more information call x8-6510, or email `mitparking@mit.edu`.

Buses, Local
See *Public Transportation*.

Cars
A car can be a great advantage, but driving in Boston involves a large set of aggravations (including Boston drivers). In addition, registration, insurance, maintenance, and gas can get pretty expensive. There is a good chance you can get by without a car in Boston and save a lot of money and aggravation. However, parking problems notwithstanding, a car is normally the best means of transportation for people living far from MIT. For information about buying a car, see *Cars* in the **Shopping** chapter.

Auto Theft Prevention
Keeping your car is a non-trivial problem, since thieves abound. Boston has the highest auto theft rate in the country. Even daylight thefts are amazingly frequent; professionals can steal a car in less than five minutes. If your car is stolen, damaged or broken into, immediately notify the Campus Police and your insurance company, in that order.

Some of the easiest ways to prevent your car from being stolen are to park in well-lit areas, always remember to lock the windows and doors, never leave the keys inside the car and never leave potentially valuable items (such as CD players, computers, or even large purchases made at clothing stores) in plain sight. Steering, clutch or ignition locks will slow down (but not stop) a thief. Try installing an alarm, especially if your car is new or otherwise desirable. However, be attentive to locking your car properly when you have one; car thieves listen for an alarm that indicates that the driver has left his door open. The Campus Police can also advise you on anti-theft systems for your car that will qualify you for a discount on Massachusetts Comprehensive Car Insurance. Some of the more common anti-theft devices in addition to alarms include kill switches (which prevent your car from being started once activated) and tracking systems which allow the state and local police to locate your car.

Even if your car is not stolen, it is still vulnerable to random acts of vandalism. If you have a car, it is well worth getting a permit to use in one of MIT's parking lots or garages if you can get one (which is expensive). Memorial Drive seems to have the most frequent problems with vandalism. If your car is damaged on Memorial Drive, you can report the crime to the MIT Police but you will have to call the State Police to get the police report.

Driver's License
In order to get a license to drive in Massachusetts you will have to go to a Registry of Motor Vehicles branch. The closest is in Boston at 630 Washington Street (MBTA: Chinatown). Driver's license renewals can be done at the RMV branch at the Cambridgeside Galleria Mall

at 100 Cambridgeside Place in Cambridge, but to get one for the first time you need to go to the Boston branch. If you don't already have an out-of-state license you have to take both the written test and the driving test. Otherwise, you just have to cough up the cash. After a $68.75 fee in both cases you have a genuine Massachusetts license. More licensing and legal information can be obtained at www.massrmv.com in excruciating detail.

So you don't own a car and don't plan to drive — why should you want a driver's license, anyway? In Massachusetts, the cost of car insurance is based on the number of years with a clean driving record — 'no record', meaning getting your license immediately before getting insurance, can count pretty heavily against you (to the tune of several hundred dollars). Since an out-of-state clean record counts like an in-state clean record, newcomers to Massachusetts should consider getting a driver's license in their home state or as soon as practical upon arrival at MIT, even if they don't plan on immediately driving or having a car. Similarly, international students may benefit from getting a US driver's license sooner rather than later. However, getting a Massachusetts driver's license may affect your state of residence, which could in turn affect other things (*e.g.* parents' taxes), so you should check the rules for your state.

Insurance

Massachusetts auto insurance always seems to be in a state of flux. However, one thing that remains constant is the cost; it is among the highest in the nation. Insurance has changed somewhat over past years. It has fluctuated between the "fault" and the "no-fault" systems. Your best bet for getting accurate information is to contact the insurance broker of an insurance company. Campus Police may also be helpful.

If you are insured in another state, you must have the equivalent of the minimum insurance required by Massachusetts state law. In addition, at the beginning of the new year when you renew your policy, you must inform your insurance company that your car is now principally garaged in Massachusetts. This will result in you having to pay Massachusetts insurance rates. Please note that you should give your company the name of the city you are actually living in as rates vary by city (Boston being the highest and Cambridge one of the next highest). While you might be tempted not to report to your insurance company that your car is in Massachusetts, *you would be running a serious risk.* The company will not normally catch you, but if you get into a collision, they can easily find out in the process of the investigation and refuse to pay you anything. Thus, you may effectively have no insurance coverage at all.

If you are insured in another state, you will save money (cancellation fees and the like) by insuring with the same company in Massachusetts if they have agents here. Likewise, you will do well to insure with a nationwide company if you are not a permanent Massachusetts resident. Check around with a few agents and see what they have to offer, since auto rates in Massachusetts are fixed by law. Note that Allstate no longer sells insurance in Massachusetts.

Registration

All student-owned cars must be registered with the Parking Office (E32-105, x8-6510) annually, even if you don't have an MIT parking permit. More information about parking and transportation is available at the web.mit.edu/parking/ site.

Massachusetts Registration: In order to register a car in Massachusetts you must have the required minimum insurance and pay an excise tax of 5% based on the value of the car. Also, cars registered in Massachusetts must pass an annual auto inspection which includes an emissions test. Tests can be done at most service stations that have repair facilities. Emissions tests generally run by numbers on your license plate. Inspections run on a yearly basis. Warning: Massachusetts now seems to have a policy of aligning all registrations to a certain date — if you don't register your car exactly a year before that date, your registration will lapse in less than a year, so make sure you know when your registration runs out to avoid serious problems if you get pulled over with it expired.

Out-of-State Registration: Rules vary depending on which state you are from, but the following generally applies: If you are from outside Massachusetts you will probably do well to keep your out-of-state registration. According to state law you must register your car within thirty days of becoming "gainfully employed" here. (Graduate students receiving a stipend or having a fellowship or assistantship may fall under this category.) Otherwise, you will probably be able to keep your registration, provided you don't become a legal resident of Massachusetts. (Registering to vote or getting married may affect your status.) In any of these cases check with Campus Police or the Registry of Motor Vehicles.

Questions about Massachusetts vehicle laws and regulations concerning out-of-state cars (including insurance) may be addressed to the Campus Police (x3-1212).

A useful information sheet should be included in your registration material each term.

Carpools

You can reduce pollution, save on gas and other expenses, and perhaps make some friends if you join or organize a commuter carpool. Carpooling also gets you a significant discount on MIT parking permits. The classified ads in *Tech Talk* and the Parking and Transportation Office (x8-6510) are handy for locating rides/riders.

Car Rental

Most companies require a major credit card and won't rent to anyone under 21 (25 at airport locations), but several nearby agencies are rumored to rent on a cash basis to students 18 and over with an MIT ID. All require a valid driver's license. Shop around for the best deal since rates vary considerably. Which agency offers the lowest price depends in part on when and where you'll be traveling, how long you'll be gone, and how many miles you'll be driving. Some offer week-long, weekend, or overnight rates, some have unlimited free mileage, and some restrict travel to within New England. For a short trip, a cheap "rent-a-wreck" from a small, local firm may be all you need, while you may want to rent from a reputable national agency for a long journey. With a national company, you can rent one-way, although usually this is prohibitively expensive. In general, the places closest to MIT (including branches of national agencies) have the lowest rates, airport locations the highest, with Hertz and Avis the most exorbitant.

Before you sign any rental agreement, *read it* thoroughly. Check who else is authorized to drive the car and make sure the odometer reading written down is correct and that any damage to the body of the car has been noted. People have rented cars with malfunctioning heaters, burned out lights, flat spare tires, and no jack, even from well known national agencies — so take the time to look over the car carefully. Don't be intimidated by an impatient salesperson; you're the one who will be driving and will be responsible for this many-thousand-dollar metal heap. Note that many credit cards let you waive the rental company's insurance.

ZipCar

An alternative to renting a car for MIT staff and graduate students is **ZipCar**, a car-sharing company with whom MIT has agreed to trade parking for discounted car usage. See www.zipcar.com for more info, but the basic idea is you reserve a car (located in various parking areas on campus and around town) for the time you need it and then just go and borrow it. You need to be registered in advance in order to have the proximity card for unlocking the car.

Registration for MIT-sponsored members costs $20, which is then refunded as driving credit. This plan has no monthly committment, no driving discount and no monthly rollover. (Extra value plans are also available.) Zipcar has an hourly charge of $8.50-$12.50 plue 18 cents per mile after 125 miles. Daily rental rates start at $65 with the same mileage rates. This compares favorably with car rental agencies, especially since you don't have to rent the car for the entire day if you just need to make a quick trip. Unfortunately, it is still only for students over the age of 21, as ZipCar is working out insurance costs for younger drivers. Also, make sure you apply for membership in advance of your first rental, as there is a week or so of delay. ZipCars are often tightly scheduled, especially at the last minute or on weekends. Be sure to schedule ahead accordingly or consider using cars from other T accessible locations such as Quincy, Alewife, or JFK/UMass.

Driving Around Boston

At first, having access to a car may give you a feeling of exhiliration as you contemplate the freedom of movement you now enjoy. This feeling will last approximately 2.5 minutes. This is about how long it will take you to either get lost in a maze of twisty one-way roads that look alike or hit a traffic jam. Boston driving was always confusing, and now with the Big Dig changing roads around at whim, it's *dynamically* confusing.

If you don't know where you're going, always call ahead or get directions from an online service like www.mapquest.com or maps.yahoo.com. Make sure your car has at least one set of maps even if you have directions (See Maps below) and a second person to read those maps and navigate for you if possible. (Reading maps while driving in Boston traffic is as dangerous as it is difficult.) Having a copy of the yellow pages and a cell phone is also a good idea so you can call for help if you are lost or break down.

If you do know where you're going, you should still be prepared for the possibility that the roads have moved over night. If you're driving at night, be prepared for the possibility that the roads are closed instead.

Many intersections in and around Boston which *should* have stoplights do not. Some of those that do also have pedestrian-operated lights, but watch out for pedestrians who blithely cross against the light and expect you to come to a screeching halt. The area is full of them. (MIT students are among them, as pedestrian behavior at 77 Mass. Ave. illustrates.) Watch also for pedestrians crossing at any random point, which happens most frequently around a college (such as MIT), but is pandemic.

Many things that should be intersections are rotaries instead. A rotary is a one-way traffic circle of death with no traffic signals of any kind. Cars in the rotary have the right of way, so incoming cars must yield. You can exit a rotary at any point as long as you don't cause an accident.

Boston drivers are unbelievably bad, even for a large American city. On any given day, you can see the entire repertoire of wrong turns, U-turns, nerve-wracking lane changes, light crashing, weaving, speeding (too fast or too slow), plus some new tricks, such as charging up the left side of a street at 60 mph in order to be able to make a left turn against the oncoming traffic before the light goes red. The traffic pattern at red lights is that people keep zipping through 1 1/2 seconds after the light turns red but don't move when it turns green for about the same time (which balances things). Massachusetts has one of the lowest auto fatality rates in the country, but may be #1 in "fender-benders."

Driving, Distance

If you own a car, driving can be the most convenient way to get where you're going if your destination is far away. However, if you are traveling alone, driving can be extremely expensive and tiresome. Riders and drivers can find each other through the APO ride board on the second floor of the Student Center. Want ads in *Tech Talk* and *The Boston Phoenix* also work.

If you don't own a car and can't get a ride with someone else, renting a car may be the least expensive, most convenient option. See above.

One way to get a car for a long distance trip is to call one of the auto delivery services listed in the Yellow Pages under Automobile Transporters. They have cars that need to be taken to many parts of the country, and they will pay some expenses.

Parking

Parking is a problem, but it's not too bad if you don't mind walking long distances and feeding meters. Meter-maids patrol until 6pm Monday—Saturday, so if you neglect to pay up you're very likely to get tagged. A parking ticket in Cambridge costs $15; Boston is more. Car thieves are as prevalent as bicycle thieves, so keep your car locked and put tempting articles out of sight, preferably in the trunk. There are many garages in the theater and shopping districts, but they fill early and cost a lot, especially in the evening; go early or take the T.

Parking on certain Cambridge streets is banned from 7am-10am due to Environmental Protection Agency regulations. However, cars with resident parking stickers are allowed to park on streets within one half mile of their owner's residence. To obtain a City of Cambridge parking permit, you must have proof of residency and your car must be registered in Massachusetts. You cannot obtain or renew a Cambridge resident parking permit if you have unpaid parking tickets. The parking permit costs $8 a year. For more information see www.ci.cambridge.ma.us/~Traffic/

Many Cambridge streets have rules against "storage" — if you don't move your car every day, you will get a ticket. If enough storage tickets pile up the car will be towed. In addition, if you are parking on the street, keep watch for street cleaning and snow emergencies. On street cleaning mornings (once a month April—December) the tow trucks patrol the streets of Cambridge like enormous, loud, greasy vultures, so a lapse in attention can prove costly.

If you live in an apartment, your landlord may provide off-street parking. If he promises to provide it, be sure it says so in your lease. You may be able to rent garage space nearby. (Rates run around $40 a month.) Otherwise, you'll have to park in the street if it is legal. (In Brookline it is illegal to park in the street overnight, so make sure you get a parking space.)

On-campus parking

MIT parking is very highly sought after, as space is limited. Several permit options are available, although the most common type will allow you to park in a specific lot or garage 24 hours a day. Faculty and some staff members are assigned parking permits through their Department Parking Coordinator. Volunteer and Invited Visitor Parking Permits are intended for volunteers, alumni and retired employees. Apply at the Parking Office. Rates vary but most parking permits cost $518. Carpooling, regardless of what type of permit you have, can greatly reduce cost.

Undergraduate commuting students are eligible for a parking permit in the West Lot. Apply at the Parking Office and bring proof of off-campus residency. Graduate commuting students should apply to the Parking Coordinator in their academic departments. It is still possible to get a parking sticker if you live on-campus, but you have to be lucky. The various housing offices have parking coordinators, but you will probably save time just going straight to the Parking Office. If you are a freshman, there is no hope of getting a permit. Student resident permits currently (August 2004) cost $480 and student commuter permits are $333. Carpooling in either case can save money.

Trading parking stickers between Regular Commuter permits is allowed; check the ads in *Tech Talk*. You will have to take your old stickers to the parking office and pay a small fee for the switch. Parking stickers can be replaced for a new vehicle for a fee (which is waived if the car is stolen). Parking can also be canceled all together. In both cases, bring your old sticker (or its pieces) to the Parking Office. In the case of a canceled parking permit, you should have the money that you paid for the rest of the year returned to you.

Parking regulations are enforced by both the Parking Office and the Campus Police. You cannot renew your parking permit if you have any unpaid parking tickets (although the people getting the tickets are usually the ones without permits). If they notice you illegally parking and you have four or more unpaid tickets, they'll tow you. If you park in the street, blocking fire-lanes, pedestrian access, delivery access or street cleaning, they'll tow you. If you park in the MIT permit parking zones on dorm row without a permit, they'll tow you. On a slow night in McCormick, watching the tow trucks remove every car can be entertainment for all.

There is some "open" parking around campus, however. Open parking is street parking that does not have meters and does not require a permit. All of Memorial Drive is open parking, as are parts of Vassar (when it's not being dug up) and Ames Streets. It will be relatively easy to find a place to park on Memorial Drive after 10pm. It will be almost impossible to obtain any form of street parking between 8am and 6pm. There are a few locations on and around campus, such as Ames Street immediately next to East Campus, that allow parking only with a City of Cambridge resident parking permit, so be careful of this when choosing a parking space that looks "open" if you don't have one.

Most MIT parking lots are open to MIT affiliates without an MIT parking permit on Institute Holidays, on weekends and after 5pm on weekdays. Those that do not allow parking without a permit during these times will have a sign indicating this. The presence of a parking attendant does not necessarily mean that an MIT lot is closed to MIT affiliates after business hours. However, be wary of the parking garages at night. They have been known in the past to be high-risk areas for theft and assault.

Parking stickers are usually issued at the beginning of each term. The Dean's office (7-133) has some stickers they will give out if you show good cause. The Campus Activities Office (W20-500) handles stickers for special exceptions. Campus Police (x3-1212) has information on good places to park around the Institute and can issue temporary or guest parking permits. Departments also can issue guest parking permits, but they have a limited supply for the year so make sure it's really important before you ask for one.

Parking in winter

During the winter, snow removal is slow and inefficient, especially on the weekends; side streets often don't get plowed. There are also emergency parking bans on many major streets during snowstorms. If you park in the street, be sure you are familiar with the regulations which apply to that location.

If your car is parked in Cambridge, make sure that you will know if any official "snow emergency" is declared. At such times, all parked cars must be removed from Memorial Drive and other locations marked by a red-and-white "Snow Emergency" sign. You can use the Westgate West parking lot overnight, but you must move your car in the morning. The 24-hour Cambridge parking ordinance is enforced during snow because it is easy to determine how long you have been parked.

Radio stations WEEI, WBZ, and WRKO will broadcast announcements of snow emergencies. (See *Radio* in the **Media** section.) Also, you can call the appropriate municipal Departments of Traffic and Parking. In Cambridge the number is 617-349-4747.

Traffic reports

WBZ (1030 AM) has the best and most regular traffic reports from a helicopter. It is reported that WEZE (1260 AM), WRKO (680 AM), WEEI (850 AM), WMJX (106.7 FM), and others also report on traffic. All can be invaluable to someone with little knowledge of the area and a car radio.

Boston traffic is heavy even during non-rush hours. During rush hours (7-9 AM, 3:30-7 PM) and especially on Friday it becomes ridiculous. As you become familiar with the area, you should notice and use shortcuts and circuitous routes which will avoid the major jam-up areas. Example: Bay State Road is a good way to bypass Kenmore Square if you're going west from Beacon Street onto Commonwealth Ave.

One of the best tools available for driving in the greater Boston area is www.smartraveler.com. This site has traffic reports for many different cities; choose Boston from the dropdown menu on the first page. This takes you to a map with hotlinks for all the major highways and some surface roads out to 495; clicking on any highway brings up a traffic report for that road, broken out into useful chunks. There are traffic cameras and details about construction and road closings due to special events. The site also reports problems in the MBTA system, such as when a station is closed and operating shuttle buses instead of trains. When you're enroute, you can call 617-374-1234 to get the same traffic and weather updates.

Tollroads

There are some toll roads in and around Boston. Some examples are the Callahan/Sumner Tunnels (from/to the airport), the Tobin Bridge (to Revere), and the Mass. Turnpike (Interstate 90). Tolls for the Mass. Turnpike are assessed according to the number of miles you travel plus an additional dollar on occasion for good measure. Commuter passes (most prominently the electronic "Fast Lane" or "EZ Pass" systems) are recommended if you have to use tollroads often.

Geography

Boston Geography

It is impossible to find your way around the Boston area without a map. It is only slightly less impossible to find your way around with a map, but any advantage helps. The streets in the older sections follow former cowpaths and shorelines and make very little sense to newcomers. Occasional grids exist, *e.g.*, in Back Bay and South Boston, but even here confusion reigns — the numbering changes from street to street. To really understand Boston's street layout, you need to realize that its roads run from "square" to "square". Learn where each square is, and the streets just fall into place. Peculiarities to note:

1. Most streets are not clearly marked. Main streets are almost never marked; you can go out of your mind reading the name of each tiny side street without ever finding out which highway you are on. One key to finding your way in Back Bay: side streets there go in alphabetical order, starting with "A" (Arlington) at the Public Garden and ending at "K" (Kilnarnoch) in the Fenway.

2. The Charles River is *not* a good direction index. It bends from north to south and back. The only certain thing about it is that if you follow it downstream or upstream far enough you'll get to MIT. Then you can ask someone for directions.

3. Main streets likewise weave back and forth. Massachusetts Avenue is a primary example, weaving its way from Lexington through Cambridge into Boston. If you don't believe this, try figuring out how Mass. Ave. and Memorial Drive both lead to Harvard.

4. House numbers on a street do not go by 100 per block but sequentially, with random inconsistencies. The average is about 30 numbers per block, meaning that 300 numbers is far away. Some streets have odd or even numbers on the same side, numbers increasing on one side and decreasing on another!

5. What appears to be one roadway can sometimes have more than one name. For example, the same pavement is Winter Street north of Washington Street but Summer south of it. Water turns to Milk in a similar maneuver. A favorite trick is for a street to change names as it crosses a town line. Cambridge Street in Allston turns into River St. as soon as it enters Cambridge. Mass. Ave. in Cambridge changes into White Way near Porter Square and then to Cambridge St.

Not only that, but the same name is used for different streets in different towns or even different sections of the same town. All of the streets mentioned above are repeated again and again in various locations. Boylston St. in Cambridge has no relation to Boylston St. in Boston, nor do any of the myriad Harvard and Washington Streets have anything in common. In another variation, the street names stay the same, but the numbering system starts all over again, normally in the opposite direction. For instance, 840 Mass. Ave. in Boston is nowhere near 840 Mass. Ave. in Cambridge.

6. Town names are no less confusing than street names. Present-day Boston includes the old townships of Allston, Brighton, Charlestown, Hyde Park, Roxbury, West Roxbury, Jamaica Plain, Mattapan, South Boston, Dorchester, East Boston, and Roslindale. At the core of all this is Boston Proper, which includes all the neighborhoods of the North End, West End, South End, Downtown, Chinatown, Beacon Hill, and Back Bay. In addition there are unofficial terms, such as Readville, South Cove, Columbia Point, and Orient Heights, in common use. The various governments, the post office, the telephone company, and the local people all differ concerning which of these terms should be used. (But note that Brookline, although an inner suburb, is *not* a part of Boston.)

7. Adjacent areas often have similar names. For example, Newton Center, West Newton, Newton Lower Falls, Newton Upper Falls, and Auburndale (how did *that* get there?) are all parts of Newton.

8. When traveling to an unfamiliar place, pick an easily-visible landmark near where you want to go or know the name of the nearest square (roads tend to run from square to square) and head for that. For example, in Cambridge, it is easier to find the general location of MIT by looking for the Green Building. It is also much easier to ask strangers for directions to landmarks than to out-of-the-way places.

Maps

Maps are an indispensable aid to travel in the Boston area. Good, free maps are difficult to come by. The Cambridge and Boston Chambers of Commerce sporadically publish maps and may have a few available. The Cambridge City website often has useful maps. Currently `gis.ci.cambridge.ma.us/bustransit/index.html` has both a good bus map and a detailed city map in `pdf` format. The Information Office (7-121, x3-4795) and many dorm desks have maps you can consult.

For a few dollars, the Coop sells several good maps of Cambridge and Boston, including *The Arrow Street Guide of Boston and Surrounding Communities*, the *Rand-McNally Map of Boston and Neighboring Communities*, and *Car-free in Boston and all Massachusetts*. This last is an excellent book with all sorts of transit, biking, and walking maps as well as tips on using mass transit, taxicabs, and bicycles. The *Boston Bike Map* by Rubel Maps, `www.bikemaps.com`, is also great for pedestrians and bicyclists, and *Streetwise Boston* is useful as it shows the T Stops in relation to the streets. The Park St. T station usually has maps and schedules of all T and bus routes.

Mopeds

Mopeds are a good compromise between a motorcycle and a regular bike. The requirements are that you have an RMV moped sticker affixed to the moped, an automobile driver's license, and that you drive the moped at no more than 30 miles per hour. Otherwise, treat it like a bicycle. Get a Kryptonite moped lock so you can keep your moped. A reasonable moped costs approximately $600-$900.

Motorcycles

Motorcycles must be registered with Campus Police. Check with Campus Police (x3-1212) for details. State law requires that you have a certain minimum amount of insurance and proper headgear for both driver and passenger, in addition to the inevitable license (procedures and costs essentially the same as an automobile license). There are several motorcycle organizations in the area. Check with other owners or dealers. Wear a helmet! (It's state law.)

Public Transportation

Bus

Bus fare on most lines is 90 cents. On some longer-distance lines, the fare is based on a zone system, with additional zones costing 65 cents each. Express Bus and Night Owl Bus Routes cost extra. Some lines (especially many leaving from the Harvard station) make you pay as you get off, not as you board. Exact change is required on all lines. Most of the major bus routes in Cambridge radiate from either Harvard or Central stations on the Red Line.

The line most often used by MIT people is the Harvard-Dudley bus (MBTA Bus #1), which stops at several rapid transit stations as it threads its way on Mass. Ave. through Cambridge and Boston. (Make sure you don't take the limited stops bus.) The buses are said to travel in packs: three at a time and then none for an hour. Allow extra time in case you have to wait. The bus starts at Harvard Square (Red Line), runs along Mass. Ave. through Central Square (Red), and passes the MIT Building 7 entrance. From MIT it travels into Boston via the Harvard Bridge, then continues along Mass. Ave. It stops at Auditorium (Green), Symphony (Green), and Northampton. Finally, there is a short leg south on Washington Street to Dudley, where the bus turns around for the return trip. If you are unsure whether or not you should get off at a certain stop, it can be useful to ask the bus driver, as they are often only too happy to help you find your destination.

See the section on *Wellesley*, in the **Colleges** chapter, for information on the free MIT/ Wellesley Exchange Bus, as well as the Wellesley Senate bus which runs on the weekend (but isn't free).

Commuter rail

Commuter intermediate-distance rail service to points north and west of Boston is available at North Station. Lines to the north and west of Boston will stop at Porter Square before heading into North Station. Lines to the south and west of Boston originate at South Station. The MBTA rapid transit lines make stops at both of these stations. The commuter rail (or Purple Line) is most useful for weekend day trips out of the city. Unless you are using it to commute in from the suburbs during normal commuting hours, the schedule is erratic, so plan ahead and check www.mbta.com for times. The commuter rail also goes all the way to Providence, Rhode Island, which can make it very cheap and convenient to see concerts and shows in Providence, provided they're early enough in the evening.

Shuttles

There are several shuttle services that aren't affiliated with the MBTA. Some of them are free to the general public, some are free with your MIT ID, and some cost a nominal fare.

MIT operates a free weekday shuttle service from 7:15am to 7:15pm around campus called the Tech Shuttle. It circles the perimeter of MIT from Westgate to Sloan, with a number of stops along the way. During the summer the Tech Shuttle visits each stop every 20 minutes, and during the winter, each stop is visited every 10 minutes. More information can be found at web.mit.edu/parking/techshuttle.html

EZRide operates between Cambridgeport and North Station, including stops at Kendall Square and the MIT Museum, and a few other locations near MIT. It's free with an MIT ID, or $1 without (there are discounts for seniors, children and people with disabilities). It is designed for commuters, so its hours are limited to rush hour — every 12 minutes from 6:24am to 10:48am and 3:12pm to 8:12pm, only on weekdays and excluding holidays. Visit www.ezride.info or call 617-8EZ-INFO for all the details.

The free Cambridgeside Galleria bus runs between the Kendall Square T-stop, the Cambridgeside Galleria mall, and the Kendall Square movie theatre. It is limited in hours, from 9am to 6pm Mon-Sat, and 12pm to 6pm Sun. It's also a convenient way to get to the Museum of Science, which is a few blocks past the Galleria.

The LMA M2 Cambridge Shuttle runs from Harvard down Mass Ave to MIT, across the Harvard Bridge, and over to the Longwood Medical Center. It costs 85 cents for the general public (75 cents when you buy 10 tickets at a time), but the tickets must be purchased in advance from a few select offices. See www.masco.org/transit/ptsM2.htm for details. You can ride the shuttle free if you have an ID for a Boston-based Harvard graduate school. The temp IDs for these are green index-card-type-things, so if you ever feel like bumming a ride to Longwood, flashing a green index card with some writing on it can usually get you on the bus.

There are several shuttles run by Partners Healthcare. The two of most interest are MIT/ MGH and MIT/Brigham & Women's Hospital. You can get schedules online at www.partners.org/ourhosp/ourhosp_shuttle.html. They run from about 7am to 7pm and depart from in front of the Student Center, and are free.

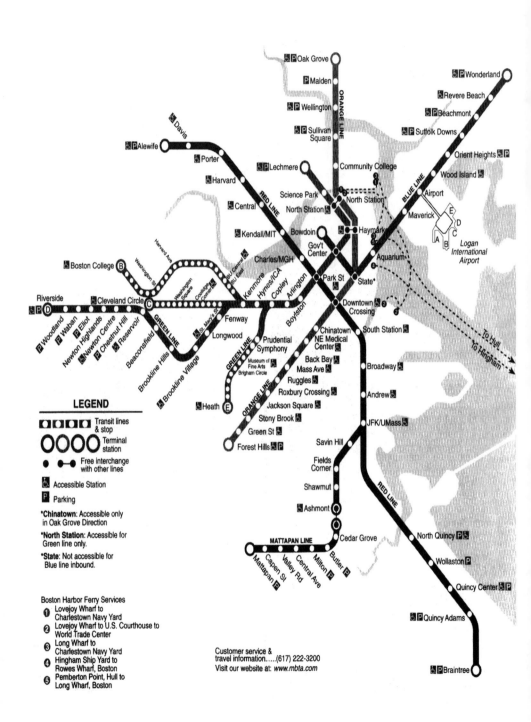

LEGEND

▪▪▪▪ Transit lines & stop

○○○○ Terminal station

●─●●─● Free interchange with other lines

♿ Accessible Station

P Parking

*Chinatown: Accessible only in Oak Grove Direction

*North Station: Accessible for Green line only.

*State: Not accessible for Blue line inbound.

Boston Harbor Ferry Services
1 Lovejoy Wharf to Charlestown Navy Yard
2 Lovejoy Wharf to U.S. Courthouse to World Trade Center
3 Long Wharf to Charlestown Navy Yard
4 Hingham Ship Yard to Rowes Wharf, Boston
5 Pemberton Point, Hull to Long Wharf, Boston

Customer service & travel information......(617) 222-3200
Visit our website at: www.mbta.com

The T

Boston has one of the oldest mass transit systems in the country. It is operated by the **Massachusetts Bay Transportation Authority** (MBTA), usually known as the "T". Park Street station, in a tunnel which has been declared a National Historic Landmark, is the oldest subway station in the nation. The T uses rapid transit cars, streetcars, electric buses (trackless trolleys), conventional buses, and diesel-powered commuter rail cars.

The subway consists of four main lines, each of which is identified by a color. The Red Line, which has two branches at its southern end, the Green Line, which branches into four variations (rhymingly labeled B through E), the Orange line, and the Blue line. The four Lines cross in the middle of Boston. See the T map on the previous page. (Note that the map is symbolic and bears little resemblance to actual directions or distances.) MIT is located on the Red Line. The two closest T stops to the MIT campus are Kendall, located in Kendall Square next to the MIT Coop, and Central, located up Mass. Ave. from MIT.

In addition to the four subway lines, a rapid-transit bus line known as the Silver Line has recently opened and is considered part of the subway system for fare purposes. The Silver Line replaces service terminated decades ago, so it is important politically even if no tunnels were dug for it. It currently runs from Dudley Square to the New England Medical Center, near Chinatown. The link from South Station to Logan Airport is expected to open in 2004.

Tokens for the subway are $1.25 each and are available at every station. Most subway stops have a booth for making change and/or selling tokens, but don't count on them late at night. Make sure you have exact change if you plan to use the above ground transport.

Where the Green Line is above ground (past Boston University), it is free outbound and requires exact change inbound. The D (Riverside) line has extra charges that depend on the distance traveled. There is an extra $1 charge for Red Line service to Quincy Center, Quincy Adams and Braintree. Inbound service from Mattapan costs an extra 75 cents.

MIT subsidizes T Pass costs for students and employees; applications for passes are available at the Parking and Transportation Office (E32-105) or online at `web.mit.edu/parking/studentapp.html` on the Parking Office site. The passes vary in price and services offered, all of which is enumerated on the application. As of July 2004, one must still fax a copy into the office if using the online application. Efforts are underway to complete the online application system, but despite the appearance of functionality, you will not receive your T Pass if you do not turn in a physical application.

As of August 2004 a monthly bus pass is $12, a monthly subway pass is $22 and a combo pass will set you back $35.50, which appears to be a worse deal than buying the two passes separately. (We don't understand this either.) T passes (without an MIT subsidy) are also available the first ten business days of each month at the Harvard and Park St. stops.

The T schedules are based around time leaving each terminus. The first trains leave their respective terminals between 5am and 6am, except Sundays, which start about a half hour later. The last trains leave their terminus between 12:15 AM and 12:45 AM. This means that the last train you can catch varies depending on which direction you are going, and which end of the line you're on. Schedules late at night tend to be erratic; there may be cutbacks in runs, the driver may not feel like stopping; things are generally bad. Be careful when riding late at night, or you may be left stranded.

232   Transportation

On a good note for those late night drunks on the town, Friday and Saturday nights until 2:30 AM, the MBTA has started to run a "Night Owl" bus service with 10 routes that run parallel to subway lines and popular bus routes. However, these lines only run every half hour or so, and have very few buses inbound, so be careful if you're trying to get from the outer Red Line area back to MIT, or trying to make a transfer downtown.

Complete system maps, showing all bus and subway routes, and bus schedules, are available at many bookstores and online at www.mbta.com. For the information superhighway impaired, the MBTA information backroad is 617-222-3200.

Taxis
Taxis can be convenient since they avoid many of the usual problems associated with cars. However, they are expensive ($1.75 for the first quarter mile and then $.30 for each 1/8 mile, $24 per hour of waiting time) and are least available when you need them most. During rush hour they tend to be quite hard to find and will sometimes take a half hour to answer a call. Just before a holiday or bad weather they are almost impossible to find quickly; if you want a cab at such times you should call not less than an hour beforehand. Some taxi company phone numbers are:

Ambassador-Brattle Taxi and Cambridge Taxi Co. — 617-492-1100
Checker Cab of Cambridge — 617-497-9000 or 5-8294 from Harvard internal phones
Yellow Cab of Cambridge — 617-547-3000
Yellow Cab of Boston — 617-876-8294

During peak times, try a taxi company from an outside phone (phone numbers in Yellow Pages). They tend to respond more quickly if they don't think you're a student. Taxis can often be found in front of 77 Mass. Ave., near the Kendall Square T stop, and (almost always) outside the Hyatt-Regency (right next door to Next House).

Cab drivers are generally talkative, opinionated, and nonviolent if you tip them 10-15%.

An alternative to traditional taxi services is **PlanetTran**, an environmentally friendly livery service based exclusively on the use of hybrid electric/gas cars like the Toyota Prius. They currently offer a 10% discount to MIT faculty, staff, and students who use the service. The cost from campus to Logan is $26 with the discount, plus tip and tunnel tolls from Logan to campus. There is no Logan pickup fee charged by PlanetTran to the customer (usually $2.25), because Massport offers a 50% discount for using alternative fuel vehicles. To make a reservation, sign an online petition to allow the operation of hybrid taxis in Cambridge, or to just learn more, call 1-888-PLNT-TRN or visit www.planettran.com.

Trains
Amtrak (www.amtrak.com, 1-800-USA-RAIL) is the national passenger rail service, operating trains to 46 states and Canada. Trains provide a reasonably comfortable way to travel, with plenty of leg room, space to walk around, snack or meal service, smoking stops for the addicted, and (on newer cars) standard AC power outlets for your laptop. Prices are generally competitive with buses, one notable exception being the Boston-New York City route (see *Buses*). Students can get a 15% discount on all tickets with a Student Advantage card (www.studentadvantage.com).

Boston is the northern terminus of the Northeast Corridor, one of the few stretches of track that Amtrak actually owns. Here the *Acela Express* hits maximum speeds of 150 mph, getting to New York in 3.5 hours and to Washington, DC in 6.5 hours. Less expensive *Regional* trains are more frequently used by students, getting to New York an hour slower. The *Lake Shore Limited* runs once a day, overnight to Chicago.

Westbound and southbound trains depart from South Station (MBTA Red Line) and from Back Bay Station, 145 Dartmouth St., behind the John Hancock Tower in Copley Square (MBTA Green and Orange Lines). During holiday seasons unreserved trains can be standing-room only, and it is always easier to find a good seat at South Station (where the trains originate) than at Back Bay. Note: The *Downeaster*, with four daily round-trips to Portland, Maine, is the only Amtrak train which departs Boston from North Station (MBTA Green and Orange Lines). Schedules change every 2-3 months, so check the website for the latest timetable.

Chicago is the hub of the American rail network; connect there for scenic transcontinental trains to Seattle, San Francisco, and Los Angeles. For trips south to New Orleans and Florida or points between, it is faster to connect at New York or Washington. The *Auto Train* provides a unique experience, picking up you (and your car) in Virginia and dropping both off in Florida the next morning, refreshed and ready to tackle Space Mountain. On long-distance trains, Amtrak operates on track owned by freight railroads, so be prepared for delays. Sleepers are available but priced similarly to hotel rooms.

Amtrak often has very cheap tickets on less-traveled segments; check the Rail Sale section of the Amtrak website for these discounts. Most western trains are double-deckers, from which you can get incredible views of mountains, prairies, and oceans (white with foam). Amtrak's funding is subject to battles in Congress, so these opportunities may not be around forever.

SafeRide

If you need an escort across campus, or to a number of off-campus locations, use the free SafeRide service operated by the MIT Parking and Transportation Office (x8-6510). It is composed of a set of vans that travel in set routes over the campus and to many of the ILGs across the river. There are four vans: Cambridge East and West and Boston East and West. The routes take about 20-25 minutes. Maps and schedules can be obtained from Campus Police or from the front desks in most dorms, and also linked from SafeRide's web.mit.edu/parking/saferide.html web page. SafeRide operates 7 days a week, from 6 PM to 3 AM Sunday through Wednesday and 6 PM to 4 AM Thursday through Saturday.

Walking

Hitchhiking

Although hitchhiking may be a popular way to get around, it is illegal in Boston, Cambridge, and other cities. Enforcement, however, seems to be left up to the whim of the particular policeman. Your hair length, number of holes in your clothes (and face), and the policeman's disposition must be taken into account. Usually, the police will ask violators to stop and will not bother to issue tickets. Laws and penalties vary from one jurisdiction to the next.

Unfortunately, police are not the only hazard to hitchhikers. There have been a number of students (drivers and hitchhikers) shot or robbed. It takes a lot of nerve for even a gorilla to hitchhike in some neighborhoods.

If you haven't hitchhiked before, Boston isn't the place to start. If you plan on hitchhiking anyway, remember that you are taking your life into your own hands. It's usually worth the money spent to avoid playing Russian Roulette.

Actual Walking

Compared with many other cities, Boston is a city of microscopic distances, and walking is often the easiest form of transportation. During rush hour it may be faster than driving, especially from here to Harvard Square. Another advantage of walking is that you get a chance to meet people and see shops and activities you would otherwise miss.

If you are walking at night, find a friend or two to go with you, especially if you are going off campus or into an unknown area. Otherwise, use your common sense. Boston and Cambridge have high crime rates. Use only well-lit, well-traveled streets; don't take shortcuts. Even if you plan to avoid the notorious Combat Zone (which doesn't really exist any more, but treat it as a back-in-the-day reference to anywhere sketchy), remember that just walking along Memorial Drive to look at the river by moonlight can be deadly. The Campus Police can give you information about danger zones around the MIT campus.

Sightseeing

Every once in a while you may feel like playing tourist. MIT is located near many museums and sights in and around the fun-filled city of Boston. There are many wonderful ways to get away from the Institute when the pressures of the term are getting to you. (It's also a good, neutral thing to do to keep parents occupied.)

Resources

The *Boston Phoenix* is Boston's larger free alternative weekly released on Thursdays. Besides the usual cartoons and local politics, it has a complete listing of the week's events, as well as criticism and reviews of larger concerts and plays. The *Weekly Dig* is a smaller alternative weekly, available on Wednesdays, which also publishes weekly events listings, as well as reviews of smaller and more obscure shows and releases. *Calendar*, published in the Thursday *Boston Globe*, is yet another source of event listings. You may be fooled into thinking *Stuff@Night* to be a source of information on events, but beware — it is little more than a vehicle for night club advertisements. There are many more general guides to Boston available from travel agencies, most hotel lobbies, the Boston Chamber of Commerce, and other groups. A wide variety of topical (*e.g.*, dining out, hiking, biking) and general guidebooks to Boston and Cambridge are available at most bookstores.

For free maps, brochures on most tourist attractions, and information on current happenings in the city, visit one of the following information booths. The Greater Boston Convention and Visitor's Bureau (1-888-SEE-BOSTON; www.bostonusa.com) operates the **Boston Common Information Center** on the Common near the Park Street T station, which is also where the Freedom Trail (see below) starts. It is open daily Monday-Saturday 8:30am -5pm , Sunday 10am -6pm . You can also stop by their headquarters at the plaza level of the Prudential Plaza, open Monday-Saturday 9am -8pm , Sunday 10am -6pm . The **National Park Service Visitor Center** (617-242-5642), located across from the Old State House on 15 State Street, near State Street T, operates 7 days a week from 9-5.

The MIT Activities Committee (MITAC) is also a good resource for tourist information regarding Boston. Their office is located in building 32, and is open Tues-Fri 11am-4pm. MITAC frequently provides discounts on admission to local events and performances. They have a somewhat barren list of "things to do in New England" at web.mit.edu/mitac/travel.html and a more useful list of available discounts at web.mit.edu/mitac/events.html.

Other Information Kiosks:

At Faneuil Hall Marketplace between Quincy Market and the South Market Building. It's outdoors and staffed in the spring, summer, and fall Monday through Saturday 10am to 6pm, Sunday noon to 6pm.

In Harvard Square, Cambridge, near the T entrance at the intersection of Mass. Ave., John F. Kennedy Street, and Brattle Street is another booth (www.cambridge-usa.org). It's open Monday through Saturday 9am-5pm, Sunday 1-5pm.

In Boston near the Theatre District, there is an information kiosk run by the Commonwealth Dept. of Commerce (617-727-3201), open only on weekdays 9-5, located at 10 Park Plaza.

Tours of Boston

Most of the sights in Boston are within walking distance and can be covered in a day. A word of caution regarding wandering in Boston: Boston is a big American city and therefore has some dangerous neighborhoods, particularly after dark. Roxbury, Mattapan, parts of Dorchester, parts of the South End, and the areas around Northeastern University (south of Symphony Hall) are bad places to be at night. The North End, Charlestown, and South Boston are dangerous for minorities and nonconformists ("freaks") after dark. Certain sections of Cambridge are also pretty grubby, though not so bad as some of the preceding areas. *Don't* go wandering off in these areas unless you know what you are doing. This warning applies especially to students and staff who may not be used to the concept of dangerous neighborhoods in a city. Also, watch your wallet in crowded areas such as Faneuil Hall and Harvard Square.

There are many bus and boat tours of Boston which are good for orientation, fun, and packing off the parents for a few hours when they come to town. Check out the amphibious **Duck Tours** (617-267-3825, www.bostonducktours.com), which embark at Prudential Center and the Museum of Science, and the **BeanTown Trolley** (617-720-6342, www.beantowntrolley.com), which stops at Kendall. Information about various cruises around the Boston Harbor, including the Lighthouse and Whalewatch Cruises, is available at www.bostonboats.com. MITAC offers discounts on some walking and boating tours, such as the Duck Tours or the Charles Riverboat Sightseeing Tours (charlesriverboat.com). For more information, check the MITAC events and discounts page (web.mit.edu/mitac/events.html), the Yellow Pages under "Sightseeing Tours" for more information, or grab a brochure from one of the booths in Kendall Square.

The Freedom Trail

One of the most popular ways to become familiar with the sights of Boston and brush up on your American history is to walk the Freedom Trail. The Freedom Trail — marked along its entire route by a large red stripe running down the center of the sidewalk — is a 2.5 mile path that runs from the Boston Common to the Bunker Hill Monument. Along the way are 16 historical sights relating to America's struggle for independence — the State House, Park Street Church, Granary Burying Ground, Kings' Chapel, the site of the first Public School, the Old Corner Book Store, Old South Meeting House, Old State House, Boston Massacre site, Quincy Market, Faneuil Hall, the Paul Revere house, Old North Church, Copps' Hill Burial Ground, *U.S.S. Constitution*, and Bunker Hill monument. Ninety-minute tours begin at the Visitor Center at 15 State Street and cover the heart of the Freedom Trail from the Old South Meeting House to the Old North Church. Tours leave at regular intervals during the spring, summer, and fall, weather permitting. Call 617-242-5642 for daily schedule or tour reservations.

Many of the sites close at 4:30pm, so start at least 3 hours earlier to allow enough time. The trail starts at the Boston Common, near the Park Street T Station. Then just follow the red path. It's a good idea to stop at the Information Kiosk and get a guide and a map, but it will cost you $1.50. Most of the attractions are free, but a few of the major sites will charge a small admission fee. Many will give you discounts for an MIT ID.

The **Boston Common** is the oldest public park in the U.S., and is located in the center of Boston. You can no longer graze your cow there (if you have one), but it is a pleasant grassy park filled with a wide variety of people and activities every day of the year. One of the best spots for people watching and squirrel fishing.

Free tours of the gold-domed **State House** (617-727-3676) on Beacon and Park at the edge of the Common are given Mon-Fri 10am -4pm .

Old South Meeting House (310 Washington at Mild St.; 617-482-6439; MBTA: State) is one of Boston's three remaining 18th century Anglican churches. It is now a National Historic Landmark. The Boston Tea Party began at "Old South." Across the street from the Gift Shop is **Ben Franklin's Birthplace**. Hours: daily 9:30am-5:00pm April through October. Open 10:00am-4:00pm weekdays; 10:00am-5:00pm, weekends November through March. Admission: Students $4, General $5.

The **Old State House** (corner of Washington and State; 617-720-1713; MBTA: State), the center of colonial government, is the city's oldest surviving public building, now a museum open to visitors. It was in front of this building that the Boston Massacre occurred. Hours: 9-5. Admission: students, $4, general $5.

Quincy Market and **Faneuil Hall** (MBTA: Government Center) are a great mix of old and new on the Freedom Trail. These newly refurbished structures are now the Greatest Place on Earth to be with full wallet and an empty stomach. The buildings accommodate booths and booths and booths of food, food, and more food as well as lots of "cute" shops designed to part you from your money. A native Bostonian once said that Heaven smells like Quincy Market, and this statement has rarely been disputed. But the area is, of course, a tourist trap, so be prepared to pay for its appetizing offerings. Faneuil Hall houses Durgin Park Market Dining Room (888-766-6528), which is a historical sight itself. Most shops in the Marketplace are open Mon-Sat 10-9 and Sun 12-6.

The **Paul Revere House** (19 North Square in the North End; 617-523-2338; MBTA: Haymarket), built in 1676 and now restored to its original appearance, is the oldest dwelling in Boston. Hours: 9:30-5:15 (4:15 in winter until April 15) daily. Admission: $2.50 student (with ID), general $3.

Built in 1723, the **Old North Church** (193 Salem St, 617-523-6676, www.oldnorth.com; MBTA: Haymarket) is the oldest church building in Boston, and today continues to serve a thriving Episcopal congregation. The belfry of the Old North Church is the very tower in which lanterns were hung ("one if by and and two if by sea") to inform Paul Revere of the British advance as he began his famous midnight ride to rouse Lexington and Concord. Today MIT students climb the very same belfry to practice change ringing. Hours: daily summer 9am-6pm, winter 9am-5pm).

The **U.S.S. Constitution** (617- 242-5670; MBTA: Haymarket, then take the #92 or #93 bus to Charlestown City Square or take the Orange Line to Community College) received her nickname, "Old Ironsides," during the War of 1812, when cannonballs bounced off her stout wooden sides in a battle with HMS Guerrière. The Constitution mostly stays put, but remains capable of sailing under her own power and is the world's oldest commissioned warship. "Old Ironsides" is on the Freedom Trail but located in the Charlestown Navy Yard. Hours: summer daily 10:00am-4:00pm, winter Thu-Sun 10:00am-4:00pm. Tours of the ship are free every half hour from 10:30am to 3:30pm. Also in the Navy Yard is the *U.S.S. Constitution* Museum (617-426-1812). The Museum is free and open 9:00am to 6:00pm in the summer; 10:00am to 4:00pm in the winter. Entry is free.

   Bunker Hill Monument (617-242-5641; MBTA: Community College on the Orange Line) is at the end of the Freedom Trail. The 221-foot landmark is free to anyone interested in climbing 294 dark, damp steps. It offers a great view of Charlestown, Boston, the Harbor, and the rivers. Worth the climb if you can make it. Hours: 9-4:30 daily. A 10-minute walk away at the **Bunker Hill Pavilion** (55 Constitution Road, Charlestown; 617-241-7575; on the Freedom Trail), the Battle of Bunker Hill is recreated through sight, sound, and other theatrical effects. Hours 9:30-4.30 Summer, 9:30-4 Spring and Fall, Closed December-March. Admission is free.

Black Heritage Trail

   Another do-it-yourself walking tour of Boston, this one explores the history of Boston's black community as a center of the abolitionist movement. The **Museum of Afro-American History** (8 Smith Court; 617-739-1200) and the **Boston African American History Site** (46 Joy Street; 617-742-5415, call for group and scheduled guided tours) offers self-guided tour maps that begin on the Boston Common and end at Beacon Hill. Hours: 10-4 every day in the summer, closed Sundays from Labor Day to Memorial Day.

Harborwalk

   The Boston Harborwalk (www.bostonharborwalk.com) is the newest walking tour and, as such, is not completely finished. It is similar to the Freedom Trail, but the Harborwalk follows a blue stripe and focuses on the city's maritime past. It winds through the downtown districts, stretching along the East Boston, Charlestown, North End, Downtown, South Boston and Dorchester neighborhoods from Chelsea Creek to the Neponset River. The southern stretch is also lined with some nice beaches. Check out the *Beaches* section in the **Athletics** chapter.

Some Other Interesting Places

   The **Back Bay** was a sewage-saturated swamp filled over 100 years ago to produce some 580 acres of residential area. The broad, straight avenues that cross the area are, shockingly for Boston, laid out in a rational (alphabetical) manner. The **Back Bay Fens** (near Fenway Park, Simmons College, and the Museum of Fine Arts) is a nice park with ducks to feed (and very polluted water). It is not, however, a safe place to be wandering at night. There are also some Victory Gardens left from World War II, which are still maintained by private citizens. Boylston Street has many boutiques and other stores, and Newbury Street is a bustling boutique avenue with art galleries, restaurants, ice cream stores and record shops. Commonwealth Avenue between Mass. Ave. and the

Public Garden is a divided roadway with a shaded mall down the middle. The Boston bank of the Charles River is great for picnics and sunbathing. The tree-lined **Esplanade**, a long string of linear islands, is great for walking trips and relaxation. During the summer, the Boston Pops and other groups give free concerts at the Hatch Shell there.

Christian Science Center

Just southwest of the Prudential is a collection of modern buildings associated with the "Mother Church" of this religious group. Tours of the buildings are given when they are not in use, and the reception given to non-members is low-key and friendly. Of special note are the Mapparium, a huge stained-glass globe which allows you to view things "from the center of the Earth," and the Sunday School, an unusual architectural work. There is also a large reflecting pool outside the Christian Science Center (617-450-3793). The pool and buildings are located just a walk down Mass. Ave. at the corner of Huntington (Symphony stop on the #1 bus). Open: Monday-Saturday 10-4, Sundays 11:15-2. General admission to the Mapparium is $5, while students get in for $3.

City Hall

The City Hall at Government Center (617-635-4000, open Mon-Fri 8:30-5, MBTA: Government Center) in the heart of Boston is what some would describe as "an architectural abomination that makes MIT's recently-constructed Stata center and Simmons dormitory look elegant and tasteful." Tours are given on weekdays, but call for a time.

Copley Place

Copley Place is a beautiful mall complete with marble floors, a waterfall, and upscale boutiques (Neiman-Marcus, Tiffany, and Godiva Chocolate, to name a few). It is connected by a covered skybridge to the mall at Prudential Center. This is a good place for eating, people watching, and shopping indoors. Nearby are the somewhat less commercial attractions of Copley Square — namely, Trinity Church and the main branch of the Boston Public Library, which is the oldest circulating public library in America.

Kenmore Square

Slightly further west, at the intersection of Beacon Street, Comm. Ave., Brookline Ave., and three other streets, is the driver's nightmare called Kenmore Square. The area caters to BU and Northeastern students. It is built up and becoming more so, with shops ranging from hamburger joints to boutiques and nightclubs. It's a nice place to visit on foot if you like watching crowds of people, particularly if you like watching drivers in hysterics.

Chinatown

Boston's Chinatown is America's third largest. It is located between Beach, Harrison, Tyler, and Hudson Streets, and it's a great place to eat or visit. It's on the Orange Line, but it is a short walk down Washington Street from Downtown Crossing/Park Street, or down Beach Street from South Station. There are many Chinese grocery shops, bakeries, and late-night eateries here. From time to time, there are street celebrations featuring fireworks and dancing dragons sponsored by community groups. On weekend mornings, most restaurants serve dim sum, a meal consisting of tea and small delicacies.

Davis Square

Davis Square (MBTA: Davis) is the hippie-yet-quickly-gentrifying neighborhood Harvard Square was 20 years ago. Full of coffeeshops, great restaurants and bars, and used book, record and clothing stores, this is a great Red Line stop to explore when MIT is grinding you down.

Harvard Square

Harvard Square has a lot of visual appeal for a walking tour, with huge crowds of all descriptions, a tremendous variety of stores, and solicitors of all (and we do mean all) types looking for your support. The architecture around Harvard is also interesting, ranging from staid Colonial to futuristic. The banks of the Charles are pretty pleasant here, with less pollution than the area around MIT and big grassy areas on either side. Tour **Harvard** yourself or pretend to be a prefrosh and take a structured tour from the Holyoke Information Center, 1350 Mass. Ave. (617-495-1573). They also offer tours for the general public twice daily (10,11:15,2 and 3 Mon-Sat). This is the office to approach for a (free) map of the Harvard campus.

You may also want to visit the **Cambridge Common** just north of Harvard Yard where Washington took control of the Continental Army in 1775. There are often free impromptu concerts on the Common, and there are scheduled concerts on most summer Sunday afternoons at 2pm .

Public Garden

Just west of the Boston Common, across Charles Street, is the 24-acre Public Garden. Here, visitors will find many labeled trees, rare flowers, lots of birds, and a pond. In the summer, for $2, you can ride on the swan boats in the pond. It's a wonderfully romantic way to be silly. In the winter, bring your skates and enjoy some outdoor skating. If it's a view you're looking for and not a tour, climb a building.

Mount Auburn Cemetery

Mount Auburn Cemetery (580 Mt Auburn St, 617 547 7105, www.mountauburn.org) is a beautiful place to wander without having to worry about cars. The city is visible from the top of one of the hills, and a number of interesting people are buried there, including everyone's favorite mathematician/architect, Buckminster Fuller. The cemetery is open from 8am to 5pm every day, and is open until 7pm from May to September. Pets are not permitted, and visitors are requested to be respectful of the grounds. Either MBTA bus #71 or #73 from Harvard Square will drop you off right outside the entrance on Mt Auburn St, at the corner of Aberdeen Ave.

Prudential Center

"The Pru" or Prudential Center (800 Boylston, 617-859-0648, MBTA: Prudential) is 52 stories of glass and steel. For $7 you can get a panoramic view of the city from the 50th floor observation deck. With pay telescopes, you can see New Hampshire and the White Mountains on a clear day. Hours: 10am-9pm every day. Several blocks away at Copley Square is the **John Hancock Building**, New England's tallest building. Designed by renowned architect and MIT graduate I. M. Pei, the Pru's windows originally had a dismaying tendency to detach themselves from the building and plummet to the ground during high winds. The Observatory deck at the top, which used to feature a fascinating narrated exhibit of Boston in the Revolutionary War in addition to its lofty view, is sadly closed for the foreseeable future due to terrorism hysteria. Prospects for reopening are grim.

Harbor Islands

The islands off Boston Harbor have several neat forts, fort ruins and other good stuff to see on a relaxing day trip.

The Great Outdoors (or, "the Yellow Face, She Burns!")

Should you tire of Boston's urban squalor, the surrounding countryside is full of places to hike, picnic, boat, and otherwise enjoy nature. Detailed information about outdoor recreation (including canoeing, fishing, hiking, mountain biking, and swimming) is available in the **Athletics** chapter. Information about all public parks and reservations in the Boston area can be found at `www.mass.gov/mdc`. Information about a few of the reservations nearest to Boston follows:

Harbor Islands

The islands off Boston Harbor (`www.bostanislands.org`) feature beaches with beautiful views, historical ruins, wildlife preserves, and some easy hiking. A ferry can take you from a wharf near the Boston Aquarium to Georges Island, site of Fort Warren. From Georges Island, water taxis to various smaller islands are available free of charge. A round-trip ferry ticket costs $10, and group rates are available. See the *Beaches* section of the **Athletics** chapter for more information about these and other oceanside destinations.

Blue Hills

The Blue Hills Reservation (1904 Canton Ave., Milton 617-698-1802), located about 11 miles from Boston, was one of the first reservations set aside for public recreation. The Blue Hills reservation consists of 6,500 acres of woods, meadows, and ponds, crossed by more than 200 miles of trails. Unfortunately, the reservation's Milton location makes it almost inaccessible to those without a car. Should you make it there, however, be sure to climb to the top of Big Blue Hill for an excellent view of Boston from the **Blue Hill Weather Observatory and Science Museum** (617-696-0389).

Trailside Museum

The Trailside Museum (1904 Canton Ave., Milton, 617-333-0690) is located in the Blue Hills Reservation, and is thus virtually inaccessible without a car. Should you make it to the Blue Hills, however, the museum may be worth visiting. It features exhibits about native New England (squirrels, rabbits, deer, more squirrels, foxes, etc). The museum is managed by the Massachusetts Audubon Society. Hours: Wed-Sun and holidays 10-5. Admission: $3; children under 12, $1.50.

Arnold Arboretum

(125 Arborway, Jamaica Plain at the junction of Jamaicaway, Rte. 1 and the Arborway, MBTA: Forest Hills, 617-524-1718, `arboretum.harvard.edu`) is a beautiful 265-acre park filled with over 6000 labeled varieties of trees, vines, and flowers. "No bicycling or picnicking, except on Lilac Sunday in May". On most days, simply walking through the park and taking pictures can fill hours. Hours: Weekdays 9-4, Sat 10-4, Sun 12-4. Admission: free.

Critter Watching

Aquarium

The New England Aquarium (State St. at Atlantic Ave., on the waterfront in Boston, 617-973-5200; www.neaq.org, MBTA: Aquarium) has impressive marine exhibits, including an enormous cylindrical tank with glass walls 2.5 inches thick in which sharks, groupers, sea turtles, and other large marine life live together, calmly ignoring the stares of visitors. Dolphin/sea lion shows daily. Tickets to whale watching tours and IMAX movies are also available. Winter Hours: Mon-Fri 9am-5pm, Sat, Sun, and holidays 9am-6pm. Summer Hours (July 1 to Labor Day): Mon-Thu 9am-6pm, Fri-Sun and holidays 9am-7pm. Admission: $15.95 for adults although tickets are a mere $6 if you purchase them in advance from the MITAC office in building 32. Admission is free for members (who pay an annual fee of $45/individual or $80/family.)

Franklin Park Zoo

(Blue Hill Ave. & Columbia Rd., Dorchester; MBTA: Forest Hills, then #16 bus to entrance) is filled with hundreds of animals and birds and thousands of children every day. There are many exhibits of Australian and African animals. The **Children's Zoo**, also in Franklin Park, allows children to mix with and feed small, tame animals. The Butterfly Landing is open from June to September. The area is dangerous at night but reasonably safe during daylight. Hours: Apr-Sep 10am-5pm daily, weekends 10am-6pm ; Oct-Mar 10am-4pm daily. Admission: adults $9.50, children $5. Call 617-541-LION for recorded information or visit www.zoonewengland.com.

Museums

Museum of Fine Arts

Boston is richly endowed with museums, but one of the best is the Museum of Fine Arts (465 Huntington Ave., Boston by the Fenway; MBTA: Museum of Fine Arts stop Green E Line, 617-267-9300, www.mfa.org). This museum boasts one of the finer collections of Oriental art in the Western World, excellent selections of Mediterranean and Renaissance art, and some fine French impressionistic works. They also have an impressive collection of American art, most notably the works of Winslow Homer and other colonial artists. There are often special shows, for which you must pay extra, of selected classical and contemporary artists in some of the more secluded galleries. The museum also holds concerts, films, lectures, classes, and children's events. The MFA is worth repeated and thorough trips. Hours: Mon & Tues 10am-4:45pm; Wed 10am-9:45pm; Thurs & Fri 10am-5pm; Sat & Sun 10am-4:45pm, selected galleries only Thurs-Fri 5am-9:45pm. Admission: free with an MIT student ID with 10% discount in the gift store; for adults $15 (good for two visits in 30 days), kids under 17 free during non-school hours.

Isabella Stewart Gardner Museum

The Gardner (280 The Fenway, one block from MFA, 617-566-1401, www.gardnermusuem.org, MBTA: Museum of Fine Arts stop) is patterned after a sixteenth-century Venetian palace. It was once the home of the flamboyant Mrs. Jack Gardner and is stocked with her collection of nearly 200 pieces of Renaissance Italian art, with a scattering of items from other lands and periods. The artwork is placed in strange combinations and juxtapositions and is often poorly illuminated; her will stipulated that nothing be changed. The collection includes paintings, sculpture, tapestries, furniture, ceramics, rare books and manuscripts. There is a beautiful indoor garden growing all year at the core of the building. In the fall, an excellent series of chamber music concerts is given Sundays at 1:30), and there are jazz performances on the first Saturday of every month at 1:30. Museum hours: Tues-Sun 11-5, also open some Monday and holidays. Admission: students $5 (student ticket for both concert and museum is $10); adults $10 ($11 on weekends). In memory of the museum's benefactress, all people named Isabella (exact spelling required) are admitted for free. Call 617-734-1359 for recorded information on upcoming concert programs.

Institute of Contemporary Art

The ICA (955 Boylston St., Boston, 617-266-5152, www.icaboston.org, MBTA: Hynes Convention/ICA) sponsors exhibits by contemporary artists, lectures, and special events such as children's art shows. Hours: Sat-Sun 11-5, Wed-Fri 12-5, Thurs 12-9. Admission: $7, $5 for students; free Thursdays 5-9.

Science Museum

The Museum of Science (Science Park, on the Charles River Dam between East Cambridge and Boston, 617-723-2500; www.mos.org; MBTA: Science Park) exhibits objects of a scientific bent, notably a step-by-step model of an appendectomy, a beehive, an alcohol cloud chamber, and strobe displays. They also have the impressive Theatre of Electricity, containing a two-megavolt Van der Graaf generator and other hands-on exhibits. The renowned **Hayden Planetarium** is also part of the museum. Planetarium and OMNIMAX shows are $8, with some discounts for later showings. The museum is always looking for student volunteers — for more information call 617-723-2500. Cost: MIT students get in free to the exhibits with MIT ID, general admission $13. Hours: Summer July 5 to Labor Day Sat-Thurs 9am-7pm; Fri 9am-9pm. Day after Labor Day to July 4 Sat-Thurs 9am-5pm; All Fridays 9am-9pm.

Museum Wharf

Following the milk-bottle-shaped signs downtown should bring you to the forty-foot Hood Milk Bottle (where one can, unsurprisingly, buy ice cream and frozen yogurt) and to Museum Wharf (300 Congress St., Boston, 617-426-8855; MBTA: South Station; www.bostonkids.org), the home of a rather unusual museum. The **Children's Museum** (300 Congress St., Boston, 617-426-8855, www.bostonkids.org; MBTA: South Station) is designed to let children 2-12 years of age learn about the world around them through "hands-on" activities. In a series of immersive exhibits, the curious can learn about other cultures, various environmental concepts, arts and crafts, or simply play in the massive mazes and jungle gyms. They have an educational miniature golf game, too! Hours: daily 10-5, Fri 10-9. Admission: adults $8, seniors and children $7, children under one $1. Fri night from 5-9, everyone pays $1.

The **Boston Tea Party Ship and Museum** (Congress Street Bridge; 617-338-1773; MBTA: South Station or via the free Tea Party Courtesy Shuttle from the Old State House; www.bostonteapartyship.com) is a full-sized working replica of the Beaver II, one of the ships raided by the colonial "Indians" in the protest against British taxes. Hours: 9-5 in Fall and Spring, 9-6 in summer. Admission: $7 with student ID. Unfortunately, due to fire, the museum is still closed for the 2004 season.

JFK Birthplace

Across the BU Bridge, and very near the ZBT fraternity house, is the John F. Kennedy Birthplace (83 Beals St., 617-566-7937; www.nps.gov/jofi; MBTA: Green Line C to Coolidge Corner). This restored house should send just about everyone's family through oceans of nostalgia. If you wish to learn more about the Kennedy family, however, the **JFK Library** (617-514-1600; www.jfklibrary.org; MBTA: JFK/UMass) is out in Dorchester. Admission to the Birthplace is $3. Hours: Wed-Sun 10-4:30 daily, guided tours every half-hour from 10-3:30pm , closed mid-Nov. to March.

Harvard University Museums

Following are brief descriptions, which in no way do justice to the museums. All are fascinating and merit repeated visits.

The **Harvard Museum of Natural History** (617-495-3045, www.hmnh.harvard.edu/) encompasses the following three museums and is affiliated with the fourth. They are part of the same complex (entrances at 26 Oxford St. and 11 Divinity Ave.). Unless otherwise noted, there is an admission charge of $7.50 adult/$6 student, free Sun 9-12, free after-school Wednesdays 3 to 5pm September through May. Harvard ID holders and one guest are also admitted free. The Harvard Hot Ticket (good for one year) is available for $10 adults/$8 students to visit each of the Harvard museums. Hours are 9-5 daily:

- *Museum of Comparative Zoology* (617-495-3045) features dinosaurs and stuffed animals.

- *Botanical Museum* (617-495-2365) features a renowned display of glass flowers.

- *Mineralogical Museum* (617-495-3045) offers mineral exhibits.

- *Peabody Museum of Archaeology and Ethnology* (617-496-1027) is an anthropological museum with many Indian artifacts.

The **Harvard University Art Collection** (617-495-9400) is distributed among the following museums. The Harvard Art collections are open from Mon-Sat 10am-5pm, and Sun 1-5pm, except where noted. They are closed most major holidays. The museums are free Saturday mornings until noon.

- *Fogg Art Museum* (32 Quincy St. near Broadway,), built in the style of an Indian Palace, houses Harvard's extensive permanent art collection in addition to a wealth of temporary exhibits.

- *Busch-Reisinger Museum* (32 Quincy St., enter through the Fogg), a reconstructed Gothic cathedral, displays medieval German art.

- *Sackler Museum* (485 Broadway at Quincy St.) is devoted to Oriental and Islamic art.

- *Semitic Museum* (6 Divinity Ave., 617-495-5631), a museum featuring Mideast cultural exhibits. Hours: Mon-Fri 10-4, some Sundays 1-4. Admission: free.

- *Carpenter Visual Arts Center* (617-495-3251) at Harvard (24 Quincy St.) is the only building in North America designed by Le Corbusier. It is affiliated with the Peabody, but usually contains art exhibits. You can often watch artists at work, too.

Other Museums

If you are feeling particularly adventurous, the **Massachusetts Museum of Contemporary Art** (87 Marshall Street, North Adams; 413-664-4481; www.massmoca.org) may be 130 miles from Boston, but it is well worth the trip. Beyond the exhibits — which are generally novel and intriguing — Mass MoCA is dedicated to presenting the art making process including rehearsals, sculptural fabrication, and developmental workshops. Hours: daily 10am- 6pm in the summer, closed Tuesdays in the fall and winter, 11am-5pm. Admission: $10 for adults, $8 for students.

You will probably want a car to get to the **De Cordova Art Museum** (51 Sandy Pond Road, Lincoln, 781-259-8355, www.decordova.org), although it's a pleasant one-hour bike ride from MIT or a two-mile walk from the Lincoln commuter line train station. The trip is worthwhile; the museum is in a beautifully remodeled house set among 30 acres of parkland. It presents lectures, exhibitions by local artists, classes, films, and other educational activities. Hours: Tues-Sun 11-5, and selected Mondays. Admission: $6 for adults, $4 for those with college ID; there is an additional charge for the concerts on Sunday. Free admission to the sculpture park, open during daylight hours.

The Museum of Printing (800 Massachusetts Avenue, North Andover, 978-686-0450, www.museumofprinting.org) is a must-see for anyone interested in the evolution of the printed word. They have an amazing collection of printing machinery ranging from early hand presses, to (working!) Linotypes, to the first phototypesetters and the dawn of the digital age. Exhibits show how letters have been made from the time of Gutenberg to the present, with one of the most fascinating collections being the Merganthaler international font library, meticulously hand-drawn by artisans over the first half of the 20th century. The manager of the museum is extremely personable and a delight to speak with, and will often give you a remarkable guided tour if you strike up a conversation. Unfortunately, a car is required to get out there — see the website for directions. Hours: Wed-Sat 10-5 and by appointment. Student admission $3, regular adult admission $5, members free with 10% discount at museum shop (membership $25 per year individual, $50 per year family).

The Museum of Bad Art (MOBA, 580 High Street in Dedham Center, Dedham, 781-326-0409; MBTA: Orange Line to Forrest Hills, www.museumofbadart.org) is a gallery featureing "art too bad to be ignored." It is located in the basement of the Dedham Community Theater and is staffed and curated by volunteers. Expect to spend your visit inspecting the worst artwork Salvation Army stores have to offer, leavened by MOBA's tongue-in-cheek commentary. Hours: Mon-Fri 6-10pm, Sat-Sun 1-10pm. Free admission.

Museums at MIT

The **MIT Museum** (2nd floor, 265 Massachusetts Avenue, building N52, 617-253-4444; web.mit.edu/museum/) has displays pertaining to the history of science, technology and MIT, important MIT figures such as Harold "Doc" Edgerton, special exhibits such as holography, robotics and 2003's "The Winning Hand: Images

From The MIT Radiation Laboratory Negative Collection", and fascinating kinetic sculptures by Arthur Ganson. The MIT Museum also has two galleries separate from the main museum: the Compton Gallery and the Hart Nautical Gallery. Tue-Fri 10-5, Sat-Sun 12-5, closed Mondays and holidays. Admission is free with MIT ID, general admission $5. The MIT Museum can also be booked for meetings and special events.

The **Compton Gallery** (first floor of Building 10, open 9:30am-5pm weekdays) is part of the MIT Museum, has free admission and an information line (617-253-4444). Recent exhibits include scenery and props from MIT theatrical productions, architectural models, drawings and photographs of Simmons Hall, and "Hacks are Back!". Exhibits change every month or so.

The **Hart Nautical Museum** (building 5 at 55 Mass. Ave, open daily 9-8, 617-253-4444) houses detailed wooden models of ships and pictorial reports on advances in ocean engineering. Admission is free.

The **List Visual Arts Center** is home to the **Hayden Gallery** (atrium of the Media Lab building E15, 20 Ames St, 617-253-4680, web.mit.edu/lvac/www/) and houses temporary exhibits of works by contemporary artists. It is widely considered one of the better galleries in Boston. The List's gallery hours are Tue-Thu, Sat and Sun 12-6pm, Fri 12-8pm. A free map is available at the Visual Arts Center if you wish to take a self-guided tour of the public artworks and buildings around campus, or visit the website at web.mit.edu/lvac/www/collections/map.html to print your own. Group guided tours of exhibitions and of the outdoor public sculptures may be arranged by calling 617-253-4400. The List also offers an annual Student Loan Art Program, where students may enter a lottery (usually held in September) to borrow art from the List collection for display in their dorm rooms for one year.

The **Wiesner Student Art Gallery** is located on the 2nd floor of the Student Center (W20) and is open 24 hours a day. The gallery is only for student exhibitions, whether they be academic, co-curricular or projects supported by the Council for the Arts. Exhibit applications are available at The Council for the Arts at MIT (E15-205), the Student Art Association (W20-429), and the Campus Activities Complex (W20-500).

There are also numerous exhibits of varying types tucked in Main Campus and the Infinite Corridor that can be worth wandering past:

Displays along the Infinite Corridor and other first-floor hallways generally relate to MIT's history, programs and environment. Hallways on higher floors and those in out-of-the-way places show interesting aspects of work done in their respective regions. For instance, the fourth floor of building 4 outside of the late Doc Edgerton's strobe lab (affectionately called Strobe Alley) is full of strobe photographs and related devices.

Outdoor sculptures dot the campus, particularly around Hayden Library, Killian Court, and in front of the Med Center. Most notable is the Great Sail sculpture by Alexander Calder, which is located in front of the Dot, outside the Green Building (building 54).

Art Galleries

Lastly, there are a fair number of contemporary art galleries in and around Boston. Some are traditional, while others are very avant-garde. They are fun to visit and a few host a variety of performances, concerts, and screenings as well. Unfortunately, clashes over zoning laws have recently forced several of the most innovative galleries, including the **Oni Gallery** and the **Berwick Research Institute** (www.berwickinstitute.org) to close or go on indefinite hiatus. The most notable remaining local avant garde gallery is the **Zeitgeist Gallery** (1353 Cambridge St., Inman Square, 617-876-6060, www.zeitgeist-gallery.org), which has a fantastic array of events. Nearby, the **Gallery Bershard** (99 Dover St., 617-629-9500) focuses primarily on local, up-and-coming artists. The **Fort Point Art Community**, an organization for the large artcommunity of the Fort Point Channel neighborhood, operates its own gallery (300 Summer St. M1, 617-423-4299, www.fortpointarts.org), focusing on works created by members of the FPAC. Exhibits by more established and traditional artists tend to occur in the galleries and salons of Newbury Street. The **Chase Gallery** (129 Newbury St., 617-859-7222, www.chasegallery.com), the **Martin Lawrence Galleria** (77 Newbury St., 617-369-4800, www.martinlawrence.com/), and the **Pepper Gallery** (38 Newbury St., 617-236-4497, www.peppergalleryboston.com) are all good places to start. For complete listings of galleries and current showings in the Boston area, try the *Boston Phoenix* or the *Weekly Dig*.

Entertainment

Boston, being both a real city and a multi-college town, offers an unparalleled selection of theater groups, concerts, professional and amateur sports, bars, clubs, and other ways to entertain yourself.

Resources

There are many newspapers which carry listings for plays and movies. Perhaps the best is the *Boston Globe Calendar* (www.boston.com/globe/calendar/); it contains listings for most movies and professional plays in the Boston area, and capsule reviews of the movies. Unfortunately it doesn't have much about movies and plays showing at colleges. Another good source, with pretty much the same information as the *Calendar*, is the *Boston Phoenix* (www.bostonphoenix.com). It contains capsule reviews of plays as well as movies. For information on things showing in New York, the Sunday issue of the *New York Times* is your best bet.

The Tech carries fairly extensive arts listings and, along with *Tech Talk*, covers all MIT events. For Harvard events, the best newspaper for listings is probably the *Independent*, which you can find at the Mount Holyoke Information Center on Mass. Ave. It also reviews plays showing at Harvard. *The Crimson*, also available at Harvard, features a fairly literate, though at times pretentious, art section (formerly in their weekend rag, called *What Is To Be Done* in a strange nod to Vladimir Lenin). Posters can also be found at the Loeb Drama Center and scattered around campus. Often events will be announced only by poster so it is a good idea to look every now and then. Also, near the beginning of each play season, you may be able to find a copy of the *Drama Calendar*, which contains listings for most plays to be shown that season.

Other colleges list their events in their newspapers, as well as at various places around campus. For example, BU has listings of events on Commonwealth Avenue.

The MIT Activities Committee (MITAC) coordinates cultural and recreational activities for the MIT Community. Activites include hayrides, whale watching, sporting events, theatre and musical performances and more. They offer discounted tickets for skiing, golfing, movies and the New England Aquarium, and very frequently also offer discounts for Six Flags New England and other area attractions. MITAC is currently in the basement of Walker Memorial (50-005) but will move to the Stata Center (Building 32) and become part of a second Information Center location on the first floor near the Gates Lobby. Their current hours are Tuesday-Friday 11am-4pm. They accept cash, check (with MIT ID) and credit cards. You must present a valid MIT ID for all MITAC purchases. For more information email mitac-office@mit.edu or check out their website at web.mit.edu/mitac/. Their Walker Memorial number is x3-7990.

Music

Boston is one of the best cities for live music in the US. With some searching, you can hear good live music 7 days a week. Check out the *Boston Phoenix* and the *Weekly Dig*, free in newsstands everywhere (or at www.bostonphoenix.com and www.weeklydig.com respectively), for all the show listings you can read. The concert schedule maintained by WMBR (www.wmbr.org/cr.php) is usually the most up-to-date and complete listing of indie/punk/metal shows, and is read on the air at 9:15am and 11:30am on WMBR 88.1 FM every weekday morning. For local rock shows all around New England, check www.justanotherscene.com for listings and venue information. For only Boston and Providence shows, check www.bostonconcerts.com. If you're too lazy or too spontaneous to do any of the above, just walk through Central Square and keep your ears open.

Classical Music

The Boston Symphony Orchestra (BSO, www.bso.org), led by newly appointed James Levine, is one of the world's finest orchestras. This year is Levine's inaugural year and "audiences will have the rare opportunity to experience artistic synergy at its most exciting." Levine is the first American-born music director to grace the BSO. Also exciting for the 2004-2005 season, is the opportunity to hear the massive Aeolian-Skinner organ after a two-year, extensive renovation.

Concerts are given in Symphony Hall, perhaps the best hall in the United States (corner of Mass. Ave. and Huntington Ave., Boston; MBTA: Symphony), on Friday afternoons, Saturday nights, and assorted Tuesday and Thursday nights. They are divided into several series, which are sold on a subscription basis at Symphony Hall. There is also a set of eight open rehearsals. These feature unreserved seating, informal dress, a half hour lecture on the works to be performed, and a run-through and rehearsal of the coming Friday-Saturday pair's program.

Here are some ways to acquire tickets: First, you can buy a subscription for a series at Symphony Hall. This is rather expensive, but a good buy if you're planning on going to a lot of concerts. It offers a guaranteed location and renewal rights, if you know you'll be free and interested in going to all the concerts; you can sell the extra ones, but they are nonrefundable if you take them to the box office. For tickets to a particular concert, you can try the Symphony Hall box office (617-266-1200). They often have seats for sale for weeknight series, but they are at full marked price. Occasionally, an MIT community member will be unable to use his subscription seats on a given night; check the Music Library bulletin board for such announcements. Also, try the box office a few hours before a performance; subscription holders unable to attend often turn their tickets in for resale at the last minute. This is often the easiest way to get tickets, although they are still sold at full price. Symphony Hall also offers tickets cheaply through "rush seats" — a limited number of tickets are put on sale for only $8. To obtain rush tickets, you must go to Symphony Hall and buy them, in cash, when the tickets go on sale. Because there are only a limited number of tickets, it is important to get there well in advance. For more information on buying tickets, go to bso.org/genC/ticketingInfo.jhtml. The best way to obtain tickets is through the Council for the Arts at MIT. They have recently initiated a new student ticket program which allows students to attend BSO concerts for free. Passes are limited, however, and it is a good idea to contact the Arts Office as soon as possible. For more information, visit web.mit.edu/arts/general/BSO.html.

The **Boston Pops Orchestra**, directed by Keith Lockhart, performs from mid-April through mid-July. Pops programs are long streamers which can sometimes be found around MIT. The seats on the floor of Symphony Hall are replaced by tables and the suit-and-tie patrons by noisy champagne drinkers, but it's all in the Pops' style. If you go, try to sit in the second balcony in order to avoid the noise from the floor. "Tech Night at the Pops" (an annual tradition) is generally attended by alumni, and tickets are available through the Alumni Association. You, too, can sing "Arise All Ye of MIT" to the strains of the Boston Pops! For more information about the BSO or the Boston Pops, visit their website at www.bso.org.

Other professional orchestras in town include the **Pro Arte Chamber Orchestra** (www.proarte.org), the **Boston Classical Orchestra** (www.bostonclassicalorchestra.org) and the **Boston Philharmonic** (www.bostonphil.org). These orchestras perform mostly standard orchestral repertoire, which includes a mix of Classical, Romantic and 20th Century works. In contrast, **Metamorphosen Chamber Orchestra** (www.metamorphosen.org) performs mostly contemporary works.

Boston probably has more decent choral music than anywhere else in the country. The **Handel and Haydn Society**, which has been around since the early 1800's, gives ten performances a year. The highlight of its season is its annual performance of Handel's Messiah in Symphony Hall at Christmas time. Christopher Hogwood, the artistic director of the society, is rather famous. The H&H's name is narrower than the repertoire of the Society, whose programs include works by other Baroque and Classical composers as well. For more information, visit www.handelandhaydn.org. Less well known, but no less fine, are the **Cantata Singers** (www.cantatasingers.org) and the **Cecilia Society** (www.bostoncecilia.org). The Cantata Singers primarily perform Baroque works although they occasionally include contemporary pieces. The Cecilia Society has a broader repertoire.

The **Boston Celebrity Series** brings dozens of superb performers (e.g., Berlin Philharmonic, Emerson String Quartet, Murray Peheria, Isaac Stern) to Boston. They perform mostly in Symphony Hall and Jordan Hall. Check for a flyer, which is available in the Music Library, or check out their website www.celebrityseries.org.

The **Boston Ballet** is Boston's resident ballet group (www.bostonballet.com). The season runs from October to May and often features outstanding guest dancers.

The **Boston Modern Orchestra Project** (BMOP, www.bmop.org) is a full orchestra dedicated dedicated exclusively to performing works of the twentieth and twenty-first centuries and features an MIT professor (Prof. Elena Ruehr, whose latest opera was performed in Feb. 2003) as their composer in residence. Tickets are often available for BMOP through the Council for the Arts.

Local schools of music often present recitals by students and staff which can be excellent and are usually free of charge. The **New England Conservatory** (290 Huntington Ave., Boston) publishes a monthly listing of performances there. Also check out their concert listings on their website: www.newenglandconservatory.edu. Of special note is NEC's Symphony Orchestra, which is directed by MIT's own Dante Anzolini. Also try the **Berklee College of Music** (www.berklee.edu) and the **Longy School of Music** (www.longy.edu).

At MIT there are several sources of live music. The Humanities Department sponsors free noon-hour chamber music concerts on Thursdays in the Chapel. Periodically, (usually on Fridays at noon) there are concerts in Killian Hall (Building 14). The Music Department sponsors a series of evening concerts throughout the year, and the concerts are generally free and open to the public. Visit the Music Office (4-246) to get on their mailing list.

Of special interest are the following groups that not only provide excellent performances throughout the year but also offer the opportunity to participate. The **MIT Symphony Orchestra** is open to MIT and Wellesley students and alumni. Its repertoire combines standard classical works with a significant amount of contemporary music. The award-winning **Festival Jazz Ensemble** and **Concert Jazz Band** are student jazz groups that perform at concerts at MIT as well as at other local colleges. In addition, the Festival band travels to jazz festivals throughout the year. The **Concert Choir** is a mixed chorus, open to students and the entire MIT community. Two performances a year are given with professional orchestras and soloists.

The **MIT Concert Band** is open to the entire MIT community. It is devoted entirely to original works written for wind ensemble and commissions a new work every year. The band presents four concerts at MIT and one at Wellesley annually, and goes on a winter concert tour during the last week of IAP. The **Chorallaries** are a mixed, *a cappella*, popular music singing group comprised of undergraduate and graduate students. They give frequent concerts at MIT, and also sing at local schools and at colleges throughout the country. They are renowned on campus for their "Concert in Bad Taste" every spring, in which they perform naughtier songs with varying degrees of musicality. This is somewhat of a cult classic and people camp out in the hall by 10-250 for up to 24 hours in advance to secure a seat. The **Logarhythms** are an all-male close-harmony *a cappella* group of about 12 people. The Logs sing barbershop, pop, and Tech melodies to high school, alumni, and college audiences. Each year they give four concerts at MIT as well as several at other colleges. The **Muses** are a more recent, all-female *a cappella* group. The **Cross Products** are a Christian *a cappella* group. The **Toons** are a joint MIT/Wellesley *a capella* group. **Techiya** is a Jewish, Hebrew and Israeli *a cappella* group. Finally, **Resonance** is a coed, secular *a cappella* group. The **MIT Chamber Music Society** is also open to all members of the MIT community. This group provides coaching by music faculty and staff for all kinds of chamber ensembles. Groups whose work leads to performance can receive credit for 21M.445. The Society sponsors concerts in the Music Library and in La Sala de Puerto Rico in the Student Center, as well as an evening series in Kresge Auditorium. Other musical groups include the **Chamber Chorus** and the **Gospel Choir**.

For most of the above events there are standard sources of information that can be checked regularly. The MIT Music Library maintains a bulletin board with concert announcements, and the music department has boards on the second floor of Building 4 and in the Infinite Corridor. There are concert listings in several papers, including *The Boston Phoenix, Boston After Dark*, the *Boston Sunday Globe*, and The Globe's *Calendar* section (on the net and in the Thursday *Globe*). Also check WCRB's magazine *Classical Radio Boston* and the *Boston Review of the Arts*.

During the summer there are performances by various groups in many of the city's parks and along the Esplanade in the Hatch Shell. The **Boston Pops Esplanade Orchestra** plays free during the first two weeks of July, but crowds can be very large. The BSO moves to Tanglewood in western Mass. for the summer.

Electronica

For a big city, Boston's electronica scene is rather depressing — unless you just want to get all glittered up and go dancing to loud music. There are a lot of club nights that feature DJs of moderate ability, but they shift from club to club on a frequent basis. Your best bet for grooving in your shiny pants with a massive crowd is to head over to Lansdowne Street in Boston, where you'll find **Avalon** (617-262-2424, 15 Lansdowne St.; www.avalonboston.com), **Axis** (617-262-2437, 13 Lansdowne St.), **Embassy** (617-536-2100, 36 Lansdowne St.), **Karma** (617-421-9595, 9 Landsdowne St.), and so on and so forth. To go there, take the Green Line to Kenmore Square and follow all the beautiful people.

If you're into the goth/industrial scene, do not despair more than usual: **Man Ray** (617-864-0400, 21 Brookline St., Cambridge, www.manrayclub.com) is a 15-minute walk from campus, though you need to be 18+ or very cute. It's open Wed-Sat, with a different theme every night. Wednesdays are goth/industrial and quite nice, as are Fridays, but more crowded. Dressing up is required.   For those willing to stray farther at night**An Tua Nua** (617-262-2121, 835 Beacon St., Boston) has a goth night (18+) every Monday with a cheap cover.

There are some other (smaller) venues that regularly feature electronic music: the **Phoenix Landing** (617-576-6260, 512 Mass. Ave., Central Sq.) has consistently had several nights of Trance, Drum 'n' Bass, and House, and Wednesday nights' Anitya at **Vertigo** (617-723-7277, 126 State St., Boston) comes recommended to psychedelic trance fans for its "mind-boggling" decorations, cozy atmosphere and lack of dress code, and a $5 cover. **The Enormous Room** (617-491-5550, 567 Mass. Ave., Central Sq.) is a small spot for lounge, funk, hip-hop, and electronic deejays. For quality deep or soulful house, **The Milky Way** (617-524-3740, 403-405 Center St., Jamaica Plain) does Mercury Lounge every Wednesday and **An Nua Tua** does the Atmosphere party on Sunday nights. Also keep an eye out in the fall and winter for the monthly Soul Revival parties, held last year at **Villa Victoria** in the South End.

If you're looking for the hipster dance scene, try the **Pill** (which alternates between four bars on a regular schedule, available at www.thepillboston.com), **Start** (currently at Axis on Saturday nights).

Big name acts and DJs do come to play Boston while on tour, such as Digweed, Orbital, Van Dyk, Oakenfold, etc. However, the city of Boston proper lacks large venues (except for Avalon, which sucks), so you might want to look at the listings for the Worcester **Palladium** (508-797-9696, 261 Main St., Worcester; www.thepalladium.net). You'll need to take the commuter rail to get there, unless you can find a ride.

Folk

The center of the Boston folk scene is **Club Passim** (617-492-7679, 47 Palmer St., Harvard Sq.; www.clubpassim.org), which attracts nationally famous performers and charges $5 to $20 depending on the performer and the night. **Kendall Café** (617-661-0993, 233 Cardinal Medeiros Ave., Kendall Sq.; www.thekendall.com) is great for up-and-coming artists; it's a bar and thus 21+, but they usually don't card until you buy a beer. **The Lizard Lounge** (617-547-0759, 1667 Mass. Ave., near Harvard Sq.) has folk music some evenings, slam poetry others. **The Cantab Lounge** (617-354-2685, 738

Mass Ave, Central Sq.; www.cantablounge.com) has open-mike folk on Mondays, bluegrass on Tuesdays, and a blues jam on Wednesdays and Sundays. Otherwise, listen to WERS's CoffeeHouse show (6-10am, ouch!) or check the *Dirty Linen Gig Guide* (www.dirtynelson.com/linen/special/bystate1.html) for the latest listings.

The **Boston Bluegrass Union** (www.bbu.org) holds concerts and runs bluegrass and country music festivals. You can get on their mailing list online. Sandy's Music, (617-491-2812, 896A Mass. Ave.; www.sandysmusic.com) holds weekly "Old Timey Jam" sessions, check the website or talk to Sandy for more information.

Jazz

The **Regattabar** (617-876-7777, Charles Hotel, Harvard Sq.; www.concertix.com) and **Scullers** at the Doubletree Guest Suite Hotel (617-562-4111, www.scullersjazz.com) both attract world-class jazz acts, but you pay for what you get. The Regattabar is a fairly posh venue rather than your typical jazz dive. **Ryles Jazz** (617-876-9330, 212 Hampshire St., Inman Sq.; www.rylesjazz.com), **The Good Life** (617-868-8800, 720 Mass. Ave., Central Sq.; www.the-goodlife-us.com), and **Wally's Cafe** (617-424-1408, 427 Mass. Ave., Boston; www.wallyscafe.com) are all cheaper, but the quality of music varies more. The "original" **House of Blues** located in Harvard Square, closed in September, 2003. It may reopen if a suitable alternate location can be found. See www.hob.com for more details. **The Lizard Lounge** (617-547-0759, 1667 Mass. Ave., near Harvard Sq.) has amazing jazz on Monday nights, with a $10 cover. **Zuzu**, part of the Middle East complex, has stuff on Wednesdays, and the **Middle East** itself (617-864-EAST, 480 Mass. Ave., Central Sq.; www.mideastclub.com) often has sporadic jazz and jazz-fusion stuff, especially Upstairs and on the Corner.

Rock, Local

Boston has a lot of good local rock bands (and more bad ones), and correspondingly many venues for them to play in. In nearby Central Square, **The Middle East** (617-864-EAST, 480 Mass. Ave., Central Sq.; www.mideastclub.com) and **TT The Bear's** (617-492-BEAR, 10 Brookline St., Central Sq.; www.ttthebears.com) are two of the best spots in town. **The Paradise** (617-562-8800, 967 Comm. Ave., Boston), **Bill's Bar** (617-421-9678, 5.5 Lansdowne St., Boston; www.billsbar.com), **The Abbey Lounge** (617-441-9631, 3 Beacon Street, Inman Square; www.schnockered.com/abbey/abbey.htm), **The Skybar** (617-623-5223, 518 Somerville Ave., Somerville; www.esporecords.com/skybar.html), and **The Choppin' Block** (617-734-4177, 724 Huntington Ave., Boston; www.geocities.com/patrickwilson_ig/patrickwilson.html) also have lots of good shows. Though not exclusively rock, **The Milky Way** (617-524-3740, 405 Centre St., Jamaica Plain; www.milkywayjp.com) has hosted some of the best Boston shows of the past three years (and bowling, to boot), while **The Lizard Lounge** (617-547-0759, 1667 Mass. Ave, Cambridge) has become more rock oriented than anything else in recent times. Both venues are 21+. Finally, **The Druid** (617-497-0965, 1357 Cambridge St., Cambridge; www.celticweb.com/druid/) and the **Zeitgeist Gallery** (617-876-6060, 1353 Cambridge St., Cambridge; www.zeitgeist-gallery.org) have strung together a decent number of smaller, more intimate shows in the past year or so. See also the *Bars, Clubs, and Dancing* section later in this chapter, since many of them occasionally have live music.

Rock, National

Most of the major concerts occur at **Tweeter Center** in Mansfield (www.tweetercenter.com/boston/), the **Centrum** in Worcester (www.centrumcentre.com), or the **Fleet Center** (www.fleetcenter.com) in downtown Boston. Tickets can be bought at the box office or at Ticketmaster. The official Ticketmaster box office is located at The Orpheum (1 Hamilton Place). Tickets can be purchased Mon-Sat from 10am to 5pm or charged over the phone at 617-931-2000 or through www.ticketmaster.com. NEXT Ticketing (617-423-6000) also sells tickets to some of the big concerts in town. The **Palladium** in Worcester (508-797-9696, 261 Main St., Worcester; www.thepalladium.net) gets most of the medium-to-large heavy metal shows in Massachusetts. **Suffolk Downs** (Rt. 1A, East Boston) is used for huge concert festivals, and sometimes individual bands or performers. Easily accessible off the Blue Line. **Tsongas Arena** (300 Arcand Ave., Lowell) and **Gillette Stadium** (60 Washington St., Gillette) also host big stadium shows. The **Orpheum Theatre** (617-482-0650, Washington St., Boston) and **Avalon** (617-262-2424, 15 Lansdowne St, Boston; www.avalonboston.com) sometimes get big acts.

World

Johnny D's (617-776-2004, 17 Holland St., Davis Sq.; www.johnnyds.com) has different world music every night of the week; most shows are 21+. Though primarily jazz, **Ryles** (617-876-9330, 212 Hampshire Street, Inman Square; www.rylesjazz.com) sometimes features world music as well. **The Plough and Stars** (617-441-3455, 912 Mass. Ave., Harvard Sq.) is an Irish pub with folk and blues music and occasional Irish music on traditional instruments. You might also try **The Druid** (617-497-0965, 1357 Cambridge St., Cambridge; www.celticweb.com/druid/) or **The Burren** (617-776-6896, 247 Elm St., Davis Sq.; www.burren.com). **The Western Front** (617-492-7772, 343 Western Ave., Cambridge) has lots of good reggae at cheap prices.

Movies

Films at MIT

The **Lecture Series Committee** (LSC, lsc.mit.edu) shows popular films at MIT and sponsors lectures by famous personalities (e.g., Douglas Adams and Leonard Nimoy) from time to time. On Friday, Saturday, and Sunday nights, an entertainment series features recent films in 26-100 or 10-250. Unlike many other college film groups, LSC shows movies in 35mm, the same format used in commercial movie theaters. Most Hollywood films are presented in 6-channel DTS Digital Sound, and other films are often in Dolby Stereo. LSC also shows classic and foreign films in a Classics series, and a few times a term will show a sneak preview of an upcoming movie before its release date. To complete the moviegoing experience, LSC sells soda, candy, nachos, and fresh-popped popcorn at their movies.

The MIT audience adds an extra dimension to films. Everyone should go to at least one LSC movie, if only to figure out why "IN STEREO!" is an in-joke. Admission is $3.00; schedules and term calendars can be picked up at Registration or at LSC movies, or looked up on the web site (lsc.mit.edu). LSC movies can also be listed by typing 'finger @lsc' at the athena% prompt. Frequent LSC moviegoers can get six admissions for the price of five by buying a Multipass; up to four can be used for a single movie.

There are several other MIT groups that show movies. The Humanities Department often holds free showings of movies that are related to class discussions. In recent years, 21L.011, the introductory film class, has collaborated with LSC to present a free 35mm series of films shown for that class. The international student organizations often show the better movies from their home countries. MIT showings are usually announced on the bulletin boards and in *Techcalendar*.

Local Theatres

Whatever your taste in movie (or movie theatre) is, Boston and Cambridge have it. Choose from the huge multiplex, reclining chair stadium seating, escalators galore, digital surround sound, exclusively blockbuster showing theatres to the smaller, few screens, repertory, arty foreign film theatres complete with staff that will laugh at your Dziga Vertov jokes. Also, although the T stops running at 12:30am, the movies do not; some of the theatres listed below have weekend midnight showings. As mentioned before, *The Phoenix* is a wonderful resource for movie listings, as is www.bostonmovietimes.com. It's still not a bad idea to call the theater to make sure the listings are correct since movie times can change without notice. Same goes for ticket prices.

AMC Fenway 13 — (617-424-6266; www.amctheatres.com; 401 Park Drive Ste 7; MBTA: Fenway) One of the big multiplexes. Tickets are $9.50 for adults, $7.50 for students and $7.50 for the first show of the day. Tickets are avaliable online with a dollar service charge.

Boston Public Library — (617-536-5400; www.bpl.org; 700 Boylston St, MBTA: Copley) Yes, it's the public library and yes it shows films, usually about one a week. The BPL shows classic films and very very indie films. The films are shown in the Rabb Lecture Hall, which is in the Johnson Building on the lower level. Best of all, it's free. Worst of all, it confines itself to video presentation and usually not in the Original Aspect Ratio.

Brattle Theater — (617-876-6837; www.brattlefilm.org; 40 Brattle Street; MBTA: Harvard) The Brattle is one of few remaining repertory theaters combining recent independent films with retrospectives of classic cinema often in beautiful new or archival prints. The Brattle is a non-profit run by its members, but membership fees are fairly high. The schedule runs on a day to day basis so check the calendar often. Tickets are $9 for adults and $7.50 for students.

Coolidge Corner — (617-734-2500; www.coolidge.org; 290 Harvard Street; MBTA: Coolidge) Originally built as a 1930s movie palace, the non-profit Coolidge also has 70mm capability with 6-track magnetic sound, allowing the area to share in revivals of epics such as Lawrence of Arabia. Not to be missed are the weekend midnight showings of cult classics, underground cinema and film geek favs. The Coolidge boasts that they show movies "the way they were meant to be seen," and they aren't lying. Seriously, check them out. Tickets are $9 for adults, $6 for members and $7 for any show before 2 pm.

Harvard Film Archive — (617-495-4700; www.harvardfilmarchive.org; 24 Quincy Street; MBTA: Harvard) Located in the basement of Harvard's Carpenter Center, the

HFA stores more than 8,000 films and strives to perserve as many films as they can. Unlike at most theatres, the screen is not parallel to the seating. Thus, the best seats are on the left side. Film calendars can be found online or scattered around Cambridge. Tickets are $8 for adults and $6 for students.

Kendall Square Theatre - (617-621-1202; www.landmarktheatres.com; One Kendall Square; MBTA: Kendall) Located close by on Binney Street, the Kendall was the nation's largest arthouse at the time of its construction. The 9-screen theater blends art house films with multiplex management with mixed results depending on your taste. The concessions stand includes an espresso bar and food from local bakeries. Tickets are $9.25 for adults, $7.50 for students and $6.50 for the first show of the day on weekends and before 6pm weekdays. Tickets can also be purchased in advance from the MITAC.

Loews Boston Common — (617-423-5801; www.enjoytheshow.com; 175 Tremont Street; MBTA: Park Street or Boylston) The most popular multiplex among MIT students. Tickets are $9.75 for adults Mon-Thurs, $10.25 for adults Fri-Sun (their "adult premium" ticket), $8.75 for students Mon-Thurs, and $6.50 for the first show of the day. This place is huge. Bigger does not mean better.

Loews Copley Place 11 — (617-266-2533; www.enjoytheshow.com; 100 Huntington Ave; MBTA: Copley) The black sheep of the multiplexes in Boston. Tiny screens combined with seating that slopes downward instead of upward to create a unique experience for your eyes and neck. Tickets are $9 for adults, $6.50 for students Mon-Thurs and $6.50 for matinee.

Loews Harvard Square — (617-864-4581; www.enjoytheshow.com; 10 Church Street; MBTA: Harvard) The neglected member of the Boston Area Loews family. Not nearly as fancied up as the other Loews but host to the weekly Saturday midnight Rocky Horror Picture Show showing. Tickets for all shows are $9.00 for adults and $6.25 for matinee.

Museum of Fine Arts — (617-369-3306; www.mfa.org/film/; 465 Huntington Ave; MBTA: Museum of Fine Arts) The MFA has a nice screening room on the lower level of the museum. They show a wide range of films heavy on the (surprise!) artsy side. They routinely have film festivals showing movies you won't find anywhere else. Tickets are $9 for adults and $8 for MFA members, students and seniors.

Somerville Theater — (617-625-5700; www.somervilletheatreonline.com; 55 Davis Square; MBTA: Davis) Somerville Theater is a second-run theatre, meaning if there was a movie you heard about a month or so ago but missed in the above multiplexes, chances are you can find it at Somerville. Because of that, ticket prices are much cheaper. Tickets are $6 for adults, and $4 for matinee before 6pm Mon-Thurs.

Wang Center — (617-482-9393; www.wangcenter.org; 270 Tremont St; MBTA: Boylston) In the Theatre District, the Wang Center started out as a movie palace but its current cinematic involvement is limited to a token dozen classic films a year. One of the few places (if not the only one) where one can see Ben-Hur on a screen 40 feet wide.

IMAX

Boston has now reached the exalted status of a two-IMAX city. The **Museum of Science** joined the IMAX bandwagon early, and for more than a decade has featured an OMNIMAX (also known as IMAX Dome) theater which surrounds the viewer with a wraparound screen. Seeking a way of distinguishing itself, the **New England Aquarium** recently built an IMAX-3D theater, bringing the action to you with polarized 3-D glasses. The Museum of Science sticks to documentaries, but the Aquarium doesn't deem it beneath its dignity to pad its pockets by showing Hollywood films enlarged and re-mastered for IMAX. Matrix fans rejoice.

If you have a car, you can also find an IMAX theater in (of all places) a **Jordan's Furniture** store in Natick (1 Underprice Way, off Route 9; 508-424-0088; www.jordansimaxtheatre.com). Next time your parents come to town, they can buy you a chair and watch a movie in the same store.

Video Rentals

Another possibility is to rent movies. Your best bet is generally **Hollywood Express** (617-864-8400, 765 Mass. Ave. in Central) which has an extremely impressive selection, especially of old hollywood classics and nearly-forgotten independent movies, a database containing all their store's possessions, five day rentals and three locations (two of which, Central and Porter, are easily accessible on the Red Line; the third is in Twin City Plaza — the mall with the Star Market beside McGrath Highway — a longish but not arduous walk from MIT). Conveniently, they allow you to return films at any of their three locations, and offer a discount on the rental of five movies. There is also a **Blockbuster** in Central Square, similar to pretty much every other Blockbuster in the country in that it has an extremely narrow selection of non-Hollywood "blockbusters."

Spectator Sports

Boston has major league baseball, basketball, football and hockey teams, along with an impressive number of collegiate, semi-professional, and special groups. For quick information about yesterday's local and national games, call the Boston Globe Score Board anytime (617-265-6600).

The **Red Sox** (www.redsox.com) specialize in frustrated but fanatical fans. They play at Fenway Park, which is near Kenmore Square; convenient by foot or subway, guaranteed traffic jam by auto.

The **Celtics** (www.nba.com/celtics/) have been NBA World Champions 16 times in 40+ years. The Celts play in the Fleet Center, located by North Station and the old Boston Garden and easily accessible by T. Buy your tickets early, especially if you want to see them play the Bulls, Rockets, or Knicks. (www.fleetcenter.com)

The **New England Patriots** (www.patriots.com) have plenty of rude fans and fea-ture expensive tickets. Home games are played at Gillette Stadium in Foxborough. For information and tickets, call the club at 1-800-543-1776. Round trip fare to the stadium from South Station is around $3-5.

The **Boston Bruins** (www.bostonbruins.com), like the Celts, play in the Fleet Center. Tickets are available by mail at the beginning of the season, and at the box office starting a few weeks before the game if they are any left. Watch the papers for announcements of sale dates or call the box office at 624-1000.

The **Boston Marathon**, run each year on Patriots' Day (in mid-April), draws large numbers of both competitors and spectators. Information starts appearing in the papers a month before the race. The race goes through Wellesley and Kenmore Square, and finishes at the Boston Public Library on Boylston Street.

For women, there is the ten kilometer **Bonne Belle** road race in October on the Monday closest to Columbus Day. The race starts and finishes at the Common, and the course goes down Memorial Drive, past the MIT dorms.

The **Head-of-the-Charles Regatta** is the largest single-day rowing regatta in the world and draws crews from all over the world, including MIT. It is held the second-to-last Sunday in October (which is during Parents' Weekend). The race starts at the B.U. boathouse and finishes at the Cambridge Boat Club. The bridges along the river are good places to watch the race.

Another sporting event in Boston is horse racing, which draws bigger crowds than any other sport. **Suffolk Downs** racetrack (617-567-3900, www.suffolkdowns.com) features harness racing in the fall and flat racing in the spring. It is easily accessible by car or by MBTA as is **Wonderland (781-284-1300, www.wonderlandgreyhound.com)**, the greyhound racing center. During the summer there is harness racing at **Foxboro**, located south of Boston on Rt. 95.

The meat of spectator sports around Boston lies in the collegiate teams which compete in every imaginable sport, including tiddly-winks. The collegiate events which draw the greatest crowds include football at Harvard and Boston College, basketball at the same two schools, and hockey and crew races in general. This specific listing is not meant to belittle anything not mentioned, merely to point out the most obvious popular events.

Theater

There are a number of excellent theater groups at MIT. **Dramashop** (W16-018; x3-2908) puts on a wide variety of plays, while the **MIT Musical Theatre Guild** (W20-453; x3-6294) does musicals. The **MIT Community Players** (x3-2530) also produce plays. The **MIT Gilbert & Sullivan Players** (x3-0190) are noted for the quality of their productions. The **Shakespeare Ensemble at MIT** (W20-423; x3-2903) specializes in productions of Shakespeare and scenes from modern plays. If you wish to actually get involved in drama, one of these groups would be good to contact. Look for posters for auditions around campus and announcements in *The Tech* and *Tech Talk*. The Theater Arts Office (x3-2877) is an excellent source of performing arts information.

Dramas abound at Harvard University, ranging in price from free to $20 for big productions. The seasons run from October to December and from March to May. There are typically over 40 productions covering the entire range of theater. Large productions are shown on the Mainstage of the **Loeb Drama Center** (617-547-8300, 64 Brattle

St., Cambridge). Also in the Loeb is the **Experimental Theatre**, which shows plays weekly for free. You can pick up tickets up to one day in advance. Its wise to go early, as the tickets tend to go rather quickly. Despite the name, the plays shown are not always experimental, but rather high-quality productions of plays ranging from musicals to Pinter. Perhaps the most notable troupe at Harvard is the **Hasty Pudding Theatricals** (www.hastypudding.org). The Pudding features high-budget, high-glamour, student-written, no-holds-barred burlesque shows and is notable both because it is the oldest drag show in the country and because it goes on tour to New York City and Bermuda every year. Harvard also has a Gilbert and Sullivan company which does one production per term at the **Aggasiz Theatre** in Radcliffe Yard; they tend towards slapstick rather than real musical theatre, though.

Most plays are shown at the various Houses at Harvard, generally in common rooms, basements, or dining halls, which explains the huge number of productions. Despite the unprofessional atmosphere, the quality of the plays tends to be excellent. Tickets are sometimes available at the Holyoke Information Center; otherwise you can get them at the door maybe a half hour before the show begins.

Other colleges in the area also show plays. Brandeis University produces plays at their **Springold Theater** (781-736-3400) of a very high quality, comparable to Harvard. Wellesley, Boston University, Tufts, Emerson, etc., all have drama groups of varying quality. Try them out and see.

There are also many active professional theaters in the Boston area. The nationally famous **American Repertory Theatre** (617-547-8300) shares the Loeb Drama center with Harvard. They specialize in world premieres, as well as radical reinterpretations of classic plays. Prices are high, but you can usually get "student rush" seats. If there are seats left before the show begins, you can get them for a bargain by showing your school ID. Call ahead and ask about the potential availability of such tickets. If you plan to see everything in one season (which covers the whole school year), buy a student pass in the early fall, which entitles you to see five plays and lets you get virtually any seat you want for most performances. Student passes also come with discount coupons for other theaters. Other professional theaters often have student rush and / or student passes; check with the theater. Another feature of the American Repertory Theatre is volunteer ushering. You can sign up to usher a play and see it for free. This is a lot of fun.

Other good theaters are the **New Erlich Theater** at the Boston Center for the Arts (617-426-5000, 539 Tremont St., Boston; www.bcaonline.org), the **Charles Playhouse** (617-426-6912, 76 Warrenton St., Boston;), the **Lyric Stage** (617-437-7172, 140 Clarendon St., Boston; www.lyricstage.com) and the **Huntington Theater Company** (617-266-0800, 264 Huntington Ave., Boston; www.bu.edu/huntington/) at Boston University. All typically produce modern classics and some older plays. The **Mobius** (617-542-7416, 354 Congress St., Boston; world.std.com/~mobius/) specializes in experimental work. The **Shubert** (617-424-9393, 265 Tremont St., Boston), the **Wilbur** (617-423-4008, 246 Tremont St., Boston) and the **Wang Center** (617-482-9393, 270 Tremont St., Boston; www.wangcenter.org), all in the theater district near the Boylston MBTA stop, are Broadway-style with steep ticket prices. Sometimes Broadway shows preview at one of these. There are many other theaters in Boston as well. Check the theater listings.

Arcades and Billiards

Boston Billiards (617-536-POOL) is located at 126 Brookline Ave in Boston. Open 7 days a week until 2am.

Flat Top Johnny's (617-494-9565, www.flattopjohnnys.com) is located in One Kendall Square close to the Cambridge Brewing Company. They offer pool tables and a limited menu of appetizers, sandwiches and salads. Nothing spectacular, but it's nearby. Women play pool for half price on Tuesday nights. Flat Top Johnny's was voted Best Boston Pool Hall by Boston Magazine in 2003. Open Mon-Fri 12pm-1am, Sun 3pm-1am.

Good Times Emporium (617-628-5559) is located on 30 Sturtevant Street in Somerville just behind the Sullivan Square Home Depot. It is open 365 days a year from 10am-1am and features 100,000 square feet of billiards, batting cages, arcade games, bumper cars, laser tag, go-karts, and even a carnival ride. It also has a bar and limited menu. After 8pm you must be 18+ or be accompanied by a legal guardian.

Jillian's (617-437-0300; MBTA: Kenmore; www.jilliansboston.com), located at 145 Ipswich Street in Boston, is a 70,000 square foot entertainment complex including 2 restaurants, 30 pool tables, darts, table tennis, foosball, and a 16 lane bowling alley. The video games have been removed and now it's more of a night club than an arcade, but they still have billiards. Monday-Sunday 11am - 2am, Sundays 12pm-2am. Sunday through Thursday, 18+ after 8pm. Friday and Saturday, 21+ after 8pm.

The **Stratton Student Center (W20)** also has an arcade. The Game Room is open daily from 8am-12am and provides diversions such as air hockey, bubble hockey, Dance Dance Revolution, pool tables, video games and pinball. It also has tables where you can eat snacks purchased from LaVerde's and work on problem sets. Not as large (or expensive) as the other arcades in the area, but the location can't be beaten.

Bars, Clubs, Concerts and Dancing

There are countless bars, clubs and music venues in Boston and Cambridge. This is only a sampling of those that are more popular with MIT students. Check the newspapers or the *Boston Phoenix* club directory (www.bostonphoenix.com/listings/music/CLUB_DIRECTORY.asp) for listings of the types of music at clubs on a given night.

Remember, the legal drinking age in Massachusetts is 21. Any night of the week, though, you can find an 18+ night at some club. Call around, or check the newspapers. Massachusetts has also instituted an indoor smoking ban, which applies to pretty much everywhere except the occasional cigar club.

All Asia Cuisine & Cocktail Bar (617-497-1544, 332 Massachusetts Ave, Cambridge) Very close to campus, from time to time has very good live music.

Axis (617-262-2437, 13 Lansdowne St., Boston; MBTA: Kenmore) Rock, techno/hiphop, indie/punk and other types of music. Two floors. Recorded and live music. Cover ranges from $5 to $8.

Avalon (617-262-2424,15 Lansdowne St., Boston; MBTA: Kenmore; www.avalonboston.com) Rock, techno/hiphop, indie/punk and others. The crowd has accurately been described as "skanky." Use discretion.

Bill's Bar (617-421-9678, 5.5 Lansdowne St.; MBTA: Kenmore) Hip-hop, funk, reggae, others; has a cool college crowd and features live bands many nights.

Cask 'N' Flagon (617-536-4840, 62 Brookline Ave., Boston; MBTA: Kenmore) Rock music, college and townie crowd. Usually no cover.

Cactus Club (617-236-0200, 934 Boylston) Features a nice atmosphere and a twentysomething crowd.

Crossroads (617-262-7371, 495 Beacon St., Boston; www.crossroadsirishpub.com) Just over the Harvard Bridge. A favorite of MIT fraternities. Food and/or drinks. No cover. Guinness Stout on tap.

Dick's Last Resort (617-267-8080, 55 Huntington Ave. in the Pru; www.dickslastresort.com) Features rude service. Dick's is a great place to go on your birthday — you get extra harrassment from the waitstaff, and they'll even make you a balloon hat.

Jake Ivory's (617-247-1222, 9 Lansdowne St., Boston; MBTA: Kenmore; www.jakeivorys.com). Features live "dueling pianos" every night. The show is a lot of fun — everyone should go at least once.

Karma Club (617-421-9595, 9 Lansdowne St., Boston; MBTA: Kenmore) Techno/industrial, features dancing most nights.

Mercury Bar (116 Boylston, 617-482-7799). A "yuppyish" bar.

Middle East Restaurant and Club (617-492-9181, 472 Mass. Ave., Cambridge; MBTA: Central; www.mideastclub.com). A very vibrant scene with Boston's best local bands, national acts, and Middle Eastern food. Free shows in the Bakery.

Miracle of Science Bar + Grill (617-868-2866, 321 Massachusetts Ave, Cambridge) Terrific laboratory-inspired decor. Great MIT hangout spot, but beware the after-work biotech crowd. Drinks and food are reasonably priced, amazing cheeseburgers. Their weekend breakfasts are tasty but expensive.

Muddy Charles Pub (50-110, X3-2158). Open in Walker during lunch and in the evening on weeknights. The pub serves beer, wine and munchies.

O'Brien's (617-782-6245, 3 Harvard Ave., Allston; obriens.purp.org) Small venue; indie, punk, experimental, 18+.

Orpheum (617-679-0810, 1 Hamilton Place, Boston; MBTA: Park St.) Medium sized, restored theater, events range from ballet to rock.

Paradise Rock Club (617-562-8800, 969 Comm. Ave., Boston) New wave, rock, folk, blues, and country every night. A great, intimate setting. Also doubles as M-80, a dance club with Euro and Asian nights.

People's Republik (617-492-8632, 876 Massachusetts Ave, Cambridge; MBTA: Central) How can you go wrong with a Cold War-themed bar? With capitalist prices. ($4 for a draft beer) Plenty of seating, and now serving lunch daily. The bartenders are very good and it's a great stop for a group outing.

Phoenix Landing (617-572-6260, 512 Mass. Ave., Cambridge; MBTA: Central) Books mostly small and local bands. Nice bartenders, buying a drink for someone entitles you to a card that you give that special someone that they trade in for a drink

The Plough and Stars (617-441-3455, 912 Mass. Ave.) Small Irish pub between Central and Harvard Square. Live music nightly; you don't want to miss the incomparable "Bad Art Ensemble" on Wednesdays. Soccer on weekends, Irish accents every night. Be prepared to sneak between the musicians to use the bathroom.

The R&D Pub. The newest pub on campus, located in the fourth floor of the Stata Center, building 32. Slated to open the week of August 30th, 2004. The R&D pub will be open from 4pm to 10pm M-F serving beer, wine and light fare.

The Roxy (617-338-7699, 279 Tremont St., Boston; www.roxyboston.com [horrible website, worth seeing]) — Live music, occasionally national acts.

Thirsty Ear Pub (x8-9754), run by graduate students and located in the basement of Ashdown House (Building W1). The Thirsty (as its commonly called) features a wide selection of beers (imported and domestic), munchies, music, and competitive prices. It is also available for rental to private parties (call for details). Although the Thirsty was shut down at the end of the 2003-2004 school year, Deans Benedict and Colbert, the Office for Campus Dining and the Ashdown House Executive Committee are working hard to reopen the doors for September 2004. We'll drink to that!

Thirsty Scholar Pub (617-497-2294, 70 Beacon St, Somerville) A spacious hangout just off Inman Square, popular with Harvard students. Its ambience is definitely more concerned with thirst than with scholarship, as the multiple widescreen TVs will capture your attention wherever you look. The bar boasts a huge selection of beers, and the seating layout allows for both pairing off with your special one, and for discussing life with a group of friends.

T.T. The Bear's Place (617-492-0082, 10 Brookline & Mass. Ave., Cambridge; MBTA: Central; www.ttthebears.com) Smaller venue, books local and national bands, and is owned by the same people as the Middle East.

Vertigo (617-723-7277, 126 State St., Boston) Different themes on different nights of the week; Anitya on Wednesdays comes recommended as perhaps the only place to hear psychedelic trance in Boston and Cambridge outside of your home or the occasional radio show. The crowd is very friendly, and rarely tops 75 so expect to become acquainted with everyone. 21+, $5 cover, no dress code.

Comedy

There are a few good comedy clubs in the area. Some have no cover or minimum, others do. Discount coupons are frequently distributed in papers and on Mass. Ave.

The Comedy Connection (617-248-9700, 245 Quincy Market, Faneuil Hall; www.comedyconnectionboston.com) Small, fairly intimate set up. National level acts every night of the week. Cover around $10, though for bigger name comics the cover may run a bit higher. Tickets can be bought in advance.

Back Alley Theatre (617-576-1253, 1253 Cambridge St., Inman Sq.) Home to ImprovBoston. Catch TheatreSports Boston every Friday night, where two local improv troupes duke it out. Also popular, on Thursday nights, is Sitcom!, where the audience creates the basis of the sitcom the troupe will then perform. Cover is $10 for students, $12 otherwise.

The Improv Asylum (617-263-1441, 216 Hanover St., Boston; www.improvasylum.com) An improv place in the North End near Faneuil Hall. Tickets range from $15-$20, depending on the night.

Nick's Comedy Stop (617-423-2900, 100 Warrenton St.; www.nickscomedystop.com) In the theatre district, and features free ticket giveaways. You can sign up a friend, who may win 30 free passes.

Coffeehouses

Coffeehouses are pleasant places to study, talk, relax. Some have music every night; others simply have tea, cake, and a pleasant ambience.

1369 Coffeehouse (617-576-4600, 757 Mass. Ave., Cambridge; MBTA: Central; www.1369coffeehouse.com) Popular with students and relatively close to the MIT campus. Relaxed atmosphere and a good range of coffees and baked goods. Name derived from their other slightly cozier location at 1369 Cambridge Street in Inman Square, 617-576-1369.

Café Algiers (617-492-1557, 40 Brattle St., Cambridge; MBTA: Harvard) — Cozy basement coffeehouse, with interesting coffees. At random times, guitar pickers visit and perform for free.

Café Pamplona (12 Bow St., Harvard Square) is an unassuming, relaxing coffeehouse. Excellent espressos, peace and quiet.

Carberry's Bakery & Coffee House (617-576-3530, 74 Prospect St., MBTA: Central) Famous for their pastries and breads, though soups, sandwiches, and salads are available also. Nice outdoor seating when the weather permits, and cozy and pleasant on the inside.

Diesel Café (257 Elm St., MBTA: Davis) — where the funky college kids of Davis Square go to hang out. Large location, sofas and a pool table in the back. Open Sunday to Thursday until midnight, Friday and Saturday till 1am.

Greenhouse Coffeeshop & Restaurant (617-354-3184, 3 Brattle St.; MBTA: Harvard) — A coffeehouse/restaurant in a greenhouse. What will they think of next? No music, but a great place to go to talk.

The Other Side Café (617-536-9477, 407 Newbury St.) — Hard to find (it's across Mass. Ave. from the Virgin Megastore) but features a relaxed atmosphere with good recorded music, and in addition to coffee, serves smoothies and health and vegetarian oriented food. Their Italian creme sodas are especially delicious.

The Nameless Coffeehouse (617-864-1630, 3 Church Street; MBTA: Harvard, www.namelesscoffeehouse.org) Has folk singers and contemporary rock musicians. The performers are volunteer, and range in quality from poor to excellent. New acts every half-hour, so be patient if you don't like what you hear. No cover charge. Open weekends. Refreshments including hot cider and cookies served free, but donations are requested.

Someday Cafe (617-623-3323, 51 Davis Square; MBTA: Davis) Relaxed, full of comfy couches facing big windows perfect for reading or just watching the people and bustle of Davis Square. Check out the bathroom, it's fun.

Tealuxe (617-441-0077, 0 Brattle St, MBTA: Harvard and 617-927-0400, 108 Newbury St; www.tealuxe.com) Technically not a coffeehouse, but must be visited by anyone with even a passing interest in tea. Relaxing atmosphere and over 70 varieties of tea available for purchase.

When in doubt, check the *Boston Phoenix* for current information. Almost every college in the area has its own coffeehouse during the academic year, with the obvious exception of MIT which didn't consider its 24-hour student coffeehouse valuable enough to preserve. Harvard's coffeehouses can be quite good.

SUBMIT

TO VooDoo

Voo Doo, the MIT Journal of Humor, is a peer-reviewed journal that is published twice yearly in both print and electronic versions, and in special editions as the need arises. Original manuscripts are invited in the form of writing, illustrations and comics, as well as any other format. Submissions should be sent to voodoo@mit.edu or Room 50-309. Voo Doo publication credit is highly sought after in the academic community and is a valuable addition to any resumé.

ISSEL ANNE LIM '05

Shopping

Although it may not seem so at first, Boston is a real town and real people live here. Almost anything that real people need can be bought in the area. Chances are, you can get to what you want to buy on the T, the bus or a combination of the two (see **Transportation**). Occasionally, however, a car is useful. We have given public transportation directions to places in the suburbs when we could. If we did not give directions, call the store. Most stores are quite willing to give you decent directions; after all, they are expecting you to give them your money. Ask for a student discount wherever you go. Many places offer them if asked but won't bring the matter up themselves.

If you don't find what you are looking for here, ask around. Quite probably, someone you know has gone through the process of purchasing what you now want to buy. You can ask around to check a store's reputation. If you're just planning to window shop, check the *Shopping Districts and Malls* section of this chapter.

Anime

There is an anime club at MIT (`web.mit.edu/anime/www/`) which has a large collection for lending. A viewing schedule is located on their web site. If you wish to buy your own anime, the following are good sources:

Suncoast Motion Picture Co. (617-252-9035, `www.suncoast.com`) in the Cambridgeside Galleria has over 100 DVD anime titles in stock. Their VHS collection is usually special order, generally taking 3-5 business days. The prices are a little high compared to Best Buy, but their anime selection is larger, they have a membership program which gives you 10% of the value purchased in store credit, and there are "triple point weekends", usually every 4-6 weeks, which give 30% back.

Tokyo Kid (617-661-9277, `www.tokyokid.com`), located in the Garage Mall in Harvard Square at 36 John F. Kennedy St., has over 1000 anime titles in both DVD and VHS format. They rent a large portion of the titles they sell (and they have those cool figurines that you know you've always wanted). Hours are Mon-Thur noon-7pm, Fri-Sat noon-8pm, Sun noon-6pm.

Appliances

Get advice from a knowledgeable person or organization before making a major purchase. *Consumer Reports* (`www.consumerreports.org`) has information on appliances; they also produce a Buyer's Guide Issue. Both of these can be found at the Humanities Library. **Best Buy** (`www.bestbuy.com`) also has buyer's guides for major appliances.

When purchasing appliances, the best and most convenient stores are **Sears** (617-252-3500) and Best Buy (617-577-8866), both located in the Cambridgeside Galleria (see *Department Stores*). For a fee, both stores offer home delivery, installation, and in some cases, haul-away service on a one-to-one basis. Sears has an excellent return policy and is willing to replace goods that arrive damaged either from the factory or from the delivery process.

Art and Drafting Supplies

There are several good options in the area. **Pearl Arts and Craft**, located in Central Square at 579 Mass. Ave., Cambridge (617-547-6600), has an extensive collection and reasonable prices, with a 10% student discount. Pearl is pretty much the only place around that stocks a decent variety of architectural modeling and drafting supplies. Hours are Mon-Sat 9am-7pm, Fri 9am-8pm, Sun noon-6pm. **University Stationery**, across from Random Hall (311 Mass. Ave., 617-547-6650) also gives a student discount, is pretty well stocked, and has excellent prices even before the discount. They are only open until 5pm, though. For art supplies, **Utrecht** (333 Mass. Ave., across the bridge in Boston, 617-262-4948, and 1030 Mass Ave, Cambridge 617-495-0250, www.utrechtart.com) at the Symphony T-stop has two floors and is a good alternative to Pearl. Utrecht also offers a 10% discount to students which they don't advertise. If you sign up on their mailing list they will send you coupons and special discounts in the mail. Hours are Mon-Fri 8:30am-7:30pm, Sat 10am-6pm, Sun noon-5pm. **Bob Slate Stationery** (617-547-1230), at 1288 Mass. Ave. in Harvard Square, has art supplies as well as stationery and office supplies. **Artist Supply** (580 Mass. Ave, 617-354-3636) is right across the street from Pearl and is worth checking out because they sometimes have better deals on art supplies. Also see *Stationery and School Supplies* in this chapter.

Bicycles

Bicycles and accessories can be purchased from several stores in the area; check the Yellow Pages. **Cambridge Bicycle**, right next to MIT (259 Mass. Ave.), carries frames, bikes, and components, with a bit of attitude and hot employees. **Broadway Bicycle School** (broadwaybicycleschool.com), a half mile from campus, offers bicycle repair, rents tools and space, and has incredible used-parts bins. **Ace WheelWorks** in Davis Square, (145 Elm Street, Somerville, www.wheelworks.com) is renowned for being the best no-nonsense bike store in the city. Other cycle stores include **International Bicycle Centers** (www.internationalbike.com), which mainly appeals to higher-end customers who want the newest gear and tech, and **The Bicycle Workshop** (259 Mass. Ave., 617-876-6555). For more information, especially about purchasing a used bike from the Campus Police, and theft prevention devices, see the **Transportation** chapter.

Hint: Buy a Kryptonite Lock and make sure to secure the front wheel whenever you lock your bike; you would be amazed at how many times you see bikes missing the front wheel, or front wheels missing a bike, not to mention the number of people who carry around bolt cutters.

Books

This is a very, very, very incomplete list. There are literally (OK, figuratively) millions of places to buy books in Boston and Cambridge. One of the best places is Harvard Square, which probably boasts more excellent bookstores than street performers, panhandlers and layabouts. Besides Harvard Square, there are many quality bookstores scattered less densely throughout Boston. The Yellow Pages, friends, and an afternoon to go wandering are among the best ways to find new ones.

General

Like any other city, Boston has its share of large bookstore chains. **Borders Books and Music** is located on the 2nd floor of the Cambridgeside Galleria next to Best Buy (617-679-0887) and at 10 School Street in Downtown Crossing (617-557-7188). The closest **Barnes and Noble** bookstores are in the Prudential Center (617-247-6959), on Washington Street (617-426-5184), and in Kenmore Square (617-267-8484). You are unlikely to get discounts or find staff who truly understand your intense and desperate need for that special, hard-to-find book on obscure Japanese noise labels, but they will offer a numerically large selection and the opportunity to browse happily for hours.

Conversely, in the People's Republic of Cambridge, with its "support local business" mantra and elitist intellectualism, the largest bookstores are great: **Wordsworth** (617-354-5201, www.wordsworth.com, 30 Brattle St.; MBTA: Harvard) discounts everything except textbooks and has author readings almost daily. Good rare-book search service.

The **Harvard Coop** (617-499-2000, www.thecoop.com), 1400 Mass. Ave.; MBTA: Harvard. A good selection of text, reference, fiction, and nonfiction. Reasonable selection of foreign language books and dictionaries. More convenient **MIT Coop** branches reside in the Student Center and Kendall Square, with smaller selections to offset their proximity. Despite its size, the Kendall Square Coop has a reasonable selection of technical books and also features a sci fi/fantasy selection that has a different focus than many other stores in the area. Worth checking out. The Student Center Coop has an amusing range of MIT T-shirts.

Harvard Book Store (1-800-542-READ, www.harvard.com), 1256 Mass. Ave.; MBTA: Harvard. Perennially voted best bookstore in the Boston/Cambridge area. Wide selection of new books, particularly fiction, philosophy, psychology, critical theory, women's studies, philosophy, artsy photography and classics. They also have a great selection of 'remainders', perhaps better known as "good books for dirt cheap because the publishers don't love them anymore". They have a good staff, sales on new books, good prices on the rest, plus a frequent-buyer's card, and a basement full of used books. The bookstore also organizes talks by authors, both big and small, and offers a weekly email newsletter with a schedule and sale announcements. Hell, if you're too lazy to haul your ass to Harvard Square, you can also shop online from their website (Harvard University sued them for the domain name but lost).

Special Interest
Ahab Rare Books (617-547-5602), 5 JFK St. #401; MBTA: Harvard. Antiquarian, literature, religious, Americana, autographs.

The Avenue Victor Hugo Bookstore (617-266-7746, www.avenuevictorhugobooks.com), 353 Newbury St., Boston, across from Virgin Records. New, used, rare and old books, magazine back issues to 1850, discounted old editions of collected works. Great selection of fiction. Somewhat more expensive than many used bookstores, and in some genres (notably sci-fi) new seems to outnumber used. Not for people allergic to cats. Their physical store is on the process of closing as of the summer of 2004, but they will still be open online.

Brattle Bookshop (617-542-0210, www.brattlebookshop.com), 9 West St.; MBTA: Park St. Ancient books and "antiquarian" paraphernalia. Lots of history and nonfiction. First editions abound.

Calamus Books (617-338-1931, www.calamusbooks.com), 92B South St.; MBTA: South Station. Gay/lesbian/bisexual/transgender bookshop, founded by a guy who used to work at Glad Day.

Commonwealth Books (617-338-6328, www.commonwealthbooks.com), 134 Boylston St., Boston; MBTA: Park St and 526 Commonwealth Ave, Boston; MBTA: Kenmore Sq. Antique and used books, primarily history, architecture, some amount of obscure literature, philosophy, and religion. By their own admission, mostly attractive to the "scholar or collector".

The Compleat Strategist (617-267-2451, www.thecompleatstrategist.com), 201 Mass. Ave., Boston. Gaming (D&D, Gurps, White Wolf etc.).

Curious George Goes to Wordsworth (617-498-0062, curiousgeorge.wordsworth.com), 1 JFK St., Harvard Square. Basically the children's books department for the larger Wordsworth up the street (except larger than it might otherwise be), Curious George has a good selection of stuff and is a friendly place to browse. Picture books and other books for younger readers are kept upstairs (along with a variety of plush and other toys); juveniles (8-12), series, and some "young adult" books are kept downstairs, along with older and more educational toys.

Glad Day Gay Liberation Bookstore (617-267-3010, www.gladdaybookshop.com), 673 Boylston St., Boston; MBTA: Copley. Very complete gay, lesbian, queer bookstore with an adult bookstore in the back half.

The Globe Corner Bookstore (617-497-6277, www.globecorner.com), 28 Church St., Cambridge; MBTA: Harvard. Specializes in travel guides and maps.

Grolier Poetry Book Shop (617-547-4648, www.grolierpoetrybookshop.com), 6 Plympton St.; MBTA: Harvard. "Minimum of prose." Poetry, to the ceiling. Special and mail-order; poetry contest; readings; bulletin board.

Harvard University Press Display Room (617-495-2625), 1350 Mass. Ave., Harvard Square. Harvard Press books and a roomful of classics.

Israel Book Shop Inc. (617-556-7113, www.israelbookshop.com), 410 Harvard St., Brookline. Excellent selection of Jewish religious books. Horrible staff.

Kate's Mystery Books (617-491-2660, www.katesmysterybooks.com), 2211 Mass. Ave.; MBTA: Davis. Like Grolier except for mystery books. Lots of readings and signings.

Micro Center (617-234-6400, www.microcenter.com), 730 Memorial Drive, Cambridge. Has a good selection of technical books covering math, engineering, physics and computer science. You can also get some good deals on old, but not quite useless, books. They have a paltry but present sci-fi and fantasy section.

MIT Press (x3-2889, mitpress.mit.edu/bookstore/), Building E38, 292 Main St., Kendall Square. All MIT Press publications, plus a selection of books by MIT authors from other publishers. Excellent postcards and T-shirts, cool staff.

New England Mobile Book Fair (617-527-5817), 82 Needham St., Newton; MBTA: Newton Highlands. A vast and disorderly (and determinedly stationary) warren of books and shelves - an excellent place for browsing. Books are organized somewhat haphazardly, and generally by publisher, although the salespeople have an uncanny knowledge of Where Things Are. If you have the time to browse, possibly worth the trip.

New Words Bookstore (617-876-5310, www.centerfornewwords.com), 186 Hampshire St., Cambridge. Women's books. They have readings Thursdays at 7:00pm.

Out of Town News (617-352-7777), right by the Harvard T (0 Harvard Sq., in fact), great selection of newspapers and magazines from all over. Also try Nini's Corner right across the street.

Pandemonium (617-547-3721, www.pandemoniumbooks.com), 36 JFK St., The Garage; MBTA: Harvard. Science fiction and fantasy, as well as some horror and used videos. They also stock many role-playing materials, dorky-yet-amusing T-shirts referencing Cthulhu and the word "fnord", and various deserving comics. The staff is generally composed of knowledgeble and helpful geeks. They also stock second-hand books — though given the relative paucity of good used sci-fi bookstores, these are generally somewhat well picked-over. A discount is available for MITSFS members.

Quantum Books (617-494-5042, www.quantumbooks.com), 4 Cambridge Center (behind the Marriott). Excellent technical/science/computer bookstore. Friendly and helpful staff. Offers textbooks for many MIT courses, including freshman subjects, and claims convincingly to always have official course texts cheaper than the Coop. They take TechCash.

Revolution Books (617-492-5443), 1156 Mass. Ave., Harvard Square. Don't think they have books about any radical thinker or theory - the store is run by the RCP - Revolutionary Communist Party. Even Georg Lukacs is banned. Marxism; Political economy; Central America; Africa; Women; Third World culture. Much space also devoted to small-press polemics, zines, and t-shirts. The people-watching can be amusing.

Sasuga Japanese Bookstore (781-891-5055, www.sasugabooks.com), 96 Clematis Avenue; Waltham, MA Books and manga in Japanese. Slim selection of English books about Japan. Moved away from Cambridge in May 2004 to Waltham (15 minutes away by car), focuses on internet sales now, but they are open to the public from noon to 6pm on Saturdays. MIT Anime Club members get discounts.

Schoenhof's Foreign Books, Inc. (617-547-8855, www.schoenhofs.com), 76A Mt. Auburn St., Harvard Square. Foreign language bookstore with amazing language learning selection. Takes special orders for in print titles. Prices can be high, so call for a quote before making the trip to Harvard.

Seven Stars (617-547-1317), 731 Mass. Ave., Central Square. Eastern religions, New Age books, crystals and other hokey, holistic scheisse.

Trident Booksellers (617-267-8688, www.tridentbookscafe.com), 338 Newbury St., Boston. Left-leaning bookstore with interesting magazine and non-fiction section. Also has free wireless access and a cafe; open till midnight.

Textbooks

The most obvious places to buy your textbooks are **The Coop** in Kendall Square and **Quantum Books** in Cambridge Center. They're so close to each other that if you're too lazy to visit both and price check, you have too much money. Textbooks are organized by course number and are easy to find. However, they are crowded at the beginning of the term, so go early. The prices are basically list, because there's less markup on textbooks. (Blame the publishers, who think they have everyone cornered.)

The good news is that they don't always have you cornered. The first place to try to find books is from people you know who have taken the class. They may be willing to loan or sell you their books. Next try the **APO Book Exchange** (x3-3788, web.mit.edu/apo/www/bookexchange.html). Also at the beginning and end of term, ads to sell textbooks are often posted on bulletin boards around campus. Many classes, particularly literature and other humanities classes, have books which can be found in normal new or used bookstores. The Coop sells used textbooks at a discount, and **Harvard Book Store** (see above) has a good selection of used textbooks, cheap, and other used bookstores occasionally do too - call around. Websites for cheap and/or used textbooks (such as www.mit411.com and half.com, eBay's used bookstore) abound and some professors will discreetly recommend them.

One potential problem with used textbooks is that they may be an older edition of the book than the professor is using. For some classes this matters; for many it doesn't. Just be careful that the $75 you're saving isn't really just $15 down the drain.

Used Books

Used books are wonderful things. Luckily there are many used bookstores in the area. Some are:

Buck A Book — Like the name says. The selection is completely disorganized and seems to be mostly useless for almost everything except romance, but some have reported good finds. Check it out if you like browsing or lurid descriptions of rippling man-flesh. Many locations, one being 30 JFK St., Cambridge, in Harvard Square.

Harvard Book Store (see above) also has a wonderful used book selection downstairs.

House of Sarah Books (617-547-3447), 1309 Cambridge St. Small selection but interesting books. Strong in religion and fiction. Whole section of women in religion worth browsing.

McIntyre & Moore Booksellers (617-629-4840, www.mcintyreandmoore.com), 255 Elm Street; MBTA: Davis. Has "academic" books, literary criticism, history, philosophy and general stock. You'll almost always find a jewel hidden in the stacks at a good price.

Rodney's Bookstore (617-876-6467), 698 Mass. Ave., Central Square. Large size with eclectic selection. Lots of local history, arts, childrens, and sailing/navy.

Many of the "special interest" bookstores also carry used books in their particular fields. The MIT chapter of **APO** hosts a Book Exchange (web.mit.edu/apo/www/bookexchange.html) twice a year, usually during the first week of the Fall and Spring academic terms. Books are sold on behalf of the owner after the owner sets the price. Anyone may buy books from the exchange and the selection typically includes textbooks, fiction, non-fiction and reference books. It's rumored that the MIT Science Fiction Society sells off redundant titles every once in a while at the book exchange.

Building Supplies

See *Hardware and Building Supplies*.

Calculators

You should probably look online for anything really fancy (HP or Texas Instruments). However, you don't necessarily need something that fancy; you should consult with upperclassfolk before deciding that you do. If you're going to get a more ordinary calculator you should go to CambridgeSide Galleria's **Best Buy** or **Circuit City** or, if you're really lazy and don't mind paying too much, to **The Coop**. Also, people sometimes sell their calculators in *Tech Talk*, or at www.mit411.com.

Cars

Buying a car is often a person's first big purchase, and, if not done carefully, can easily become a person's first big monetary mistake. First, think about your driving habits, your needs and your budget. This will help focus your search for a car that will be best for you. Next, you should do some research before walking into a dealership. The safety of your car is probably its most important feature. Look for features like front and side airbags, safety crash cages and check to see if your car is prone to rolling over or flipping. You should also make sure you look for theft rates when choosing the car to buy. Some vehicles are designated "high-theft" and Massachusetts Law requires insurance companies to charge an "extra risk" premium or refuse collision and comprehensive coverage to those vehicles if they do not have a minimum anti-theft or auto recovery device. Information that will also be of interest includes car models, options, costs, frequency-of-repair records, safety tests and gas mileage.

You can read comparisons and find all sorts of other information including options, safety ratings and advice for new car buyers from **Consumer Reports** (www.consumerreports.org/Categories/CarsTrucks/), **Vehix** (vehix.com) or **Edmund's** (edmunds.com). **AAA** (aaa.com) has information on every aspect of buying and owning a car although you may have to be a member to get access to the information. Finally, before even considering walking onto a car dealer's lot, read *Don't Get Taken Every Time* by Remar Sutton. Despite the hokey title, this really is an outstanding book. Remar Sutton, a former car dealer himself, details *everything* you need to know (in a very readable fashion) to insure that you get a good deal.

Financing your car will ultimately increase the cost of the car because you have to pay interest and other loan costs. If you choose to finance your car, avoid offers that involve a large down payment and high annual percentage rate (APR) as these can be finanicially risky if the car is repossessed or destroyed in an accident. You may wish to pay cash for a less expensive car instead.

After buying your car, you should get some maps (especially a US Road Atlas and a map book for Eastern Massachusetts), a AAA membership, and a cell phone if you don't already have one. These will prevent you from getting lost, give you 24 hour emergency roadside assistance, and allow you to call the police or AAA in the event of an emergency.

New Cars

Take time to shop around and be prepared to bargain with the salesman; his first price usually isn't the best he can offer. Prices tend to be up to 30% lower in the suburbs. It is possible to buy a car and have it registered in your home state (if you're not from Massachusetts), thereby saving the sales tax (5%) and excise tax (2.5%). This may affect insurance rates, which are discussed later. Do *not* let the dealer affix an inspection sticker; have the car inspected yourself. If it does not pass, the dealer must repair it for free.

Used Cars

Be very careful. Used car dealers are generally disreputable and overpriced; national dealers are not much more reputable than local dealers. Dealers are not required by law to give buyers the right to return a car after it has been purchased. They are, however, required to post a Buyer's Guide in every used car they offer for sale (unless they sell less than 6 cars a year). You will want to get all promises in writing, keep the Buyer's Guide after the sale and ask to have the car inspected by an independent mechanic before you buy it. The Federal Trade Commission puts out *Buying a Used Car: A Consumer Guide from the Federal Trade Commission* which is available online (`www.ftc.gov/bcp/conline/edcams/automobiles/index.html`) or through the MIT Police. If you are seriously considering buying a used car, get this booklet and read it carefully. Twice.

If you do not wish to buy from a dealer, check *Tech Talk*, *The Phoenix*, and *The Boston Globe* for potential sellers. (Buying from a stranger is risky, but the risks are different from those encountered when purchasing from an experienced salesman.) If you do buy from a dealer, first consult the Better Business Bureau. Occasionally, used cars go out over the mailing lists reuse-sell and reuse (only for free cars - believe it or not, it happens!) and the newsgroup `athena.forsale`.

The US government, too, sells cars. The **General Services Administration** (GSA) operates and maintains vehicle fleets for federal agencies. Each year they sell between 35,000 and 45,000 pre-owned vehicles at public auction in commercial auction houses across the US (including Massachusetts). Most sedans are compacts or midsize and are sold at three to four years of age with low mileage (sometimes as low as 10,000-15,000 miles). Minivans and light trucks are sold when they are six years old and have about 60,000 miles on them. All of these vehicles follow a strict preventative maintenance program: they are all serviced regularly and are sold in excellent condition. (If you have the time and money to spend on auction cars, this is a really good way to get a slightly used car and is highly recommended.)

The GSA also sells vehicles for other government agencies and occasionally sells vehicles that were seized in government operations (however, these may not have been maintained as well and you may not know what you are getting). For more information see `www.gsa.gov` or `www.gsaauctions.gov`.

Enterprise Rent-A-Car also has used car sales. They have haggle-free buying (so you save money but can't save more by being clever), they take trade-ins, and each vehicle must pass a 109-point certification before being sold. They come with a 1-year warranty and they offer an incentive program if you convince your friends to buy an Enterprise used car as well. Some people swear by them, so check it out.

Maintenance

Car maintenance can be a problem. Many garages are shady if not outright dishonest. Find a reputable garage and stick with it; ask someone who has been around for awhile. Dealerships can be more reliable for quality repairs than independent shops, but also more expensive; and, like all automotive repair shops, they may try to convince you to get service or repairs that are not yet necessary. There are several tire companies in the Cambridge area that sell tires at large discounts; watch for ads in the MIT newspapers. Wholesale clubs such as **BJs** and **CostCo** tend to also sell tires.

Clothing

New Clothing

In general, new clothing stores can be found at all of the major shopping malls in the area. Check out the *Shopping Malls and Districts and Department Stores* sections of this chapter. Boston's better (read: more expensive) clothing stores are for the most part along Boylston and Newbury Streets from Boston Garden to the Prudential Center. These include **Sak's Fifth Avenue** (617-262-8500) at the Prudential Center, **Brooks Brothers** (617-261-9990) at 75 State St., and several smaller stores. **Filene's Basement** (617-542-2011) in the basement of Filene's at Downtown Crossing is a great place to shop, as everything there is reduced. Some of the merchandise is seconds or irregulars, and you should be sure you know why it's irregular before you buy it. Beware: unless things have changed, there is only one dressing room for women, and none for men. Wear clothing which you can try other clothing on under or over. It gets very crowded on Saturdays; the best time to go is during the day during the week. For more creative styles, try the stores on Charles St. at the foot of Beacon Hill and in or near Harvard Square. Newbury St. and Harvard Square have a bunch of "hip" and trendy clothing stores that target over-bankrolled college students. For example, **Allston Beat** (Newbury St.) sells whatever is fashionable among college students; **Ozone** (338 Newbury St.) has hipster Paul Frank/Von Dutch with a dash of raver clothing, and of course **Urban Outfitters** (corner of Newbury St. and Mass. Ave. in Boston, also in Harvard Square) specializes in mid-priced trendy stuff (clothes, books, housewares) that gets relatively inexpensive when it goes on sale (there is also a clearance section in the basement). **H&M** (350 Washington St, in Downtown Crossing, Cambridge Galleria location coming soon) has cheaper trendy stuff and is worth checking out.

Used Clothing

Used clothing is a cheap way to get funky things which you might usually refuse to pay more money for. Many stores that sell used clothing sell it sometimes (but not always) for less money than their new clothing. **Oona's** (617-491-2654) at 1210 Mass. Ave. near Harvard or 1110 Boylston St. in Boston has creative-styled used clothing. Cheaper sources of used clothing include **Salvation Army** stores, one of which is at 382 Mass. Ave. in Central. The misleadingly named **Dollar-A-Pound+** at 200 Broadway in

Cambridge sells used clothing by the pound ($1.50/lb., $0.75/lb. on Fridays). It's an experience. Upstairs from Dollar-A-Pound+ is **The Garment District** (617-876-5230), which is worth visiting when you make it to Dollar-A-Pound+. **Planet Aid** (two locations: 30 JFK St., Harvard Square and 306 Newbury St., Boston; www.planetaid.org) is a nonprofit organization.

Clothing Repair and Dry Cleaning

Alpha Cleaners and Tailor, located at W20-006 in the basement of the Student Center, offers alterations and dry cleaning Monday through Friday 9am-5pm. Their service is excellent and the prices are very good. Average turnaround time is 2-3 days. In the Galleria, **The Men's Wearhouse** (617-494-0900) will mend most suits, as well as rent tuxedos. In Kendall Square there is **Arrow Dry Cleaners** (290 Main St., 617-354-4088) who mend clothing, dry clean, and repair shoes.

Costumes and Creative Attire

There are plenty of resources in Cambridge and Boston for attention-grabbing apparel. **Boston Costume** (69 Kneeland Street, Boston, MBTA: Downtown Crossing; www.bostoncostume.com) sells and rents full costumes and accessories. Wigs and drag-queen glam can be had at **Dorothy's Boutique** (190 Mass. Ave., Boston, 1-866-253-9335; Mon-Sat 9:30am-6:30pm). For Rennaisance/Goth style, **Gypsy Moon** (1607 Mass. Ave., MBTA: Porter; www.gypsymoon.com) has high quality stuff. For Goth, Punk & Fetish try **Hubba Hubba** (534 Mass. Ave., Central Square) or **Hootenanny's** (The Garage, Harvard Square). For a military look, the **Army Barracks** (328 Newbury St.) has surplus dress uniforms, hats, boots, gas masks and so on.

Comics

First off, even if you have just a passing interest in comics, read Scott McCloud's *Understanding Comics*. (His *Reinventing Comics* is also worth a read).

OK, now that you're sufficiently hyped up, rejoice: there are incredible comic book shops around MIT. Unlike a lot of comic shops, the owners are not fat, geeky misanthropes and they don't yell at you for reading comics off the shelves (even for hours on end).

Million Year Picnic (617-492-6763), 99 Mt. Auburn St.; MBTA: Harvard. Prides itself on having the largest collection of independent and underground comics in Boston. Besides that, they stock the largest collection of European comics in Boston, as well as a vast and eclectic collection of graphic novels, adult comics, translated manga, DC/Vertigo/Marvel, and comic related T-shirts cramped in a very small store. Pretty good back stock if overpriced. Staff sometimes snooty or rude, but then again if you were an aging hipster forced to have hours-long conversations with the loonies around Harvard Square, you'd be too. Have been known to keep subscriptions for up to six months between pickups.

Comicopia (617-266-4266), 464 Commonwealth Ave. #13; MBTA: Kenmore. Run by an MIT alumnus, this store has the best customer service around — they're friendly and won't look down on you even if you collect *X-Men*. Superb collection that beats MYP (except as above), especially in translated manga, paperback and hardcover collections in a spacious and chill store. All the cards, statues, posters, and knick-knacks anyone could care for.

New England Comics (617-354-5352), 14A Elliot Street; MBTA: Harvard, among others. Publisher of *The Tick* and thus has a complete collection of related paraphernalia. Besides that and a very good subscription service, nothing here that beats the above two stores — mostly mainstream American stuff. The only store that might bitch you out for reading comics off the shelf. Back issue stock used to be supreme but is now disappointing.

Newbury Comics (617-491-0337), 36 JFK St., Cambridge; MBTA: Harvard, among others. Despite its name, mainly sells CDs and is reviewed in the *Music* section. Small selection of mostly mainstream stuff and quite expensive.

Sasuga Bookstore (see above, under Books) Japanese bookstore with decently large collection of recent *untranslated* manga, anime videos and DVDs, anime CDs and a nice selection of weekly manga magazines. Store understands value of catering to anime / manga-obsessed gaijin and will special-order anything that's in print.

Boston hosts the annual Great American Comic Book Expo every October, focusing mostly on DC/Vertigo/Marvel stuff. Around Cambridge and Somerville, both towns with an abnormally high appreciation of the comic medium, there's usually an expo/convention/festival of some sort once a year, mostly focusing on independent and underground comics.

If you like creating your own comics instead of merely reading them, get in touch with *Voo Doo* magazine (see the **Media** chapter), which is always looking for comic talent (both writing and illustrating). On the other hand, if you can muster a decent semiweekly serial comic (bonus points if it can be relevant to the MIT experience), contact *The Tech* and rid them (and us) of one of their many embarrassments. Million Year Picnic will carry your 'zine/comix if you ask nicely.

Computers

The four best places to acquire computers at MIT are the mailing list `reuse`, which offers free older computers from people who no longer want them; the **Apple Store**, in the CambridgeSide Galleria or online at `store.apple.com`, for cool computers that work; **Best Buy**, in the CambridgeSide Galleria, for cheap computers; and **PCs for Everyone** (617-395-7200, `www.pcsforeveryone.com`), across the street from the Galleria, for custom computers or for parts so you can do-it-yourself. For accessories and media, the **Micro Center** (617-234-6400, 727 Memorial Drive) is your run-of-the-mill computing megastore with typical prices.

To purchase through MIT go to `web.mit.edu/ecat/`. Their prices aren't always the best, but MIT does have some institutional discounts. In particular, MIT students get a reasonably significant discount from Apple; follow the link from the ECAT web page for instructions on how to make sure you get it.

Before buying software, first make sure that you can't just get it for free from MIT. Common places to look include `web.mit.edu/software/` and `web.mit.edu/is/products/vsls/`. Your department may also have purchased site licenses for software specifically related to your field. Check out your departmental website or talk to your department's network administrator for details. The **MIT Computer Connection** may also be able to get you discounts on software purchased through `dell.com` or `govconnection.com` — see the *Computers* section in the **MIT Facilities** chapter for more information on buying and using computers at MIT.

For software pricing, the **Coop** is pretty good; students get educational discounts on most software. The Coop's selection is not that great, but if you ask, they will sometimes order out-of-stock items. Another good place to get educational versions of popular, expensive software packages is BU's **University Computers** (617-353-1800, 533 Commonwealth Ave., Boston; MBTA: Kenmore; `www.universitycomputers.com`). You'll need your student ID. The best place to shop for educational versions of software online is probably **JourneyEd** (`www.journeyed.com`); you have the hassle of having to fax them proof that you're a student, but once you have an account it's usually cheaper than going to a real store even including shipping (be careful though — their default shipping option is FedEx, so you'll get slugged more than you expect for shipping unless you change it to a cheaper, slower option).

Copying and Printing
There are copying machines everywhere, particularly on campus. Most offices have one, and there are several in the library. There is also **CopyTech** (Buildings 11, W20 and E52, among other locations). If you have a very large job, they can help you find something that fits your budget; also ask **LSC** or **APO** for advice. (See the **MIT Facilities** chapter for more details.) For smaller jobs (if you try not to look too suspicious) most office workers will not question you when you come in to use their copy machine.

Kinko's (617-494-5905) is at 600 Technology Square and they, too, have other offices. **BFF Printers** (previously TypoTech; 617-492-6300) at 1120 Mass. Ave. has many services, including doing blueprints. **Minuteman Press** (5 Cambridge Ctr., 617-876-3688) does high-end press work and duplication.

If you want to put out something in a large print run, like a newspaper, magazine or book, there are a plethora of printers in the area who will usually give you wildly varying quotes for a particular job — too many to list here, with the exception of **Turley Publications** (`www.turley.com`, 413-283-8393, ask for Keith Sikes) who consistently delivers rock bottom quotes on jobs using newsprint stock, such as zines. Your best bet is to look around campus for publications similar to your physical specs; people on campus typically select the printer who can deliver the appropriate quality for the lowest cost, and they usually list the printer they used inside one of the covers, so you will at least get a place to start.

Department Stores
Name any type of merchandise, and there's probably a department store somewhere in Boston that sells it. Below is a list of some of the more common department stores in the area and their closest locations.

Best Buy: Cambridgeside Galleria (617-577-8866); **Bloomingdales**: Chestnut Hill Mall (617-630-6000); **Filenes**: Cambridgeside Galleria (617-621-3800), Downtown Crossing (617-357-2100), Belmont Center, Chestnut Hill, Square One Mall; **K-Mart**: Sullivan Square, Somerville (617-628-9500), 400 Western Ave., Brighton (617-562-4492); **Lord and**

Taylor: Prudential Center (617-262-6000), South Shore Plaza, Burlington Mall, North Shore, Natick Mall; **Macy's**: Downtown Crossing (617-357-3000), Braintree, Burlington Mall, North Shore, Peabody Mall, Natick Mall; **Marshalls**: Downtown Crossing (617-338-6205), Boston, Dorchester, Medford, Watertown; **Neiman Marcus**: Copley (617-536-3600); **Pier 1 Imports**: Porter Square (617-491-7626), Brookline, Everett; **Sak's Fifth Avenue**: Prudential Center (617-262-8500); **Sears**: Cambridgeside Galleria (617-252-3500), Square One Mall, Saugus, Braintree, Burlington Mall, Natick Mall; **Target**: 180 Somerville Ave. (617-776-4036), Everett, Watertown Mall; **TJ Maxx**: Brookline (617-232-5420), Medford, Alewife. See *Shopping Malls and Districts* for directions to many of these.

Drugstores

There are several drugstores in the area. Most convenient to those near East Campus is **Kendall Drugs** (617-876-8680), in Kendall Square. More rationally priced drugstores include **CVS** (617-354-4130) on Mass. Ave. in Central Square, the CVS in Harvard Square (with a pharmacy) and the CVS in the Cambridgeside Galleria (without a pharmacy). The CVS in Porter Square (617-876-4037) is open 24 hours, including pharmacy. The CVS at Charles/Mass. General Hospital (MGH) is also open 24 hours (617-227-0437), but the pharmacy has limited operations, 8am to midnight. The **MIT Pharmacy** (E23, x3-1324, M-Th 8.30am-7pm, F 8.30am-5pm, 24-hour scrip refill hotline x3-0202) has some interesting items, but not a great selection. Verify that your health insurance is accepted at the MIT Pharmacy if you have outside insurance; MIT subsidizes all prescriptions, but it still may cost more than your co-pay. A **Brook's Pharmacy** is located next to the Star Market on McGrath Highway. Many grocery stores in the area also have pharmacies, but the University Park Star Market does not.

Electronics

The most interesting place to buy electronic equipment is **E.L.I. Incorporated** (617-547-4005, www.eli.com) at 288 Norfolk St., Cambridge. This place has a constantly changing inventory of surplus devices, parts, components, and junk, especially junk. Remember to bargain, particularly for more expensive pieces. Downstairs from E.L.I's is a place which sells new chips.

There is also a **Radio Shack** (617-547-7332) on Mass. Ave. in Central Square and one in the Cambridgeside Galleria (617-577-0024). They are decent but not particularly impressive (not to mention infuriatingly incompetent); they're most appropriate for consumer components such as speaker wire and things of that sort.

If you have a car, the biggest and best-stocked place to go is "You Do It" Electronics (www.youdoitelectronics.com, 781-449-1005, 40 Franklin St., Needham; hours M-F 9am-9pm, Sa 9am-6pm, Sunday closed). In addition to all sorts of parts for the hobbyist, they sell many kits and pro audio-visual and lighting equipment.

Many MIT people who use hard-core quantities of electronic components order them online from wholesalers such as **DigiKey** (www.digikey.com), **Jameco Electronics** (www.jameco.com), and **Hosfelt Electronics** (www.hosfelt.com).

For used electronic equipment and parts of all kinds, subscribe to the reuse mailing list, and see the **Swapfest** section of this chapter for details on the monthly electronics flea market. Good online retailers for surplus (*i.e.* cheap, usually new but sometimes used) parts include **C & H Sales** (www.candhsales.com) and **Electronic Goldmine** (www.goldmine-elec.com), both very popular with robot builders and other tinkerers.

The **Equipment Exchange and Storage Warehouse** (WW15-197, 617-253-5611, web.mit.edu/property/www/ww15.htm) is located at 350 Brookline Street, Cambridge, MA. The warehouse is open Monday through Friday, 10:30am-2:30pm. The Equipment Exchange and Storage Warehouse has surplus lab, computer and office furniture. Preference is given to people wishing to reuse items at the Institute. There is no charge for items that are transferred back on campus. You must arrange for your own transportation and/or moving. Items not claimed for transfer are sold to the general public for reasonable prices.

Eye Care

Routine eye examinations and services for eyeglasses and contact lenses are available in several nearby establishments. The **MIT Medical Eye Service** offers comprehensive eye care including contact lenses. Appointments can be made for routine eye examinations, contact lens fittings, or evaluations with one of the staff optometrists. These visits are fee-for-service. Contact lenses can also be ordered from the Eye Service. If you are experiencing an eye problem which requires urgent care, you should call Urgent Care x3-1311. Visits that are not considered "routine" are often covered by the MIT Student Health Fee.

The Medical Department also offers eyeglass services at **MIT Optical** in the basement of the Stratton Student Center (W20-027), reachable at x8-LENS (x8-5367). They are open M-F 9am-6pm. An MIT ID is required and there is a 25% discount for students, meaning that prices there will be lower than anywhere else in the private sector. They have a good selection of lens types (generally much better than the private sector) and can order anything that you want. They don't have contact lenses, you have to go to the Med Center for them.

LensCrafters (closest outlets in the Cambridgeside Galleria and on Boylston St. in Boston) lets you choose your frames and then will make your glasses in about an hour at the same location. Most stores have an optician so you can get your eyes checked before you buy your glasses. If you have forgotten your prescription, they can call the Med Center to get it for you. They also carry contact lenses and will adjust your glasses for free pretty much forever after you buy them.

Other options in the area include **Four Eyes** (somewhat inexpensive) and **Cambridge Eye Doctors** (nicer frames), both in Harvard Square. Many of the wholesale clubs in the area (*e.g.* **BJs**, **Costco**) also sell frames, eyeglass lenses and contact lenses and offer free adjustments. Some may even offer optical exams.

Need contacts and don't want to go through the Med Center? Try 1-800-CONTACTS or www.1800contacts.com. You give them the name and phone number of your optician and your prescription and they'll ship you your contacts. Easy to use, excellent return policy.

Fabrics

Good fabric stores do exist in the Boston area; they're just hard to find. Many of them hide out in Chinatown. **Winmil Fabrics** (617-542-1815) at 111 Chauncy St. in Chinatown has mostly remnants and basics. They're cheap, if they have what you want, and they have the best service — they'll also stock fabrics for you on request. **Sew Low** (within walking distance at 473 Cambridge St.) is warehouse-style and requires a bit of searching to find what one is looking for, but has dirt-cheap prices and some nice finds. They also play Christian radio at full volume. **Sew-fisticated** (also walkable at Twin City Plaza, the mall on McGrath Highway with the Star Market, 617-625-7996) has some interesting fabrics at decent prices. They'll treat you like dirt for free. **Van's Fabric** in Chinatown (14 Beach St., 617-423-6592; MBTA: Downtown Crossing) has gorgeous Vietnamese and Chinese brocades and silks. Note that their fabrics tend to be 30" wide! **Clement Textile** (617-542-9511) at 54 Kneeland St. has some good stuff but mostly junk. You should unfold and check anything you intend to purchase here before you pay for it to be sure it is in decent condition. **Windsor Button** (617-482-4969, www.windsorbutton.com) at 35 Temple Place has buttons, buckles, trims, embroidery stuff, notions, fake flowers, beads, etc. An out-of-town shop, **Fabric Place** (508-872-4888) in Framingham and Woburn is good for decorating fabrics, including drapery and upholstery materials, and basics. It has retail prices and a helpful staff.

Florists

There are two florists down Mass. Ave. from MIT: **University Florist** (617-492-5700) on the corner of Main St. and Mass. Ave. and on Mass. Ave. in Central Square. Both are decent and friendly. **Kendall Flower Shop** (617-661-8180) in Kendall Square is an award-winning FTD florist which delivers in the greater Boston area. There are a couple of florists in Harvard Square too: **The Brattle Square Florist** (617-876-9839) at 31 Brattle St. is very good and is reputed to never have an imperfect flower. **Winston Flowers** (617-541-1100) has a very good selection of rare and imported flowers and plants, although they can be rather expensive. The absolute fastest and cheapest flowers are available outside the Kendall Square T-stop, Mon-Fri 8am-7pm in Spring, Summer and Fall (no weekends). Winter hours depend on the weather; the stand is never open in January. Also keep in mind that grocery stores have flowers.

Food

Bakeries
See listings under the Bakery category in the **Restaurants** chapter.

Co-ops
The **Harvest Food Co-op** (617-661-1580) on Mass. Ave. in Central is the area co-op. In additional to the Central Square location there is also a Harvest Co-op in Jamaica Plain. To be a member you must make a $200 refundable equity deposit, paid either all at once or over time. In exchange for the equity you get a 2% discount. If you become a worker in addition to this you get a larger discount — an 8% discount for 3 hrs/month or 18% for 2 hrs/week. Note that you don't need a membership to shop at the Harvest Co-op, although it will save you money. Harvest also stocks a lot of packaged products, supplements, and fresh and deli items that aren't available at the bigger supermarkets, so it is worth browsing at least once.

There are also smaller co-ops which operate on the block level or out of a church or community center. The theory behind these is that when more people buy food together, they can buy bulk and it will be cheaper. Ask your neighbors if you live off campus and are interested in this possibility, and find out if one exists in your neighborhood.

If you are interested in buying food in bulk yourself, there are a number of warehouse "price club" stores in the area. These places typically charge a yearly membership fee and then allow you to purchase bulk products, from food to clothing, housewares and car supplies (though there is typically not a great selection within a particular subcategory). The closest one to MIT is **BJ's** in Medford (278 Middlesex Ave., 781-396-0451, www.bjs.com) which has a $40 annual membership fee. **Costco** (www.costco.com, $45 annual membership) also has several locations in Massachusetts, including one in Everett, about 2 minutes away from BJs. You can get to both via the last stop on the Orange Line; CostCo is just a bit closer if you're going to take the T. The closest **Sam's Club** is in Natick. You're really best off trying to get to all of these places by car (think about how you're going to carry wholesale quantities of stuff back on the T), but since they can be especially handy when planning a party, you will probably be able to find someone to take you if you express it in that context.

Ethnic Food

Cambridge and Boston are home to a number of ethnic food markets. **Shalimar Food & Spices** (617-868-8311), at 571 Massachusetts Ave. in Central Square, has a wealth of Indian food supplies including spices, beans, nuts, frozen meals and breads, and essentials like curry, tandoori, and vindaloo paste. There are several small Indian markets in the Boston/Cambridge area. These markets, including Shalimar, are the cheapest places for spices of any kind in the area.

For Japanese food, groceries, and boutiques, be sure to check out the markets in the **Porter Exchange Mall** at 1815 Mass. Ave. near Porter Square — sometimes referred to as a miniature Japan Town. There is also **Yoshinoya** (617-491-8221) at 36 Prospect St., right in Central Square. **Lotte Food** (297 Mass. Ave., 617-661-1994) is a Korean grocery store extremely close to campus, in Central Square near where Landsdowne St. crosses Mass Ave.

Take the T to Chinatown on the Orange Line and you'll find many small Chinese markets. The infamous **Super 88** (617-541-5624), at 50 Herald Street, offers an enormous selection of Eastern cooking options. The Super 88 in Dorchester, at 101 Allstate Road in the South Bay Shopping Center, is even bigger than the Chinatown branch. You can get there by T: take the Orange Line to Andrews. It's next to the Home Depot. There's also one on the Brookline/Allston border at 1095 Commonwealth Avenue (Green Line to Packard's Corner or SafeRide to ZBT and walk down Naples Road).

For Kosher food, take the MBTA Green Line to Coolidge Corner. Many of the shops in this area — including **The Butcherie** (617-731-9888) at 428 Harvard St. and **Ruth's Kitchen** (617-734-9810) at 401 Harvard St. — are Kosher. Check with the MIT Hillel for more information. Watertown, about a 10-minute bus ride from Harvard Square, has a number of Middle Eastern markets as it is home to a large Lebanese community.

Grocery Stores

Which grocery store is most convenient for you will depend, of course, on where you live. There are several decent ones in the area. There is a **Star Market** (617-494-5250) located right at the edge of campus in University Park at 20 Sidney Street. There is also a Star Market at the Porter Square T stop on the Red Line, and one on McGrath Highway opposite Sav-Mor Liquors, as well as other branches in the Boston/Cambridge area. Of particular interest may be the sole remaining 24-hour Star Market, located at 33 Kilmarnock St. in Boston, near the intersection of Brookline and Boylston streets just past Fenway Park (MBTA: Green Line to Fenway; also walkable or easily bikeable). Star Market is a subsidiary of Shaw's Supermarkets and participates in a cardholder plan whereby you receive "discounts" on certain items for having a unique card. This card tracks your purchase pattern, but does not have your name printed on it, so if you give yours to a friend and they lose it, you can get another one free of charge. If you're paranoid, you can also just give false details when you fill out the form (available at the customer service desk), as they don't check them. Since you're undoubtedly being overcharged without it, it's worth having one if you plan on doing any shopping at these stores.

A more upscale supermarket with tastier food and correspondingly higher prices (though less than you might expect to pay for specialty items), and also a wine and beer selection, can be found in **Trader Joe's** — the closest one is at 727 Memorial Drive (towards Harvard, 617-491-8582) across the parking lot from the Micro Center. There's also a smaller Trader Joe's at 899 Boylston St. (across the bridge, parallel to Newbury St.) that sells the more popular goods but no liquor. Open 9am-10pm daily. For gourmet foods, **Cardullo's** (6 Brattle St., Harvard Square) sells expensive imported goods and culinary delights such as truffle oil.

Harvest Co-op (617-661-1580) is an organic and whole foods supermarket. They carry locally grown produce in the Spring-Summer-Fall months, and host a farmers' market in the parking lot each Monday until late November (a similar one is held in Harvard Square on Sundays). A **Whole Foods Bread and Circus Market** (617-876-6990), at 320 River Street in Cambridgeport, was opened in the Fall of 2001. Whole Foods is probably the cheapest place for organic products in the Boston area. They have both organic and non-organic produce. The non-organic is competitively priced and is as good as or often better than that at "normal" groceries. They also have a decent selection of ethnic and "healthy" foods other than produce — in addition to meats, fish, and cheeses, Whole Foods also boasts a bakery and prepared foods section with perhaps the best salad bar in the area. There is another Bread and Circus (617-492-0070) at 115 Prospect St. in Central Square. For many Italian foodstuffs such as fresh cheese, visit the North End.

There is a small grocery store, **LaVerde's** (617-621-0733), in w20. It is a bit more expensive than the larger markets, but hey, it's in w20. LaVerde's has a limited (though impressive in some areas) selection but also has a sub and sandwich counter, and many people often get their lunch or dinner right there. Recently, MIT allowed LaVerde's to take the MIT card, making it more convenient for students who need a way to get their parents' money off the card without having to buy prepared food. It is the only place on campus open 24 hours (Sun-Thu during fall and spring term, 7am-11pm Friday, Saturday and during the summer). They also deliver and provide catering with just 24 hours notice (Excellent cookie platters).

MacGregor Convenience (also takes the MIT card) is located on the ground level of MacGregor. They have all the caffeinated goods you need in order to stay up all night long, including caffeinated water. **Baker Dining** also has a small convenience store that is open till 2am, as does **Pritchett** (upstairs in Walker, open only until 9pm). There used to be resident-operated convenience stores in Eastgate and Westgate, but no longer.

Haymarket

Haymarket is an open market, something you don't see too often around here. You should go there at least once in a while at this holy Institute, for the experience if nothing else. There is a Haymarket stop on the Green Line, or you can easily walk there from Government Center (also on the Green Line). If you continue down the street to the left of Faneuil Hall when coming from Government Center, you'll run right into it.

Haymarket is open Friday and Saturday more-or-less all day. Official hours are 6 AM to 6 PM and tend to be longer, especially in the summer. The hours vary with the booth. Some booths will stay open very late Saturday to try to sell the last of their produce; it gets cheaper in the evening, but remember: it's the last pickings, and it's been sitting out all day. Even earlier, prices are usually much better than those in the groceries, and the produce can be better, but beware. The produce you look at is not necessarily what will be put in your bag. Make them let you pick your own fruit or vegetables, or check what they put in the bag and refuse to pay for bruised or overripe produce. This happens less often if you go to the same people often enough that they recognize you.

There are wholesale-retail meat stores in nearby buildings, Quincy Market, and around Faneuil Hall. However, this is often not high-class stuff. Again, once you know the butcher you can get good bargains, but until then be careful. During the summer you should make sure the merchants you frequent have good refrigeration.

There are also grocery, cheese, canned goods, leathercraft, and other types of stores in the area. Be careful and watch your wallet, backpack, or purse. Pickpockets aren't stupid. Also, bring your money to Haymarket in the form of $1 bills or change, *not* tens or twenties.

Furniture

New Furniture

For generally useful and inexpensive items such as bookcases and storage options, you may want to try **K-Mart** or **Home Depot**. Assembly will be required, but the cost will be pretty low. Furniture from **Target** or from **Economy Hardware** (617-864-3300, 438 Mass. Ave., Central Sq.) tends to be overpriced, but Economy usually has discount coupons in the books that you'll see handed out on campus periodically. Making furniture is also an option; see *Hardware and Building Supplies*, below, for more details. Your friends and neighbors may make fun of you for it, but you'll be the one laughing when you have something unique and cool.

Stores that sell "real furniture" include **Putnam Furniture** (556 Mass. Ave., Cambridge), **Bernie and Phyl's** at 1 East Street in Cambridge, **Bob's Discount Furniture** and **Jordan's Furniture** in Natick or Waltham. All of these options will be fairly expensive. However, the Jordan's Furniture in Natick is probably the most bizarre and entertaining furniture store you'll ever see, and thus worth the trip. It has its own restaurant, ice cream parlor, animatronic FX show, virtual reality pirate game, and a genuine OmniMax cinema. The entire store has been decorated in a Mardi Gras theme.

Used Furniture

Check bulletin boards around campus and ads in *Tech Talk* for people selling their own furniture. Mailing lists like `reuse` are also good resources for furniture, or just walk around your building during move-out time asking for what people don't want (a tried and true method). The best time to do this is generally in the spring, as students graduate and move out permanently. There is also the **MIT Furniture Exchange** (WW15, x3-4293, `web.mit.edu/womensleague/fx/`) for MIT students. They both buy and sell used furniture. The hours are from 10am-4pm Tuesday and Thursday, and 10am-1pm on the first Saturday of every month. They are located at 350 Brookline, beyond Next House.

The Salvation Army (617-354-9159) at 382 Mass. Ave. sells cheap used furniture, but you should be sure to check the quality. **Sadye & Co.** (617-547-4424) at 182 Mass. Ave. has some antique furniture which they usually display outside, but tends to be somewhat expensive (though not unreasonable for antiques).

Beds and Futons

Before choosing between a bed and a futon, consider how long you will own it and how much you want to spend. A futon can always be used as a couch later on, but it is well worth it to spend the money up front to get a good futon mattress. You'll notice the difference in a month once the padding starts to compress. There are a number of futon stores along Mass. Ave., and all of them are expensive. To get an inexpensive futon, try **K-Mart** or any of the discount futon stores in the area.

Most of the major department stores (**Sears**, **Filenes**, **Macy's**, etc.) have furniture departments that sell mattresses. The difference between stores, in terms of brands and quality, is negligible. They all offer approximately the same sale prices and they all deliver. If you want to save money on your mattress, you may want to try the wholesale clubs like **BJs** and **CostCo**. You will certainly get a lower price, but you'll have to find a way to transport your new bed home.

Finally, there is **Big John's Mattress Factory** (617 876 6344) at 121 First St. near the Cambridgeside Galleria. This low-key shop looks a bit grungy but they have a good selection and make excellent mattresses at a very good price. They make the mattresses in the same building the store is in, so they don't sell name brands, but it means that you can order a custom mattress in almost any size. They deliver the next morning. Some people swear by them.

Gardening

Some students find it relaxing to plant a small garden on their windowsill, balcony, fire escape or porch. **Home Depot** has an extensive and inexpensive garden shop; see *Hardware and Building Supplies* for directions. **Mahoney's Garden Centers** have a Cambridge location at 880 Memorial Drive (617-354-4145, www.mahoneysgarden.com) which is easy to get to, and another location in Winchester which is much larger and better. There is another garden supply store at the intersection of Prospect and Washington Streets in Union Square, Somerville. Try to avoid buying plants from grocery stores and other unlikely venues — they are often sick before you take them home and will die quickly, leaving you with disappointment and less money.

Haircuts

The **New Tech Barber** (617-621-0848) in the basement of the Student Center is a barber and styling salon for men, women and children. Walk-ins are accepted and there is almost never a wait. Hours are M-F 8:30am-6pm, Sat 11am-4pm. **Technicuts** (617-225-2887) is also located in the Student Center for the rare occasions when there is a wait at New Tech. **Coop HairStyling** is located in the Kendall Square MIT Coop (617-577-8878). **Judy Jetson's** (1765 Mass. Ave.; MBTA: Porter) has pricier but funky hairstyling, dealing in unnatural colors, bleaching, braiding, *etc.* The **Kendall Barbers** (283 Main St., 617-876-1221) are the closest option on the east side of campus. For other off-campus locations, there is a useful listing of local beauty salons and hairdressers online at www.cambridge.zami.com/Beauty_Salon/

Hardware and Building Supplies

The best store for real hardware within walking distance is **Pill's Hardware** (617-876-8310) at 743 Mass. Ave. in Central Square. They sell fasteners by the pound and plenty of other useful items. Closer and more of a combination hardware and furniture store is **Economy Hardware** (617-864-3300), a few blocks up Mass. Ave. in Central (438 Mass. Ave.); prices range from a great deal to highway robbery. Their selection of paint is fairly extensive and reasonably priced; a good close place to go if you're thinking of repainting your room.

Dickson Bros. (617-876-6760) at 26 Brattle St. in Harvard Square has a good selection, but they are in Harvard Square and their prices will on the whole reflect this (some things are cheap, though). Many students are familiar with Dickson Bros. key duplication services. **Inman Square Hardware** (617-491-3405) is at 1337 Cambridge St. in (surprise!) Inman Square. **Sears** (617-252-3500) in the Cambridgeside Galleria has a decent selection of reasonable quality tools.

If you have a big job, or are just the kind of person who buys your hardware in bulk, the **Home Depot** chain has a number of enormous warehouse-type hardware stores in the area. If you have a car, the easiest one to get to is at 75 Mystic Ave. in Somerville (617-623-0001). Otherwise, the one at South Bay Center (617-442-6110, 5 Allstate Road, Boston; take the Red Line to Andrew) is most convenient by public transportation. There is also one in Everett (Orange Line to Wellington) a couple of miles from the Somerville store, and in the Arsenal Mall (#70 bus from Central Square). The closest **Lowe's** is in Woburn (781-376-5500) and you'll need a car to get there.

There are also many specialty supply stores in the area. **Boulter Plywood** (24 Broadway, Somerville, 617-666-1340,) stocks some interesting products including bending plywood and marine plywood. **Admiral Metals** (11 Forbes Rd., Woburn, 781-933-8300, www.admiralmetals.com) incorporates an outlet store called The Metal Source that sells metal by the pound for when you need stock right away, and also has online ordering. Most plastic distributors in the area are part of GE Polymers — one of the better ones is **Modern Plastics** (56 Pulaski St., Peabody, 800-634-8189 or 978-531-3154) — call before you leave and your plastic may be ready by the time you get there. **Altec Plastics** (116 B St, South Boston, 617-269-1400) sells plexiglas and acrylics for laser cutting and other art projects. For plumbing supplies, **Metropolitan Pipe** (303 Binney St., 800-MET-PIPE) is within walking distance but not very friendly or helpful. **F.W. Webb** (237 Albany St., Boston, 617-367-1326) is less convenient but has much better service. Tell them you're from MIT. For large orders, they will come to you.

There is a whole world of industrial supply catalogs for almost every area. Look for ones like www.mcmaster.com, www.granger.com, www.berg.com and www.digikey.com. In these cases, you will be getting convenience in exchange for cost, but it is sometimes worth it.

Kitchen Supplies
A good place to start looking for kitchen supplies would be **Sears** or the **Filene's Home Store** (617-621-3800) in the **Cambridgeside Galleria**. **Dickson Bros.** in Harvard Square also has some kitchen supplies. **Crate and Barrel** (617-876-6300) at 48 Brattle St. in Harvard Square has some creative dishes, glasses, and pottery. They are often expensive, but there is a bargain room on the lowest level which usually has very good buys. **China Fair** (2100 Mass Ave; 617-864-5030; MBTA: Porter) has great prices and an extensive selection of china, pyrex and sturdy dishes. If you'd rather just get rudimentary kitchen necessities insanely cheaply, so that it's not a big deal when your roommate steals them, **Dollar-A-Pound+** (200 Broadway in Cambridge), **Goodwill** (520 Mass Ave. in Central) and the **Salvation Army** (382 Mass. Ave. in Central) have crockery and silverware for pennies. For more exotic kitchenware, there's **Kitchens Etc** (MBTA: Alewife, in the strip mall on Alewife Brook Parkway near the station) which is a large store that only sells cooking supplies.

Liquor
There are many liquor stores in the Boston area carrying the popular brands of beer and liquor along with some assortment of wine. Prices vary, but the larger stores generally have lower prices.

In order to buy alcohol in Massachusetts, as virtually everywhere else, you must prove you're 21. This law is enforced to varying degrees by the different liquor stores, but things get noticeably tighter around election time, and the closer you get to Harvard Square. It helps to have a Massachusetts ID, many stores have been known to refuse to sell to people with ID from other states or countries (most annoyingly, Blanchard's in Allston won't even let you in the store with anything but a Mass. ID). It is also worth noting some stores will card people who come with you even if they are not buying anything.

The following stores either have convenient locations or above average selections and services.

Kappy's Liquors (781-395-8888), 10 Revere Beach Pkwy, Medford. Huge warehouse of alcohol. Also has other stores, including a smaller one at 215 Alewife Brook Pkwy, Cambridge (617-547-8767), just down the road from the Alewife T stop on the Red Line.

Libby's Liquor Market (617-354-3678), 575 Mass. Ave., Central Sq. has a convenient location and reasonable selection. Prices are somewhat higher than the big places. They used to offer an MIT discount before the silliness of recent years; maybe if enough people ask them about it they'll bring it back.

Martignetti's (617-782-3700) at 1650 Soldier's Field Road Extension, Brighton, was supposedly at one point the world's largest liquor store and has a huge selection of anything ever fermented or distilled; the wine and beer selections are particularly impressive. Prices are some of the lowest around. They have a second outlet, smaller but closer, at 64 Cross St. in Boston's North End (617-227-4535).

Marty's Liquors (617-782-3250) at 193 Harvard Ave., Allston, has lots of unadvertised discounts and an excellent selection of unusual beers and other esoteric libations.

Sav-Mor Liquors (617-628-6444) at 13 McGrath Hwy, Somerville, has a reasonably large selection and competitive prices. There is a Star Market across the highway, so it's a convenient way to buy liquor and mixers cheaply.

The Wine and Cheese Cask (617-623-8656) at 407 Washington Street, Somerville, is the best place in the area to go for wine and its gourmet food accompaniments. Great selection from around the world, and its knowledgeable staff will be happy to make a recommendation.

Many of the more up-market or alternative supermarkets such as **Bread & Circus**, the **Harvest Co-op** and **Trader Joe's** sell wine and beer. See the *Food* section for details.

Music

CDs and Records

There are lots of music stores around MIT. The walk from Building 7 down Mass. Ave. to the area around Harvard Square is a goldmine of stores catering to practically every taste. Harvard Square itself has six stores within blocks of each other, and the intense competition keeps selection high. (Since the vast majority of consumers are academic yuppies more concerned with availability than value, the prices around Harvard are pretty high.) Newbury Street also has some good stores.

Note: Besides Newbury Comics and the chain megastores, almost every store discussed below has around 40%-95% of their stock in vinyl. Obtaining a record player will easily quadruple your available selection of music, and finding a vinyl of a once-popular album is usually a lot cheaper than getting the CD reissue.

Along Mass. Ave.:

Satellite Records (617-536-5482, `www.satelliterecords.com`), 49 Mass. Ave. A store for the rich and aspiring DJ. Dance-oriented Techno, House, Trance vinyl and DJ equipment; insanely expensive. Snotty, unhelpful staff.

Skippy White's (617-491-4500), 538 Mass. Ave. Store named after the owner, a white guy obsessed with "black" music since the 60s. Specializes in R&B, soul, reggae, swing, gospel and oldies but the prices are high and CDs are disorganized. The vinyl collection is cheaper, more comprehensive and actually organized. About 10,000 old 45s of blues, R&B and soul collecting dust in the back.

Cheapo Records (617-354-4455), 645 Mass. Ave. Vinyl selection is extensive, over 10,000 LPs and 25,000 45s with a lot of it still in boxes or unorganized on shelves. A disc digger's paradise. Vinyl has lots of rockabilly, world, soul, jazz, country, bluegrass, folk, vocals, Caribbean, blues, reggae, rock from 60s to 80s, old-school hip-hop, and vinyl sets. CD selection is decent with older rock, blues, and soul. Prices medium to high but not really "cheapo." Staff interesting and insane.

Mojo Music (617-547-9976), 904 Mass. Ave. Vinyl has good selection in classic rock, folk, country, jazz, soundtracks, world, comedy, techno, hip-hop 12"s and blues for damn cheap to medium price. The CD selection is less extensive but has a comprehensive selection of independent local record labels. Few items over $10.00.

Looney Tunes (617-247-2238), 1001 Mass. Ave. Extensive selection of classical, folk, vocal, older rock (70s at the latest), and jazz vinyl. Also check out the soundtrack vinyl. CD selection has a good amount of indie rock and jazz. Interesting 7" collection. Prices range from cheap to pretty expensive.

Phase Four (617-497-4024), 1208 Mass. Ave. A small but interesting collection of rock and jazz, both new and used. LPs and CDs for cheap. Bootlegs and rare imports. An extensive collection of Atari 2600 games.

Harvard Square:

Planet Records (617-492-0693), 54 JFK St. #B. Planet Records is one of the best in Harvard Square. Used to have a monstrous record selection until their old store burned down. Their CD collection is extensive, well organized, and easy to look through. Occasionally missing things that most stores would have in spades, but their tendency to have several albums by that obscure artist that you just found out influenced all your favorite musicians more than compensates for this occasional flaw. A respectable selection of mid- to high-priced vinyl, usually in near-flawless shape.

Newbury Comics (617-491-0337), 36 JFK St.; **Tower Records** (617-876-3377), 95 Mt. Auburn St.; **HMV Music Superstore** (617-868-9696), 1 Brattle Square. Big chains that specialize in taking your money. Be prepared to spend $12-$18 for a new CD at these places. Newbury has a good collection of indie, "alternative" music, a decent hip-hop section, all manner of band T-shirts, dumb toys, dumb decorations and other things 13-year-olds buy to feel cool and "punk rock." Still, if you desperately need a CD by a mainstream or sidestream artist and are willing to pay too much, Newbury seldom disappoints. Has a smattering of electronic vinyl. The used section is good to browse but still overpriced. Tower Records and HMV, besides their classical and international sections for HMV, and jazz and blues section in Tower, have lesser variety than Newbury for similarly (or often more) ridiculous prices. These are often good places to shop for VHS/DVD copies of that television series you used to love as a kid.

Twisted Village (617-354-6898, www.twistedvillage.com), 12B Elliot St. It's possible you've never heard of a single artist in this store. Hard-to-find off-stream psych, prog, rock, avant-garde, noise, experimental, improv, jazz and modern composers. Some incredibly rare stuff. Does mail order for no extra cost. Equal amounts of vinyl and CDs. Used section is decent. Prices medium to high, but where else are you going to find this stuff? Great place to introduce yourself to new artists. Usually has a nice selection of adverts for local art performances. Staff always willing to chat.

In Your Ear! (617-491-5035), 72 Mt. Auburn St #A. Vinyl has lots of 60s rock, jazz, and indie rock with a smattering of experimental/noise. Good Elvis collection. Nice collection of indie and punk CDs. Prices are pretty cheap to medium.

CD Spins (617-497-7070), 54 Church St. Strictly used CDs. Quality of collection varies, but if you're willing to dig, you might find something for damn cheap.

Newbury St.:
Boston Beat (617-247-2428), 279 Newbury St. Mostly import CDs with a marginal progressive house and trance selection on vinyl. A relatively stagnant selection of vinyl seems to be held over from the previous owners. Average import prices.

Mars Records (617-441-0307), 299 Newbury St. Good selection of indie rock, electronic, and punk on both CD and vinyl. Surprisingly, the best hip-hop LP collection around. A nice collection of no-wave and obscure offstream 45s. Staff know what you're talking about and are willing to recommend. Prices medium to high.

Newbury Comics (617-236-4930), 332 Newbury St. Reviewed above. Same type of selection but smaller selection of kitschy toys and much larger selection of DVDs than the Harvard location.

Virgin Megastore (617-896-0950), 360 Newbury St. Large Location. Lots of mainstream music. Good public bathrooms if you are stuck in Newbury St. too long.

Other places:
Disc Diggers (617-776-7560), 401 Highland Ave., Somerville; MBTA: Davis. Over 10,000 used CDs with a fast turnaround rate due to furious discounting. Basically the Filene's Basement of CD stores. No CD costs more than $10 and it's quite possible you

can find what you want for about $3 or under. Perfect for patient browsers, who make up most of the clientele. Mostly rock CDs but they have something in every genre.

Knowname Records (857-540-9266) Corner of Huntington and Mass Ave, Boston; MBTA: Symphony. Hours: noonish to 8pm (generally, although during the summer they appear to be closed on sundays) The only authoritative jungle/drum & bass/UK garage/breakbeat record store in Boston. Although two record listening stations overlook scenic Huntingon Ave, ask whoever's working to hear your tracks on the PA before deciding. On average, expect to pay about ten dollars per plate. Knowname stocks a moderate selection of DJ related hats, t-shirts, and other trinkets at above-moderate prices. The comfortable couch in front is for significant others to lounge on while you decide which records you will eventually buy ... this week.

Nuggets (617-536-0679), 486 Commonwealth Ave.; MBTA: Kenmore Square on the Green Line. Tons of vinyl and a decent amount of CDs, focusing on sidestream and offstream rock and all kinds of jazz. A wall of 45"s in the back and a large $1-per-CD section. Nearly guaranteed to find something you want here and some obscenely good deals in the $1-per-CD section. Staff is snotty.

Stereo Jack's (617-497-9447), 1686 Mass. Ave., Cambridge; between Harvard and Porter T stops on Mass. Ave. Vintage jazz of all stripes, on CDs, LPs, and 78s, stacked and piled in a tiny space. Very friendly owner who can talk you up no matter what your experience level. Good prices except on the rareties.

Musical Instruments and Equipment
There are many different types of music makers, and different stores suit them individually. The following is a list that will be of interest to most 'college-type' musicians; i.e., the "I've always wanted to play guitar" sort. If you're looking to buy a grand piano, check the Yellow Pages.

Daddy's Junky Music (617-247-0909, www.daddys.com), 159 Mass. Ave. Just a few blocks from the Harvard Bridge in Boston, Daddy's is about 20 minutes away by foot or on the T (Red Line to Park Street, Green Line to Hynes/ICA). Daddy's has a better selection of used gear than any major store in the area, and prices are mostly negotiable. The store can be somewhat disorganized, however, and tag prices for new merchandise are usually a bit higher than other stores. Make sure to test everything out thoroughly, as some of the equipment (especially drums and used gear) has been in the store a long time, receiving less than tender treatment. The staff is generally friendly and helpful, though, and the careful shopper should be able to get some nice deals. Their repair service can be really spotty; i.e. they forget to call you back, repair the wrong thing, etc.

Guitar Center (617-738-5958, www.guitarcenter.com), 750 Commonwealth Ave., Boston. About 25 minutes away by foot or 20 on the T (Red Line to Park St., Green Line B to BU Central), has an excellent selection of mid-range and higher-end gear. They do not sell any high-school band type instruments, but have a better selection of guitars, basses, drums, and keyboards than any of the other stores. They also carry very nice DJ and pro audio equipment, along with a modest stock of used merchandise. There are a few slimy salesmen on the floor, particularly in the guitar department, and they will often push you around and turn their backs if you don't want to pay their price. Sidestepping these types pays off, however, as a helpful salesperson will often make very good deals on very nice gear.

Sandy's Music (617-491-2812, www.sandysmusic.com), 896A Mass. Ave. Bills itself as "Cambridge's Funkiest Music Store", which isn't far from the truth. Has an eclectic selection of instruments ranging from old-time acoustic, such as banjos and mandolins, to various aging electric things. Owned and operated by a cool bearded man named Sandy who knows everything there is to know about folk music and, undoubtedly, a million other things. About a 15 minute walk from 77 Mass. Ave., situated next to Mojo Records; a good place to buy the tuning fork or pitch pipe that's required for some music courses at MIT. Generally very reasonable prices. Hosts an "Old Timey Jam" every Monday at 8; probably a good way to meet local non-MIT musicians.

Photography

Calumet (www.calumetphoto.com), 65 Bent Street near the Cambridgeside Galleria, is large and well-stocked with photographic supplies such as paper, film reels, tripods, chemicals, plastic neg. holders, etc., and has a good selection of new cameras. **SBI Photo** (57 JFK St., Harvard Square) is smaller but has better prices and a helpful staff. **Ferenti Dege** (1300 Mass. Ave., Harvard Square, www.f-d.com) sells digital and analog cameras, film and simple darkroom and photography supplies. For the rare cases where you can't find what you want at those stores, try **E. Philip Levine Inc.** (23 Drydock Ave., Boston); it's a bit far, but it has everything you could possibly want for non-digital photography. They are also the best place to go to get a broken camera repaired. **Hunt's Photo and Video** (100 Main St., Melrose) requires a 20 minute drive, but will have all your darkroom needs — from film to enlargers, this place has it all.

Inside the Galleria, one can find all types of digital cameras to play with in the **Apple Store**, **Best Buy** and **Sears**. There is also a **Ritz Camera** there. A good place to go if you have a car is **Hunt's Photo and Video** (781-662-8822, 100 Main St., Melrose) — they have a very large selection of stuff for moderate prices and fairly helpful employees. For those who buy in bulk and want to compare prices, or need to see every possible product available, go to **B&H** at www.bhphotovideo.com. And of course there is always **eBay** for those that don't mind the risk (www.ebay.com). Most photo stores also sell used lenses, so keep your eyes open for ones that will fit on your camera. Always be sure to ask if the number on the price tag is the best the seller can do.

CVS in Central or Harvard Square does inexpensive 1 hour color processing. **LaVerde's** in the Student Center has a Konica dropoff point, and there is a Kodak dropoff in the Best Buy at the Galleria.

Colortek (617-451-0894, www.colortek.org) is the most visible professional photo lab in the area, with a drop box at the Kendall Deli and several retail locations in Boston (727 Atlantic Ave., MBTA: South Station, Mon-Fri 8:30am-7pm; 251 Newbury St., Mon-Fri 9am-6pm; 636 Beacon St., Mon-Fri 10am-7pm, Sat 10am-6pm). Colortek used to be known as 'Colorwreck' for butchering slide film (E-6). Others disagree; judge for yourself. But they do good work on color negatives (C-41) and prints.

A trio of professional labs services the high-end market. Although these labs cater to people who make their living off their photographs, prices are similar to Colortek's, though locations are somewhat less convenient. The labs are **Boston Photo** (355 Boylston St., Boston, MBTA: Boylston; www.bostonphoto.com), **Spectrum Select** (51 Melcher St., Boston, 800-320-0222), and **Zona Photo Labs** (561 Windsor St., Cambridge, 617-628-2545). The three are practically identical in quality, service and price — many people stick with just one out of habit or convenience. All the pro labs, including Colortek, offer the standard minilab services including digital prints and black-and-white processing.

In terms of rental darkrooms in the city, good luck. If you want to develop and print, take advantage of MIT's facilities. The Art Association's darkroom has no responsibilities except fees attached, *The Tech*'s darkroom is not often used because the paper mostly uses digital cameras and access is only given to the newspaper staff, and *Technique*'s darkroom is the most used and thus best equipped but entrance entails working for the yearbook. All are located in the Student Center. Some MIT dormitories, such as East Campus and Random Hall, have fully-functional, free darkrooms for both B&W and color film.

For those with only a budding interest in photography, letting the newspaper or yearbook supply the equipment and taking on an assignment in exchange is probably the cheapest way to get hold of a nice camera. *The Tech* provides professional Nikon digital cameras and lenses and *Technique* provides 35mm Pentaxes and film. Classes are also offered by the Art Association, but they cost money.

A fun event in October is the **Photographica** show in Waltham (a car is necessary) which features working and sometimes ancient camera equipment. This a great place to pick up cheap medium format or 75mm cameras. Usually, *Technique* takes a group to this event. Contact technique@mit.edu for details.

The **Musuem of Fine Arts** (to which MIT students have free admission) always has some photographs up and both the *Boston Phoenix* and the *Weekly Dig* list ongoing photo exhibitions in the area. MIT students also have membership benefits of the **Photographic Resource Center** (www.bu.edu/prc/) which organizes classes, exhibitions, and portfolio viewings in the Boston area. Also, the **Boston Photo Collaborative** (www.bostonphoto.org) offers much of the above in an informal, local atomsphere and hosts a fun photo critique night every two weeks.

Outdoor Gear

So you joined MITOC and want to be a European naturist ice climber, or perhaps you've decided that you simply must go biking in a blizzard, or you want to go 15 miles into the woods and have sex — or hell, maybe you just want to be able to deal with the spastic weather in this town. Now what? You need clothes and equipment, that's what. Most outdoorsy clothes and gear are expensive, no doubt about it, but you often get what you pay for. You can rent stuff from the MIT Outing Club (web.mit.edu/mitoc/) until you've saved up enough money to buy your own. MITOC is a good place to ask for information on stuff to do or what specific kind of equipment to get. By the way, don't be put off if you come across a few elitist condescending jerks in MITOC, — most of them are more than happy to help you figure things out.

For buying outdoor stuff, the internet is usually your friend, but some things you really need to try on in a store. Where to go? Well, there aren't too many choices. Luckily, they tend to be good, though each suited for slightly different things. **Hilton's Tent City** (272 Friend St., Boston; MBTA: North Station) is the best: good and cheap, though the selection can be strange. Halfway down an alley by the elevated Green Line, Hilton's has four floors packed full of random gear, reasonably well sorted by type, and attended to by knowledgeable outdoorsy punks. Anyone looking for trendy pseudo-hiker urban wear will be sorely disappointed (and good riddance!). A lot of their stock is a model year old, but that's why it's cheap. They have, among zillions of other things, one of the best selections of winter gloves around. This is also *the* place to go for tents. Hours are Mon-Fri 9am-9pm, Sat 9am-6pm, Sun 12n-6pm.

REI (Recreational Equipment Inc., 401 Park Drive, Boston, 617-236-0746, www.rei.com) is a large outdoor equipment chain, but is also a co-op, so you have the chance to buy a membership for a one-time fee (the membership will not expire as long as you make a purchase at least once a year). They have the best assortment of climbing gear, and lots of other basic stuff, as well as ski and snowboard repair. Hours Mon-Sat 10am-9pm, Sun 11am-6pm. **EMS** (Eastern Mountain Sports, a.k.a. Expensive Mountain Stuff) is another chain, with nearby locations at 1041 Comm. Ave., Boston (617-254-4250, Mon-Fri 10am-9pm, Sat 10am-7pm, Sun 12n-6pm), One Brattle Square, Harvard Square (617-864-1540, Mon-Thu 10am-8pm, Fri-Sat 10am-9pm, Sun 11am-6pm), and 855 Boylston St., Boston (617-236-1518, Mon-Sat 10am-8pm, Sun 12n-6pm). They carry pretty much all the outdoor gear you might expect (hiking, climbing, kayaking, camping *etc.*) as well as more wear-around type trendy clothing (particularly the Boylston St. location, which carries little else). Prices are largely aimed at the yuppie set, hence the nickname.

Printing

See *Copying and Printing.*

Shoes

Teddy Shoes (617-547-0443) at 548 Mass. Ave. in Central Square is decent and pretty cheap, although they are small. Small can be nice though, as sometimes bargaining is possible. There are some shoe stores at Downtown Crossing, and the department stores there such as **Filene's** (including the Basement) and **Macy's** carry shoes. The Cambridgeside Galleria has many shoe stores including **FootAction USA** (617-577-0155), **Payless Shoe Source** (617-225-0517) and **Lady Foot Locker** (617-225-2245). **Parade of Shoes** in Downtown Crossing is a decent discount store. A great shoe store that often has sale prices is **Berk's** (50 JFK St., Harvard Square, 617-492-9511) — they carry Doc Marten's, imports, sandals, etc. For comfortable shoes try the **Rockport Store** (83 Newbury St., MBTA: Copley). For discount sneakers, running shoes and walking shoes, try the **Saucony Outlet** (walking distance at 1066 Cambridge St., Cambridge, 617-547-4397) or the **New Balance Outlet** (61 North Beacon St., Allston, www.newbalance.com). Another shoe store is **Taha** (617-267-8432) at 727 Boylston St., Boston.

There are a couple of choices in terms of shoe repair. Kendall Square has **Arrow**, see the *Clothing Repair* subsection. On 42 Prospect St. in Cambridge there is **Jimmy's Shoe Repair** (617-868-8838), which has been there longer and is a chain.

Shopping Districts and Malls

Downtown Crossing is located at the intersection of Winter and Washington Streets and is at the center of Boston's shopping district. Easily accessible by T, this area hosts **Filene's** and **Macy's**, as well as **The Corner Mall** and **Lafayette Place**, fancy shopping centers with expensive fare. There are also many other stores in these few blocks, not all of which are expensive, and several carts selling scarves, clothing, jewelry, and other wares. The area is closed to cars - mostly. Every once in a while its wise to check behind you, there may be some vehicle approaching slowly.

Classy, exotic, and trendy stores tend to cluster in **Harvard Square**, Boston's **Back Bay** (especially around Newbury St. and Commonwealth Ave.), and at **Copley Place** and **Quincy Market**. These are fun places to look around and occasionally buy things. Lower priced, more pedestrian merchandise can be found in **Central Square** and in other not-so-touristy areas.

Chinatown is found on Essex and Beach Streets, on the Orange Line (Chinatown stop, of all things). Chinatown is consumed by the moon festival once during the summer and you can buy anything under the sun from street merchants. The Italian **North End**, located across the expressway from Haymarket on the Green Line, boasts a large number of great Italian restaurants and pastry shops of all sorts. Portuguese and Italian specialties and the best bargains in town can be found in **East Cambridge** between Lechmere and Harvard Square.

Shopping Malls

Boston has its share of shopping malls, and a few are located close to campus. The **Cambridgeside Galleria**, a fairly large mall, is located across from the Museum of Science. You can walk there or take their free van ("The Wave") from Kendall Square. The van leaves Kendall approximately every 20 minutes and operates Mon-Sat 9am-6pm, Sun 12n-6pm. It has stores of all varieties and price levels, including a **Best Buy**, **Sears**, **Filene's**, and a rather large food court. **Copley Place** and the **Prudential Center** are two interconnected upscale malls in the Back Bay, where it is often more fun to window shop than to buy. The most inexpensive malls in the area are the **Arsenal** and **Watertown Malls**, located across from each other in Watertown. Take the #70 bus from Central Square to get there.

If for some reason you can't find what you are looking for nearby, there are a quite a few large malls residing in suburbia. These include the **Burlington Mall** (781-272-8667, I93-N to I-95S by car), the **Chestnut Hill Mall** (617-965-3037) at 199 Boylston St. in Newton, and the **Natick Mall** (508-655-4800, MassPike I-90W by car). To get to the Burlington Mall without a car, take the Red Line to Alewife and then take the #350 bus. To get to the **Dedham Mall**, take the #35 bus from the Forest Hills stop (Orange or Green Line). There are also several shopping centers located along Routes 9 and 128 and both North and South Shore shopping centers.

Stationery and School Supplies

Perhaps your first instinct is to buy notebooks and things at **The Coop**. If you insist that all your stuff identify you as an MIT student, this is probably a good idea. Otherwise you might want to go to **University Stationery** (617-547-6650) on 311 Mass. Ave. across from Random Hall. They are friendly and either have or can find almost anything. They also offer a 10% discount to students which you may not even have to ask for. **Office Max** (www.officemax.com) offers free delivery on orders of $50 or more. Their closest storefront is in Twin City Plaza on McGrath Highway near the Star Market. **Staples** (www.staples.com) also offers free delivery on order over $50. Their closest store fronts are on 25 Court St., Boston, at Landmark Center near Fenway, or 57 JFK St. in Harvard Square. **Office Depot** (www.officedepot.com) offers free delivery on orders of $50 or more. They don't seem to have any stores in the area. The Cambridgeside Galleria also has several shops, such as **CVS**, which have cheap school supplies. Finally, MIT **CopyTech** has basic school supplies and thesis/resume supplies. Also see *Art and Drafting Supplies* in this chapter for high-end stationery.

Stereo Equipment

Experience has shown that salespeople at some stereo stores are more than willing to lie to make a sale. Remember that there are MIT students who are real experts. Ask around your living group before you buy anything. Never buy without comparison shopping, and never tell salespeople that you are just shopping around. They'll refuse to give their lowest prices in order to protect their competitor's "lowest price around" guarantee. Whenever you are told "rock-bottom dealers' cost", you're probably still looking at 100% markup. Local dealers should give a full "buyer protection" warranty. Watch for discontinued lines, which are usually good buys. Remember that you have to listen to the equipment in your room, not their sound room.

One way to buy stereos is to check bulletin boards and ads in *Tech Talk* for students selling theirs. Sometimes equipment gets sold because it is dying, but also sometimes it gets sold because the owner has bought a better system or is moving and doesn't want to or can't take the stereo with him or her. Stereo equipment shows up on reuse fairly frequently.

For new stereo equipment, Cambridge/Boston is not a great place to shop. **Best Buy** carries a lot of equipment of varying quality and sales people that run the gamut from infuriatingly moronic to tolerably helpful. **Cambridge SoundWorks** (also in the Galleria), has high end consumer stuff for high end consumer prices with a staff slightly better on average than Best Buy's. **Q Audio** (617-547-2727) at 95 Vassar St. buys and sells used equipment and has a good reputation. Their salespeople are knowledgeable, but can be snotty. **Bose** (www.bose.com) offers a discount to MIT students if you are looking for expensive, overhyped equipment with an MIT cachet.

Swapfest

The MIT Radio Society, in conjunction with the MIT UHF Repeater Association, the MIT Electronics Research Society, and the Harvard Wireless Club, sponsors a Swapfest on the third Sunday of each month, April through October. This is a place to buy, sell, and swap amateur radio, electronic, and computer equipment. Hams and non-hams alike are welcome. Swapfest is held at MIT's Albany Street Garage at the corner of Albany and Main Streets in Cambridge. The gate opens for buyers at 9am. There is a small admission fee. Flyers are everywhere during term. The place to sell that collectible old mini-mainframe you picked up on reuse.

Videos

Suncoast (617-252-9035) in the Galleria has a fair selection and is willing to special order. Also in the Galleria, **Best Buy** sells movies too and is the best place to find the new releases on sale. **Virgin Megastore** (617-896-0950) on 360 Newbury Street has an impressive selection of interesting videos, most notably a surprising number of those small-distribution television shows that you thought everybody had forgotten about. **Newbury Comics** (at the Newbury location) has a big selection of DVDs new and used. **Hollywood Express** (617-864-8400, 765 Mass. Ave., Central Square, other locations in Twin City Plaza and Porter Square) and **Blockbuster** in Central Square also have videos for sale, as do all of the wholesale clubs such as **BJs**, **CostCo** and **Sam's Club** — see Co-ops under *Food* for locations.

For video rental, see the **Entertainment** chapter.

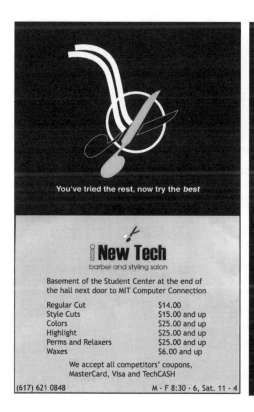

Restaurants

Previous editions of this book began this section with "Admit it: Lobdell is not always edible." Despite the improvements to on-campus dining in recent years, that sentiment remains axiomatic. Fortunately, Boston isn't totally devoid of gastronomic goodness. This section is a compilation of some of the restaurants in the MIT and greater Boston area, especially those important to the so-called "MIT Experience."

Information on hours, credit cards, etc. was taken from menus, web sites, and restaurant employees; it is (of course) subject to change. The year in parentheses following each entry's description indicates the last time the basic information, such as address and phone number, or description was checked or updated. If you have any corrections to the reviews or to any other information, please send them to us. We will be eternally grateful. For those places with credit cards explicitly listed, the abbreviations are as follows: AE = American Express; CB = Carte Blanche; D = Discover; DC = Diner's Club; MC = Master Card; V = Visa. Those places that accept the MIT card are explicitly noted as such.

In addition to the actual address of the restaurant, most of the entries include brief directions and recommended modes of transportation. Boston and Cambridge can be confusing places to navigate, but they are surprisingly small and accessible by bicycle or foot once you know your way around. In particular, it's often faster to walk or bike to many locations on the Green Line than to take the T. From 77 Mass. Ave., the #1 bus offers a quick way to get across the river or into Central and Harvard Squares. Please note: Kendall Square (where the T-stop is) is not the same as One Kendall Square, which is about five minutes walk away, past Technology Square on Broadway Street.

There are countless web-based resources for reviews and menus, including (in no particular order):

MIT alum William Chuang	web.mit.edu/wchuang/www/menus/
mit411.com	www.mit411.com
Boston Phoenix	www.bostonphoenix.com/boston/food_drink/
Boston Citysearch	boston.citysearch.com
Zagat's Online	www.zagat.com
Green Line Menus	www.greenlinemenus.com
Tufts Life	www.tuftslife.com/dining/
Boston.com	www.boston.com/ae/food/
DiningInMass	www.dininginmass.com/617/617.htm
Boston Vegetarian Society	www.BostonVeg.org/restaurants/
Amazon.com	www.amazon.com/restaurants/

Unofficial Guide to Life at Harvard	www.unofficialharvard.com
campusfood.com	www.campusfood.com
DiningIn	www.diningin.com

In addition to listing restaurants and menus, both campusfood.com and DiningIn allow you to order food for delivery from many restaurants online, but you still usually need to provide a phone number for the delivery guy to call.

Catering

Caterers come in handy whenever you need to feed a large group of people without too much hassle, such as for student group meetings, study breaks, and private parties. You generally get what you pay for in terms of quality of food and effort saved. If you are on a tight budget, you may want to consider supplementing a catered event with food from a grocery store or wholesale club.

There are a number of good caterers in the Cambridge area. If you are ordering party platters or à la carte, it is usually best to order based on the number of items you want. If you are ordering from a restaurant or getting boxed lunches, just order by the types of dishes and number of people you will have — you would tell them that you want these N types of pasta for M people and they will figure out how much food you get. They will almost always give you more food than you can eat, which is useful for making up for food lost from event crashers.

Most caterers will deliver free of charge. Their highest margins are on beverages and on paper products ($8 for a half gallon of orange juice!), so you may want to go to a grocery store or a wholesale club and pick these up ahead of time if you can. Some of the better deals require you to pick up the food. See the *Cars* section of **Transportation** for information about ZipCar if you don't have anyone in your organization with a car.

As a rough estimate, expect to pay at least $10 per person for a catered meal. Order your food as early as you can, although many operations only need 24 hours advance notice. When specifying where and when you want the food delivered, keep in mind that the vultures will descend as soon as they can. In other words, you can impress your guests by having the food ready before they arrive and take advantage of the ten minutes people will spend eating to say what you want to say, or you can keep your guests hostage waiting for food while you say what want to say. Even better, just order food and don't say anything at all.

When choosing food, remember that individuals you have invited may have dietary restrictions, food allergies, *etc*. Always include a vegan option or at least a vegetarian option. Not everyone will drink soda, so make sure water or juice is available. If you can, have people specify dietary restrictions when they RSVP, but if you can't ahead of time, just cover all the bases.

Your caterer probably won't clean up afterwards if they just drop off the food. Have plenty of garbage cans on hand and be ready to clean up afterwards.

The following three caterers are not restaurants, but they are good choices for catering:

LaVerde's Market

LaVerde's Market in the Student Center also offers catering. Almost anything you can get normally at LaVerde's you can get catered. This includes deli platters, salads (green, pasta, potato, etc.), hot entrees (lasagna, barbeque chicken, etc.), bagels, excellent cookie platters and desserts. They also do a healthy trade in coffee catering — you tell them when and where you want coffee and it appears. You leave the empty containers where you found them (or close by if the room will be locked) and they come and take them away again. LaVerde's is an especially attractive choice since they are on campus and can fill catering orders with just 24 hours notice. During term, they are open 24 hours a day Sunday through Thursday and 7am-11pm Friday and Saturday. LaVerde's is generally lauded for being very responsive to student needs; if you have a suggestion for how to make the store better, they are happy to listen and often quick to act.

MIT Catering

web.mit.edu/dining/catering/
web.mit.edu/dining/catering/mitfacultyclub/mit_catering_menu.html

MIT Catering, provided by Aramark, is very nice, convenient and pricey. Since Campus Dining has diversified its providers to include Sodexho and Bon Appetit, the MIT Catering menu seems to have decreased dramatically although the quality is still very good. In general, MIT Catering offers a variety of continental breakfasts and breakfast platters as well as a variety of boxed/bagged lunches, salads and party platters for lunch. They also offer desserts, snacks and beverages. Kosher options are available, although very expensive. Delivery is included on weekdays. Service utensils, paper goods and equipment are included. Place orders at least two business days in advance. Payment via credit card, interdepartmental requisition, cash or check.

Shaw's/Star Market Catering

www.shaws.com

Shaw's/Star Market Catering is about average in terms of catering quality and price, which is to say that they serve good to very good food at reasonable to expensive prices. They offer hot and cold breakfast platters, boxed lunches, deli platters, appetizers, salads, calzones and pizza, hot entrees and side dishes, desserts and bakes goods and floral arrangements. They prefer a minimum of 24 hours notice, although they do offer same-day delivery based on availability. Service utensils, paper goods and equipment available for a minimal charge. Pay with cash, check (you need a Rewards Card), or credit card. Cancellation fees may apply if you cancel within 24 hours. It is recommended to ask for your food to be delivered at least a half an hour before your event, as they have a tendency to be late in delivering the food.

In addition to the above caterers, many restaurants listed in this section will cater and delivery the food, especially if it's a large order. Among the tried and true are **Anna's Taqueria, Cinderella's, India Samraat, Mu Que Ca, Picante, Rebecca's Café, Red Bones,** and **Royal East**. Other places to try are **Andrew's Catering** (kosher), **Blue Ribbon, Bob the Chef's, Milk Street Café** (kosher), and **Pho Lemon**. Also, it doesn't hurt to ask your favorite restaurant if they cater.

Restaurant Listings

For your convenience, we've indexed the restaurants in several different ways. More complete descriptions follow in alphabetical order.

Within Easy Walking Distance

1369 Coffeehouse
All Asia Café
Amelia's
The Asgard
Asmara
Atasca
Au Bon Pain
Baraka Café
Bertucci's
Bisuteki Japanese Steak House
The Blue Room
Boca Grande
Brookline Lunch
Burrito Max
California Pizza Kitchen
Cambridge Brewing Company
Cambridgeside Galleria Food Court
Carberry's
Characters Bar & Grill
The Cheesecake Factory
Chicago Pizza
Cinderella's Italian Cuisine
Crossroads Restaurant and Lounge
Cuchi Cuchi
Desi Dhaba
Dunkin' Donuts, Baskin Robbins
Emma's Pizza
Fresco's
Ghandi
Helmand
Hi-Fi Pizza and Subs
Hsin Hsin
India Pavilion Restauran
India Samraat
Izzy's
Jerusalem Café
Kendall Square Food Court
King & I
Korea Garden
La Groceria Ristorante Italiano
La Luna Caffé
Legal Sea Foods
Lobdell
Mary Chung
McDonald's
Middle East Restaurant
Miracle of Science

Moody's Falafel Palace
Oleana
Pad Thai Café
Papa Razzi
Paris Crêperie
Pho Lemon
Picante Mexican Grill
The Plough and Stars
Pu Pu Hot Pot
Rangzen
Rebecca's Café
Rotisserie House
Royal East
Royal India
Shalimar Indian Grocery Store
Shalimar of India Restaurant
Spinnaker Italia
Stefani Pizzeria
Sweet 'n' Nasty
Toscanini's Ice Cream
Wendy's

Free/Cheap Delivery

All Asia Café
Ankara Café
Bertucci's
Brown Sugar Café
Chicago Pizza
Cinderella's Italian Cuisine
Domino's Pizza
Geoff and Drew's Late Night Incredible Cookies
Ghandi
Haveli
Hi-Fi Pizza and Subs
Hsin Hsin
India Samraat
La Luna Caffé
Nan Ling
New Asia
Pad Thai Café
Paris Crêperie
Pho Lemon
Pizza Ring
Pu Pu Hot Pot
Quan's Kitchen
Sicilia's Pizzeria
Stefani Pizzeria

Sweet Chili
Thailand Café
Tommy's House of Pizza
Wing-It
Wing Works
The Wrap

Open Before 8am
1369 Coffeehouse
Au Bon Pain
Aujourd'hui
Bova's
Bickford's
Brookline Lunch
Carberry's
Fresco's
Greenhouse Coffee Shop
International House of Pancakes
Krispy Kreme
Kupel's
LaVerde's Market
Mike's City Diner
Milk Street Café
Rebecca's Café
Rosie's Bakery and Dessert Shop
S&S Deli and Restaurant
Someday Café
South Street Diner
Sunny's Diner
Victoria's Diner

Open Past 11pm
Algiers Coffee House
Ankara Café
Anna's Taqueria
The Asgard
Asmara
Bickford's
The Black Rose
Bob the Chef's
Bova's
Buddha's Delight
The Cheesecake Factory
Chicago Pizza
China Sun
Christina's Ice Cream
Christopher's
Cinderella's Italian Cuisine
Crossroads Restaurant and Lounge
Cuchi Cuchi
Dali Restaurant and Tapas Bar
Denise's Ice Cream
Domino's Pizza

Finale
Fugakyu
Geoff and Drew's Late Night Incredible
Cookies
Ginza
Greenhouse Coffee Shop
Grendel's Den
Gyuhama
Herrell's
Hi-Fi Pizza and Subs
Hong Kong Restaurant
International House of Pancakes
John Harvard's Brew House
Kaya
Kentucky Fried Chicken, Taco Bell
Krispy Kreme
LaVerde's Market
Marche
Middle East Restaurant
Midwest Grill
Miracle of Science
Moody's Falafel Palace
Nan Ling
New York Pizza
Penang
Pinocchio's Pizza
Pizza Ring
Pizzeria Regina
Pizzeria Uno
The Pour House
Punjabi Dhaba
Pu Pu Hot Pot
Quan's Kitchen
Redbones
Royal India
Rudy's Café
Sabur
Sake
S&S Deli and Restaurant
Shabu Zen
Sicilia's Pizzeria
Someday Café
South Street Diner
Sunset Grill & Tap
Taiwan Café
Tommy's House of Pizza
Toscanini's Ice Cream
Trident Café
Urban Gourmet
Vinny Testa's
Wing-It
Wing Works

American

The Asgard
Au Bon Pain
Bickford's
Blue Ribbon BBQ
The Blue Room
Bob the Chef's
Brookline Lunch
Bugaboo Creek Steak House
California Pizza Kitchen
Cambridge Brewing Company
Characters Bar & Grill
Charlie's
The Cheesecake Factory
Christopher's
Darwin's Ltd.
Durgin Park
East Coast Grill
Eat
Evoo
Fire and Ice
Fresco's
Gargoyles on the Square
Greenhouse Coffee Shop
Grendel's Den
Hi-Fi Pizza and Subs
Hilltop Steak House
International House of Pancakes
Jake's Boss BBQ
Jimmy's Steer House
John Harvard's Brew House
Mike's City Diner
Milk Street Café
Miracle of Science
Mr. and Mrs. Bartley's Burger Cottage
Outback Steak House
Pizzeria Uno
The Pour House
Rebecca's Café
Redbones
Rotisserie House
S&S Deli and Restaurant
South Street Diner
Sunny's Diner
Sunset Grill & Tap
Top of the Hub
Urban Gourmet
Victoria's Diner
Village Smokehouse
Wendy's
Wing-It
Wing Works
The Wrap

African

Addis Red Sea
Asmara

Bakery

1369 Coffeehouse
Au Bon Pain
Bova's
Carberry's
Central Bakery
Geoff and Drew's Late Night Incredible Cookies
High Rise Bread Company
Kupel's
L.A. Burdick
Mike's Pastries
Rebecca's Café
Rosie's Bakery and Dessert Shop

Brazilian

Midwest Grill
Mu Que Ca

Brewpub/Bar

The Asgard
The Black Rose
Cambridge Brewing Company
Characters Bar & Grill
Crossroads Restaurant and Lounge
Hong Kong Restaurant
John Harvard's Brew House
Miracle of Science
Pizzeria Uno
The Plough and Stars
The Pour House
Rudy's Café
Sunset Grill & Tap
Village Smokehouse

Caribbean

Izzy's

Chinese

All Asia Café
Buddha's Delight
China Sun
Chinese Eatery
Hong Kong Restaurant

Hsin Hsin
King Fung Garden
Ling Garden
Mary Chung
Nan Ling
New Asia
Pu Pu Hot Pot
Quan's Kitchen
Royal East
Taam China
Taiwan Café

Coffeehouse

1369 Coffeehouse
Algiers Coffee House
Au Bon Pain
La Luna Caffé
Rebecca's Café
Someday Café
Toscanini's Ice Cream
Trident Café

Dessert

Ben and Jerry's
Bova's
Carberry's
The Cheesecake Factory
Christina's Ice Cream
Denise's Ice Cream
Dunkin' Donuts, Baskin Robbins
Emack & Bolio's
Finale
Geoff and Drew's Late Night Incredible
Cookies
Herrell's
J.P. Licks
Krispy Kreme
L.A. Burdick
Mike's Pastries
Rosie's Bakery and Dessert Shop
Sweet 'n' Nasty
Toscanini's Ice Cream

Fast Food & Food Courts

Bruegger's Bagels
Burger King
Cambridgeside Galleria Food Court
Chili's
Chinese Eatery
Dunkin' Donuts, Baskin Robbins
Kendall Square Food Court
Kentucky Fried Chicken, Taco Bell

Krispy Kreme
Lobdell
McDonald's
Porter Exchange Food Court

French

Arrow Street Crêpes
Aujourd'hui
The Elephant Walk
Harvest Restaurant
L'Espalier
Marche
Mr. Crêpe
Paris Crêperie

Greek

Fresco's
Greek Corner
Steve's Greek Cuisine

Indian

Bombay Club
Desi Dhaba
Diva Indian Bistro
Ghandi
Haveli
India Pavilion Restaurant
India Samraat
Passage to India
Punjabi Dhaba
Royal India
Shalimar Indian Grocery Store
Tanjore

Irish

The Black Rose
The Plough and Stars

Italian

Amelia's
Artu's
Bertucci's
Bova's
Carmen
Chicago Pizza
Cinderella's Italian Cuisine
The Dish
Domino's Pizza
Dom's Restaurant
Emma's Pizza
Hi-Fi Pizza and Subs
La Groceria Ristorante Italiano
La Luna Caffé
Maggiano's Little Italy
New York Pizza
Papa Razzi
Pinocchio's Pizza
Pizza Ring
Pizzeria Regina
Pizzeria Uno
Polcari's
Ristorante Marino
Sicilia's Pizzeria
Spinnaker Italia
Stefani Pizzeria
Tommy's House of Pizza
Vinny Testa's

Japanese & Korean

Bisuteki Japanese Steak House
Blue Fin
Fugakyu
Ginza
Gyuhama
Jae's Café
Kaya
Korea Garden
Koreana
Porter Exchange Food Court
Roka
Sake
Shabuso
Shabu Zen
Sweet Chili
Sushi Corner

Kosher & Halal

Kupel's
Milk Street Café

Moby Dick's
Taam China

Meat

Bisuteki Japanese Steak House
Blue Ribbon BBQ
Bob the Chef's
Bugaboo Creek Steak House
Durgin Park
East Coast Grill
Hilltop Steak House
Jake's Boss BBQ
Jimmy's Steer House
Kaya
Midwest Grill
Outback Steak House
Redbones
Rotisserie House
Shabuso
Shabu Zen
Village Smokehouse
Wing-It
Wing Works

Mediterrainian

Baraka Café
The Dish
Oleana
Sabur

Mexican

Anna's Taqueria
Boca Grande
Border Café
Burrito Max
Casa Mexico
Fajitas & Ritas
Picante Mexican Grill
Rudy's Café
Tacos Lupita
Taqueria La Mexicana
Tu Y Yo

Middle Eastern

Algiers Coffee House
Ankara Café
Baraka Café
Brookline Lunch
Helmand
Jerusalem Café
Lala Rokh
Middle East Restaurant

Moby Dick's
Moody's Falafel Palace
Oleana
Sepal

Portuguese & Spanish
Atasca
Casa Portugal
Cuchi Cuchi
Dali Restaurant and Tapas Bar
Iruna

Seafood
Atasca
East Coast Grill
Legal Sea Foods
Mu Que Ca

Thai, Vietnamese & Other Asian
All Asia Café
Brown Sugar Café
Chilli Duck
The Elephant Walk
Grasshopper

Hu Tieu Nam Vang
Jae's Café
King & I
New Asia
Pad Thai Café
Penang
Pho Lemon
Pho Pasteur
Spice
Sweet Chili
Thailand Café

Tibetan
House of Tibet
Rangzen

Vegetarian
Buddha's Delight
Grasshopper
Grendel's Den
Trident Café
Veggie Planet

AUTHENTIC CANTONESE CUISINE

Royal East

RESTAURANT

617.661.1660

782 MAIN STREET
CAMBRIDGE

Restaurant Descriptions

AE = American Express; CB = Carte Blanche; D = Discover; DC = Diner's Club; MC = Master Card V = Visa

1369 Coffeehouse
1369 Cambridge St. (Inman Square)
Walk or bike
Mon-Thu 7am-10pm, Fri 7am-11pm, Sat 8am-11pm, Sun 8am-10pm.
617-576-1369

757 Mass. Ave. (Central Sq.)
Walking distance
Mon-Fri 7am-11pm, Sat 8am-11pm, Sun 8am-10pm
617-576-4600

Coffeehouse, Bakery. Cutesy coffee shops in Inman and Central Squares, Cambridge. Chill, relaxed vibes and decent prices. They serve an assortment of coffee and espresso drinks, yummy blended drinks, and a bunch of baked goods. Many young people come in, either with friends or by themselves to study or partake of the board games and occasional newspapers. (2004)

Addis Red Sea
www.addisredsea.com
544 Tremont St., Boston (Back Bay)
Orange Line to Back Bay

Mon-Wed 5pm-10:30pm, Thu 5pm-11pm, Fri 11am-3pm & 5pm-11pm, Sat noon-11pm, Sun noon-10pm
617-426-8727

African. The atmosphere of this Ethiopian restaurant is excellent. They serve you food on the traditional mesob (table), and have a great selection of dishes to eat with injera (flatbread), including at least 8 that are vegetarian. Great to mix and match dishes too with a couple of combo options. The waiters were also knowledgeable about the culture and food. Check out the honey wine, Zilzi Tibs, and Gored Gored. Reservations accepted for parties of six or more. Price range $8-$13. (2003)

Algiers Coffee House
40 Brattle St., Cambridge (Harvard Square)
Red Line or #1 bus to Harvard
Sun-Thu 8am-midnight, Fri-Sat 8am-1am
617-492-1557

Middle Eastern, Coffeehouse. Generally overpriced but has a few specialties worth paying for: hummous, a good range of tea and coffee (especially the chamomile tea and Arabic coffee), and the ability to leave you alone for hours while you read or study. The coffee house itself is a beautiful piece of Islamic architecture that seems at least a century old. Located right next to the Brattle Theatre. A perfect place for feeling intellectual. Accepts check, AE, DC, MC, V. (2003)

All Asia Café
334 Mass. Ave., Cambridge
Walking distance
Sun-Mon 3:30pm-10:30pm, Tue, Thu, Sat 5pm-10:30pm, Fri 4pm-10:30pm
617-497-1544

Chinese, Thai. Fairly new place preparing a variety of Asian styles. Free delivery with minimum order of $15, music many weekend nights. Campusfood.com has been known to have student discounts. Accepts AE, D, MC, V. (2003)

Amelia's
ameliastrattoria.com
111 Harvard St, Cambridge
Walking distance, near One Kendall Square
Closed Sunday

617-868-7600

Italian. This is a great Northern Italian place, specializing in reasonably-priced, freshly-made Italian dishes native to the region of Abruzzo. A little bit too yuppie, but the food is good and there is an extensive wine cellar. It's one of those places to go when your relative is paying. (2003)

Ankara Café
472 Comm. Ave., Boston (Kenmore Square)
Green Line to Kenmore
Mon-Fri 8am-midnight, Sat-Sun 9am-midnight
617-437-0404 or 800-696-3069

Middle Eastern. Also known as Angora Café, but it's not the Angora Café of angoracafe.com. Vaguely Middle Eastern, best known for pita roll-ups and many available flavors of frozen yogurt. Also pizza and calzones (including interesting ingredients like tuna), but don't be surprised if yours is swimming in olive oil. Not good for large groups. Free delivery, w/min $7 order. Accepts MC, V. (2003)

1369 COFFEE HOUSE

Perennially voted "Cambridge's Best Coffee House."

Inman Square
1369 Cambridge St.
(617) 576-1369

Central Square
757 Massachusetts Ave.
(617) 576-4600

www.1369coffeehouse.com

Anna's Taqueria
www.annastaqueria.com

822 Somerville Ave., Porter Sq. Galleria
Red Line to Porter Square
Daily 10am-11pm
617-661-8500

236A Elm St., Davis Sq., Somerville
Red Line to Davis Square
Daily 10am-11pm
617-666-3900

1412 Beacon St., Brookline
Green Line C to Summer Ave
Mon-Wed 10am-11pm, Thu-Sun 10am-11:30pm
617-739-7300

Mexican. Because it's good, open late-ish and cheap, Anna's is extremely popular despite being well off campus. There are other options, but most people just want a Super Burrito (Carnitas, Chicken, and Veggie are all great; the Steak tends to be tough), possibly with extra cheese, and all the other good stuff. It's a hot, dense, nutrient-rich, foil-wrapped food pellet. Vegetarians have a few options, but are mostly out of luck. The "grilled vegetables burrito" contains rice, and the rice contains chicken broth. They do have refried beans you could substitute for the rice, and everything is made to order, right in front of you, so you can give instructions as they make it. It's still good enough that even hardcore veggies have been known to make exceptions. Anna's is excellent for catering, as long as you watch out for that vegetarian thing. Cash only. (2004)

Arrow Street Crêpes
One Arrow St., Harvard Square
Red Line or #1 bus to Harvard Square
Tue-Sat 11am-11pm, Sun 11am-8pm

French. Voted best crêpes in Boston. It has an extensive menu of filled crêpes, including both sweet and savory fillings. Among the best are the BHA (bananas, honey and almonds) and the chocolate Nutella with strawberries. Each crêpe runs about $2-$6. There is also a short menu of waffles and assorted other breakfast foods. As an extra treat, Tosci's icecream is available in-store. At the time of this writing, the restaurant did not have a telephone. (2004)

Artu's
6 Prince St., Boston (North End)
Daily 11am-11pm
617-742-4336

Italian. Artu's is in the basement of the building and has little standing room inside, so be prepared to wait outside for a bit if you don't have a reservation. Once you get seated, though, you'll find that the wait is well worth it. Insanely good Italian food. Try the crostini appetizers, the gnocchi, or the wonderful tortellini in a subtle sage sauce. Artu's is not very big, so keep your group under about 6 people. It's pricey for a student budget ($25-30 per person plus drinks) but if you can get your parents to pay for it, definitely go. The entrees cost about $11-19. (2003)

The Asgard

www.classicirish.com/
asgard_about.html

350 Massachusetts Avenue, Cambridge
(Central Square)
Walking distance
Daily 11am-1am

617-577-9100

American, Brewpub/Bar. If you like your food pseudo-Irish (basically, it's standard American bar fare with Irish names — try to read "Galway Buffalo Wings" or "Irish Quesadilla" with a straight face) in a setting reminiscent of Braveheart, then this is the place for you. Large oak chairs and tables bring you back to medieval times, but the good selection of beers will remind you of the present. Sometimes featuring live music, also from today's world. Fear the Tuesday Trivia Night. Accepts major credit cards. (2003)

Asmara

739 Mass. Ave., Cambridge (Central Square)
Walking distance
Sun-Thur 11:30am-10:30pm, Fri-Sat
11:30am-11:30pm

617-864-7447

African. Ethiopian/Eritrean food, which is traditionally eaten on the injera (flatbread) with which it is served. Reasonably priced, entrees run $10-14. Nicer than it looks from the outside. The service is friendly and the food is good. Expect to make a bit of a mess; the Zil Zil Tibbs is good for beginners. Cash only. (2003)

Atasca

www.atasca.com

50 Hampshire Street, Cambridge
Walk or bike
Mon-Sat 11:30am-11pm, Sun noon-10pm
617-621-6991

279A Broadway, Cambridge
Walk or bike
Tue-Sat 5pm-11pm, Sun 5pm-10pm

617-354-4355

Portuguese, Seafood. Portuguese food, including a wide variety of seafood prepared in many different ways. Half of the menu is Tapas style, where the table orders several dishes and shares them. The food is very good. If fish is not your style, try the Bife Ö Alfacinha, which is steak drowned in a garlic cream sauce and cooked surrounded by potatoes. (2003)

Au Bon Pain

www.aubonpain.com

 Many locations including:

254 Main St., Kendall Square
Walking distance
Mon-Fri 6am-9pm, Sat-Sun 7am-7pm
617-491-9751

1630 Mass Ave, Cambridge
Walking distance

American, Bakery, Coffeehouse. Commonly known as "ABP" (and occasionally "Urban Pain" or simply "The Pain"), there are many locations throughout the area, including two just in Kendall (Coop Food Court, and down the block toward the Charles). Yuppie sandwiches and pastries place, somewhat overpriced. A few items stand out, especially the Arizona Chicken (with extra chili-Dijon sauce), but if you're in Kendall for lunch you really should try Rebecca's instead. Good people-watching from in front of the Harvard Square restaurant — plus it's featured in the movie "Good Will Hunting." Also at that location is a lively chess scene, weather permitting. Baked goods are often half-price in the late afternoon, roughly 4-6pm. Hours vary, but most non-food-court locations are open until 9pm weekdays and 7pm weekends. (2004)

Aujourd'hui

200 Boylston Street, Boston
2nd floor of Four Seasons Hotel
Mon-Thu 6:30am-11am & 11:30am-2pm
& 5:30pm-10pm, Fri-Sat until 10:30pm,
Sun 11:30am-2pm & 6pm-10pm

617-351-2071

French. Prix fixe, three course dinner, absolutely wonderful food. Attire is dressy: jackets are preferred, ties are optional. Reservations required, credit card required for parties of 6 or more, cancellations require 48 hours notice. Also distinguished by having the best selection of single malt Scotch whisky in the city. Accepts major credit cards. (2003)

Baraka Café

80 Pearl St., Cambridge
Walking Distance, 3 blocks outside
Central Square
Tue-Sun 11am-3pm, 5:30pm-10pm

617-868-3951

Middle Eastern, Mediterranean. The Baraka Café is a small (7 tables, 20 seats) well-hidden North African (Tunisian, Moroccan, Algerian) restaurant with a delightful cook/owner by the name of Alia. The Cherbat is a very tasty lemonade with rose petals, spices, and a hint of orange. The Melfouf, comprised of kebabs of chicken, beef, and sausage over peppers and pommes frittes, is simply outstanding. Seafood specials appear regularly, and a number of vegetarian dishes are available. Alia is a superb dessert chef as well, and chocolate lovers must try the flourless chocolate torte. Entrees are $12-$20. Cash only. (2003)

Ben and Jerry's

36 JFK Street, Cambridge (Harvard Square)
Red Line or #1 bus to Harvard Square

617-864-2828

Also in the Cambridgeside Galleria

Dessert. Ben and Jerry's sells ice cream. Surprisingly enough, they sell Ben and Jerry's ice cream. It doesn't compete with Tosci's or the rest of the ice cream places described here, but it does have one thing in its favor. It has Free Cone Day. That's right, every once in a while, every Ben and Jerry's storefront gives out as many ice cream cones as their workers can scoop. The line tends to be rather long on these days, though. (2003)

Bertucci's

www.bertuccis.com
Multiple locations including:

799 Main St., Cambridge
Walking distance
Mon-Thu 11am-10pm Fri-Sat 11am-11pm,
Sun noon-10pm
617-661-8356

22 Merchants Row, Boston (Faneuil Hall)
Green Line to Government Center
Mon-Thu 11am-10pm Fri-Sat 11am-11pm,
Sun noon-10pm
617-227-7889

21 Brattle St., Cambridge (Harvard
Square) Red Line or #1 bus to Harvard
Square Mon-Thu 11am-10pm Fri-Sat
11am-11pm, Sun noon-10pm
617-864-4748

Italian. Good pizza and other Italian dishes. The pizzas have fresh toppings and are cooked in wood-burning ovens; the "gourmet" style has patches of fresh mozzarella. A small pizza serves one or two people (depending on how hungry they are) nicely. The free rolls are also very good; when ordering delivery, it can be worth getting Bertucci's just for the rolls. Don't miss the excellent seasonal lemonade. $8-12 for lunch or dinner. Accepts AE, D, DC, MC, V. (2004)

Bickford's

www.bickfords.com

349 Broadway, Somerville
Sun-Thu 7am-midnight, Fri-Sat 7am-1am
617-591-9733

Route 1, in Saugus Drive Open 24/7
781-233-3375

American. Traditionally a breakfast place, Bickford's is under new management, and is pretending to reinvent itself as an actual fine dining experience. Don't believe it for a second. It's like Denny's with decent food, it's like IHOP without all the sketch. Most locations are open late; some of the more distant ones are 24/7. Try to avoid this place on weekend mornings, when the locals stop by for breakfast after church. Try the Big Apple and an infinite cup of coffee, or the giant meal combo of fifteen thousand eggs, seven thousand pancakes, thirteen pounds of bacon, infinite coffee, and a cute little glass of juice. (2003)

Bisuteki Japanese Steak House
777 Memorial Dr., Cambridge
Walk, bike, or drive
Mon-Thu 5pm-10pm, Fri-Sat 5pm-11pm, Sun 4pm-10pm
617-492-7777

Japanese, Meat. It's best to go in groups of 8 because that's how many fit around the cooking table. The food isn't authentic, (with a name like that, how could it be?) but the dinner (about $15) is entertaining since the chef cooks in front of you. The food is okay, but you're paying for the show and nice atmosphere. Has many fruity cocktails. Accepts AE, CB, DC, MC, V. (2003)

The Black Rose
www.irishconnection.com/
blackrose.html

160 State St., Boston
Mon-Fri 11am-2am, Sat-Sun 9am-2am
617-742-2286

Irish, Brewpub/Bar. Traditional Irish food and a great Irish pub atmosphere. The service is as excellent as the food. Be sure to try the Guinness Pie. They serve traditional Irish breakfast on weekend mornings. Expect a wait, especially around St. Patrick's Day or when tourists are in season. Accepts MC, V. (2003)

Blue Fin
bluefin.boston.swbd.net

1815 Mass. Ave., Porter Exchange
Red Line to Porter Square
Mon-Sat noon-4pm & 5pm-10:30pm, Sun noon-10pm

617-497-8022

Japanese. Decent sushi on a college student budget, especially for groups who order large assortments. Best cheap sushi on the Red Line. The fish and tempura are good, avoid the cooked meat dishes. Open Accepts MC, V. (2003)

Blue Ribbon BBQ
www.blueribbonbbq.com

908 Massachusetts Ave., Arlington
Mon-Sat 11:30am-9pm, Sun noon-8pm

781-648-7427

American, Meat. Among the best BBQ in Boston, with a variety of southern styles. The dry-rubbed Memphis ribs are amazing and the Kansas City burnt ends, pulled pork and Texas sliced beef brisket are all worth trying, along with the home-made pickles and BBQ sauces. Surprisingly cheap since there is no table service — you pick up your food from the counter and dig in. Their vegetarian options are great too — but be careful, as many of the vegetable sides not explicitly listed as vegetarian actually contain some meat. Also has an outlet in West Newton, and in the Bread & Circus in Cambridge. Catering available, call 617-899-6000. Accepts MC, V. (2003)

The Blue Room
One Kendall Square
Walking distance
Mon-Thu 5:30pm-10pm, Fri-Sat 5:30pm-11pm, Sun 11am-2:30pm & 5:30pm-10pm
617-494-9034

American. A moderately expensive (entrees start around $18) sit-down restaurant during most of the year, The Blue Room runs an excellent outdoor barbecue/grill, selling meat-heavy hot sandwiches from its courtyard, downstairs from 1 Kendall Square. There is usually a meat choice, a fish choice and a veggie choice. The veggie choice is usually avocado quesadillas, which are not recommended. The flank steak and salmon are quite good, as are their sides. The outdoor grill shares table space with other restaurants. (2003)

Bob the Chef's
www.bobthechefs.com

604 Columbus Ave., Boston
Green Line to Symphony
Tue-Wed 11:30am-10:00pm, Thu-Sat
11:30am-midnight, Sun 11:00am-9:00pm

617-536-6204

American, Meat. Bob's has great Southern food, and if you catch them on the right day, a live jazz in the back. You could, if so inclined, try the chit'lings. Go for the ribs and the glorifried chicken, if you enjoy clogging your arteries. The cabbage and mac & cheese sides alone are worth the trip down to the South End. (2003)

Boca Grande
149 First St., Cambridge
Walking distance, or take The Wave to the Galleria
Mon-Fri 11am-9pm, Sat 11am-8pm
617-354-5550

1728 Mass. Ave., Cambridge (Porter Square)
Red Line to Porter Square
Mon-Sun 11am-10:30pm
617-354-7400

Mexican. Inexpensive Mexican take-out, very popular with the local corporate clientele. All orders are ready-made in the open kitchen, so you can see everything that's going into your burrito or taco. Try the grilled chicken. The First St. location takes cash only, whereas the Porter Square location accepts AE, CB, D, DC, MC, V. (2004)

Bombay Club
www.bombayclub.com

57 JFK Street
Red Line or #1 bus to Harvard Square
Daily 11:30am-11:00pm

617-661-8100

Indian. Bombay Club is a popular Indian restaurant in Harvard Square. The food, while better than anything you can get delivered, is a bit pricey for the quality. It's a good place to go with your parents — they will feel rich and special. If you go with your friends, you run the risk of feeling a bit out of place, though the appetizers are excellent. The atmosphere is very nice, though most people there are either not college students, or Harvard students wearing nice clothes. Expect to spend about $20 on a meal. (2003)

Border Café
32 Church St., Harvard Square
Red Line or #1 bus to Harvard
Mon-Sat 11am-1:45am, Sun noon-12:45am

617-864-6100

Mexican. Yuppie but good Cajun/Mexican. Prices vary but can get expensive. Good fajitas. Gets extremely crowded on weekends and for dinner during the week, so start a tab at the bar and have a few excellent margaritas, or just go for lunch. Accepts V, MC, AE. (2004)

Bova's
www.northendboston.com/bovabakery/index.html

134 Salem St., Boston (North End)
Open 24/7

617-523-56011

Bakery, Dessert, Italian. Bova's is one of the few 24-hour stores in Boston. Which is a good thing, since this family-run bakery has delicious Italian pastries and freshly baked bread. There is nothing like getting a cannoli at 5am, after spending the last n hours working on a problem set. It's actually better to visit Bova's in the wee hours of the morning, if you're travelling by car, because the North End is usually entirely devoid of parking space. If you're visiting before 1am, they also serve calzones, sandwiches, and pizza. (2003)

Brookline Lunch
9 Brookline St., Cambridge (Central Square)
Walking Distance
Daily 7am-5pm

617-354-2983

American, Middle Eastern. This is perhaps the best breakfast in Central Square, serving the usual American breakfast fare such as eggs and home fries, as well as sandwiches, all in huge portions for rock-bottom prices. In addition to standard American diner fare, the menu offers some exceptional Middle Eastern favorites. It's owned by a very friendly family of Palestinian immigrants and sometimes, when business is not too heavy, one of their young daughters will wait your table. A pleasant hole-in-the-wall breakfast nook, it at once affords a homey atmosphere and relatively secluded diner booths. It's a perfect place to slowly wake up from a hangover, and its cheap prices allow for a filling meal costing under $4. Cash only. (2004)

Brown Sugar Café
www.brownsugarcafe.com

129 Jersey St., Boston (Fenway)
Green Line B/C/D to Kenmore Square
Mon-Thu 11am-10pm, Fri 11am-11pm,
Sat noon-11pm, Sun noon-10pm
617-266-2928

1033 Commonwealth Avenue, Boston
(Boston University)
Green Line B to Babcock
Mon-Thu 11am-10pm, Fri 11am-11pm,
Sat noon-11pm, Sun noon-10pm
617-787-4242

Thai. Papaya Salad, Old Lady Spicy, Mango Curry, and Noodles Aspar are among the many favorites available at this top-notch Thai restaurant. Try the young coconut juice or Thai iced tea to cool your palate. Thankfully, it's not as expensive as the great food and pleasant atmosphere might lead you to believe. There is online ordering for both pickup and delivery, but they suggest calling if you want them to actually process your order. Only the BU location delivers to MIT, and then only with a $20 minimum paid in cash. Still, it's probably the best Thai food you can get delivered to campus. Accepts D, DC, MC, V. (2004)

Bruegger's Bagels
www.brueggers.com

Multiple locations, including:

1876 Mass. Ave. (south of Porter Sq.)
617-576-6163
644 Beacon St., Boston
617-262-7939
375 Longwood Ave., Boston
617-731-8993
211 Congress St., Boston
617-423-7105
7 School St., Boston
617-367-4702

Fast Food. Don't mistake these bagels for "real" bagels, if you're one of those people who has a specific definition of "real". They have an assortment of bagel flavors, an assortment of cream cheese flavors, and the ability to turn a bagel into a pretty good sandwich, deli-style. (2003)

Buddha's Delight
5 Beach St., Boston (Chinatown)
Orange Line to Chinatown or Red Line
to Downtown Crossing
Sun-Thu 11am-10pm, Fri-Sat 11am-11pm
617-451-2395

404 Harvard Street, Brookline
Green Line C to Coolidge Corner
Sun-Thu noon-11pm, Fri-Sat noon-
midnight
617-739-8830

Vegetarian, Chinese. Everything on the normal-looking Chinese menu turns out to be entirely vegan (with the exception of the excellent fruit smoothies, made with condensed milk). The "Buddhist temple cuisine" surprisingly effectively simulates chicken, beef, shrimp, and more from seitan (wheat gluten) and tofu (soy) and is served with excellent sauces and very fresh vegetables. Some dishes taste like Chinese, while others are more unusual; there's a "barbecue platter" with fresh spring roll skins which is a good split for two. Satisfying even to meat-eaters, and of course empowering for oppressed vegans. Lunch around $7, dinner $13. Accepts V, MC. (2004)

Bugaboo Creek Steak House
www.bugaboocreeksteakhouse.com

617 Arsenal Street, Arsenal Mall,
Watertown
Mon-Thu 11:30am-10pm, Fri-Sat
11:30am-10:30pm, Sun noon-9pm
617-924-9000

American, Meat. What the Outback is to pseudo-Australian, Bugaboo Creek is to pseudo-Canadian, only with the addition of animatronic, talking Northern fauna and flora and at least one "Buga-buga-birthday" song per visit. If you can get past the Disney aspects, the food is pretty good, particularly the Wild Pepper and Black Magic steaks and the Snowbird chicken. Other oddities abound, such as the Wedge Salad — the place is probably worth a visit for amusement alone. Prices are pretty cheap by steak standards; about $20 will get you bloated like a fat American businessman. Accepts V, MC, AE, DC, D. (2004)

Burger King
502 Mass. Ave., Cambridge (Central Square)
645 Comm. Ave., Boston

Fast Food Burgers, fast and cheap. What else can you say about Burger King? The paper crowns give a special ambiance? The menu is Clever and Satisfies Everyone's Tastes, It's A Special Place For The Entire Family? (2003)

Burrito Max
642 Beacon St., Kenmore Square
Walk or Green Line to Kenmore Square
Daily 11:30am-11pm

617-266-8088

Mexican. Burrito Max! Burrito Max! Burrito Max! Big servings, which are technically burritos. It's really only worth consideration by lazy Beacon Street residents. Burritos are often heavy on the avocado, but they are very generous with portions and will make your Burrito Max! to order. They'll sometimes stick more than half an avocado in your burrito if you're sober and female. Burrito Max! Burrito Max! Burrito Max! (2003)

Buzzy's Fabulous Roast Beef
Central Square, Cambridge
Charles Circle, Boston

Just as Deli Haus gets a memorial entry, Buzzy's deserves one too. Closed in Spring 2002, Buzzy's was a source of hot roast beef, dubious chicken, and superlative onion rings any time of the day or night. Especially refreshing after a bright exothermic experiment. A plague upon developers' heads who claim that the yuppified, limited-hours burger joint in their expensive new building could ever replace Buzzy's. Where will the cops, cabbies, and students get their meat at 4am now? (2003)

California Pizza Kitchen
www.cpk.com

Cambridgeside Galleria
Walk or take the Wave to the Galleria
Mon-Thu 11:30am-10pm, Fri 11am-11pm, Sat 11:30am-11pm, Sun 11:30am-10pm
617-225-2772

Prudential Center
Green Line to Prudential
Mon-Thu 11:30am-10pm, Fri 11am-11pm, Sat 11:30am-11pm, Sun 11:30am-10pm
617-247-0888

American. CPK is aptly named. It has many varieties of pizza, which are all California-yuppie. Jambalaya. Rosemary chicken and potato. You could probably get a pepperoni pizza but it might come with goat cheese on it. Once you reset your expectations, however, the food is very good, and the location is excellent. Try the two soups in a bowl and the focaccia checca (bread and garlicky tomatoes). (2003)

Cambridge Brewing Company
www.cambrew.com

One Kendall Square, Cambridge
Walking distance
Mon-Thu 11:30am-10pm, Fri-Sat 11:30am-11pm, Sun 3pm-10:30pm

617-494-1994

American, Brewpub/Bar. As the name implies, the big draw here is the beer. Most varieties are good; definitely try the Hefeweizen if it's up that day. In the fall, try the Pumpkin Ale. Much of their food is Froofy Yuppie, because Froofy Yuppies spend a lot of money at microbreweries. (Calamari Fritte anyone? How about Wild Mushroom Tortellini with Gorgonzola Garlic Bread?) This phenomenon means that vegetarians do all right; they should try the hummus. Fortunately, CBC also remembers its other fans, the kind who want bar food and beef. The buffalo wings have been called the best in town, and the burgers are large and messy and wonderful. It's great for large groups, even without reservations, although they appreciate a little warning. Accepts major credit cards. (2003)

Cambridgeside Galleria Food Court
Walk or take The Wave shuttle from Kendall Square

Food Court, Fast Food Every Galleria must have a food court, and ours is no exception. Along with the Taco Bell and the Burger King, the Sbarro and the D'Angelos, there is Indian, Japanese, and French food. There's an Au Bon Pain and a CinnaBon. Best of all, there's a smoothie bar. Everyone loves smoothies, especially when they come with that special little kick — try the Energy Pellet. This food court is open generally when the Galleria is, although some of the restaurants close down their grills early. Also note that the Cheesecake Factory, Papa Razzi's, and the California Pizza Kitchen are not part of the food court, and have their own hours. (2003)

Carberry's
www.carberrys.com

74 Prospect St., Cambridge (Central Square)
Walk, Red Line to Central Square, or #1 bus
Mon-Sat 6am-8pm, Sun 7am-7pm
617-576-3530

187 Elm St., Somerville (Davis Square)
Red Line to Davis Square
Mon-Sat 6am-8pm, Sun 7am-7pm
617-666-2233

Bakery, Dessert. Excellent local bakery that offers pastries, breads, and sandwiches for eat-in, take-out, or catering. Truly a treat and not a bad place to study, either. Menu available online, but somewhat dated. Every once in a while all surplus items are half-price; check for this in the evenings, especially Saturday evening. Accepts AE, MC, V.

Carmen
33 North Square, Boston (North End)
Orange or Green Lines to Haymarket
Tue-Fri 11:30am-2:30pm & 5:30pm-11pm, Sat 5:30pm-11pm, Sun 5:30pm-10pm
617-742-6421

Italian. A little bit on the pricey side, Carmen is exactly what you imagine when you hear the words 'cute Italian place' — olive oil served in a little plate before dinner, the tiny exposed-brick space manageable by a single waitress, and the owner drinking red wine with frequent clients at the miniature bar. The food is almost Italian, and as great as the atmosphere. Accepts AE, DC, MC, V. (2004)

Casa Mexico
75 Winthrop St., Cambridge (Harvard Square)
Red Line or #1 bus to Harvard Square
Daily 10am-10pm
617-491-4552

Mexican. Among the best authentic-style Mexican around. They make a great mole sauce. Try the coffee. They serve excellent margaritas by the pitcher. Entrees around $13, good quality, reasonable but not enormous portions. Accepts AE, DC, MC, V. (2003)

Casa Portugal
1200 Cambridge St., Cambridge
Walk, bike, or drive — near Inman Square
Mon-Thu 11:30am-10:00pm, Fri-Sat 11:30am-11pm, Sun noon-10pm
617-491-8880

Portuguese. A homey restaurant; the serving dishes are Portuguese ceramics, the staff is a family and the atmosphere is friendly rather than excessively formal. With the large entrees costing over $15, a meal can easily cost up to $30 per person, including wine, which is worth it for such a great example of traditional Portuguese cuisine. Reservation recommended. Accepts AE, D, DC, MC, V. (2003)

Central Bakery
www.centralbakery.com
732 Cambridge St., Cambridge
Walk or bike.
Open every day
617-547-2337

Bakery. Central Bakery has good bread and fair desserts. There are many other bakeries on Cambridge Street, so start here and keep walking. (2003)

Characters Bar & Grill
2 Cambridge Center, Kendall Square
Walking Distance
617-252-4408 x6707

American, Brewpub/Bar. Located inside the Marriott, this hotel restaurant/bar mostly serves burgers, good bar sandwiches and appetizers (excellent buffalo wings) and huge, if not all that interesting, salads. Some vegetarian options. Accepts AE, D, DC, MC, V. (2004)

Charlie's
10 Eliot St., Cambridge

American. Last time this reviewer was here, we sat next to this obscenely fat woman and a charming (in a horrifically vulgar way) gentleman clad only in a ripped-up, black Led Zeppelin shirt. They flirted all night over cigarettes and PBR, and then, as midnight struck, he leaned over and tried to kiss her. She reeled back and clubbed him in the face and stormed out. Oh, and they have good fries and meatloaf. (2003)

The Cheesecake Factory
www.thecheesecakefactory.com
Cambridgeside Galleria
Walking distance, or take The Wave shuttle from Kendall Square
Mon-Thu 11:30am-11pm, Fri-Sat 11:30am-12:30am, Sun 10am-11pm
617-252-3810

American, Dessert. Huge portions of fresh-made food; quality varies a bit, but is usually above mediocre. The menu is extensive to the point of being overwhelming, but just about everything is good; some highlights include the Avocado Egg Rolls, Jambalaya Pasta, Chicken and Biscuits, and the Chinese Chicken Salad (piled a foot high with crispy, airy, fried chow mein noodles). Generally more expensive than it's worth, but many dishes will make two meals. Desserts are wonderful, especially the eponymous cheesecake (dozens of varieties, but purists will be happy with the plain's thin top layer of sour cream). They don't take reservations for groups of less than seven, so expect a wait, especially on weekends; fortunately you can take a pager (somewhat limited range, so get a time estimate) and wander the Galleria. Accepts AE, D, MC, V. (2004)

Chicago Pizza
www.cambridgepizza.com
239 Mass. Ave., Cambridge
Walking Distance
Sun-Thu 10am-1am, Fri-Sat 10am-2am
617-497-5555

Italian. Although primarily a pizza place, Chicago Pizza also offers salads, subs, grinders, pasta and wings. Pizza is greasy but good. The calzones are huge. The prices are reasonable. Watch out for drunken louts from the Cambridgeport Saloon near closing time. Online ordering available. Delivery starts at 12:30pm. Accepts credit cards with $10 minimum. (2004)

Chili's
www.chilis.com
100 Huntington Avenue, Boston (Copley Place)
Green Line to Copley
617-859-0134

Fast Food. Tex-mex chain store — burgers, BBQ, quesadillas etc. Nothing done particularly well but reliably edible. Large portions should fill you up without massive expense. (2004)

Chilli Duck
829 Boylston, Boston
Green Line to Prudential Center
Daily 11:30am-11pm

617-236-5208

Thai. Chilli Duck is one of those "hidden gem" restaurants. It serves Thai cuisine, and is a great value for what you get. Absolutely delicious! The restaurant is very well-decorated and clean. It's a small restaurant, but its larger tables can accommodate 8-10, while booths in the back seat couples for a more quiet, romantic setting. Accepts AE, D, MC, V. (2003)

China Sun
7 Holland St.
Red Line to Davis Square
Mon-Thu 11am-11pm, Fri-Sat 11am-midnight, Sun noon-11pm

617-625-6068

Chinese. Popular mostly because of its convenient location (practically across the street from the Davis Square T-stop). Comparable to Pu Pu Hot Pot in Central Square, except that the food in China Sun is better (less deep frying, better sauces). In theory, you can eat in for their lunch or dinner specials, but the strength of China Sun is its quick and cheap take-out service. It caters to carnivores, vegetarians and omnivores with its grand selection. For vegetarians, try the General Gau tofu (which is better than the chicken counterpart of various other restaurants), cold sesame noodles, and vegetarian Peking Ravs. For carnivores, try their regular Peking Ravs and beef dishes. However, you must be warned — if you eat in, they do serve French fries. If you want a meal for less than $10, go to China Sun. (2003)

Chinese Eatery
44-46 Beach Street, Boston (Chinatown)
Red Line to Downtown Crossing or
Orange Line to Chinatown
Open late

Food Court, Chinese. Dirt cheap, all-Asian (mostly Chinese, some Vietnamese) food court. Located right in the middle of Chinatown on the second floor of the the northeast corner of Beach and Harrison Streets, this somewhat grimy cafeteria gives a glimpse of a world usually hidden from view. Before deciding on which stall to order from, make a quick survey of the half-dozen or so crufty vendors sitting atop huge vats of MSG and choose your fate wisely. The food, of course, is great and varied. Off in the corner a bubble tea vendor manages to maintain a fairly constant stream of Chinatown teens slurping down tapioca balls through huge straws while sporting their latest haircuts, shoes, and cell phone paraphernalia. Cash only. (2004)

Christina's Ice Cream
1255 Cambridge St., Cambridge (Inman Square)
Walk or bike
Sun-Thu 11:30am-11pm, Fri-Sat 11:30am-midnight

617-492-7021

Dessert. Christina's is not Tosci's (the popular Cambridge cluster of stores with branches in Central and Harvard squares), and that is OK. They make ice cream that is a bit thicker but also very good at similar prices. It's a good place to go for dessert, and if you're already on the east end of campus it's not much farther out than Tosci's and will bring you to an area you probably don't know as well. Worth checking out — you might like it better than Tosci's. Cash only. (2003)

Christopher's
1920 Mass. Ave., Cambridge (Porter Square)
Red Line to Porter Square
Mon-Sat 11:30am-midnight, Sun 10:30am-midnight

617-876-9180

American. Christopher's is all about the atmosphere and style. It's homey. Serves Southwestern and Tex-Mex food (though the Shepherds's pie is recommended), as well as sandwiches, burgers, and salads. It's set such that a person feels comfortable when eating a fajita. Service is inversely proportional to the number of people at a table, however. Not a place for large mobs. However, it is a popular neighborhood hangout and a pleasant place to linger over a beer or coffee and dessert. Meals are in the $6-$15 range. (2003)

Cinderella's Italian Cuisine
901 Main St. at Mass. Ave., Cambridge
(Central Square)
Walking distance
Sun-Wed 11am-1am, Thu-Sat 11am-2am

617-576-0280

Italian. "Cindy's" is the place for cheap, good, garlicky Italian. The food is good and the calzones are bigger than your head. The Linguine Carbonara and Chicken alla Pignoli are excellent choices from their huge selection of pastas, and the Garlic Cheese Bread will have garlic seeping from your pores for hours. Cindy's is special and beloved for its ultra-fast delivery to specific rooms on campus — delivery can come in under 10 minutes. Cindy's has been known to deliver pizza for 50 people inside half an hour. The fact that they're open late is just a special bonus. Free delivery with $8 minimum order. Accepts AE, D, MC, V. (2003)

Crossroads Restaurant and Lounge
495 Beacon St., Boston
Walk, Green Line to Auditorium, or #1 bus to Beacon St.
Mon-Sat 10:30am-2am, Sun 11am-2am

617-262-7371

Brewpub/Bar. The food is in general not exceptional, but fries, onion rings, and buffalo wings are great. Try a JenJen. People mainly go there to drink at the bar. You'll probably find people you know from MIT, especially the nearby frats. Breakfast is served all day. Open Accepts AE, DC, MC, V. (2003)

Cuchi Cuchi
www.cuchicuchi.cc

795 Main Street, Cambridge
Walking distance
Mon-Sat 6pm-11pm, bar until 12:30am

617-864-2929

Spanish. The third in a series of Tapas restaurants, including Dali's and Tapeo, Cuchi Cuchi offers much of the same style without the lines. Unlike its sisters, Cuchi Cuchi does not offer an entree menu. Instead, you order a variety of appetizers and share them around the table. The food is extremely high quality, and priced accordingly. Have some sangria or a giant cocktail to drink, and make sure someone at the table gets the handmade bonbons for dessert. Poor for groups, this is an excellent date location as long as both parties enjoy unusual food. (2003)

Dali Restaurant and Tapas Bar
www.dalirestaurant.com

415 Washington St. at Beacon St., Somerville
Drive or walk from Harvard
June-August 6pm-11:30pm, otherwise 5:30pm-11pm. Bar until 12:30am.

617-661-3254

Spanish. Authentic Spanish menu, both entrees and Tapas (small appetizers often combined to make a full meal — including marinated herbed olives, artichoke hearts in saffron batter, and several beef and shellfish dishes). Don't miss the seasonal offerings, including the Catalanese dishes, but save room for dessert and Sangria. Expect to wait, but it'll be worth it. Go with a group, order a bunch of stuff, and try tiny bites of everything. Reservations are not accepted. Tapas run $4-7 each, entrees around $15. Accepts AE, DC, MC, V. (2004)

Darwin's Ltd.
148 Mt. Auburn Street, Cambridge
Walk from Harvard, or drive

617-354-5233

American. A small take-out delicatessen patronized by those in the know. Best known for their fresh sandwiches (many of which are named after the streets intersecting with Brattle St.), they also sell homemade soups, desserts and prepared foods to go. A small grocery section features produce, specialty foods, and wine and beer. The line tends to be long, but the food is well worth the wait. (2003)

Deli Haus Restaurant
Kenmore Square, Boston

Deli Haus closed down over three years ago, but we still commemorate it with a memorial entry. Awesome greasy inexpensive food, open to the wee hours, loud non-pop music, rude punk-themed waitstaff, Velvet Elvis on the wall. You either loved the atmosphere or you hated it, but no one left without an opinion. A haven for many from the tribulations of the Institute. R.I.P. Intrepid students resurrect the experience once a term in the Senior Haus basement — watch for the announcement and don't miss a taste of history. (2004)

Denise's Ice Cream
4 College Ave #A, Somerville (Davis Square)
Red Line to Davis Square
Sun-Thu noon-11pm, Fri-Sat noon-midnight

617-628-2764

Dessert. Denise's is for many people The Other Ice Cream Shop. It's homemade, it's high-quality, it has surly, bitter waitstaff, and it's got killer sundaes. Unlike Tosci's, it doesn't do the coffee thing, but there's plenty of good coffee in Davis. Unfortunately, they just got bought by J.P. Licks, so the selection has gone down, and they don't have my favorite two flavors anymore. But if the weather is good, take your ice cream outside to the benches and watch all the Davis Square weirdos do their weird things. (2003)

The Dish
www.southenddish.com

253 Shawmut Ave., Boston (South End)
Orange Line to Back Bay, corner of Shawmut and Milford
Mon-Thu 5pm-10pm, Fri-Sat 5pm-11pm, Sun 11am-10pm

617-426-7866

Mediterranean, Italian. Another great place to for celebrating something (or someone) special. The Dish is not cheap, but reasonably priced, and the olive-oil and basil scented food is so great that you might come out considering a permanent relocation to Southern Europe. Try the amazing brick-oven pizza or the delicious grilled salmon. Open for brunch on Sundays. A dog-friendly patio offers outdoor seating. Accepts AE, DC, MC, V. (2004)

Desi Dhaba
401 Mass. Ave., Cambridge (Central Square)
Walking distance

617-547-4121

Indian. A relatively new contender; it's Yet Another Indian Place In Central Square. The food is a bit on the sweet side, which may or may not be bad depending on your taste. The lunch buffet looked bad enough that no one was willing to eat it, but that's probably from being out for hours — the fresh food was reasonably good and the same price as everywhere else in Central. A definite win over Shalimar, but probably inferior to India Pavilion, despite being a bit cheaper. $10-$15 per meal. (2003)

Diva Indian Bistro
246 Elm St, Somerville, (Davis Square)
Red Line to Davis Square
Daily 11:30am-11pm

617-629-4963

Indian. Pricier than most Indian places in the area, and you get what you pay for. With excellent tandoor dishes and reasonably good vindaloo (though not as spicy as some would like), the food at Diva is worth the price if you can afford it. The presentation and ambiance match up; the sauce is even drizzled in a stylish manner on the plates, and the front wall is missing when the weather is nice. $25-$40, more like $20-$30 if you get their combinations which also offer better variety. Accepts AE, MC, V. (2003)

Domino's Pizza
www.dominos.com

Multiple locations including:

1310 Boylston, Boston
Sun-Wed 11am-2am, Thu-Sat 11am-3am
617-424-9000

201 Elm St., Davis Square, Somerville
Sun-Thu 11am-midnight, Thu-Sat 11am-1am
617-629-2929

Italian. Acceptable pizza, but pretty expensive. The Boylston location has free delivery to MIT and accepts the MIT meal card. (2004)

Dom's Restaurant
10 Bartlett Place, Boston
Daily 5pm-10pm

617-367-8979

Italian. An excellent little hole in the wall in the North End, seating is cramped but the food is worthy of a visit. Dom himself may come by your table to discuss a sauce or suggest a wine for your meal. Can be expensive. Accepts AE, MC, V. (2003)

Dunkin' Donuts, Baskin Robbins
www.dunkindonuts.com

Everywhere. No, really. Ok, these are the closest locations:

1 Broadway, Cambridge
100 Cambridgeside Place, Cambridge (Cambridgeside Galleria)
1001 Cambridge St. Shell, Cambridge
715 Boylston St., Boston
222 Broadway, Cambridge
616 Mass. Ave., Cambridge
153 Mass. Ave., Boston

Drive, walk, it doesn't matter.

Fast Food. Founded in Boston, MA in 1950, this national chain features a strong following of loyal patrons addicted to its coffee and donuts. Others feel less strongly, but given the ubiquity of their locations it's hard to live in Boston and not appreciate their presence. Bagels, breakfast sandwiches, iced coffee and other specialty drinks are also offered. Absurdly clean bathrooms. Some locations in the area are open 24 hours (such as the location at the intersection of 3rd St. and McGrath Highway in Cambridge and the location in Porter Square across from the T stop). The locations that make the donuts are willing to provide hundreds of donuts on two days' notice. Many DD locations have a Baskin Robbins grafted onto them. Donuts and ice cream! It's a brilliant combination! Sugar and... sugar! Unfortunately, most of these locations do not have the full 31 flavors. However, Baskin Robbins does occasionally offer Free Cone Day, usually within a week of the Ben and Jerry's Free Cone Day. The nearest merged stores are the 1 Broadway and Central Square locations. (2003)

Durgin Park
340 Faneuil Hall Marketplace, Boston
Green Line to Government Center
Mon-Thu 11:30am-10pm, Fri-Sat 11:30am-11pm, Sun 11:30am-9pm

888-766-6528

American, Meat. The classic Boston restaurant, "established before you were born". Rude waitstaff, noisy atmosphere, visible kitchen. Serves an impressive prime rib — think Flintstones — and other New England specialties, though rumor says the quality used to be better. Meat. MEAT. MEAT!!! Long waits on weekends, and rather expensive, but everyone should try it once. Accepts AE, D, DC, MC, V. (2003)

East Coast Grill
www.eastcoastgrill.net

1271 Cambridge St., Inman Square
Mon-Thu 5:30pm-10pm, Fri-Sat 5:30pm-10:30pm, Sun 11am-2:30pm & 5:30pm-10pm

617-491-6568

American, Meat, Seafood. New American cuisine by chef Chris Schlesinger, including barbecue, some of the best seafood in Boston, and a raw bar. Service and atmosphere are good, and prices are within reason for the quality. Accepts AE, MC, V. (2004)

Eat
www.eatrestaurant.com

253 Washington St., Union Square
Drive or take a bus to Union Square
Wed-Thu 6pm-10pm, Fri-Sat 6pm-10:30pm, Sun 5:30pm-9:30pm

617-776-2889

American. Eat has great slightly upscale, yet homestyle, food in a casual, comfortable, but still-feels-like-going-out-to-eat atmosphere. The menu changes each season, but everything the reviewers have ordered has been very nice. There's always at least one vegetarian entree. (2003)

The Elephant Walk
www.elephantwalk.com

2067 Mass. Ave., Porter Square
Red Line to Porter
Sun-Thu 5pm-10pm, Fri-Sat 5pm-11pm
617-492-6900

900 Beacon St., Boston
Green Line C to St. Mary Street
Hours same as Porter location plus lunch Mon-Fri 11:30am-2:30pm
617-247-1500

French, Cambodian. Upscale (entrees up to $25-$35) menu is split between Cambodian and French dishes. Usually excellent (and unique, especially the spicy Cambodian side) though a few people report occasional lapses in service quality. The Cambodian food is cheaper and often more interesting than the French, but stick with the French side of the menu for dessert. Good place to take parents, or a date after the symphony; the atmosphere is elegant without being intimidating. Note that the hours listed above are the times they will seat you; your meal can extend beyond the hours listed. Available for private parties during the day on weekends. Accepts AE, D, DC, MC, V. (2004)

Emack & Bolio's
www.emackandbolios.com

290 Newbury St.
Walk, Green Line to Hynes, or #1 Bus to Hynes

Dessert. An import from New York, Emack & Bolio's is a smoothie and juice bar as well as an ice cream shop. They have somewhat small servings and no place to sit, but their smoothies and their soft-serve ice cream are very good. (2003)

Emma's Pizza
40 Hampshire St., One Kendall Square, Cambridge
Walking distance
Tue-Sat 11:30am-8pm, Sun 3pm-8pm

617-864-8534

Italian. The best thin-crust pizza around. You pay for the quality ($16-$20 for a large pie) but it is worth it. Lots of unique topping options (try the sweet potato) and even multiple sauces (including a delicious spicy rosemary). Also has panini sandwiches which are more economical. No delivery, unfortunately. Small seating area, so can tend to have a long wait at peak times, but inside is cozy, well-lit and rigidly cell-phone-free — a good place for an informal date. Accepts AE, MC, V. (2003)

Evoo
www.evoorestaurant.com

118 Beacon St., Somerville, at Kirkland Ave
Drive or walk from Harvard
Mon-Thu 6pm-10pm, Fri 6pm-11pm, Sat 5pm-11pm

617-661-3866

American. Evoo is further proof that fancy restaurants do exist in Cambridge. It is the ultimate in international bistros. Just the mushroom "cheesecake" appetizer is enough to water your mouth. It is a soft mousse with porcini mushrooms blended in a creamy texture. Each dish is meticulously designed with care by the head chef. Feel free to sample a lobster-pumpkin bisque or mint-cured rack of lamb. A Chinese dish of Shiitake mushrooms is served in the shape of a carton. Meals are not in the single digits. In fact, they are among the most expensive in the Cambridge area (ranging from $15 to $26 a course). It is not recommended for large mobs. However, it is recommended for taking that special somebody on an anniversary dinner. (2003)

Fajitas & Ritas

www.fajitasandritas.com

25 West St., Boston Common
Red Line to Park Street
Mon-Tue 11:30am-9:00pm, Wed-Thu
11:30am-10:00pm, Fri-Sat 11:30am-
11:00pm, Sun 2:00pm-8:00pm

617-426-1222

Mexican. A Mexican place which specializes in, well, Fajitas and Margaritas. They do both well; they also serve nachos (one of the cheaper meals you can have there), quesadillas that receive mixed reviews, and burritos that are pretty good but no better than what you could get at Anna's or Boca Grande. Their side dishes are quite good, though; some people order 2 or 3 corn muffins every visit and their chili is excellent for the price. $8-$10 if you're not drinking, add $4-$7 for a drink if you are. Fun environment: they encourage writing on the walls. Look for your friends' names. Available for private parties until 2am. (2003)

Finale

www.finaledesserts.com

30 Dunster St. at Mt. Auburn, Cambridge
Red Line or #1 bus to Harvard Square
Mon 11am-10:30pm, Tue-Wed 11am-
11:30pm, Thu-Fri 11am-12:30am, Sat
2pm-12:30am, Sun 2pm-10:30pm
617-441-9797

One Columbus Ave. at Park Plaza,
Boston
Green Line to Arlington
617-423-3184

Dessert. Finale is particularly great — it's primarily a very upscale dessert restaurant, but also does meals. The white chocolate risotto was to die for, but in the past you couldn't order it separately from a general chocolate plate for two (not that the chocolate plate was bad, at all). Beautiful presentations, delicious desserts. (2003)

Fire and Ice

www.fire-ice.com

50 Church St., Harvard Square
Red Line or #1 bus to Harvard Square
Mon-Thu 11:30am-10pm, Fri-Sat
11:30am-11pm, Sun 10am-10pm
617-547-9007

205 Berkeley St., Boston
Green Line to Arlington or Copley
Mon-Thu 11:30am-10pm, Fri-Sat
11:30am-11pm, Sun 10am-10pm
617-482-3473

American. All you can eat, for yuppies. For about $20 (cheaper for lunch) you get as much meat and vegetables as you can stir fry — if you've been living on Ramen, be careful not to make yourself sick. If you're an accomplished stir-fryer, you may be unimpressed; otherwise, the big grill where you can combine your own ingredients and sauce is a lot of fun, and the ingredients are good quality. It can get slow at peak times, and is noisy. Dinner starts at 4pm and costs $15, lunch ends at 4pm (3pm on Sunday) and costs $8. Accepts AE, D, DC, MC, V. (2004)

Fresco's

134 Mass. Ave. (Central Square)
Walking distance
Mon-Fri 7am-5pm

617-491-8866

Greek, American. Simple breakfast and Greek food, just a block up Mass. Ave. from the Student Center. The fish and chips is made from fresh fish dipped in crumbs right before frying, not pre-frozen sticks of fish. Cash only. (2004)

Fugakyu

www.fugakyu.net

1280 Beacon St., Brookline
Green Line C to Coolidge Corner
Daily 11:30am-1:30am

617-734-1268

Japanese. A large Japanese restaurant that stands out in the crowd of Boston's wide selection of sushi offerings, but is not as stellar as its Citysearch 'Best Sushi' award of years past might suggest. Prices are on the high side, but reasonable nonetheless considering the amount of food you get. Private, traditional-style dining rooms are available and recommended so as to avoid the feeling you are in a chain restaurant. Make reservations ahead of time or plan on spending time in the small 1980s-Tokyo-esque bar until a table opens up. The overall ambiance is worth experiencing and the service is truly excellent. Be sure to try the deep-fried tempura green tea or red bean icecream for dessert. Accepts AE, D, DC, MC, V. (2004)

Gargoyles on the Square
219 Elm St., Somerville (Davis Square)
Red Line to Davis Square
Tue-Sun 5:30pm-10pm, Fri-Sat 5:30pm-10:30pm

617-776-5300

American. A good place for a celebration. Great atmosphere and delicious contemporary American food, the kind where the chef tries interesting and creative things that look nice on the plate and taste great. The menu changes seasonally and usually has a mix of more creative entrees and a few classics for the less adventurous. There's always at least one vegetarian entree. (2003)

Geoff and Drew's Late Night Incredible Cookies
www.geoffanddrews.com

617-787-8555 or 866-EAT-LATE

Bakery, Dessert. Giant 12-inch diameter frosted cookies delivered still-hot to your dormitory room. They bake them fresh, so be prepared to wait a while. Also offering cookies and brownies by the dozen, they will bring you ice cream, milk, coffee, hot chocolate and cakes. A little overpriced and a little greasy but worth it for those sugar cravings during late night study sessions. Free delivery 8pm to midnight Sun-Thu. (2003)

Ghandi
704 Mass. Ave. (Central Square)
Walking distance or Red Line to Central Square
Daily noon-11pm

617-491-1104

Indian. The lunch buffet ($5.95 all you can eat 11:30am-3pm) is considered the best among the many Indian restaurants in Central. Almost no variety (6 dishes that seldom change), but it's always good — the Chicken Tikka Marsala is heavenly for that price. Staff is very friendly. Free delivery. Accepts AE, D, DC, MC, V. (2004)

Ginza
1002 Beacon St., Brookline
Green Line C to St. Mary Street
Mon-Thu 11:30am-2:30pm & 5pm-10pm, Fri 11:30am-2:30pm & 5pm-1:30am, Sat noon-1:30am, Sun noon-10pm
617-566-9688

16 Hudson St., Chinatown, Boston
Orange Line to Chinatown or Red Line to Downtown Crossing
Mon 11:30am-2:30pm & 5pm-1:30am, Tue-Fri 11:30am-2:30pm & 5pm-3:30am, Sat 11:30am-3:30am, Sun 11:30am-1:30am
617-338-2261

Japanese. The debate over the best sushi in Boston will never end, but the most common winner of the top spot is Ginza. Incredibly fresh fish, including an impressive lobster sashimi that's still twitching when they take it back to make miso soup from the legs. Don't miss the ice cream tempura, with crisp flaky batter around ginger and green tea ice creams. Make reservations for large parties or during the weekend rush. Accepts AE, DC, MC, V. (2004)

Grasshopper
1 North Beacon Street, Allston-Brighton
Drive or bike
Mon-Thu 11am-10pm, Fri-Sat 11am-11pm, Sun noon-10pm

617-254-8883

Vegetarian, Vietnamese. Excellent vegan Vietnamese food. The people are extremely nice and the food will make even the most resolved carnivores wish they could eat like this every day. Small place but very clean and cute table decorations. Good value, huge portions, especially for lunch. Lunch specials $5-7, dinner entrees $6-12. Accepts AE, DC, V, MC. (2004)

Greek Corner
2366 Mass. Ave., Cambridge (Davis Square)
Drive or Red Line to Davis Square
617-661-5655

Greek An unassuming Greek restaurant with great food and good prices, $8-$10 for most entrees. Take-out available. Favorites include roast or baked lamb with potatoes and rice, moussaka, gyros sandwich, and the appetizer sampler. There are other perks to Greek Corner, such as the retsina (white wine flavored with pine sap) and galaktobourikos (filo dough pastry filled with custard). Have the avgolemono soup (lemon, chicken, rice). Worth the hike. (2003)

Greenhouse Coffee Shop
3 Brattle St., Harvard Square
Red Line or #1 bus to Harvard Square
Sun-Thu 7am-11pm; Fri-Sat 7am-midnight
617-354-3184

American. Decent burgers and sandwiches, known for their chocolate chip pancakes. A good place to go if you're in Harvard Square looking for a coffee shop with decent food. Coffee shop style dessert selection. Cash only. (2004)

Grendel's Den
89 Winthrop St., Harvard Square, Cambridge
Red Line to Harvard
Daily 11am-midnight
617-491-1160

American, Vegetarian. This small underground bar in Harvard Square is best known for its deeply discounted food during happy hour (with a beverage purchase). The food is quite good, ranging from sandwiches and pizzas to fondue and falafel. Vegetarian options abound. It also has an outdoor cafÇ in the summer (although they cannot serve you alcohol if you're seated there.) Grendel's can be very crowded during dinner and on weekends. Remember that it is a bar, and you may be turned away if anyone in your party is under 21. (2003)

Gyuhama
827 Boylston St
Green Line to Prudential
Daily noon-2:30pm, 5:30pm-1:30am
617-437-0188

Japanese. Gyuhama is best known around MIT for "Midnight Sushi" — they are open very late almost every night, though they occasionally close randomly so calling first is a good idea. Their food is excellent. They serve a great variety of sushi you won't find anywhere else, and excellent eel, despite it being 1am. Plus they offer a variety of plum wines and sake. The catch: Expect to pay about $30 a person. (2003)

Harvest Restaurant
www.harvestcambridge.com
44 Brattle St., Harvard Square
Red Line or #1 bus to Harvard Square
Sun-Thu noon-10pm, Fri-Sat noon-11pm
617-868-2255

French. Trendy "Nouvelle-French" food for an intellectual group. Artfully prepared and presented. You pay for the quality and atmosphere: about $25-40 for dinner. If you're someone who values game in season, try it out, otherwise your money is better spent elsewhere. Try the specials. Lunch ends at 2:30pm and dinner starts at 5:30pm, although the bar is open between meals. Accepts AE, D, DC, MC, V. (2004)

Haveli
1248 Cambridge Street, Cambridge
Drive or bike
Daily noon-11pm
617-497-6548

Indian. One of Cambridge's better Indian choices, once again outside of the Central Square haven for Indian Food. Good quality, average prices, including luncheon specials until 3pm. Try the lunch buffet. Free delivery with $10 order. Accepts AE, D, DC, MC, V. (2003)

Helmand

143 First Street, Cambridge
Walking distance, or take The Wave to
the Galleria
Sun-Thu 5pm-10pm, Fri-Sat 5pm-11pm

617-492-4646

Middle Eastern. Afghan food may not be well-known, but Helmand is becoming a favorite among the MIT community. A good place for a celebration (or to take parents) at a reasonable price. The entrees are very good, from a good selection of vegetarian dishes to the rack of lamb. Make sure to order appetizers and bread for the full experience; try at least one item made with pumpkin. Entrees range from less than $10 up to $19 for the mouthwatering beef tenderloin. For those of you following world politics, the owner of the restaurant is the brother of Hamid Karzai, the US-backed interim ruler of Afghanistan. You might consider making reservations if dining during the weekend. Accepts AE, MC, V. (2004)

Herrell's

www.herrells.com

15 Dunster Street, Cambridge (Harvard
Square)
Red Line to Harvard Square
Sun-Thu 10am-midnight, Fri-Sat 10am-
1am; Winter: daily 11am-midnight

617-497-2179

Dessert. One of several ice cream stores in Harvard Square, Herrell's is known locally for setting up shop at random local events in a large red double-decker bus. Situated in an old bank building, you can sit in the bank vault and eat your ice cream in air conditioned comfort. Though somewhat expensive, they have a mindboggling array of flavors (jalapeno? pumpkin? girlsenberry?) and excellent milkshakes (or frappes, or whatever they're called.) Huge selection of toppings available. Features "smoosh-ins" (you take melty ice cream out, smoosh in things like M&Ms and then refreeze). Low- and non-fat frozen yogurt, sugar-free, and "no moo" vegan options are also available. (2003)

Hi-Fi Pizza and Subs

496 Mass. Ave., Central Square
Walking distance
Mon-Thu 9am-3am, Fri-Sat 9am-4am,
Sun noon-3am

617-492-4600

American, Italian. Extremely greasy pizza and subs. Not particularly good, but still popular at 1am after the surrounding clubs close, when it's the only food source still open (also a standard stop on a Mass Ave barcrawl, for the same reason). Unlike many pizza parlours, serves draught beer. Free delivery (minimum $7 order) on weekdays until midnight, weekends 'til 2am. (2003)

High Rise Bread Company

56 Brattle St., Cambridge (Harvard Square)
Red Line to Harvard Square
Mon-Fri 8:30am-5pm, Sat 9am-5pm, Sun
10am-4pm
617-492-3003

208 Concord Ave., Cambridge
Buses 72, 74, 75, 78 from Harvard Square
Mon-Fri 8am-8pm, Sat 8am-5pm, Sun 8am-
3pm
617-876-8766

Bakery. Expensive sandwiches ($7-$10), but they're worth it. The canonical example of east coast Artisan baking. Also sells very high quality baked goods. Go at least once. Weekend brunch, lunch and dinner. Accepts MC, V with $10 minimum. (2004)

Hilltop Steak House

www.hilltop-steak-house.com

855 Broadway (Route 1 US South), Saugus
About a 15 minute drive.
Mon-Thu 11am-10pm, Fri-Sat 11am-
11pm, Sun 11:30am-10pm

781-233-7700

American, Meat. This place is a classic. It seats about a billion, but sometimes has a wait that can be long. Lots of food — salad, huge portions of red meat, etc., at reasonable ($12-$20) steak house prices. Rare means raw. Everyone should go here at least once. Look for the giant cactus sign. A stand at Fenway Park sells their goods as well and, for the truly devout, they have their own butcher shop. This is where the famous cow on the dome came from. Accepts AE, MC, V. (2004)

Hong Kong Restaurant
1236 Mass. Ave., Harvard Square
Red Line or #1 bus to Harvard Square
Sun-Thu 11:30am-2am, Fri-Sat 11:30am-2:30am
Bar closes at 1am Sun-Wed, 2am Thu-Sat
617-864-5311

Chinese, Brewpub/Bar. "The pink eyesore of Harvard Square", except now it's painted yellow. Located a bit down Mass. Ave. back toward MIT. Good variety of relatively authentic Chinese food at $7-12 per person, and a big bar upstairs — make sure to have a Scorpion Bowl (this is the traditional first stop for a Mass. Ave. barcrawl). Packed with drunk students on the weekend, but the restaurant is separated enough from the bar to allow for a quiet meal. The wait staff is friendly and apparently everlasting. Accepts major credit cards. (2004)

House of Tibet
235 Holland St., Somerville (Teele Square)
Red Line to Davis Square
Tue-Sun 11:30am-3pm & 5pm-9:30pm
617-629-7567

Tibetan. Tibetan food is kind of a hearty cross between Indian and Chinese. For excellent prices, you'll find yak cheese, lentils, potatoes, cabbage, and peas. The steamed bread will make you weep with joy. The lentil soup comes with many entrees, but if you want a good hearty soup, try the Mother's Soup. Other unusual offerings include salted buttered tea (vaguely like popcorn except liquid and tea) and hot apple cider with cottage cheese. This works surprisingly well. They have cloth hanging in the doorway, which does not mean that the restaurant is closed. If you feel Tibetan after dinner, stop into the shop next door and buy something woolen. (2003)

Hsin Hsin
25 Mass. Ave., Boston
Walk or #1 bus over Harvard bridge
Daily 11:30am-10:30pm
617-536-9852

Chinese. Decent, cheap Chinese food. The best deals are the dinner specials, which include soup and an appetizer. Order the scallion pancakes for an appetizer. Delivery for $2 from 5:30pm-10:30pm. Accepts major credit cards. (2004)

Hu Tieu Nam Vang
7 Beach St., Boston (Chinatown)
Orange Line to Chinatown or Red Line to Downtown Crossing
Daily 8am-10pm
617-422-0501

Vietnamese. This hole-in-the-wall Vietnamese restaurant is a perfect place for students to find a cheap, good meal. The main attraction is Pho (pronounced "fuh"), a beef noodle soup that fills you for $5. The fresh fruit milkshakes, available in more flavors than you can shake a durian at, are excellent. Highly recommended. (2003)

India Pavilion Restaurant
17 Central Sq., Cambridge
Walking distance
Daily noon-11pm
617-547-7463

Indian. Good, authentic Indian food. Dinner is about $10. Portions are small, so you may want to get an appetizer. The restaurant is often crowded, and you should expect a wait on Friday and Saturday nights. Friendly service. Try Thali (vegetarian) or Vindaloo (very hot) dishes and the Mango Lassi. No delivery, but you can order take-out. Accepts AE, D, DC, MC, V. (2004)

India Samraat
www.indiasamraat.com
51A Massachusetts Ave., Boston
Walking Distance
Mon-Fri noon-2:30pm & 5pm-10:30pm, Sat noon-10:30pm, Sun 3pm-10:30pm
617-247-0718

Indian. Popular catering choice for MIT events — the delivery guys are very friendly and helpful. If you order a few times they'll remember you. Food can be expensive but reasonably good. The online menu has pictures to help you choose. MIT, BU, and Northeastern students get free delivery with a valid student ID, otherwise delivery to MIT incurs a $2 charge. Minimum delivery order is $30 noon-5pm and $20 5pm-10pm. The website allows for online ordering. Accepts AE, CB, D, DC, MC, V. (2004)

International House of Pancakes
1850 Soldiers Field Road, Brighton
Bus #64 (toward Oak Square) from Central Square (i.e. "drive")
Open 24/7
617-787-0533

American. Average American breakfast food for about $5-10. Fine if you feel like eating breakfast food, but the real reason to go is that it's open 24 hours (if it's a sane hour, you'll be happier with S&S or even Bickford's). Expect to find lots of local students, weird folk, and a police presence late at night, as it's pretty much the only thing open after 3am. (2003)

Iruna
56 JFK St., Cambridge (Harvard Square)
Red Line or #1 bus to Harvard Square
Mon-Fri 11:30am-2pm & 6pm-9:30pm,
Sat 11:30am-4pm & 5pm-10pm
617-868-5633

Spanish. This restaurant has one of the most interesting and appetizing selections of food in Harvard Square. Many variations of Spanish tortillas, a basic variety of tapas and other Iberian dishes. For under $12 you can get a good meal. Try the Carne Guisada, the soups, and the homemade sangria. Frequently crowded, so reservations are recommended. Accepts CB, D, DC, MC, V. (2004)

Izzy's
169 Harvard St., Cambridge
Walking distance, Corner of Harvard & Windsor
Mon-Fri 10am-8:30pm, Sat 10am-8pm
617-661-3910

Caribbean. Authentic so-so Puerto Rican food. They have daily menus with a list of about 6-8 specials, soup/salad and usually rice included. Favorite dishes include montanero (steak with egg), fajitas (beef/chicken cooked with onion and sweet peppers), and oxtail. The side of sweet plantains (considerably better than the tougher "fried plantains") comes with selected dishes and is worth buying on its own. If you want good Puerto Rican food, go to Puerto Rico; until then, this is the best (and only) you'll get in Cambridge. It's a good place to have a cheap lunch between classes — most choices cost around $6-8. (2002)

Jae's Café
520 Columbus Ave, Boston (South End)
5-10 minutes from Prudential on Green Line
Mon-Thu 11:30am-4pm & 5pm-10:00pm,
Fri-Sat 11:30am-4pm & 5pm-11pm, Sun noon-9pm
617-421-9405

Thai, Korean, Japanese. A pan-Asian extravaganza. Maybe a little pricey for things like Pad Thai, but good adventurous sushi and a good variety of tasty food from all over Asia. Accepts AE, D, DC, MC, V. (2004)

Jake's Boss BBQ
3492 Washington St., Jamaica Plain
Mon 4pm-10pm, Tue-Wed 11am-10pm,
Thu-Sat 11am-11pm, Sun 11am-10pm
617-983-3701

American, Meat. Another of the great Boston barbecue joints, and in some people's opinion, the best. Try the Burnt Ends, brisket, or either kind of ribs, with all the classic sides. Not much ambiance (order from the counter, grab a vinyl-tableclothed table and plenty of napkins), but if you're a BBQ fan or a homesick Southerner, try this place. Not for vegetarians. (2003)

Jerusalem Café
245 Mass. Ave., Cambridge (Central Square)
Walking distance
Daily 8am-9pm
617-441-8689

Middle Eastern. A genuinely charming place that is nicely decorated with plants, interesting chairs, funny Arabic posters and a beautiful pipe. The only waiter is a pleasant mother of 6 small children (they scuttle around in the back) who also cooks most of the time. An interesting mix of traditional Middle Eastern foods and standard American breakfast, everything's tasty and the dinner entrees are quite large. The chicken moutarde and calves' liver are standouts; anything with roasted chicken (e.g. the Cashew Chicken Salad) is also good. And it's cheap — $7 for an entree. Breakfast served all day. Accepts AE, DC, D, MC, V. (2004)

Jimmy's Steer House
1111 Massachusetts Ave., Arlington Drive

781-646-4450

American, Meat. The most mouthwatering Teriyaki steak ever. They do chicken and seafood as well (both excellent). The key to the meal is the spinach rice pilaf. The parking lot is a bit small. This place has great food at very reasonable prices. This is your basic steak house done right, the way you think a steakhouse should be — without surprises. A perfect first (and second) date restaurant. (2003)

John Harvard's Brew House
www.johnharvards.com

33 Dunster St., Cambridge (Harvard Square)
Red Line or #1 bus to Harvard Square
Mon-Wed 11:30am-1am, Thu-Sat 11:30am-2am, Sun 11:30am-12:30am

617-868-3585

American, Brewpub/Bar. The experts disagree on John Harvard's; some say it's average microbrew beer with good food, others say average food with good beer. In either event, the range of beer selection has gone a little downhill from the glory days, but if you want to try some beers you can't get anywhere else and use them to wash down some at least reasonable American pub fare, you can do a lot worse. Being in Harvard Square, they are extremely careful about checking IDs — expect to get carded, and if your ID is from outside Massachusetts, expect to have it refused. Last call for drinks is a half hour before closing. Accepts AE, D, DC, MC, V. (2004)

J.P. Licks
352 Newbury St

617-236-1666
Green Line to Hynes Convention Center

Dessert. Boston supposedly has a surprisingly high ice cream store to resident ratio; J.P. Licks, a local chain, is one of the many good parlours around the city which support this theory. Decorated with a memorable cow-pattern motif, J.P. Licks makes good homemade ice cream in a variety of sometimes bizarre flavors (cucumber?!). A generous small cone is $2.95. J.P. Licks is good for small- and medium-sized groups; they will, however, yell at you if you try to fit too many people in their teacup-shaped table. Always busy and always fast. There are several locations; one of the most central is on 352 Newbury Street. (2003)

Kaya
www.kayausa.com

1924 Mass. Ave., Porter Square
Red Line to Porter Square
Sun-Wed 11:30am-1am, Thu-Sat 2am
617-497-5656

581 Boylston St, Boston
Green Line to Copley
Daily 11:30am-2am
617-236-5858

Korean, Japanese, Meat. Good Korean barbecue, though a bit expensive. Be sure to get one of the tables where you grill your own meat. If you ask nicely, you can get a private room. Best with a big group. The sushi is good but overpriced for the quality (if you're willing to pay these prices for sushi, go to Ginza or Sweet Chili), so stay with the meat. See also Shabuso. Accepts AE, D, DC, MC, V. (2004)

Kendall Square Food Court
Next to the Marriott Hotel
Walking distance

Fast Food, Food Court. This court is mostly for the business types who work in the Square. It has an Au Bon Pain, because the one across the street is somehow insufficient. It's got a burger joint, a Sbarro's, and cheap Chinese. It also has a cafeteria-type place, with a salad bar, a sandwich bar, and a dessert bar, that charges you by weight. In front of one place in particular, if you hover by the counter, make eye contact, or even run past at high speed, you will often be offered a small chuck of possibly-chicken on a stick to taste. No matter what else you had hoped to buy for lunch, once you have tasted the evil sauce there is no turning back. Hey, if business critters can eat it, so can you. (2004)

Kentucky Fried Chicken, Taco Bell
168 Hampshire St., Cambridge (Corner of Prospect & Hampshire)
Walk or bike
Sun-Thu 10:30am-11pm, Fri-Sat
10:30am-midnight
617-547-8615

2072 Mass. Ave. (Porter Square)
Red Line to Porter Square
Sun-Thu 10:30am-11pm, Fri-Sat
10:30am-midnight
617-868-1498

Fast Food. Generally found as "Kentaco Bell" (for some reason, though, there don't seem to be any Kentaco Huts around). Deep fried chicken and insulting Mexican food. Isn't America great? The biscuits don't suck. (2004)

King & I
www.kingandi-boston.com

145 Charles St., Boston
Walking distance or Red Line to
Charles/MGH
Mon-Thu 11:30am-9:30pm, Fri-Sat
11:30am-10:30pm, Sun 5pm-9:30pm

617-227-3320

Thai. Nice, light food, but still with a lot of taste. Expect about $7-10 for a main course. Delivery available for large (>$100) orders made in advance. Menu available online. Accepts AE, D, MC, V. (2004)

King Fung Garden
74 Kneeland St., Chinatown, Boston
Orange Line to Chinatown or Red Line
to South Station
Daily 11am-10pm

617-357-5262

Chinese. Better known as "Brezhnev's," and a long-time TEP hangout, this tiny place packs about 15 into a converted corner gas station. Mostly devoid of atmosphere, the employees speak almost no English (but they occasionally appreciate a lesson). The northern (Shan Xi) cuisine is rare in Boston and very good, including the best three-course Peking Duck in Chinatown (order in advance). Also great scallion pancakes and chow mein. All the "secret" specials are written on the wall in Chinese, so having a translator is a big bonus. Quite inexpensive; a full meal can range from less than $5 to about $15. Cash only. (2004)

Korea Garden
20 Pearl St., Cambridge (Central Square)
Walking distance
Mon-Wed 5pm-10pm,Thu-Sat noon-
10pm, Sun 3pm-10pm

617-492-9643

Korean. A small, cozy restaurant serving good, authentic Korean food run by a very nice husband and wife team, the former of which has an amazing ability to happily mumble at you or to himself. The lunch buffet is decent for about $7. Dinner is about $12. This is the best place in town to get Bi Bim Bop. Be sure you get it in the stone pot; it makes all the difference in the world, even if it does cost an extra dollar or two. Better than Koreana, but doesn't have the barbecue tables. Plenty of vegetarian options. Reservations available. Accepts V, MC. (2004)

Koreana
154-156 Prospect St., Cambridge
Walking distance, corner of Prospect & Broadway

617-576-8661

Korean. Authentic Korean food in a somewhat tacky atmosphere. Go in a large group so you can get one of the barbecue tables, and cook your meat in front of you. It helps to have someone Korean along to help you decipher the menu. (2003)

Krispy Kreme
krispykreme.com

Prudential Building Food Court
800 Boylston Street, Boston, MA 02199
Green Line to Prudential Center
Walk-in open 5am-11:30pm
617-262-5531

35 Revere Beach Parkway, Medford, MA 02155
Drive or long bike ride
Walk-in open Sun-Thu 5am-2am, Fri-Sat 5am-3am
Drive-through open 24/7
781-393-8888

Fast Food, Dessert. Krispy Krack! Yum yum yum. Many people contend that Krispy Kreme are not real donuts, that they're overpriced, that all those people who tell you they're the best shit ever are just lying. You might be one of those people. Or you might be one of those people who thinks the Krispy Kreme is the only true donut, and that all others are merely pale imitations, poor reflections of the Kreme glory. The truth lies somewhere in between. All agree, however, that Krispy Kreme is best hot and fresh off the machine. Some have suggested that 7.354 seconds in a microwave will return a cold donut to its former hot and steamy goodness. However, if given the opportunity, be sure to check out the Medford store, where you can see the entire production line from dough to mouth. It is an amazing feat of engineering sure to be appreciated by MIT students. Plus, as long as the crowds keep lining up, they'll keep giving away free donuts from the machine. At least until the novelty wears off, it's likely that Krispy Krack will be an efficient bribe for many people you know. (2004)

Kupel's
421 Harvard St., Brookline
Green Line C to Coolidge Corner
Mon-Wed 8am-8pm, Thu 6am-10pm, Fri 6am-7pm, Sun 6am-8pm

617-566-9528

Bakery, Kosher. This classic, New-York-style bagel place under KVH supervision is a great lunch stop. A full-service bakery, Kupel's makes breads, cakes, and pastries as well as giant bagel sandwiches. Kupel's is very inexpensive and serves large portions. Visit on a Sunday morning and get a newspaper as well. Accepts MC, V. (2004)

L.A. Burdick
52D Brattle St., Cambridge (Harvard Square)
Red Line or #1 bus to Harvard Square
Tue-Sat 8am-11pm, Sun-Mon 8am-1pm

617-491-4340

Dessert, Bakery. The chocoholic's wet dream (or worst nightmare?). You must try the Hot Chocolate (available in Dark, Milk, and White); it's like a solid bar melted into a cup. Also excellent pastries. The chocolate mice are adorable. Their chocolate can be ordered online. (2003)

La Groceria Ristorante Italiano
www.lagroceriarestaurant.com

853 Main St., Cambridge (Central Square)
Walking distance
Mon-Fri 11am-10pm, Sat 4pm-10pm, Sun 1pm-9pm

617-497-4214 or 617-876-4162

Italian. Good food in a nice atmosphere. About $7-10 for lunch and up to $20 for dinner. It can be very busy on the weekends, which definitely affects speed of service. The fettuccine and Veal de Plume are recommended, although everything is pretty good. Reservations for parties of 6 or more; semiformal attire recommended. Accepts AE, CB, D, DC, MC, V. (2004)

Lala Rokh

www.lalarokh.com

97 Mt. Vernon Street, Boston
Walk, Red Line to Charles/MGH, or
Green Line to Arlington
Mon-Fri noon-3pm & 5:30pm-10pm, Sat-
Sun 5:30pm-10pm

617-720-5511

Middle Eastern. A Beacon Hill gem hidden in the basement of a residential brick-lined street, this gastronomical delight specializes in exotic Persian dishes that can be found nowhere else in Boston (except, perhaps, an Iranian friend's kitchen). For something really special, try the Fesenjaan (duck smothered in walnut and pomegranate sauce) or the Zareshke Pollo (aromatically spiced chicken served over saffron-flavored rice and barberries). The quality of the food is attested to by the long waits; reservations are essential on the weekends. Unfortunately, the food is priced to match its uniqueness. Expect to spend $20-25 without drinks. Valet parking available. (2003)

La Luna Caffé

www.lalunacaffe.com

403 Mass. Ave., Cambridge (Central Square)
Walking distance
Mon-Sat 8am-11pm, Sun 8am-10pm

617-576-3400

Italian, Coffeehouse. An Italian caffé with delicious panini sandwiches, salads, wraps and other dishes, homemade gelato, Italian sodas, all variations of hot or cold coffee drinks, slushes, and smoothies. Extremely convenient from campus. Slightly classy decor with friendly European ambiance. Has tables facing the sidewalk with large windows that open out onto the street — a great place to sit but you can also get everything to go. Meals all roughly $5. Delivery after 5pm. (2003)

Legal Sea Foods

www.legalseafoods.com

Multiple locations including:

5 Cambridge Center, Cambridge (Kendall Square)
Walking distance
Mon-Thu 11am-10pm, Fri-Sat 11am-10:30pm, Sun 4pm-10pm
617-864-3400

20 University Rd, Cambridge (Harvard Square)
Red Line or #1 bus to Harvard Square
Mon-Thu 11am-10pm, Fri-Sat 11am-10:30pm, Sun 4pm-10pm
617-491-9400

Seafood. Delicious seafood — just about everything is recommended. You must have the clam chowder. Dinner can cost about $20. Try the less expensive but also very good take-out, including fish and chips; some appetizers, such as the fried calamari, are large enough for a meal. Big menu and big wine list. The non-fish options are somewhat limited, but the steak is good, and there's always the burger. The hot chocolate pudding cake is transcendent. Try Legal's at least once; it is an MIT and Boston institution. Take your parents. Reservations for parties of 6 or more. Accepts AE, D, DC, MC, V. (2003)

L'Espalier

www.lespalier.com

30 Gloucester St, Boston
Green Line to Symphony or Hynes
Mon-Sat 5:30pm-10pm

617-262-3023

French. Superb gourmet French food. The 7 course tasting menu (one menu for meat-eaters and another for vegetarians) is amazing. If you get the tasting menu, your meal will probably last around 3 hours — it's very expensive but worth it for that special occasion, like your parents saying they want to take you to "a nice restaurant" and making mistakes like saying "money doesn't matter." Have some wine. Reservations required. Jacket and tie preferred. Accepts AE, DC, MC, V. (2003)

Ling Garden

63 White St., Belmont
Drive or take the #73 bus from Harvard Square
Sun-Thu 11am-10pm, Fri-Sat 11am-11pm

617-484-1118

Chinese. Great food, with pleasant, professional wait staff and a quiet atmosphere. The service is fantastic, fast, and very attentive and the portions are large. Beer and wine available. All in all a wonderful little restaurant for quick Chinese food. Try the Hawaiian Pineapple Chicken or the Tong An Province Chicken. They have a thriving take-out and delivery (local to Belmont) business. They will cater for large functions to MIT at very reasonable prices! Don't miss the dim sum on Sunday afternoons. (2003)

Lobdell
Student Center
Walking distance

Food Court. This food court is described in Campus Dining in Miscellaneous. It's got the same inconvenient hours, the same odd selection, the same overpriced food as all other food courts, but hey, it's your local campus food court. (2003)

Maggiano's Little Italy
www.maggianos.com

4 Columbus Ave., Boston
Green Line to Arlington, near Park Plaza Hotel
Mon-Thu 11:30am-2:30pm & 5pm-10pm, Fri 11:30am-2:30pm & 5pm-11pm, Sat noon-11pm, Sun noon-9pm

617-542-3456

Italian. This impressive Italian restaurant is, surprisingly, a chain, although you wouldn't guess from the food or the atmosphere. The food is excellent, although a little on the pricey side ($12-33 per entree), but if you are in a crowd the family style ($23/person) will bring you an all-you-can eat five-course feast. This feature makes it probably the best location in Boston for a very large group. Accepts AE, CB, D, DC, MC, V. (2004)

Marche
www.marcheusa.com

The Prudential Center
800 Boylston Street, Suite 001
Green Line to Prudential
Daily 11:30am-midnight

617-578-9700

French. An intriguing concept with a slightly disappointing implementation, Marche is still worth a visit if you're in the area. The restaurant is modeled after a French marketplace complete with umbrellas over the tables despite the indoor location. Patrons stroll through themed food stations, constructing their meal piece-wise cafeteria-fashion. But unlike cafeterias, the kitchens and the chefs are on display as well, adding to the perception of freshness. The food is of varying quality and not as unique as its presentation. Occasionally, you may find a large selection of soups (the Hungarian mushroom is amazing), and there are always some delicious cakes and crêpes. It's a bit pricey for what you get; expect to spend $10-15 for a light lunch. (2003)

Mary Chung
464 Mass. Ave., Central Square
Walking distance
Mon, Wed-Thu, Sun 11:30am-10pm, Fri-Sat 11:30am-11pm

617-864-1991

Chinese. For as long as anyone can remember, Mary's has been an entrenched establishment central to life at MIT. You will always run into someone you know at Mary's. This is because the food is very, very good, with plenty of spicy meats and a decent number of vegetarian options. Meals are served in three courses: soup, appetizer and main dish. Suan La Chow Show (wontons over spicy soup and bean sprouts) is a perennial favorite; those who can't take the heat often choose the Wonton Soup instead. Pan Fried Peking Ravioli are almost always ordered. Popular main dishes include General Gau's Chicken ("Gau"), Dried Cooked Sliced Beef ("DCSB"), and Dun Dun Noodles ("DDN," vegetarian or available with shredded chicken). For less spice, try the Mongolian Beef ("Embarrassing Beef", order it to hear why) or the Orange Sauce Chicken. Generally runs $12-$20 for a full meal. If you go with older folks from around MIT, don't be surprised if a method of ordering involving hand signals pops up. Weekend Dim Sum is served until 2:30pm; while not particularly "authentic", the dishes are excellently done. It's the only time they serve scallion pie, but more importantly it's the only local source for the exquisite Sweet Sesame Rice Balls, a.k.a. Eyeballs, for reasons that will be obvious when you try them. Other Dim Sum favorites include Yu-Hsiang Eggplant and the Steamed Vegetable Dumplings (not on the menu, but often available on weekends). Important notes: Mary's is closed on Tuesdays (hence the theory that any day on which Mary's is closed is therefore a Tuesday), they don't accept credit cards, and they don't deliver, although take-out is an option. (2004)

McDonald's
Many locations including:

463 Mass. Ave, Central Square
Walking distance

14 McGrath Hwy, Somerville
Drive or bike

Fast Food If you need us to describe McDonald's, you don't want to eat there. Service (if you can call what you get at McDonald's that) at the Central Square location is horrid. The drive-thru at the McGrath location is open 24 hours, with a very limited menu at night. Hours vary by location, but most close early enough to be annoying. (2003)

Middle East Restaurant
www.mideastclub.com

472 Mass. Ave., Cambridge (Central Square)
Walking distance
Sun-Thu 11am-midnight, Fri-Sat 11am-1am

617-492-9181

Middle Eastern. $6-12 for excellent-sized servings of Middle Eastern food. Fair falafel, lentil soup is worth a try. Also a nightclub; there are often performers there, both during the week and on weekends. Accepts AE, MC, V. (2003)

Midwest Grill
www.midwestgrill.com

1124 Cambridge St., Inman Square
Walk or bike
Sun-Thu 11:30am-11pm, Fri-Sat 11:30am-midnight

617-354-7536

Meat, Brazilian. Brazilian barbecue or, perhaps more accurately, "Meat on Swords." Servers circulate with beef, pork, chicken, and sausage on huge skewers. A large buffet of salads and side dishes includes many appealing choices (excellent mashed potatoes) if you have room for more. The chicken hearts, while very good, are not for everyone. Skip a meal or three before going. There are even a few choices for vegetarians not scared off by the sheer volume of meat wandering the aisles. Live music at night can make it very noisy. Reservations available (and recommended) for 8 or more. Expect to pay $20-25 per person. Accepts all major credit cards. (2004)

Mike's City Diner
1714 Washington St., Boston (South End)
#1 bus or Silver Line to Worchester Square
Daily 6am-3pm

617-267-9393

American. This South End grease heaven is the closest you'll find to a true urban city diner. Get a booth or share the bar with hardhat clad construction workers. Once you're done deciphering the waitresses' heavy Boston accent, you're well on your way to a gigantic and fresh tasting breakfast. Homesick Southeners will be happy to know that Mike's offers grits, that bland vehicle for salt and butter, in addition to home fries. The proprietor of Mike's (Mike?) also owns Victoria's Diner in Back Bay. Cash only. (2004)

Mike's Pastries
www.mikespastry.com

300 Hanover Street, Boston (North End)
Green Line to Haymarket
Sun-Thu 8am-9:30pm, Fri-Sat 8am-11pm

617-742-3050

Bakery, Dessert. The best Italian bakery in the North End, Mike's Pastries rivals any bakery in the country for both quality and price. All pastries are made on the premises. Cookies, cakes, pies, marzipan, tiramisu, chocolate covered strawberries, cannoli, creme puffs, rum cakes, Napoleons — it doesn't matter. It's all amazing. Now you can order it online and have it shipped to those unfortunate enough not to live near Mike's. Don't expect to find parking within 10 blocks. Don't expect the line to be anything but a mob scene. But it's well worth the trip; visiting Mike's is an experience in itself. Cash only. (2004)

Milk Street Café
www.milkstreetcafe.com

50 Milk St., Boston
Mon-Fri 7am-3pm
617-542-3663

Post Office Square Park, Boston
Red Line to Downtown Crossing
Mon-Fri 7am-5pm
617-350-7275

American, Kosher. Serving fish, dairy, and vegan fare, the Milk Street Café is located in the heart of Boston's business district not far from Downtown Crossing. From April to October, a hamburger and hot dog stand opens outside the Post Office Square location. Breakfast and lunch are both excellent, although somewhat pricey. Quiche is a specialty in both locations. Under ORCM supervision. (2003)

Miracle of Science
321 Mass. Ave., Central Square
Walking Distance
Daily 11:30am-1am

617-868-2866

American, Brewpub/Bar. The first thing you'll notice when you enter this small bar is that it's really loud. Don't go here if you want to carry on a detailed engineering conversation, but it's a good place to take a date, if you want to avoid uncomfortable silences. It's quieter during the afternoon though, so lunch is a good option too. The beer selection is reasonable and the food is pretty good — in particular, the veggie burger is well worth checking out, even for carnivores. Has the best bottled sauces in Cambridge on the tables, including everything from Jamaican to mango and tamarind sauces. (2003)

Moby Dick's
269 Huntington Ave, Boston
Walk or Green Line to Symphony

617-236-5511

Middle Eastern, Halal. A wonderful Persian cheap eats kabob place near Northeastern and the MFA. With its tile floors and booth seating, the atmosphere reflects the price but also adds to the feeling of authenticity (the restaurant is owned by an Iranian immigrant). The lamb, beef, and chicken kabobs are good and served with a generous portion of saffron-enhanced rice. For the really hungry, order a side of mast-o-khiaar (yogurt and cucumbers) and finish with a glass of Persian tea. For those devout Muslims amongst you, this is also one of the few Halal restaurants in town. Expect to spend $10-$15 for a meal that can feed two. (2003)

Moody's Falafel Palace
25 Central Square, Cambridge (Central Square)
Walking distance or Red Line to Central Square
Daily 11am-midnight

617-864-0827

Middle Eastern. Great place for a cheap and filling lunch. The falafel is the best thing there. Sometimes they forget to add the tahini sauce, so make sure you ask for it. The schwarma comes in lamb and chicken, but the chicken is better. Moody's has ample vegetarian options. The building is a former White Castle hamburger stand and has been featured in Zippy the Pinhead cartoons. The baklava is also decent. The location is very small, so if you bring a group be prepared to take it out to a nearby bench. (2003)

Mr. and Mrs. Bartley's Burger Cottage
www.mrbartleys.com

1246 Mass. Ave., Cambridge (Harvard Square)
Red Line or #1 bus to Harvard Square

617-354-6559

American. Bartley's has been a Harvard Square icon since 1961. It's got soul. No longer inexpensive, but still excellent. Big variety of burgers (hockey-puck shaped, but the resemblance ends there: they're happy to cook yours rare; make sure to give instructions), delicious frappes and Lime Rickeys. They can make any burger with turkey or veggie patties. You must try the sweet potato fries. There is outdoor seating available when weather permits. M-W, Sat: 11am-9pm, Th-F 11am-10pm, Su closed; cash only. (2003)

Mr. Crêpe
83 Holland Street, Somerville (Davis Square)
Red Line to Davis Square
Tues-Fri 9am-9pm, Sat-Sun 9am-10pm

617-628-1500

French. Amazing crêpes taken to a new level. Elaborate, gourmet dinner and dessert crêpes made while you watch. Pricey but filling. The crêpes are thicker than at other places. Try the blackberry and chocolate crêpe. Try the soup, too. The potato soup looks plain but it is wonderful. The potato soup and a chicken, feta, spinach, tomato, and basil crêpe makes for fine hang-over food. (2003)

Mu Que Ca
www.muquecarestaurant.com

1093 Cambridge St, Cambridge
Walk, bike, or drive
Tue-Sat 11am-9pm, Sun noon-5pm

617-354-3296

Brazilian, Seafood. As the name implies, this small restaurant's best dish is moqueca, a seafood stew derived from Brazilian native indian, African and Portuguese cuisines. Their vegetarian version of moqueca, which substitutes plantains for seafood, is amazing. The owners, Antonio and Fafa, are very friendly and go out of their way to make sure you enjoy your meal. Try the fried plantain and a fruit smoothy. The restaurant itself is small, but comfortable enough for a sit-down meal. At the heart of Cambridge's Brazilian enclave, Mu Que Ca is a favorite stop for the local Brazilian community to catch up on Brazilian TV while waiting in line for a taste of home. Mu Que Ca is a great option for catering large events. See the website for a menu. Accepts AE, D, MC, V. (2004)

Nan Ling
179 Mass. Ave., Boston
Green Line to Hynes Convention Center
Mon-Sat 11am-3am, Sun noon-3am

617-247-0393 or 617-247-1835

Chinese. Typical late-night, last-resort greasy Chinese food fare, i.e., even sketchier than Quan's. But it's just about the only place that will deliver past 2am during the week, so it earns an established place in MIT cuisine. Recommended dishes include the moo shi varieties and broccoli with garlic sauce. Add $1.50 for delivery. Accepts MC, V with $15 minimum order. (2004)

New Asia
1105 Mass. Ave., Cambridge
Red Line to Harvard Square
Daily 11:30am-10:30pm

617-491-1873

Chinese, Thai. A friendly little Chinese and Thai restaurant about halfway between Harvard and Central. The decor is very pink, but the service and food are both good. Drinks are very generously sized and mixed strong. Real strong. Their egg drop soup is some of the best to be found and there are options for vegetarians and vegans. Dinner entrees run between $5 and $10; there's a luncheon buffet 11:30am-2pm Monday-Friday for $6.50. Minimum order for delivery is $15. (2003)

New York Pizza

435 Mass. Ave., Boston
Green Line or #1 bus to Symphony
Open until 2am on weekends, midnight
during the week

617-266-7020

Italian. Giant, fresh thin-crust slices of the best New York pizza in Boston, hands down. Serves giant slices. (2003)

Oleana

www.oleanarestaurant.com

134 Hampshire St., Cambridge
Walk, bike, or drive
Sun-Thu 5:30pm-10pm, Fri-Sat 5:30pm-11pm

617-661-0505

Mediterranean, Middle Eastern. You have not lived a full life until you've eaten at Oleana. Both the Vegetarian Tasting Menu and the Grilled Lamb Steak w/ Turkish Spices & Fava Bean Moussaka are required eating. Everything is excellent and made on-site by chef and owner Ana Sortun, pastry chef Maura Kilpatrick, and their duo of crack-commando ninja sous chefs, Wilton and Nookie. If you go, make sure you are prepared to splurge and get appetizers, a main course, wine, and dessert. Before the food arrives, you'll be wondering why you just depleted your bank account; after you're done, you'll be wondering why they don't charge more. In other words, a perfect place to take parents as their graduation gift to you. Private lunch engagements, seasonal outdoor seating, reservations, and online menu are all available. This is the best Cambridge has to offer. Accepts AE, MC, V. (2004)

Outback Steak House

www.outbacksteakhouse.com

672 Fellsway, Medford
Drive or Orange Line to Wellington Circle

781-306-1300

American, Meat. Member of a reasonably large steakhouse chain; good, cheap steaks — the Outback Special 12oz. sirloin for about $13 is excellent value — salads, shrimp and regular American steakhouse fare (don't be fooled by the over-the-top "Australian" imagery, this place is about as Aussie as Ronald Reagan). Be careful of taking genuine Australians to this place as they may have a seizure, caused by either laughter or anger, depending on their temperament. Despite their professed image, the beer selection is lousy — typical American plus the dreaded Foster's. But you can call ahead, idle your car in the parking lot, and they'll bring your food out to you. (2003)

Pad Thai Café

1116 Boylston St., Boston
Walk, bike, or Green Line to Hynes Convention Center
Mon-Fri 11:30am-10:30pm, Sat-Sun noon-10pm

617-247-3399

Thai. This place is perhaps the perfect student-oriented Thai restaurant; cheap, good food with a minimum of fuss or wait. It generally caters to Berklee School of Music students, but is so close to MIT that it is bound to become a favorite. To get there, follow Mass. Ave. across the Harvard Bridge, then hang a right on Boylston. It will be on the left about a block down Boylston. It's generally faster to walk than take the T. Recommended dishes include the Pad Kee Mao, curries, and specials of the day. Delivery after 5:30pm with a $2 additional charge. Cash only. (2004)

Papa Razzi

www.paparazzi-restaurant.com

Cambridgeside Galleria
Walking distance, or take The Wave shuttle from Kendall Square
Sun-Thu 11:30am-10:00pm, Fri-Sat 11:30am-11:00pm

617-577-0009

Italian. Upscale Italian chain. Prices could be worse ($11-$20), but portions tend to be small. The food is generally great, down to the thin garlic breadsticks and the fresh warm focaccia brought with the menus. Take-out available, but no delivery. The bar stays open an hour longer than the kitchen closing time listed here. Accepts AE, CB, D, DC, MC, V. (2004)

Paris Crêperie
326 Cambridge St., Boston
Walk or Red Line to Charles/MGH

617-589-0909

French. This restaurant combines a sidewalk café feel with excellent crêpes. Penang duck, s'mores, chicken parmigiana, apples and brie or make-your-own are just a few of the choices. The smoothies and chai teas make wonderful sides. They'll even deliver for a minimum order of $10. Price range is $3-$7. (2003)

Passage to India
1900 Massachusetts Ave., Cambridge
(Porter Square)
Red Line to Porter Square
Mon-Sat 11:30am-3pm & 5pm-10:30pm,
Sun 5pm-10:30pm

617-497-6113

Indian. Many people consider P2I the best Indian restaurant in Cambridge. Similar menu to the Central Square Indian restaurants, but higher quality, with a few unique items and slightly higher prices. Accepts MC, V. (2003)

Penang
57 JFK St., Cambridge (Harvard Square)
Daily 11:30am-11:30pm
617-234-3988

685-691 Washington St., Boston
(Chinatown)
Daily 11:30am-11:30pm
617-451-6373

Malaysian. A chain of Malaysian restaurants, with two branches in the Boston area, they serve the unique cuisine of their homeland, a blend of Malay, Chinese, Indian, and Thai cooking. The Roti Canai is a must-try appetizer, and for a main dish, there are many choices including Mango Chicken, and a wide variety of seafood. For dessert, don't miss the ABC. Harvard location designed in a High-Tech style, with lots of shiny pipes and ducts and things. Accepts MC, V. (2003)

Pho Lemon
www.pho-lemon.com

228 Broadway St., Cambridge
Walk or bike
Daily 11am-10pm

617-441-8813 or 617-441-8812

Vietnamese. Considering this is the only Vietnamese restaurant near MIT, it is fortunate indeed that it is so good. As usual with Vietnamese cuisine, try the soups. For only $6.25, the Pho Xe Lua (beef noodle soup train car) will fill you up like you've never been filled before. All of the banh hoi (steamed vermicelli) dishes are quite good. Eating Vietnamese food is not complicated, but it does require some knowledge of how to assemble your meal before you start eating it. The staff is very friendly and will happily give you instructions if you ask. For dessert, get one of the fruit milkshakes; try the durian shake if you're feeling adventurous, otherwise the jackfruit shake is a reliable standby. Free delivery after 5pm with $15 minimum order. Available for catering. Accepts AE, MC, V. (2004)

Pho Pasteur
www.phopasteur.us

35 Dunster St., Cambridge (Harvard
Square)
Red Line or #1 bus to Harvard Square
Mon-Wed 11am-10pm, Thu-Sat 11am-
11pm, Sun 11am-10pm
617-864-4100

682 Washington St., Boston (Chinatown)
Orange Line to Chinatown or Red Line
to Downtown Crossing
Daily 9am-11pm
617-482-7467

Vietnamese. Although both locations have the same name and owners, they should almost be considered separately. The Harvard Square location is more uppity than the Chinatown location and the food isn't quite as good, although the pho (noodle soup) is the best (only?) you're going to get near Harvard Square. The Chinatown location is less expensive and the main dishes (including the pho) can be quite good, if you know what to order. Try out the canh chua (hot and sour soup), bun chao tom (shrimp cake vermicelli), and bun X xao sa ot, where X can be ga (chicken) or tau hu (tofu). Unless you know Vietnamese, please spare the world any attempt at pronouncing these dishes; pointing or calling them by their numbers on the menu works fine. There are more vegetarian options than listed on the menu, you just have to ask. The pho is cheap and filling $6-9 without tip. Menu available online. Accepts AE, MC, V. (2004)

Picante Mexican Grill
www.picantemex.com

735 Mass. Ave., Cambridge (Central Square)
Walking distance, Red Line or #1 bus to Central Square
Sun-Thu 11am-10:30pm, Fri-Sat 11am-11:00pm
617-576-6394

217 Elm St., Somerville (Davis Square)
Red Line to Davis Square
Mon-Wed 11am-10:30pm, Thu-Fri 11am-11pm, Sat 10am-11pm, Sun 10am-10:30pm
617-628-6394

Mexican. Good quick Mexican, much broader menu than Anna's or Boca Grande. Excellent enchiladas, especially with mole sauce. Bigger variety of burritos than Anna's (across the street in Davis), though they're a bit dry compared to Anna's steamed tortillas. The Burritos de Papas is a vegetarian brick with spicy potatoes. Don't forget to try the limeade. Good for catering events too, with free delivery for orders over $36. Note that the rice is not vegetarian, as it contains chicken broth. Accepts AE, D, MC, V. (2004)

Pinocchio's Pizza
74 Winthrop St., Harvard Square
Red Line to Harvard Square
Sun-Thu 11am-1am, Fri-Sat 11am-3am
617-876-4897

Italian. Voted the best pizzeria around Harvard Square by locals, and justly so. When asked why they don't deliver, they smugly reply that they are so busy with walk-in business that they don't have time for delivering. Their crusts are amazing. For $4.25 you can get two perfectly cooked Sicilian slices with the best ingredients. Tomato & basil and spinach slices especially recommended. Also has good subs and whole pizzas for kinda cheap. Extremely crowded during rush times, so order quickly! Accepts MC, V. (2004)

Pizza Ring
212 Western Ave, Cambridge
Sun-Thu 11am-1am, Fri-Sat 11am-2am
617-864-1800

Italian. The canonical cheap-but-reasonably-good pizza. They exist physically somewhere in the depths of Cambridgeport, but delivery is the standard interaction. If you catch them at the right time of day, they'll even deliver in as little as 20 minutes. A "double-decker" gets you two pizzas for about $10, and they deal well with adjusting toppings to half-pizza detail. The breadsticks are quite decent (but they won't deliver them unless you order pizza), but the Chicken Rings (processed chicken in the form of a ring, microwaved and served with Sweet and Sour Sauce) are to be avoided unless you're desperate. Accepts AE, D, MC, V. (2004)

Pizzeria Regina
11 Thatcher St., Boston (North End)
Green Line to Haymarket
Mon-Thu 11am-11:30pm, Fri-Sat 11am-midnight, Sun noon-11pm
617-227-0765

Italian. A top contender for best thin-crust pizza in Boston. It's been around for over 75 years, and you can tell that it hasn't changed a bit. It's still a hole in the wall little joint in the heart of Little Italy. They even make their own sausage that you can find only on their pizzas. You should attempt to go there early or on off nights, as there's usually a long line out the door during peak times. Of course, that's a the perfect excuse to grab a cannoli at a local bakery to make the wait less painful. If you just want the pizza but don't want to make the trip to the North End, then head to your nearest Polcari's (Tech Square), where they've joined forces and serve the pies. Check the Polcari's website for locations of spin-off and embedded Pizzeria Reginas. No delivery or reservations. Cash only. (2004)

Pizzeria Uno

www.pizzeriauno.com

Many locations including:

820 Somerville Ave, Porter Square
Galleria, Porter Square
Red Line to Porter Square
Mon-Sat 11:30am-12:30am, Sun noon-
12:30am
617-864-1916

645 Beacon St., Kenmore Square, Boston
Green Line to Kenmore Square
Mon-Sat 11am-12:30am, Sun noon-
12:30am
617-262-4911

22 JFK St., Harvard Square
Red Line or #1 bus to Harvard Square
Sun-Thu 11am-12:30am, Fri-Sat 11am-
1am
617-497-1530

Italian, American, Brewpub/Bar. A greasy deep dish pizza standby. Who cares if it's not "authentic Chicago pizza" as long as it's good; the crust is so buttery (doesn't look greasy, but your hands will be covered with it) and flaky that it's closer to pie crust than pizza. Like many things from Chicago, this stuff can kill you. The other things on the menu are okay; the potato-skin pizza appetizer (same crust) is fun and decadent. Allocate a while for your meal as the service is almost always slow. The Harvard Square location has karaoke every Monday night from 8:30pm to closing, all-you-can-eat every Tuesday night for $7.99 from 5pm to closing, and trivia night every Sunday night from 8:30pm to 10pm. Accepts AE, CB, D, DC, MC, V. (2004)

The Plough and Stars

www.ploughandstars.com

912 Mass. Ave., Cambridge (Central
Square)
Walk or Red Line to Central Square

617-441-3455

Irish, Brewpub/Bar. An Irish bar that's been in Central Square since 1969, the Plough and Stars also serves a most excellent lunch — the secret is that the kitchen is in the basement below the pub. The cuisine is a mixture of Caribbean, Southern, and European entrees — expect to see meatloaf offered on the same day as calamari and Jamaican chicken — all served in huge portions. Their Cuban sandwich is the best I've had outside the tropics (and I grew up there), and their black beans and rice are also done just-right. If you see garlic mashed potatoes or grits anywhere on the menu, get them. Lunch daily is 11:30am-2:30pm, with brunch Sundays from noon-3pm. The lunch menu changes daily, and usually has about 5 different options ($7-9) as well as soup & salad ($4). You might occasionally see soccer matches on the TV, too. (2003)

Polcari's

www.polcaris.com

300 Tech Square, Cambridge (Kendall
Square)
Mon-Thu 11am-10pm, Fri 11am-11pm,
Sat noon-11pm, Sun noon-10pm

617-577-0555

Italian. Good Italian food at reasonable prices. Includes a bar and a branch of the critically acclaimed Pizzeria Regina. (Of course, if you want the real thing, head to the original Pizzeria Regina in the North End). They deliver to MIT buildings if the order is large enough, but the fact that they're so close to campus and they accept the MIT card still qualifies them for one of the highest (quality)*(convenience) products around. Accepts MIT card, AE, D, MC, V. (2004)

Porter Exchange Food Court
Porter Square
Red Line to Porter Square

Japanese, Food Court. The Porter Exchange building, which also contains Giuseppe's and Bluefin, is home to a row of six Japanese eateries. They serve a wide variety of food at a wide variety of prices, though two good rules of thumb are "around $8-$12" and "cheaper than Blue Fin." For sushi, there is the Kotobukiya sushi bar, which is fresher, tastier and cheaper than getting your sushi from Star Market. Order by the vending machine; they'll make a hand roll of anything you ask for for less than $3. Sapporo Ramen will give you generous portions of quality ramen that will make you unable to enjoy the ramen you buy from Star Market (this is a good thing), and they offer smaller portions and vegetarian broth (though you have to ask). The others serve a combination of Korean BBQ, which is adequate, traditional meat/vegetable and rice/noodle dishes, and more specialized foods. CafÇ Mami is adorable and has a stack of Japanese manga for people to read while eating. The una don at Ittyo is excellent, as are the croquettes at Tampopo. Definitely worth a shot; between the six restaurants everyone will be able to find something they like. Casual eating environment, also a decent place to stop before work in Porter Square and pick up food to take with you — it's prepared fast. (2003)

The Pour House
909 Boylston St in Boston
Green Line to Hynes or #1 Bus to Hynes
Daily 8am-2am

617-236-1767

American, Brewpub/Bar. The Pour House is a good, cheap American restaurant and bar with a very laid-back atmosphere. Seat yourself, and try one of the tasty burgers for $4-$6 (and double-deck it for $1 more). The beer is all bottled, but it's a decent selection. Get there before 9pm if you're under 21 or you may be carded at the door. Lots of seating, but it's often pretty full. (2003)

Punjabi Dhaba
225 Hampshire St., Cambridge (Inman Square)
Walk, bike, or Red Line to Central Square then walk
Daily noon-midnight

617-547-8272

Indian. Owned by the same people who run the decade-old "India Pavillion," this is Cambridge's own quintessential hole-in-the-wall Indian joint. Forget about white tablecloths, dim lighting, and subtle music and get ready for screeching Bollywood movies, stainless steel cafeteria trays and quite possibly the best Indian food Boston has to offer. Huge helpings of fresh-made food keep the masses coming in at all hours. One of the few places that will actually make the food as spicy (or not) as you want. Any of the combination platters (~$8) will keep you full for at least 12 hours. If you catch the proprietor on a good day, he'll keep you laughing until you vomit. Cash only. (2004)

Pu Pu Hot Pot
www.pupuhotpot.com
907 Main St., Cambridge (Central Square)
Walking distance
Sun-Thu 11:30am-11pm, Fri-Sat 11:30am-11:30pm

617-491-6616

Chinese. Pu Pu completes the triumvirate of MIT's favorite Chinese restaurants, although it isn't as preferred as Mary Chung or Royal East. On the other hand, Pu Pu has more vegetarian options, doesn't use MSG (monosodium glutamate), and they offer free delivery with a $10 minimum order (+$1 if outside Cambridge). Offerings include good scallion pancakes, excellent Tofu with Spicy Ginger, good beef dishes, and well-done Chow Foon. Lunch runs $6-8 and dinner $9-12, although more often than not, you can order the "luncheon & weeknight special" at any time of day... just pretend you know what you are doing. The menu can be found on their website. Accepts MC, V. (2004)

Quan's Kitchen

www.quanskitchen-boston.com

1026 Commonwealth Ave, Boston
Sun-Wed 11am-2am, Thu-Sat 11am-2:30am

617-232-7617 or 617-232-0585

Chinese. "Sketchy" is the first word that comes to many peoples' minds, but it's a hell of a lot better than their only competition in post-midnight Chinese delivery (Nan Ling). They won several awards ten years ago, but recently seem to have been relegated to simply the only good late-night option. The Beef Chow Foon (a.k.a. "Beef Worms") is surprisingly good. The website is somewhat out-of-date. Small fee (~$1) for delivery. Accepts MC, V. (2004)

Rangzen

24 Pearl Street, (Central Square) Cambridge
Walking distance
Mon-Sat 11:45am-3pm and 5:30pm-10pm

617-354-8881

Tibetan. The Tibetan word for independence, Rangzen offers hearty Tibetan food. Specialties include light fried appetizers, and rich entrees featuring potatoes, chick peas, mushrooms, and a variety of meats. Several vegetarian options are available. Good food and a relaxing ambiance make this a great place for a quiet date. Be sure to check out the $7.55 lunchtime buffet. Accepts AE, D, DC, MC, V. (2004)

Rebecca's Café

www.rebeccascafe.com

Multiple locations including:

290 Main St., Cambridge (Kendall Square)
Walking distance
Mon-Fri 7am-4pm

617-494-6688

American, Bakery, Coffeehouse. This is a somewhat expensive, somewhat yuppie, but very good bakery/café. It's best known for its excellent corporate catering, which, if you're lucky, you may find leftovers of scattered about the Institute hallways. Good for lunch; particularly good for dessert. Make sure to get the 15% student discount. Accepts AE, MC, V. (2004)

Redbones

www.redbonesbbq.com

55 Chester St., Somerville (Davis Square)
Red Line to Davis Square
Mon-Thu 11:30am-10:30pm, Fri-Sat 11:30am-11:30pm, Sun noon-10:30pm
Late night menu every night until 12:30am.

617-628-2200

Meat, American. Pretty good barbecue, crowded room, sometimes rude staff. For rib selection (more varieties than most Northerners knew existed!), go here; for sheer volume, the all-you-can-eat lunch special (one kind of ribs, chicken, steak and sausage plus sides) can't be beaten. The best thing on the menu though is the fried catfish sandwich. Some things, like the buffalo shrimp appetizer, are a rip-off. Great selection of beers on tap. Not for vegetarians. Bike delivery to the general Davis Square area. (2003)

Ristorante Marino

www.marinoristorante.com

2465 Mass. Ave., Cambridge
Drive, or walk for a while from Porter Square
Mon-Thu 11:30am-10pm, Fri 11:30am-10:30pm, Sat noon-10:30pm, Sun noon-9pm

617-868-5454

Italian. Excellent Italian food, originating in the Abruzzo region. While the food is a bit more expensive than most restaurants around, it is more than worth the money. Most of the food is grown by the owners and is organic. The lunch buffet is incredible, and includes brilliantly wonderful Çclairs. All of the food is very, very good. Try any of the raviolis, and save room for dessert. You will be happy and full when you leave. Stop by for takeout, too; they have a market with some of their best offerings available by the pound. (2003)

Roka

1001 Mass. Ave., Cambridge
Red Line to Harvard Square
Mon-Fri 11:30am-2:30pm & 5:30pm-
10pm, Sat 11:30am-2:30pm & 5:30pm-
11pm, Sun 5:30pm-10pm

617-661-0344

Japanese. Roka is halfway between Central and Harvard Squares on Mass. Ave. The decor is a little strange, with shiny black and red neon lights. The dinner menu is fairly standard Japanese, as are the prices — expect sushi to cost about $20. Rumor has it the box lunches (bento) are not bad. Unfortunately, the overall quality of the food is fairly low and you're better off trying out somewhere else if you're looking for good Japanese cuisine. Accepts AE, CB, DC, MC, V. (2004)

Rosie's Bakery and Dessert Shop

www.rosiesbakery.com

243 Hampshire St., Cambridge (Inman Square)
Mon-Thu 7:30am-7pm, Fri 7:30am-
7:30pm, Sat 8am-7:30pm, Sun 8:30am-
6pm

617-491-9488

Bakery, Dessert. Arguably the best bakery goods in the Boston area, with prices that reflect it. Everything is good, but the carrot cake, cream cheese brownies, and velvet underground cake are especially recommended. They also serve Haagen-Dazs ice cream and beverages. Online shopping available. The goodies are worth the walk to Inman square. (2003)

Rotisserie House

736 Mass. Ave., Cambridge (Central Square)
Walk, Red Line to Central Square, or #1 bus
Mon-Sat 11am-10pm

617-661-0607

Meat, American. Located between Cantab Lounge and 7-11, this small joint offers cheap, homemade roast chicken, sandwiches and side dishes, all of which put Boston Chicken to shame. You can eat there several times a week and have a different meal costing around $5 each time, with a different special everyday. The guys who run it are super nice, and the food is excellent for the money. Favorites include take-out chicken sandwiches, the leg and thigh meal with a side of broccoli and a side of carrots), chicken sandwiches, gyros, and much more. Usually a bit crowded. The most expensive meal is $34 for a two-family meal deal, but you should expect more like $4-8 for a main course. Cash only. (2004)

Royal East

782-792 Main St., Cambridge
Walking distance
Sun-Thu 11:30am-10pm, Fri-Sat 11:30am-11pm

617-661-1660

Chinese. Best place to bring a big group for standard Chinese. Standbys like ravs (pan-fried Peking Ravioli) and Gau (General Gau's Chicken) are well done, as are the scallion pancakes and chicken velvet and corn soup. The menu is much bigger than what's printed — ask for what you want and chances are they'll make it. Their seafood is fresh — if you order the Alaskan King Crab, they will pull it out of the tank and bring it over to you for inspection before cooking it up. Alaskan King Crabs are very large, spiky, and have lots of legs. Watching one whisk by you as you down some tea can be startling. They often have vegetarian specials, involving rarely-found veggies in varied, and delicious, sauces. Royal's handles large groups exceptionally well, and if your group is more than about 25 people, they'll give you the back room. About $7 for lunch and $10 for dinner. Rumored not to deliver but actually they do, for free if you order enough stuff (~$100). Accepts AE, DC, MC, V. (2003)

Royal India

313 Mass. Ave., Cambridge
Walking distance
Tue-Thu 11am-11pm, Fri-Sat 11am-11:30pm, Sun 11am-11pm

617-491-8333

Indian. Located almost directly across from Random Hall, Royal India provides fine northern Indian (Bengali) cuisine at reasonable prices. The lunch buffet, at $5.95, is quite good; it varies daily (though in a decently steady pattern) and usually features a solid Aloo Ghobi, exquisite lentils, and a assortment of others, Goat Curry being an unexpected (and very tasty) surprise. The Chicken Korma is highly recommended, as are the soups. In the evenings, Royal India serves unique Bengali specials. It's inexpensive, quick, and good. (2003)

Rudy's Café

www.rudyscafe.com

248 Holland St., Somerville
Mon-Wed 5:00pm-midnight, Thu-Sat 11:30am-1:00am, Sun 11:30am-midnight

888-470-4024

Mexican, Brewpub/Bar. Rudy's is something of a Mexican restaurant, but, really, it's a tequila bar, without that bar vibe. The food is good anyway, with the usual array of Tex-Mex food. Try the black bean nachos, and then try a tequila flight. If you're spice sensitive just ask them to leave off everything red and they'll usually get it right. Good for medium-size groups, but 25 people would be a bit of a strain. (2003)

Sabur

www.saburrestaurant.com

212 Holland St., Somerville
Red Line to Davis then walk up Holland 5-10min
Mon-Fri 5pm-1am, Sat-Sun 11am-1am

617-776-7890

Mediterranean. A Bosnian-owned restaurant offering "exotic Mediterranean cuisine", including Bosnian-influenced cooking as well as a range of other Mediterranean influences, all presented beautifully. The open-hearth roast, veal medallions, seared tuna, and grilled Balkan sausages are delicious. Nice place for a special occasion, well-decorated and good atmosphere. Try the Turkish coffee, and all of the desserts. Brunch is also nice. (2003)

Sake

670 Broadway, Saugus 01906 (Route 1 North)
Across from Hilltop Steak House
Mon-Thu 11:30am-11pm, Fri-Sat 11:30am-midnight, Sun noon-10pm

781-233-3858

Japanese. Despite all outward appearances of being exactly the kind of sushi joint you would never want to step into, Sake is an incredible find, serving up some of the most authentic Japanese food around. Between his previous career in Japan and his current job at Sake, the head chef has decades of sushi preparation experience. The menu also features standard dishes, such as tempura, udon and soba. Private rooms are available for small dinner parties. To get there, take Route 1 North from Boston and look for the large, cactus-shaped Hilltop Steak House sign on your left. Sake will be directly across the highway on your right. Accepts AE, DC, D, MC, V. (2004)

S&S Deli and Restaurant

www.sandsrestaurant.com

1334 Cambridge St., Cambridge (Inman Square)
Walk, bike, or drive
Mon-Wed 7am-11pm, Thu-Sat 7am-midnight, Sun 8am-midnight

617-354-0620

American. S&S offers American and (non-kosher) Jewish deli food at moderate prices ($8-13). They serve their entire menu all day, making it possibly the only place in Cambridge to get French toast at 10pm. Weekend brunch has an expanded menu that includes a good Eggs Benedict. Good atmosphere but often crowded, and service can be slow. Great desserts. Catering and delivery available. Accepts AE, CB, D, DC, MC, V. (2004)

Sepal

17 Nichols Ave., Watertown
Drive or #70 bus from Central, near
Arsenal Mall off Arsenal St.
Mon-Sat 11am-9pm, (June-September
only Sun 1pm-8pm)

617-924-5753

Middle Eastern. It's a bit hard to get to Sepal, but if you want good Palestinian food and great service, this is the place. Their falafel is wonderful, and their dinner combinations offer good soup, salad, bread, and meat. At least half of their menu dishes are vegan, also, making this a great restaurant for the whole hippie family. They also make great sandwiches, but MIT students are less likely to want to go out to Watertown for lunch. The best part is you can get a good meal for under $20. Despite what the internet might tell you, this is not an all-vegan restaurant; a few years ago, the owner branched out into the meatier reaches of the culinary universe. (2003)

Shabuso

www.kayausa.com

1366 Beacon St. Brookline
Green Line C to Coolidge Corner
Daily 11:30am-3pm, 5pm-11pm

617-738-2244

Korean, Japanese, Meat. This is one of the three Kaya restaurants, just with a different name. In addition to Korean barbecue, this location serves shabu shabu. See the Kaya entry for details. (2004)

Shabu Zen

www.shabuzen.com

16 Tyler St., Boston
Orange Line to Chinatown or Red Line
to Downtown Crossing
Sun-Wed 11:30am-11pm, Thu-Sat
11:30am-midnight

617-292-8828

Japanese, Meat. One of the few shabu-shabu restaurants in the Boston metro area. That in and of itself should be enough to get your two little legs running there. Don't get the appetizers; they're pricey and substandard. Meat combo with beef and pork, a side of sirloin (c5), enoki mushrooms, tofu skin, and a lychee drink is the recommended meal. (2003)

Shalimar Indian Grocery Store

www.kashmirspices.com

571 Mass. Ave., Cambridge (Central
Square)
Walking distance
Mon-Sat 10am-9pm, Sun 11am-8pm

617-868-8311

Indian. Not the restaurant by the same name. There's a counter in back that sells Indian fast food of medium to poor quality for under $6. Good for a quick dinner. Accepts AE, D, MC, V. (2004)

Shalimar of India Restaurant

www.shalimar-of-india.com

546 Mass. Ave., Central Square
Walking distance
Mon-Fri 11:30am-3pm & 5pm-11pm, Sat-
Sun noon-11pm

617-547-9280

Indian. Vies with Gandhi Restaurant for title to the best Indian restaurant in Central Square. Offers a great lunch buffet for around $7. Good range of vegetarian options. Try the Mango Lassi to get an overview of the restaurant's strengths, then move on to the Tandoori and Chicken Do Piazza. The staff could be friendlier. Accepts AE, MC, V. (2004)

Sicilia's Pizzeria

Member of: www.campusfood.com
840 Commonwealth Ave, Boston
Green Line B to BU West (walk 2 blocks
toward Boston)
Daily 11am-3am

617-566-0021

Italian. Probably the best stuffed pizza around; an inch thick, lots of cheese and sauce, good flaky crust that's not dripping with butter like Uno's deep dish. Try the Sicilia's Original, stuffed spinach and mushroom, or the stuffed garlic pizza. $1 delivery charge, but take the estimate of 30-40 minutes with a grain of salt. Best of all, they're open late. Accepts AE, D, MC, V. (2004)

Someday Café
51 Davis Square
Red Line to Davis Square
Mon-Thu 7am-11pm, Fri 7am-midnight,
Sat 8am-midnight, Sun 8:00am-11:00pm

617-623-3323

Coffeehouse. Someday provides good coffee, tea, and hot chocolate with eclectic seating, and an eclectic crowd. Their pastries are overpriced and not very good, but they have Tosci's ice cream, nifty furniture, and don't mind people hanging out indefinitely. There are always lots of newspapers lying around, and it is air conditioned on hot days Excellent for people-watching. Recently bought by Tosci's owner. (2003)

South Street Diner
178 Kneeland St., Boston
Red Line to South Station
Open 24/7

617-350-0028

American. Now the last surviving 24-hour diner in inner Boston, the South Street diner is a classic of the genre but its newfound late-night isolation may make it hard to get a table. Energetic, tattooed, surly waitresses, an eclectic jukebox (Johnny Cash to the Sex Pistols), and prices not jacked up to gouge the post-club crowds are the highlights of this establishment. Tends to be especially crowded after the bars close on Friday and Saturday nights. Try the milkshakes. (2003)

Spice
24 Holyoke St., Cambridge (Harvard Square)
Red Line to Harvard Square
Mon-Thu 11:30am-10pm, Fri-Sat 11:30am-10:30pm, Sun noon-10pm

617-868-9560

Thai. Spice is small and loud. Depending on your tastes, you may find it cozy or a bit cramped — either way, the cash register will get on your nerves for the first ten minutes. The food is very good, though; their Pad Thai is quite good and they offer a deep-fried soft shell crab that is simply excellent, though spicy. Their Thai Iced Tea is also popular. $15-$25 per meal on average, though the Pad Thai is cheaper and still very tasty. (2003)

Spinnaker Italia
575 Memorial Drive, Cambridge
Walking distance
Mon-Thu 6pm-9:30pm, Fri-Sat 6pm-10pm

617-876-7746

Italian. Standard American Italian. Good view on revolving platform, but you pay for it. The food is okay; portions are small. Crowded for Sunday Brunch. Located in the Hyatt Regency Hotel next to Tang. Accepts AE, CB, DC, MC, V. (2003)

Stefani Pizzeria
783 Main St., Cambridge
Walking distance
Mon-Sat 11am-10pm, Sun noon-10pm

617-491-7823

Italian. The top choice when you want greasy pizza done right. About $5 for a small pizza, which feeds one person nicely. The subs are better, especially on Phoenician bread. Small place. Free delivery with minimum $7 order. Accepts AE, CB, D, DC, MC, V. (2004)

Steve's Greek Cuisine
316 Newbury Street, Boston
Green Line to Hynes Convention Center

617-267-1817

Greek. Reasonably authentic Greek cuisine, with the best Yiros (what Americans call a "Gyro") around. Not as pricey as you might expect for Newbury Street, but appetizers are on the expensive side — the sizzling marinated octopus is worth trying, however. (2003)

Sunny's Diner
7 Lansdowne Street
Walking distance
Mon-Sat 6am-3pm, Sun 8am-2pm

617-491-9550

American. A small diner, and one of the best breakfast places around. For $5 you can get a good amount of food. Sunny's breakfast and lunch menus are simple, but they cover all the important things. You can make a light breakfast out of an egg-and-cheese sandwich, or you can go all out with various combos involving generous portions of pancakes, french toast, breakfast meats, home fries, and eggs. Rather sketchy looking from the outside, the place is usually filled with locals. Sunny's Diner is a favorite breakfast spot for construction workers and hungry MIT students after tooling all night. It's one of the first breakfast places to open. On Tuesdays only you can ask for delicious homemade falafel and hummus, which the Egyptian short-order cook secretly prepares and keeps in the back room. Accepts MC, V. (2004)

Sunset Grill & Tap
www.allstonsfinest.com

130 Brighton Ave, Allston
Green Line B To Harvard Ave.
Daily 11:30am-1am

617-254-1331

American, Brewpub/Bar. The food here is OK (make sure to get the beer battered onion rings to prepare your stomach for the onslaught), but the real reason to go here is the impressive array of beers — they boast 380 microbrews, with 112 beers on tap, though inevitably at least one of the ones you want will be unavailable, making every selection an agonizing choice. Be sure to check out the beer-based desserts. If you're lucky, perhaps you can convince them to make a Guinness float. Expect crowds and a long wait for a table. Accepts AE, D, MC, V. (2004)

Sushi Corner
18C Essex St, Melrose
20 minute drive along the Fellsway or train to Melrose
Sun-Thu 11:30am-2:30pm & 4:30pm-9:45pm, Fri-Sat 11:30am-2:30pm & 4:30pm-10:30pm

781-662-1278

Japanese. Fantastic sushi at amazing prices. They have a wide selection of sashimi, nigiri, and maki rolls with top-quality fish. There are many vegetarian options as well. They also have plenty of delicious Japanese items for the non-fish eaters, including noodle bowls and tempura. The place is pretty small and the chef is friendly, usually offering suggestions on the freshest fish of the day. The prices are quite reasonable (slighly lower than Bluefin/Ginza/Fugakyu but the same quality of sushi). However, the thing to go for is definetely the sushi buffet. For $26, you get all-you-can-eat (while in the restaurant) of whatever nigiri or maki your heart desires. The one downside is that the buffet is only offered Sunday-Thursday. But if you have a car and some money, this is definitely a place to check out. Hint — they're not quite on Essex St. Check around the corner in the Shaw's parking lot to find it. Accepts MC, V. (2004)

Sweet Chili
www.sweetchili.com

1172-1178 Cambridge St., Cambridge (Inman Square)
Walk or bike
Sun-Thu 11:30am-10pm, Fri-Sat 11:30am-11pm

617-864-4500

Thai, Japanese, Korean. Excellent pan-Asian food, including one of Boston's best sushi bars. Very friendly staff and nice atmosphere. Take-out, delivery, and catering available. Entrees $8-15. Switches from lunch to dinner at 3pm. (2003)

Sweet 'n' Nasty
www.sweet-n-nasty.com

90A Mass. Ave., Boston
Walking distance, just over the Harvard Bridge
Mon-Fri 10am-7pm, Sat 11am-6pm, Sun noon-5pm

617-266-7171

Dessert. Ever wanted chocolate genitalia? Erotic cakes? A store that sells homemade sweets AND sex toys? Dude! (2003)

Taam China

423 Harvard St., Brookline
Green Line B to Harvard Ave. or Green
Line C to Coolidge Corner
Sat-Thu 11am-10pm, Fri 11am-3pm

617-264-7274

Chinese, Kosher. Serving reasonably priced, high quality kosher Chinese food under the supervision of Rabbi Aaron Hamaoui, Taam China provides a nice Saturday night dinner. The Pu-Pu meat platter served with a large bowl of fire excites the pyromaniacally inclined, while there are plenty of tofu and vegetable dishes for vegetarians. Accepts AE, MC, V. (2004)

Tacos Lupita

13 Elm Street, Somerville (Porter Square)
Red Line to Porter Square
Daily 11am-11pm

617-666-0677

Mexican. If you're considering going to Anna's in Porter, do yourself a favor and walk across the shopping center, take a right down Elm Street. A few blocks down you'll find the best Mexican/Salvadorean food around. The food makes up for the hole-in-the-wall atmosphere. It's authentic, fresh and cheap. Tacos, gorditas, huaraches, mulitas, soups, plates, and of course mind-blowing burritos. The pork and rice are especially good, and there's an assortment of sodas from Mexico including apple! If you're adventurous, try the lengua or mondongo. Burritos for $2.75, most under $5, plates for $7-8. Cash only. (2004)

Taiwan Café

34 Oxford St., Boston (Chinatown)
Red Line to Downtown Crossing or
Orange Line to Chinatown
Daily 11am-1am

617-426-8181

Chinese. Consistently ranks among the favorite Chinese restaurants of the Chinese student population. The menu sports excellent steamed dumplings and basil eggplant, as well as a healthy sprinkling of jellyfish, tongue, intestine, and stomach dishes. Service is fast without being pushy and the wait staff can offer suggestions. A good place to go with a large group of people. Be warned, the phone is often answered in Chinese. Cash only. (2004)

Tanjore

www.tanjoreharvardsq.com

18 Eliot St., Cambridge (Harvard
Square)
Red Line or #1 bus to Harvard Square
Daily 11:30am-3pm & 5pm-11pm

617-868-1900

Indian. Offers a wide variety of food from the cuisines of the Indian subcontinent. Selections include Dosas and Utappams (stuffed crêpes and pancakes from the south), snack food and seafood from Bombay and Goa, and Mughlai style vegetable and meat dishes from Northern India. As usual, service is buffet-style during lunch-time hours. Delivery available for large (read $100+) orders. Accepts AE, D, MC, V. (2004)

Taqueria La Mexicana

www.lataqueria.com

247 Washington St., Somerville, (Union
Square)
About one mile up Prospect, from
Inman Square
Daily 11am-10pm

617-776-5232

Mexican. If you can find it and avoid the horrid Tortas, it's the best taqueria you'll find in Massachusetts. The flautas and enchiladas potosinas are especially good and the tamales are superb. Probably the only taqueria around MIT to serve homemade tortilla chips. A wide range of ingredients and food for a taqueria, especially if you can read the small Spanish menu posted near the cash register. A full meal costs $6-10. Accepts AE, MC, V. (2004)

Thailand Café

Member of: www.campusfood.com

302 Mass. Ave., Cambridge
Down Mass. Ave., next to Random Hall
Sun-Thu 11am-10pm, Fri-Sat 11:30am-
11pm

617-492-2494

Thai. Yet another Thai restaurant run by Chinese people. The combination somehow produces VERY fast, reliable service and Thai food that is slightly more greasy and less flavorful than one would hope. Cheap and convenient, Thailand Café has been a staple of the MIT diet for quite some time. The Crazy Noodles are excellent and the Fisherman's Fury is pretty good. Luncheon specials (comes with a cup of hot spicy tofu soup) are around $6, dinner is more expensive. Delivers within 2 miles (includes MIT) with a $10 minimum. Orders for delivery start at 5pm and stop 15 minutes before closing. Accepts AE, MC, V. (2004)

Tommy's House of Pizza
Member of: www.campusfood.com
49 Mount Auburn St., Harvard Square
Red Line or #1 bus to Harvard Square
Mon-Fri 11am-2am, Sat noon-2am, Sun 11am-2am

617-497-4849

Italian. "Tommy's happens to be God and Jesus to the nightshifted (in particular, nightshifted stoners) because it delivers high-grade pizza with sesame crusts until 3am." Unfortunately the hours seem to have changed but it's still decent pizza with flavored crusts (sesame, poppy, garlic, onion, or salt). Only the sesame is available by the slice. Reasonably inexpensive, too. Order for delivery before 1:30am, with $8 minimum. Accepts AE, D, MC, V. (2004)

Top of the Hub
www.topofthehub.net

800 Boylston Street, Prudential Tower-52nd Floor, Boston
Green Line E to Prudential or Green Line B/C/D to Hynes
Mon-Thu 11:30am-2:30pm & 5:30pm-10pm, Fri 11:30am-2:30pm & 5:30pm-11pm, Sat 11:30am-2:30pm & 5pm-11pm, Sun noon-2pm & 5pm-10pm

617-536-1775

American. One of the best views you'll ever find, but you pay for it. Average American food, though great coffee and desserts. Live jazz featured nightly. Special brunch on Sundays. Accepts AE, D, DC, MC, V. (2004)

Toscanini's Ice Cream
www.tosci.com

899 Main St., Cambridge (Central Square)
Walking distance
Sun-Thu 11:30am-11pm, Fri-Sat 11:30am-midnight

617-491-5877

Dessert, Coffeehouse. Tosci's (pronounced "toss-keys") is the ice cream store that cares. The best ice cream around Boston is close to MIT and comes in all sorts of innovative flavors. Try a weird one, it'll taste exactly like whatever it's named — Guinness ice cream, Champagne Sorbet. Cocoa Pudding is the best chocolate; Sweet Cream is what ice cream is before you add flavoring. If there's a flavor of ice cream you've been itching to try, suggest it, and chances are, they'll make it up, at least once. The basics and extra toppings are good too, particularly the hot fudge. The coffee is excellent, often grown organically, and their loose tea selection is impressive. Tosci's is also often available at LSC movies and occasionally in local grocery stores (try Bread & Circus). Recently, Gus, The Man, bought Someday Café in Davis Square, which now also sells Tosci's. (2003)

Trident Café
388 Newbury St.
Green Line or #1 bus to Hynes Convention Center
Daily 9am-midnight

617-267-8688

Coffeehouse, Vegetarian. Coffee shop but also serves plenty of food. Feels like Berkeley in Boston. Really yummy food, with many veggie options, but way expensive. Being on Newbury St., it has a rather yuppie atmosphere, and well, the prices are going to bring the yuppie people in. The upside is that it's open relatively late, but other than that, it's really just not worth the money to go there often. It is attached to a bookstore and provides alterna-books for reading while you eat. (2003)

Tu Y Yo

www.tuyyomexicanfonda.com

858 Broadway, Somerville (Davis Square)
Red Line to Davis Square
Mon-Thu 5pm-10pm, Fri-Sat 4pm-11pm, Sun 4pm-9pm

617-623-4511

Mexican. The sign on the door clearly states "NO we do not have 'burritos'." This is authentic Mexican food, using family recipes from 75-100 years ago. Delicious meat and fish for about $10 an entree, served with the best beans and rice you've probably ever had. If you're over 21, you'll want to try the sangria as well. Tu Y Yo is the kind of authentic Mexican food you've probably never tried — home cooked dishes from several generations of Mexican family recipes. A few appetizers are based on flour or corn tortillas, and entrees are served with a side of rice and some black beans, but that's about where the familiar Mexican parallels end. A few of our favorites are Pulpo Pichirillo (octopus with olives and onions), Pollo Yunkaax (chicken stuffed with cuitlacoche in a spinach sauce), and Bisteces en Salsa Borracha (beef and cactus leaves). For dessert, the flan is fabulous. (2003)

Urban Gourmet

688 Broadway, Somerville (Ball Square)
Red Line to Davis Square, then walk
Mon-Fri 3pm-midnight, Sat-Sun noon-1am

617-628-2322

American. True to its name, this place serves staples of the American city (sandwiches, pizza, salads) with exotic ingredients and true culinary flair. The food here is so good that it's surprising it doesn't cost more — most prices are $6-$12 for a filling meal. The specialty hot sandwiches are fantastic, particularly the Pork Adobo, and the pizza is excellent: slow-cooked with a satisfyingly crunchy crust even in the middle (no sag of the slice here). The salads are worth it — generous in size and ingredients, and come with the dressing properly tossed-in instead of just dumped on top. Also has commendable pasta and a range of other entrees, as well as daily specials. Delivery is available. Accepts AE, V, MC. (2003)

Veggie Planet

www.veggieplanet.net

47 Palmer St., Cambridge (Harvard Square)
Red Line or #1 bus to Harvard Square
MOn-Sat 11:30am-10:30pm, Sun 11am-10:30pm

617-661-1513

Vegetarian. Here you'll find good vegetarian and vegan food served in a lively, if somewhat small setting. Actually located in Club Passim, so you stand a chance of catching a live band while you enjoy your meal. Everything is fresh and cooked to order. Cash only. (2004)

Victoria's Diner

1024 Mass. Ave., Boston (Back Bay)
Red Line to Andrews Station
Daily 6am-10pm
617-442-5965

American. Standard diner fare, featuring breakfast all day, lunch and dinner specials, free parking, and a back room that can seat loads of people. Owned by the same person as Mike's City Diner in the South End. Accepts AE, MC, V. (2004)

Village Smokehouse

www.villagesmokehouse.com

1 Harvard Street, Brookline
Sun-Wed 4-10pm, Thu 11:30am-10pm, Fri 11:30am-11pm, Sat noon-11pm
617-566-3782 (617-LONESTA...
Bostonian for 'Lonestar')

Meat, American, Brewpub/Bar. This place serves "Texas Style" BBQ — which means meat, beans and cornbread, and lots of it. The spicy Texas sausage is very good and the pork babies' back ribs are delicious, perhaps the best in town. Has a smaller and cheaper lunch menu for those on a budget. Sometimes the service can be a little slow. Also has a full bar that stays open later than the restaurant. (2004)

Vinny Testa's
www.vinnyhtestas.com

867 Boylston St., Back Bay, Boston, MA 02115
Mon-Wed 11:30am-11pm, Thu-Sat 11:30am-midnight, Sun noon-10pm
617-262-6699

1700 Beacon Street, Brookline, MA 02146
Mon-Thu 11:30am-10:30pm, Fri-Sat 11:30am-11:30pm, Sun noon-10pm
617-277-3400

Italian. Good Italian food, with big entrees intended to be served family-style. Used to be the canonical place for very large groups (20 or more), but portion sizes have dropped as prices rose; Maggiano's is a much better choice for your birthday dinner. Expect to wait 20-60 minutes at popular times unless you make a reservation. (2004)

Wendy's
598 Mass Ave, Cambridge (Central Square)
Walking Distance

Fast Food. Standard quintuple-bypass fare. What's with those square burgers anyway? At least that way you know they weren't shat by some beast as it died. No parking available. Often very long lines during lunch, probably due to it being perceived as somehow less ghetto than the other Central Square fast food joints. It must be the Frosty, or the Baked Potato of Doom. Anyway, their competition caused the other fast food joints in Central to open dollar menus and the lines move pretty quick. (2003)

Wing-It
www.wing-it.com

1153 Commonwealth Ave, Allston
Green Line B to Fordham Rd. (half block back toward Boston)
Mon-Fri 4pm-midnight, Sat noon-2am, Sun noon-midnight

617-783-BIRD (617-783-2473)

American, Meat. Take-out chicken wings, with over 20 flavors including Buffalo, Jamaican Jerk, Sweet & Sour, Lemon Pepper, pterodactyl and Suicide (very hot). An MIT tradition, try the boneless for tons of meat and less mess. Delivers to campus, but slowly. Expect a 45 minute wait or more. Delivery is free with $10 minimum. Orders stop 15 minutes before closing. Accepts AE, MC, V. (2004)

Wing Works
201 Elm St, Davis Sq
Mon-Thu 4pm-11pm, Fri-Sat 11am-midnight, Sun noon-10pm

617-666-9000

American, Meat. The other wings place, for when you're trapped outside the Wing-It delivery range and desperately need some wingz. Anyway, it's wingz. They've won awards, they're pretty cheap, and hey, they'll deliver you wingz. Have some. (2003)

The Wrap
www.thewrap.com

137 Massachusetts Ave. (Berklee)
Daily 10am-11pm, Delivers Mon-Sat noon-10pm, Sun noon-8pm
617-369-9087

247 Newbury Street
Daily 10am-11pm, Delivers Mon-Sat noon-10pm, Sun noon-8pm
617-262-2200

71 Mt. Auburn Street (Harvard Square)
Daily 10am-11pm, Delivers Mon-Sat noon-10pm, Sun noon-8pm
617-354-5838

American. Homogenized ethnic food or healthy alternative to fast food? You decide. The Wrap offers wraps (who would have guessed), as well as burritos, salads, soups, and smoothies. The smoothies are tasty. The food is fairly quick and there's a small seating area. Not upscale, but a step up from fast food. Free wireless access in the Newbury St. store. $2 charge for delivery. MIT is on the edge of their delivery zone, so ask nicely when requesting delivery. (2003)

SIPB

IN A NUTSHELL

A Freshman's Quick Reference

W20-557   *Student Information Processing Board*

SIPB (pronounced ``Sip-bee") is the Student Information Processing Board, the volunteer student group concerned with computing at MIT. We are available for telephone (x3-7788), email (sipb@mit.edu) or in-person (W20-557) consulting at almost any time of day or night; have one-of-a-kind meetings every Monday evening at 7:30 pm; write documentation of all sorts; hack; run a wide variety of servers (including AFS servers; we also created www.mit.edu); and generally have a good time. We also act as an advocate for student computer users and student computer access on campus. Come see us!

Media

Radio

Boston is one of the largest radio markets in the country. The programming offered by the commercial stations is wider than what you'll find in most cities and features new music, rock, Top 40, and Muzak. Boston also has a large number of public, network, and college stations, generally commercial-free, featuring music not played by the majority of commercial stations (jazz, classical, folk, metal, etc.). WGBH is the local public outlet. Eight college stations are listed here, mostly at the low end of the FM dial. WMBR (MIT), WHRB (Harvard), WBUR (BU) and WERS (Emerson) are the most easily received on campus.

The MIT radio station, **WMBR** (50-030, x3-8810, `wmbr.org`) broadcasts on 88.1 FM to the entire Cambridge and greater Boston area. Monthly schedules are sent out free upon request. If you're interested in becoming a member and volunteering at the station, email `recruitment@wmbr.org` or stop by the station during Recruitment Office Hours: Mondays 6-8pm in September. The station also sets aside one hour a week for people who have no radio experience, or DJs who want to try out experimental shows. Details can be found on `http://wmbr.org/shows/vr.html`

If Boston's stations don't satisfy you, or if you are homesick, you can listen to numerous out-of-town AM stations at night. Continuous news can be heard on WCBS (880 kHz) and WINS (1010 kHz) from New York or WBBM (780 kHz) and WLS (890 kHz) from Chicago. Numerous other clear channels around the US and Canada can be heard at night; most of the powerful stations are between 640 and 900 kHz, 990 and 1220 kHz, and 1500 and 1580 kHz. Reception, however, is irregular at best. Incidentally, WBZ-AM (1030 kHz, Boston) can be heard in 38 states at night.

AM Stations

The following table lists some Boston AM stations, their call letters, frequencies, and a brief description of each.

(Note: this list is accurate as of August 2004, but may not be complete. There may be more radio stations on your dial than are listed here. `www.radio-locator.com` and `www.bostonradio.org` were used, in part, to compile this list.)

WEZE	590	(Boston) Religious.
WRKO	680	(Boston) "The Talk Station" (*i.e.* no music).
WJIB	740	(Cambridge) Instrumental Pop and light Oldies.
WEEI	850	(ESPN/Boston) "The Sports Station", English Red Sox broadcasts.
WROL	950	(Boston) Religious, ethnic, Spanish Red Sox broadcasts.
WBZ	1030	(Boston) Daytime: News. Night: Talk. Weekends: Sports Talk. Bruins broadcasts.
WBIX	1060	(Natick) Business and news.
WILD	1090	(Boston) Urban, Rhythmic.

WITT	1150	(Boston) News, Talk.
WMKI	1260	(Boston) "Radio Disney."
WXKS	1430	(Everett) Nostalgia, Standards.
WNTN	1550	(Newton) Many different types of ethnic programming and English-language variety.
WUNR	1600	(Brookline) Various ethnic.

FM Stations

WBUR (90.9) interferes with the reception in the BU area and on the west side of campus; WBCN (104.1) has its transmitter on top of the Prudential Tower and can be found across the dial at times. Station logos are included in the description when available.

WMBR	88.1	(20hr) MIT/Cambridge. WMBR is Walker Memorial Basement Radio, staffed by students, alums, staff and non-MIT people. Their transmitter is atop Eastgate. Music runs the gamut from raw and primitive black metal to techno to rock to world music. Program guides are available at the station, at wmbr.org, or by calling x3-8810. WMBR also streams its audio on the web at wmbr.org so you can listen from your computer. E-mail recruitment@wmbr.org to join.
WERS	88.9	Emerson College Radio. Classical, rock, folk, hip-hop, jazz, nu-metal, etc.
WGBH	89.7	National Public Radio/Boston. Classical on mornings and weekends, jazz all night. Live music (BSO and New England Conservatory concerts) and good tapes (BBC, CBC), organ recitals. Program guide and streaming available at www.wgbh.org.
WZBC	90.3	Boston College/Newton. Mostly rock from 7am to 4pm on weekdays. Otherwise, show formats run the gamut, depending on the DJ. Current program schedule and live webcast available at wzbc.org.
WBUR	90.9	National Public Radio News/Talk. Talk, news, news analysis, public affairs, BBC World Service, etc.
WMFO	91.5	Tufts U/Medford. A wide variety of programming that changes every season. You can view the program schedule or listen to the webcast at wmfo.org.
WUMB	91.9	Folk Radio. A public radio station with folk and roots music every day of the week. They have fixed announcers and mostly national shows on the weekdays, and locally engineered shows on the weekends. wumb.org for their program schedule and streaming audio.
WBOS	92.9	Dorchester/Boston. Modern adult contemporary (rock, 80s & 90s).
WQSX	93.7	Lawrence. General rock and roll, oldies-based.
WJMN	94.5	Boston. "Jam'n," Hip-Hop, R&B, dance, rap.
WHRB	95.3	Harvard U/Cambridge. A lot of Jazz and Classical during the day, plus the indie/punk oriented Record Hospital from 10pm to 5am. Blues and Country/Western on the weekends, too. Big classical-

music programs ("orgies") during Harvard reading period. Program guide available at www.whrb.org/pg/.

WTKK	96.9	Talk.
WBMX	98.5	"Mix." Pop music "without the rap and hard rock."
WPLM	99.1	Easy listening (soft rock, adult contemporary, soft oldies).
WKLB	99.5	Lowell, Country.
WZLX	100.7	Boston. Classic rock, 60s through 90s.
WFNX	101.7	Boston Phoenix/Lynn. Boston's pioneer alternative rock station, with jazz on Sunday mornings.
WCRB	102.5	Waltham. BSO, Pops, and Tanglewood concerts Friday-Sunday evenings. The classical music station with commercials. Few commercials 1-6am. Occasional simulcast with WGBH-TV. "What did I hear?" service available online.
WODS	103.3	Boston. Oldies.
WBCN	104.1	Boston. Modern Rock, with Howard Stern in the mornings. New England Patriots Football.
WRBB	104.9	Northeastern U/Boston. Talk, variety, all kinds of music. wrbbradio.org for a schedule and streaming audio.
WROR	105.7	Framingham. Oldies and 80s with DJ personalities.
WMJX	106.7	Boston. "Magic 106" plays soft rock and adult contemporary.
WAAF	107.3	Worcester. Hard-core rock. Also listed as "Active Rock".
WXKS	107.9	Medford. Kiss-108. Contemporary hits leaning toward dance beat. Sometimes they'll play the same song three times in one hour. "Boston's #1 Hit Music Station."

Television

Clear reception of all Boston VHF channels is very difficult to achieve on campus, thanks to ghosts bouncing off the Muddy Charles. If you're seeing double, you can try one of the more distant stations listed below; they may be a little fuzzy but will be ghost-free. For the final solution, see *MIT Cable Television*, below.

Station	Channel	Affiliation	MIT Cable	Description
WGBH	2	PBS	23	Public TV. Some simulcasts with WCRB-FM. Boston
WBZ	4	CBS	24	Standard CBS fare. Boston
WCVB	5	ABC	25	Standard ABC fare. Boston
WLNE	6	ABC		Standard ABC fare. Providence, RI
WHDH	7	NBC	26	Standard NBC fare. Boston
WJAR	10	NBC		Standard NBC fare. Providence, RI
WPRI	12	CBS		Standard CBS fare. Providence, RI

WFXT	25	Fox	28	Fox Television, movies. Boston
WUNI	27	Univision	29	Spanish programming. Worcester/Boston/Providence
WLWC	28	UPN		UPN, Providence, RI
WSBE	36	PBS		PBS, Providence, RI
WSBK	38	UPN	30	Reruns, old movies, news, sports, UPN programming. Boston
WGBX	44	PBS	31	Educational. Associated with WGBH. Boston
WLVI	56	WB	32	Reruns, old movies, and sports, plus WB programming. Cambridge
WUTF	66	TeleFutura	33	Spanish programming. Marlborough
WBPX	68	Pax TV	34	Variety of "feel good TV" syndicated programming. Boston

MIT Cable Television

MIT has a cable TV system with cable drops in all dormitories, lobbies 7 & 10, and various other locations. The control center is located in the basement of Building 9, in 9-050. Channels 8, 9, 10, 11, and 12 have included live and taped lectures, foreign and classic films, student projects, and rebroadcasts of commercial (usually news) programs. NASA TV is on channel 6, channel 16 is the International Channel, channel 17 is China Central Television (CCTV-4), channel 18 is Deutsche Welle TV, channel 19 is French TV5, channel 20 is the Israeli Network, channel 21 is the Weather Channel. The MIT Student Cable Group (x3-7431) has channel 36. Other channels carry rebroadcast local TV as listed above. Some cable channels are offered as well, including MTVU (MTV's attempt to retain street cred by broadcasting "college rock" videos on their ostensibly low budget exclusively college network, channel 35) The Cartoon Network (38), C-SPANs 1 and 2 (40, 41), TNT (46), and USA (47). For a full listing, check web.mit.edu/org/m/mitcable/www/channels.html. The Library Access to Music Project (LAMP) occupies channels 63-78, allowing you to listen to self-chosen selections from the MIT music libraries. This service is, however, temporarily suspended for legal reasons at time of writing. Visit lamp.mit.edu to find out more. Earthshaking developments that the major networks are carrying (space shuttle incidents, unapproved terrorism) are routed to the lobby monitors in Lobby 10.

People interested in working at MITV should contact the Student Cable Programming Group (9-030, x3-7431, mit-student-cable@mit.edu). MIT Cable TV also relays Boston TV channels 24 hours a day. If your TV or VCR is not cable ready (practically all of them are these days), you can receive all the MIT channels and perfect reception of all stations marked wtih an MIT cable number above, by purchasing a cable converter and connecting it to a cable outlet. Converters are available from the MIT Cable TV office, 9-050.

If you're looking for even more channels with which to waste all that free time you have, you can subscribe to MIT digital cable, which costs $14 a month. Visit `www.fallsearth.com/campus/2139/` for more information.

Newspapers

The three daily Boston newspapers are the **Boston Globe**, the **Boston Herald** and the **Boston Metro**. In addition, there are many good national papers available.

The *Globe* is a liberal, Democratic newspaper that nevertheless has a tendency to publish reactionary, sensationalistic articles about MIT students; hence its nickname 'The Glob' on campus. It is a local newspaper once trying to become a national one until it was bought by the *New York Times*, but it has a great sports section and over a page of comics, and the "Calendar" section (on Thursdays) has a fairly complete schedule of events and things to do around Boston. The paper's website at `www.boston.com/globe/` contains much of the written material.

The *Herald* (`www.bostonherald.com`) is fond of banner headlines, and tends toward sensationalism. If all you care for is sports, turn to the *Herald*.

The *Metro* is a free daily newspaper that started up recently and is given out on the T and in newspaper machines all over the place. It is owned by a Swedish company that has started up similar *Metro* publications in other cities around the world, with the sole intention of putting in as little effort as possible to make the newspaper, grabbing a large market share by giving it away for free, and profiting from advertising revenue as a result. The news stories are mostly edited down to 1-3 paragraphs of 1-3 sentences each from Reuters wire copy, and the rest are poorly written and atrociously edited. Most of the publication is made up of advertisements, but on the other hand it is free and at least gives you something to do when riding the T on the rare occasions that there are no weirdos to stare at.

The **Boston Phoenix** (`www.bostonphoenix.com`) is a local example of the "alternative" press. It regularly publishes "muck-raking" articles about world, national, and local affairs. Reviews of entertainment products and programs, complete listings of the week's events, and some incredible classified ads are also featured. It has excellent listings of events about Boston. New issues come out once a week on Thursdays in those red bins. Free.

The Weekly Dig ("The Best Little Paper in Boston," `www.weeklydig.com`) is another small alternative paper which prides itself on hip language, cartoons that take a comparative media degree to understand, and opinion columnists that have never felt that strange sensation that many of us call "doubt." Appears on Wednesdays, free and a fun read nonetheless.

Stuff @ Night (`www.stuffatnight.com`), a free glossy newspaper focusing on nightlife, is really little more than a vehicle for nightlife-related ads. Another aim of this paper seems to be featuring a sufficient amount of hip models to smother any bud of self-esteem that might have developed in the reader since picking up the previous issue.

The **Cambridge Chronicle** (`www.townonline.com/cambridge/`) and other smaller weekly publications such as the **Tab** are oriented toward local communities. There are some foreign-language weeklies for minority groups in Boston.

Many living groups subscribe to out-of-town newspapers as well as locals. **The New York Times** and **The Wall Street Journal** are favored since they arrive on the issue date. **The Washington Post** arrives a day late. The **Out of Town News Agency** in Harvard Square carries a wide selection of national and international papers, as well as magazines.

USA Today is a national newspaper full of pretty color pictures and charts aimed at people with the attention span of sixth graders. The sports section is not bad.

Finally, several political groups have weekly papers which they are continuously hawking. These are usually quite biased and polemical but make interesting reading and occasionally break stories before the regular newspapers do. They sometimes ask for a donation, occasionally in an intimidating manner. The best response is often to politely give the paper back.

On-Campus Newspapers and Magazines

The most important campus periodical to watch out for is **Voo Doo**, MIT's only intentionally humorous publication. All the other magazines and newspapers are somewhat amusing, but they don't do it on purpose and you will find yourself laughing at them not with them. *Voo Doo*'s erstwhile publisher Phos puts out an issue every term, the timing depending on the rate submissions are received or the temperment of the editor. Due to their small print run, issues of *Voo Doo* usually become treasured collectors' items, so be sure not to dally in picking one up when an issue comes out. Occasionally *Voo Doo* will also put out other written material besides the regular issues, throw wild parties, or host 24-hour telethons on Student Cable. *Voo Doo* welcomes submissions of articles, comics, advertisements, illicit trysts, and live human organs (`voodoo@mit.edu, web.mit.edu/voodoo/www`).

There is one main student newspaper published at MIT. **The Tech** (W20-483, x3-1541) has news, sports, arts reviews, and an ever-increasing plethora of ill-informed opinion rants, and is distributed on campus Tuesdays and Fridays during the school year. It has provided continuous news service to MIT since 1881 and is even more pleased with itself about this than you probably think. *The Tech Index*, a microfiche topic and person index of articles that have appeared in *The Tech*, along with microfiche of the newspaper itself from 1881-1995, has been scanned in and digitized and is fully searchable and available for use by the MIT community. Call *The Tech*'s office for details. Their website at `www-tech.mit.edu` is also erratically updated so if you visit it a few days after the original publication date you can usually read the articles.

Counterpoint (x5-8922) is an MIT/Wellesley political opinion magazine, which publishes sophomoric articles on all sides of campus and national issues. It used to publish an extremely honest (and thus very offensive in some cases) guide to all of the ILG's in the fall, but now it has softened up a little and is less useful. These days most of Counterpoint's content is provided by the Wellesley contingent, and thus concentrates on what Wellesley students find worth remarking upon, which turns out to be pretty much what you'd expect.

The Thistle (W20-413, x3-0399, `web.mit.edu/thistle/www/`) is an alternative newspaper which comes out once in a while. First published in June 1987, the *Thistle* provides campus, local, national, and world news from a very left perspective, as well as opinion, art and venomous political diatribes by students and community members, though in recent years it has become less distinctively MIT-oriented and more of a carbon copy of the other activist papers found around the People's Republic of Cambridge. Unlike most newspapers, however, the *Thistle* is distinguished by being operated as a collective. There are no editors-in-chief. All decisions are made by the group and in theory everyone has equal say.

All of the above publications are given out free on campus and will accept letters, articles, and advertising.

Rune (`web.mit.edu/rune/www/`) is a student-run campus arts and literature magazine. Once each year, it publishes a collection of recent student art and composition. Submissions are encouraged throughout the year. Back issues can be found online, although the website is not updated very frequently.

Tech Talk (5-111, x3-3094, `web.mit.edu/newsoffice/tt/`), the MIT house newspaper, is distributed free on campus most Wednesdays during the academic year. Once intended as a basic campus news resource aimed at staff members, it has been reinvented as a brightly-colored, vapid public relations spin sheet apparently targeted at visitors to MIT. However, it does still contain some useful information such as a calendar of the week's events, arts news and campus interest announcements, classified ads, and a listing of available MIT jobs. Ads are accepted from the entire MIT community.

Other MIT Periodicals

Technology Review (`www.techreview.com`) carries articles on contemporary technology in addition to news about alumni and MIT. It is published monthly or bimonthly and copies are available to MIT students at most dorm desks; subscriptions are available off-campus for a fee.

MURJ (`web.mit.edu/murj/www/`), the MIT Undergraduate Research Journal is published once per semester and includes news articles on research at MIT and around the world, short summaries of student work, detailed lab reports and feature essays about controversial topics. Near the end of term, the journal can be found online and in most major buildings. To contact, email `murj-public@mit.edu`.

I/S (`web.mit.edu/is/isnews/`) is a news publication from Information Systems and Technology, the office which handles the technical requirements of computing on campus.

Opendoor (`alum.mit.edu/ne/opendoor/`) is a publication from MIT's Alumni Association. Features articles on current research and other activities of the Institute.

EMILY COFER '04

Colleges Around Boston

There are more than a quarter million students in the Boston area: 100,000 male and 150,000 female. The following list provides terse coverage of local schools. Wellesley College has a special relationship with MIT, and is discussed in greater detail at the end of the section.

The following schools, listed with their information numbers, are also nearby and may be of interest.

Art Institute of Boston, Boston	617-585-6600
Babson College, Wellesley	781-235-1200
Bentley College, Waltham	781-891-2000
Berklee College of Music, Boston	617-266-1400
Boston Architectural Center, Boston	617-262-5000
Boston Conservatory of Music, Boston	617-536-6340
Bunker Hill Community College, Watertown	617-228-2422
Curry College, Milton	617-333-0500
Eastern Nazarene College, Boston	617-773-6350
Fisher College, Boston	617-236-8800
Katherine Gibbs School, Boston	617-578-7100
Lasell Junior College for Women, Newton	617-243-2000
Longy School of Music, Cambridge	617-876-0956
Massachusetts Bay Community College, Wellesley	781-239-3000
Massachusetts College of Art, Boston	617-879-7000
Massachusetts College of Pharmacy, Boston	617-732-2800
Mt. Ida College, Newton	617-928-4500
New England Conservatory of Music, Boston	617-585-1100
Olin College of Engineering, Needham	781-292-2222
Pine Manor College, Chestnut Hill	617-731-7100
Regis College, Weston	781-768-7000
Suffolk University, Boston	617-573-8000
Wentworth Institute of Technology, Roxbury	617-989-4590
Wheelock College, Boston	617-734-5200

The following five colleges, in Western Massachusetts, are further away (2 hours by bus, $45 round trip including student discount).

Amherst College, Amherst	413-542-2000
Hampshire College, Amherst	413-549-4600
Mount Holyoke College, South Hadley	413-538-2000
Smith College, Northampton	413-584-2700
UMass Amherst, Amherst	413-545-0111

Boston College

(9,000 undergraduates, 4,510 graduate students) Located at Chestnut Hill near Newton, with direct access to Boston via the T, Boston College is a large Catholic university and 73% of the undergraduates live on campus. BC offers a broad, liberal arts curriculum; the most popular majors are finance, English, and communications. (617-552-8000, www.bc.edu)

Boston University

(17,860 undergraduates, 11,122 graduate students) Boston University's campus extends along the Back Bay, across the Charles River from MIT. It offers both graduate and undergraduate courses in all fields and draws students from across the nation and around the world. It is a private institution with Methodist ancestry. 66% of the students live on campus, and most of the rest are scattered throughout Boston, Brookline, and Cambridge. A cross registration program exists between BU and MIT. (617-353-2000, www.bu.edu)

Brandeis University

(3,057 undergraduates, 1,795 graduate students) Brandeis is located in Waltham, nine miles west of Boston, and offers both graduate and undergraduate liberal arts courses. 82% of the students live on campus and most of the rest live in either Waltham or Cambridge. Brandeis has a very large Jewish student population. It is located at the end of the #70 Bus line from Central Square. (781-736-2000, www.brandeis.edu)

Emerson College

(3,518 undergraduates, 1,011 graduate students) Emerson College is located on Beacon Street between Arlington and Clarendon Streets. It is a specialized private school concentrating in communication (speech, drama, mass communication, education). Freshmen and sophomores (52% of the student body) live on campus. (617-824-8500, www.emerson.edu)

Emmanuel College

(1,578 undergraduates, 88% female) Emmanuel is a Catholic liberal arts college. 77% of the students live on campus. (400 The Fenway, Boston, 617-277-9340, www.emmanuel.edu)

Harvard University

(6,637 undergraduates, 13,495 graduate students) Probably the most renowned university in Harvard Square, Harvard offers graduate and undergraduate education in virtually every field. The student body comes from all over the world. On October 1, 1999, **Radcliffe College**, the women's division of Harvard, and Harvard officially merged. The Radcliffe Institute for Advanced Study was created as one of ten Harvard Schools. Harvard is located 2 miles up Mass. Ave. from MIT, and most students live on or near the campus. Maps of Harvard are available at the Information Center. (617-495-1000, www.harvard.edu, www.radcliffe.edu)

Lesley University

(1,071 undergraduates, 5,384 graduate students, including many part time students) Lesley is a private college located right behind Harvard Law School. Lesley specializes in education, arts, human-services, and management. 77% female. (617-868-9600)

Massachusetts Institute of Technology

(4,173 undergraduates, 6,139 graduate students) A small technical school, located in Cambridge along the banks of the Charles River. Graduate and undergraduate education centered around science and technology. Most undergraduates live on-campus. Said to have the largest percentage of foreign students (8% of undergraduates, 38% of grad. students) in the country. (617-253-1000, `web.mit.edu`)

Northeastern University

(14,144 undergraduates, 4,363 graduate students) Northeastern is a private research university. Located in Boston's cultural district between the Museum of Fine Arts and Symphony Hall. 46% of students live on campus. (617-373-2000, `www.northeastern.edu`)

Simmons College

(1,300 female undergraduates, 2,007 graduate students) Simmons is a compromise between a liberal arts and a professional school, and specializes in the sciences. The most popular major is nursing. 75% of the students live on campus. The school is convenient to Kenmore Square and the Gardner and Fine Arts museums. (617-521-2000, `www.simmons.edu`)

Tufts University

(4,910 undergraduates, 4,522 graduate students) Tufts University is located on Walnut Hill in Medford and maintains a medical and dental school on Harrison Ave. in Boston. It is a private institution offering the usual range of curricula. 75% of the undergraduates live on campus. **Jackson College** is the women's counterpart of Tufts. You can travel by bus from Harvard Sq. or Lechmere. (617-628-5000, `www.tufts.edu`)

University of Massachusetts, Boston Campus

(10,071 undergraduate, 2,648 graduate students) This state college offers a liberal arts undergraduate program. No residential facilities. (617-287-5000, `www.umb.edu`)

Wellesley College

Wellesley College is about fifteen miles from MIT, straight out the Mass. Pike., a small (2,300) women's liberal arts school. After spending time by the Charles, it is very refreshing to experience grass, trees, hills, a lake, and the silence that comes from having much space between you and the nearest car. There's a 182-foot bell tower (known as Galenstone Tower) that can be climbed on weekdays from which a wonderful view of the countryside and the Boston skyline can be seen.

There are other attractions as well.

Wellesley is officially linked with MIT by the MIT-Wellesley cross-registration program, rendering classes and athletic programs open to MIT students. There are other ways to get involved in Wellesley activities but you have to be enterprising: they usually aren't well publicized here. There are opportunities to live on the campus for a term (or sometimes a year) along with other exchange students, mostly from MIT. Check with the Exchange Office at either school for more information. Beware: if you are a man you will be called a co-ed!

Getting There

Although it is 15 miles from Cambridge, Wellesley is not hard to reach. A free bus service runs approximately once an hour, Monday through Friday, and is part of the cross-registration program (you must have your MIT ID).

Bus schedules are available in 11-120, the Student Services Center or online at
`www.wellesley.edu/Housing/exchangesched.html`

In addition, there is a bus sponsored by the Wellesley Senate that runs on Friday nights and all day Saturday and Sunday (`www.wellesley.edu/Housing/senatesched.html`). Tickets for the Senate Bus are sold (~$1.75) at the Cafe Hoop at Wellesley College, Out of Town News in Harvard Square, LaVerde's in the MIT student center, and at the Marlboro Market located on Mass Ave. If you have to resort to the MBTA, the Green Line (Riverside-D) goes to Woodland, the nearest T-stop to Wellesley, with a $20.00-$25.00 taxi ride from Woodland to Wellesley. Lastly, you can take the MBTA Commuter Rail's Framingham/Worcester line from South Station to Wellesley Square ($3.00, or $4.00 on board), with a $4.00 taxi ride to campus.

Lake Waban

There is a fairly large lake on the campus. Popular activities include walking along the perimeter, swimming, and boating. In late spring and early fall there is a lifeguard on duty at the beach by the boathouse. There are also canoes, sailboats, and windsurfing boards for free rental. A Wellesley Small Craft Permit, MIT sailing card, or an equivalent (like a WSI certificate) are needed to rent the boats; canoes are available with a Wellesley or MIT Swimming Certificate. Call the boathouse (781-283-2190) or visit `www.wellesley.edu/CampusMaps/Buildings/boat.html` for more information.

Green Growing Things

Wellesley is full of real green vegetation — it is certainly a refreshing sight. Especially in early spring and late fall the campus is full of flowering trees and multi-colored foliage. There is an extensive Arboretum and Botanical Garden, which includes a spring, winding stream, and paramecium pond, as well as all kinds of labeled exotic trees and shrubs, and lots of flowers. Visit any day of the year between 8:00am and 4:00pm. If you have questions call the Friends of Horticulture Visitor Center at 781-283-3094 or visit `www.wellesley.edu/FOH/home.html`

Whitin Observatory

The Observatory is located on a hill behind the Science Center. It is equipped with 6", 12", and 24" telescopes, a spectrohelioscope, a radio telescope, a number of 8" telescopes, and an astronomy library. For use of the facilities call the Observatory at 781-283-2726 or visit `www.wellesley.edu/Astronomy`

Jewett Arts Center

Jewett, which forms one side of the Academic Quad, houses the Arts and Music Departments. In the Art building are studios, study rooms, the Art Library, and a student sculpture court. The Music building has practice and listening rooms, the Music Library, and Jewett Auditorium. Connecting the two halves is the Davis Museum. Admission and parking is free; exhibits change every month or two. Call 781-283-2051 for more information or see `www.wellesley.edu/Music/facilities.html#Jewett` for hours.

Music

For those interested in singing, there are several opportunities for MIT students. The Wellesley College Choir and the more selective Toons are open to women who want to try out. The Toons is also open to MIT men. There are other groups on campus, most notably the Wellesley Widows and the Tupelos, both of which sing *a capella* and give a variety of performances. Also, black women who are interested in singing can find out about Wellesley's Ethos Choir by contacting the Black Students' Association in Harambee House (781-283-2133, `www.wellesley.edu/Music/home.html`).

If you are interested in chamber music, see the Chamber Music Society (`www.wellesley.edu/Music/CMS/Home.html`). Additionally, the Carillon Guild, reachable at 781-283-3900 x2244, is always interested in students who want to learn how to play the carillon in the Great Tower above Green Hall. Call the Music Office at 781-283-2077 for more information.

Theater Performances are put on by Shakespeare House and by the Wellesley College Theater in Alumnae Hall. Call Nora Hussey, the head of the Theater Department, at 781-283-2029 for more information. (`www.wellesley.edu/Activities/homepage/shakespeare`, `theatre.wellesley.edu`)

Radio
WZLY (91.5 FM, `www.wzly.net`) is Wellesley's all-student radio station, located in Schneider Center. Those interested in broadcasting or working there should call the station for details. Shows are usually 1.5-2 hours long, and the material is up to the broadcaster (subject to approval). The request line is 781-283-2690 and the business line is 781-283-2791.

Schneider
One of the oldest and most interesting buildings on Wellesley's campus, Billings Hall has been expanded and renovated and now fronts Schneider College Center. Open seven days a week from 8am to 1am (during the academic year), it is the main stop for the MIT-Wellesley Exchange Bus and contains facilities for off-campus students (lounge, mailboxes, kitchen, computer, phone), the student-operated "Cafe Hoop" (a small coffee house) and Molly's Pub (light refreshments), a kosher kitchen and Hillel lounge, the Info Box, and an entertainment stage/dance floor. It also has a cafeteria-style grill and limited deli and various student and College organizations. Sometimes there are live bands at Molly's.

Near Schneider is Harambee House, a social and cultural center for black students. Contact Carol Estridge (781-283-2133) for more information. Also, near Schneider are TZE and ZA, the pseudo-sororities nominally devoted to the Arts, but infamous for their parties.

General Information
For further information on almost anything at Wellesley, including students' telephone numbers and information on activities and events, call the student-staffed Info Box at 781-283-2670. You can also call Information Services at 781-283-2096 or the main number at 781-283-1000.

MIT History

I doubt not that such a nucleus-school would, with the growth of this active and knowledge seeking community, finally expand into a great institution comprehending the whole field of physical science and the arts with the auxiliary branches of mathematics and modern languages...

—William Barton Rogers, 1846

In 1835 William Barton Rogers was elected to the professorship of Natural Philosophy at the University of Virginia, a chair founded by Thomas Jefferson only ten years earlier. Rogers, a graduate of William and Mary College, was intensely involved in the emerging science of geology, although he had an enduring interest in all scientific subjects. During Rogers' eighteen years at the University of Virginia, he became increasingly troubled by bigotry, anti-intellectualism, and sporadic support from the state. In 1845, Rogers, then chairman of the Faculty, was further shaken by severe rioting and was forced to make a decision to close the school for a week.

Discouraged by his experiences in Virginia, Rogers went on a geological expedition to New England, attending the Boston meetings of the Association of American Geologists and Naturalists (later the American Association for the Advancement of Science). Rogers found himself enamoured of the region, writing of the "contrast between the region in which I live and the highly cultivated nature and society of glorious New England." In the advanced intellectual and industrial climate of Boston, he felt, a new type of education could be fostered. Rogers left Virginia for Massachusetts in 1853. His dreams finally achieved substance when, on April 10, 1861, the governor of the Commonwealth of Massachusetts signed the act to incorporate the Massachusetts Institute of Technology. Four days later Fort Sumter was attacked (one suspects that the two events were unrelated). Although the Civil War delayed Rogers' plan, construction of MIT's first building began in 1863, in a landfill area of the Back Bay, in the estuary of the Charles River.

On February 20, 1865, the first class of fifteen students finally entered MIT. President Rogers taught Physics, as part of a six-man faculty. These first years proved to be hard on Rogers' health, and he suffered from a slight stroke in 1868. John D. Runkle was appointed Acting President and in 1870 succeeded him. Runkle's presidency saw the gradual development of MIT into "Boston Tech." Fiscal problems still plagued the young Institute, and at one time MIT came perilously close to becoming part of Harvard. Harvard's President Eliot (a former MIT professor) broached the topic of a merger during Runkle's presidency, and continued to press the issue during the later presidencies of James Crafts and Henry Pritchett. Eliot's advances, however, were repeatedly rebuffed by Runkle and late the MIT Corporation. Problems with money continued, and in 1873 tuition was doubled (to a staggering $200). President Runkle resigned in 1878, although he continued to teach mathematics until 1902.

Following the resignation of John Runkle, Brigadier General Francis A. Walker became president in 1881. In 1882, Walker asked William Rogers (who was by that point rather frail) to award diplomas at the May graduation exercises. The ceremony proved overly taxing to Rogers' delicate condition; he collapsed on the podium and died.

MIT continued to grow during the latter part of the nineteenth century, and by 1900 there were 1277 students. In 1906 it became apparent that MIT was fast outgrowing its Copley Square lodgings, despite the addition of several new buildings. A site committee was formed to search for "Technology's new home." Plans ranged from a golf course in Allston to building an island in the Charles River, until the current site in Cambridge was settled upon. Excavations for the buildings began in September 1913, and the first of 25,000 piles was driven into Cambridge soil on December fourth of that year.

A neo-classical motif was chosen by designer William Welles Bosworth '89, who could hardly contain himself with his plans for "a great white city of majestic proportions that will fitly express the noble ideas of its purpose and the dignity of its work." The central feature of the new complex was the Great Dome, towering 147 feet above street level. Five thousand tons of steel and fifty thousand cubic yards of concrete later, the new Technology was complete.

During its first 60 years, MIT's curriculum focused almost exclusively on architecture and engineering. In 1930 President Karl T. Compton undertook to strengthen the position of science at MIT and to encourage the growth of the graduate school. The next decade saw a steady increase in both graduate work and research. World War II brought further expansion of research programs and the establishment of the Radiation Laboratory, a major center for American development of radar. For the national interest during the war the Institute assumed management of major research enterprises such as the Instrumentation Laboratory. These programs fostered a close working cooperation between the Government and the Institute, laying the groundwork for the development of facilities such as the Research Laboratory of Electronics and the Laboratory for Nuclear Science.

The Instrumentation Lab, known primarily for its work on inertial navigation systems and ballistic missiles, designed key guidance and control systems for the Apollo lunar and command modules. Due to increasing anti-war sentiment among the student body during the Vietnam War, the Instrumentation Lab ceased to be an MIT research program. In 1973 it became a separate, nonprofit research corporation and was renamed the Charles Stark Draper Laboratory, after the lab's founder and inventor of inertial navigation. Nevertheless, MIT's major role in defense research continues today. One recent defense initiative is the Institute for Soldier Nanotechnologies, which opened in May 2003, and is funded in part by a $50 million grant from the US Army.

When World War II ended, MIT continued to hold a central position in education and research. To its traditional curricula in architecture, engineering and science, the Institute added programs in fields such as management, economics, political science, psychology and linguistics. In recent years, MIT's Media Lab has achieved world renown for its unique approach to merging art and technology. While MIT began to integrate humanities and the social sciences into its offerings, its core commitment to technological progress remained strong.

In 1951, the Lincoln Laboratory was created as a federally-funded research center. Located in Lexington, the lab quickly established a reputation for pioneering work in advanced electronics and air defense systems. The Millstone Hill radar, completed in 1957, utilized the first all solid-state, digital computer. It was the first American facility to detect and track the Soviet Sputnik satellites.

MIT-trained astronauts have participated in some of the most challenging and historically significant US space missions: the first lunar landing, the first docking of two spacecraft in orbit and the first long-duration mission on board the International Space Station. NASA has chosen more MIT graduates to become astronauts than graduates of any other private educational institution (only the US Air Force Academy, the US Naval Academy and the US Naval Postgraduate School have had more).

In the late 1950s, computers were big, expensive, and for serious work only. But at MIT, some members of the Tech Model Railroad Club began programming for the fun of it, using available machines in the middle of the night. The computer hacker was born. Project MAC (which stood for both Machine-Aided Cognition and Multiple Access Computer) was founded in 1963, and eventually evolved into the Artificial Intelligence Lab (AI) and the Laboratory for Computer Science (LCS). The AI Lab of the '60s and '70s was later described as "pure hacker paradise," and it played an important role in the computer revolution.

In the early 1980s, an AI Lab hacker named Richard Stallman founded the GNU Project to create free and open software, which ultimately led to the Linux operating system, the Apache web server, and the rest of the Open Source movement. On July 1st, 2003, the AI Lab and LCS merged into what is now known as CSAIL and shortly thereafter moved into the spacious Stata Center.

During the 1970s and 1980s, increased research in cell and molecular biology, microbiology, and immunology resulted in the establishment of the Center for Cancer Research. The Whitehead Institute of Biomedical Research was established in 1982, and its Center for Genome Research served as the flagship for the Human Genome Project. Today, while research into cancer or the human genome continues, increasing collaboration between the Biology Department and other departments at MIT has spawned novel research in areas such as biophysics, computational biology, and synthetic biology.

Entrepreneurial MIT graduates have always had a significant economic impact on the nation; this was especially true during the booming 1990s. According to a study conducted by MIT and BankBoston in 1997, "...if the companies founded by MIT graduates and faculty formed an independent nation, the revenues produced by the companies would make that nation the 24th largest economy in the world, placing MIT above Thailand and below South Korea."

The recent flurry of ambitious building projects could be considered a testimony to MIT's optimism for the future... or perhaps the fruit of dot-com era hubris. Latest expensive additions to the "Evolving Campus" include the Zesiger Sports and Fitness Center, the Sidney-Pacific graduate dorm, the sponge-like Simmons Hall (an undergraduate dorm), and the Ray and Maria Stata Center (home of CSAIL). Other projects, such as the Picower Center for Learning and Memory, the McGovern Insitute for Brain Research, and the oft-delayed expansion to the Media Lab, remain in various states of planning or construction. Visit the website (`web.mit.edu/evolving/`) for more information.

MIT was among the first universities to establish programs of study in applied physics, meteorology, food technology, naval architecture, and marine engineering, and electrical, aeronautical, and sanitary engineering. The Institute was a leader in developing the modern profession of chemical engineering, and the nation's first degree in architecture was given here. Today, while justifiably known for its engineering prowess, the Institute is also home to stellar programs in most of the sciences, not to mention well-respected programs in other disciplines, such as economics or linguistics.

Today, the MIT campus covers 154 acres extending for more than a mile along the Charles River. The MIT community includes more than 4,000 undergraduates, 6,000 graduate students, and 950 faculty. Fifty-seven present and former members of the faculty have won the Nobel Prize. MIT employs about 9,400 individuals on campus, including research, library, administrative, and support staff.

Books on the History of MIT

All of the following books can be checked out from the MIT Libraries (`libraries.mit.edu`). Most are available by request at the MIT Press Bookstore, and some may be available at the Coop.

Hackers: Heroes of the Computer Revolution, by Steven Levy. Penguin Books, 1984. Describes the MIT computer hackers of the 1950s and 60s, starting with the Tech Model Railroad Club and describing the early days of the AI Lab. This book is a classic for the aspiring hacker.

The Life and Letters of William Barton Rogers is a book in two volumes edited by his wife with the assistance of William T. Sedgwick. Houghton-Mifflin Company, Boston and New York, 1896. The definitive biography of MIT's founder.

Mid-Century: The Social Implications of Scientific Progress, by John E. Burchard. The Technology Press and John Wiley & Sons, Inc., New York, 1950. A verbatim account of MIT's great Mid-Century Convocation, March 31, and April 1—2, 1949.

M.I.T. in Perspective, by Francis E. Wylie, Little, Brown & Co., Boston, 1975. A glossy coffee-table account of MIT and its progeny; not comprehensive, but interesting, with lots of pretty pictures.

Q.E.D.: MIT in World War II, by John E. Burchard. The Technology Press, 1948.

Richard Cockburn MacLaurin, by Henry Greenleaf Pearson, a biography of MIT's sixth president. MacMillan Company, New York, 1937.

Scientists Against Time, by James Phinney Baxter III. MIT Press, 1968. An account of the scientific developments of WWII, with a large section on the activities of the Radiation Labs.

Technology's War Record is an interpretation of the contribution made by MIT, its staff, former students, and undergraduates to the cause of the Allies in World War I. Published by the War Records Committee of the MIT Alumni Association, 1920.

When MIT Was Boston Tech, by C. Samuel Prescott. The Technology Press, Cambridge, 1954. A history of MIT from its founding in 1861 through its move to Cambridge in 1916.

For more information on MIT's history, contact the MIT Museum (x3-4444).

MIT Songs (and Such)

The Engineers' Drinking Song (Lady Godiva)
Words by many many people. Compose some yourself.

Godiva was a lady who through Coventry did ride
To show the royal villagers her fair and pure white hide.
The most observant man of all, an engineer of course,
Was the only man who noticed that Godiva rode a horse.

CHORUS:

We are, we are, we are, we are, we are the engineers.
We can, we can, we can, we can demolish forty beers.
Drink rum, drink rum, drink rum all day and come along with us.
For we don't give a damn for any old man who don't give a damn for us!

She said "I've come a long, long way, and I shall go as far
With the man who takes me from this horse and leads me to a bar."
The men who took her from her steed and lead her to her beer
Were a bleary eyed surveyor and a drunken engineer.

(chorus)

My father was a miner from the Northern Malamute,
My mother was a mistress in a house of ill repute.
The last time that I saw them, these words rang in my ears,
"GO TO MIT, YOU SON-OF-A-BITCH, AND JOIN THE ENGINEERS!!!"

(chorus)

Princeton's run by Wellesley, Wellesley's run by Yale
Yale is run by Vassar, and Vassar's run by tail
Harvard's run by stiff pricks, the kind you raise by hand.
But MIT's run by engineers, the finest in the land.

(chorus)

MIT was MIT when Harvard was a pup.
And MIT will be MIT when Harvard's time is up.
And any Harvard son of a bitch who thinks he's in our class
Can pucker up his rosy lips and kiss the beaver's ass.

(chorus)

An artsman and an Engineer once found a gallon can,
Said the artsman "Match me drink for drink, let's see if you're a man."
They drank three drinks, the artsman fell, his face was turning green,
But the Engineer drank on and said "It's only gasoline."

(chorus)

The Army and the Navy went out to have some fun.
They went down to the taverns where the fiery liquors run.
But all they found were empties, for the engineers had come,
And traded all their instruments for gallon kegs of rum.

(chorus)

Venus was a statue made entirely of stone.
Without a stitch upon her, she was naked as a bone.
On seeing that she had no clothes, an engineer discoursed:
"Why the damn thing's only concrete, and should be reinforced!"

(chorus)

Rapunzel let her hair down for two suitors down below,
So one of them could grab a hold and give the old heave-ho.
The Prince began to climb at once, but soon came out the worst,
For the Engineer rode the elevator and reached Rapunzel first.

(chorus)

Caesar set out for Egypt at the age of fifty three,
But Cleopatra's blood was warm, her heart was young and free.
And every night when Julius said goodnight at three o'clock,
There was a Roman engineer waiting just around the block!

(chorus)

An engineer once staggered in though the Roderick Gate,
He was carrying a load you would expect to ship by freight.
The only things that kept him upright and on his course,
Were the boundary conditions and the coriolis force.

(chorus)

Ace Towing roams the streets of Cambridge each and every night,
They tow cars and stow cars and hide them out of sight;
They tried to tow Godiva's horse, the Engineers said "Hey!"
Then towed away their towing truck, and now the Ace must pay!

(chorus)

Sir Francis Drake and all his ships set out for Calais Bay.
They'd heard the Spanish rum fleet was headed on their way.
But the engineers had beat them by a night and a half a day
And though as drunk as ptarmigans, you still could hear them say:

(chorus)

A maiden and an engineer were sitting in the park,
The engineer was working on some research after dark.
His scientific method was a marvel to observe —
While his right hand wrote the figures, his left hand traced the curves.

(chorus)

My father peddles opium, my mother's on the dole.
My sister used to walk the streets, but now she's on parole.
My brother runs a restaurant with a bedroom in the rear.
But they don't even speak to me 'cause I'm an engineer.

(chorus)

Some engineers were working on the dome to pull a hack.
The CPs picked them up as they were done and heading back.
The cops detained, the deans complained, the hackers went to trial —
But professors Hal and Gerry paid their fine in true Tech style.

Arise Ye Sons of MIT
Music and lyrics by John B. Wilbur '26
(The closest thing MIT has to an old Alma Mater.)

Arise all ye sons of MIT, in loyal brotherhood.
The future beckons unto ye and life is full and good.
Arise and raise your steins on high; tonight shall ever be
A mem'ry that will never die, ye sons of MIT.

Once more thy sons, oh MIT, return from far and wide
And gather here once more to be renourished by thy side,
And as we raise our steins on high to pledge our love for thee
We join thy sons of days gone by in praise of MIT.

Oh loyal sons of MIT, when clouds of war burn red,
In foreign land on distant sea, your battle line is spread,
To you we raise our steins on high wherever you may be
And join your voices from the sky, ye sons of MIT.

Arise All Ye of MIT
(The closest thing MIT has to a new Alma Mater.)

Arise all ye of MIT, in loyal fellowship.
The future beckons unto ye and life is full and good.
Arise and raise your glass on high; tonight shall ever be
A mem'ry that will never die, for ye of MIT.

Thy sons and daughters, oh MIT, return from far and wide
And gather here once more to be renourished by thy side,
And as we raise our glasses high to pledge our love for thee,
We join all those of days gone by in praise of MIT.

e to the u du dx!
(a.k.a. the Tech Cheer)

e to the u du dx, e to the x dx!
Cosine! Secant! Tangent! Sine!
3 point 1 4 1 5 9!
Integral, radical, μ dv
Slipstick, slide rule, M.I.T.!

WE ARE HAPPY — TECH IS HELL
T-E-C-H-N-O-L
O-G-Y!

M.I.T. RAH! RAH! RAH!
M.I.T. RAH! RAH! RAH!
M.I.T. RAH! RAH! RAH!
Technology! Technology! Technology!

Take Me Back to Tech

I wish that I were back again at Tech on Boylston Street,
Dressed in my dinky uniform so dapper and so neat.
I'm crazy after calculus, I never had enough;
It's hard to be dragged away so young,
It was horribly awfully tough!

Hurrah for Technology, 'ology 'ology oh,
Glorious old Technology, 'ology 'ology oh!

Back in the days that were free from care in the 'ology varsity shop,
With nothing to do but analyze air in an anemometrical top.
The differentiation of the trigonometric pow'rs
The constant pi that made me sigh in those happy days of ours.

Hurrah for Technology, 'ology 'ology oh,
Glorious old Technology, 'ology 'ology oh!

Take me back on a special train to that glorious institute,
I yearn for the inspiration of a technological toot.
I'd shun the quizzical physical profs the chapel and all that,
But how I'd love to go again on a scientific bat.

Hurrah for Technology, 'ology 'ology oh,
Glorious old Technology, 'ology 'ology oh!

M-A-S-S-A-C-H-U-S-E-T-T-S
(and)
I-N-S-T-I-T-U-T-E-O-F-T-E
(but)
C-H-N-O-L-O-G and Y comes after G
(and what does that spell?)
The Massachusetts Institute of Technology!
Hey!

The Ballad of 5.60
(To the tune of "The Battle Hymn of the Republic")

Free energy and entropy were whirling in his brain
With partial differentials and greek letters in their train
While delta, sigma, gamma, theta, epsilon and pi
($\Delta\Sigma\Gamma\Theta E\Pi$)
Were driving him distracted as they danced before his eye.
Glory, glory dear old thermo...
      Glory, glory dear old thermo...
            Glory, glory dear old thermo,
                  We'll pass you by and by.

Heat, Content, and fugacity revolved within his brain
Like molecules and atoms that you never have to name.
And logarithmic functions doing cakewalks in his dreams,
And partial molar quantities devouring chocolate creams.

They asked him on the final if a mole of any gas
In a vessel with a membrane through which Hydrogen could pass
Were compressed to half its volume what the entropy would be
If two-thirds delta-sigma equalled half of delta-P.
($2/3\ \Delta\Sigma = 1/2\ \Delta P$)

He said he guessed the entropy would have to equal four
Unless the second law should bring it up a couple more
But then, it might be seven if the Carnot law applied,
Or it might be almost zero if the delta-T should slide.

The professor read his paper with a corrugated brow.
For he knew he'd have to grade it and he didn't quite know how
'Til an inspiration in his cerebellum suddenly smote,
And he seized his trusty fountain pen and this is what he wrote:

Just as you have guessed the entropy, I'll have to guess your grade,
But the second law won't raise it to the mark you might have made.
For it might have been a 100 if your guesses all were good,
But I think it must be zero 'til they're rightly understood.

Glory, glory dear old thermo...
      Glory, glory dear old thermo...
            Glory, glory dear old thermo,
                  We'll try again next term.

M.I.T.
(To the tune of "Let It Be")

When I find myself in times of trouble,
Charles Vest comes to me,
Speaking words of wisdom: MIT.
And now I find I'm losing
What's remaining of my sanity.
I'm told that that's expected: MIT
MIT, MIT, what have you done to me?
I think that I'm OD'ing; too much technology.

And even though the night is cloudy
There's a light that shines on me.
It must be a laser: MIT.
And if the light proves dangerous
I'll go to the infirmary
Provided it is open: MIT.
MIT, MIT, computer running free
Athena's at the stem of everything I see.

I wake up to the sound of lectures
Some professor's telling me
du/dh=BS - du(dt).

Although the course seems difficult
The catalogue says it's elementary
Everything's so simple: MIT.
MIT, MIT, you weren't true to me.
You promised me an education, and gave me misery.

And when I'm doing a problem set
I find they're all too hard for me.
There will be an answer: MIT.
I'll go and threaten the tool next door
And he will do them all for me.
Cheating is so simple: MIT.
MIT, MIT, I'm as desperate as can be.
If a B's a bit too much I'll settle for a C.

I gaze at the towering building
And emotion sweeps all over me,
Standing on the campus: MIT.
How many times I've thought of jumping
From the buildings that I see.
That is not the answer: MIT.
MIT, MIT, you don't agree with me.
A dome is not a home: MIT.

MIT Commandments

I am Athena thy Goddess
Thou shalt not have false gods before me.

0x1 — Thou shalt not take the name of OLC in vain
0x2 — Thou shalt not eat at Lobdell
0x3 — Thou shalt keep holy the hour of Star Trek
0x4 — Honor thy professors, for they are the source of grades
0x5 — Thou shalt not decrease entropy
0x6 — Thou shalt not connect PWR to GND
0x7 — Thou shalt not sex toads
0x8 — Thou shalt not exceed the speed of light
0x9 — Keep holy the month of IAP for it is a time of rest
0xA — IHTFP
0xB — Thou shalt not sleep
0xC — Thou shalt consume caffeine
0xD — Thou shalt not take pass/fail in vain
0xE — Thou shalt not covet thy neighbor's HP
0xF — Thou shalt not divide by zero

Hacking

Roof and tunnel hackers specialize in knowing How to Get Around MIT. They take great pride in knowing where the most interesting nooks and crannies of the Institute can be found and how to get to classic hacking spots such as the top of the Great Dome. It's fun to find your way into a rumored hacking location such as the bricked-in shower or the Tomb of the Forbidden Ladder, or, better yet, to be the first to discover a particular "tomb" (an interesting, out-of-the-way, unused spot). The greatest challenge, however, is to do so without leaving a trace of your actions.

Another activity under the aegis of the term "hacking" is what is known as "pulling a hack". A hack, in this sense, differs from ordinary college pranks in that emphasis is placed on cleverness, timeliness, the ability to overcome technical obstacles, and the avoidance of damage to the object being hacked. Some of the best known hacks in recent years have been the transformation of the Great Dome into R2D2, the One Ring around the Great Dome, the astronaut on the dome celebrating the 30th anniversary of the moon landing, the Magic Pi-Ball on the Green Building, the cracking of the dome by a 48-unit weight, the human maze in Lobby 7, the parachuting beavers at the 2001 Commencement, the Wright Brothers flyer which appeared on the dome on the 100th anniversary of the first powered and controlled flight and the elevator to secret floors that appeared in the rubble of Building 20. Most famous, however, of recent hacks, was the life-size fiberglass model campus police car placed on the Great Dome, complete with a dummy CP and boxes of Dunkin' Donuts. It's considered a challenge to make your hack difficult for Physical Plant workers to remove (therefore ensuring its longevity), although should your hack manage to evade the attentions of PhysPlant, it is considered classy to remove it after a suitable length of time.

Hacking is an MIT tradition, with a strong emphasis on ethics and ingenuity. You can learn more about hacks by visiting the MIT Museum and asking to see the folders on student pranks in the student activities file. They have several inches of photos and newspaper clippings dating back to 1910, and they welcome any information about current hacks. They hold a talk and slide show every IAP, and have published a number of excellent picture histories of hacks. The latest book, by "Institute Historian T. F. Peterson", is called *Nightwork: A History of Hacks and Pranks at MIT*. An online gallery of hacks is also available at the IHTFP Hack Gallery: `hacks.mit.edu`.

Roof and tunnel hacking dates back many years. The oldest known piece of graffiti is from a plumber on the fourth floor of Building 10, dated 1915, found in 1985 by hackers known as Heretic and Circumscribed Triangle. Various groups offer tours during orientation and CPW for interested freshmen, the most notable of which are the Orange and Tangerine Tours (run by Jack Florey and his associates) and the Spelunkers' Tours (run by the "Caving Club"). During the rest of the year, the "Coffeehouse Club" — an informal group that meets regularly to go exploring — meets at the location of the late, lamented 24-hour Coffeehouse.

Hacking Groups

There are and have been many hacking groups at MIT. Many are associated with living groups, but there are a few that are somewhat random collections of people.

Jack Florey

Jack Florey's Old No. 5 East Roof and Tunnel Hackers is based just under the roof of East Campus's east parallel. Jack is best known for running the Orange tours during Rush week. (If you need to find your way to Baker House, Jack is the person to ask.) Jack's strength has generally been exploration. While his numbers have varied from year to year, Jack remains a prominent figure in the hacking community.

James E. Tetazoo III

The Third East Traveling Animal Zoo is based in East Campus. They were probably the best hackers during the late seventies, and continue to amuse East Campus residents and the Institute with their wacky antics. During the dedication of building 66 (the triangular building inhabited by Course 10), they lowered an anchor over the bow, dropped a banner christening the "USS Tetazoo," broke a bottle of champagne across the point, and blasted "Anchors Aweigh" on their stereos. In exploring they were the first group to sign in under the steps of 77 Massachusetts Avenue. James Tetazoo's *No Knife: A study in mixed media earth tones, number three* appeared overnight at an exhibit in the List Visual Arts Center and recieved rave reviews. This objet d'art consisted of a grey commons tray set with two spoons, a plate, a bowl, a tumbler and a fork ... but no knife.

Order of Random Knights

ORK is a small tightly-knit hacking group based in Random Hall. They are mainly an exploring group and are best known for discovering one of the missing half stories in Building Ten. ORK's most famous hack was the die hack that appeared in Lobby 7 several years ago.

Technology Hackers Association

Reputed to have once been the largest group on campus, THA pulled off several widely known hacks requiring lots of manpower such as the Massachusetts Toolpike in 1985 and the Home on the Dome in 1986.

Delta Kappa Epsilon

DKE is famous for the balloon hack at the November 1982 Harvard-Yale football game. That hack received more publicity than any other hack in the history of MIT. See *Technique '83* for details. DKE had tried to hack the game before, most memorably in the late 1940s when they buried explosive cord in a pattern that would spell out "MIT". Unfortunately, Harvard discovered the hack and set up a trap. They arrested several students wearing coats lined with batteries. A dean, who had been informed about the hack after the arrest, went down to bail the students out. He pointed out to the detective that the battery-lined coats were only circumstantial evidence. At this point the dean opened his own battery-lined coat and declared that "all Tech men carry batteries."

Larry West (defunct)

Conglomerated around the 41st floor of the Western Front of East Campus, back in the day. Archnemesis to James Tetazoo and self-appointed champion of Elvis and φρεδ , Larry was an instigator and participant in much mischief around the Institute.

Blue Goose, Incorporated (defunct)

Blue Goose was founded in 1978 at Nu Delta. They were well known as expert explorers, and their name can be found in many of the more obscure nooks and crannies of the Institute.

Smoots

Although not technically a hacking group, every year Lamda Chi Alpha still repaints the Smoots, which mark the distance along the Harvard Bridge. Just what is a Smoot? Oliver Smoot was an unfortunate pledge of that fraternity in 1959 (the first year the marks were painted) who was immortalized as a unit of measure during a pledge event.

Society of Institute Nihilists

This group has no members and never will.

Hacking Ethics

This hackers' code of conduct is taken from that enshrined by anonymous hackers on a mural within the Tomb Of The Unknown Tool.

- The safety of yourself, of others, and of property should have highest priority. Safety is more important than pulling off a hack or getting through a door.
- **Be subtle**; leave no evidence that you were there.
- Brute force is the last resort of the incompetent.
- Leave things as you found them or better. Cause no permanent damage during hacks *and* while hacking. If you find something broken, call F-IXIT.
- Do not steal anything; if you *must* borrow something, leave a note saying when it will be returned and remember to return it.
- Do not drop things without a ground crew to ensure that no one is underneath.
- Sign-ins are not graffiti and should not be seen by the general public. Sign-ins exhibit one's pride in having found an interesting location and should be seen only by other hackers. Real hackers are not proud of discovering Lobby 7, random basements, or restrooms. Keep sign-ins small and respect other hackers' sign-ins.
- Never drink and hack.
- Never hack alone. Have someone who can get help in an emergency.
- Know your limitations and do not surpass them. If you do not know how to open a door, climb a shaft, *etc.*, then learn from someone who knows before trying.
- Learn how not to get caught; but if you do get caught, accept gracefully and cooperate fully.
- Share your knowledge and experience with other hackers.
- Above all, exercise **common sense**.

Hacking Tips

The following tips are based on a document by Keshlam the Seer, Knight of the Random Order. The editors take no responsibility for its content.

Evasion and Escape

The Eleventh Commandment: Don't get caught. Thou shalt honor it and keep it wholly. On the other hand, if you *are* caught, the least you can do is accept it with dignity, and have respect for your captor.

Always have two ways to run. If someone comes one way, you can go the other. If possible, run along a path that has many side branches. Your pursuer will pause to check them. Change floors often. Don't start running when someone spots you. Walk around a corner and *then* run. Remember that the person who sees you must first decide that you are doing something wrong, and running is an admission of guilt. "It's amazing what you can get away with if you don't look like you're getting away with anything."

It is usually better to talk to a Campus Police officer than to try to run away. If nothing else, ask questions like "Where's the nearest bathroom?" The proper blend of interest, respect, and a willingness to follow up on the things that are said can do wonders.

If you can become invisible, people give up hunting for you and go away. Keep track of hiding places that you can get into quickly and quietly. If someone is chasing you, don't hide unless you can convince them you kept running.

People are usually unaware of anything above them unless it moves or otherwise calls attention to itself. When hacking, remember to look up periodically.

Planning a hack

When planning a hack, concentrate on the tools and materials. People are awfully good at figuring how to do something, but they have a hard time imitating a roll of tape. Some feel that the best way to get the manpower needed for a hack is to get several people involved in the planning stage, but it is wise to remember that too many cooks can spoil the soup.

Plan your deployment in excruciating detail, in order to keep the actual "critical time" during which you are actually putting the hack in position to a minimum. Anything that can be prepared ahead of time should be. The night before lasts, at most, eight hours, and no matter how careful your planning may have been, many of these will be consumed by unforeseen delays.

Exploring

Try to account for all the space in a building. If a bump in one wall does not line up with a dent on the other side, then there is a space that needs exploring.

Move as quietly as possible. If you can see or hear trouble before it hears you, then retracing your steps should bring you to safety. Trouble tends to come from behind. Walking past someone may arouse suspicion (especially if you're carrying something odd, like lots of rope), and by definition those people are behind you. Periodically check your back side. Enter and exit an area using different routes.

Write your sign-in in places that you are proud to have reached, and include the date. This makes the order of re-discovery clear. Other hackers judge you by where they've seen your logo. Use it as a sign of approval and accomplishment.

Always carry a flashlight, but don't panic if you're without one. The human eye is very sensitive if you give it time to adjust. In an emergency use your digital watch to light the way.

General Advice

Brute force is the last refuge of the incompetent. Carrying master keys is extremely stupid and unnecessary. Things are not always as they appear. This is true of locks, doors, walls, and people.

ISSEL ANNE LIM '05

Moah 'Bout Boston

Those of you unfamiliar with Boston may think that you are coming to just another American city that uses English as its native tongue. If so, you are due for something of a shock. So, as another of its continuing services, HowToGAMIT has persuaded a true native Bostonian to compile this

Guide to the Language of Boston
Together with Commentary
on the Strange Customs Thereof
with Pronunciation Guide
and a Glossary of Native Vocabulary

Introduction

The accent of Eastern New England is characterized as a "twang." This means that the speech is quick and clipped. Rumor has it that in Northern Maine it's so clipped that it sometimes dies off into pure silence. This, however, is not a problem in Boston. A "twang" also means it has a tendency to be nasal. An example of a nasal sound in English is the "ng" at the end of "looking." Now try applying this to a vowel and you've almost got it.

Of course, not all New England accents are the same. People in Western New England talk almost like the rest of the country, and many suburbanites are altogether too affected by the bland language of national TV. Proper Bostonians talk almost like Britishers, and Mainiacs have a delightful accent all their own.

It's only in Boston and nearby that one can hear the sweet dulcet tones of pure Bostonian English. While it may at first sound grating and harsh, even cacophonous to the inexperienced ear, you will soon grow to love it. Just keep telling yourself that.

Specific Characteristics

The disappearing "R"

This is the most distinctive aspect of Bostonese. The combination "or" is pronounced "awe." In extreme cases it is pronounced very nasally (approximately "woh") as in "Dorchester" (pronounced "Dwohchestah"). Note, however, that "or" and "er" at the end of a word are pronounced "ah." JFK talked about "vigah." No one in Boston thought that strange. The classic example is "I parked my car in Harvard Yard," pronounced "I pahked my cah in Hahvahd Yahd."

The reappearing "R"

Having discarded so many r's, Bostonions must put them somewhere, and they often end up pronouncing the words ending in "a" as though they ended in "er". Hence "Cuber" (Cuba) and "bananer" (banana).

The mysterious extra syllable

Many words which you think have one syllable appear to have two. This is even more common in Maine than in Boston. Example: "there" (*they-ah*), "door" (*doe-ah*), and "Revere" (*Re-ve-ah*).

The broad "A"

The words "calf," "half," and "laugh" rhyme and have the same "a" sound as in "father." This is known as a "broad A" and in extreme cases may appear in words like "glass" and "grass."

"Phantom" Negatives

Bostonians often insert negatives in places never intended, with the meaning only to be figured out in context. Example: Bostonian 1: "I wicked wanna go to Glostah to get some clams!" Bostonian 2: "So don't I!" The second Bostonian just expressed agreement. Go figure.

Localities

Boston — (*BAH-ston*), a city north of Quincy.
    Eastie — East Boston.
    Southie — South Boston.
Quincy — (*QUIN-zee*), a city south of Boston.
Worcester — (*WOOS-tah* or *WISS-tah*), second largest city in Massachusetts (and New England). (**Westawoosta** — no-man's-land.)
Gloucester — (*GLOSS-tah*), a seaport north of Boston.
Medford — (*MEH-fuh*), a city north of Boston.
Revere — (*Re-VEE-ah*), a city north of Boston.
Peabody — (*PEE-buh-dee*, <u>not</u> *PEE-bdee*, <u>not</u> *Pee-BOD-ee*, <u>not</u> *PU-ber-ty*), another city north of Boston.
P-Town — Provincetown, a town on the cape.
North End — a part of Boston which lies East of the West End, which in turn no longer exists. The North End is known for its Italian restaurants.
Down East — Maine.
Cradle of Liberty — (1) Boston; (2) Faneuil (*FAN-yul*) Hall.
Athens of America — Boston.
Hub of the Universe — Boston.
Midwest — area around Worcester, Mass.
West — area around Springfield, Mass.
Edge of Civilization — The Connecticut River.
Indian Country — land west of the Berkshire Hills.
New York — (*NooYawk*), city, a suburb of Stamford, Connecticut.
Ireland — (*EYE-ah-land*), lawtsa Bostonians are from theah.

Food

Tonic — generic term for "soft drinks" (also acceptable). **Soda** ("*soder*") is gradually filtering into usage from visitors. **Pop** is not used.
Frappe — (*FRAP*), what you think of as a milkshake.
Milkshake — milk and flavored syrup, shaken up. Contains no ice cream..
Hoodsie — a small ice cream in a paper cup.
Jimmies — sprinkles for ice cream.
Steamed Clams — the world's best food.
Fried Clams — the world's biggest crime to the world's best food.
Clam Chowder — absolutely heavenly treat; contains no tomato — often called *chowdah*.

Manhattan-Style Clam Chowder — tomato soup. Rumored to contain some clams, but this has never been substantiated.

Scrod — whatever they tell you it is, usually fish. If you paid more than $6/pound, you got scrod (see **Glossary**).

Government

The Great and General Court — The official name of the legislature; what the legislature likes to call itself.

Those Crooks on Beacon Hill — What everyone else call the legislature.

Governor's Council — A popularly-elected group of nine wheeler-dealers who must approve appointments by the Governor. About 20 years ago they almost had a quorum in the state prison.

Town — Main unit of local government throughout New England. Every square inch of Massachusetts is part of some city or town. Counties have insignificant power.

Town Meeting — An assembly of voters in a town. It runs the local government and is presided over by a moderator.

Selectmen — A board of local magistrates (generally 3 to 5) who run the day-to-day affairs of the town, according to the instructions of the town meeting.

Commonwealth — What Massachusetts is. There are 46 states and four commonwealths (Ma., Pa., Va., and Ky.) in the United States.

Highway Terms

Motorist — someone granted a license to hunt pedestrians and bicyclists.

Pedestrian — a hazardous occupation.

Bicyclist — a suicidal occupation.

Crosswalk — strange paintings on some city streets, the significance of which is unknown to the natives.

Expressway — a "freeway", to furriners.

Rotary — A traffic circle; a counterclockwise ring of speeding death.

Traffic Light — a signalling device for drivers; green means go, yellow means go, and red means two more can go. Red and yellow together mean to stop in all directions — pedestrians crossing. Blinking green means to be prepared for the light to turn red.

Bang a — to take a, as in "bang a left" or "bang a U-ey."

Miscellaneous

Harvard — (*Hah-vahd*), a small liberal arts college up the creek.

Blue Laws — laws left over from the Puritan days, which say that anything you want to do on Sundays, you can't.

Yankee — (1) to a foreigner, an American; (2) to a Southerner, a Northerner; (3) to a Northerner, a New Englander; (4) to a New Englander, a Vermonter; (5) to a Vermonter, someone who eats apple pie for breakfast.

Fankees — the Fuckin' Yankees. A baseball team.

Common — a park in the center of a city or town. Generally has public buildings and churches clustered around it.

Bubblah — a water fountain.

Barrel — a wastebasket.

Garbage — "wet" trash. If it can compost, it's garbage. Otherwise, it's rubbish.

Nawtheastah — (also *Naw-E-stuh)* a storm that blows in from the ocean.

Townie — a young native of more backward parts of the Boston area. Characterized by their Trans Ams (in males of the species), big hair (in females of the species), and use of phrases such as "That would be wicked pissah" and "Let's go down Joey's for a tonic."

Hahyadooin' — A greeting. Best answered with a nod and "howyadoin?" in return.

Wanna go? — Do you want to fight?

A Whole Nothah — A totally different thing.

Wicked — (adj.) very. Ex.: Aerosmith is wicked awesome!

Wicked pissah — something really good.

Wicked fuckin' pissah — just about the best thing in the whole world.

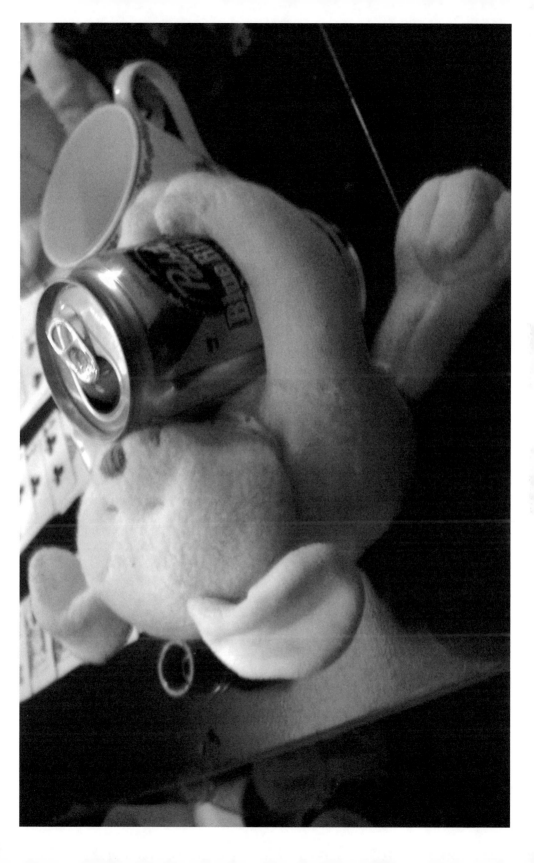

Glossary

The following is a dictionary of MIT words, phrases, and acronyms. Terms commonly identified by either acronyms or names are listed here by acronym. Alphabetically, acronyms are listed as words. A useful resource, if you should come across an acronym not listed here, is the 'whats' database on Athena; type "`add sipb ; whats <acronym>`" for expansions of a huge collection. MIT also keeps a somewhat up-to-date internal acronym list on the web at `web.mit.edu/acronym/`.

Admin — Administrator. Someone hired to fix things that aren't broken. The fastest-growing ethnic group on campus.

AI — Artificial Intelligence.

All Tech Sing — An annual event that used to be held every spring during Spring Weekend (archaic).

alum — *n*. (1) Short for alumnus or alumna. (2) A potassium aluminum sulfate or an ammonium aluminum sulfate, used especially as an emetic and as an astringent and styptic.

Alumni Association President's Court — A nice place to sit, if you can find it.

anal — Uptight, obsessive-compulsive.

ARC — Academic Resource Center. Administers orientation, UROP, and anything else vaguely academic that doesn't fall under a specific department.

ASA — Association of Student Activities. Coordinating body for student activities, clubs, *etc.* Handles things often covered by administrators at other schools, such as office and bulletin board allocation.

armadillo — A small set of drawers common to a select few dorms.

Athena — The MIT computing environment. People who complain that it is too complex are often **millennials** (*q.v.*).

back in the day — (1) A very long time ago, archaic. (2) An indeterminate time ago, usually equal to the time since the speaker was a freshman, when things were much more **hardcore** (*q.v.*).

Barton — MIT Libraries online catalog.

Bathroom — Arts and Media Technology Building (E15, The Media Lab). Also known as the "Pei Toilet" (after architect I. M. Pei).

bazorg — The nickname of the "extra extra large" 20 oz. coffees sold at the 24-hour Coffeehouse before its closure. Regarded by purists as a heresy, as traditionally the largest item in the hierarchy was named **blooter** (*q.v.*).

BCS — Brain and Cognitive Sciences (Course IX).

Beast from the East — Resident of Second East, East Campus.

beaver — The MIT mascot, engineer of the animal kingdom.

Big Dome — See **Great Dome**.

Big Sail — The official name of the steel sculpture by Alexander Calder south of the Green Building, one of the few art pieces on campus that is also functional. Starting place of the annual spontaneous **Tuition Riot** (*q.v.*). Usually called the Great Sail.

Big Sail, Working Model — A preliminary scaled-down version of the Big Sail. Used to reside on Mass. Ave. in front of Building 9, until they found out it was worth something and moved it to the Media Lab atrium. Often called the Little Sail.

Big Screw — A 36", solid aluminum, left-handed thread, wood screw presented by APO during Spring Weekend to the faculty or staff member voted most deserving.

blood on concrete — Irreverent nickname for MIT's cardinal red and steel gray school colors.

blooter — (1) *adj.* Any person or object of unbelievably large size, *e.g.*, "That's a blooter corn muffin you have there." (2) *n.* The nickname of the 16 oz. "extra large" coffees sold at the 24-hour Coffeehouse prior to its forced shutdown.

blow off — *v.* (1) To **flush** (*q.v.*). (2) To **punt** (*q.v.*).

Bomber — Resident of Burton Third.

Bonsai Kitten — *n.* (1) A domestic cat grown in a constrictive container to acheive a visually pleasing shape. (2) A mistaken belief or deliberate red herring; *e.g.*, "That story about Senior Haus exploding turned out just to be a bonsai kitten".

Brass Rat — Ugly hunk of gold some MIT students and **alums** wear on a finger.

Bridge Circuit — *n.* (1) A running course along the Charles River which includes the BU, Harvard, and/or Longfellow Bridges. Not to be confused with a circuit bridge. (2) A series of card contests where people play rubbers.

Bronze Bunny — Sculpture in Lowell Court (building 1), also called the "Bunny Shrine". Officially named "Three Piece Reclining Figure, Draped."

Bruno — A unit of volume resulting from a piano falling six stories onto Amherst Alley from the roof of Baker House.

BSO — Boston Symphony Orchestra.

BSU — Black Students Union.

bummer — Post-choke or post-screw description of said **choke** or **screw**; in general, something not good.

bug — *n.* (1) A natural or introduced flaw, often the cause of a **crash** (*q.v.*). (2) One of our cherished friends inhabiting MIT dorms, who does not pay tuition, nor, more relevantly, rent.

busted — *pp.* (1) Arrested. (2) Broken.

by definition — *av.* (1) Clearly, obviously. (2) Necessarily. (3) "I can't remember why."

Cambridge Tool & Die — Local nerd shop; not to be confused with Tool & Die, which the MIT humor magazine **Voo Doo** was named for a few years, **back in the day**.

Camp Cambridge — MIT.

CAES — Center for Advanced Educational Services.

CAP — Committee on Academic Performance. (2) *v.* To place on academic probation; *e.g.* "I got capped because I spent too much time **punting**."

caveat emptor — Let the buyer beware.

CAVS — Center for Advanced Visual Studies (N52-390).

CGSP — Committee on Graduate School Policy.

Chancellor — Administration bigwig position, currently held by Phillip L. Clay. Responsible for "overseeing" all student life, undergraduate and graduate education, and research policy.

chaus — Nickname of the former 24-hour student-run Coffeehouse on the 3rd floor of the Student Center. Still used as a meeting place.

cheese graters — Nickname of the ridiculous metal booths in Lobby 7 that replaced the low-key, "messy" functionality of drop posters and publications shelves with the lofty architectural form of giant, obstructive kitchen implements.

ChemE — *[pronounced "kem-ee"]* Chemical Engineering (Course X).

Cheney Room — Margaret Cheney Room (3-310), for women students only.

Chocolate City — Top three floors of New House 1.

choke — *v.* To snatch defeat from the jaws of victory.

CivE — *[pronounced "siv-ee"]* Civil Engineering (Course I).

clue — *n.* The technical knowledge needed to carry out a task, or useful knowledge in general. A prerequisite for **pants** (*q.v.*).

cluster — A room of public access **Athena** terminals.

clusterbate — Access privates in a room of **Athena** terminals.

CMI — Cambridge-MIT Institute.

CMS — Comparative Media Studies.

COC — Committee on Curricula.

COD — Committee on Discipline.

Compton Lecture Hall — Room 26-100.

Concourse — An experimental freshman program. Prof. Rose (x3-3230) has more information.

Coop — Co-operative store. Located in Kendall Square, Harvard Square, and other locations. The main source of MIT-logo merchandise.

Course — *n.* (1) Department major. (2) Subject (*e.g.*, 5.11). Note: the Registrar's Office has declared (2) an invalid definition.

CP — Campus Police.

crash — *v.* (1) To sleep in a place where one does not pay rent, such as a friend's apartment. (2) To join a party without being invited. (3) To cease functioning, as in a computer system.

cretin — A fool.

crock — *n.* (1) Something that has been botched, *e.g.*, "What a crock." (2) Bucket, *e.g.*, "This is a crock of shit." (3) The comic rock opera performed at TEP during Rush.

crunch — (1) *n.* What happens at the end of the term. (2) *v.* To process mindlessly, as in "number crunch".

cruft — Old equipment; junk. Being able to take cruft and make it work again, or do something new and useful, is a badge of honor.

crust — An old person, particularly an **alum**; often stated explicitly, as in "crusty alum". Crust can be notorious for trying to **hit on** (*q.v.*) **frosh** (*q.v.*).

CSAIL — (1) Computer Science and Artificial Intelligence Laboratory. Formerly two separate labs, the MIT AI Laboratory and the Laboratory for Computer Science (LCS) were combined in July 2003. (2) Transaction of C shells by the cshore.

CSR — Center for Space Research (building 37).

CSS — Counseling and Support Services. Also known as the "Counseling Deans".

CUP — Committee on the Undergraduate Program.

DAPER — Department of Athletics, Physical Education and Recreation.

Dean — Occupier of administrative supervisory position. See **Admin**.

defrosh — *v.* To temper enough of one's irritating characteristics with the acquisition of **clue** (*q.v.*). Usually occurs some time during freshman year, but extreme cases may be delayed into graduate school and beyond.

Deke — Delta Kappa Epsilon fraternity.

dl — See **Dormline**.

D-Labs — See **Draper**.

dope — *n.* (1) Marijuana, rarely other drugs. (2) Trace impurity added to pure substance to alter properties. (3) *adj.* Outdated popular parlance equivalent to "cool" or "rad". (4) Moron (archaic).

DormCon — Dormitory Council. The central dormitory governing and coordinating body.

Dormline — Old MIT dormitory telephone system. (Also **dl**). Now replaced by 5ESS. "This is MIT. Collect and third-number calls will not be accepted at this number."

Dot — The circle of grass between the Green Building and the **Big Sail**. A popular place to eat lunch, play frisbee or hold Oddball Olympics. Officially named McDermott Court.

Double-E — See **EE**.

down — *adj.* (1) Feeling depressed, said of a person. (2) Non-working, **gronked** (*q.v.*), said of a computer.

Draper — Formerly Instrumentation Labs. Works on inertial guidance systems, radar, etc. Divested by MIT due to student protest two decades ago. Hires many MIT students.

drop — (1) *v.* To de-register for a subject during a term. (2) *n.* Network access point. (3) *n.* Type of sodium experiment performed by Third East.

Drunkle — Runkle, Senior Haus (**back in the day**).

DSL — (1) Dean for Student Life (4-110, x3-4052). (2) Digital Subscriber Line; **alums** often use this to get Internet when they can't suck the Institute's digital teat anymore.

DUE — Dean for Undergraduate Education (4-110, 3-6056).

DUSP — *[pronounced "dusp"]* Department of Urban Studies and Planning (Course XI).

dweeb — *n.* Similar to **nerd** (*q.v.*), but more disparaging.

DYA — Domestic Year Away.

EAPS — *[pronounced "eeps"]* Earth, Atmospheric and Planetary Sciences (Course XII).

EE — Electrical Engineering (Course VI-1).

EECS — *[pronounced "eeks"]* Electrical Engineering and Computer Science (Course VI).

EIT — [*rhymes with "fight"*] (1) The Engineer in Training exam, given each year to students en route to becoming professional engineers. (2) An exclamation which originated at TEP, used when someone is unfairly destroyed. Can be used as virtually any part of speech, *e.g.*, "I got eited on my 18.03 test."

elephant — A large piece of furniture resembling a wardrobe; common to a few dorms.

emeritus — Retired from regular service with honor. See **professor**.

entrée — French word meaning "appetizer". Inexplicably used by Americans to refer to a main course.

-er joke — A set of jokes common on campus, *e.g.*, "Fiddler on the Roof? But I just met her!"

ESG — Experimental Study Group. An alternative freshman program located at 24-612. Associate Director Holly Sweet (x3-7786) has more information.

ESP — Educational Studies Program. Runs **HSSP** (*q.v.*).

FAC — Friday Afternoon Club.

FADC — Friday Afternoon Drinking Club. Synonymous with **FAC**.

feed the tree — Shed blood on the Senior Haus tire swing. The tree (a.k.a. The Angry God) is not pleased until it has drunk from you.

Fiji — Phi Gamma Delta. Dissolved at MIT after the death of Scott Krueger.

FinBoard — Finance Board. The undergraduate body charged with proposing and administering the Undergraduate Association budget and funding student activities.

First-year — A freshman, at Wellesley.

Fishbowl — A former **Project Athena** workstation cluster located off the Infinite Corridor in building 11, where the Student Services Center now resides. Some claim that the building 12 cluster is a recreation.

5ESS — MIT's new and improved phone system (c. 1988). Now short for 5ESS-2000.

5 O'Clock Club — Daily event at which the commuter students used to hang out in the basement of Walker after classes, *way* **back in the day**.

flushed — (1) *pp.* Turned down or out. Disappointed in some endeavor, usually involved with selling oneself. Examples: "I got flushed at the mixer," "I just got flushed by [fill in fraternity name here]". (2) *adj.* Having a reddish hue on one's face from heat, exertion, or embarrassment. Example: "I got flushed at the mixer." (3) *pp.* Disposed of. When said of a person, this connotes dismissal or expulsion. Example: "I got flushed at the mixer."

flame — (1) *n.* A savage castigation of someone in a public forum, usually e-mail or usenet. Usually written with the intention of amusing or outraging uninvolved readers. (2) *v.* To write the aforementioned devastating attack. Certain mailing lists exist specifically for this purpose. (3) *v.* To speak obnoxiously and/or at great length.

Flammschmeisser — A gas-fired device used for spreading burning iron particles when creating a hoax crop circle.

FPC — Faculty Policy Committee.

frappe — In New England, a snack made up of milk, syrup, and ice cream. Called a "**milkshake**" in the English-speaking world.

Fred — East Campus. Ask a resident for the story.

frosh — *n.* (1) Freshman. (2) Freshmen.

FSILG — Fraternity, Sorority or Independent Living Group.

Fuck Truck — The Wellesley Senate Bus.

funnelator — Home-made catapult device for launching water balloons, eggs, rotting **turkey** carcasses *etc.* So named because the simplest example consists of two lengths of surgical tubing connected to a funnel which holds the projectiles. See also **mariah**.

furry fish — Cat; references the general rule that fish were the only pets officially permitted in dorms, except for the ones that require them for rodent control.

fuxxor — (1) *n.* A meddling or incompetent fool. Frequently written in **leetspeak** for added effect. (2) *v.* To **shaft** something such that it becomes **gronked**. (3) *int.* Expression of frustration or disappointment, *e.g.* "My fuxxor of a 6.270 partner just fuxxored our robot! Fuxxor!"

G — Graduate student.

GAMIT — Gays, Lesbians, Bisexuals and Transgenders at MIT (unrelated to this book).

geek — A **nerd** in Course VI. (Q: What's the difference between a geek and a nerd? A: A geek has **double-E**.)

generate — To create; to come up with.

ghost — (1) *n.* A dorm resident who lives unseen by neighboring students, often deliberately. (2) *v.* To sublet a room from its official occupant.

GIR — General Institute Requirement. A class that all undergraduates must pass in order to get their degree.

glitch — A bug; cause of sporadic **gronkedness** (*q.v.*).

GPA — Grade Point Average. MIT's is out of 5.0, as opposed to most places which grade on the 4.0 scale. **Harvard**'s answer to this is grade inflation.

grease — Indicator of one's clout within the governing body of an organization.

Great Dome — The dome on top of building 10. Bigger (and harder to get to) than the **Little Dome**.

Great Sail — See **Big Sail**.

Green Line — *n.* (1) One of Boston's four subway lines. (2) Former access method to the roof of the Green Building.

gritch — (1) *v.* To complain. (2) *n.* Complaint. Not to be confused with **glitch**, which is sometimes the cause of a gritch.

Grogo — Mascot of Technique, the MIT yearbook. A big ape.

gronked — Kaput, non-functioning.

GRT — Graduate Resident Tutor.

grunge — To throw away, especially an item in a public space. "The **Grunge Crew** grunged my shopping cart!"

Grunge Crew — People hired to clear hallways and clean empty rooms in dorms, especially prevalent just after Spring term.

grungy — *adj.* (1) Grubby and dingy. What you feel like after studying for 20 hours straight in 85 degree heat. (2) The opposite of elegant; long, boring, complicated, painful, but often necessary. "This 18.03 problem set is disgustingly grungy." Grungy work is often called "grungework".

GSC — Graduate Student Council. The governing body for graduate students as a group (50-110, x3-2195).

hack — (1) *n.* A trick or prank. For example, having a balloon pop up out of the field in the middle of the Hahvahd-Yale football game or getting elected **UAP** are fine hacks. (2) *n.* An inelegant shortcut to get something done quickly, for example in a computer program. (3) *v.* To use or operate something in a manner outside its design or published documentation; see **kludge**. (4) *v.* To explore ordinarily inaccessible or unknown places; equivalent to "go hacking". (5) *v.* To apply oneself with utmost dedication in order to understand or become proficient in something. Example: a computer hacker. Also connotes fanaticism.

hacker — *n.* (1) One who hacks. (2) One who pulls hacks. (3) One who goes hacking.

Hacker Heaven — A summer program at **LCS**.

Hahvahd — The big red-brick school, both Up The Street and Up Chuck River; little liberal arts school.

Hahvahd Bridge — The Mass. Ave. bridge from MIT to Boston, which measures 364.4 **Smoots** + 1 ear in length.

hand-wave — *v.* To attempt to explain something one doesn't actually understand or that doesn't make any actual sense, or to gloss over a question for which one wasn't prepared. Sometimes performed by **professors** when taken by surprise.

hardcore — *adj.* (1) A state of extreme desirability; an indicator that a situation or thing is superior to normal. Example: "A hardcore week of hacking." (2) An extreme dedication to a cause, often characterised by the willful disregard of personal hardship or risk. Example: "A week of hardcore hacking." (3) Generally extreme or excessive. Example: "That week of hacking was hardcore."

HASS — Humanities, Arts and Social Sciences. Undergraduates need some of these classes in order to graduate.

HASS-D — Humanities, Arts and Social Sciences Distribution. Undergraduates need some of these classes in order to graduate also. Not the same as regular **HASS** (*q.v.*).

haxxor — (1) *n.* Derogatory term for self-conscious **hackers** who go to great lengths to ensure that you notice that they carry a multitool and wear all black. (2) *v.* To **hack** something in a trivial or inept fashion.

Hell — *n.* (1) MIT. (2) The underground steam tunnel from Vassar Street towards building 13.

hit on — *v.* Attempt to seduce; flirt with. Principal activity of many upperclassmen during the month of September. In more **sketchy** instances, the term **slime** is used.

HNC — Area of Senior Haus corresponding to the Holman, Nichols and Crafts entries **back in the day**.

hosed — *adj.* (1) Bogged down with work, when referring to a person. (2) Bogged down with packets, when referring to the network.

HowToGAMIT — The abbreviated, conversational name for this book. Not to be confused with **GAMIT** (*q.v.*). We hope you found this book useful; if so, it needs people like you to help put it out. Send e-mail or add yourself to `htgamit@mit.edu`.

HSSP — High School Studies Program, in which MIT students design and teach their own courses to high school students. Run by **ESP** (*q.v.*).

Hub — (1) Boston. (2) Something you shouldn't plug in to **MITnet**.

Huntington Hall — Room 10-250.

IAP — Independent Activities Period. The month of January at MIT, and the most fun time to be on campus.

IFC — Interfraternity Council. The central coordinating and governing body of the **FSILG**s (*q.v.*). Counterpart to **DormCon** (*q.v.*).

IHTFP — (1) I Hate This Fucking Place. (2) I Have Truly Found Paradise. (3) It's Hard To Fondle Penguins. (4) I Help Tutor Freshman Physics. (5) I Have To Forever Pay. (See **TDM**.)

Infinite Corridor — A quarter-mile hallway through the heart of the Institute. At one time the longest continuous straight corridor in the world.

infinitely — Exceedingly, really, quite, *e.g.*, "infinitely screwed up."

The Institute — Affectionate name for MIT. See **Hell**.

Institute Professor — A prestigious honor conferred on particularly outstanding **professors** (*q.v.*).

instructor — *n.* (1) Person who stands in front of students and lets fall pearls of wisdom. (2) Academic rank in the lower echelons of the junior faculty.

Interphase — An intensive summer academic program for minorities, designed to ease the transition from high school to MIT.

intuitively obvious — *adj.* (1) Too simpleminded to deserve explanation. (2) More often, too abstruse to explain, if the speaker even understands it at all.

I/S — MIT Information Systems. Among other things, the people who run **Athena**. Now officially known as **IS&T**.

IS&T — Information Services & Technology. The newer, more corporate sounding and less efficient way to refer to **I/S**. See **PhysPlant**.

"Is this the way to Baker House?" — Classic line said by a freshman to a Campus Police officer when caught in the steam tunnels.

Jack Florey — *n.* (1) Mythical resident of Fifth East, East Campus. (2) A hacking group associated with Fifth East.

James E. Tetazoo — *n.* (1) Mythical resident of Third East, East Campus. (2) A hacking group associated with Third East.

J. Arthur Random — Mythical resident of Random Hall.

jock — *n.* (1) An athletic supporter. (2) An athletic supporter. (3) Anyone who does a lot of something.

JudComm — Judicial Committee, a generic term signifying a group of students charged with enforcing student laws. Usually attached to a **living group**.

JYA — Junior Year Abroad.

k — One thousand (of anything).

Killian Court — The large courtyard in the middle of main campus, surrounded by buildings 1-4, building 10, and Memorial Drive. Called the Great Court until it was named for former MIT President Killian after his retirement.

Kiss of Death Award — The Baker Award, given to professors who teach well. A surprisingly high percentage of Baker Award recipients are subsequently denied tenure. Damned shame, too.

kludge — *[rhymes with "stooge"] n.* (1) A Rube Goldberg-style device which appears unlikely to work but does anyhow. (2) A method by which something is effectively but inelegantly made to perform a function for which it was not designed. (3) Something complex that doesn't work, *e.g.*, this definition.

Kresge — The hump between the Oval and the athletic field. Used for lectures, theatre, movies, concerts, conferences, and — less frequently — skiing.

Krotus — Malevolent deity of Fifth East, East Campus.

Lambchops — Lambda Chi Alpha fraternity.

LCS — Laboratory for Computer Science. Now part of **CSAIL** (*q.v.*).

lecturer — *n.* (1) One who lectures. (2) Low, low academic rank.

leetspeak — The practice of replacing typed alphabetic letters with alternate characters that more or less visually resemble said letters, originally advocated by **haxxors** who considered themselves "elite". Many variants exist but are now almost always used to convey derisive or satiric intent.

Little Dome — The dome on top of building 7. Smaller than the **Great Dome**, but easier to see from Mass. Ave.

Little Sail — See **Big Sail, Working Model.**

living group — The place where you live (may not apply for some people found in the Student Center).

L-Lab — Lincoln Laboratory, a special MIT-affiliated laboratory located in Lexington. Its specialties include optics, radio physics, data systems, radar, and re-entry systems.

loser — One who bans flags.

LSC — Lecture Series Committee. A student organization that puts on movies, lectures, and other entertainment for the MIT community.

mariah — A long piece of laboratory rubber tubing filled with water; useful in waterfights. Also spelled "moriah."

MBA — Master of Business Administration. A degree pursued by many **Sloanies** (*q.v.*).

MBTA — Massachusetts Bay Transit Authority. Operates the Boston area mass transit during the day, well, not too horribly. Known as the "T".

MechE — *[pronounced "mek-ee"]* Mechanical Engineering (Course II).

MEng — *[pronounced "emm-enj"]* Masters in Engineering.

MGH — Massachusetts General Hospital.

milkshake — Snack made with milk and syrup, but no ice cream. If you want a "milkshake," order a **frappe** (*q.v.*).

millennial — Derogatory term for modern resume-padding, cookie-cutter university students who exhibit the desire to be spoon-fed and a general lack of uniqueness and idiosyncrasy. Entered popular discourse through an infamous article penned by Dean of Admissions Marilee Jones in the faculty newsletter.

MIT Community — *n.* (1) Nearly 20,000 students, faculty, researchers, staff, and employees at MIT. Sometimes used more expansively to include their families and also alumni. (2) An indefinable, probably mythical item invented by **Admins** (*q.v.*) to justify the implementation of various private projects and testing of politically-inspired social theories.

MITERS — MIT Electronic Research Society.

MITFCU — MIT Federal Credit Union. Not pronounced "*MIT-fuck-you*" despite possible temptation, as the Credit Union is actually very cool.

MITnet — The Institute's campus computing network.

MITOC — MIT Outing Club.

MITSFS — MIT Science Fiction Society. Pronounced "mittsfiss" or "mitt-siffs," but never "misfits."

MITV — MITelevision.

moat — The wet thing wrapped around the Chapel. A good place to throw obnoxious people.

MOF — Most Obnoxious Freshman. Awarded at Senior Haus during **Steer Roast** (*q.v.*).

MRS — Model Rocket Society.

MTG — Musical Theatre Guild.

mumble — *n.* A verbal expression used to replace actual mumbling.

munge — *v.* To mangle, mutilate, or mess up badly.

Mystery Hunt — The famous annual weekend-long puzzle competition held during **IAP** (*q.v.*).

n — A random number with various connotations. There are n ways to beat (or get screwed by) the system.

nerd — [pronounced "gnurd"] *n.* (1) Someone with a high level of expertise in an esoteric, usually technical field. A badge of honor at the Institute, *e.g.*, "Nerd pride". (2) Someone who studies too much. See **tool**.

NGL — Nobody Gets Laid.

nonoptimal — *adj.* (1) In need of improvement. (2) Horribly bad.

nontrivial — (1) Very difficult. (2) Impossible. (See **trivial**.)

nuke — (1) *n.* Nuclear power plant. (2) *n.* Nuclear weapon. (3) *v.* To attack with a nuclear weapon, *e.g.*, "Nuke 'em 'til they glow." (4) *adj.* Damage caused by a microwave oven, *e.g.*, "Nuke alert!", or by a **jock** (*q.v.*), *e.g.*, "My knee's nuked thanks to him." (4) *v.* To cook in a microwave oven, *e.g.*, "I'll just nuke some dinner."

NukeE — *[pronounced "nuke-ee"]* Nuclear Engineering (Course XXII).

ODSUE — Office of the Deans of Students and Undergraduate Education. Umbrella administrative office responsible for managing the myriad of bureaucracies attempting to control student life on campus.

OE — Ocean Engineering (Course XIII).

Orange Tour — A guided excursion to some of the Institute's less-publicized architectural sights. To get on one, ask a **hacker**.

ORK — Order of Random Knights, a hacking group based in Random Hall.

OSP — Office of Sponsored Programs. An administrative apparatus overseeing outside research grants and works at MIT.

pants — *n.* (1) A condition or thing that is notable in the event of its absence. Often refers to the ability to get things done effectively and competently, *e.g.*, "My TA helped me find my pants after office hours." (2) What people are ultimately trying to get into when they **hit on** someone, *e.g.*, "My TA helped me find my pants after office hours."

petition — (1) *n.* A form used to request something unusual with regard to academics, such as placing out of all your upper-class requirements. (2) *v.* To fill out a petition form, submit it to the proper authorities, and satisfy other protocols associated with that kind of activity. (3) *v.* To request a delay on an Incomplete, an administrative means of procrastination.

PhysPlant — Contraction of Physical Plant, what the maintenance and janitorial staff used to be called. Now officially renamed Department of Facilities, but everyone still says PhysPlant because it's just better.

placement — The process of career counseling, graduate school counseling, and finding a job (summer, temporary, or permanent). Often occurs at the Placement Office (12-170).

Player — Resident of Burton Four.

policy — *n.* (1) A predefined set of procedures for handling certain situations or processes. (2) What **Admins** use as an excuse after a failed attempt to **hand-wave**.

postdoc — Someone who already has a Ph.D. but is still here.

postgrad — Graduate student.

powertool — (1) *n.* An electrically operated tool. (2) *v.* What one has to do to catch up on the entire term in any given course the night before the final exam in that course.

pox card — Derisive nickname for **RFID** proximity access cards. Refers to the inherent security flaw associated with such devices, namely that the transmission of identifying data can be both triggered and collected without the knowledge or consent of the holder.

prefrosh — Those happy few who can still decide whether or not to come to MIT.

professor — *n.* (1) Person teaching a course. (2) Academic rank with three levels (assistant, associate, full) comprising the main body of the faculty. (3) Institute Professor: Academic post recognizing exceptional distinction. Institute Professors can work as they wish on research and teaching, without regard for formal boundaries and duties. (4) Professor Emeritus: Faculty member who has reached 70 (mandatory retirement age) but who is working (legally) at up to 50% of his or her former load.

Project Athena — A project to integrate computers into MIT academics; the origin of the current **Athena** system.

Provost — The senior academic officer, who assists the President of the Institute in addition to carrying on projects of his own.

prox card — Contraction of Proximity Card. See **pox card**.

punt — (1) *v.t.* To determine after analytical deliberation not to do something, said something often academic in nature. (2) *v.i.* To be in the process of not doing something.

putz — (1) *v.* To do something in a ridiculous manner or for no justifiable reason. (2) *n.* One who putzes. (3) *n.* A resident of Second West, East Campus.

quantum mechanics — People who repair quanta.

RA — (1) Research Assistant. Usually a graduate student employed by a department, receiving pay plus a tuition allowance for research. Often funded by outside grants. (2) Resident Advisor. **FSILG** equivalent of a **GRT** (*q.v.*).

RAC — Room Assignment Chair. Student representative, usually elected, that determines who lives where in a dorm, floor or entry.

random — (1) *adj.* Any. (2) *adj.* Indeterminate, sometimes connoting number. (3) *adj.* Without order, garbled. (4) *n.* Average person.

Randomite — Resident of Random Hall.

RBA — Residence-Based Advising. A program to prevent freshmen in McCormick and Next from transferring dorms or participating in **REX**.

Red Staple — Sculpture by Tang Hall. Officially named "For Marjorie."

REX — Residence EXploration. Politically correct new term for Dorm Rush, a phrase which apparently terrorized parents with its connotations of potentially dangerous haste. The revamped acronym instead conjures family-friendly images of Greeks named Oedipus.

RFID — Radio Frequency Identification.

rip-off — *n.* (1) A theft. (2) Something so outrageously expensive as to be almost a theft, *e.g.*, "Tickets to Bruins' hockey games are a real rip-off."

RLE — Research Laboratory of Electronics, an interdisciplinary lab in building 36.

RMS — *n.* (1) Root Mean Square, the square root of the mean squared deviation of a signal from a given baseline or fit. (2) Richard M. Stallman, AI Lab denizen and founder of the GNU free software project.

ROTC — *[pronounced "rot-see"]* Reserve Officer Training Corps. Military officer training program operating within MIT and some other colleges.

SAA — Student Art Association.

SAFO — Student Activities Finance Office.

SAO — Student Accounts Office.

Sala — La Sala de Puerto Rico. Large all-purpose room in the Student Center donated by Puerto Rico.

SCA — Society for Creative Anachronism.

SCEP — Student Committee on Educational Policy.

screw — (1) *n, v.* Bad thing, such as the Institute Screw or "screwed to the wall." (2) *v.* What nuns don't do.

scrod — (1) *n.* A baby codfish popular to eat in Massachusetts. Example: "I got scrod at the Dining Hall." (2) *v.* Past tense of **screw**. Example: "I got scrod at the Dining Hall."

secretary — One who is paid starvation wages to run everything.

Secret Ninja Courtyard — The courtyard bounded by buildings 8, 6, 2 and 4. Also known as the Atomic Courtyard.

Secret Ninja Parking Lot — The parking lot bounded by buildings 7, 5, 3 and 1.

SGS — Strategic Games Society.

SH — (1) Senior Haus. (2) Student House.

shaft — (1) *v.* To damage or otherwise **screw** something up. (2) *v.* To drop something from a great height, in particular the roof of Random Hall. (3) *n.* An enclosed vertical tunnel, such as where elevators or pipes run. (4) *v.* To climb a vertical tunnel, for example while hacking.

shrink — Psychiatrist.

SIPB — *[pronounced "sip-bee"]* Student Information Processing Board.

sketchy — Insalubrious.

slime — (1) *n.* Term applied to the guest each **LSC** member gets to admit to the movies for free. (2) *v.* Particularly egregious attempt by upperclassmen or **crust** to **hit on** a **frosh**, especially before November.

Sloanie — *n.* (1) Member of the Sloan School of Management (Course XV). (2) Someone who can't do math.

SLP — Student Life Programs. Administrative group in charge of student activities and associated social function prevention and other meddling. The people you have to see to fill out pages of forms if you want to throw a party.

slug — Resident of Fourth East, East Campus.

Smoot — A unit of length equal to the height of Oliver Smoot '62, most commonly used for the **Harvard Bridge** (364.4 Smoots plus 1 ear).

snow — (1) *v.* To impress someone, such as a date. (2) *v.* To confuse favorably with a profusion of detail. (3) *n.* Brown, cold particles that cover sidewalks and gutters through Boston winters. Rumored to contain water.

Sponge — Nickname for Simmons Hall dormitory, based on its reputed ability to soak up beer.

Sport Death — Philosophy at Senior Haus. Ask a resident for an introduction.

Squanch — *n.* (1) Resident of Third East, East Campus. (2) A short fellow with a picket sign and a wilted flower.

squat — *v.* To circumvent a housing lottery by opting to stay in the same place. Depending on a dorm's **RAC** (*q.v.*) **policy** (*q.v.*), possession may be ten-tenths of the law.

Squinto — Nichols 2, 3 and 4 of Senior Haus (**back in the day**).

Stratton House — *n.* (1) Student Center (3rd, 4th, and 5th floors). (2) Not just a **living group**, a way of life.

Steer Roast — annual Senior Haus party at which said animal is actually roasted, amid various other activities. Tradition dates back to the mid-sixties.

structural — (1) Presently holding something else up, such as a ceiling. Example: "Don't lean on that, it's structural." (2) Able to hold something else up, such as a person. Example: "Don't lean on that, it's not structural."

Stud Center — Student Center.

Stud House — Student House.

subject — One or two professors, **n** students, a room, a formal curriculum, a formal subject number, and a formal grade, except when it isn't.

suboptimal — See nonoptimal.

SWE — Society of Women Engineers.

TA — Teaching Assistant. Usually a grad student employed by a department, receiving pay plus a tuition allowance for teaching duties. Funded by the Institute.

Tangerine Tour — smaller than an **Orange Tour**, for **prefrosh**.

TDM — Too Damned Much. Refers to tuition.

TEAL — Technology Enabled Active Learning. A new, futuristic method of teaching freshman physics that attempts to use technology to replace learning.

Tech — MIT (archaic). Now called the **Institute** (*q.v.*).

The Tech — A student-written and published newspaper that appears in Lobby 7 and other random places on Tuesdays and Fridays (except summers and Institute holidays).

TechCASH — Official name of the declining-balance retail payment system attached to the MIT card. Preferred by the Institute to the more accurate but less diplomatic term "parents' cash".

Technology — Very archaic name for the Institute. See **Tech**.

Tech Square — *n.* (1) Member of the MIT Square Dancing Club. (2) Group of buildings located northeast of MIT, location of the offices of the **MITFCU** and numerous tech companies.

Tech Talk — The official MIT newspaper published every Wednesday (except summers and Institute holidays).

Terrascope — An alternative freshman program involving earth studies. Located at 16-177, contact Debra Aczel (`daczel@mit.edu`).

TFM — See **TDM**.

THA — Technology Hackers Association, a hacking group not affiliated with any particular **living group**.

Tin Rat — Hunk of steel that is a modern alternative to the **Brass Rat** (*q.v.*). Slightly less ugly and heavy, and comes in a tasteful gray to match the concrete and the sky.

TMRC — *[pronounced "tumurk"]* Tech Model Railroad Club.

tomb — An enclosed space, often created when a new building is put next to an old one without fully coordinating the floorplans. They tend to be named by the first **hackers** to find them.

tonic — Soda, New England style.

tool — (1) *v.* To study. (See **powertool**.) (2) *n.* One who studies to an extreme. Connotes over-concentration on problem sets. Supertool: an extreme extreme. (3) *n.* MIT student. Slightly derogatory. See **nerd**.

Towers — 5th and 6th floor "penthouse" suite area of Senior Haus.

Towers Bug — Particular variety of house centipede often encountered in **Towers** (*q.v.*).

Transparent Horizons — Pile of scrap metal left by Louise Nevelson in the East Campus courtyard, best appreciated by facing away from it. Tends to be buried whenever there is enough **snow** to do so.

trash — To destroy or vandalize, especially during a riot.

trivial — *adj.* (1) Obvious. Often said sarcastically. (2) Easy to do.

Tuition Riot — Traditional "spontaneous" demonstration held to celebrate a tuition increase. See **TDM**.

turkey — (1) A chestnut-stuffed, giblet-jammed Tom gobbler. (2) One lacking common sense.

'Tute — MIT. See **Institute**.

twinkie — A person belonging to the loose social group surrounding the Assassins' Guild, **SIPB**, **MITSFS**, **SGS**, also APO and **LSC** to a lesser extent. Often characterized by punting a lot in myriad ways, usually involving games of some sort, usually as nerdy as possible.

U — Undergraduate.

UA — Undergraduate Association. Organization of all MIT undergraduates (W20-401).

UAC — Undergraduate Association Council. Undergraduate governing, coordinating, and information-distributing agency.

UAP — Undergraduate Association President.

UAVP — Undergraduate Association Vice President.

UMOC — Ugliest Manifestation On Campus, a contest to raise money for charity by showcasing unpleasantness. Frequently won by Random Hall's many-year-old milk. Originally named Ugliest Man On Campus, back in the unenlightened days before it was realised that women and non-humans could be ugly too.

urchin — Term, among others, for anyone (especially a high school student) who hangs around and makes a pest of himself, frequently causing objects of value to sprout legs and walk away.

UROP — Undergraduate Research Opportunities Program. A source of credit and dollars for many undergrads.

voodoo — Shamanistic religion originating in Haiti; notorious for cult-like behaviour and turning some of its members into zombies.

Voo Doo — MIT's humor magazine; notorious for cult-like behaviour and turning some of its members into zombies.

W1MX — MIT amateur ("ham") radio society and repeater.

Waffle Haus — Nickname for Simmons Hall dormitory, based on its reputed ability to soak up whipped cream.

wanking — (1) *n, v.* Self-indulgent pontification. (2) *v.* What nuns probably don't do.

WHOI — Woods Hole Oceanographic Institute.

WMBR — Walker Memorial Basement Radio, MIT's radio station at 88.1 FM.

Women's League — Service and social organization for all MIT women. Once upon a time named Tech Matrons.

wonky — Askew.

WYSIWYG — What You See Is What You Get. Generally refers to publishing software that attempts to provide an accurate screen preview of the printed output. Mockingly renamed WYSIAYG ("What You See Is All You Get") by typesetting language aficionado Leslie Lamport, for the lack of control of detail below the resolution of the screen. Other derivatives include WYSIWYP, such as Mountain Dew or $6 pitchers of Budweiser at the Muddy.

Z-Center — Zesiger Center, the newly-constructed athletics complex.

Zebe — Zeta Beta Tau fraternity brother.

Index

Advertisers' Index

Support the people who support HowToGAMIT!